无忧雅思网 八大雅思学校 十五大留学移民公司 联合指定用书

江涛英语

MW01711302

80天攻克雅思

Conquer IELTS In 80 Days

（第三版）

丛书主编 北京外国语大学 江 涛

本册主编 孟 飞 江 涛

朗读 雅思考试口语考官 Guy Taylor

国际汉语水平考试主播 范明

核心词汇

3小时MP3

石油工業出版社

80天攻克 IELTS 核心词汇

从书顾问委员会

从书编委会

IELTS 核心词汇丛书 序

泡沫

从前有一个人，家里有很多蚊子，于是就到集市上买驱蚊药，不料却碰上个卖蚊符的。这个卖蚊符的大吹特吹自家祖传的蚊符是如何神灵，如何有效果，家中只要有一张蚊符，蚊子便不敢骚扰。这个人便花高价买了一张，心想从此一劳永逸也还值得。于是回家后，把先前的蚊香、蚊帐通通扔掉，贴上了蚊符，一心想睡个好觉。结果事与愿违，蚊子对蚊符视而不见，一晚上的功夫把这人叮了365个包。第二日，此人气势汹汹地冲到集市上找那个卖蚊符的理论，卖蚊符的却反问他把蚊符贴在什么地方了，此人回答：当然是墙上了！卖蚊符的笑了，说：昨天你走的时候没听清楚，我的蚊符只有贴在蚊帐里才管用！

儿时听到这个寓言的反应是这个买蚊符的人可怜又可笑，而现今回味起来，更多的是无奈。记得还有一次去外地讲课的途中碰到一个推销名牌护肤品的大姐，她一语道破美容业的天机：什么深海淤泥、深层护理啊！我每天就拿自来水给你拍半个小时，也保证你的皮肤弹性不紧绷！广告的夸张和失真同样没有放过教育，为了争夺生源，各大培训机构竞相创造独霸武林的名师或是日进千里的神功大法，但我并不想就此发表谁之过的言论，只想提醒大家一句，在学习的路上，尤其是在语言的习得过程中，抛弃了自身的勤学苦练，一切的名师和诸如逆向顺向、追踪位移、模板美文的解题技巧都只能是空谈！

缘起

前年还在戴尔国际英语学校的时候，便有出版社来找我编一套雅思丛书，那时的我说实在话，还不清楚学生需要的究竟是什么，教与学的差距究竟有多大，再加上终日为事务所缠，便委婉地拒绝了。我一向很反感应试教育的学术化和培训老师的专家化、大师化，然而，时至今日，在离开戴尔后的这两年中，在接触了各地的各类考生后，我才开始惊诧原来崇拜的背后包含着的是当代大学生如此的不自知、不自信和追从心理。三年前我对新东方的一句话感触颇深——一堂让自己感动的课才能感动学生。而现在，我坚信：**一个能让学生自己崇拜自己的老师才能算得上是一个优秀的老师。**

于是，去年秋天的某一天，一个我自认为在培训界中有划时代意义的工程破土了。原来我想把这套书的名字定成《80天傻瓜攻克雅思》，就像傻瓜相机、傻瓜电脑，“傻瓜”的意思是连傻瓜都会操作，潜台词是：何况我们这些正常人呢？无奈反对的人太多，他们最有说服力的理由便是：你这是在侮辱学习者的智慧！最好把“傻瓜”二字去掉！我笑而从之，去掉便去掉，我在前言里说明白！

狮子和蚂蚁骄傲的理由

我有一个怀才不遇的朋友，他告诉我为什么蚂蚁会不痛苦，而狮子会孤独。蚂蚁目光短浅，体积微小，而狮子体积庞大，目光长远，进而知世界之大，从而倍感己之渺小。而我则认为，狮子和蚂蚁都应是骄傲的，因为狮子有思想，而蚂蚁有朋友。

倘若把给此书提意见的老师和朋友也算上的话，可以开一个小型学校了。在编写此套丛书的过程中，我们也借鉴和吸收了很多已出版书中的精华，正应了那句话：我来晚了，所以我必须得站在巨人的肩膀上。正是因为这一点，我才敢拍着胸脯讲，别的书中有的优点，我们有，而我们有的优点，别的书未必有，那我们这套书有哪些独特的优点呢？

阶梯性：全套书基本上分为三个阶梯，不同水平段的同学可以选择从不同的阶段开始练习，即便如此，我还是强烈建议大家踏踏实实从第一天的练习开始，毕竟来考雅思的同学必须面对自身英语水平相对薄弱的现实。

仿真性：本书所有的练习题都或多或少地来源于真题，例如在阅读分册中，我们是根据历次雅思考试出现的话题，到英文材料中找到其原文，再根据雅思的命题规律，由外教和考官重新命题，如多次考到的厄尔尼诺现象、儿童孤独、蜘蛛的习性……

趣味性：在编写此套书的过程中，所有的编者一致并且多次互相强调该书的趣味性。在此插入我的一句“名言”——如果学习对于你来说是一种痛苦的话，最好的办法是把学习材料撕掉。而学习的快感来源于两处，即每天看到自己进步的成功感和学习过程中对生活的体验。

而这套书有什么缺点呢？——缺点就是我们说了实话！

首先，从书的名字上我们就打破了短期见效的培训神话，也打击了大多数考生的投机心理。因为我始终坚信：与其一击不中，卷土重来，不如稳扎稳打，一刀拿下。有些培训学校打出了一期不过，免费重读或无效退款的广告，我劝那些为之所动的同学为自己考虑考虑，浪费的钱财谁来补给？逝去的青春谁来赔偿？

其次，智者千虑，必有一失！在二校和三校的过程中，我们都陆续地发现一些疏漏和错误，因此，在成书中也必定会存在一些毛病，我们真诚地欢迎所有的读者给我们指出我们的错误和不足，并提出您的宝贵意见。请相信我们的诚意和虚心！

五位我钦佩和感谢的人

俞敏洪——是他让许许多多像我这样除了英语之外一无是处的人喝得上美酒，穿得起西服，并且有了时间和空间去思考。感谢他创造了一个曾经让我梦寐以求的地方，尽管这个地方现在成为了我的靶子。

王中伟——是他当时不拘一格地提升我早熟地当上了戴尔国际英语学校的副校长，我视他为怪才或称他为“刘邦”。我对培训产业的切实体会启蒙于他，也是他让我在嗅到了鲜花甜美的同时，也尝到了汗水和眼泪的复杂滋味，我感谢他，尽管我们最终分道扬镳。

冯小平——文都的董事长，感谢他在这两年来为我提供了一个宽广的平台，让我得以走遍祖国的各大省市，积累了第一手的各地学生的资料，让我颇有一种要救学生于水火之中的冲动，尽管他并不是十分看好雅思。

刘　玮——这套书的责任编辑，她的执着和认真是我选择石油工业出版社的直接原因，尽管我对她在这一年中无数次的催稿、校稿电话躲闪不及。

我的女友——感谢她在这几年中对我的工作一如既往地怀疑、肯定和再怀疑。她的美影响了我对整个世界美的看法，也感谢她对于此套书付出的汗水和努力，仅仅是因为她爱我的原因，尽管我时常对她的唠叨和牢骚颇为不满。

2003.6.1于北京

2011年2月28日购于卓越网

陈小桂

IELTS 核心词汇 本书前言

近几年来,英联邦国家成为国人出国选择的热门,国内掀起了雅思学习和考试的热潮。而如何快速有效地记忆单词，成为广大考生及其他英语学习者的一大问题。大家急需一本与雅思考试紧密挂钩，能迅速提高学生听说读写能力的单词书。应江涛先生之邀编写了本词汇书。

本书在编写方面做了一些新的尝试：首先是把词汇分为80天进行学习，已达到目标明确、短期高效的目的。而80天中又分为三部分。

编者从Webster's Universal College Dictionary （韦氏国际大学辞典）中颉取并结合历届雅思考试出现的单词收集了10000个左右词汇，首先删去其中中学教育已涉及的词汇，然后请（美）龙泰先生、（英）Martin Green 先生对其中过于偏僻或已失去时代价值的词汇进行删减，最后获得3000词汇。然后承美国莱斯大学Eve Bower女士再从中选出2000个在大学学习和海外生活中最常用的单词，编者对其进行了精心炮制。其余1000个词汇作为提高和巩固使用。

▶ 第一部分 ◀

1至65天，记忆最重要的2000个单词。编者首先对单词进行分类，一般的单词书是按照字母顺序编排的，查找起来容易，但记忆时就会使人陷于枯燥。本书打破了字母顺序，按单词间的语义联系编排。尽量使学生可以联系记忆，国内外的众多语言学家都很推崇这一做法，编者希望这也能给雅思学员以帮助。

本部分第一大特色，是编者联系雅思考试，对每一个单词进行演绎。其中例句是一大特色，雅思考试强调考生要灵活使用长句，但是传统辞典普遍存在着例句较短、较旧的问题，远不能达到雅思考试的要求。编者从**最新海外报纸、杂志和网站上精心挑选立意新颖、句式灵活多变的长句型例句，**参考多部权威词典，精心为每个单词炮制和翻译了两个例句，（美）Eve Bower女士也为之倾注了很多精力，为本书制作了很多精彩的例句。第一个例句，用于提高大家的阅读能力，把单词放在一定的语言环境中，让学生猜出它们的情景意，培养语感，提高阅读能力，同时也可以加深对单词的印象。第二个例句放在最后，题名为“大头例句”，是编者精心打造和选择的或语义诙谐、或立意新颖、或句式优美的句子，便于大家背诵记忆，用于提高学生的口语和写作水平。

本部分的第二大特色，是对每个单词进行了**词根分析**。将长词化为短词来记。并给了学生一把学习英语单词内部结构的金钥匙。俗话说“理解的才是记忆的”，通过对单词内部结构的理解来记住单词是本部分的另一目的。

本部分的精华部分，编者将其命名为**“大头巧记”**，实有自嘲之意。编者学习和教授英文多年，积累了很多记单词的经验和想法，也走了很多弯路。编者认为自己走更多的弯路，花更多的时间寻找巧妙记忆的方法，就可以使读者朋友少走些弯路，记单词时少花些时间。编者通过词形联想、词音联想、拆分单词、词源记忆等多种方法，尽最大努力将单调的记忆变成愉快的消遣，以求根本解决单词记忆难的问题。最多的时候，在一个单词记忆方法的寻求上花掉过一个多小时的时间，编者感觉头大如斗，于是自名为“大头”以自嘲。在单词的记忆方法上，编者进行了一项大胆尝试，化抽象记忆为具体画面记忆。给读者一个场景或形象，而将字母直接传达为图像的方法被大多数学者所推崇。经试验证明，人脑对具体的图像记忆力要强和轻松的多，对以形象思维能力著称的汉语人群尤其如此。如:

mimic （模仿） [大头巧记] mimi, 咪咪， 猫的声音，猫模仿老虎的动作。

aesthetic （美学） [大头巧记] 学科的词很多以 tic 结尾，属共同特征。所以只要记住 aesthe 表美学即可，aes，反过来写是 sea，海洋，the，定冠词，the sea，大海，把大海反过来，何等壮观，具有美学特性。

希望编者的努力可以为广大的英语学习者提供方便，或一些记忆上的新思路。

本书还提供了另一种记忆方法：**“习语记忆”**。编者为某些单词精选了几个实用诙谐的习语，以提高读者记忆的兴趣，同时也为口语、写作和听力提供一些素材。

总之，本书是要通过多种记忆方法综合记忆，不断强化，已达到让学生完全掌握该部分单词的目的。

第二部分

66至70天为较难的提高词汇，1000多个，共分5天记忆。该部分主要为雅思阅读服务，也可提高学生们的词汇量。只要求大家记住词性和词意。也就是所说的“见面认识”即可。要求大家集中记忆，“临阵磨枪”。可以通过视觉（看）、听觉（读）、嘴部感觉（说）和手部感觉（写）来循环综合记忆。最大限度地在雅思考试前期增大单词量，提高阅读能力。

第三部分

编者根据雅思考试常涉及的内容，制作了10个专题，分10天记忆，即71至80天。每个专题提供100至200个最常用单词。目的是在雅思考试的最后前10天熟悉专题，扩充词汇量。记忆要求比前面又低一些，只要求对单词有印象，大体记得意义。并在几个相关专题后面提供了相应的阅读材料，扩展学生视野，巩固相关词汇。

IELTS 前言

三个部分，区别对待，互相补充，以求在最短的时间内达到最好的效果。该书的编写过程历时近一年，其间得到众多朋友的帮助。在此，我首先要感谢我的未婚妻Eve Bower女士的帮助和支持；还要感谢江涛先生在编写过程中的指导、审校和在经济上的支持；北京外国语大学高级翻译学院赵利光老师、(美)Christian 女士和北京外国语大学任仲奇先生在翻译上的帮助；北京外国语大学王心先生、陈光先生在词语分类和材料选择方面的帮助；(美)Caroline Catts小姐在英语部分校对工作方面的帮助；北京外国语大学高级翻译学院潘琛东先生在各方面的支持，等等。

最后，我用哈奇森的一句话与大家共勉，祝各位考生成功！

Wisdom denotes pursuing of the best ends by the best means.

—— *Hutcheson*

明智是指用最好的办法寻求最好的目标。

——哈奇森

孟 飞

2003年6月16日于北京

IELTS 核心词汇

目录

第一阶段 基础篇（1–65 天）

目录

Day 1~65

IELTS 核心词汇

第1阶段

基础篇

-ed读音：1. 一般[t]
2. t/d后读[id]
3. 元音或浊辅音后[d]
[d][g][v][z][r][m][n].

etc. 读 etcetera，也可读 and so forth

contract.
/kən'trækt/ 收缩，感染
/'kɒntrækt/ 合同，订约

contrast
/'kɒntræst/ 对比

bureaucracy n. 官僚

bureaucratic adj.

official. n. 官员
adj. 官方的，正式的

officer n. 工作人员

'regal adj. 帝王的.
'legal adj. 法律的，合法的

Day 1~65 快乐指南

大家好，我是Sof，中文名索夫——你们的向导，有什么问题请发邮件至Sofielts@Yahoo.com.cn

在这里我要给大家介绍一位新朋友——“大头”！他是我最好的哥们儿，名字听起来怪怪的，学习英语时也是怪招不断，不过效果却极为不错哦，本人也跟他学了不少高招，哈哈！在这65天里，他将陪伴大家为雅思考试打下坚实的词汇基础。希望大家会喜欢他！

大家好，我是大头，很开心认识大家，在这65天里，我们要掌握雅思考试中最重要的一部分单词。每天30个单词左右，为了方便大家记忆，我把相关的单词放在了一起，这样大家可以放开自己的想象力，联系记忆，我试过这种方法，效果棒极了！ :-)我是不是有点儿王婆卖瓜——自卖自夸，不过精彩的还在后面呢！

为了在学习单词的同时培养阅读、写作、口语及听力各方面的能力，我对每个单词进行了展开：刚开始就开门见山，抛出一个例句，让大家猜一猜单词在句中的情景意，培养语感，锻炼大家的阅读能力，同时也诱导我们改变传统的被动记忆方式，主动参与单词的记忆，加深对单词的印象。然后我对每个单词进行了词根分析，化长为短，颇得“分个敌人，分而歼之”的军事思想，哈哈，可能又要有人说大头“shameless”了 :-)不过这确实可以帮助大家通过对单词内部结构的理解来记住单词。下面这个部分可以说是我的“得意之作”，不能说“呕心沥血”，也算得上“殚精竭虑”了；大头我使尽了全身解术，通过词形联想、词音联想、拆分单词、词源记忆等多种方法，尽最大努力将单调的记忆变成愉快的消遣，愉快学习一直是我学英语的信条，其中不乏妙招，但怪招、奇招也随处可见；黑猫白猫，抓住老鼠就是好猫；很多人会笑我奇怪，但是只要能让大家对单词印象更深，记得更快、更牢、更轻松愉快，吾愿足矣！

紧接着，我将单词的各个主要意项罗列出来，让大家来记忆学习。然后是另一个例句，这一个尤为关键，名字叫"大头例句"，哈哈！雅思考试强调考生使用句子要活，要新，要多用长句；但是传统辞典的例句较短、较旧，远不能达到大家的要求，而课堂上学到的也只是杯水车薪。这个准备必须从平时日积月累，大头从最新海外报纸、杂志和网站上精心挑选，并参考多本权威词典为大家选了很多立意新颖、句式灵活多变的例句，还请一些海外的朋友为大家专门炮制了很多面向雅思口语和写作的精彩长句。这些句子，或幽默好玩，或句式严谨，或用词灵活，或立意新颖；大家一定要好好利用哦！

最后我还为大家留了些习题，目的还是要加深大家对单词的印象，句子都来自于例句部分，所以答案可以自己寻找，这就要求大家反复多次回去复习，更重要的是锻炼大家根据句子猜词意的能力。千万不要“再回首恍然如梦”，要用心哦！

不过还是要提醒大家，该部分的每一个词都很重要，大家一定要完全掌握，不仅要认得，还要会用，要和它们交朋友，成为很好的朋友，没有了它们的支持，你的雅思可是很难令人满意的哦。:-)

所以我们每天交30个新朋友，但也不要忘老朋友，每天记得不多，越是要记得很好。“愿我们到处都有好朋友！”

enter：进入
'exeund：退场
eksiʌnt

Day 1

abject *adj.* /ˈæbdʒekt/

Tom's company was bankrupt during the Great Depression; then, he was in *abject* poverty.

[猜一猜]A 可怜的　B 反对的　C 健康的　D 惊人的

[翻　译]汤姆的公司在大萧条期间破了产，那时他一贫如洗。

[分　析] ab + ject
away + throw → 被扔到一边的 → 可怜的，卑鄙的

[大头巧记]object，物体，东西，去掉 o (own，拥有)，换上了 a (ask，要)，从有东西到要东西的变化，确实可怜。

[近义词]**miserable** 悲惨的，可怜的
wretched 可怜的，肮脏的

[词义扩展]*adj.* ①卑鄙的；下贱的 *an abject trickster* 卑鄙的骗子 ②不幸的；可怜的 *abject poverty* 一贫如洗

advocate *vt.* /ˈædvəkit/

Some experts strongly *advocate* building more private colleges.

[猜一猜]A 肯定　B 主张　C 花费　D 研究

[翻　译]有些专家极力主张建立更多的私立大学。

[分　析] ad + vocate
朝向 + 呼吁，倡导 → 主张

[联　想]**vocation** *n.* ①职[行]业，业务，使命；②(对某种职业的)适合性，才能
commercial vocation 商务行业
have no [*little*] *vocation to* [*for*] *arts* 不[不大]适合搞文艺
另：**avocation** *n.* (个人)副业，业余爱好
advocacy *n.* 主张

[词义扩展]*n.* 辩护者；律师；拥护者；替人说情者 *an advocate of feminism* 拥护或提倡女权主义的人

[大头例句]He was called Devil's advocate at the meeting. 在会上他被称为魔鬼的拥护者。(在英文中喻吹毛求疵的人，爱抬扛的人或爱提反面意见的人)

brutal *adj.* /ˈbruːtl/　brute adj.残忍的 n.畜生，残忍的人

The police have arrested the *brutal* sniper who commited Wednesday night's fatal shooting of a man at a gas station just south of the nation's capital.

[猜一猜]A 凶残的　B 可爱的　C 愤怒的　D 贪婪的

[翻　译]警方已经抓住了周三晚上在国家首都南部的一个加油站制造致命枪击案件的凶残罪犯。

[分　析] berut + tal
brut (禽兽) + 形容词词尾 → 像禽兽一样的 → 凶残的

[词义扩展]①粗暴无礼的 ②严酷的；无情的 *a brutal winter* 严冬 ③令人不快又无可否认的 *speak with brutal honesty* 坦白地说

[大头例句]The brutal treatment can never bend her to betray her nation. 残酷的拷打永远不能使她屈服而背叛自己的国家。

clumsy *adj.* /ˈklʌmzi/

You are so *clumsy*! Look, you've knocked over my cup of coffee again!

[猜一猜]A 粗暴的　B 笨拙的　C 品质坏的　D 惹人厌的

[翻　译]你真是笨手笨脚，看，又把我的咖啡打翻了。

[分　析]clums + y
麻木 + 形容词词尾 → 有麻木性质的 → 笨拙的

[词义扩展]*adj.* 愚笨的，粗陋的，(文体)臃肿的

[大头例句]I made a clumsy but well-meaning attempt to comfort you. 我想要安慰你们的意图虽然愚笨但却是好意的。

dignity *n.* /ˈdigniti/

The *dignity* of the occasion was lost when he cut in with an unrefined joke.

[猜一猜] A 愉快　B 紧张　C 火药味很浓　D 庄严

[翻　译] 他突然插进一则粗俗不堪的笑话,使当时的庄严气氛丧失殆尽。

[分　析] dign + ity
有价值的 + 名词词尾 → 有价值的东西 → 威严,尊严,庄严,光荣

[大头巧记] dig + nity
挖掘 + 名词词尾 → 挖掘 → "钻研"是一种高尚的品格。

[词义扩展] *n.* 高职位,光荣,神圣

[大头例句] A man's dignity depends not upon his wealth or rank but upon his character. 人的真正价值不在财富或地位,而在他的品格。

ferocious *adj.* /fəˈrəuʃəs/

The *ferocious* tiger tore the lamb apart with its teeth.

[猜一猜] A 微小的　B 饱的　C 残忍的　D 热烈的

[翻　译] 那只残忍的老虎用牙齿把小羊羔撕了个粉碎。

[分　析] feroc + ious
凶猛 + 形容词词尾 → 凶猛的,残忍的

[词义扩展] 非常的,激烈的
a ferocious bore 非常讨厌的家伙

[大头例句] Many people were killed in the flooding caused by last night's ferocious storm. 很多人在昨天凶猛的暴风雨造成的洪水中丧生。

hound *vt.* /haund/

The police are always *hounding* him.

[猜一猜] A 买断　B 敌视　C 怀疑　D 追踪

[翻　译] 警方一直在追捕他。

[大头巧记] hound,源于古英语 hund,猎狗,hound 本身也有猎犬的意思。→ 用猎狗追踪。

[词义扩展] *n.* ①卑鄙的人 ②热衷于(某事)的人 *rock hound* 地质学家

[大头例句] She was sick of being hounded by the press. 她厌恶于媒体对她的追踪。

idle *adj.* /ˈaidl/

His words were just *idle* threats; you don't have to take them too seriously.

[猜一猜] A 无来由的　B 善意的　C 认真的　D 故意的

[翻　译] 他的话只不过是吓人的空话,你不必太认真了。

[大头巧记] id(ea) (litt)le 没有什么主意的 → 闲着的,懒的,无根据的

[词义扩展] *vt./vi.* 虚度;(机器)空转;消磨时间
Don't idle! 不要吊儿郎当!

[大头例句] This country will not remain idle if its friends are attacked. 如果它的盟友被攻击的话,这个国家不会坐视不管的。

lavish *vt.* /ˈlæviʃ/

He thought he would win her over by *lavishing* her with expensive gifts.

[猜一猜] A 吸引　B 显露　C 遗忘　D 慷慨地给予

[翻　译] 他本以为给她大量的贵重礼物就可以赢得她的芳心。

[分　析] lav + ish
洗浴 + 词尾 → 像洗浴池中的水那么多的慷慨给予 → 挥霍

[词义扩展] *adj.* 慷慨的,过度的,大量的

[大头例句] Skyscrapers become lavish consumers and wasters of electric power. 摩天大楼成为电力的消费大户,甚至成为电力的浪费者。

nasty *adj.* /ˈnæsti/

I don't like the colour they've chosen for their new carpet — it looks really *nasty*.

[猜一猜] A 令人厌恶的　B 单调的　C 暗淡的　D 颜色绚丽的

[翻　译] 我不喜欢他们所选的新地毯的颜色——看

起来很恶心。

[大头巧记] nasal(鼻子的) → nasty(鼻涕般的) → 污秽的，恶心的

[大头例句] Though she smiled as she said it, there was a nasty tone in her voice that let me know for sure how angry she was. 她说话的时候虽然笑着，但她声音中那令人不快的音调却让我清楚地认识到她很生气。

miser n. /ˈmaizə/

He really is a *miser*: for my birthday, he gave me a piece of grass because he said it was the cheapest thing he could find!

[猜一猜] A 坏人　　B 小丑　　C 吝啬鬼　　D 好心人

[翻　译] 他真是个吝啬鬼：我过生日的时候，他送给我一根草，说是因为那是他能找到的最便宜的东西！

[大头巧记] 和 **moneygrubber**(守财奴)同义。

[大头例句] You should not be such a miser fowards children. 你不应该对孩子这么吝啬。

optimism n. /ˈɔptimizəm/

There is a touch of *optimism* in every worry about one's own moral cleanliness.

[猜一猜] A 悲观　B 自省　C 乐观　D 良心

[翻　译] 在对自身道德纯净度的每次焦虑中，都存在一种乐观因素。

[分　析] optim + ism
最好 + 词尾 → 把什么都想成最好的 → 乐观，乐观主义

[大头巧记] 和 **pessimism**(悲观)联合记忆。

[大头例句] The optimism of the postwar years inspired them to rebuild their hometown. 战后岁月里的乐观思想鼓舞他们重建家园。

renowned adj. /riˈnaund/

The coast is *renowned* for its beautiful beaches.

[猜一猜] A 有声誉的　　B 开发的　　C 旅行的　　D 财源的

[翻　译] 这个海岸因其美丽的海滩而享有盛名。

[分　析] re + nown + ed
一再 + 名字 + 形容词词尾 → 名字一再出现的 → 有名的，有声誉的

[大头巧记] re + (k)nown + ed
一再 + 知道 + 形容词词尾 → 名字一再被人所知 → 有名的

[大头例句] Internationally renowned artist Jiang Tao will have an exhibition this Saturday afternoon, after which time he will speak briefly about his artistic philosophy. 国际知名艺术家江涛将于本周六下午举办展览会，此后他将简单陈述自己的艺术哲学。

rigorous adj. /ˈrigərəs/

Capital spending is *rigorously* controlled.

[猜一猜] A 拘谨的　　B 争论的　　C 严格的　　D 松弛的

[翻　译] 资金的花销被严格控制。

[分　析] rigor + ous
王 + 形容词词尾 → 像君主一样统治的 → 严格的，一丝不苟的，严酷的

[大头例句] A rigorous course load in school will not only challenge your abilities and help you know your limits as an individual, but it will provide valuable preparation for the work force, in which you will almost certainly have more responsibilities than time. 学校里严峻的课程负担不仅是对你能力的挑战，帮助你了解自己作为个体的极限，还会为你的工作能力提供有价值的准备，在工作时你一定会有忙不完的职责。

talented adj. /ˈtæləntid/

She is really a *talented* writer.

[猜一猜] A 自私的　　B 荒谬的　　C 天才的　　D 肤浅的

[翻　译] 她确实是个天才的作家。

[分　析] talent + ed
天才 + 形容词词尾 → 天才的，有才能的

vigorous *adj.* /ˈvigərəs/

We need a *vigorous* campaign to reduce deaths on the roads.

[猜一猜]A 不实际的 B 挑剔的
C 有力的 D 让人高兴的

[翻 译]我们需要一个有力的措施来减少马路上的死亡事件。

[大头巧记]**vigor 精力，活力**
vigorous 精力旺盛的，有力的

[大例头句]They demanded more vigorous action to tackle the disease. 他们要求采取更有力的行动来应付这种疾病。

virtuous *adj.* /ˈvəːtjuəs/

Sam's *virtuous* and superior tone was beginning to irritate me.

[猜一猜]A 道德的 B 美丽的
C 诱人的 D 天真的

[翻 译]萨姆道学而高傲的腔调开始让我不舒服。

[分 析]virtu + ous
道德 + 形容词词尾 → 道德的，善良的，有效力的

[大头巧记]联系反义词 **vicious**（不道德的），**nefarious**（邪恶的）记忆。

[大例头句]Thomas was a virtuous man and a leader in the community. 托马斯是个有德之人并在社团中担任领导。

vulgar *adj.* /ˈvʌlgə(r)/

Educated people should avoid using *vulgar* language.

[猜一猜]A 普通的 B 奉承的
C 欺骗的 D 粗俗的

[翻 译]受过教育的人应避免说粗话。

[分 析]vulg + ar
庸俗 + 形容词词尾 → 粗俗的，普通的，通俗的。

wisdom *n.* /ˈwizdəm/

I wonder where your *wisdom* has gone.

[猜一猜]A 智慧 B 嫉妒 C 计划 D 痛苦

[翻 译]不知道你的智慧到哪里去了。

[分 析]wis + dom
英明 + 名词词尾 → 智慧，学识，名言，贤人

[习语记忆]**cut one's wisdom teeth** [喻] 开始成熟起来

Learn wisdom by the follies of others. [谚] 从旁人的愚行中学到智慧。

No wisdom like silence. 智者寡言。

That's good wisdom which is wisdom in the end. [谚]聪明到底才算真。

[大例头句]The conventional wisdom is that governments should lead rather than simply reflect public opinion. 大多数的意见认为政府应该领导而不是仅仅反映公众的主张。

spiritual *adj.* /ˈspiritjuəl/

Music provides an immensely satisfying *spiritual* experience for many people.

[猜一猜]A 迷人的 B 不容置疑的
C 精神上的 D 奇怪的

[翻 译]音乐为很多人提供了无限的精神满足的体验。

[大头巧记]**spirit 精神**
spiritual 精神上的

[词义扩展]*adj.* 神的，宗教的，高尚的
spiritual songs 圣歌

[大例头句]As a priest, I'm responsible for your spiritual welfare. 作为一名牧师，我有责任让你精神安宁。

vegetarian *n.* /ˌvedʒiˈteəriən/

My wife is a *vegetarian*, but she is ok with my eating meat.

[猜一猜]A 基督徒 B 天主教徒
C 伊斯兰教徒 D 素食主义者

[翻 译]我妻子是素食主义者，但是她不在乎我吃肉。

[分 析]veget + arian （vegetable 蔬菜）
植物 + …的人 → 只吃植物的人 → 素食主义者，食草动物

[词义扩展]*adj.* 素食的

习题：在下面的空格中填入本单元出现的单词。

1. You are so __________! You've knocked over my cup of coffee again!
2. He thought he would win her over by __________ her with expensive gifts.
3. The coast is __________ for its beautiful beaches.
4. Tom's company was bankrupt during the Great Depression; then, he was in __________ poverty.
5. She was sick of being __________ by the press.
6. Some experts strongly __________ building more private colleges.
7. The __________ of the occasion was lost when he cut in with an unrefined joke.
8. They demanded more __________ action to tackle the disease.
9. My wife is a __________, but she is ok with my eating meat.
10. Educated people should avoid using __vulgar__ language.
11. As a priest, I'm responsible for your __________ welfare. n. 幸福. 福利(事业)
12. The __________ treatment can never bend her to betray her nation.
13. The __________ tiger tore the lamb apart with its teeth.
14. He really is a __________: for my birthday, he gave me a piece of grass because he said it was the cheapest thing he could find! threaten v. 恐吓
15. His words were just __________ threats; you don't have to take them too seriously.
16. I don't like the colour they've chosen for their new carpet — it looks really __________.
17. The__________ of the postwar years inspired them to rebuild their hometown.
18. She is really a __________ writer.
19. Capital spending is__________ controlled.
20. Tomas was a __________ man and a leader in the community.
21. I wonder where your __________ has gone.

Day 2

abase *v.* /ə'beis/

A man who betrays(出卖) a friend *abases* himself.

[猜一猜] A 享受 B 有利于 C 降低 D 烦恼

[翻　译] 一个人出卖了朋友也就降低了自己。

[分　析] a + base

to (去) + 底部 → 变得较低,降低自己

[大头巧记] ab(离开) + ase(American Stock Exchange 美国证券交易所) → 身无分文地离开证券交易所 → 自己的身份降低了。

[联　想] 词尾去 e, abas (打倒) 音近词: abash 使…羞愧, 使…脸红, 使局促不安

[近义词] **degrade (使降级)**

[词义扩展] *v.* 贬, 降低 (地位, 价值, 身分); 自卑, 自贬; 下降

[大头例句] I will not abase myself by dating a girl like that. 我不会自贬身份去和那样的女孩子约会。

altitude *n.* /'æltitjuːd/

The plane flew at an *altitude* of 20,000 metres.

[猜一猜] A 高度 B 航线 C 距离 D 区域

[翻　译] 飞机在两万米的高空飞行。

[分　析] alt + itude

high + 名词词尾 → 高度

[词义扩展] *n.* (海拔)高度

[大头例句] It is difficult to breathe at the high altitudes of Tibet. 在西藏海拔很高的地方呼吸比较困难。

ascend *v.* /ə'send/

The fire balloon *ascended* to a height of 500 feet in a graceful curve.

[猜一猜] A 漂浮 B 启动 C 舞蹈 D 上升

[翻　译] 热气球以优美的曲线攀升到500英尺的高度。

[分　析] as + cend

to + climb → 爬,攀登,上升

[词义扩展] *vi.* 追溯到 *vt.* 登上(王位)

[大头例句] Ascending to the morality of the time, we can see how the famous philosophy inspired the revolution. 回顾当时的道德观念, 我们可以明白这个著名的哲学理论是如何激发了一场革命的。

alight *vi.* /ə'lait/

The queen *alighted* from the carriage.

[猜一猜] A 明亮 B 跳起 C 减轻 D 下来

[翻　译] 女王从马车上下来。

[分　析] a + light

表强调 + 轻的 → 减轻, 卸掉包袱 → 从…下来

[词义扩展] *vi.* ①飞落下来并停住 *The bird alighted on a twig.* 那只鸟飞下来落在细树枝上。② 下车 *We planned to alight in Shanghai.* 我们原计划在上海下车。③凑巧碰到 *alight on a happy solution* 偶然发现一个皆大欢喜的解决方法

adj. 发亮(的); 燃着(的) *The lamp was still alight until the next morning.* 直到第二天早晨,灯还亮着。

acme *n.* /'ækmi/

He reached the *acme* of his career in his forties.

[猜一猜] A 低潮 B 顶点

C 机遇 D 成功

[翻　译] 四十多岁的时候,他达到了自己事业的顶峰。

[大头巧记] act me, 去掉 t — top, 不再有顶点的情况下表现自我,达到了自己的最高点。

[近义词] **crown; peak; summit; top; zenith**

[词义扩展] *n.* ①【古生】顶峰期;【生】极盛期 ②弧点, 最高点 ③聚变期

acme of science 科学尖端

the acme of one's hope 最高的愿望

[习语记忆] **be [reach] the acme of perfection** 十全十美，尽善尽美

[大头例句] On the acme of success, you feel the same cold as on the acme of the mountain. 高处不胜寒。

bounce *v.* /bauns/

After *bouncing* over the potholes for a whole afternoon, our car finally arrived at the campsite.

[猜一猜] A 通过 B 跳动 C 损坏 D 抛锚

[翻　译] 在坑坑洼洼的路面上晃荡了整整一个下午，我们的车终于到达了宿营地。

[大头巧记] b(eat) the ounce(雪豹)，打了雪豹以后有两种可能：(1)它跳着跑开；(2)你跳着跑开。

[词义扩展] *v.* ①（球）跳起，（使球）弹起 *The boy was bouncing a ball.* 小男孩在拍皮球。②跳上跳下 *Just at that moment her husband bounced into the room.* 就在这时她丈夫猛然冲进房来。③（支票）遭银行退票

n. ①（球）跳起；弹回 *The ball has plenty of bounce.* 球的弹力很好。②活泼；顽皮 *Her brother has a lot of bounce.* 她的弟弟很活泼。③〈经〉（股市价格的）回弹，反弹

[大头例句] If your business accepts checks for payment, eventually a bad one will bounce through. 如果你的经营业务以收取支票作为付款方式的话，最终很可能会有透支支票出现。

compass *n.* /ˈkʌmpəs/

The *compass* is one of the four most important inventions in Chinese history.

[猜一猜] A 火药 B 指南针 C 印刷术 D 造纸

[翻　译] 指南针是中国历史上的四大发明之一。

[分　析] com + pass
完全地 + 通过 → 环绕，界限，指南针

[大头巧记] 折：com(e) pass，过来通过的时候需要用指南针辨别方向。

[词义扩展] *n.*①[常用复]圆规 ②范围，界(限)，境界 ③迂回的路，绕行 ④圆周

v. ①获得，达到 ②图谋，计划 ③(在辩论中)兜了一圈又回到原处 ④完全了解

[大头例句] Suddenly we compassed the enemies on all sides. 我们突然从四面八方将敌人包围了。

climax *n.* /ˈklaimæks/

It is time to bring the matters to a *climax* now.

[猜一猜] A 高潮 B 结局 C 障碍 D 实施

[翻　译] 到了把事情推向高潮的时候了。

[分　析] cli + max
倾向于 + 最大程度上 → 最大程度的倾向 → 高潮，顶点

[词义扩展] *vi.&vt.*(使)达到顶点[高潮]

[大头例句] Her determination and hard work climaxed during her appointment as chairwoman. 她的决心和努力在被指定为主席时达到顶点。

decline *v.* /diˈklain/

The culture of China has not *declined* in spite of Western influence and repeated wars.

[猜一猜] A 衰落 B 断裂 C 发展 D 专横

[翻　译] 虽然有西方的影响和屡次的战争，中国文化并没有因此而走向衰落。

[分　析] de + cline
向下 + 倾斜，弯曲 → 向下倾斜

[大头巧记] dec 谐"低"，line(线)，低的线 → 下降

[词义扩展] *vt.&vi.* ①下降，下倾 ②衰退，衰落 *The empire that had declined still occupied a vast territory.* 业已衰落的帝国仍然占有庞大的疆土。③谢绝，婉谢 *I declined their offer of help.* 我婉言拒绝了他们提供的帮助。

*n.*①下倾，下垂 ②下跌，下落 ③衰落，衰退

descend *v.* /diˈsend/

Ahead of us is a rough path *descending* like a steep stair into the plain.

[猜一猜] A 向下延伸 B 通向 C 向上延伸 D 展示

[翻　译] 在我们的前方是一条小路，像陡峭的楼梯般向下面延伸进入平原。

[分 析] de + scend
向下 + 爬 → 向下延伸 → 下来，下降

[词义扩展] v. ①(财产等)传给，遗传 ②转而说到，涉及 ③降低身份去做 ④突然去访问，袭击 *Men are descended from ape-men.* 人是由类人猿转变而来的。

[大头例句] He traces his descent from an old Norman family. 他有古诺曼底人的血统。

enhance *v.* /inˈhɑːns/

She had a sweetness to her face, a warmth that was *enhanced* by luminous dark eyes.

[猜一猜] A 表现 B 装饰 C 装饰 D 提高

[翻 译] 她的面容甜美，因那双明亮的黑眼睛而充满热情。

[分 析] en + hance
使 + 高 → 使提高，增加

[词义扩展] v. 夸张，宣扬

[大头例句] The measures taken should considerably enhance the residents' quality of life. 这些措施的实行应当在相当程度上提高居民的生活质量。

democracy *n.* /diˈmɔkrəsi/

The main task of that organization is to promote *democracy* in developing countries.

[猜一猜] A 稳定 B 发展 C 医疗 D 民主

[翻 译] 这个组织的主要任务就是推进发展中国家的民主进程。

[分 析] demo + cracy
人民的 + 政体 → 人民性的政体 → 民主政体

[大头巧记] 音译记忆，德莫卡拉希，就是陈独秀所说的德先生——民主。

[词义扩展] n. ①民主，民主主义，民主国家 *economic democracy* 经济民主 ②Democracy[美]民主党 *the democracy* 老百姓

[大头例句] We have to do something to popularize democracy to the world. 我们必须为民主的普及做点事情。

gravity *n.* /ˈɡræviti/

Anything that is dropped falls towards the centre of the earth because of the pull of *gravity*.

[猜一猜] A 拉力 B 动能 C 保护 D 重力

[翻 译] 物体脱手即向地心方向跌落是由于重力吸引的缘故。

[分 析] gravi + ty
重的 + 名词词尾 → 重力，重量，万有引力

[词义扩展] n. 认真，庄重，重要[危险，严重]性 *keep one's gravity* 不苟言笑

[大头例句] Offenders should be punished in proportion to the gravity of their offences. 罪犯应该根据他们罪行的大小而被给予相应的惩罚。

hoist *vt.* /hɔist/

The sailors *hoisted* the flag and the ship was ready to start on a long voyage.

[猜一猜] A 收起 B 换过 C 升起 D 卸下

[翻 译] 水手们升起船上的旗帜，轮船准备好出发远航。

[词义扩展] n. 升起，起重机

[大头例句] The publicity hoisted ticket sales to 12,500 in two days. 宣传使得售票量在两天内增加到12500张。

inferior *adj.* /inˈfiəriə/

This design is *inferior* to the one the British company proposed, so we would not accept it.

[猜一猜] A 相联系的 B 较好的
C 差的 D 一样的

[翻 译] 这个设计方案比英国公司所提议的那个差，所以我们不会使其通过。

[分 析] infer + ior
低的 + 表示比较级 → 劣质的，差的，下等的

[词义扩展] n. (地位，能力)低下的人，部下，晚辈，次品

[习语记忆] **inferior by comparison** 相形见绌

[大头例句] No inferior products should be allowed to pass. 决不允许放过任何次品。

hierarchy *n.* /ˈhaiərɑːki/

He was taught to put honesty first in his ***hierarchy*** of values.

[猜一猜] A 表现 B 趋向 C 层次 D 发展

[翻　译] 他被教导要把诚实放在他自己的价值层次的首要地位。

[分　析] hier + archy

神圣 + 统治 → 宗教统治 → 等级制度 → 层次

[词义扩展] *n.* 动、植物学的分类(纲，目，科，属等)；统治集团

[大头例句] He reached a high level within the Soviet political hierarchy. 他达到了苏联政治等级内的高层。

likelihood *n.* /ˈlaiklihud/

Do you think there is any ***likelihood*** of his agreeing to it?

[猜一猜] A 疑问 B 可能性 C 原因 D 影响

[翻　译] 你认为他有同意此事的可能性吗？

[分　析] likeli + hood

可能的 + 名词词尾 → 可能性，可能

[大头例句] In all likelihood the vase was made in China. 这个花瓶十有八九是中国产的。

plummet *vi.* /ˈplʌmit/

The president's popularity has ***plummeted*** since the war began.

[猜一猜] A 直线上升 B 直线下降 C 保持稳定 D 大起大落

[翻　译] 战争爆发以来，总统的声望直线下降。

[大头巧记] 原意为铅锤，引申为直线下降。

[大头例句] The stock market's 1929 plummet was one of the most influential events of the twentieth century. 1929 年股市的暴跌是 20 世纪最具影响的事件之一。

radar *n.* /ˈreidə/

We located an aircraft by ***radar***.

[猜一猜] A 雷达 B 智慧 C 激光 D 探测

[翻　译] 我们通过雷达对飞机进行定位。

[大头巧记] 本词属于音译词：radar，雷达。

pitch *v.* /pitʃ/

We ***pitched*** a camp in the woods for the night.

[猜一猜] A 制作 B 搭 C 铺开 D 离开

[翻　译] 我们在林地搭帐篷过夜。

[词义扩展] *n.* 程度，斜度，沥青，市场 *v.* 投，用沥青涂 *The hill pitches steeply.* 小山陡峭。

[习语记忆] **Touch pitch, and you will be defiled.** 近朱者赤，近墨者黑。

[大头例句] In British society, for a sales pitch to have massive appeal, it has the tripleponged challenge of needing to be innovative, entertaining, and memorable. 在英国社会，一个销售市场如果要具有很大的吸引力的话，新颖、有趣和有纪念意义是需求量的三大挑战。

superior *adj.* /sjuːˈpiəriə/

Towards the end of the game Agassi's ***superior*** strength began to show.

[猜一猜] A 出众的 B 愤怒的 C 傲慢的 D 慷慨的

[翻　译] 在比赛接近尾声的时候，阿加西出众的能力开始显示。

[大头巧记] **super** ***adj.*** 超级的

superior n. 高手，上级 ***adj.*** 出众的

另：和 **inferior**(下等的，次的)对应记忆。

[大头例句] I'll report you to your superior officer. 我要向你的上级官员告发你。

trend *n.* /trend/

We've seen a ***trend*** towards more violent films this year.

[猜一猜] A 合同 B 趋势 C 经验 D 危害

[翻　译] 今年我们看到暴力影片有增多的趋势。

[大头巧记] 和 **tendency**(趋向)联系记忆。

[词义扩展] *vi.* 伸向，转向，趋向

[大头例句] Rambo set the trend for a whole wave of violent action movies.《兰博》(史泰龙的代表作)为暴力动作片的浪潮带了个头。

underneath *adv./prep.*/ˌʌndəˈniːθ/

They looked down from the bridge at the water *underneath.*

[猜一猜] A 在下面 B 不驯的 C 奔流 D 污染

[翻 译] 他们从桥上观看桥下的水。

[分 析] under + neath

neath adv. 在…之下.

在…下 + 向下 → *prep.* 在…下面

adv. 在下面

[大头巧记] 联系记忆 **beneath** ***adv./prep.*** 在下面

[习语记忆] **treachery lying underneath a mask of friendliness** 口蜜腹剑,笑里藏刀

[大头例句] Underneath you will see soft silky fur, very different from the fur on the animal's back. 在底下你将看到柔软的丝般的皮毛,它和动物背上的皮毛很不同。

习题:在下面的空格中填入本单元出现的单词。

1. The stock market's 1929 __________ was one of the most influential events of the twentieth century.
2. He reached the __________ of his career in his forties.
3. Her determination and hard work __________ in her appointment as chairwoman. 任命
4. The main task of that organization is to promote __________ in developing countries.
5. Suddenly we __________ the enemies on all sides.
6. The culture of China has not __________ in spite of Western influence and repeated wars.
7. The measures taken should considerably__________ the residents' quality of life.
8. It is difficult to breathe at the high __________ of Tibet.
9. Ahead of us is a rough path __________ like a steep stair into the plain.
10. The lamp was still __________ until the next morning .
11. __________ you will see soft silky fur, very different from the fur on the animal's back.
12. __________ to the former century, we can see how the famous philosophy inspired the revolution.
13. *Rambo* set the__________ for a whole wave of violent action movies.
14. We located an aircraft by __________.
15. Do you think there is any __________ of his agreeing to it?
16. We'll __________ a camp in the woods for the night.
17. I will not __________ myself by dating a girl like that.
18. Anything that is dropped falls towards the centre of the earth because of the pull of __________.
19. The sailors __________ the flag and the ship was ready to start on a long voyage.
20. This design is __________ to the one the British company proposed.
21. If your business accepts checks for payment, eventually a bad one will__________ through.
22. He reached a high level within the Soviet political __________.
23. Towards the end of the game Agassi's __________ strength began to show.

Day 3

abate *v.* /ə'beit/

I began my sailing when the storm *abated*.

[猜一猜] A 开始 B 分开 C 加强 D 减弱

[翻 译] 当风暴减弱的时候我开始了我的航程。

[分 析] a + bate

to (去) + to beat, (打) → 打击某物 → 使它减弱

[联 想] **abet** *vt.* 唆使，鼓动，怂恿，助长

abet the commission of a crime 教唆犯罪

abut *vi.&vt.* 邻接，毗连；靠紧，接近 *My house abuts on the Summer Palace.* 我的家和颐和园挨着。

amate *v.* 使挫折，使懊恼

[近义词] **curtail; decrease; do away with; lessen; moderate; put an end to; reduce**

[词义扩展] *v.* ①减弱；减轻；减低 *We should abate the economic burden of the peasants.* 我们应该减轻农民负担。

②消除；停止 *It is difficult to abate polluting in developing countries.* 在发展中国家停止污染是很困难的。

augment *v./n.* /ɔːg'ment/

He *augmented* his income by translating English poems in his spare time.

[猜一猜] A 骗取 B 增加 C 赚取 D 消遣

[翻 译] 他在空闲的时候翻译英文诗来增加收入。

[分 析] aug + ment

增加 + 名词词尾 → 增加，扩大（可活用为 *vt./vi.*）

[大头例句] Internet medical sources should augment, not replace doctors' advice. 网上医学资料应该增加，而不是替换掉医生的建议。

aggregate *adj.* /'ægrigeit/

Due to your effort, the *aggregate* sales in our market have increased a lot.

[猜一猜] A 一般的 B 部分的 C 总共的 D 减价的

[翻 译] 由于你的努力，我们公司的销售总量已经有了很大的提高。

[分 析] ag + gregate

朝向 + 收集 → 收集在一起 → 总共的

[大头巧记] 记住其主体部分 gregate，拆为 GRE gate，GRE 考试的门前聚集了很多人。

[词义扩展] *vt.* ①结合；集结；(使)聚集 ②共计，计达 *The money collected at that bank will aggregate a billion dollars.* 那家银行的进账将达十亿美金。

[大头例句] The population of the world will soon amount to 6 billion in the aggregate. 世界人口总量不久就将达到60亿。

deduct *vt.* /di'dʌkt/

The tax will be *deducted* from your wages directly.

[猜一猜] A 计算出 B 推断出 C 偿还 D 扣除

[翻 译] 税钱将直接从你的薪水中扣除。

[分 析] de + duct

去掉 + 引导 → 引导去掉 → 减少 → 扣除

[词义扩展] *v.* 追溯；(演绎地)推论

[大头例句] Nothing will be deducted from your pay without your consent. 没有你的许可，我们不会从你的报酬中扣除任何费用。

diminish *v.* /di'miniʃ/

The delay may well have *diminished* the impact of their campaign.

[猜一猜] A 挑起 B 消除 C 减小 D 转移

[翻 译] 延期可能已经大大地减小了他们竞选运动的影响。

[分 析] di + mini + sh

减少 + 小 + 形容词词尾 → 缩小，变小，减

少。

[大头巧记] mini，迷你型，把某物变成迷你型，变小。

[词义扩展] v. 贬低 *He likes to diminish the ability of others.* 他喜欢贬低别人的能力。

[大头例句] His illness diminished his strength. 他的病让他浑身无力。

gauge *v.* /geidʒ/

> I *gauge* the distance to the office building to be about 200 metres.

[猜一猜] A 估计 B 设计 C 标明 D 决定

[翻　译] 我估量到办公楼大约有200米的距离。

[大头巧记] 注意它与 **gouge** /gaudʒ/ 的区别，**gouge** 意为：**圆凿，欺骗，敲竹杠**。

[词义扩展] n. 标准尺寸，(铁道)轨距，测量仪器，(电线)直径 v. 估计，评价

[大头例句] New orders are a gauge of how well manufacturers are doing. 新规则是制造商经营情况的衡量标准。

maximum *adj.* /ˈmæksiməm/

> Though you have completed all of your assignments for this course, the *maximum* final grade you can expect is 80% because your attendance has been so poor.

[猜一猜] A 最终的 B 主课的 C 辅修的 D 最高的

[翻　译] 虽然你完成了本课程的所有的任务，可是你能得到的最高的期末成绩是80分，因为你的出勤率太低了。

[大头巧记] 数学上表示最大值的符号"max"即是maximum的简写。

[词义扩展] n. 最大量，最大数，极点 *reach a maximum* 达到顶点

[大头例句] 20 kg of luggage is the maximum we allow on the flight. 我们所允许的带上飞机的最高重量是20千克。

minority *n.* /maiˈnɔriti/

> With only a *minority* of the total vote, George W. Bush was elected 43rd president of the United States.

[猜一猜] A 多数 B 半数 C 少数 D 足够

[翻　译] 乔治·布什仅以总选票中的少数当选为美国的第43任总统。

[分　析] minor + ity

更少的 + 名词词尾 → 少数，少数民族，未成年

[大头巧记] 和它的反义词对比记忆：**majority** /məˈdʒɔriti/ **n. 多数，成年**。

[习语记忆] **be in a minority of one** 得不到任何人的支持

[大头例句] The nation wants peace; only a minority wants the war to continue. 全国人民想要和平，只有少数人希望继续打仗。

minus *prep.* /ˈmainəs/

> *Minus* the amount spent on food and clothing, I earned a total of 7,000 pounds for my work in London.

[猜一猜] A 算上 B 减去 C 为了 D 负担

[翻　译] 减去花在吃穿上的钱，我在伦敦工作总共挣了7000英镑。

[大头巧记] 联系其反义词 **plus(加上)** 一起记忆。

[词义扩展] *prep.* 零下…度 *n.* 负号 = minus sign *adj.* 负的，减的

minus 20 degrees 零下20度

[大头例句] 10 minus 7 leaves 3. 十减去七剩三。

majority *n.* /məˈdʒɔriti/

> In its purest form, democracy is governance by the decision of the *majority*.

[猜一猜] A 群众 B 市民 C 多数 D 少数

[翻　译] 民主的最纯粹形式是通过多数人的决策来进行管理。

[分　析] major + ity

大多数的 + 名词词尾 → 多数，大半，多数派，法定年龄

[大头巧记] **major** *n.* 专业，主修课 → **majority** *n.* 多数。另：**minority** *n.* 少数，少数民族

[大头例句] Wilson won with an overall majority of 60 percent. 威尔逊以60%的大体多数选票胜出。

minimal *adj.* /ˈminiməl/

My boyfriend prefers that I wear only a *minimal* amount of makeup, as he says it allows my natural beauty to shine through.

[猜一猜] A 特殊的　B 漂亮的　C 最少的　D 进口的

[翻　译] 我的男友更喜欢我只用最少量的化妆品，他说这样可以让我的自然美焕发出来。

[大头巧记] **mini 迷你型，袖珍型 → minimal 最少的，最小限度的。**

[大头例句] Alcohol has a particularly unpleasant effect on me when I have a minimal amount of food in my stomach. 当我的胃中只有极少量食物时，喝酒就会使得我非常难受。

numerous *adj.* /ˈnjuːmərəs/

Those birds have become more *numerous* lately.

[猜一猜] A 无聊的　B 众多的　C 流行的　D 警惕的

[翻　译] 近来那种鸟变得越来越多了。

[分　析] numer + rous
数字 ＋形容词词尾 → 数目众多的

[大头例句] Scientists have documented numerous advantages to the non-smoking lifestyle including prolonged life expectancy, decreased incidence of illness, younger-looking appearance, and decreased risks during pregnancy. 科学家们已经证明了无烟生活方式众多的好处，包括延长生命，减少发病率，拥有更年轻的外表和降低怀孕期间的风险。

multiply *v.* /ˈmʌltiplai/

3 *multiplied* by 5 is 15.

[猜一猜] A 加　B 减　C 乘　D 除

[翻　译] 三乘五等于十五。

[分　析] multi + ply
多的 ＋动词词尾 → 变成多倍的 → 乘

[词义扩展] *v.* 增加，繁殖 *Within the last 20 years, both sales and profits have multiplied.* 在过去的二十年里，销售和赢利都有很大增加。

[大头例句] Rabbits are famous for their high rate of fertility: given just a few short years, they seem to multiply and an original two can easily become thirty or more! 兔子以高繁殖率而著称，仅短短几年的时间，他们就几乎能从最初的两只轻松地变成30只或更多！

multitude *n.* /ˈmʌltitjuːd/

The *multitude* may laugh at his music, but we college students know better.

[猜一猜] A 犯罪者　B 一般人　C 受教育者　D 边缘人口

[翻　译] 平常人可能会笑话他的音乐，可我们大学生知道不是那么回事。

[分　析] multi + tude
多的 ＋名词词尾 → 多数人，群众一般人

[大头巧记] **altitude 高度；latitude 纬度；multitude，多的范围 → 多数**

[词义扩展] *n.* 大量，众多 *hide a multitude of sins* 隐藏很多的罪恶

[大头例句] In today's economy, students who fluently speak more than one language face a multitude of job opportunities. 在今天的经济中，能够熟练地讲一种以上语言的大学生面临着大量的工作机会。

nought *n.* /nɔːt/

Unfortunately, all their plans came to *nought.*

[猜一猜] A 无　B 成功　C 辉煌　D 实践

[翻　译] 不幸的是，他们所有的计划结果都是一场空。

[分　析] no + ught
没有 ＋thing → 没有东西 → 无，零

[大头例句] I misplaced the wallet which contained all my savings from the last three months; it seems all my hard work was for nought. 我忘记我把钱包放在哪里了，里面有我过去三个月所有的积蓄，我所有的努力工作都好像成了一场空。

maintain v. 维持 /menteɪn/

maintenance *n.* /ˈmeintinəns/

These two countries were trying their best at the *maintenance* of the good cooperation between them.

[猜一猜] A 利润　B 可能　C 投资　D 保持

[翻　译] 这两个国家正在尽他们最大的努力以保持两国间良好的合作关系。

[分　析] main + ten + ance
手 + 拿住 + 名词词尾 → 用手拿住 → 维持,保持,抚养

[大头巧记] 本词是 maintain 的名词形式。注意 maintain 中的第二个"ai"组合到了名词形式中变成了"e"。

[大头例句] The maintenance of international peace and security is everyone's responsibility. 维持国际和平与安全是每个人的责任。

quantitative *adj.* /ˈkwɔntitətiv/

The differences are not measurable in *quantitative* terms.

[猜一猜] A 性质的　B 谨慎的
C 专业的　D 数量的

[翻　译] 这些差别是不能用数量来衡量的。

[分　析] quantita + tive
数量 + 形容词词尾 → 数量上的,定量的

[大头巧记] 注意和 **qualitative/ˈkwɔlitətiv/**(性质的)区别记忆。

redundant *adj.* /riˈdʌndənt/

5,000 miners were made *redundant* when the tin market collapsed.

[猜一猜] A 流失的　B 多余的
C 后悔的　D 安置的

[翻　译] 罐装市场倒闭后,5000 名矿工成为多余劳力。

[分　析] re + dund + ant
一再 + 波动 + 形容词词尾 → 一再出现 → 多余的,过剩的

sufficient *adj.* /səˈfiʃənt/

Will the growth in output be *sufficient* to meet the increased demand?

[猜一猜] A 充足的　B 明智的
C 重要的　D 幸运的

[翻　译] 产量的增加足够满足增长的需求吗?

[分　析] suf + fici + ent
下面 + 做 + 形容词词尾 → 下面做好了的 → 充足的

[大头例句] We can only prosecute if there is sufficient evidence. 我们只有在证据充足时才会提出起诉。

习题:在下面的空格中填入本单元出现的单词。

1. Poor plumbing __________ from the value of the house.
2. We should __________ the economic burden of the peasants.
3. __________ the amount spent on food and clothing, I earned a total of 7,000 pounds for my work in London.
4. Wilson won with an overall __________ of 60 per cent.
5. My boyfriend prefers that I wear only a __________ amount of makeup, as he says it allows my natural beauty to shine through.
6. Scientists have documented __________ advantages to the non-smoking lifestyle including prolonged life expectancy, decreased incidence of illness, younger-looking appearance, and decreased risks during pregnancy.

7. In today's economy, students who fluently speak more than one language face a __________ of job opportunities.
8. He __________ his income by translating English poems in his spare time.
9. Due to your effort, the __________ sales in our market has increased a lot.
10. I __________ the distance to the office building to be about 200 metres.
11. The delay may well have __________ the impact of their campaign.
12. We can only prosecute if there is __________ evidence.
13. I misplaced the wallet which contained all my savings from the last three months; it seems all my hard work was for __________.
14. With only a __________ of the total vote, George W. Bush was elected 43rd president of the United States.
15. 20 kg of luggage is the __________ we allow on the flight.
16. The children are learning to __________ and divide.
17. 5,000 miners were made __________ when the tin market collapsed.
18. These two countries were trying their best at the __________ of the good cooperation between them.
19. The differences are not measurable in __________ terms.

Note 前事不忘后事之师 *Remember the past and it will guide your future.*

Day 4

abeyance n. /əˈbeiəns/

From May 1st 2004, the law will go into *abeyance*.

[猜一猜] A 服从　　B 制定
C 修改　　D 暂时无效

[翻　译] 从2004年5月1日起，这个法令要暂时无效。

[分　析] a　+ beyance
at，对　+ baer，目瞪口呆 → 对某物目瞪口呆，当然要先暂时中止

[词义扩展] n. 中止，暂搁，保留，未定；【律】(所有权等的)未定

abdicate v. /ˈæbdikeit/

As a member of this club, you can't *abdicate* your responsibilities.

[猜一猜] A 吞噬　B 放弃　C 感激　D 尊敬

[翻　译] 作为这个俱乐部的成员，你不能放弃你的责任。

[分　析] ab　+ dicate
(away)离开 + 发表宣言 → 宣布离开 → 放弃

[大头巧记] 谐音法：abdicat，我不离开的

[近义词] **abandon; give up; quit**

[词义扩展] *vt.* 放弃(权利)，让位，辞职
abdicate a chance 放弃一个机会
abdicate the throne in sb.'s favour 让位给某人

abort vi/n. /əˈbɔːt/

The official *aborted* the take off because of the fog.

[猜一猜] A 买下　B 减少　C 回避　D 取消

[翻　译] 由于雾的缘故，那个官员取消了起飞。

[分　析] ab　+　ort
away from + to arise, grow → 停止了生长 → 夭折，流产，此处引申为取消

[联　想] **abortion** *n.* ①流产 *induced abortion* 人工流产 ②失败；夭折 *Their government's attempt to ameliorate working conditions proved an abortion.* 他们的政府试图改善工人工作条件的努力完全失败了。
abortive *adj.* ①无结果的；失败的 *It would be an abortive effort to try to close this wide price gap.* 设法缩小这样大的价格差距将是徒劳的。②早产的；发育不完全的

abrogate vt. /ˈæbrəugeit/

This law has been *abrogated* because of the new situation.

[猜一猜] A 公认　B 承认　C 改善　D 废除

[翻　译] 因为新的形势，这个法律已经被废除了。

[分　析] ab + rogate
去掉 + 要求 → 要求去掉 → 废除

[大头巧记] abroad 出国；gate 大门。出国的大门如果没有 a—aim(目标)和 d—dollar(美钞)的话，就要废止了。

abscond vi. /æbˈskɔnd/

The police are looking for the man who *absconded* with the bank's money.

[猜一猜] A 旅游　B 潜逃　C 犯罪　D 拖欠

[翻　译] 警方正在寻找那个携银行款潜逃的人。

[分　析] ab + scond
远离 + to put → 远远地放置自己 → 潜逃，逃跑

[大头例句] My wife gave me some money to buy her some makeup, but I absconded with it. I was dying to smoke. 妻子给了我一些钱让我帮她买化妆品，我却"携款潜逃"了，因为我太想抽烟了。

barrier n. /ˈbæriə/

The police put a *barrier* across every road out of the the city to find the suspects connected to the shooting.

[猜一猜]A 岗哨　B 摄像机　C 启示　D 路障

[翻　译]警察在出城的每条路上都设置了路障，以寻找与枪击案有关的嫌疑人。

[分　析]bar　+ rier

横木 + 词尾 → 用横木做成的障碍物

[词义扩展]*n.* 障碍，妨碍因素，界线

vt. 用栅围住

[大头例句]The visit of the president removed the barrier between our two countries. 总统的来访消除了我们两国间的障碍。

breakdown *n.* /ˈbreikdaun/

The *breakdown* in health has little influence on his strong will.

[猜一猜]A 崩溃　B 打倒　C 解决　D 保持

[翻　译]健康的崩溃没有对他那坚强的信念产生什么影响。

[大头巧记]词组：break down 毁掉，分解

[词义扩展]*n.* ①衰弱 ②细目分类

[大头例句]He has suffered from his nervous breakdown for more than two years. 他患神经衰弱症已经两年多了。

bankrupt *n.* /ˈbæŋkrʌpt/

Many companies went *bankrupt* because of their poor management during the economic depression.

[猜一猜]A 亏损　B 停业　C 破产　D 借贷

[翻　译]在经济衰退期间，很多公司因经营不善而破产。

[分　析]bank + rupt

银行 + 破坏 → 破产

[词义扩展]*n.* 破产者 *vt.* 使破产；使穷困

adj. 完全丧失

[大头例句]Zhong's wife's extravagance bankrupted him quickly. 钟某妻子的奢侈生活很快就使他破产了。

cease *v.* /siːs/

At last the factory *ceased* production for lack of capital.

[猜一猜]A 增加　B 停止　C 规划　D 参考

[翻　译]由于缺乏资金，这家工厂最终停了产。

[大头巧记]拆 c(ertain) ease，必然的轻松来源于停止工作。

[词义扩展]*n.* ［通常只与 without 搭配］停止，终止 *I am working without cease to finish my papers on time.* 我不停地工作，以按时完成我的论文。

[大头例句]Our love should never cease. 我们的爱永无休止。

deter *v.* /diˈtəː/

We'll see whether the negotiated disarmament can *deter* war or not.

[猜一猜]A 区分　B 推迟　C 阻止　D 孤立

[翻　译]裁军协议能否阻止战争，我们将拭目以待。

[分　析]de　+ ter

表否定 + 恐吓 → 用恐吓手段使某事不发生 → 使不敢，威慑，阻拦，不许

[大头例句]It's this edge that gives nuclear weapons their power to deter. 就是这个优势给了核武器与众不同的威力。

drawback *n.* /ˈdrɔːbæk/

The main *drawback* of the scheme is its expense.

[猜一猜]A 特点　B 成分　C 缺点　D 优点

[翻　译]这个计划的惟一的缺点就是它的花费。

[分　析]draw + back

拉　+ 向后 → 向后拉，拖后腿 → 缺点

[词义扩展]*n.* 退税（进口货物再出口时海关退回税款）

[大头巧记]One drawback of New York in the summer is the heat. 纽约夏天的一个缺点就是热。

doom *n.* /duːm/

He predicted *doom* for any country that did not act immediately.

[猜一猜]A 灭亡　B 失败　C 发展　D 改革

[翻　译]他预言任何一个国家如果不马上行动起来就会有灭顶之灾。

[词义扩展]*vt.* 注定，判决

[大头例句] The invention of the train doomed the canals to extinction. 火车的发明注定了运河的消亡。

halt n. /hɔːlt/

Traffic was brought to a *halt* by the demonstration.

[猜一猜] A 混乱 B 暂停 C 苦恼 D 危险

[翻 译] 交通因示威游行而暂停了。

[大头巧记] 形近词：**hold 控制** *hold back* 阻止；**halt 停止，中止，暂停。**

[词义扩展] *vt./vi.* 停止，立定，踌躇，犹豫 *The search halted overnight, then resumed early Thursday morning.* 搜寻工作在前天晚上停止了，随后在周四早上又恢复了。

[大头例句] No one can halt the advance of history. 谁也阻挡不了历史的前进。

handicap n. /ˈhændikæp/

Poor eyesight is a *handicap* to a student.

[猜一猜] A 通病 B 小毛病 C 标志 D 障碍

[翻 译] 视力不好对学生来说是一个障碍。

[大头巧记] 词源记忆：hand in cap，旧时的一种赌博游戏，因参加者将罚金置于帽中而得名。赢者在下一次发牌时必须加注(罚金)，并将其置于帽中，这样来给输者以翻本的机会。后引申为给与优胜者不利条件以使竞赛机会均等。再引申为障碍之意。

[词义扩展] *vt.* 使不利，妨碍 *Some applicants were handicapped by their poor level of English.* 一些申请者可怜的英文水平给他们带来很多不利。

[大头例句] Lack of money handicapped him in his business badly. 缺少资金对他的生意十分不利。

hinder adj./v. /ˈhində/

The travelers were *hindered* by storms throughout their journey.

[猜一猜] A 顺利 B 迷路 C 阻碍 D 打扰

[翻 译] 旅行者们一路上被暴风雨所阻碍。

[大头巧记] **hind (后面的)，hinder，** 后面的东西在拉后腿 → **阻碍，妨碍。**

[大头例句] "Go and join the army," said his wife. "I won't hinder you." "去参军吧，" 他妻子说："我不会阻拦你的。"

impede v. /imˈpiːd/

The deep snow *impeded* our making an early start.

[猜一猜] A 鼓励 B 妥协 C 妨碍 D 引发

[翻 译] 深雪阻碍了我们早点动身。

[分 析] im + pede

里面 + 脚 → 把脚放到…里面 → 妨碍，阻止。

[大头例句] The darkness was impeding my progress. 黑暗在阻碍我的前进。

meddle v. /ˈmedl/

I don't mean to *meddle* in your personal affairs, but I really do believe you should not be seeing this other man while your husband waits for you at home.

[猜一猜] A 管闲事 B 催促 C 漠然 D 紧张

[翻 译] 我不想故意干涉你的私事，但是我确实觉得在你的丈夫在家等你的时候你不应该和别的男人约会。

[大头巧记] 通过同音词"**medal(奖牌)**"记忆它的另一个义项"摸弄"。*Don't meddle with my medal* 不要胡乱摸弄我的奖杯。

[大头例句] Who has been meddling with my papers? 谁动了我的文件？

neutralize v. /ˈnjuːtrəlaiz/

We need a policy of *neutralizing* possible conflicts before they arise.

[猜一猜] A 消解 B 掀起 C 暴露 D 调查

[翻 译] 我们需要一个在可能的矛盾出现之前将其消解掉的政策。

[分 析] nertral + ize

中性 + 动词词尾 → 中和掉 → 消解，压制

[联 想] **neutralise** /ˈnjuːtrəlaiz/ *v.* 使中和

[大头例句] To neutralize the spicy taste in one's mouth after eating some Chinese dishes, drinking milk is an effective agent. 为了消除吃完某些中餐后口中的辣味，喝牛奶是一种有效的

方法。

mansion *n.* /ˈmænʃən/

To the south of the *mansion*, there is a tennis court; to the east there is a swimming pool.

[猜一猜] A 俱乐部　　B 大厦
C 足球场　　D 体育馆

[翻　译] 在这座大厦的南边有一个网球场，东面是一个游泳池。

[大头巧记] manse(牧师住宅) → 很大的房子 → 大厦，官邸，公寓楼。

[大头例句] The expansion plan for the mansion includes ten new bedrooms, four new bathrooms, and two new kitchens! 该大厦的扩建计划包括十个新卧室、四个新洗手间和两个新厨房。

marble *n./adj.* /ˈmɑːbl/

Many of the most regal structures in ancient Rome were built using *marble*, and until this day, they have not begun to decay.

[猜一猜] A 木料　　B 大理石
C 火山岩　　D 青石

[翻　译] 古罗马时代的大多数王室建筑是用大理石建成的，直到今天还没有开始朽败。

[习语记忆] **lose one's marbles** 失去理智
go for all the marbles [俚]全力以赴

[大头例句] Chinese checkers is a game that uses many different colors of marbles. 跳棋是一种用许多不同颜色的石弹子玩的游戏。

permeate *v.* /ˈpəːmieit/

Our thinking is *permeated* by our historical myths.

[猜一猜] A 升华　B 集中　C 开放　D 渗透

[翻　译] 我们的历史神话渗透我们的思想。

[分　析] per + mea + (a)te
全部 + 通过 + 动词词尾 → 渗透，弥漫，透入

[大头巧记] 拆：per+me+ate，每一个我吃的东西，都渗透着农民的汗水。

[大头例句] Some of the more traditional cultures of the world highly resent the way America's culture has permeated and sometimes begun to replace their own ways of life through means such as McDonald's and blue jeans. 世界上一些较传统的文化很憎恶美国文化通过像麦当劳和蓝色牛仔裤对他们进行渗透，有时甚至开始取代他们原有的生活方式。

pierce *vt.* /piəs/

A nail *pierced* the tire of our car.

[猜一猜] A 刺破　　B 阻隔
C 燃烧　　D 弄出斑点

[翻　译] 一个钉子将我们的车胎扎了一个洞。

[分　析] pier + ce
穿过 + 词尾 → 穿破，刺破

[大头巧记] piece(一块东西)，用“r”将它刺破。

[词义扩展] 洞察，打动，响彻
pierce a disguise 识破伪装

[大头例句] Many frustrated parents fear the milder forms of teenage rebellion: pierced navels, eyebrows, and other assorted parts of the body. 很多父母对青年人温和方式的反叛很郁闷：在肚脐、眉毛和其他身体各种部位打眼儿穿孔。

surrender *v./n.* /səˈrendə/

No terms except unconditional and immediate *surrender* can be accepted.

[猜一猜] A 明确　B 良心　C 投降　D 猛击

[翻　译] 除去无条件立即投降，其他条件一概无法接受。

[分　析] sur + render
下面 + 给 → 放下武器 → 投降

[词义扩展] *v./n.* 交出，放弃，投降
Never surrender. 决不投降。

[大头例句] Critics feel that Paul has surrendered his artistic identity in his later films. 评论家们觉得保罗在他后来的影片中失去了自己的艺术特性。

习题：在下面的空格中填入本单元出现的单词。

1. The __________ in his health has little influence on his strong will.
2. Many companies went __________ because of their poor management during the economic depression.
3. At last the factory __________ production for lack of capital.
4. Some applicants were __________ by their poor level of English.
5. “Go and join the army,” said his wife. “I won’t __________ you.”
6. As a member of this club, you can’t__________ your responsibilities.
7. The official __________ the take off because of the fog.
8. This law has been __________ because of the new situation.
9. To the south of the __________, there is a tennis court; to the east there is a swimming pool.
10. Some of the more traditional cultures of the world highly resent the way America’s culture has __________ and sometimes begun to replace their own ways of life through means such as McDonald’s and blue jeans.
11. Many frustrated parents fear the milder forms of teenage rebellion: __________ navels, eyebrows, and other assorted parts of the body.
12. I don’t mean to __________ in your personal affairs, but I really do believe you should not be seeing this other man while your husband waits for you at home.
13. No terms except unconditional and immediate __________ can be accepted.
14. To __________ the spicy taste in one’s mouth after eating some Chinese dishes, drinking milk is an effective agent.
15. From May 1st 2004, the law will go into __________.
16. The police are looking for the man who __________ with the bank’s money.
17. We’ll see whether the negotiated disarmament can__________ war or not.
18. No one can __________ the advance of history.
19. The invention of the train __________ the canals to extinction.
20. The main __________ of the scheme is its expense.
21. The police put a __________ across every road out of the city to find the suspects connected to the shooting.
22. The darkness was __________ my progress.
23. Many of the most regal structures in ancient Rome were built using __________, and until this day, they have not begun to decay.

Day 5

antibiotic *n./adj.* /ˌæntibaiˈɔtik/

That factory is famous for it's production of *antibiotics*, which are exported to many countries.

[猜一猜] A 洗衣机　B 抗生素　C 防毒软件　D 水处理设备

[翻　译] 这家工厂以其抗生素产品而扬名，这些抗生素被出口到很多国家。

[分　析] anti + bio + tic
反 + 生命 + 词尾 → 抗生素，抗生的

[大头巧记] 记住 bio 词根的另一个词：**biology(生物学)**

[大头例句] Antibiotics are very important during war. 在战争期间抗生素很重要。

artery *n.* /ˈɑːtəri/

Arteries carry blood away from the heart to the cells, tissues, and organs of the body.

[猜一猜] A 动脉　B 静脉　C 心血管　D 毛细血管

[翻　译] 动脉将血液从心脏输送到身体的各细胞、组织和器官。

[分　析] arter + y
管道 + 名词词尾 → 动脉

[词义扩展] *n.* 干线，要道；中枢

[大头例句] This road is one of the main arteries that lead to Tibet. 这条公路是通往西藏的主干线之一。

bacterium (*pl.* bacteria)

n. /bækˈtiəriəm/

Bacteria in the soil break down the dead leaves.

[猜一猜] A 蘑菇　B 昆虫　C 细菌　D 肥料

[翻　译] 土壤中的细菌分解落叶。

[大头巧记] bac(k)(回去)，ter（…的人），使…回到其原来状态的"人"→ 生物圈的降解者——细菌。

[大头例句] Bacteria consist of only a single cell, but don't let their small size and seeming simplicity fool you. 细菌只是由一个单细胞组成的，但是可别让它微小的尺寸和表面上的简单欺骗了你。

bruise *v.* /bruːz/

The fruit on sale here has already been *bruised* by careless packing.

[猜一猜] A 碰伤　B 腐烂　C 压碎　D 没有味道

[翻　译] 这里待售的水果在包装时不小心被碰伤了。

[词义扩展] *n.* 青肿，瘀伤 *v.* ①植物损伤碰伤 ②削弱或损害 ③捣碎，研细 ④(尤指精神上)伤害

[大头例句] What you just said bruised my feelings. 你刚刚说的话伤害了我的感情。

capsule *adj.* /ˈkæpsjuːl/

He has already sent out his *capsule* biography to pursue a new development in his career.

[猜一猜] A 系列的　B 详尽的　C 简略的　D 官方的

[翻　译] 他已经寄出了自己的简历，以寻求事业上的新发展。

[大头巧记] capsule 有"瓶帽"的意思，拆 cap sule → cap sue 帽子要控告瓶帽侵犯其姓名权。

[词义扩展] *n.* ①荚，胶囊，瓶帽 ②太空舱 ③摘要 *adj.* 简略的，小而结实的
vt. 压缩，节略，以瓶帽密封

[习语记忆] **in a capsule** [口]简明扼要的；概括地

[大头例句] The doctor suggested that he take two capsules a day. 医生建议他一天吃两粒胶囊。

chronic *adj.* /ˈkrɔnik/

We suffered a *chronic* shortage of food in that period.

He is a medical practitioner.
他是执业医生。 n. 执业者

[猜一猜]A 短期的 B 长期的
C 无聊的 D 痛苦的

[翻 译]在那段时期我们经历了长时间的食物短缺。

[分 析]chron + ic
时间 + 形容词词尾 → 长时间的,慢性的

[词义扩展]adj. ①慢性的 chronic colitis 慢性结肠炎 ②一贯的 a chronic smoker 一贯抽烟的人

[大头例句]The movie was pretty chronic, but we had a good laugh. 电影很长,但是我们笑得很开心。

clinical adj. /ˈklinikəl/

The undergraduate training in our medical college is divided between study and ***clinical*** practice.

[猜一猜]A 医药的 B 课外的
C 临床的 D 实习的

[翻 译]我们医学院的本科培训分为学习研究和临床实习。

[分 析]clinic + al
门诊部 + 形容词词尾 → 在门诊工作的,直接接触病人的 → 临床的

[词义扩展]①冷静的,慎重的,极度客观的 clinical judgement 客观的判断
②[新闻用语]训练有素的

[大头例句]They played excellent football and their passing was clinical. 他们足球踢得极好,传球非常出色。

cocaine n. /kəˈkein/

It is harmful and illegal to take ***cocaine.***

[猜一猜]A 鸦片 B 可可豆
C 赌博 D 可卡因

[翻 译]吸食可卡因对身体有害并且也是非法的。

[大头巧记]汉语名称是它的音译,根据发音很容易记忆。

deteriorate v. /diˈtiəriəreit/

The nation's economy is ***deteriorating*** at a rapid pace these years due to the overissue of bonds.

[猜一猜]A 发展 B 恶化 C 巨变 D 动荡

[翻 译]由于公债的过度发行,这个国家的经济近几年来迅速恶化。

[分 析]deterior + ate
更坏 + 动词词尾 → 变坏,恶化

[词义扩展]①败坏(风俗);使变坏 ②退化;堕落

[大头例句]The weather deteriorated overnight. 天气经过一个晚上,变得很糟。

diagnose v. /ˈdaiəgnəuz/

The general practitioner ***diagnosed*** the illness of my classmate as influenza.

[猜一猜]A 混淆 B 否认 C 诊断 D 照顾

[翻 译]这位全科医生诊断我的同学的病为流行性感冒。

[分 析]dia + gnose
通过 + 得知 → 判断,分析,诊断

[大头巧记]拆:dia (lo)g nose,对鼻子进行问话 → 诊断。

[词义扩展]v. 找出毛病

[大头例句]The teacher finally diagnosed the student's learning disability. 老师们最终找出了学生们学习上的问题。

epidemic adj. /ˌepiˈdemik/

Violence is reaching ***epidemic*** levels in some films and TV shows.

[猜一猜]A 泛滥的 B 夸大的
C 血腥的 D 变态的

[翻 译]在一些电影和电视剧中,暴力已经快到泛滥的程度了。

[分 析]epi + dem + ic
in + 人们 + 形容词词尾 → 在人们之间的 → 流行的,泛滥的

[词义扩展]n. 流行[传染]病,(风尚等的)流行,蔓延

[大头例句]An epidemic of petty crime has hit the area. 轻微犯罪的蔓延已经危及这个地区。

gasp v. /gɑːsp/

The swimmer came out of the water and ***gasped*** for breath.

[猜一猜]A 喘气 B 抬头 C 开口 D 划动

[翻 译]游泳者钻出水面,急切地喘了口气。

[大头巧记] **gas**(气体),**gape**(打呵欠) → **gasp**(喘气)。

[词义扩展] *v.* 气喘吁吁地说

I literally gasped at how beautiful it was. 它的美丽真是让我大吃一惊。

[习语记忆] **breathe one's last gasp** 断气;死亡

[大头例句] This is the last gasp of economic activity in this depressed part of the country. 这是这个国家经济萧条地区经济活动的最后一丝喘息。

genetic *adj.* /dʒiˈnetik/

Doctors believe the condition is caused by a ***genetic*** defect.

[猜一猜] A 生理的　B 心理的　C 心脏的　D 基因的

[翻　译] 医生们相信这种状况是由基因缺陷导致的。

[大头巧记] gene 音译为"基因";**genetic 基因的,遗传学的**。

[大头例句] The genetic makeup of an organism is encoded in its DNA. 从 DNA 中可以看出一个有机体的遗传基因的构成。

germ *n.* /dʒəːm/

It's a ***germ*** that causes sore throats.

[猜一猜] A 细菌　B 病毒　C 器官　D 药物

[翻　译] 这是一种让人喉咙疼的细菌。

[词义扩展] *n.* 种子,幼芽,起源,萌芽

[大头例句] We just know a little about the germ of life. 我们对生命的起源所知甚少。

ghastly *adj.* /ˈgɑːstli/

Robbing graves is ***ghastly***.

[猜一猜] A 害羞的　B 喜出望外的　C 可怕的　D 不安的

[翻　译] 盗墓是可怕的。

[大头巧记] **ghost**(鬼),**ghastly**,见了鬼的 → **可怕的,苍白的,令人不快的**

[大头例句] We had a ghastly time at the party. 在舞会上我们玩得很不愉快。

gown *n.* /gaun/

The doctor in the hospital wore a ***gown*** over his ordinary clothes.

[猜一猜] A 证件　B 听诊器　C 保护罩　D 长外衣

[翻　译] 医院里的医生在他平常穿的衣服外边罩一件大褂。

[词义扩展] ①大学礼服,法衣,(律师,法官)礼服 ②大学全体师生

[大头例句] She looks gorgeous in her white wedding gown. 她穿着白色的婚纱,看起来漂亮极了。

hectic *adj.* /ˈhektik/

There was nothing feverish or ***hectic*** about his vigor.

[猜一猜] A 忙乱的　B 无理的　C 危害的　D 坚定的

[翻　译] 他精力充沛但却毫不忙乱或狂热。

[分　析] hect + ic

许多 + 形容词词尾 → 有很多事要做的 → **繁忙的,忙乱的**

[词义扩展] *adj.* 发红的,发烧的,兴奋的

hectic cheeks 通红的双颊

[大头例句] The hectic trading on the stock exchange there reminded me of the years I spent in London. 那儿闹哄哄的股票交易让我记起了在伦敦的那几年。

herb *n.* /həːb/

There was an ***herb*** garden behind our house.

[猜一猜] A 月季花　B 假山　C 草本植物　D 盆景

[翻　译] 在我们家后面曾有一个百草园。

[词义扩展] *n.* 药草,香草

aromatic herbs 芳香草料

hygiene *n.* /ˈhaidʒiːn/

Wash regularly to ensure personal ***hygiene***.

[猜一猜] A 精神　B 紧张　C 卫生　D 健康

[翻　译] 经常洗澡以保证个人卫生。

[大头巧记] 源于希腊神话中的健康女神 Hygeia 海基亚。

[大头例句] Good personal hygiene is essential to limiting the incidence of infectious disease. 良好的个人卫生对于控制传染性疾病发生很重要。

immune *adj.* /iˈmjuːn/

The criminal was told he would be *immune* from punishment if he helped the police.

[猜一猜] A 判刑的 B 增刑的 C 免除的 D 邪恶的

[翻 译] 罪犯被告知,如果他协助警方,就可以免受惩罚。

[分 析] im + mune

没有 + 公共 → 不公共的 → 不受影响的,免除的

[大头巧记] immune 可谐音为"疫苗",联系到它的另外一个意项:免疫(性)的,有免疫力的。

[大头例句] Japan was by no means immune from continental influences. 日本决不可能不受大陆的影响。

muscular *adj.* /ˈmʌskjulə/

The player is big and *muscular.*

[猜一猜] A 灵活的 B 肌肉发达的 C 经验丰富的 D 谦虚的

[翻 译] 这个运动员长得魁梧强壮。

[大头巧记] **muscle** ***n.*** 肌肉

muscular ***adj.*** 肌肉发达的

[大头例句] A body with a high degree of muscular tone may be heavier but appear slimmer than another body with a higher concentration of fat. 肌肉高度发达的身体可能比脂肪度多的身体重点儿,但看上去却瘦些。

x-ray *n./v.* /ˈeks-rei/

The doctors took some *X-ray* pictures of my broken leg.

[猜一猜] A 谜语 B 圣徒 C X 片 D 奇妙

[翻 译] 医生给我受伤的腿拍了几张 X 光片。

[大头例句] The problem was only discovered when her lungs were X-rayed. 只到给他的肺做 X 光片,才发现了问题所在。

surgery *n.* /ˈsəːdʒəri/

Cancer usually requires *surgery.*

[猜一猜] A 外科手术 B 药物治疗 C 祈祷 D 坚强

[翻 译] 癌症通常需要外科手术。

[大头巧记] **surge** 汹涌;**surgeon** 控制病人波涛汹涌般病情的人 → **外科医生**;**surgery** 外科手术,外科。

[大头例句] Doctor Corday will be in surgery all morning. 考戴尔医生整个上午都会在手术室。

习题:在下面的空格中填写本单元出现的单词。

1. The doctor suggested that he take two__________ a day.
2. The undergraduate training in our medical college is divided between study and __________ practice.
3. The swimmer came out of the water and __________ for breath.
4. It's a __________ that causes sore throats.
5. That factory is famous for it's production of __________, which are exported to many countries.
6. The criminal was told he would be __________ from punishment if he helped the police.
7. The __________ trading on the stock exchange there reminded me of the years I spent in London.

8. The __________ makeup of an organism is encoded in its DNA.
9. The general practitioner __________ the illness of my classmate as influenza.
10. A body with a high degree of __________ tone may be heavier but appear slimmer than another body with a higher concentration of fat.
11. She had a __________ expression on her face.
12. The doctors took some __________ pictures of my broken leg.
13. This road is one of the main __________ that lead to Tibet.
14. __________ consist of only a single cell, but don't let their small size and seeming simplicity fool you.
15. Cancer usually requires __________.
16. She looks gorgeous in her white wedding __________.
17. There was a __________ garden behind our house.
18. Good personal __________ is essential to limiting the incidence of infectious disease.
19. The fruit on sale here has already been __________ by careless packing.
20. The movie was pretty __________, but we had a good laugh.
21. The nation's economy is __________ at a rapid pace these years due to the overissue of bonds.
22. It is harmful and illegal to take __________.
23. Violence is reaching __________ levels in some films and TV shows.

Note 前事不忘后事之师 *Remember the past and it will guide your future.*

Day 6

ambassador n. /æmˈbæsədə/

He was appointed *ambassador* to Britain.

[猜一猜] A 代理 B 记者 C 参赞 D 大使

[翻 译] 他被任命为驻英国大使。

[分 析] ambassad + or

embassy 大使馆 + …者 → 管理大使馆的人 → 大使

[词义扩展] n. 使者，代表

[大头例句] He is working as an ambassador of peace in the Middle East. 他在中东做和平大使的工作。

assassination n. /əˌsæsiˈneiʃən/

The *assassination* of President Kennedy made many people feel sorrow.

[猜一猜] A 卸任 B 上台 C 宣战 D 暗杀

[翻 译] 肯尼迪总统被暗杀让很多人感到悲痛。

[大头巧记] ①assassi 谐"我杀谁"(用西安话) → 谋杀

②ass+ass+in+ate → 一头驴，两头驴，走进去，吃了你 → 暗杀

[词义扩展] n. 中伤，诋毁

[大头例句] Character assassination always makes people annoyed. 人格诋毁总是让人讨厌的。

bilateral adj. /baiˈlætərəl/

Although they have already signed a *bilateral* peace treaty, armed conflicts still happen at times.

[猜一猜] A 暂时的 B 长期的

C 最终的 D 双边的

[翻 译] 虽然他们已经签署了双边和平协议，但武装冲突还是不时地发生。

[分 析] bi + later + al

two + side + 形容词词尾 → 两边的，双边的

[大头例句] The bilateral relationship could be so calm despite the tumult in international diplomacy, which is testimony to the strength and stability of the alliance. 尽管在国际交往中有所吵闹，但两者的双边关系能够如此平静，这证明了他们联盟关系的力量和稳定性。

brew v. /bruː/

Political strikes are *brewing* in many cities to oppose the new social security policy.

[猜一猜] A 消退 B 酝酿 C 升级 D 蔓延

[翻 译] 很多城市正酝酿着政治罢工，来反对新的社会保障政策。

[词义扩展] vt. & vi. ①酿造(啤酒) ②冲(茶或咖啡) ③酝酿；孕育 n. 酝酿物

[大头例句] As you brew, so you must drink.

[谚]自酿苦酒自己喝。

bulletin n. /ˈbulitin/

It's said that we can see the latest *bulletin* about the President's health in today's newspaper.

[猜一猜] A 新闻 B 信息 C 攻击 D 公告

[翻 译] 据说在今天的报纸上我们能看到关于总统健康情况的公告。

[分 析] bullet + in

发票，账单 + 名词词尾 → 账单，报告你的财务状况 → 公告，报告，告示

[大头巧记] bullet是一个独立的单词，意为"子弹"，bullet in像子弹一样钻进去，当然什么秘密都可以知道，可以把他们公报了。

[大头例句] My papers were published in our school bulletin. 我的论文在校刊上发表了。

bureaucracy n. /bjuəˈrɔkrəsi/

The new Premier promised to reorganize the government's *bureaucracy*.

[猜一猜] A 经济体制 B 社会福利制度

C 官僚作风 D 教育弊病

[翻 译] 新任总理发誓要整顿政府的官僚作风。

[分　析] bureau　+ cracy
政府的局,处 + 统治 → 官僚政治,官僚作风

[大头例句] We all hate bureaucracy. 我们都恨官僚主义。

civic *adj.* /ˈsivik/

We enjoy our *civic* rights, meanwhile, we should perform our *civic* duties.

[猜一猜] A 政治的　B 公民的
C 很多的　D 多样的

[翻　译] 我们享有我们的公民权,同时,我们也应该履行我们作为公民的义务。

[大头巧记] 同源词:**citizen** /ˈsitizn/ ***n.*** 市民,公民

[词义扩展] *adj.* 城市的;市民的

[大头例句] The study showed that most teens felt little sense of civic pride or responsibility. 研究显示,大多数青少年对于市民的自豪感和责任心没有多少感觉。

colony *n.* /ˈkɔləni/

The Chinese *colony* in London gained respect from the local people for their hardwork and intelligence.

[猜一猜] A 学者　B 学生
C 侨民　D 手工业者

[翻　译] 在伦敦的中国侨民用自己的勤劳和智慧赢得了当地居民的尊敬。

[分　析] colo　+ ny
耕种 + 名词词尾 → 耕种的地方 → 殖民地,侨民聚居区,侨民

[词义扩展] *n.*【生】集群,菌落
a colony of termites 一群白蚁

[大头例句] Britain used to have a lot of colonies around the globe. 英国曾经在世界各地拥有很多殖民地。

budget *n.* /ˈbʌdʒit/

A new computer will not be part of my *budget* this semester.

[猜一猜] A 任务　B 目标　C 预算　D 眼光

[翻　译] 一台新的电脑不在我这个学期的预算之内。

[词义扩展] *n.* ①预算,预算报告,预算金额
a government budget 政府预算
②[喻]一束,一捆(信件等);一组(新闻)
She has a budget of billets-doux in her mail box. 在她的信箱里有一大堆情书。
v. 做预算,做好安排
adj. 廉价的

[大头例句] Now you can have your own car via a budget plan. 现在通过分期付款,你可以拥有自己的汽车。

credentials *n.* /kriˈdenʃəls/

The new ambassador presented his *credentials* to the president.

[猜一猜] A 请愿书　B 弹劾　C 奇想　D 国书

[翻　译] 新大使向总统递交了他的国书。

[大头巧记] **credit**,信任,信用 → **credential**,让人相信的东西,凭证 → **credentials**,国书,信任状

[大头例句] The company is looking to enhance its environmental credentials. 这家公司正在设法改善自己环境方面的名誉。

diploma *n.* /diˈpləumə/

The professor achieved her *diplomas* in both education and linguistics in Britain.

[猜一猜] A 文凭　B 兴趣　C 外交　D 成功

[翻　译] 这位教授在语言学和教育学上的文凭都是在英国得到的。

[分　析] di　+ ploma
两次 + 对折 → 对折的纸 → 文凭,毕业证书

[大头巧记] 同源形近词帮助记忆:**diplomat** 外交家,要有 **diploma** 文凭。

[词义扩展] ①公文 ②特许证 ③荣誉证书

[大头例句] The council's peace-prize was given to him along with a diploma. 委员会向他颁发了和平奖并附有一张奖状。

ethnic *adj.* /ˈeθnik/

She is keen on *ethnic* dance.

[猜一猜] A 交际的　B 拉丁的

C 传统的 D 民族的

[翻　译]她热衷于民族舞蹈。

[分　析]ethn + ic

民族 + 形容词词尾 → 人种的，种族的，异教徒的

[词义扩展]*adj.* 源于某种文化传统的

[大头例句]The country's population consists of three main ethnic groups. 这个国家的人口包括三个主要的民族。

frontier *n.* /ˈfrʌntiə/

The *frontiers* of medical knowledge are being pushed further outwards as time goes on.

[猜一猜]A 技术 B 研究 C 新领域 D 限定

[翻　译]医学知识的新领域正随着时间向前推进。

[分　析]front + ier

前面 + 名词后缀 → 新领域，尖端

[词义扩展]*n.* 国界，边界

adj. 国境的，边界的 *frontier line* 边界线

[大头例句]We are dedicated to experimentation, to pushing back the frontiers. 我们专注于试验，来开辟新的领域。

grease *vt.* /griːs/

Grease the tin with butter before baking the cake.

[猜一猜]A 装满 B 加热 C 晾干 D 涂油

[翻　译]烘蛋糕之前先在罐子上涂上一层黄油。

[大头巧记]gr(ow) ease，增长安逸，涂油润滑，使更加不费力。

[词义扩展]*n.* 油脂，贿赂

accepted some grease to fix the outcome of the race 接受贿赂来操纵比赛结果

[习语记忆]**Elbow grease gives the best polish.** [谚]苦干出好活。

fry in one's own grease 自作自受

[大头例句]My wife coated the pan with grease. 我妻子在平底锅里涂上油脂。

guideline *n.* /ˈgaidlain/

We should know more about the *guidelines* for the completion of tax returns.

[猜一猜]A 界限 B 领导

C 指导方针 D 价值取向

[翻　译]我们应该了解更多关于那些指导完成退税的方针。

[分　析]guide + line

指导 + 线 → 指导你行动的一些路线 → 指导方针，准则

[大头例句]The Department of Education has issued new national guidelines for science teachers. 教育部颁发了新的关于理科老师的国家指导方针。

ideology *n.* /ˌaidiˈɔlədʒi/

The dominant free-market *ideology* of the late 20th century is facing a challenge now.

[猜一猜]A 法规 B 政策

C 意识形态 D 冒险

[翻　译]20世纪晚期占统治地位的自由市场的意识形态现在正面临挑战。

[分　析]ide(a) + ology

主意，想法；+ …的学 → 关于想法的学问 → 观念学，思维方式，意识形态

[大头例句]Our ideology differs. 我们的意识形态不同。

impose *v.* /imˈpəuz/

This new tax is *imposing* an unfair burden on employers.

[猜一猜]A 帮助 B 用于 C 强加 D 加强

[翻　译]新的税收是把一个不公平的负担强加在雇主身上。

[分　析] im + pose

上面 + 放置 → 把…强加在…上，硬塞

[词义扩展]*vi.* 利用，欺骗，施加影响，征税

impose a tax on imports 征收进口税

[大头例句]Don't impose yourself on people you don't like. 不要勉强和你不喜欢的人在一起。

municipal *adj.* /mju(ː)ˈnisipəl/

The government makes great efforts to strengthen *municipal* construction.

[猜一猜]A 多方面的 B 本年度的

C 市政的　　　　　　D 郊区的

[翻　译]政府做出很大努力来加强市政建设。

[分　析]muni + cip + al

服务 + take + 形容词词尾 → 为公众服务的 → 市政的

[大头例句]Upon election, the municipal leader had little political experience; however, his background in law provided him some necessary tools for dealing with city affairs. 对于选举，这位市政领导没有什么经验，但是他在法律上的背景为他处理城市事务提供了必要的手段。

layer *n.* /ˈleiə/

If there had not been a hard *layer* of rock beneath the soil, they would have completed the job in a few hours.

[猜一猜]A 集合　B 布置　C 层　D 晶体

[翻　译]如果土壤下面没有坚硬的岩层，他们早就在几个小时内完成这项工作了。

[大头巧记]**lay(铺设),layer**,铺设形成之物 → 层

[词义扩展]*n.* 阶层，计划者，产蛋的鸡 *a good layer* 产蛋多的鸡　*v.* 分层堆积

[大头例句]She layered the aubergine slices with tomatoes, garlic, and parsley. 她把茄子片和西红柿、大蒜、欧芹分层放在一起。

oath *n.* /əuθ/

He swore an *oath* to support the king.

[猜一猜]A 意志　B 理想　C 宣誓　D 神圣

[翻　译]他宣誓支持国王。

[大头巧记]谐音"怄死"→ 不明不白的发誓，怄死我了！

[习语记忆]**left-handed oath** 没有约束力的誓言

[大头例句]Lying under oath is not a trivial offense. 在法庭上撒谎罪行不轻。

preach *v.* /priːtʃ/

He was always *preaching* exercise and fresh air.

[猜一猜]A 倡导　B 预示　C 亲近　D 谣传

[翻　译]他总是倡导运动和呼吸新鲜空气。

[分　析]pre + ach

在…之前 + 宣扬 → 在众人前宣扬 → 布道，倡导

[大头巧记]拆：p(riest) reach，牧师到了以后开始传教，宣扬，倡导。

privilege *n.* /ˈprivilidʒ/

Cheap air travel is one of the *privileges* of working for the airline.

[猜一猜]A 回报　B 荣誉　C 偏见　D 特权

[翻　译]很便宜地乘飞机旅行是在航空公司工作者的特权。

[分　析]privi + lege

分开 + 法律 → 不受法律限制的 → 特权

[大头巧记]读音联想：priest village，村子里面的牧师有特权。

[词义扩展]*vt.* 给…特权，特免 *privilege sb. from arrest* 特免某人不受逮捕

[大头例句]Even in today's world of high mobility across national borders, for a student to have the opportunity to study abroad is a privilege indeed. 即使在现今的世界中，国与国之间人员流动灵活性很强，对于一个学生来说，获得一个在国外学习的机会确实还是一种特殊的荣幸。

习题：在下面的空格中填写本单元出现的单词。

1. Although they have already signed a __________ peace treaty, armed conflicts still happen at times.
2. He is working as an __________ of peace in the Middle East.
3. It's said that we can see the latest __________ about the President's health in today's newspaper.
4. If there had not been a hard __________ of rock beneath the soil, they would have completed the job in a few hours.
5. Don't __________ yourself on people you don't like.
6. The Department of Education has issued new national __________ for science teachers.
7. The study showed that most teens felt little sense of __________ pride or responsibility.
8. Britain used to have a lot of __________ around the globe.
9. A new computer will not be part of my __________ this semester.
10. The __________ of President Kennedy made many people feel sorrow.
11. Political strikes were __________ in many cities to oppose the new social security policy.
12. The new Premier promised to reorganize the government's __________.
13. The company is looking to enhance its environmental __________.
14. The __________ of medical knowledge are being pushed further outwards as time goes on.
15. My wife coated the pan with __________.
16. Cheap air travel is one of the __________ of working for the airline.
17. He swore an __________ to support the king.
18. He was always __________ exercise and fresh air.
19. The dominant free-market __________ of the late 20th century is facing a challenge now.
20. The government makes great efforts to strengthen the __________ construction.
21. The country's population consists of three main __________ groups.
22. The professor achieved her __________ in both education and linguistics in Britain.

Day 7

artillery *n.* /ɑːˈtiləri/

Her husband served in the *artillery* as a captain in the Gulf War.

[猜一猜] A 部队 B 间谍 C 敢死队 D 炮兵

[翻　译] 在海湾战争中，她的丈夫在炮兵中担任上尉。

[大头巧记] art ill (v)ery，非常坏的艺术，用大炮把它的头"v"轰下来。

[大头例句] The news that his wife had been murdered knocked him down like heaven's artillery. 他的妻子被谋杀的消息像晴天霹雳般把他击倒了。

assault *n.* /əˈsɔːlt/

During the Second World War Japan made a surprise *assault* on Pearl Harbor.

[猜一猜] A 出现 B 袭击 C 事件 D 战争扩大

[翻　译] 在第二次世界大战期间，日本偷袭了珍珠港。

[分　析] as + sault
to + sail → 跳上去打 → 袭击，攻击

[词义扩展] *v.* 袭击，伤害

[大头例句] Sexual assault is a serious social problem in America. 性骚扰在美国是个很严重的社会问题。

ammunition *n.* /ˌæmjuˈniʃən/

Writing is his *ammunition* against the autocracy.

[猜一猜] A 原因 B 武器 C 方法 D 反抗

[翻　译] 写作是他用来反对独裁政府的武器。

[分　析] am + muni + tion
to + 防御 + 名词词尾 → 用于防御的东西 → 军火，弹药

[大头例句] To make it worse, the only ammunition I could then use against the bear was rocks. 更糟的是，那个时候我惟一能够用来抵御熊的武器是石头。

atlas *n.* /ˈætləs/

The world *atlases* that were newly put up on the wall attracted many people's attention.

[猜一猜] A 地图 B 灭火器 C 招贴画 D 说明

[翻　译] 最近贴在墙上的世界地图引起了很多人的注意。

[大头巧记] 源于希腊神话人物 **Atlas(阿特拉斯)**，宙斯罚他把天扛在肩上，他能俯视大地，所以用他的名字表示地图、地图集。

[大头例句] Unlike the previous atlas, this version is largely digital. 和以前的地图集版本不同的是，这个版本的数字化程度很高。

armour *n.* /ˈɑːmə/

A firm faith is your only *armour* to resist temptations.

[猜一猜] A 武器 B 盔甲 C 希望 D 原因

[翻　译] 坚定的信仰是你抵御各种诱惑的惟一护身符。

[分　析] arm + our
军队 + 名词词尾 → 盔甲，装甲部队

[大头巧记] 反过来看 our arm(我们的武器) → 盔甲

[词义扩展] *vt.* 为…装甲；为…穿盔甲
armour a car 将汽车装甲

[大头例句] The soldiers have buckled on their armour. 士兵们已经做好了战斗准备。

allocate *vt.* /ˈæləukeit/

Even though the Red Cross had *allocated* a large sum for the relief of the sufferers of the disaster, many people perished.

[猜一猜]A 筹集 B 赠送 C 拨出 D 收容

[翻 译]尽管红十字会拨出了很大一笔钱救济灾民，但是仍有很多人死亡了。

[分 析] al + locate

添加 + 放置 → 配给，拨出

[大巧头记]记住 loc 这个词根，由此引发开去，如 **local**（地方的）；**location**（位置）；**locate**（使…位于）。

[联 想]**allot** *v.* 分配，分派 *Each speaker is allotted ten minutes.* 每一个发言者被指定用十分钟时间。（和 *allocate* 同义）

[词扩义展]①（常与 to 连用）分配；配给 *We must allocate the shares.* 我们必须分好股份。

②划拨；拨出 *He allocated a room to be a study.* 他划出一个房间来做书房。

[大例头句]You are not a machine. Allocate some time for recreation! 你不是机器，给自己留些时间娱乐吧！

breakthrough *n.* /breikˈθruː/

The scientists have made a great ***breakthrough*** in human cloning.

[猜一猜]A 反对 B 禁令 C 突破 D 协议

[翻 译]科学家们已经在人类克隆上取得了很大的突破。

[大巧头记]词组：break through 突破

[词扩义展]*n.*（价格等的）猛涨

[大例头句]Before Christmas the allied forces made several new military breakthroughs in France. 圣诞节前，盟军在法国取得了几个新的军事突破。

collision *n.* /kəˈliʒən/

Two pilots and three passengers were killed in the midair ***collision*** of two light planes.

[猜一猜]A 事故 B 灾难 C 绑架 D 相撞

[翻 译]这次两架轻型飞机的相撞使得两名飞行员和三位乘客丧生。

[大巧头记]形近词：**collusion**（共谋），勾结在一起策划撞机事件。

[词扩义展]①（利益、意见的）冲突 ②振动，跳跃，颠簸 ③打击，截击（空中目标）

[大例头句]The affair is described as a collision between personality and principle. 这件事被认为是个性和原则的冲突。

disposable income 可支配收入

dispose *v.* /disˈpəuz/

I am ***disposed*** to agree with you as far as the selection of the location of the new theatre.

[猜一猜]A 欣赏 B 强制 C 倾向于 D 抗议

[翻 译]就新剧院的选址问题，我倾向于你的观点。

[分 析] dis + pose

分离 + 放置 → 摆脱，干掉，倾向于

[词扩义展]*v.* 安排，排列，安放

[大例头句]Man proposes, God disposes. 谋事在人，成事在天。

errand *n.* /ˈerənd/

I've got a few ***errands*** to do in the town.

[猜一猜]A 朋友 B 差事 C 购物 D 零售

[翻 译]我有几件事要进城办。

[分 析] err + and

漂泊，跑腿 + 名词词尾 → 跑腿的事 → 差事，使命

[习记语忆]**go on a fool's errand** 白白受累，无谓奔走

[大例头句]I'm about to send you out on an errand. 我马上有一件差事给你办。

escort *v.* /isˈkɔːt/

The Queen was ***escorted*** by the directors as she toured the factory.

[猜一猜]A 邀请 B 陪同 C 领导 D 建议

[翻 译]女王由主任们陪同参观了工厂。

[分 析] e + scort

无实意 + 引导 → 引导，护卫，陪同

[词扩义展]*n.* 护卫队，护航舰，晚上陪女友外出的男人 *Christina's escort arrived to take her out for the evening.* 克里斯蒂娜的男伴来陪她出去参加晚会。

[大头例句] Her bodyguards escorted her through the airport. 她的保镖护送她穿过机场。

fleet *n.* /fliːt/

The *fleet* is manoeuvring in combination with the air unit.

[猜一猜] A 舰队　B 炮兵　C 后勤部队　D 空军部队

[翻　译] 舰队正在和航空部队进行联合演习。

[大头巧记] **float(漂浮),fleet,**漂浮在水面的舰队。

[词义扩展] *n.*(汽)车队 *adj.*快速的,浅的 *vt.*消磨 *vi.*疾驰,飞逝 *adv.*浅

[大头例句] Survivors were taken to the hospital in a fleet of ambulances. 生还者被救护车队送往医院。

itinerary *n.* /aiˈtinərəri/

The captain was describing the *itinerary* of the journey.

[猜一猜] A 路线　B 目的　C 故事　D 技能

[翻　译] 队长正在描述旅行路线。

[分　析] itiner + ary

旅行 + 词尾 → 旅程,旅行计划,旅行日记

[词义扩展] *adj.*巡回的,旅行的

an itinerary pillar 路标

lurk *v.* /ləːk/

Unaware of the poisonous snakes that *lurked* inside, we proceeded through the dark, slimy cave unafraid.

[猜一猜] A 悬挂　B 潜伏　C 游动　D 被困

[翻　译] 我们没有觉察到那条潜伏在里面的毒蛇,仍然毫无畏惧地在黑暗而泥泞的洞穴中行进。

[词义扩展] *v.* 偷偷地行动,不为人知

n. 潜伏,埋伏

Why is that woman lurking around? 那个女人为什么鬼鬼祟祟的?

[大头例句] That night, danger seemed to lurk behind every tree. 那天晚上,每棵树后似乎都隐藏着危险。

mediate *v.* /ˈmiːdieit/

After fifteen minutes of constant squabbling, the mother decided to intervene and *mediate* the disagreement between her two young sons.

[猜一猜] A 搞清楚　B 减小　C 指责　D 调解

[翻　译] 不停地争吵了十五分钟之后,妈妈决定要介入来调解她两个小儿子间的争论。

[分　析] media + te

媒体 + 词尾 → 作为引起…的媒介 → 居中调停,仲裁

[词义扩展] *adj.* 靠媒介的,间接的

mediate inference 间接推理

[大头例句] Iran mediated an agreement between the two African countries last September. 去年9月,伊朗居中调停两个非洲国家达成了协议。

missile *n.* /ˈmisail/

With the rapid development of *missile* technology, world peace is either ever more secured or ever more in danger.

[猜一猜] A 核武器　B 导弹　C 信息　D 生物

[翻　译] 随着导弹技术的飞速发展,世界和平处于更加安全或更加危险两者之间。

[分　析] miss + ile

发送 + 物体 → 投射物 → 导弹

[大头例句] The motive for the missile attack was not initially clear. 最初,导弹攻击的动机是不明确的。

notify *v.* /ˈnəutifai/

We've *notified* our policyholders of the changes affecting their policies.

[猜一猜] A 通报　B 注意到　C 说服　D 强迫

[翻　译] 我们已经通报给我们的投保客户,这些变化会影响他们的投保。

[分　析] not + ify

知道 + 使… → 使知道 → 正式通知

[大头巧记] **notice** *n.* 通知

notify *v.* 发布通知,通告

[大头例句] It is common practice for this bank to notify its customers when new investment options become available. 该银行习惯于在新的投资选择成为可能时通知它的客户。

objective *n.* /əbˈdʒektiv/

My *objective* this summer will be learning to swim.

[猜一猜]A 梦想 B 目标 C 价值 D 盛事

[翻 译]我今年夏天的目标是学习游泳。

[大头巧记]**object** *n.* 物体，宾语

objective *adj.* 客观的，宾格的 *n.* 目标联系 **subjective**(主观的)记忆。

[大头例句]Gathering more information is helpful to take an objective view of a situation. 收集更多的信息有助于对形势做出客观的看法。

reinforce *v.* /ˌriːinˈfɔːs/

The news *reinforced* our hopes.

[猜一猜]A 加强 B 摩擦 C 强调 D 显示

[翻 译]这个消息增强了我们的希望。

[分 析] re + inforce

再次 + 强化 → 再次强化 → 加强，增援，加固

[大头例句]To reinforce her point that young people open themselves to serious dangers when they engage in pre-marital sex, the teacher invited a young woman who was recently found to be HIV-positive. 为了强化她的观点：年轻人应该直面发生婚前性行为所产生的严重危险，该老师邀请了一位女性，她不久前被发现HIV呈阳性。

scheme *n.* /skiːm/

I should say this is a imaginative *scheme*.

[猜一猜]A 事务 B 条件 C 计划 D 尴尬

[翻 译]应该说，这是一个富有创意的方案。

[大头巧记]sch(ool)+eme(像猪的鼻子和眼睛)→在好的学校里，猪也能学会做计划。另：注意它和**schema**(轮廓)的区别，**scheme** 有"阴谋"之意。

[词义扩展]*n.* 阴谋，图解

v. 计划，图谋 *scheme their revenge* 谋划他们的报复

[习语记忆]**Bubble Scheme** 空头计划

in the scheme of things 在某事发展过程中。

[大头例句]The interior rooms of the White House are decorated in a series of distinct color schemes such as The Green Room, one of the most well-known, which features painted walls, furniture, and antiques in many complementary shades of green. 白宫里的房间用一系列截然不同的色彩调配装饰，例如绿屋——其中最著名的之一——其特色就是其墙面、家具和古董都是用互补的深浅不一的绿色搭配的。

supervise *v.* /ˈsjuːpəvaiz/

His job was to *supervise* the loading of the ship.

[猜一猜]A 选择 B 监督 C 中止 D 处理

[翻 译]他的工作是监督轮船的装载。

[分 析] super + vise

在上面 + 看 → 监督，管理，指导

[大头巧记]super(man)+vise → 超人在监督我们的签证(以防签证官作弊)。

[大头例句]The teacher supervised our drawing class. 该老师负责我们的图画课。

习题：在下面的空格中填入本单元所学的单词。

1. To make it worse, the only __________ I could then use against the bear was rocks.
2. During the Second World War Japan made a surprise __________ on Pearl Harbor.
3. A firm faith is your only __________ to resist temptations.
4. The scientists have made a great __________ in human cloning .
5. The affair is described as a __________ between personality and principle.
6. I am __________ to agree with you as far as the selection of the location of the new theatre.
7. The __________ is manoeuvring in combination with the air unit.

8. The captain was describing the __________ of the journey.
9. The news that his wife had been murdered knocked him down like heaven's __________.
10. The world __________ that were newly put up on the wall attract many people's attention.
11. Even though the Red Cross had __________ a large sum for the relief of the sufferers of the disaster, many people perished.
12. The queen was __________ by the directors as she toured the factory.
13. I've got a few __________ to do in the town.
14. After fifteen minutes of constant squabbling, the mother decided to intervene and __________ the disagreement between her two young sons.
15. Unaware of the poisonous snakes that __________ inside, we proceeded through the dark, slimy cave unafraid.
16. With the rapid development of __________technology, world peace is either ever more secured or ever more in danger.
17. It is common practice for this bank to __________ its customers when new investment options become available.
18. His job was to __________ the loading of the ship.
19. To __________ her point that young people open themselves to serious dangers when they engage in pre-marital sex, the teacher invited a young woman who was recently found to be HIV-positive.
20. I should say this is a imaginative __________.
21. Gathering more information is helpful to take an __________ view of a situation.
22. The news __________ our hopes.

Day 8

aesthetic *adj.* /iːsˈθetik/

The Summer Palace has great *aesthetic* value.

[猜一猜] A 科学的 B 考古学的 C 美学的 D 哲学的

[翻 译] 颐和园有很高的美学价值。

[联 想] **aesthetics** *n.* 美学 **aesthete** *n.* 审美学家 注意：aesthetic 与其变体 esthetic 的意思基本相同。

[大头巧记] 学科的词很多以 tic 结尾，属共同特征。所以只要记住 aesthe 表示"美学"即可。aes，反过来写是 sea（海洋），the（定冠词），the sea（大海），把大海反过来，何等壮观，具有美学特性。

[词义扩展] *adj.* 美感的，审美的，有审美能力的 *n.* 审美能力，美学标准

[大头例句] Aesthetic faculty is an important standard in the interview. 在面试中，审美水平是一个重要标准。

antagonism *n.* /ænˈtægənizəm/

The inherent *antagonism* of capitalism and socialism is the basic conflict in the world.

[猜一猜] A 对立 B 调和 C 竞争 D 演变

[翻 译] 资本主义和社会主义之间固有的对立是现今世界的基本矛盾。

[分 析] ant + agon + ism
反 + 打斗，比赛 + 名词词尾 → 对着打的 → 对立

[词义扩展] *n.* 对抗，敌对

[大头例句] The antagonism the old soldier felt towards Japanese still exists. 那个老兵对于日本人的敌对情绪仍然存在。

ballet *n.* /ˈbælei/

Her sister had spent 4 years in the Royal *Ballet* School before she became a famous dancer.

[猜一猜] A 踢踏 B 艺术 C 芭勒 D 芭蕾

[翻 译] 她姐姐在成为一名著名的舞蹈演员以前，曾在皇家芭蕾舞学校学过4年。

[词义扩展] *n.* ①芭蕾舞，舞剧 ②芭蕾舞剧团 ③芭蕾舞音乐
ice ballet 冰上芭蕾舞 *water ballet* 水上芭蕾舞

[大头例句] We are going to the ballet with our tutors this evening. 我们今天晚上将和我们的辅导老师去看芭蕾。

comic *adj.* /ˈkɔmik/

Most of the TV viewers expect a *comic* ending.

[猜一猜] A 戏剧性的 B 悲剧的 C 意味隽永的 D 喜剧的

[翻 译] 大多数电视观众都期待着一个喜剧结尾。

[大头巧记] 同源词记忆：**comedy** /ˈkɔmidi/ *n.* 戏剧

[词义扩展] *n.* ①喜剧演员 ②连环画杂志，连环漫画 *adj.* 滑稽的，连环图画的

[大头例句] Most Sunday papers have comics, which children enjoy. 多数星期日报登载滑稽或笑话，这是孩子们所喜欢的。

confront *vt.* /kənˈfrʌnt/

The defendant was *confronted* with incontrovertible evidence of guilt.

[猜一猜] A 习惯 B 说服 C 面对 D 贬抑

[翻 译] 被告被传来面对他确凿的罪证。

[分 析] con + front
和 + 前面 → 共同面对 → 对抗，使面临

[大头例句] A soldier has to confront danger and death. 军人必须勇敢而冷静地面对危险和死亡。

engrave *v.* /inˈgreiv/

The champion's name is supposed to be *engraved* on the trophy.

[猜一猜] A 写 B 雕刻 C 画 D 出现

[翻 译] 冠军的名字本应该刻到奖品上的。

[分 析] en + grave
使 + 雕刻 → 刻上，雕上

[词义扩展] *v.* 铭记，牢记

[大头例句] The experience was engraved into his memory. 这次经历铭刻在他的记忆里。

episode *n.* /ˈepisəud/

South Africa may remain one of history's most tragic ***episodes.***

[猜一猜] A 情景 B 条件 C 事件 D 规定

[翻 译] 南非可能是保留历史上最悲惨的事件之一的地方。

[分 析] epi + sode
旁边 + 进入 → 从旁边插入 → 插曲，一个事件

[大头例句] After this episode, relations between us were strained. 这个事件之后，我们之间的关系紧张起来。

gorgeous *adj.* /ˈgɔːdʒəs/

Maria was there, looking ***gorgeous*** as usual.

[猜一猜] A 漂亮的 B 聪明的 C 平静的 D 傲慢的

[翻 译] 玛丽亚在那里，看上去和平常一样美丽。

[大头巧记] **gorge（喉咙）, gorgeous** ***n.***，什么东西让你张大嘴，呈饥渴状，答曰：美女。

[词义扩展] *adj.* 华丽的，豪华的，辉煌的，宜人的
gorgeous weather 宜人的天气

[大头例句] The pianist's gorgeous technique impressed me deeply. 那位钢琴家精湛的技艺给我很深的印象。

horticulture *n.* /ˈhɔːtikʌltʃə/

The best major in this college is ***horticulture*** and not architecture.

[猜一猜] A 建筑学 B 园艺学 C 教育学 D 饭店管理

[翻 译] 这个大学里最好的专业是园艺学，而不是建筑学。

[分 析] horti + culture
花园 + 文化 → 关于花园的文化 → 园艺学，园艺。

[大头例句] Horticulture is the science or art of cultivating fruits, vegetables, flowers, or ornamental plants. 园艺学是有关种植水果、蔬菜、鲜花或装饰性植物的学问或技巧。

ivory *n.* /ˈaivəri/

He bought an antique knife with an ***ivory*** handle.

[猜一猜] A 松木 B 青铜 C 白金 D 象牙

[翻 译] 他买了一把佩象牙手柄的古刀。

[词义扩展] *n.* 象牙制品，象牙色 *adj.* 象牙制成的，象牙色的，乳白色的 *ivory tower* 象牙塔，与世隔绝的境地

[大头例句] Her ivory skin is very attractive. 她乳白色的皮肤很有魅力。

mantle *n.* /ˈmæntl/

In the living room, there is a mirror hung above the ***mantle.***

[猜一猜] A 衣架 B 壁炉架 C 书柜 D 大理石

[翻 译] 在起居室里，壁炉架的上方挂着一个镜子。

[大头巧记] man + tle
男子 + 词尾 → 显示男子气概之物 → 斗篷，覆盖物，壁炉架

[词义扩展] *v.* 覆盖，掩藏；【地质】地幔
a mantle of snow 一层雪

[习语记忆] **one's mantle descends to sb.** 衣钵传给某人（《圣经》）

[大头例句] Clouds mantled the moon. 云把月亮遮住了。

microfilm *n.* /ˈmaikrəufilm/

Many old government documents can be found in the library's ***microfilm*** collection, stored in the basement.

[猜一猜] A 缩影胶片 B 小型电影 C 微型世界 D 微软公司

[翻 译] 很多旧的政府文件在这所图书馆收藏的储存在地下室里的缩影胶片中都可以找到。

[分　析] micro　+ film

微型的 + 胶片 → 缩影胶片

[大头巧记] **microphone(麦克风);microwave oven(微波炉);microscope(显微镜);Microsoft(微软公司)microfilm(微缩胶片)。**

[词义扩展] *vt.* 微缩拍摄

[大头例句] The spy was caught when she was microfilming the documents about the secret plan. 这个间谍在微缩拍摄关于该秘密计划的文件时被抓住了。

prominent *adj.* /ˈprɔminənt/

A single tree in a field is ***prominent***.

[猜一猜] A 孤独的　　B 奇怪的

C 困惑的　　D 显眼的

[翻　译] 田地里一棵孤零零的树是很显眼的。

[分　析] pro　+ min　+ ent

向前 + 伸出 + 形容词词尾 → 显眼的,杰出的

[大头巧记] 拆:pro mine, 在我的前面的 → 显眼的

[大头例句] A prominent Texas politician before making the leap to the presidential stage, George Bush is, perhaps, the most famous Houstonian in the world today. 在跃居总统宝座之前，杰出的得克萨斯政治家——乔治·布什也许是当今世界上最著名的休斯顿人。

refine *vt.* /riˈfain/

Reading good books helps to ***refine*** one's speech.

[猜一猜] A 理解　B 反驳　C 干涉　D 使精美

[翻　译] 阅读好的书籍有助于一个人的言谈文雅。

[大头巧记] re　+ fine

一再 + 好 → 一再让它好 → 使精美。

[词义扩展] *vt.* 精炼,净化,提纯

[大头例句] In order to make most kinds of candy, sugar has to be refined and made into a more workable form. 在做大多数糖果的时候，糖必须被精练,做成一种更可塑的形式。

script *n.* /skript/

The ***script*** was delivered to the director ahead of schedule.

[猜一猜] A 计划书　　B 剧本

C 构思　　D 演员表

[翻　译] 剧本已提前送交导演了。

[词义扩展] *n.* 笔迹,手迹,书写字母,笔试卷

cursive script 草书

[大头例句] I received a love letter from her in her neat script. 我收到了她一封字迹工整的情书。

sculpture *n.* /ˈskʌlptʃə/

Works to be shown include ***sculptures*** by Houdon.

[猜一猜] A 手稿　B 瓷器　C 绘画　D 雕塑

[翻　译] 将要展出的展品中包括乌东的雕塑作品。

[分　析] sculpt + ure

雕刻　+ 名词词尾 → 雕刻作品,雕刻术

[词义扩展] *v.* 雕刻,刻蚀

sculpture a statue out of ivory 雕刻象牙雕像

[大头例句] Michelangelo's renowned sculpture David is considered to be one of the most exquisite depictions of the male physique. 米开朗基罗享誉之作品——大卫像被认为是对男性体格最优美的描绘之一。

solemn *adj.* /ˈsɔləm/

The ***solemn*** statement of the central government on this issue was featured in full in the newspapers.

[猜一猜] A 虚伪的　　B 官僚的

C 严肃的　　D 影响深远的

[翻　译] 各报全文刊登了中央政府对这个问题的庄严声明。

[大头巧记] **sole(单独的)** → 要单独一人沐浴更衣,祈祷 → 严肃的

[大头例句] With solemn reserve, the mayor quietly announced the final death toll of the attack of the two towers in New York city. 在严肃谨慎的气氛中,市长宣布了在纽约双子楼受袭

中的最终死亡人数。

splendid *adj.* /ˈsplendid/

The *splendid* image of Lei Feng will forever live in the hearts of the people.

[猜一猜] A 猥琐的　　B 鲜明的
　　　　C 温顺的　　D 光辉的

[翻　译] 雷锋的光辉形象将永远留在人民的心里。

[分　析] splend + id
闪耀 + 形容词词尾 → 闪耀的，光辉的，极好的

[大头例句] We had a splendid time in Paris. 我们在巴黎度过了一段美妙的时光。

startle *v.* /ˈstɑːtl/

She was *startled* to see him looking so ill.

[猜一猜] A 震惊　B 后悔　C 高兴　D 悲伤

[翻　译] 看到他病到这种程度，她大为吃惊。

[分　析] start + le
惊起 + 反复 → 使吓一跳，震惊

[大头例句] You startled me! I didn't hear you come in. 你把我吓了一跳！我没听到你进来。

习题：在下面的空格里填写本单元的单词。

1. The inherent __________ of capitalism and socialism is the basic conflict in the world.
2. In the living room, there is a mirror hung above the __________.
3. Her __________ skin is very attractive.
4. We are going to the __________ with our tutors this evening.
5. The pianist's __________ technique impressed me deeply.
6. The defendant was __________ with incontrovertible evidence of guilt.
7. Most of the TV viewers expect a __________ ending.
8. The champion's name is supposed to be __________ on the trophy.
9. After this __________, relations between us were strained.
10. __________ is the science or art of cultivating fruits, vegetables, flowers, or ornamental plants.
11. __________ faculty is an important standard in the interview.
12. You __________ me! I didn't hear you come in.
13. The __________ statement of the central government on this issue was featured in full in the newspapers.
14. Many old government documents can be found in the library's __________ collection, stored in the basement.
15. A __________ Texas politician before making the leap to the presidential stage, George Bush is, perhaps, the most famous Houstonian in the world today.
16. In order to make most kinds of candy, sugar has to be __________ and made into a more workable form.
17. The __________ image of Lei Feng will forever live in the hearts of the people.
18. Michelangelo's renowned __________ David is considered to be one of the most exquisite depictions of the male physique.
19. The __________ was delivered to the director ahead of schedule.

Day 9

adulterate *vt.* /əˈdʌltəreit/

The milk has been ***adulterated*** with water.

[猜一猜]A 替换 B 增加 C 变质 D 掺杂

[翻 译]牛奶中被掺了水。

[大头巧记]adult(成年人),e(nter)(进入)rate(比率)。在美国要年满21周岁才能合法饮酒，有些人为了进入酒吧而谎称自己是成年人，所以这个时候，成年人的比率是掺了假的

[联 想]**adulteration *n.* 掺杂，掺假货**

[词义扩展]*adj.* 不道德的，通奸的；堕落的，伪的，假的 *adulterated goods* 假货

[大头例句]The alcohol tastes terrible: it might be adulterated with water. 这酒难喝死了，很有可能是掺了水的。

ambiguous *adj.* /æmˈbigjuəs/

Frustrated by ***ambiguous*** instructions, the worker could never figure out how to run the machine.

[猜一猜]A 不明确的 B 清楚的 C 简单的 D 外来的

[翻 译]被那不明确的说明书弄得沮丧万分，这个工人根本不可能搞明白怎样运行这个机器。

[分 析] ambi + igu + ous
around + to drive +形容词词尾 → drive around → 模糊不清的

[大头巧记]拆:(I) am big, u? 我个头很大，你呢？(不明确的)

[大头例句]What we are struggling for is not an ambiguous reply, but definite feedback. 我们为之奋斗的不是一个模棱两可的答复，而是个明确的意见。

bulk *n.* /bʌlk/

The great ***bulk*** of necessary work can never be anything but painful.

[猜一猜]A 垃圾 B 大量 C 群众 D 层层

[翻 译]大量的必要的工作永远都是一种痛苦。

[词义扩展]*n.* ①容积，体积 ②货舱，散装货 ③大部分，大多数 ④肥胖的人 ⑤大物体
The dark bulk of buildings against the sky look like monsters in fairy tales. 天空下的巨大建筑群看起来像童话故事里的怪物。
v. ①显得大，给人深刻印象 ②使成大量

[大头例句]Safety considerations bulked large during the design of the new car. 在设计新的汽车时，安全方面的考虑占了很大比重。

counterfeit *v.* /ˈkauntəfit/

It is against the law to ***counterfeit*** money.

[猜一猜]A 毁坏 B 赢取 C 伪造 D 消解

[翻 译]伪造货币是违法的。

[分 析]counter + feit
反 + 做 → 反着做 → 伪造，假冒

[词义扩展]*n.* 赝品 *adj.* 伪造的 *counterfeit death* 装死

[大头例句]The gold necklace her fiancé bought her is counterfeit. 她的未婚夫为她买的那条金项链是假的。

distort *vt.* /disˈtɔːt/

Human understanding is like a false mirror, which, receiving rays irregularly, ***distorts*** and discolors the nature of things by mingling its own nature with it.

[猜一猜]A 渲染 B 蒙蔽 C 歪曲 D 美化

[翻 译]人的理解如同一面假镜子，无规律地接收光线，将自己的本质和事物的本质混合起来，从而歪曲和玷污了事物的本质。

[分 析] dis + tort
分离 + 扭曲，变形 → 歪曲，曲解

[大头巧记]同源词记忆：**torture** /ˈtɔːtʃə/ ***vt.* 折磨，曲解**

[大头例句]Those newspapers' accounts of international affairs are sometimes distorted. 报纸上的国

际新闻报导有时候是被歪曲了的。

disguise *n.* /dis'gaiz/

His repeated references to his dangerous hobbies were only a *disguise* to cover up his insecurity.

[猜一猜]A 试图　B 计划　C 表示　D 伪装

[翻　译]他不时地提起他危险的嗜好只是掩饰他的不安全感的托词。

[分　析] dis + guise

改变 + 方式 → 改变做法，以掩饰某物 → 托词，伪装

[词义扩展] *n.&v.* ①伪装，化装 ②托辞，借口

He disguises himself as a soldier. 他乔装成一个士兵。

[大头例句] The soldiers disguise themselves by wearing white garments in the snow. 士兵们通过穿白色的衣服在雪地里伪装自己。

fallacy *n.* /'fæləsi/

It is a *fallacy* to suppose that riches always bring happiness.

[猜一猜]A 谬误　B 武断　C 愚蠢　D 恰当

[翻　译]认为财富总能带来幸福是一种错误的见解。

[分　析]falla + cy

欺骗 + 名词词尾 → 谬论，谬误

[大头巧记] **fall**（倒下），谬论是最终将倒下的东西。

[词义扩展] *n.*（辩论中）错误的推理

[大头例句] He said, "Love is a fallacy." 他说："爱情就是一种谬误。"

fallible *adj.* /'fæləbl/

I know I am *fallible*, but this time I know I am absolutely right.

[猜一猜]A 莽撞的　　B 易错的

C 爱骗人的　　D 行事无计划的

[翻　译]我知道我容易犯错，可是这次我知道我绝对是对的。

[分　析]falli + ble

欺骗 + 可…的 → 容易被骗的，可能犯错的

[大头例句] Everybody is fallible. 人人都难免有错。

fraud *n.* /frɔːd/

People who tell your future by means of a pack of cards are *frauds*.

[猜一猜]A 算命者　　B 特异功能

C 骗子　　D 奇人

[翻　译]用一叠纸牌为你占卜未来的人都是骗子。

[大头巧记] Frau，德语中是夫人，女士的意思，张无忌（金庸小说中人物）的妈妈告诉他女人都是会骗人的，**fraud，**骗子。

[词义扩展] *n.* 欺骗，骗局，诡计，假货

[大头例句] Police are investigating a complex fraud involving several bogus contractors. 警方正在调查一起牵涉到几个假承包人的复杂诈骗案。

glamour *n.* /'glæmə/

Her presence adds a touch of *glamour* to the government team.

[猜一猜]A 希望　B 信心　C 力量　D 魅力

[翻　译]她的到场给政府工作队增添了一点魅力。

[词义扩展] *vt.* 迷惑，迷住

[习语记忆] **cast a glamour over**

施魔法，使对…着迷

[大头例句] Most other cities cannot rival Hollywood for glamour. 大多数城市无法与好莱坞相媲美。

illusion *n.* /i'luːʒən/

This description creates the *illusion* that we can solve all our environmental problems.

[猜一猜]A 理想　B 想像　C 错觉　D 雄心

[翻　译]这个描述引起一种错觉，就是我们能够解决所有的环保问题。

[分　析]　il　+ lusion

在…里面 + 愚弄 → 在被愚弄中 → 错觉，幻想

[词义扩展] *n.* 错误的印象［概念］，假相

cherish the illusion that... 错误地认为…

[大头例句] Glass bricks in the bathroom gave the illusion of lightness and space. 洗澡间里的玻璃砖给人一种光和空间的错觉。

intricate adj. /ˈintrikət/

complex

They were frustrated by this *intricate* pattern of birds and flowers.

[猜一猜]A 复杂的　B 精美的　C 奇特的　D 模糊的

[翻　译]他们被这个复杂的花鸟图案搞得灰心丧气。

[分　析] in + tric + ate
进入 + 复杂，花招 + 词尾 → 错综复杂的，难以理解的

[大头巧记]词的中心部分:tric(k)(诡计),诡计一般都很错综复杂。

[大头例句] An intricate plot is one of the essential elements of a river novel. 复杂的情节是长篇小说的基本要素之一。

intrigue v. /inˈtriːg/

The news *intrigued* all of us, because we are all interested in golf.

[猜一猜]A 涉及　B 污蔑　C 赞扬　D 引起兴趣

[翻　译]这条新闻引起了我们大家的兴趣,因为大家对很热衷于高尔夫。

[词义扩展] *n.&v.* 阴谋,私通,勾结
intrigue against one's friend 阴谋陷害朋友

[大头例句] This film has everything: passion, political intrigue, and humour. 这个电影里什么都有:激情,政治阴谋,还有幽默。

invert vt. /inˈvəːt/

The little boy caught the insect by *inverting* his cup over it.

[猜一猜]A 罩　B 悬挂　C 推动　D 上下倒置

[翻　译]小男孩把杯子倒过来就逮住了那只昆虫。

[分　析]in + vert
反 + 翻转 → 上下颠倒 → 使倒转,转换

divert v. 转向.

mimic vt. /ˈmimik/

As a display of respect, the young performer *mimicked* the famous performance of his mentor at the comic's 60th birthday celebration.

[猜一猜]A 改善　B 模仿　C 光大　D 回顾

[翻　译]为了显示尊敬,这位年轻的演员在他的导师60岁诞辰庆典之时模仿演出了这位喜剧大师的那次著名表演。

[大头巧记]mimi(咪咪),猫的声音,老虎模仿猫的动作。

[词义扩展] *adj.* 模仿的,[生]拟态的
n. 模仿者,小丑,仿制品
mimic coloration(动物的)保护色

[大头例句] Computers with the ability to mimic human intelligence are playing a very important role in modern technology. 能够模仿人类智能的电脑在现代科学中扮演着很重要的角色。

no. talk

notorious adj. /nəuˈtɔːriəs/

Such a *notorious* person has gotten to the top of the company. That's more than I bargained for.

[猜一猜]A 平庸的　B 势利的　C 声名狼藉的　D 率直的

[翻　译]这样一个臭名昭著的家伙竟然登上了公司最高层。这个我可没料到。

[分　析] not + orious
知道 + 多的 → 众所周知的,臭名昭著的

[大头巧记]和其名词形态一起记:notoriety/ˌnəutəˈraiəti/一起记。另:famous(著名的),infamous(声名狼藉的)和notorious同义。

[词义扩展] Despite being dead for over a century, the notorious criminal's nasty reputation lives on. 尽管已经死去一个多世纪了,这个臭名昭著的罪犯的恶名仍然存在。

mist n. /mist/

Through the thick silver-blue morning *mist*, only the outline of the giant ship could be seen in the harbor.

[猜一猜]A 雾　B 烟　C 霞光　D 背景

[翻　译]透过厚厚的亮蓝色的晨雾,我们只能看到港口里那艘巨轮的轮廓。

[词义扩展] *vt.* 蒙上雾水,变得朦胧
His breath misted the mirror. 他的呼吸在镜子上蒙上了一层雾。

[大头例句] The program looks through the mists of time to examine the lives of our earliest ancestors. 这个节目透过时光的迷雾来审视我们最早的祖先们的生活。

jumble *v.* /ˈdʒʌmbl/

The rapid-fire questioning ***jumbled*** the witness's thoughts.

[猜一猜] A 侵犯　B 坚定　C 使开心　D 搞乱

[翻　译] 一连串的询问扰乱了证人的思路。

[大头巧记] **rumble** *n.* 嘈杂声;混乱的声音
jumble *v.* 混乱

[词义扩展] *n.* 混乱,旧杂品
jumble shop 廉价杂品店

[大头例句] The delightful jumble of pretty painted houses made the landscape very beautiful. 这些色彩靓丽的房屋令人愉悦的结合使这里的景色非常美丽。

plausible *adj.* /ˈplɔːzəbl/

Don't believe the ***plausible*** talk of a crafty salesperson.

[猜一猜] A 花言巧语的　B 严肃的　C 粗鲁的　D 温顺的

[翻　译] 不要相信诡计多端的推销员的花言巧语。

[分　析] plaus + ible
鼓掌 + 可…的 → 值得鼓掌的 → 看似有理的,花言巧语的。

[大头例句] In the year 1400, the idea that the Earth revolved around the sun not only did not seem plausible, but, in fact, seemed so ludicrous that one of its main proponents, Galileo, was severely punished for maintaining his belief. 在1400年的时候,地球围绕太阳转的思想不仅被认为是花言巧语,而且还如此荒唐——它的主要支持者之一伽利略因为坚持自己的信仰而受到了严厉的惩罚。

ridiculous *adj.* /riˈdikjuləs/

It is ***ridiculous*** to even think about going out in this storm.

[猜一猜] A 可笑的　B 惹人生气的　C 完美的　D 浪漫的

[翻　译] 在这种风暴中,即使想要出去溜达溜达也是可笑的。

[分　析] ridi + culous
笑 + 多…的 → 可笑的,荒谬的

[大头例句] In modern times, it seems almost ridiculous to believe that the world is flat, but with the lack of technology available hundreds of years ago, that was a logical conclusion. 现在相信地球是平的似乎近于荒唐,但在几百年前,就科技所能达到的范围来看,那是个合理的结论。

skeptical *adj.* /ˈskeptikəl/

He is always ***skeptical*** of political promises.

[猜一猜] A 遵行　B 怀疑的　C 言而无信的　D 冷漠的

[翻　译] 他总是对政治上的许诺产生怀疑。

[分　析] skeptic + al
怀疑 + 形容词词尾 → 怀疑的

[大头例句] I know I might be too skeptical, but I think this offer to earn $40,000 by simply writing your own name ten times is ludicrous! 我知道我可能疑心太重了,但是我觉得这个只要把你自己的名字写10遍就可以获得4万美元的事儿很可笑。

simulate *vt.* /ˈsimjuleit/

The delegates were shown computer models used for ***simulating*** battle conditions.

[猜一猜] A 改善　B 模拟　C 微缩　D 愚弄

[翻　译] 他们向代表们展示了用于模拟战斗环境的计算机模型。

[分　析] simul + ate
相同 + 动词词尾 → 模拟,模仿,冒充

[大头例句] Modern video games are able to simulate the experience of driving race cars or flying airplanes with incredible accuracy. 现代的视频游戏可以以难以置信的精确性模仿开赛车或驾驶飞机时的体验。

习题：在下面的空格中填入本单元的单词。

1. The human understanding is like a false mirror, which, receiving rays irregularly, __________ and discolors the nature of things by mingling its own nature with it.
2. An __________ plot is one of the essential elements of a river novel.
3. Computers with the ability to __________ human intelligence are playing a very important role in modern technology.
4. Despite being dead for over a century, the __________ criminal's nasty reputation lives on.
5. Through the thick silver-blue morning __________, only the outline of the giant ship could be seen in the harbor.
6. The delegates were shown computer models used for __________ battle conditions.
7. In modern times, it seems almost __________ to believe that the world is flat, but with the lack of technology available hundreds of years ago, that was a logical conclusion.
8. I know I might be too __________, but I think this offer to earn $40,000 by simply writing your own name ten times is ludicrous!
9. In the year 1400, the idea that the Earth revolved around the sun not only did not seem __________, but, in fact, seemed so ludicrous that one of its main proponents, Galileo, was severely punished for maintaining his belief.
10. People who tell your future by means of a pack of cards are __________.
11. His repeated references to his dangerous hobbies were only a __________ to cover up his insecurity.
12. The alcohol tastes terrible: it might be __________ with water.
13. The gold necklace her fiancé bought her is __________.
14. The delightful __________ of pretty painted houses made the landscape very beautiful.
15. Her presence adds a touch of __________ to the government team.
16. It is a __________ to suppose that riches always bring happiness.
17. This description creates the __________ that we can solve all our environmental problems.
18. I know I am __________, but this time I know I am absolutely right.
19. The little boy caught the insect by __________ his cup over it.
20. Frustrated by __________ instructions, the worker would never figure out how to run the machine.
21. The dark __________ of buildings against the sky look like monsters in fairy tales.
22. This film has everything: passion, political __________, and humour.

Day 10

abduct *vt.* /æbˈdʌkt/

The criminal who *abducted* the boy asked his parents for 5 million dollars.

[猜一猜]A 绑架　B 坚持　C 杀害　D 喜欢

[翻　译]绑架那个男孩的绑匪向他的父母勒索5百万美元。

[分　析]ab + duct

away(离开) + to lead(引导) → 把某人引着离开 → 拐骗,绑架

[联　想]**abductor** ***n.*** **诱拐者**

换词头: **conduct** ***v.*** **引导,管理**

[大例　头句]My girlfried abducted my heart and forced me to buy her 999 roses. 我的女友"绑架"了我的心,向我勒索999朵玫瑰。

accomplice *n.* /əˈkɔmplis/

The police arrested John and his several *accomplices*, but *accomplices* under duress shall go unpunished.

[猜一猜]A 老板　B 雇工

C 同谋　D 经纪人

[翻　译]警方抓走了约翰和他的几个同伙,但是胁从者不究。

[分　析]ac + com + plice

to + together + fold, 伙同 → 伙同的人 → 同谋

[大巧　头记]和 **accompany(伙计)**类似。把 pany 变成了 p(o)lice,就有了同谋的意思。

adjudicate *v.* /əˈdʒuːdikeit/

I was often asked to *adjudicate* claims for damages.

[猜一猜]A 补偿　B 击败　C 裁定　D 举证

[翻　译]我经常被邀请就损害索赔问题进行裁定。

[分　析]ad + judicate

朝向 + 判断 → 对某事进行判断,裁定

[联　想]**adjudication** ***n.*** **判决**

Adjudication was given one week ago. 判决是在上周作出的。

[词扩　义展]*vi.* 审断,裁决 (on; upon)

adjudicate (up)on a question 裁决一个问题

adjudicate on a case 判决某案子

[大例　头句]My wife and I always quarrel, but when neither of us wants to concede, we often ask our son to adjudicate. 我和妻子经常吵架,并且谁都不退让,于是常常去找儿子来裁定对错。

allure *v.* /əˈljuə/

The ostensible glory of that company *allures* the unwary investor.

[猜一猜]A 欺骗　B 吸引　C 提醒　D 改变

[翻　译]那个公司表面上的兴隆吸引了那个心存侥幸的投资者。

[分　析]al + lure

to + 诱饵 → 诱引,吸引

[词扩　义展]*n.* 诱惑力

[大例　头句]Although she is already in her forties, her charms still allure. 虽然她已经四十多岁了,可是她仍然很有魅力。

abstain *v.* /əbˈstein/

He *abstained* from telling a lie at the meeting.

[猜一猜]A 吸引　B 坚持　C 卷入　D 放弃

[分　析]abs + tain

away + to hold(拿着) → 拿开,放弃

[翻　译]他在会上毫无谎言。

[大巧　头记]**stain(污点)**,a b(ig) stain,很大的污点,当然要禁绝了。

[近义词]**refrain; withhold**

[反义词]**indulge** (沉迷于)

[词扩　义展]① 戒(烟、酒等)*to abstain from smoking / wine* 戒烟/酒

② 节制 *He abstained from speaking an the party.* 聚会时,他默不作声。

③弃权 *She abstained from voting.* 她弃权了。

[大头介绍]英文中有一俗语 abstain from beans，意思是拒绝投票(因古代雅典人选举是把各种颜色的豆子放到容器里)。

captive *n.* /ˈkæptiv/

Matt is easy to become the *captive* of girls.

[猜一猜]A 俘虏 B 跟屁虫 C 眼中钉 D 运输工

[翻 译]马特很容易成为女孩子们的俘虏。

[分 析]cap + tive

抓住 + 被…的人 → 被抓住的人 → 俘虏

[词义扩展]*adj.* 被活捉到的，被控制的，不自愿的，被迷住的

[大头例句]He was always a captive audience to those uninteresting shopping stories from his wife. 他总是没有选择地成为他妻子的那些没劲的购物故事的听众。

commit *vt.* /kəˈmit/

If you *commit* a crime you can never escape being punished.

[猜一猜]A 犯(罪) B 发现了 C 纵容了 D 恭维

[翻 译]法网恢恢，疏而不漏。

[分 析]com + mit

with + 呈交 → 委托，犯(罪)

[词义扩展]*v.*①监禁，入精神病院 *to commit somebody to jail* 将某人监禁 ②承诺，束缚 *to commit oneself to a promise* 受诺言的约束 ③托付 *commit one's soul to God* 将自己的灵魂托付给上帝

[大头例句]The study aims to find out what makes people commit crimes. 该项研究的目的是要找出人们犯罪的原因。

bait *n.* /beit/

When the Federal Gold Reserve is broken into by a criminal mastermind, the chief investigator uses human "*bait*" to lure him out into the open.

[猜一猜]A 弱点 B 黑暗 C 感召 D 诱饵

[翻 译]当联邦黄金储备局被一高智商的犯罪分子闯入之后，首席调查员利用人性的"诱饵"来引诱他浮出水面。

[词义扩展]*vt.* ①装饵 ②激怒，挑惹

vi. 中途稍事休息(或吃东西)

[大头例句]He kept asking her out, but she didn't rise to the bait. 他一直不停地邀她出去，可她就是不上钩。

deceive *v.* /diˈsiːv/

He was *deceived* into giving them all his money.

[猜一猜]A 糊涂 B 决定 C 欺骗 D 犹豫

[翻 译]他被骗得把他所有的钱都给了他们。

[分 析]de + ceive

离开 + 拿 → (悄悄地)拿走 → 诈骗，欺骗

[大头巧记]同源词巧记：receive(收到，拿来)，deceive：以欺骗的手段拿走。

[习语记忆]**He that once deceives is ever suspected.**

[谚]骗人一次，受疑一生。

[大头例句]He deceived her into thinking he could drive a car. 他骗她相信他会开车。

defraud *v.* /diˈfrɔːd/

They *defrauded* the immigrants of thousands of pounds by selling them worthless land deeds.

[猜一猜]A 赚取 B 勒索 C 欺骗 D 拖延

[翻 译]他们通过卖给移民假地契，赚取了数千英镑。

[分 析]de + fraud

变坏 + 欺骗 → 欺骗

[大头例句]She defrauded her employers of thousands of pounds. 她骗了雇主们成千上万英镑的钱。

forfeit *v.* /ˈfɔːfit/

If you do any damage to the computer even by chance, you'll *forfeit* your right to get the fund.

[猜一猜]A 负责 B 得到 C 丧失 D 申请

[翻 译]你如果把计算机损坏了，你就会丧失索回货款的权利。

[分 析]for + feit

在外面 + 做 → 拿出去 → 丧失，没收

[词义扩展] *n.* 没收物，罚款
adj. 丧失了的 *His lands were forfeit.* 他的土地都已被没收。

[大头例句] By attacking too late, they had forfeited the advantage of surprise. 由于进攻得太晚了，他们失去了偷袭的优势。

kidnap *vt.* /ˈkidnæp/

Three American journalists have been *kidnapped* by political extremists.

[猜一猜] A 杀害　B 围困　C 侮辱　D 绑架

[翻　译] 三名美国记者被政治极端分子绑架了。

[大头巧记] **kid**（小孩）；**nap**（小睡）：趁小孩睡觉的时候将其拐走 → 诱拐（儿童），绑架。

[大头例句] He was kidnapped when he was five years old. 在五岁的时候，他被人拐走了。

malice *n.* /ˈmælis/

Despite its unfortunate broken result, the little girl's venture into the cookie jar was without *malice*.

[猜一猜] A 恶意　B 技巧　C 目的　D 营养

[翻　译] 尽管不幸地打破了那个饼干罐，但这个小女孩冒险去拿它是没有恶意的。

[分　析] mal + ice
坏的 + 名词词尾 → 恶意，怨恨，预谋

[习语记忆] **with malice aforethought** 〈法〉恶意预谋

[大头例句] Bob felt a lot of malice toward his sloppy roommate. 鲍勃对他邋遢的同屋很有怨意。

maltreat *vt.* /mælˈtriːt/

The official law of most countries deems the person who *maltreats* others in the form of physical violence a lawbreaker.

[猜一猜] A 护理　B 虐待　C 诈骗　D 危害

[翻　译] 大多数国家的正式法律都认定对他人进行人身虐待是违法的。

[分　析] mal + treat
坏的 + 对待 → 虐待，滥用

[大头例句] It is forbidden to maltreat animals in this shire. 在这个郡不允许虐待动物。

obscene *adj.* /ɔbˈsiːn/

He was fined for making an *obscene* gesture at the umpire.

[猜一猜] A 挑衅的　B 慌乱的
C 下流的　D 附带的

[翻　译] 他因向裁判做下流手势而被处以罚款。

[分　析] ob + scene
向着 + 污秽 → 向着污秽 → 下流的，淫秽的

[大头巧记] 联系 **decent**（正派的）记忆。

[大头例句] The way he writes about the disease that killed her is simply obscene. 他对于死去的女孩的病的描写令人恶心。

plagiarize *v.* /ˈpleidʒiəraiz/

The author has *plagiarized* most of the book from others' works.

[猜一猜] A 推演　B 剽窃　C 引用　D 撕毁

[翻　译] 这本书的大部分内容是从别人的书上剽窃的。

[分　析] plagiar + ize
斜的 + 动词词尾 → 行得不正 → 剽窃，抄袭

[大头例句] At most universities, the penalty for even the more subtle forms of plagiarsm is permanent expulsion. 大多数大学对于即使是细微的剽窃的处罚也是永久性开除。

sabotage *n.* /ˈsæbətɑːʒ/

The secret agent was arrested on a charge of *sabotage*.

[猜一猜] A 阴谋破坏　B 窃取机密
C 制造恐慌　D 劫掠

[翻　译] 密探因犯有蓄意破坏罪而被捕。

[分　析] sabot + age
木屐 + 词尾 → 该词源于法语，早先法国农民为争取更高的工资，穿着木屐去践踏地主的庄稼 → 阴谋破坏

[词义扩展] *v.* 从事破坏活动，妨害
sabotage peace 破坏和平

[大头例句] In an effort to sabotage his nemesis' grand plan to kill all the cats in the city, the hero built a giant shelter for cats to live safely, hidden from the evil man who wanted to kill them. 他的宿敌要杀死该城所有的猫，为了破坏这个大计划，英雄建造了一个避难所，在这里，猫儿们可以安全地生活，避开那个想要杀死它们的恶魔。

smuggle *n.&v.* /ˈsmʌgl/

He was caught *smuggling* cameras into the country.

[猜一猜] A 盗窃　B 毁坏　C 走私　D 间谍

[翻　译] 他向这个国家走私照相机而被抓住。

[大巧记] **smug(自鸣得意的) → smuggle,** 走私是自鸣得意的。

[大头例句] After living in Britain, away from the beloved Chinese spices that made food so delicious to her, my teacher asked me to clandestinely smuggle some on my way back into Britain. 我的老师生活在英国后，远离了她深爱的中国调味品，在我回英国时，她让我给她偷偷地带一些。

suppress *vt.* /səˈpres/

The troops *suppressed* the rebellion by firing on the mob.

[猜一猜] A 中止　B 镇压　C 管理　D 威胁

[翻　译] 军队向暴徒开枪，镇压叛乱。

[分　析] sup ＋ press

向下 ＋ 压 → 镇压，抑制，查禁

[大头例句] The virus suppresses the body's immune system. 这种病毒抑制身体的免疫系统。

temptation *n.* /tempˈteiʃən/

The *temptation* to steal is greater than ever before — especially in large shops.

[猜一猜] A 报偿　B 诱惑　C 谨慎　D 机会

[翻　译] 偷窃的诱惑力比以往任何时候都更强烈了，在大商店里尤其如此。

[分　析] tempt ＋ ation

诱惑 ＋ 名词词尾 → 诱惑，诱惑物

[大头例句] There might be a temptation to cheat if students sit too close together. 如果学生们彼此坐得太近的话，就会有作弊的欲望。

trespass *v.* /ˈtrespəs/

I must not *trespass* too far on the patience of a good-natured critic.

[猜一猜] A 侵犯　B 妨碍　C 习惯　D 修饰

[翻　译] 我不能过于挑衅这位善良评论家的耐心。

[分　析] tres ＋ pass

横者 ＋ 经过 → 横行霸道 → 侵犯

[词义扩展] *n.* 过失，罪过

[大头例句] It would be trespassing on their hospitality to accept any more from them. 从他们那里再拿任何东西的话，就对不住他们的盛情了。

trans- 横过、贯穿

习题：在下面的空格中填入本单元出现的单词。

1. He kept asking her out, but she didn't rise to the __________.
2. He was __________ when he was five years old.
3. The criminal who __________ the boy asked his parents for 5 million dollars.
4. The troops __________ the rebellion by firing on the mob.
5. I must not __________ too far on the patience of a good-natured critic.
6. The __________ to steal is greater than ever before — especially in large shops.
7. The official law of most countries deems the person who __________ others in the form of physical violence a lawbreaker.

8. In an effort to __________ his nemesis' grand plan to kill all the cats in the city, the hero built a giant shelter for cats to live safely, hidden from the evil man who wanted to kill them.
9. At most universities, the penalty for even the more subtle forms of __________ is permanent expulsion.
10. Despite its unfortunate broken result, the little girl's venture into the cookie jar was without __________.
11. He was fined for making an __________ gesture at the umpire.
12. After living in Britain, away from the beloved Chinese spices that made food so delicious to her, my teacher asked me to clandestinely __________ some on my way back into Britain.
13. If you do any damage to the computer even by chance, you'll __________ your right to get the fund.
14. The police arrested John and his several __________, but __________ under duress shall go unpunished.
15. My wife and I always quarrel, but when neither of us wants to concede, we often ask our son to __________.
16. If you __________ a crime you can never escape being punished.
17. He was always a __________ audience to those uninteresting shopping stories from his wife.
18. Although she is already in her forties, her charms still __________.
19. She __________ her employers of thousands of pounds.
20. He was __________ into giving them all his money.
21. He __________ from telling a lie at the meeting.

Day 11

audience n. 听众，观众 接见

aisle n. /ail/

The bicycles you put in the *aisle* would block the way and bring your neighbors inconvenience.

[猜一猜] A 车间 B 门口 C 人行道 D 过道

[翻 译] 你们放在过道里的那些自行车可能会阻塞道路而给你的邻居带来不便。

[联 想] **aisle-man** ***n.*** **自动服务商店工作人员**
aisle-sitter ***n.*** **[美]坐在靠通道座位上的人，尤指剧评者**

[习语记忆] **roll/knock/lay/rock them in the aisle; have them rolling in the aisle** [口]使(观众)捧腹大笑

alley n. /ˈæli/

You can get to the theater after passing through the *alley* on your left.

[猜一猜] A 门洞 B 大街 C 小巷 D 花园

[翻 译] 穿过你左边的小巷以后，你就到那个剧院了。

[习语记忆] **up (one's) alley** 相称，合口味与某人的兴趣或才能相称的
an assignment that is right up your alley 一项正好让你去发挥才能的任务

[大头例句] My wife likes shopping around in Silk Alley. 我的妻子喜欢在秀水街购物。

arena n. /əˈriːnə/

Withdrawing from the political *arena*, he concentrated on literature studies.

[猜一猜] A 竞技场 B 职位 C 风波 D 资本

[翻 译] 退出政治角逐，他集中精力搞文学研究。

[大头巧记] 在 area 里面有标着 n(umber)的跑道，形成竞技场

[词义扩展] *n.* 舞台，界
the literature arena 文学界

[大头例句] Two boxers are fighting in the arena. 两个拳击手正在竞技台打斗。

auditorium n. /ˌɔːdiˈtɔːriəm/

The Centennial *Auditorium* provides premier facilities and services at every level.

[猜一猜] A 饭店 B 展览馆 C 娱乐中心 D 礼堂

[翻 译] 百年礼堂提供第一流的设备和各种水平的服务。

[分 析] audit + or + ium
听 + …人 + 表地点的名词词尾 → 旁听的人呆的地方 → 听众席，观众席，礼堂

[大头例句] Thousands of color-balloons rose from the auditorium. 数以千计的彩色气球从观众席上升起。

abbey n. /ˈæbi/

Westminster *Abbey* which lies in London is well known all over the world.

[猜一猜] A 修道院 B 礼堂 C 会议室 D 公寓

[翻 译] 坐落在伦敦的西敏寺举世闻名。

[联 想] **abbess 女修道院院长，abbe/abbot 男修道院院长**
另:**monk 修道士，僧侣，和尚**

[词义扩展] ①修道院；大教堂；大寺院
②全院修道士[修道女]

asylum n. /əˈsailəm/

He spent his childhood in an orphan *asylum* operated by the church.

[猜一猜] A 幼儿园 B 私立中学 C 研究院 D 救济院

[翻 译] 他的童年是在一所教会办的救济院里度过的。

[分 析] a + sylum
不 + 逮捕的权力 → 流浪汉不被逮捕 → 庇护所

[词义扩展] n. ①收容所，精神病院 ②政治避难=political asylum

[大头例句] That charity provides free legal advice and representation to refugees and asylum-seekers seeking safety from persecution in the UK. 这个慈善机构向在英国的难民和寻求政治避难的人提供免费的法律意见和陈述。

cellar n. /ˈselə/

Nowadays the ordinary house *cellar* is not as common as it was in 19 century.

[猜一猜] A 阁楼 B 花园 C 书房 D 地窖

[翻译] 现在，在一般家庭里地窖已经不像在19世纪时那样流行了。

[大头巧记] **cell 细胞，小房子；cellar 地窖**

[词义扩展] vt. 把…藏入地窖[酒窖]

[大头例句] The revitalized team came from the cellar to win the pennant. 恢复元气的团队从位列最后直升到赢得三角锦旗。

compartment n. /kəmˈpɑːtmənt/

Watertight *compartments* are one of the most valuable inventions that China contributed to the development to the world.

[猜一猜] A 印刷 B 隔间 C 公寓 D 造纸

[翻译] 水密舱是中国对世界的发展所作贡献的最有价值的发明之一。

[分析] com + part + ment
和，与 + 分开 + 名词词尾 → 分开的一个个空间 → 隔间

[词义扩展] n. ①区划，间隔 ②部分火车中的小房间 ③分立而不相属的机能、作用等
vt. 分隔（成间）*The contract has been compartmented into several parts.* 合同被分成了几个部分。

[大头例句] She found a secret compartment behind a drawer in the desk. 她在桌子抽屉的后面发现了一个秘室。

entity n. /ˈentiti/

Persons and corporations are equivalent *entities* under the law.

[猜一猜] A 内涵 B 优点 C 目标 D 实体

[翻译] 个人和企业是依法存在的对等的独立实体。

[词义扩展] n. 存在

[大头例句] The two countries fought for the right to become separate entities. 这两个国家正在为成为具有独立主权的实体而奋斗。

forum n. /ˈfɔːrəm/

The letters page of this newspaper is a *forum* for public argument.

[猜一猜] A 版面 B 论坛 C 反馈 D 精华

[翻译] 这份报纸的读者来信栏是公众意见的论坛。

[词义扩展] n. 法庭，讨论会，评论，制裁 *the forum of conscience* 良心的制裁

[大头例句] For years the club has provided a forum for political discussion. 许多年来这个俱乐部为政治讨论提供了一个场所。

framework n. /ˈfreimwəːk/

Einstein's research provided much of the theoretical *framework* for particle physics.

[猜一猜] A 重要工作 B 加班工作 C 贡献 D 框架

[翻译] 爱因斯坦的研究为粒子物理学提供了很多的框架。

[分析] frame + work
框架 + 工作 → 骨架，支架，框架

[词义扩展] n. 体制，计划 *the framework of modern government* 现代政府的体制

[大头例句] A free market economy operates within a framework of minimal state intervention. 自由市场经济在国家最小限度的干涉中运行。

funnel n. /ˈfʌnəl/

Underwater hoses *funnel* water from the reservoir to a purification plant.

[猜一猜] A 灌进 B 积压 C 喷射 D 处理

[翻译] 水中的管道将水从库灌入净化车间。

[词义扩展] n. 漏斗，烟囱，从漏斗中通过 *He poured the petrol into the car through a funnel.* 他用一个漏斗把汽油灌进汽车。

[大头例句] The crowd funneled through the hall. 群众从走廊中鱼贯而过。

furnace n. /ˈfəːnis/

He was living in an attic room that was a *furnace* in the summer.

[猜一猜] A 精装修　B 向阳　C 火炉　D 景色

[翻　译] 他住在夏天时像火炉一样的阁楼里。

[分　析] furn + ace
熔化 + 表地点的词尾 → 炉子，熔炉

[词义扩展] *n.* 严峻的考验或磨难

[大头例句] Tom endured the furnace of his friends' blame after the accident. 汤姆在事故发生之后遭到朋友严历的指责。

illuminate v. /iˈljuːmineit/

Cleverly made attacks can often serve to *illuminate* important differences between candidates, as well as entertain the voters.

[猜一猜] A 区分　B 说明　C 煽动　D 倾向于

[翻　译] 灵活的攻击往往能说明竞选者之间的重大区别，同时又能取悦于选民。

[分　析] il + lumen + ate
在…里面 + 光 + 动词词尾 → 使…在光里面 → 照明，阐明，说明

[词义扩展] *v.* 用金、银等鲜艳色彩装饰，使辉煌，使显赫，启迪，启发 *The river was illuminated by the setting sun.* 这条河被落日照亮。

[大头例句] Her face was dimly illuminated by the reading lamp beside her. 她的脸被旁边的台灯朦胧地照亮了。

instrumental adj. /ˌinstruˈmentl/

Technical innovation is *instrumental* in improving the qualities of products.

[猜一猜] A 机械化　B 控制　C 有助于　D 不利于

[翻　译] 技术革新有助于提高产品的质量。

[大头巧记] **instrument**，工具，器具。工具可以帮助人 → **instrumental**，器具的，起作用的，有助于。

[大头例句] The general was instrumental in helping both sides to reach a compromise. 这位将军在帮助双方达成妥协方面作用很大。

lace n. /leis/

She is wearing a wedding dress made of *lace*.

[猜一猜] A 纱　B 绸　C 涤纶　D 花边

[翻　译] 她穿着一件用蕾丝花边做成的婚纱。

[词义扩展] *n.* 鞋带；*v.* 系带，修饰 *Has he learned to lace his shoes?* 他学会系鞋带了吗？

[大头例句] Quacks now lace their pitch with scientific terms that may sound authentic to the uninformed. 江湖庸医现在在零售摊上加上科学字眼，以使不知情者相信他们的正统性。

lawn n. /lɔːn/

The *lawn* is interspersed with flower-beds in the shape of five-point stars.

[猜一猜] A 草地　B 广场　C 林带　D 市区

[翻　译] 草地上点缀着五角星形的花坛。

[大头例句] Let's have lunch on the lawn. 让我们在草坪上吃午饭吧。

lease v. /liːs/

Our company *leases* an office in the centre of London.

[猜一猜] A 购买　B 经营　C 开办　D 租用

[翻　译] 我们公司在伦敦市中心租了一间办公室。

[大头巧记] l(ess) ease，较少的轻松，租用的房子不是自己的，所以轻松较少。

[词义扩展] *n.* 租约，租借权，改善处境的机会 *proprietary lease* 产权租赁

[习语记忆] **new lease on life** 重新振作

[大头例句] This extra money could give some older hospitals a whole new lease onlife. 额外的钱可以给一些较老的医院一个全新的风貌。

lobby n./v. /ˈlɔbi/

They were *lobbying* for stronger environmental safeguards.

[猜一猜] A 通过　B 否决　C 游说　D 停止

[翻　译]他们在为加强环境保护而游说。

[大头巧记]lob,蹒跚地走 → lobby,多方奔走,游说,疏通。

[词义扩展]n. 门廊,门厅,(英国下院的)会客室,游说团 *a transport lobby group* 交通系统的游说团

[大头例句]I will wait for you in the lobby of your dormitory. 我会在你们宿舍的大厅等你。

lottery n. /ˈlɔtəri/

The state uses a *lottery* to assign spaces in the campground.

[猜一猜]A 人工智能　B 抓阄　C 逻辑　D 激将

[翻　译]政府用抓阄的办法来指明营地地点。

[大头巧记]lot,多,lottery,从很多中抽取一个 → 抓阄,抽彩给奖法,彩票,不可靠的事。

[大头例句]He thinks marriage is a lottery. 他觉得婚姻是缘分。

manual n./adj. /ˈmænjuəl/

You will find the instructions for the DVD player in a *manual* in the box.

[猜一猜]A 图解　B 文章　C 手写稿　D 手册

[翻　译]在箱子里的手册上你将会找到该DVD机的说明。

[分　析]manu + al

手　+词尾 → 手的,手工的,手头的,手册,指南

[大头例句]In most places, manual labor — that is, work that is done using one's hands, earns less money than work using one's mind. 在很多地方,手工劳动——也就是说用双手工作者,挣的钱比脑力劳动者要少。

pier n. /piə/

We can board the ship from the *pier*.

[猜一猜]A 市场　B 礁石　C 港口　D 海关

[翻　译]我们可以从码头上船。

[大头巧记]与 **peer(贵族)**同音。码头有很多贵族等待远行。

[大头例句]On a clear day, the opposite side of the bay is clearly visible from the edge of the pier. 风和日丽的日子里,从码头边望去,海湾的对面可以看得很清楚。

习题:在下面的空格中填写本单元出现的单词。

1. On a clear day, the opposite side of the bay is clearly visible from the edge of the ________.
2. You can get to the theater after passing through the ________ on your left.
3. Thousands of color-balloons rose from the ________.
4. Westminster ________, which lies in London, is well known all over the world.
5. Nowadays the ordinary house ________ is not as common as it was in 19th century.
6. For years the club has provided a ________ for political discussion.
7. She found a secret ________ behind a drawer in the desk.
8. In most places, ________ labor, that is, work that is done using one's hands, earns less money than work using one's mind.
9. I will wait for you in the ________ of your dormitory.
10. The bicycles you put in the ________ will block the way and bring your neighbors inconvenience.
11. Quacks now ________ their pitch with scientific terms that may sound authentic to the uninformed.

12. Cleverly made attacks can often serve to __________ important differences between candidates, as well as entertain the voters.
13. Einstein's research provided much of the theoretical __________ for particle physics.
14. That charity provides free legal advice and representation to refugees and __________-seekers seeking safety from persecution in the UK.
15. Withdrawing from the political __________, he concentrated on literature studies.
16. Underwater hoses __________ water from the reservoir to a purification plant.
17. Technical innovation is __________ in improving the qualities of products.
18. The __________ is interspersed with flower-beds in the shape of five-point stars.
19. He thinks marriage is a __________.
20. This extra money could give some older hospitals a whole new __________ on life.
21. He was living in an attic room that was a __________ in the summer.
22. The two countries fought for the right to become separate __________.

Note 前事不忘后事之师 *Remember the past and it will guide your future.*

active, 主动的
passive 被动的

Day 12

activate v./ˈæktiveit/

His braveness and intelligence have greatly attracted and *activated* others.

[猜一猜]A 感动　B 激励　C 嫉妒　D 威胁
[翻　译]他的勇敢和智慧吸引并激励了别人。
[分　析]act + ive + ate
动 + 形容词词尾 + 动词词尾 → 使…有活力,激活,激励
[联　想]**actuate vt. 开动(机械等);驱使,激励(人等)** *She was actuated by love for her mother.* 她为爱母之情所激动。
[词义扩展]vt. ①使…活动,对…起作用 ②开[起]动,触发 *His mistake activated a snowslide.* 他的错误诱发了雪崩。③创设,成立(机构等) *activated by selfish motives* 在自私动机的驱使下
[大头例句]If you are a new student in this university, you need to activate your account. 如果你是这所大学的新生,你需要开通你的账户。

chill n./tʃil/

The bad news from the war cast a *chill* on the celebration.

[猜一猜]A 骚动　B 高潮　C 愤怒　D 扫兴
[翻　译]战场上传来的坏消息使得庆祝活动很扫兴。
[词义扩展]n. ①风寒 ②寒冷;凉意
a chill in the air 凉意
vt.&vi. ①使变冷,冰冻 ②(由于害怕)战栗,心凉
adj. ①凉的;寒冷的 *a chill wind* 冷风 ②冷淡的,令人沮丧的
[大头例句]There was a chill in the air when I got out of the house this morning. 今天早晨我走出房子时空气中有一股凉意。

beam v./biːm/

The news was *beamed* to the whole globe by satellite.

[猜一猜]A 出售　B 接受　C 炒作　D 传送
[翻　译]这则新闻通过人造卫星向全世界传送。
[词义扩展]vi. 发光,照射 vi.&vt. 微笑,微笑致意 n. ①梁 ②(光)束,道,柱 ③[喻]笑容
[大头例句]Several beams of the searchlights fingered the sky over the military base. 几道探照灯光刺破军事基地的天空。

bleak adj./bliːk/

The life he had on the small island to the south of Italy was always *bleak* and difficult.

[猜一猜]A 艰苦的　B 危险的
C 无聊的　D 暗淡的
[翻　译]他在意大利南面的岛屿上度过的生活是暗淡而艰苦的。
[词义扩展]adj. 没有指望的,沮丧的
[大头例句]The future of the revolution will be very bleak indeed if we don't wake up the demos. 如果我们不唤醒民众的话,革命的前途将是非常暗淡的。

drastic adj./ˈdræstik/

His dissertation is on the *drastic* social change brought about by the French Revolution.

[猜一猜]A 奇怪的　B 剧烈的
C 缓慢的　D 深远的
[翻　译]他的学术论文是关于法国革命带来的剧烈的社会变动的。
[分　析]dras + tic
做 + 形容词尾 → 活跃的
[词义扩展]adj. 激烈的,极端的,(法律等)严厉的,强有力的 *Drastic measures will have to be taken*

to restore orders. 为恢复秩序而采取激烈措施。

[大头例句] Now the drastic measure of amputating the entire leg must be taken. 现在必须采取切除整条腿的极端措施。

dynamic *adj.* /daiˈnæmik/

Profits have doubled under his ***dynamic*** leadership.

[猜一猜] A 英明的　B 坚定的　C 充满活力的　D 正确的

[翻　译] 在他充满活力的领导下，利润翻了一番。

[分　析] dynam + ic
力量 + 形容词尾 → 充满力量的，动力学的

[词义扩展] *adj.* 动力的，动力学的，电动的，冲击的 *n.* 动力，原动力，动态 *dynamic balance* 动（力）平衡 *dynamic economics* 动态经济学

[大头例句] We're looking for someone positive and dynamic. 我们在寻找积极的有动力的人。

dreary *adj.* /ˈdriəri/

I have to do the same old ***dreary*** routine every day.

[猜一猜] A 重要的　B 恐怖的　C 枯燥的　D 振奋人心的

[翻　译] 我不得不每天都做这些老套烦人的事。

[分　析] drear + y
血 + 形容词尾 → 血腥的，沉寂的，凄凉的，阴郁的，枯燥的

[大头巧记] dr(ive) ear -y，强迫耳朵去听的 → 枯燥的。

[词义扩展] *adj.* 阴沉的 *a dreary day* 阴沉的天
n. 可怕[可憎]的人物

[大头例句] This novel portrays a dark life in a dreary town. 这部小说描写了烦闷城市里的郁闷生活。

excursion *n.* /iksˈkəːʃən/

We went on an ***excursion*** to the city the other day.

[猜一猜] A 差事　B 考察　C 游览　D 研究

[翻　译] 前几天我们到这个城市去旅行。

[分　析] ex + curs + ion
出去 + 跑 + 名词词尾 → 跑出去 → 游览，短途旅行

[词义扩展] *n.* 旅行团，游览团，离题

[大头例句] His rare excursions into poetry show his real talent. 他很少的几次涉及诗歌的创作表现出了真正的天赋。

fertile *adj.* /ˈfəːtail/

A large area of desert was reformed to turn into ***fertile*** soil in the northwest region.

[猜一猜] A 贫瘠的　B 肥沃的　C 旱田的　D 水田的

[翻　译] 在西北地区有一大片沙漠经过改良变成了肥沃的土地。

[分　析] fer + tile
结果 + 形容词尾 → 多产的，肥沃的

[词义扩展] *adj.* 能生育的，想象丰富的，富于创造的 *a fertile imagination* 丰富的想像力

[大头例句] This is surely fertile ground for experimentation. 这里确实是进行试验的沃土。

gale *n.* /geil/

The ***gale*** drove the freighter off of its course.

[猜一猜] A 轰击　B 海盗　C 浓雾　D 飓风

[翻　译] 大风把货船吹出了航道。

[词义扩展] *n.* 一阵，(租金的)定期交付
hanging gale 欠交租金

[大头例句] Gales of laughter floated up from the flat below. 一阵阵的笑声从楼下的公寓传过来。

glacier *n.* /ˈglæsjə/

I am looking forward to seeing Alaska's majestic ***glaciers.***

[猜一猜] A 哥特式建筑　B 冰河　C 原始森林　D 峭壁

[翻　译] 我盼望去看阿拉斯加宏伟的冰河。

[分　析] glac + ier
冰 + …的地方 → 充满冰的地方 → 冰川，冰河

[大头例句] In regions where average temperatures hover below zero degrees Celsius, glaciers grow with each snowstorm. 温度在摄氏零度以下盘旋的地区,每一场暴风雪都会使冰川增大。

instinct n. /ˈinstiŋkt/

Potential investors want to know that you've got strong entrepreneurial *instincts.*

[猜一猜] A 眼光　B 魄力　C 品位　D 天分

[翻　译] 潜在的投资商们想知道你具有企业家的天分。

[分　析] in + stinct

内部的 + 刺激 → 内在的刺激 → 本能,直觉,天性,天才

[大头例句] Birds learn to fly by instinct. 鸟学飞出自本能。

invincible adj. /inˈvinsəbl/

He works as a coach for an *invincible* basketball team.

[猜一猜] A 平凡的　B 国家的　C 职业的　D 无敌的

[翻　译] 他在一个无敌的篮球队做教练。

[分　析] in + vinci + ble

不 + 征服 + 可…的 → 不可征服的,无敌的

[大头例句] Difficulties like that are not invincible. 像那样的困难并不是不可征服的。

flourish v./n. /ˈflʌriʃ/

flower

The company has really *flourished* since the chief engineer joined us.

[猜一猜] A 举步维艰　B 进退两难　C 繁荣兴旺　D 倦怠

[翻　译] 自从主任工程师到我们公司来了以后,公司真正地兴旺起来了。

[分　析] flour + ish

花 + 动词词尾 → 开花,繁荣,兴旺,盛行

[大头巧记] **flour 面粉**,在中国历史上,很多人都能吃上白面的时期就是繁荣的时期。

[词义扩展] *vt.* 挥动,夸耀　*n.* 繁荣 *He flourishes his wealth.* 他炫耀他的财富。

[大头例句] She came in flourishing a photograph. 她挥舞着一张照片走进来。

flour 读音一样
flower

flush v. /flʌʃ/

The negotiators were *flushed* with the success of their final meeting.

[猜一猜] A 兴奋得意　B 感动　C 拒绝　D 庆祝

[翻　译] 谈判双方因最后一轮谈判获得成功而兴奋不已。

[词义扩展] *vi.&vt.* 冲洗,冲刷 *n.* 奔流,冲洗,兴奋,活力,旺盛 *adv.* 直接地 *He hit him flush on the jaw.* 他恰好打中他的下颚。

[大头例句] If any medicine is left over, flush it down the toilet. 如果有药物剩下的话,用马桶里冲走。

ingenious /inˈdʒiːniəs/

An *ingenious* idea suddenly came upon him when he was taking a walk with his wife.

[猜一猜] A 绝妙的　B 奇怪的　C 天生的　D 虚伪的

[翻　译] 他和他夫人散步时突然想到了一个绝妙的主意。

[分　析] in + gen + ious

内在 + 产生 + 形容词尾 → 聪明与内的,绝妙的,机灵的,灵巧的,足智多谋的

[大头巧记] **genius,天才,ingenious,有天才的,绝妙的。**注意和 **ingenuous**(坦白的,直率的)区分。

[大头例句] Shakespeare was an ingenious author. 莎士比亚是一位有创造力的作家。

jungle n. /ˈdʒʌŋgl/

We had to cut our way through dense *jungle.*

[猜一猜] A 沙漠　B 丛林　C 高山　D 城市

[翻　译] 我们必须穿过浓密的丛林。

[大头巧记] 形近词:**juggle,杂耍,骗术**。可联想到 jungle 的另一个义项:错综复杂的事物。

[词义扩展] *n.* 杂乱无章的东西,弱肉强食的社会关系 *adj.* 丛林的,野性的 *jungle law* 弱肉强食的原则

[习语记忆] **blackboard jungle** 无纪律的学校

[大例 头句] You'll never get another job — it's a jungle out there. 你再也找不到工作了，因为外面是个弱肉强食的世界。

latitude *n.* /ˈlætitjuːd/

Our position is 40 degrees north *latitude*.

[猜一猜] A 纬度　B 经度　C 海拔　D 仰望角

[翻　译] 我们的位置是北纬 40 度。

[分　析] lati + tude

宽 + …度 → 纬度，纬线

[大巧 头记] **longitude，经度，经线；altitude，高度，高等；latitude，纬度。**

[词扩 义展] *n.* 地区，自由程度；*horse latitudes*（习语）亚热带无风带

[大例 头句] He was allowed a lot of latitude in implementing company policy. 在执行公司政策方面他被赋予了很多的自由空间。

lunar *adj.* /ˈluːnə/

The Gregorian calendar is only roughly based on *lunar* cycles, unlike many calendars in the East which rely more strictly on phases of the moon.

[猜一猜] A 太阳的　B 月亮的　C 潮水得　D 星象的

[翻　译] 阳历历法只是粗略地根据月亮的周期，而不像很多东方的历法是更严格的依据月相。

[大巧 头记] **Luna，月亮女神，月亮；lunar，月亮的，月形的；lunula，新月状物；lunatic，疯狂的，疯子**（与月亮有关的人，人们认为精神病与月亮有关）。另：**solar，太阳的**。

[大例 头句] We can see a lunar eclipse tonight. 我们今晚能看到月食。

lament *v.* /ləˈment/

The royal members *lamented* the passing of aristocratic society.

[猜一猜] A 期望　B 哀叹　C 疲倦　D 绝望于

[翻　译] 王室家族成员悲叹贵族社会的消失。

[大巧 头记] **lame，跛的**，lame person 是值得我们为之悲伤的 —— **lament，悲伤**。

[词扩 义展] *n.* 悲伤，哀悼，悼词；*vt.* 痛惜，悔恨

We lamented his absence. 我们对他的缺席感到非常遗憾。

[大例 头句] "Things were better then" is an often-repeated lament. "那个时候一切都好得多。"是我们经常重复用来表示哀悼的话。

predominant *adj.* /priˈdɔminənt/

Optimism is the *predominant* feature of my character.

[猜一猜] A 主要的　B 次要的　C 无趣的　D 和睦的

[翻　译] 乐观是我性格的主要特征。

[分　析] pre + dominant

前面 + 支配的 → 在前统治的 → 支配的，主要的，流行的

[大例 头句] The students at my school are predominantly from wealthy families, though there are a few whose parents do not make much money at all. 虽然有少部分学生的父母挣钱很少，但是我们学校的大多数学生都来自富有的家庭。

thrive *v.* /θraiv/

A business cannot *thrive* without good management.

[猜一猜] A 认真　B 破败　C 兴旺　D 浅薄

[翻　译] 商业管理不好是兴旺不起来的。

[大巧 头记] 联系 **decline**（衰落），**languish**（衰弱）和 **wizened**（枯萎）记忆。

[词扩 义展] *vi.* 繁荣，茁壮成长，旺盛

[习记 语忆] **He that will thrive，must rise at five.**

[谚]五更起床，百事兴旺。

[大例 头句] I wouldn't want that much pressure, but she seems to thrive on it. 我本不想要那么多的压力，但是她似乎是要靠这种压力成功。

习题：在下面的空格中填写本单元出现的单词。

1. __________ of laughter floated up from the flat below.
2. He works as a coach for an __________ basketball team.
3. Potential investors want to know that you've got strong entrepreneurial __________.
4. If any medicine is left over, __________ it down the toilet.
5. I wouldn't want that much pressure, but she seems to __________ on it.
6. The students at my school are __________ from wealthy families, though there are a few whose parents do not make much money at all.
7. 'Things were better then' is an often-repeated __________.
8. The Gregorian calendar is only roughly based on __________ cycles, unlike many calendars in the East which rely more strictly on phases of the moon.
9. If you are a new student in this university, you need to __________ your account.
10. We went on an __________ to the city the other day.
11. This novel portrays a dark life in a __________ town.
12. A large area of desert was reformed to turn in to __________ soil in the northwest region.
13. Several __________ of the searchlights fingered the sky over military base.
14. Now the __________ measure of amputating the entire leg must be taken.
15. Profits have doubled under his __________ leadership.
16. There was a __________ in the air when I got out of the house this morning.
17. The future of the revolution will be very __________ indeed if we don't wake up the demos.
18. In regions where average temperatures hover below zero degrees Celsius, __________ grow with each snowstorm.
19. The company has really __________ since the chief engineer joined us.
20. You'll never get another job — it's a __________ out there.
21. An __________ idea suddenly came upon him when he was taking a walk with his wife.
22. Our position is 40 degrees north __________.

Day 13

attain v. /əˈtein/

His calligraphy *attained* perfection.

[猜一猜]A 发展 B 包含 C 差很远 D 达到

[翻 译]他的书法已达到完美的境界。

[分 析]at + tain

to + reach → 到达,得到

[词义扩展] vt. 获得,得到

[大头例句] Tony Blair gradually attained the position of the Prime Minister of Britain. 托尼·布莱尔逐渐地当上了英国的首相。

avail v./n. /əˈveil/

She *availed* herself of every opportunity she met.

[猜一猜]A 发现 B 认真对待 C 要求 D 有利于

[翻 译]她利用了她遇到的每一个机会。

[分 析] a + vail

加强前缀 + 值得 → 有利于

[词义扩展] vt. 有利于

n. 效用,利益

[大头例句] Nothing can avail you except your strong will. 除了你坚强的意志没有什么可以挽救你。

bachelor n. /ˈbætʃələ/

To do the job, you must have at least a *bachelors* degree in chemistry.

[猜一猜]A 学士 B 硕士 C 博士 D 专家

[翻 译]要做这项工作至少也要先取得化学学士学位。

[大头巧记] 源自古法语 **bacheler(青年人)**,单身汉,因此有生手的意思,于是具有了另一词义"学士",当代由于受到妇女运动的影响,被用作定语表单身,不限性别,且派生出 **bachlorette** 一词,指**年轻的单身女子**。

[大头例句] Your best buddy's wedding is just around the corner, and you, as the best man, are in charge of planning and organizing a kick-ass bachelor party. 你最好的伙伴的婚礼马上就要到了,你作为伴郎正在负责计划和组织一个单身汉狂欢舞会。

brilliant adj. /ˈbriljənt/

The official who found that *brilliant* solution to the problem later became the mayor.

[猜一猜]A 出色的 B 有效的 C 使用的 D 具体的

[翻 译]那位找到解决这个问题的出色方法的官员不久当上了市长。

[分 析] brilli + ant

宝石 + 形容词尾 → 像宝石一样的,闪光的,出色的

[大头例句] He made brilliant achievements in science. 他在科学方面获得了显赫的成就。

commence v. /kəˈmens/

The mass meeting will *commence* in Tiananmen Square at 8 o'clock tomorrow morning.

[猜一猜]A 开始 B 举行 C 继续 D 游行

[翻 译]明天早晨8点,群众大会将在天安门举行。

[分 析]com + mence

一起 + 说,做 → 一起说,做,倡导,开始

[词义扩展] [英] 获得学位 *commence in arts* 获文学学位

[大头例句] The lawyers are preparing for the trial, which commences in 30 days. 律师们正在为审判做准备,审判将于30天后开始。

conquer vt. /ˈkɔŋkə/

I finally *conquered* my fear of heights.

[猜一猜]A 认识 B 克服 C 清醒 D 紧张

[翻 译]我终于克服了我的惧高症。

[分　析] con　+ quer
完全 + 寻求 → 完全寻求到,征服,克服
[习语记忆] **To conquer or to die.** 不成功便成仁。
[大头巧记] The tribes were easily conquered by the Persian armies. 这些部落被波斯人轻易地征服了。

dedicate *vt.* /ˈdedikeit/

He *dedicated* his life to scientific research on ophthalmology.

[猜一猜] A 从事　B 准备　C 富有激情　D 献身
[翻　译] 他献身于眼科的科学研究。
[分　析] de　+ dicate
完全地 + 宣言 → 宣布自己完全地属于…,献身
[词义扩展] *vt.* ①专门用于 ②题献给 *He dedicated his first novel to his mother.* 他把他的第一部小说题献给他的母亲。③(为建筑物、展览会等)举行落成仪式 ④捐赠
[大头例句] He dedicated all his wealth to the study of heart disease. 他把自己所有的财富捐赠给了关于心脏病的研究。

devise *vt.* /diˈvaiz/

The Inquisition of the Medieval Ages *devised* many demonic means of torture.

[猜一猜] A 发明　B 归纳　C 揭发　D 废除
[翻　译] 中世纪的宗教法庭创造了许多骇人听闻的酷刑。
[分　析] de + vise
分开 + 看 → 辨别 → 计划,发明,设计
[大头巧记] 拆 de(ny) visa,拒绝签证,要想出办法解决
[词义扩展] *n.* 〈法〉遗赠(不动产)
[大头例句] They've devised a plan to allow students to study part-time. 他们设计出了一个方案允许学生不必整天学习。

diploma *n.* /diˈpləumə/

The professor completed her *diplomas* in both education and linguistics in Britain.

[猜一猜] A 文凭　B 兴趣　C 外交　D 成功
[翻　译] 这位教授在教育学和语言学上的文凭都是在英国得到的。
[分　析] di　+ ploma
两次 + 对折 → 对折的纸 → 文凭,毕业证书
[大头巧记] 同源形近词帮助记忆,**diplomat 外交家**,要有文凭。
[词义扩展] *n.* ①公文 ②特许证 ③荣誉证书
[大头例句] The council's peace prize was given to him, and along with it, a diploma. 委员会向他颁发了和平奖并附有一张奖状。

elite *n.* /eiˈliːt/

In addition to notions of social equality there was much emphasis on the role of *elites* and of heroes among them.

[猜一猜] A 领导　B 理论　C 政策　D 精英
[翻　译] 除了社会平等概念之外还强调其中精英们和英雄们所起的作用。
[大头巧记] 形近词 **elect,选出的,精英**。
[大头例句] Only a small group of elite mountaineers can climb these routes. 只有登山者的一小部分精英分子才能爬这些路线。

embark *v.* /imˈbaːk/

Our company is thinking about *embarking* upon a new business undertaking in Britain.

[猜一猜] A 从事　B 评论　C 停止　D 创造
[翻　译] 我们公司正在考虑在英国从事一项新的商业。
[分　析] em　+ bark
在…里面 + 船 → 乘船,开始,从事
[大头例句] We embarked at Naples. 我们在那不勒斯登船。

eminent *adj.* /ˈeminənt/

The students are expecting the arrival of an ***eminent*** scientist.

[猜一猜] A 迁移学的　B 社会学的
C 敌对的　D 杰出的

[翻　译] 同学们正期待一位杰出科学家的来访。

[分　析] e + min + ent
出来 + 投影 + 形容词尾 → 高的，巍峨的，杰出的，闻名的

[词义扩展] *adj.* (品德)优秀的，突出的
eminent souls 社会名流

[大头例句] He is one of Britain's most eminent scientists. 他是英国最著名的科学家之一。

glorious *adj.* /ˈglɔːriəs/

Our country has a ***glorious*** past.

[猜一猜] A 丰富的　B 悲伤的
C 悠久的　D 光辉的

[翻　译] 我们的国家有一段光辉的历史。

[分　析] glori + ous
光荣 + 形容词尾 → 光荣的，美丽的，辉煌的，令人愉快的

[大头例句] The cottage is surrounded by the most glorious countryside. 这栋小别墅环抱于美丽的乡村景色之中。

inherit *vt.* /inˈherit/

The new administration ***inherited*** the economic problems of the last four years.

[猜一猜] A 解决　B 减轻　C 加大　D 继承

[翻　译] 新政府继承了前四年的经济问题。

[分　析] in + herit
在…里面 + 继承人 → 继承，经遗传而得的

[大头例句] He inherited the business from his father. 他继承了父亲的生意。

lofty *adj.* /ˈlɔ(ː)fti/

The town hall's ***lofty*** tower dates from the fourteenth century.

[猜一猜] A 古式的　B 高高的
C 巨大的　D 别致的

[翻　译] 该市政厅高高的塔楼可以上溯到14世纪。

[分　析] loft + y
天空 + 形容词尾 → 高高的，高尚的，高傲的

[大头例句] I want to be a man of lofty sentiments. 我想做一个有高尚情操的人。

luminous *adj.* /ˈljuːminəs/

On the night she won the Oscar, she looked ***luminous*** in her golden gown, and was gracious in her acceptance speech.

[猜一猜] A 高尚的　B 吸引人的
C 别致的　D 发光的

[翻　译] 在赢得奥斯卡奖的当晚，她身穿金色的礼服，光彩照人，其获奖演讲也高雅庄重。

[分　析] lumin + ous
光 + 形容词尾 → 发光的，发亮的

[词义扩展] *adj.* 易懂的，启发性的。
luminous ideas 启发性思想

[大头例句] His romantic fiction is simple and luminous and quite popular among ordinary readers. 他的传奇小说简明易懂，很受一般读者欢迎。

magnificent *adj.* /mægˈnifisnt/

The ***magnificent*** scene of the waterfall is a perfect delight to the eye.

[猜一猜] A 奇妙的　B 滑稽的
C 有力的　D 宏伟的

[翻　译] 瀑布的宏伟景象真是好看极了。

[分　析] magni + fic + ent
大 + 做 + 形容词尾 → 做大 → 宏伟的

[大头巧记] **magnify**，放大，扩大。**magnificent**，宏伟的，高尚的，华丽的。

[词义扩展] *adj.* 极好的，最好的 *a magnificent place for sailing* 航海的最好地点

[大头例句] The young father stood in silent awe of the magnificent birth of his first child. 年轻的父亲沉默地肃然站立着，期待着他第一个儿子出生的美丽时刻。

mingle *v.* /ˈmiŋgl/

In the business world, it is crucial to be fluid and at

ease when *mingling* with one's superiors in a social setting.

[猜一猜] A 交际　B 工作　C 讨论　D 说服

[翻　译] 在商界，在社交场合和上司们交际的时候能够轻松而转换自如非常重要。

[大头巧记] ming，谐"名"，-le，动词词尾 → 提高名声要进行交际。

[词义扩展] *v.* 混合，混入，合二为一　*mingle water and alcohol* 使水与酒精混合

[大头例句] Leave the dessert overnight for the flavours to mingle. 把甜点放一夜，让香味混合。

outcome *n.* /ˈautkʌm/

No one can predict the *outcome* of the general election.

[猜一猜] A 时期　B 地点　C 结果　D 规模

[翻　译] 没有人能预测大选的结果。

[大头巧记] come out，出来；**outcome，结果**。

[大头例句] We are anxiously awaiting the outcome of the negotiations. 我们焦急地等待着会谈的结果。

periodical *adj./n.* /piəriˈɔdikəl/

He was doing a *periodical* cleaning of his desk.

[猜一猜] A 积极的　B 滑稽的　C 短时的　D 定期的

[翻　译] 他定期清理着桌子。

[分　析] period + ical
时期 + 词尾 → 周期的，定期的

[词义扩展] *n.* 期刊，杂志
learned periodical 学术期刊

[大头例句] "The Economist" is perhaps Britain's most widely-circulated and highly-aclaimed periodical, known for its insightful, thorough coverage of international economic players and events.《经济家》杂志也许是英国发行最广，评价最高的期刊，因其富有洞察力的，透彻地对国际经济人和事件的报道而著称。

pertinent *adj.* /ˈpəːtinənt/

He was determined to ask Mrs. Thomas a few *pertinent* questions.

[猜一猜] A 奇怪的　B 重要的　C 热门的　D 相关的

[翻　译] 他决定问托马斯夫人几个相关的问题。

[分　析] per + tin + ent
始终 + 拿住 + 形容词尾 → 始终不放手的，相关的，中肯的

[大头巧记] **continent，大陆**，大陆是互相关联的 → **pertinent，关联的**。

[大头例句] Please refrain from making comments that are not pertinent to today's discussion: we have a limited amount of time and a lot of information to cover. 请避免做与今日论题无关的评论，我们时间有限，还要涵盖很多的信息。

yearn *vi.* /jəːn/

He *yearned* to see his family again.

[猜一猜] A 渴望　B 计划　C 尊敬　D 付出

[翻　译] 他渴望看到家里的人。

[大头巧记] y(ell) to earn，喊着要得到 → **yearn，渴望**。

[大头例句] They were yearning for a baby. 他们渴望有个孩子。

习题：在下面的空格中填写本单元出现的单词。

1. He was determined to ask Mrs. Thomas a few __________ questions.
2. Your best buddy's wedding is just around the corner, and you, as the best man, are in charge of planning and organizing a kick-ass __________ party.
3. He __________ all his wealth to the study of heart disease.
4. Tony Blair gradually __________ the position of the Prime Minister of Britain.
5. We are anxiously awaiting the __________ of the negotiations.
6. The young father stood in silent awe of the __________ birth of his first child.
7. He __________ to see his family again.
8. He was doing a __________ cleaning of his desk.
9. Our company is thinking about __________ upon a new business undertaking in Britain.
10. The town hall's __________ tower dates from the fourteenth century.
11. The Inquisition of the Medieval Ages __________ many demonic means of torture.
12. The professor completed her __________ in both education and linguistics in Britain.
13. Nothing can __________ you except your strong will.
14. The mass meeting will __________ in Tiananmen Square at 8 o'clock tomorrow morning.
15. In addition to notions of social equality there was much emphasis on the role of__________ and of heroes among them.
16. In the business world, it is crucial to be fluid and at ease when __________ with one's superiors in a social setting.
17. On the night she won the Oscar, she looked __________ in her golden gown, and was gracious in her acceptance speech.
18. The students are expecting the arrival of an __________ scientist.
19. The cottage is surrounded by the most __________ countryside.
20. The official who found that __________ solution to the problem later became the mayor.
21. The tribes were easily__________ by the Persian armies.
22. The new administration __________ the economic problems of the last four years.

Day 14

alter v. /ˈɔːltə/ =change

The design of your novel must be ***altered*** to meet the new requirement.

[猜一猜]A 神圣　B 改变　C 提高　D 怀旧

[翻　译]你的小说的构思必须改变来适应新的需求。

[分　析]alter 作为词根时意思是"其他的",变为其他的 → 改变

[联　想]**alteration *n.* 改变，改动** *The alteration of your article is necessary.* 你的文章的改动是有必要的。

[词义扩展] *vt./vi.* ①改变;变更 ②阉割 *These clothes are so tight that they must be altered.* 这些衣服太紧了,必须改改。

[大头例句] The world alters almost daily, but you are still the same. 世界似乎天天在改变,而你却还是你自己。

alternate v. /ˈɔːltəːneit/

She is so sensitive and ***alternates*** between happiness and depression.

[猜一猜]A 犹豫　B 交替　C 成熟　D 经历

[翻　译]她如此的敏感,时而开心,时而沮丧。

[分　析]alter + nate

其他的 + 动词词尾 → 不断变为其他的,交替

[联　想]**alternation *n.* 交替，轮流** *They have to get used to the alternation of hope and fear.* 他们必须适应希望和恐怖的更迭。

alternative *adj.* 二者择一的 *The way was blocked, so we went by an alternative road.* 这条路被挡住了,因此我们走了另一条路。

*n.*抉择;选择余地 *We have no alternative but to go on.* 除了继续下去,我们没有选择的余地。

[词义扩展] *v.* (常与 with 连用)(使)轮流 (与between 连用)(使)交替 *adj.* ①轮流的;交替的 *alternate seasons of the year* 四季交替 ②间隔的 *He works on alternate days.* 他隔日工作。

amend v. /əˈmend/

We were asked to ***amend*** the document so as to make it more comprehensive.

[猜一猜]A 修理　B 撰写　C 修改　D 提高

[翻　译]要求我们修改那个文件,使其更全面。

[大头巧记] **mend(修理)**的变体,修理,修改,改进

[联　想]**amends *n.* 赔偿,道歉**　**amenity *n.* 宜人,舒适** *The town's local amenities are really colorful.* 这个镇上的康乐设施真是丰富多采。

[词义扩展] His wife forced him to amend his way of eating. 他的妻子强迫他改正吃饭的方式。

[大头例句] *vi.* 改良,改正 *When will you amend?* 你什么时候才会改正呢?

degrade v. /diˈgreid/

Charity without principles ***degrades*** those who receive it and hardens those who dispense it.

[猜一猜]A 使懒惰　B 使贪婪　C 使心存感激　D 使屈辱

[翻　译]没有原则的施舍使得接收者蒙羞，也使它的发放者变得冷漠无情。

[分　析]de + grade

降低 + 级别 → 降低级别,使…屈辱

[词义扩展] *v.* ①免职 ②使堕落 ③退化 ④分解，降解 *This kind of wrapping degrades in moist soil.* 这种的包装材料在潮湿的土壤中分解。

[大头例句] We should never degrade ourselves by cheating and telling lies. 欺诈和说谎话让自己堕落。

dilute v. /daiˈljuːt/

He was drinking a glass of wine ***diluted*** with water.

[猜一猜]A 稀释　B 冲洗　C 保温　D 过滤

[翻　译]他正在喝一杯加水稀释过的酒。

[分　析]di　+ lute

分离 + 冲洗 → 冲淡，变弱，稀释

[词义扩展]*adj.* 稀释的，变次的 *a dilute form of democracy* 一种不彻底的民主

[大头例句]The nurse diluted the drug with saline water. 护士用盐水冲淡了药。

diverse *adj.* /daiˈvəːs/

Prague offers visitors a series of excursions into a rich and *diverse* past.

[猜一猜]A 悠久的　B 模糊的　C 多样的　D 浪漫的

[翻　译]布拉格为旅客提供一连串的短途旅行，带领他们进入丰富多彩的历史中。

[大头巧记]**divert，转移，转向；diverse 多转移的，多变的，多样的**

[大头例句]The newspaper aims to cover a diverse range of issues. 该报纸的目标是要覆盖全方位的新闻。

evaporate *v.* /iˈvæpəreit/

The pool of water on the playground *evaporated* in the sun.

[猜一猜]A 加热　B 污染　C 蒸发　D 渗透

[翻　译]操场上水坑里的水在阳光下蒸发了。

[分　析]e　+ vapor + ate

离开 + 蒸气 + 动词词尾 → 变成蒸汽离开

[词义扩展]*v.* 使浓缩，使脱水，使消失，消灭 *evaporate apples* 使苹果脱水

[大头例句]Our fears at last evaporated. 我们的恐惧最终消失了。

evolution *n.* /ˌiːvəˈluːʃən/

He gave us a lecture on the *evolution* of human beings.

[猜一猜]A 进化　B 斗争　C 特点　D 文明

[翻　译]他给我们做了一个关于人类进化的报告。

[分　析]e　+ volu + tion

向外 + 卷　+ 名词词尾 → 向外卷开 → 发展，演变，进化

[大头巧记]revolution，革命，快速的巨变，是有 r(isk)(风险)的演变。

[大头例句]The space program is the evolution of years of research. 太空计划是多年研究的发展结果。

extinct *adj./vt.* /iksˈtiŋkt/

Some species of birds are *extinct*.

[猜一猜]A 迁徙的　B 怪异的　C 著名的　D 灭绝的

[翻　译]有几种鸟类已经绝种了。

[分　析]ex　+ tin + ct

out + 刺 + 形容词尾 → 消灭了的，绝种的

[词义扩展]*adj.* 熄灭了的；(法令等)过时的，失效的 *an extinct volcano* 死火山

[大头例句]Many jobs have become extinct with the advent of computers. 由于电脑的出现，很多工种消失了。

flexible *adj.* /ˈfleksəbl/

We can visit your company on Monday or Tuesday; our plans are fairly *flexible*.

[猜一猜]A 无足轻重的　B 简单的　C 灵活的　D 准备好的

[翻　译]我们可以在星期一或星期二到你们公司来，我们的计划是相当灵活的。

[分　析]flex　+ ible

弯曲 + 可…的 → 可弯曲的，灵活的，有伸缩性的

[词义扩展]*adj.* 柔韧的，柔顺的 *A gymnast has to be flexible above all else.* 一位体操运动员首先必须有柔韧性。

[大头例句]A more flexible approach to childcare arrangements are needed. 我们需要更加灵活的照顾孩子的方法。

fluctuate *v.* /ˈflʌktjueit/

The price of vegetables and fruits *fluctuates* according to the season.

[猜一猜]A 波动　B 上升　C 下降　D 控制

[翻　译]蔬菜和水果的价格随季节而波动。

[分　析]fluctu + ate

波 + 动词词尾 → 波动，起伏

[词义扩展]（意见等）动摇不定 *fluctuate between hopes and fears* 忽喜忽忧

[大头例句]The price fluctuates between 50 pence and 1 pound per kilo. 价格在每公斤50便士和一镑之间波动。

fluid *n.* /ˈfluːid/

Drink lots of ***fluids*** during exercise.

[猜一猜]A 汽水　B 药物　C 流食　D 奶制品

[翻　译]锻炼要多吃流食。

[分　析]flu + id

流 + 词尾 → 流体，流动性，流食

[词义扩展]*adj.* 液体的，不固定的，易变的，流畅的 *fluid capital* 流动资本

[大头例句]We were living in a fluid situation fraught with uncertainty. 那个时候我们生活在充满不稳定因素的动荡局势里。

highlight *n./vt.* /ˈhailait/

Using contrasting colours will ***highlight*** the shape and dimensions of your room.

[猜一猜]A 压低　B 渲染　C 暗示　D 突出

[翻　译]用对比色可以突出你房间的形状和尺寸。

[大头巧记]复合词，high light，高光，给某个部位高光→突出。或作名词，光线最强处，最突出部分，最精彩部分。

[大头例句]The highlight of the trip was visiting the Great Wall of China. 这次旅行的亮点就是访问中国的长城。

inclination *n.* /ˌinkliˈneiʃən/

I shall indulge the ***inclination*** so natural in old men to be talking of themselves.

[猜一猜]A 观念　B 生活　C 倾向　D 尝试

[翻　译]我将沉迷于老年人的一种自然倾向，那就是不停地谈论自己。

[分　析]in + clin + ation

朝着 + 靠 + 名词词尾 → 倾斜，弯曲，倾向

[词义扩展]*n.* 趋向，趋势，倾斜，斜面，倾角 *an inclination to grow fat* 长胖的趋势

[大头例句]The military government has shown little inclination to restore democracy. 军政府已经显示出一点重建民主的趋势。

infest *v.* /inˈfest/

The entire house was ***infested*** with mice.

[猜一猜]A 消灭　B 防范　C 成群出现　D 数不清

[翻　译]这整座房子老鼠横行。

[分　析]in + fest

进来 + 匆忙 → 匆忙进来 → 滋扰，骚扰，大批出动，成群出现

[大头巧记]in fest(ival)，在节日的时候，人们在街上大量出现。

[大头例句]He was born in a street that was infested with drugs. 他出生在一个毒品泛滥的街上。

intensify *v.* /inˈtensifai/

The press has ***intensified*** its scrutiny of the candidate's background.

[猜一猜]A 启动　B 解释　C 好奇　D 加强

[翻　译]新闻界已增强了对该候选人背景的调查。

[大头巧记]**intense**，强烈的；**intensify**，使…强烈，加强

[大头例句]The scientists have intensified their search for the new gene by working harder. 科学家们更加努力工作加紧搜寻这种新的基因。

manufacture *vt.* /ˌmænjuˈfæktʃə/

It is too expensive to ***manufacture*** most clothing domestically.

[猜一猜]A 设计　B 销售　C 制造　D 处理

[翻　译]在国内制造大多数衣物都太过昂贵。

[分　析]manu + facture

手 + 制造 → 制造，捏造，粗制滥造

[大头巧记]man-u-fact-ure，特征部分：man-fact，人类的真实就是人类可以制造。

[词义扩展]*n.*（大量）制造，工厂，产品 *quantity manufacture* 大量生产

[大头例句]To develop manufactures to the utmost, China must have new markets for her products. 不过，中国若极大地发展制造业就必须拥有销售其产品的新市场。

medieval *adj.* /medi'iːvəl/

Medieval Europe is characterized by feudalism, a system in which each person belonged to a very specific social class, and mobility was difficult, if not impossible.

[猜一猜] A 中间的　B 中世纪的
C 媒介的　D 黑暗的

[翻 译] 封建主义支配着中世纪的欧洲，在这个系统中，每个人都属于一个明确的等级，要转换它的话即使不能说完全不可能，但是很难。

[分 析] medi + eval
中间 + 时代 → 在中间的时代 → 中世纪的，老式的

[大头例句] His ideas about women are positively medieval! 他关于女性的观点已经过时了。

moist *adj.* /mɔist/

These plants do best in fertile, *moist* soil.

[猜一猜] A 肥沃的　B 热带的
C 温带的　D 潮湿的

[翻 译] 这种植物最适合在肥沃而潮湿的土壤中生长。

[大头巧记] most 中间插入"i"-ice，大多数的冰都潮湿。

[大头例句] These clothes are still too moist to fold; I don't want them to develop mildew before they have fully dried. 这些衣服由于太湿还不能折叠，在它们完全干透之前我不想它们发霉。

ponder *v.* /'pɔndə/

He and the council had already *pondered* the list of members returned to the parliament.

[猜一猜] A 预定了　B 认真考虑了
C 回绝了　D 通过了

[翻 译] 他和委员会已经认真地考虑过了重返国会的人员名单。

[分 析] pond + er
重量 + 动词词尾 → 权衡轻重，认真考虑

[大头巧记] pond，池塘 → ponder，在池塘边徘徊思考。

provisional *adj.* /prə'viʒənl/

We just provide *provisional* service in this field.

[猜一猜] A 暂时的　B 专业的
C 业余的　D 有限的

[翻 译] 我们只提供这个领域暂时性的服务。

[大头巧记] **provide**，供应，预防；**provision**，*n.* 供应品，预备；**provisional**，预备的，临时的

习题：在下面的空格中填写本单元出现的单词。

1. We can visit your company on Monday or Tuesday; our plans are fairly ________.
2. We were living in a ________ situation fraught with uncertainty.
3. I shall indulge the ________ so natural in old men to be talking of themselves.
4. The scientists have ________ their search for the new gene by working harder.
5. To develop ________ to the utmost, China must have new markets for her products.
6. We just provide ________ service in this field.
7. The design of your novel must be ________ to meet the new requirement.
8. Charity without principles ________ those who receive it and hardens those who dispense it.
9. We were asked to ________ the document so as to make it more comprehensive.
10. The newspaper aims to cover a ________ range of issues.
11. Many jobs have become ________ with the advent of computers.
12. She is so sensitive and ________ between happiness and depression.

13. He and the council had already __________ the list of members returned to the parliament.
14. The price of vegetables and fruits __________ according to the season.
15. His ideas about women are positively __________!
16. These clothes are still too __________ to fold; I don't want them to develop mildew before they have fully dried.
17. Using contrasting colours will __________ the shape and dimensions of your room.
18. He was born in a street that was __________ with drugs.
19. The space program is the __________ of years of research.
20. He was drinking a glass of wine __________ with water.
21. The pool of water on the playground __________ in the sun.

Note 前事不忘后事之师 *Remember the past and it will guide your future.*

Day 15

arrogant *adj.* /ˈærəgənt/

> His *arrogant* contempt for the weak brought him big trouble.

[猜一猜] A 傲慢的　　B 无知的
C 肤浅的　　D 形之于色

[翻　译] 他对弱者的傲慢的蔑视给他带来很大的麻烦。

[分　析] ar + rog + ant
to + to ask + 形容词尾 → 总是要求 → 傲慢的

[大头例句] Redmond is so arrogant that he is not willing to talk to others. 雷德蒙如此的傲慢，他不愿意和别人说话。

ardent *adj.* /ˈɑːdənt/

> The *ardent* hope for the future brought them through all the sufferings during the Culture Revolution.

[猜一猜] A 朦胧的　　B 突然的
C 不断的　　D 热情的

[翻　译] 对未来的向往使他们度过了文化大革命中的种种苦难。

[分　析] ard + ent
燃烧 + 形容词尾 → 燃烧的，热情的

[大头巧记] 谐音法：啊—等她 → 富有热情地等待着女孩的到来。

[词义扩展] *adj.* 炽热的，强烈的
ardent passion 热情

[大头例句] "an impassioned age, so ardent and serious in its pursuit of art" (Walter Pater) "一个热诚的年代，如此热烈而认真地追随着艺术"(沃尔特·佩特)

baffle *vt.* /ˈbæfl/

> The little girl's question *baffled* me completely and I didn't know how to reply.

[猜一猜] A 困惑　　B 揭露
C 感动　　D 刺激

[翻　译] 这个小女孩的问题完全把我难住了，我不知道说什么才好。

[词义扩展] *vt.* 使挫折，阻碍　*vi.* 徒劳地挣扎；折腾 *The sailors were baffling with the storm.* 水手们正在徒然地与暴风雨搏斗。*n.* 迷惑，隔板，防护板

[大头例句] I am always baffled by gymnasts' limitless flexibility. 体操运动员们无限的身体柔韧性总是让我想不通。

boast *v.* /bəust/

> You should never *boast* of your qualifications.

[猜一猜] A 弄虚作假　　B 失望
C 绝望　　D 吹嘘

[翻　译] 你永远不应该吹嘘自己的资格。

[大头巧记] 形近词记忆，**coast**，**海岸**，去过海岸的公鸡 c(ock)，吹嘘自己变得和熊 b(ear)，一样强大。用"b"替换"c"，得到 boast。

[词义扩展] *v.* ①自夸 ②以拥有…为自豪　*n.* ①自夸，夸口 ②可夸耀的事物 *The library boasts first editions of Shakespeare.* 这个图书馆以藏有初版的莎士比亚集而自豪。*It has never been the boast of a modest person that his intelligence is greater than others.* 谦虚的人从来不自夸他的理解力比别人好。

[大头例句] We confide in our strength without boasting of it; we respect that of others without fearing it. 我们自信于自己的力量，而不自我吹嘘；我们尊重别人的力量，但不畏惧。

bold *adj.* /bəuld/

> It is a very *bold* action that you decide to live by yourself.

[猜一猜] A 武断的　　B 勇敢的
C 令人尊敬的　　D 愚蠢的

[翻　译] 你决定自己养活自己是一个勇敢的行为。

bolt: n.螺栓.
v.闩门.囫囵吞.逃跑

[大头巧记] 形近词记忆,bald,秃头的,剃光头是个很大胆的行为。

[词义扩展] adj. 鲁莽的

n. 黑体,粗体

a. n.黄铜.厚脸皮.

[习语记忆] **as bold as brass** 厚颜无耻

[大头例句] You are normally as meek as a lamb, but on this issue you are as bold as brass. 你通常都很谦恭温顺,但是在这个问题上你却如此的厚颜无耻。

courtesy *n.* /ˈkəːtisi/

They showed us great *courtesy*.

[猜一猜] A 谦虚　B 礼貌　C 激情　D 美感

[翻　译] 他们对我们很有礼貌。

[大头巧记] **court**,法庭 → **courtesy**,在法庭上的礼貌,谦恭。

[习语记忆] **stand to the courtesy of** 有赖于…的宽容或好意

[大头例句] The hotel provides courtesy shuttle service from the airport. 该旅店提供礼貌的往返机场乘车服务。

/riːlækˈseiʃən/

ease *v.* /iːz/

relaxation

The relationship between the two countries has *eased* since the beginning of the talks on the border conflicts.

[猜一猜] A 缓和　B 建立　C 恶化　D 稳固

[翻　译] 自从开始边界争端的谈判以来,两国关系已趋缓和。

[大头巧记] **easy**,简单的,轻松的,-y 为形容词尾,**ease**,(使)轻松

[词义扩展] *n.* 舒适,悠闲,容易 *He passed the examination with ease.* 她轻松地通过了考试。

vt. 减轻(痛苦等),使舒适,使安心,放松,降低 *ease sb.'s anxiety* 减轻某人的忧虑

[大头例句] He was a compassionate doctor blessed with natural ease. 他是一个富有同情心的医生,有着一种天赋的自然的轻松。

adj

compassion n.同情

impassioned adj.热情的

ego *n.* /ˈegəu/

The critics' praises boosted the pop singer's *ego*.

[猜一猜] A 事业　B 名声　C 天赋　D 自我

[翻　译] 这些评论家的赞扬使这位歌手自我膨胀起来。

[词义扩展] *n.* 利己主义,自负

[大头例句] I hate that guy with the huge ego. 我讨厌那个自命不凡的家伙。

elegant *adj.* /ˈeligənt/

Personally I like her *elegant* manners.

[猜一猜] A 伦敦式的　B 羞涩的
C 开朗的　D 优雅的

[翻　译] 我本人很喜欢她优雅的风度。

[分　析] e　+ legant
出来 + 选 → 精心挑选的,优雅的,有风度的

[词义扩展] *adj.* 上品的,一流的

[大头例句] Their solution was much more elegant than mine. 他们的解决方法比我的出色得多。

esteem *vt.* /isˈtiːm/

I *esteem* it as a privilege to attend this meeting and give a report here.

[猜一猜] A 对待　B 认为　C 沉迷　D 希望

[翻　译] 我能参加这个大会并在这里作报告,感到十分荣幸。

[词义扩展] *vt.* 把…看做,尊敬,尊重,认为
n. 尊敬

[大头例句] She has always been held in high esteem by fellow actors. 她总是很受演员同事们的尊敬。

exclude *vt.* /iksˈkluːd/

The court *excluded* the improperly obtained evidence.

[猜一猜] A 拒绝接纳　B 惩罚
C 受理　D 参考

[翻　译] 法院不接受非正常渠道获得的证据。

[分　析] ex　+ clude
出来 + 关闭 → 把…关在外面 → 拒不接纳,排斥

anxiety /æŋˈzaiəti/
anxious /ˈæŋkʃəs/

[大头巧记] include，包括；exclude，不包括，排斥

[词义扩展] *vt.* 逐出，驱除，排除

[大头例句] We can't exclude the possibility that some warmongers will run the risk of starting a new world war. 我们不能排除有些战争贩子会冒险发动一场新的世界大战的可能性。

flee *v.* /fliː/

Citizens were forced to ***flee*** the besieged city.

[猜一猜] A 保卫　B 逃离　C 走向　D 领导

[翻　译] 居民被迫逃离这座被围困的城市。

[大头巧记] **flee，谐"离"，离开，逃离。**

[词义扩展] *vi.* 逃散，消失 *Color fled from her cheeks.* 红晕从她的双颊上消失了。

[大头例句] Police caught up with one of the gangs, but the other three fled. 警察抓住了团伙中的一个，其余的三个跑了。

genial *adj.* /ˈdʒiːnjəl/

The ***genial*** sunshine was saturating his miserable body with its warmth.

[猜一猜] A 充足的　B 新生的　C 和暖的　D 耀眼的

[翻　译] 和暖的阳光用温暖充满他痛楚的躯体。

[大头巧记] **gene，基因，genial，天生的性情** → 人性本善 → 和蔼的，亲切的，和暖的。

[词义扩展] *adj.* 愉快的，宜人的，舒适的，显示天才的 *a genial climate* 宜人的气候

[大头例句] He exchanged genial greetings with his colleagues. 他和同事们亲切地互相问候。

genuine *adj.* /ˈdʒenjuin/

All ***genuine*** knowledge originates from direct experience.

[猜一猜] A 抽象的　B 推理的　C 实际的　D 真正的

[翻　译] 一切真知都是从直接经验发源的。

[大头巧记] **gene，基因，genuine，天生的，未经琢磨的，真性情的，真正的。**

[词义扩展] *adj.* 诚恳的，纯的，纯血统的，用天然原料制成的 *a genuine signature* 亲笔签字

[大头例句] We are doing everything we can do to help people to work towards genuine democracy. 我们正在做一切我们能做的来帮助人们向着真正的民主努力。

gratitude *n.* /ˈgrætitjuːd/

I am full of ***gratitude*** to you for helping me with my English study.

[猜一猜] A 感激　B 尊敬　C 自豪　D 自信

[翻　译] 我非常感激你对我英语学习的帮助。

[分　析] grat + titude

愉快的 + 名词词尾 → 感激，感恩，谢意

[大头巧记] **grateful，*adj.* 感激的**
gratitude，*n.* 感激

[大头例句] I felt I owed a debt of gratitude to my old teacher. 我觉得欠我过去的那个老师一个人情。

integrate *v.* /ˈintigreit/

The teachers are trying to ***integrate*** all the children into society.

[猜一猜] A 介绍　B 使成为一体　C 建议　D 教导

[翻　译] 教师们正设法使所有的孩子都要与社会融为一体。

[分　析] integr + ate

完整 + 名词词尾 → 使完整，使一体化。

[词义扩展] *vt.* 【数】求…的积分
vi. 与…结合起来 (with)

[大头例句] Care will also be taken to integrate the buildings with surrounding architecture. 还要注意使这些建筑和周围的建筑融为一体。

furious *adj.* /ˈfjuəriəs/

He'll be ***furious*** at being kept waiting.

[猜一猜] A 紧张　B 着急　C 暴怒　D 不满

[翻　译] 如果让他久等，他会大发雷霆的。

[分　析] furi + ous

狂怒 + 形容词词尾 → 狂怒的，暴怒的

[词义扩展] adj. ①猛烈的，不驯的 *a furious temper* 性格暴躁 ②喧闹的，飞快的

[大头例句] His speech was greeted by furious applause. 他的讲话被报以热烈的掌声。

lenient *adj.* /ˈliːniənt/

The judge was ***lenient*** with her as this was her first offence.

[猜一猜] A 理解的　B 严厉的　C 纵容的　D 宽大的

[翻　译] 由于是初犯，法官对她宽大处理。

[分　析] len + ient
软化 + 形容词尾 → 软化的，宽大的，仁慈的

[大头巧记] **convenient(方便的)** 的尾巴 enient 前加上一个"l"-loose，很方便就可以宽松的，宽大的。

[大头例句] The prosecution complained that the sentence was far too lenient. 控方抱怨判决太宽松了。

lounge *v.* /laundʒ/

The beggar was ***lounging*** against the walls at street corners.

[猜一猜] A 懒洋洋的倚在　B 挖掘　C 直接　D 持久

[翻　译] 这个乞丐总是懒洋洋地倚在街头的墙上。

[大头巧记] 在 long（长）中加入了"u"和"e"(used to ease)，长长的用来放松自己的东西 → 长沙发，懒洋洋地倚/躺。

[词义扩展] n./v. 闲荡，漫步，混日子
n. 休息室，娱乐室，起居室

[习语记忆] **lounge about the door** 闲散过日

[大头例句] There is a growing trend among international airports to have special smokers' lounges so as to limit the general public's susceptibility to unpleasant cigarette smoke. 在国际机场里设立吸烟休息室的趋势在增长以限制一般公众对抽烟的不愉快感觉。

meek *adj.* /miːk/

A shy, ***meek***, girl, Anna was too nervous to initiate a conversation with Sam, the cutest boy in her class.

[猜一猜] A 害羞得　B 温柔的　C 甜美的　D 美丽的

[翻　译] 害羞而温柔的女孩安娜由于太紧张而无法和她班里最可爱的男孩萨姆搭话。

[大头巧记] 谐音：蜜，像蜜一样的女孩一定是温柔的，谦恭的。

[词义扩展] adj. 善忍的，缺乏胆量的，和缓的

[大头例句] She is as meek as a lamb. 她像羊羔一样的温顺。

melancholy *n.* /ˈmelənkəli/

Melancholy, though complex and often uncomfortable, is as valid a state of mind as happiness and excitement, and it deserves exploration and understanding.

[猜一猜] A 忧郁　B 邪恶　C 愤怒　D 怯懦

[翻　译] 忧郁，虽然复杂且经常不舒服，但是它也是情绪的一种正当状态，就像快乐和兴奋，它值得我们去探究和理解。

[分　析] melan + chol + y
黑色的 + 胆汁 + 词尾 → 胆汁发黑的 → 忧郁的，忧郁

[词义扩展] adj. 忧郁的，沉思的，愁思的，令人沮丧的 *a melancholy mood* 忧郁的心情

[习语记忆] **melancholy as a cat** 非常忧郁

[大头例句] That is really a bleak and melancholy landscape. 那真是一幕阴冷而忧郁的景色。

mythology *n.* /miˈθɔlədʒi/

In Greek ***mythology***, the goddess of love, Aphrodite, is said to have been "born" by emerging from the head of her father, Zeus.

[猜一猜] A 文学　B 哲学　C 政治学　D 神话

[翻　译] 在希腊神话中，爱神阿芙罗狄蒂据说是从她的父亲宙斯的头上生成的。

[分　析] myth + ology
神话 + 名词词尾 → 神话学，神话集

[大头例句] I am reading Roman mythology. 我正在读罗马神话集。

pedestrian *n.* /piˈdestriən/

In the accident, two *pedestrians* and a cyclist were injured.

[猜一猜]A 步行者　　B 警察
C 学生　　D 观光者

[翻　译]在这起事故中，有两位行人和一位骑车者被伤。

[分　析]ped + estrian
脚 + 词尾 → 步行者

[词义扩展]*adj.* 徒步的，平凡的 *He was rather a pedestrian student.* 他原是个相当平常的学生。

[大头例句]Though laws often protect pedestrians from the larger vehicles people share the roads with, legal protection is of little consolation when a traffic accident results in permanent injury. 虽然法律经常保护人车公用车道上的步行者，但是法律保护对车祸造成的永久性伤害安慰甚微。

penetrate *v.* /ˈpenitreit/

Dell is planning to *penetrate* the home-computer market with an affordable new model.

[猜一猜]A 垄断　B 打入　C 保护　D 开发

[翻　译]戴尔公司正计划以大众可承受的新机型打入家用电脑市场。

[分　析]pen + etr + ate
全部 + 进入 + 动词词尾 → 打入，穿透

[词义扩展]*v.* 渗入，弥漫，洞察 *penetrate the mystery of* 揭示…的秘密 *Western ideas penetrate slowly through the East.* 西方观念逐渐传入东方。

[大头例句]If the windows are all the way up, rain, snow, and hail rarely penetrate the average motor vehicle. 如果车窗全都摇上去的话，雨、雪和冰雹很少可以打入一般的机动车。

sacred *adj.* /ˈseikrid/

He considered it a *sacred* duty to fulfill his dead father's wishes.

[猜一猜]A 根本的　　B 神圣的
C 必要的　　D 肤浅的

[翻　译]他认为实现父亲的遗愿是神圣的义务。

[词义扩展]*adj.* 宗教的，严肃的 *sacred writings* 宗教经典 *a sacred promise* 郑重的诺言

[习语记忆]**be sacred from** 免除
hold sacred 尊重

习题：在下面的空格中填入本单元所学的单词。

1. His speech was greeted by __________ applause.
2. Redmond is so __________ that he is not willing to talk to others.
3. I am always __________ by gymnasts' limitless flexibility.
4. The critics' praise boosted the pop singer's __________.
5. Police caught up with one of the gangs, but the other three __________.
6. She has always been held in high __________ by fellow actors.
7. We can't __________ the possibility that some warmongers will run the risk of starting a new world war.
8. The __________ hope for the future brought them through all the sufferings during the Culture Revolution.
9. It is a very __________ action that you decide to live by yourself.
10. He considered it a __________ duty to fulfill his dead father's wishes.
11. In the accident, two __________ and a cyclist were injured.
12. The __________ sunshine was saturating his miserable body with its warmth.

13. I am full of __________ to you for helping me with my English study.
14. The beggar was __________ against the wall at street corners.
15. The prosecution complained that the sentence was far too __________.
16. That is really a bleak and __________ landscape.
17. In Greek __________, the goddess of love, Aphrodite, is said to have been "born" by emerging from the head of her father, Zeus.
18. Dell is planning to __________ the home-computer market with an affordable new model.
19. Care will also be taken to __________ the buildings with surrounding architecture.
20. We are doing everything we can to help people to work towards __________ democracy.
21. She is as __________ as a lamb.
22. The relationship between the two countries has __________ since the beginning of the talks on the border conflicts.
23. Their solution was much more __________ than mine.
24. The hotel provides __________ shuttle service from the airport.
25. We confide in our strength, without __________ of it; we respect that of others, without fearing it.

Note 前事不忘后事之师 *Remember the past and it will guide your future.*

Day 16

assortment. n. 分类

assorted adj./v. /ə'sɔːtid/

Xi'an is famous for its *assorted* snacks.

[猜一猜]A 著名的　B 传统的　C 各式各样的　D 特色的

[翻　译]西安以它各式各样的小吃著称。

[分　析]as + sort + ed

to + 分类 + 形容词尾 → 把各类东西放到一起，各式的，什锦的

[大头例句] I bought a tin of assorted cookies.我买了一听什锦饼干。

category n. /'kætigəri/

They were trying to rearrange the books by *categories*.

[猜一猜]A 规则　B 需要　C 集合　D 类别

[翻　译]他们正试着给这些书重新分类。

[分　析]cat + egory

下面的 + 会议 → 当作集体，看成一个类别，种，部门

[词义扩展] n.【数】范畴，类型；【哲、逻】范畴

[大头例句] Computer viruses fall into three broad categories.电脑病毒可以宽泛地分成三类。

classify vt. /'klæsifai/

In the study families are *classified* according to their incomes.

[猜一猜]A 分类　B 出版　C 古典　D 编撰

[翻　译]在该研究中家庭被按照收入进行了划分。

[分　析]classi + fy

等级 + 使…化 → 使分成等级，分等，分类。

[大头巧记] class，班级 classify，分班，分类。

commonplace n./adj. /'kɔmənpleis/

The scientists believe that soon it will be *commonplace* for people to use artificial intelligence.

[猜一猜]A 影响　B 普通　C 瞩目　D 稳定

[翻　译]科学家们相信在不久的将来人们使用人工智能将变成寻常之事。

[大头巧记] 拆：common place，普通的地方 → 普通的。

[词义扩展] n. ①口头禅，老生常谈 ②常事，平常物品

commonplace book 备忘录

vt. 把…记入备忘录，(由备忘录中)摘出

[大头例句] It is now commonplace for people to use the Internet at home. 现在人们在家上网是很寻常的事。

constitute compose

comprise v. /kəm'praiz/

The word "politics" *comprises*, in itself, a difficult study of no inconsiderable magnitude. (Charles Dickens)

[猜一猜]A 意味　B 浓缩　C 联系　D 包含

[翻　译]"政治学"这个词本身就包含了复杂广大的学问。(查尔斯·迪更斯)

[分　析]com + prise

共同 + 握取 → 一起收入，包含

[词义扩展] vt. 组成，由…组成 *The Union comprises 50 states.* 联邦由50个州组成。

[大头例句] Two essays and three assignments comprise the course. 这个课程包含两篇论文和三份作业。

component n. /kəm'pəunənt/

Each of the *components* of the computer is useful in its degree.

[猜一猜]A 品牌　B 型号　C 部件　D 软件

[翻　译]电脑的每个部件都有不同程度的作用。

[分　析] com　　　+ pon + ent
一起，合成+ 放 + 形容词尾 → 放在一起的，组成的，成分，部件

[词义扩展] *adj.* 合成的，成分的，分量的
n. 部分，成分，分力，支命题 *component of force*【物】分力

[大头例句] I was trying to break the problem down into its separate components. 我在试着把问题分解成一个个单独的部分。

encyclopedia *n.* /enˌsaikləuˈpiːdiə/

He always appears to be a walking *encyclopedia*.

[猜一猜]A 字典　　B 伟人
C 百科全书　　D 经理

[翻　译]他总是表现得好像自己是活的百科全书。

[分　析] encyclo　　+ pedia
循环的，普遍的 + 教育 → 指导教育的普通课程 → 百科全书

[大头例句] A dictionary explains words and an encyclopedia explains facts. 词典解释词义，百科全书解释事物。

decompose *v.* /ˌdiːkəmˈpəuz/

You can use a prism to *decompose* light.

[猜一猜]A 聚集　B 反射　C 折射　D 分解

[翻　译]你可以用三棱镜来分解光线。

[分　析]de　+ com + pose
离开 + 一起 + 放 → 放在一起的东西散开 → 分散，腐烂

[大头巧记] **compose，组合**，de 离开，组合在一起的东西离开 → 分散。

[大头例句] You can apply heat to decompose organic compounds. 有机组织可以通过加热来使之分解。

detach *vt.* /diˈtætʃ/

The hood fastens to the collar with studs and *detaches* easily.

[猜一猜]A 分开　B 毁坏　C 隐藏　D 易变

[翻　译]这个帽兜通过扣子固定在领子上，很容易取下来。

[分　析]de　+ tach
移出 + 连接 → 分开，解开，分离

[大头巧记] 同源词 attach，系上，附带。de 和 at 为反义词头。

[词义扩展] *vt.* 派遣 *I proposed detaching a squadron to seize the island.* 我提议派出一个中队夺取那个小岛。

[大头例句] He detached a check from the checkbook and gave it to her. 他从支票本上撕下张支票给了她。

digest *v.* /daiˈdʒest/

There was a pause while she *digested* this piece of news.

[猜一猜]A 领会　B 发现　C 公布　D 展示

[翻　译]她花了一些时间来领会这个消息。

[分　析] di　+ gest
分开 + 传送 → 分类传送出去 → 消化，融会贯通，领会

[词义扩展] *n.*分类，摘要
business condition digest 商情摘要

[大头例句] Cheese can be difficult to digest. 奶酪有时很难消化。

distinct *adj.* /disˈtiŋkt/

Those two suggestions are quite *distinct* from each other.

[猜一猜]A 矛盾的　　B 衬托的
C 误解的　　D 明显的

[翻　译]这两个建议截然不同。

[分　析] di　+ stinct
分开 + 刺 → 分别的，清楚的

[词义扩展] *adj.* 很有可能的，可能的 *There is a distinct possibility that she won't come.* 她很有可能不来了。

glossary *n.* /ˈglɔsəri/

You can find the word in the *glossary* at the back of the book.

[猜一猜]A 附录　B 说明　C 注释　D 词汇表

[翻　译]你可以在书后的词汇表中找到这个词。

[分　析] gloss　　+ ary
舌头，语言 + 名词词尾 → 词汇表，术语表

/ˈdʒiːnəs/
genus. n 种类

homogeneous *adj.* /ˌhɔməuˈdʒiːnjəs/

He bought a ***homogenous*** collection of books, all on cross-cultural awareness.

[猜一猜]A 同类的　　B 复杂的
C 多样的　　D 珍贵的

[翻　译]他收集了同类书籍，都是关于文化交叉意识的。

[分　析]homo + geneous
同　+ 属 → 同类的，相似的，纯一的，均匀的

[大巧头记] homo，同，例如：**homosexual**，同性恋的。**gene**，基因，**geneous**，基因的。**homogeneous**，同类基因的，同类的。

[大例头句] That is a tight-knit, homogeneous society. 那是一个紧密相连的同种社会。

identical *adj.* /aiˈdentikəl/

The handwriting on both cheques is ***identical***.

[猜一猜]A 真实的　　B 假造的
C 激励的　　D 相同的

[翻　译]两张支票上的笔迹完全相同。

[分　析]identi + cal
相同　+ 形容词尾 → 同一的，完全相同的

[大巧头记] identity，经常缩写为 ID，意为身份，同一。ID card，身份证。身份证明，就是证明你和你所说的是同一个人。**identical**，同一的。

[词扩义展] *adj.*【数】恒等的；【生】同卵的

[大例头句] This house is almost identical to the one where I lived as a child. 这个房子和我小时候住的那个几乎完全一样。

paradox *n.* /ˈpærədɔks/

'More haste, less speed' is a ***paradox***.

[猜一猜]A 假话　　B 真理
C 似是而非的隽语　　D 座右铭

[翻　译]"欲速则不达"是似是而非的隽语。

[分　析]para　+ dox
旁边的 + 观点 → 旁门左道的观点，矛盾，似是而非的论点，矛盾的事物

[大例头句] Many of history's most famous photographs incorporate a juxtapositioning of paradoxes; for example, the lone expeditioner climbing on the backdrop of the might of giant Mount Everest and its extreme climate. 很多历史上著名的照片都是并列的互相矛盾的事物的组合，例如，孤独的探险队员在珠穆朗玛峰及其严酷的气候背景下攀登。

parasite *n.* /ˈpærəsait/

He thinks students are just ***parasites***.

[猜一猜]A 小孩子　　B 书呆子
C 栋梁　　D 寄生虫

[翻　译]他认为学生只是些寄生虫。

[分　析]para　+ site
旁边 + 食物 → 在食物旁边的 → 寄生虫，食客，谄媚者

[大例头句] Plagued by a rare intestinal parasite, it became painful to digest food and difficult to retain the nutrients provided by the food. 由于一种肠内寄生虫的困扰，消化食物变得疼痛，且也难于保留食物所提供的营养。

summary *n.* /ˈsʌməri/

The text provides ***summaries*** of the plots of Shakespeare's plays.

[猜一猜]A 评价　B 分析　C 概要　D 影响

[翻　译]这篇文章提供了莎士比亚戏剧情节的概要。

[分　析]summ + ary
总　+ 词尾 → 摘要，概要

[大巧头记] summer，夏天太热，夏天做的事需简单、概要 summary。

[大例头句] So, in summary, we've got to try to get further funding. 所以，一句话，我们需要更多的资金。

Organic Chemistry
有机化学

习题：在下面的空格中填入本单元所学的单词。

1. He __________ a check from the checkbook and gave it to her.
2. Plagued by a rare intestinal __________, it became painful to digest food and difficult to retain the nutrients provided by the food.
3. Xi'an is famous for its __________ snacks.
4. In the study families are __________ according to their incomes.
5. Two essays and three assignments __________ the course.
6. He always appears to be a walking __________.
7. There was a pause while she __________ this piece of news.
8. You can apply heat to __________ organic compounds.
9. The scientists believe that soon it will be __________ for people to use artificial intelligence.
10. Computer viruses fall into three broad __________.
11. Each of the __________ of the computer is useful in its degree.
12. Those two suggestions are quite __________ from each other.
13. He bought a __________ collection of books, all on cross-cultural awareness.
14. Many of history's most famous photographs incorporate a juxtapositioning of __________.
15. This house is almost __________ to the one where I lived as a child.
16. You can find the word in the __________ at the back of the book.
17. So, in __________, we've got to try to get further funding.

Day 17

algae *n.* /ˈældʒiː/

The *algae* play a very important role in marine biosphere.

[猜一猜]A 珊瑚 B 飞鸟 C 沙丁鱼 D 海藻

[翻 译]海藻在海洋生物圈里扮演着极为重要的角色。

albatross *n.* /ˈælbətrɔs/

The mariner killed the *albatross* and had to wear it around his neck as a penance.

[猜一猜]A 白天鹅 B 鹦鹉 C 孔雀 D 信天翁

[翻 译]那个水手杀死了信天翁之后不得不把它挂在脖子上以示赎罪。

[分 析]al + batross

the + 白尾的海鹰 → 信天翁

[词义扩展]*n.* ①沉重的负担,包袱 ②障碍,阻碍成功的阻碍

[大头例句]Albatrosses, the world's largest flying birds, most magnificent expressions of biodiversity, yet are facing extinction due to illegal and unregulated longline fishing. 信天翁,世界上最大的飞鸟,生物多样性的完美体现,由于长期非法、盲目地捕猎,正面临着灭绝的危险。

alligator *n.* /ˈæligeitə/

Have you seen the *alligator* in the zoo?

[猜一猜]A 美洲鳄 B 美洲豹 C 非洲象 D 澳洲考拉

[翻 译]在公园里你见到美洲鳄了吗?

[分 析]al + ligator

the + 蜥蜴 → 蜥蜴似的东西 → 鳄鱼

[大头介绍]Alligator 来源于西班牙语 ellagarto,意思是"蜥蜴"。在采用 alligator 这个词之前,其发音和词形经过了好几种变化。这些变化,语言学家们称作禁忌变形,在人们惧怕的某种事物的名称里是常见的。

[大头例句]She bought the alligator which she had found three days before. 她买下了她三天前发现的那个鳄鱼皮的手提包。

almond *n.* /ˈɑːmənd/

The City of Cheng De is famous for *almond* juice.

[猜一猜]A 柠檬 B 瓜子 C 核桃 D 杏仁

[翻 译]承德市以杏仁著名。

[词义扩展]*n.* 杏树,形状物

I like almond cakes. 我喜欢杏仁饼。

alpine *adj.* /ˈælpain/

Alpine plants look very different from the ones we saw on the bank of Med.

[猜一猜]A 雨林 B 丘陵 C 平原 D 高山

[翻 译]高山植物和我们在地中海岸边看到的植物很不一样。

[大头巧记]此词还可表示阿尔卑斯山,Alps,最高峰勃朗峰,高 4810.2 米,所以 alpine 有高山的之意。

[大头例句]It's unbelievable to think I've won the first alpine medal for Britain at the Olympics. 当我想到我为大不列颠赢得了第一枚高山运动的金牌时,真是让人难以置信。

amphibian *adj./n.* /æmˈfibiən/

Frogs are *amphibians.*

[猜一猜]A 两栖动物 B 冷些动物 C 有益动物 D 有害动物

[翻 译]青蛙是两栖动物。

[分 析]amphi + bian

两面的 + life,生命 → 两栖动物

[词义扩展]*n.* ①水陆两用飞机/车 ②有双重性格的人

[大头例句]For more than one decade now, a worldwide amphibian decline seems to affect even populations in pristine habitats.十几年来，世界范围内两栖动物的衰减，似乎甚至波及到了它们在其原始栖息地的数量。

bloom *n.* /bluːm/

Her hair was caught all to one side in a great ***bloom*** of frizz, which attracted all the gentlemen in the hall.

[猜一猜]A 果实　B 花朵　C 青山　D 笤帚

[翻　译]她的头发挽在一边，象一大朵卷起的花，这引起了大厅里男士们的注意。

[词义扩展]*n.* 旺盛，青春 *v.* 使旺盛，使开花，大量出现，突然出现或膨胀

[习语记忆]**in the bloom of**，最佳时期 *She is in the bloom of beauty.* 她正值豆蔻年华。

[大头例句]After that incident the subscription selling of our magazine bloomed splendidly. 在那个事件以后，我们杂志的订阅销售量激增。

blossom *vi.* /ˈblɔsəm/

For a long time I hadn't seen her, so it really surprised me a lot that she had ***blossomed*** into a beauty.

[猜一猜]A 注意　B 花朵　C 成长　D 收养

[翻　译]我很久没有见过她了，所以当我发现她已经出落成一个美人的时候，我吃了一惊。

[词义扩展]*n.* ①花，花簇　②开花期；发育初期　③兴旺时期，前途有望的人 *The apple tree has an excellent blossom this time.* 这次这棵苹果树花开得特别好。*vi.* 开花，繁荣兴旺

[大头例句]New industries can blossom over night if we develope the new technology for our production. 如果我们研究出产品的新技术，新的工业就可以在一夜之间遍地开花。

bug *n.* /bʌg/

The police planted a ***bug*** in the suspect's room.

[猜一猜]A 窃听器　B 罪名　C 证人　D 证据

[翻　译]警方在嫌疑犯的房间里装了窃听器。

[词义扩展]*n.* ①小虫，臭虫 ②细菌，或由细菌产生的疾病 *a flu bug* 流感病菌 ③（机器、设计等的）缺陷，瑕疵 ④着迷，热衷于(某事)者
v. 凸出，变大

[习语记忆]**put a bug in sb.'s ear** 事先给某人暗示（警告）

[大头例句]My eyes bugged when I saw the love letter. 当看见那封情书时，我的眼睛睁大了。

buzzword *n.* /ˈbʌzwəːd/

"Return to the ancients" is the ***buzzword*** in the fashion industry this autumn.

[猜一猜]A 时髦话　　B 诀窍
C 主题　　D 副产品

[翻　译]"复古"是今年秋天时装业的时髦话。

[分　析]buzz + word
嗡嗡地响 + 话，词 → 嗡嗡响的话 → 大家都在说的话 → 时髦话

[大头例句]His speech in Oxford was full of buzzwords. 他在牛津大学的演说全是时髦词。

ecology *n.* /i(ː)ˈkɔlədʒi/

I am interested in the ***ecology*** of the wetlands.

[猜一猜]A 生物　B 生态学　C 景观　D 经济

[翻　译]我对沼泽地区的生态学感兴趣。

[分　析]eco + logy
家，房屋 + …学科 → 研究环境的学问 → 生态学

[大头巧记]去尾法：记住其特征部分 eco，谐音"依靠"，生物之间互相依靠的学问——生态学。

infant *n./adj.* /ˈinfənt/

Infant mortality has been dramatically reduced by modern medicine.

[猜一猜]A 不应该得的　　B 可避免的
C 婴儿　　D 贫困人

[翻　译]由于现代医学的进步，婴儿死亡率已经极大地降低了。

[分　析]in + fant
不 + 说话 → 不会说话，婴儿，幼儿。

[词义扩展]*n.* 未成年者(即未满21岁)，生手
adj. 婴儿的，幼稚的，初期的，未成年的 *an infant school* 幼儿园

[大头例句]Infants and elderly people are particularly at risk. 婴幼儿和已过中年的人尤其处在危险中。

intact *adj.* /inˈtækt/

Despite his misfortunes, his faith and optimism remained *intact*.

[猜一猜] A 原封不动的　B 坚定的
C 醒目的　D 昂扬的

[翻　译] 虽然他遭到一连串的不幸，他的信心和乐观丝毫未减。

[分　析] in + tact
不 + 接触 → 未经触动的，原封不动的，完整无损的，处女的

[大头巧记] contact，与…接触；intact，不与…接触，原封不动的

[大头例句] This great Victorian house will be preserved intact and opened to the public. 这所伟大的维多利亚女皇时期的房子会被完整地保存并向公众开放。

juvenile *adj.* /ˈdʒuːvinail/

The problem of *juvenile* delinquency presented itself for the attention of the whole society.

[猜一猜] A 暴力的　B 欺诈的
C 青少年的　D 移民的

[翻　译] 少年犯罪这个问题引起了全社会的注意。

[分　析] juven + ile
年轻 + 形容词尾 → 年轻的，幼稚的

[词义扩展] *n.* 青少年，少年读物

[大头例句] The number of juveniles arrested for violent crimes is increasing year by year. 因暴力犯罪而被捕的青少年的人数正逐年增加。

kidney *n.* /ˈkidni/

Kidneys filter the blood of metabolic wastes, which are then excreted as urine.

[猜一猜] A 孩子　B 脾　C 肾　D 肝

[翻　译] 肾脏过滤代谢产物中的血液，然后将此以尿的形式排出。

[词义扩展] *n.* 个性，脾气 *a man of the right kidney* 脾气好的人

[大头例句] Kidney transplant technology achieved big progress in the past ten years. 在过去的十年里，肾移植技术取得了很大的进展。

livestock *n.* /ˈlaivstɔk/

We call animals such as cows, sheep, and pigs that are kept on farms *livestock*.

[猜一猜] A 哺乳动物　B 牲畜
C 宠物　D 生活必备物

[翻　译] 我们把像母牛、羊、猪这样的农场畜养的动物叫做牲畜。

[大头巧记] lives，生灵，stock，储备，放牧，储备放牧的生命 → 牲畜，家畜。

[大头例句] There is a lot of livestock in his family. 他家里有很多家畜。

mammal *n.* /ˈmæməl/

Many are surprised to know that whales, creatures of the sea, are also *mammals*, as they have hair and nurse their young.

[猜一猜] A 爬行动物　B 两栖动物
C 鱼类动物　D 哺乳动物

[翻　译] 对于海洋生物鲸鱼也是哺乳动物，很多人感到很吃惊，它们也具有毛发并养育他们的幼儿。

[分　析] mamma + l
乳房 + 词尾 → 哺乳动物

[大头巧记] mammal，谐音：妈妈。靠妈妈母乳喂养的动物 → 哺乳动物。

[大头例句] Human beings also belong to the mammal species. 人类也属于哺乳动物。

metabolism *n.* /meˈtæbəlizəm/

Due to a high *metabolism*, most young people can eat anything they want without gaining very much weight; as they age, however, *metabolism* slows down, and it becomes easier to gain weight.

[猜一猜] A 境界　B 精力
C 消耗　D 新陈代谢

[翻　译] 由于新陈代谢旺盛，很多年轻人可以吃他们想吃的任何东西而不会增加很多体重；当他们年龄稍长以后，新陈代谢减缓，就更容易体重增加了。

[分　析] meta + bol + ism

改变 + 扔 + 名词词尾 → 改变某物使用后扔掉 → 新陈代谢

[大头例句] Do more exercises to speed up your metabolism. 做更多的运动，增快你的新陈代谢。

mortal n. /ˈmɔːtl/

Forgetting momentarily that he was but a mere *mortal*, the young boy dreamt of the lifestyle of Superman, leaping tall buildings without ever facing life-threatening danger.

[猜一猜] A 人　B 鬼　C 怪　D 神

[翻　译] 这个年轻人即刻忘记了自己只是一个普通人，幻想着超人的生活方式：从高高的楼上跳下而不用面对死亡威胁的危险。

[大头巧记] 行进词：**moral**，道德的；道德的载体 **mortal**，人。

[词义扩展] *adj.* ①必死的，人类的 ②非常…的

mortal combat 决斗

[大头例句] All mortals must die. 人终有一死。

organism n. /ˈɔːɡənizəm/

The global economy is a complex *organism*.

[猜一猜] A 有机体　B 问题

C 危机　D 实验室

[翻　译] 全球经济是个复杂的有机体。

[大头巧记] **organize** *v.* 组织；**organism**，*n.* 有机组织，生物体，有机体。

[大头例句] This is a microscopic organism living in the cow's stomach. 这是一种生活在牛的胃中的微生物。

zoology n. /zəuˈɔlədʒi/

One of my friends studies *zoology* in this university.

[猜一猜] A 管理学　B 组织学

C 动物学　D 社会学

[翻　译] 我的一个朋友在这所学校学习动物学。

[分　析] zoo　+ logy

动物园 + …学 → 动物学，生态

习题：在下面的空格中填入本单元所学的单词。

1. New industries can __________ over night if we deveolpe the new technology for our production.
2. The police planted a __________ in the suspect's room.
3. The global economy is a complex __________.
4. One of my friends studies __________ in this university.
5. The __________ plays a very important role in marine biosphere.
6. The mariner killed the __________ and had to wear it around his neck as a penance.
7. It's unbelievable to think I've won the first __________ medal for Britain at the Olympics.
8. For more than one decade now, a worldwide __________ decline seems to affect even populations in pristine habitats.
9. I am interested in the __________ of the wetlands.
10. She bought the __________ which she had found three days before.
11. __________ transplant technology achieved big progress in the past ten years.
12. Many are surprised to know that whales, creatures of the sea, are also__________, as they have hair and nurse their young.
13. Due to a high __________, most young people can eat anything they want without

gaining very much weight; as they age, however, __________ slows down, and it becomes easier to gain weight.

14. Forgetting momentarily that he was but a mere__________, the young boy dreamt of the lifestyle of Superman, leaping tall buildings without ever facing lifethreatening danger.
15. Have you seen the __________ in the zoo?
16. Her hair was caught all to one side in a great __________ of frizz,which attracted all the gentlemen in the hall.
17. The City of Cheng De is famous for __________ juice.
18. "Return to the ancients" is the __________ in the fashion industry this autumn.
19. The problem of __________ delinquency presented itself for the attention of the whole society.
20. This great Victorian house will be preserved __________ and opened to the public.
21.__________ mortality has been dramatically reduced by modern medicine.
22. We call animals such as cows, sheep, and pigs that are kept on farms __________.

Note 前事不忘后事之师 *Remember the past and it will guide your future.*

Day 18

alliance *n.* /əˈlaiəns/

I just interviewed the chairman of the ***alliance*** of labor unions opposing the bill.

[猜一猜]A 联盟　B 组织　C 权益　D 合同

[翻　译]我刚刚采访了反对法案的工会联盟的主席。

[分　析]alli + ance

ally,联合 + 名词词尾 → 联盟

[词义扩展] *n.* ①同盟；联盟，同盟国；同盟条约 *International Co-operative Alliance* 国际合作社联盟 ②联姻，结亲 *The two families made an alliance.* 这两家结了亲家。③类似，共同点 *There is an ancient alliance between mathematics and music.* 数学和音乐之间有古老的联系。

Holy Alliance 神圣同盟

[大头例句] Britain acts in alliance with the USA to deal with the Iraq affairs. 英国和美国统一行动以处理伊拉克事物。

align *v.* /əˈlain/

The PLA always ***aligns*** itself with the people.

[猜一猜]A 领导　B 和…站在一起　C 精兵简政　D 战斗

[翻　译]人民解放军总是和人民站在一起。

[分　析]a + lign

to + line → 排成一队，和…站在一起

[词义扩展] *v.* ①排成直线；排成行 *aligned the bikes with the wall* 使自行车沿墙排成行

②使密切合作，联合，使结盟 *We decided to align ourselves with the students.* 我们决定和学生们站在一起。

③调准；调整（电路、频率）*The wheels of my bicycle needs aligning.* 我的自行车轮子需要调整一下了。

agglomeration *n.* /əˌgloməˈreiʃən/

"To avoid the problems of large urban ***agglomerations***,the state decentralized the university system" (Bickley Townsend)

[猜一猜]A 商业　B 教育　C 聚结　D 限制

[翻　译]"为了避免大城市地聚结问题，国家把大学分散开"。(比克利·汤森)

[分　析]ag + glome+ration

朝向 + 球形 + 名词后缀 → 向球形发展的情况 → 结聚，凝聚

[大头例句] I can't bear the ugly agglomeration of clothes in your flat. 我受不了你房间那乱成一团的衣服。

analogous *adj.* /əˈnæləgəs/

This proposal was ***analogous*** to/with the one we discussed at the last meeting.

[猜一猜]A 类似　B 抵触　C 补充　D 阐释

[翻　译]这项提案与上次会议上我们讨论过的那份提案相似。

[分　析]ana + logous

根据 + 比例 → 成比例的，类似的

[大头例句] His opinions are always analogous to his wife's, so his friends think him henpecked. 他的观点总是和他妻子的看法类似，所以他的朋友都觉得他是个妻管严。

assemble *v.* /əˈsembl/

Did you know that you could make over $700.00 a week ***assembling*** just one product?

[猜一猜]A 制造　B 购买　C 销售　D 装配

[翻　译]你原来知道仅仅是组装一个产品每周就可以挣到700多美元吗？

[分　析]as + semble

to + 一起 → 使在一起，召集，装配

[大头例句] On National Day, tens of thousands of people assembled at Tian'anmen Square. 国庆节的时候成千上万的人聚集在天安门广场上。

assimilate *v.* /əˈsimileit/

As a qualified teacher, he has to help the students *assimilate* the facts, not just let them remember.

[猜一猜] A 接受 B 分析 C 总结 D 吸收

[翻 译] 作为一名称职的老师，他必须帮助学生完全地理解这些事实，而不是只让他们记忆。

[分 析] as + simil + ate
to + 相同 + 动词词尾 → 使相同，同化，吸收

[大头巧记] 根据同根词 **similar** 来记。

[大头例句] China has assimilated many outstanding cultures from all corners of the world. 中国同化了许多来自世界各地的优秀文化。

breach *n.* /briːtʃ/

Her revealing of my secret would be a *breach* of the trust between us.

[猜一猜] A 倒霉 B 惩罚 C 破坏 D 考验

[翻 译] 她对我的秘密的泄漏会破坏我们之间的信任。

[大头巧记] b(u) reach → 不 reach，产品不达到要求，是对社会主义建设的破坏。

[词义扩展] *n.* ①破坏，违反 ②(友好关系的)破裂 ③缺口，伤口
vt. ①突破；违约 ②违反；破坏

[大头例句] Their company breached the agreement first, so they ought to take full responsibility for the loss. 他们公司首先违反了协议，所以他们应该对损失承担全部责任。

coalition *n.* /ˌkəuəˈliʃən/

The aim of this party is the establishment of a democratic *coalition* government in that country.

[猜一猜] A 民主 B 统一 C 独立 D 联合

[翻 译] 这个政党的目标是在国家实现一个民主的联合政府的建立。

[分 析] co + alition
共同 + 成长 → 联合，结合，合并

collaboration *n.* /kəˌlæbəˈreiʃən/

This company is developing new medicine for cancer in *collaboration* with a university.

[猜一猜] A 领导 B 支持 C 合作 D 竞争

[翻 译] 这家公司正在和一所大学合作开发治疗癌症的新药。

[分 析] col + labrat+ ion
一起 + 工作 + 名词词尾 → 一起工作，合作

[词义扩展] *n.* ①合作作品 ②通敌，勾结

compact *adj.* /kəmˈpækt/

His apartment in Britain is very *compact*.

[猜一猜] A 宽敞的 B 狭小的 C 舒适的 D 紧凑的

[翻 译] 他在伦敦的公寓安排得很紧凑。

[分 析] com + pact
和，与 + 紧固 → 紧固地放在一起，紧凑

[词义扩展] *adj.* ①不占空间的，小型的 *a compact car* 小型汽车 ②简洁的，简明的 *a compact narration* 简明的叙述 ③结实的 *a boxer of compact build* 结实的拳击手 *v.* ①压紧 ②由…组成 *n.*契约，合同，协定

[大头例句] The two nations signed the compact to control contraband. 这两个国家签署了协定以管制走私行为。

compatible *adj.* /kəmˈpætəbl/

Compatible family relationships are very important in the growth of the children.

[猜一猜] A 比较的 B 有热情的 C 有爱心的 D 和谐的

[翻 译] 和谐的家庭关系在孩子的成长过程中很重要。

[分 析] com + pat + ible
一起 + 忍受 + 能…的 → 能够共同忍受的，能够相处的，和谐的

[词义扩展] *adj.* ①适宜的，符合的，能共存的 ②相容的，与…不矛盾的，一致的(with)

[大头例句] Success and happiness are not always compatible. 成功和幸福不总是一致的。

cooperate *vi.* /kəuˈɔpəreit/

When buyers *cooperate*, they can make large wholesale purchases at a discount.

[猜一猜] A 退出　B 加入　C 联合　D 连贯

[翻　译] 如果购买者联合起来，他们可以打折购买大批的批发商品。

[分　析] co + operate

共同 + 操作 → 共同操作，合作，协作

[大头例句] The company has agreed to cooperate in the development of this technology. 这家公司已经同意加盟开发这项技术。

correlate *v.* /ˈkɔrileit/

Research workers find it hard to *correlate* the two sets of figures.

[猜一猜] A 相关联　B 统一　C 不满　D 掩饰

[翻　译] 研究人员发现很难使这两组数字互相关联。

[分　析] cor + relate

共同 + 相关 → 和…相关，使相互关联

[大头例句] This response to the question did not correlate significantly with age or gender. 对该问题的这个反应与年龄和性别没有大的关联。

blend *vt.* /blend/

He has no difficulty *blending* his two business careers: advertising and entertainment.

[猜一猜] A 驾驭　B 发展　C 结合　D 赢利

[翻　译] 他毫无困难地把他的两个生意—广告业和娱乐业结合起来。

[词义扩展] *n.* 混合物

[大头例句] Her face shows, as she stares at me, a blend of sadness and excitation. 当她盯着我看的时候，她脸上的表情混合着悲伤和兴奋。

boycott *n./vt.* /ˈbɔikət/

The workers there are on strike to *boycott* the new foreign policy.

[猜一猜] A 抵制　B 响应　C 讨论　D 实施

[翻　译] 那里的工人正在罢工抵制新的外交政策。

[大头介绍] Boycott 是爱尔兰 Earl of Erne 伯爵的房地产经纪人，原为英军士兵，他拒绝执行新的土地政策。爱尔兰土地联盟对 Boycott 及其家人进行孤立——没有仆人，农业工人，得不到商店服务，也没有人送信。Boycott 很快就被用作这种对待方法的专有名词——联合抵制。

[词义扩展] *n./v.* 联合抵制，经济抵制

[大头例句] They put the dumped commercial products from Europe under a boycott. 他们联合抵制那些从欧洲来的倾销商品。

deposit *v.* /diˈpɔzit/

If you evaporate a little sea water on a porcelain dish; on cooling, crystals of common salt will *deposit* on the sides of the dish.

[猜一猜] A 沉淀　B 分解　C 腐蚀　D 结晶

[翻　译] 如果你将少许海水放到瓷盘中蒸发，冷却后就会有普通食盐的结晶沉淀在盘的四周。

[分　析] de + posit

向下 + 放 → 沉淀，淤积，堆积，附着

[词义扩展] *v.* ①寄存；②贮存，抵押；③留下，放下 *n.* ①沉积物 ②存款，保证金，押金 ③寄存，寄存(处)

[大头例句] He left a $1,000 deposit toward the purchase of this car. 为买这辆车他留下了1000美金的定金。

federation *n.* /fedəˈreiʃən/

The small countries joined together into a *federation*.

[猜一猜] A 大国　B 竞争　C 合作　D 联盟

[翻　译] 小国联合起来组成一个联盟。

[分　析] federa + tion

条约 + 名词词尾 → 通过条约组成的联合体，同盟，联盟，联邦

[大头巧记] **federal** ***adj.*** **联邦的** *FBI* (*Federal Bureau of Investigation.*) 美国联邦调查局

[大头例句] The International Tennis Federation organized these games. 国际网球联盟组织了本次比赛。

merge *v.* /məːdʒ/

In an effort to trim transportation costs and increase their ability to produce, the two companies ***merged*** in an agreement that was finalized last Friday.

[猜一猜] A 经营 B 激活 C 合并 D 设计

[翻 译] 为了调整运输成本，增强生产能力，这两家公司的合并协议在上周五最后敲定。

[大头巧记] 形近词：**immerge，浸入，隐没。merge，并入，结合，融合。**

[习语记忆] **merge into the background** 不显山，不露水

I kept quiet and tried to merge into the background. 我保持安静，试图不为人所注意。

[大头例句] For her, work and life merge into one another. 对于她来说，工作和生活融为一体了。

muddle *n.* /ˈmʌdl/

She was in a ***muddle***; she couldn't even remember what day it was.

[猜一猜] A 糊涂 B 困厄 C 清醒 D 繁忙

[翻 译] 她糊里糊涂，甚至记不起那是哪一天。

[分 析] mud + dle

泥浆 + 词尾 → 泥浆似的 → 混乱，糊涂

[词义扩展] *v.* 搞乱，弄糊涂

[大头例句] His intellect and decision-making ability muddled by an evening full of alcohol, it seemed unwise to persevere through the remainder of his homework and, instead, he started anew in the morning. 通晚地酗酒搞乱了他的智力和决断能力，没有选择在第二天早晨再开始，而是在当晚坚持把剩下的家庭作业做完，这种举动显得他很不明智。

multilateral *adj.* /ˌmʌltiˈlætərəl/

The leaders signed a ***multilateral*** treaty to maintain the peaceful situation in Asia.

[猜一猜] A 核控制 B 多边的 C 多项的 D 最高级的

[翻 译] 这些领导们签署了多边协议来维持亚洲的和平环境。

[分 析] multi + later + al

多的 + 侧面 + 形容词尾 → 多边的，多国的

[大头例句] Some of the most successful peace treaties in history have also been the most complex: many feature multilateral agreements that require strict adherence by many different parties in order to be successful. 一些历史上最成功的和平协定同时也是最复杂的：很多是以多边协定为其特征，这些协定需要很多不同的党派严格坚持才能获得成功。

习题：在下面的空格中填入本单元所学的单词。

1. Their company __________ the agreement first, so they ought to take full responsibility for the loss.
2. The aim of this party is the establishment of a democratic __________ government in that country.
3. Evaporate a little sea water on a porcelain dish; on cooling, crystals of common salt will__________ on the sides of the dish.
4. I just interviewed the chairman of the __________ of labor unions opposing the bill.
5. His opinions are always __________ to his wife's, so his friends think him henpecked.
6. This company is developing new medicine for cancer in __________ with a university.
7. The two nations signed the __________ to control contraband.

8. __________ family relationships are very important in the growth of the children.
9. He has no difficulty __________ his two business careers: advertising and entertainment.
10. The workers there are on strike to __________ the new foreign policy.
11. We decided to __________ ourselves with the students.
12. I can't bear the ugly __________ of clothes in your flat.
13. China has __________ many outstanding cultures from all corners of the world
14. On National Day, tens of thousands of people __________ in Tian'anmen Square.
15. Research workers find it hard to __________ the two sets of figures.
16. The company has agreed to __________ in the development of this technology.
17. The leaders signed a __________ treaty to maintain the peaceful situation in Asia.
18. In an effort to trim transportation costs and increase their ability to produce, the two companies __________ in an agreement that was finalized last Friday.
19. The small countries joined together into a __________.
20. She was in a __________; she couldn't even remember what day it was.

Note 前事不忘后事之师 *Remember the past and it will guide your future.*

Day 19

abominate *vt.* /ə'bɔmineit/

Manager Bower *abominates* sin.

[猜一猜]A 憎恶 B 领导 C 介入 D 成就

[分 析]ab + omin + ate
away + omen, 前兆 + 动词词尾 → 感到前兆而离开, 看到它出现的势头就走 → 憎恶,痛恨

[翻 译]鲍沃尔经理憎恶邪恶。

[大头巧记](put) a bom(b) in ,ate (it).把炸弹放到里面炸它,吃它,所以恨之入骨。

[联 想]反义词: **adore 崇拜,爱慕**

adore *v.* /ə'dɔː/

She *adores* going to karaoke, and she has a wonderful voice.

[猜一猜]A 喜欢 B 讨厌 C 经常 D 曾经

[翻 译]她很喜欢卡拉 ok, 并且她有一个很好的嗓子。

[分 析] ad + dore
朝向 + 祈祷 → 向…祈祷 → 崇拜, 引申为喜欢

[联 想]**adorable *adj.* 可爱的; adoration *n.* 尊重,敬慕; adoring *adj.* 表示爱慕的**
The time I saw her adoring look I fell in love with her. 当我看到她那充满爱意的目光时,我就爱上了她.

[大头例句]I adore your adoring look and adorable smile. 我喜欢你爱慕的目光和你可爱的笑脸。

affectionate *adj.* /ə'fekʃənət/

She is *affectionate* to me.

[猜一猜]A 挚爱的 B 亲切的
C 冷漠的 D 粗俗的

[翻 译]她非常的爱我。

[分 析]affection + ate
友情,爱情 + 动词词尾 → 挚爱的,充满感情的

[大头巧记]记住 affection,影响,而最能够影响人的,是感情。

[词义扩展]*adj.* 充满深情的,有感情的,慈爱的 *an affectionate mother* 慈母 ;*be on affectionate terms with* 和…交情极好 ② A-yours= yours affectionately 你挚爱的,英美人的家人写信时的结束语。

[大头例句]Donald Duck is on affectionate terms with Mickey Mouse. 唐老鸭和米老鼠是铁哥们。

afflict *vt.* /ə'flikt/

Although he had already compensated the child for the loss of his boat, he was still *afflicted* with a conscience.

[猜一猜]A 明晰 B 同情
C 折磨 D 充满感情

[翻 译]虽然他已经对那个孩子的船做出了补偿,他还是感到良心上在受折磨。

[分 析] af + flict
朝向 + 打, 击 → 打击某人 → 给其带来痛苦,折磨

[联 想]**flick *n.* ① 电影, 影片 ②轻弹, 轻击** *By a flick of his whip, the horse started its journey.* 他用鞭子轻轻打了一下,马儿就开始了行程。 *vt.* 拂去, 轻击 *flick the dust from one's shoes* 从鞋子上轻轻拂去灰尘
[关于 flick 的习惯用语]
flick-knife (=switch-blade knife) **弹簧刀**
flick on (通过轻按)**咯哒地一声打开**(开关等)

[词义扩展]*vt.* 使苦恼, 痛苦, 折磨 *afflicted with arthritis* 苦于关节炎

[习语记忆]**be afflicted at** 因某事而受折磨

[大头例句]The Monkey King was being afflicted by his master's taking the hind leg off a donkey. 美猴王正在受他师傅喋喋不休的折磨。

agape *adj.* /ə'geip/

She was staring at me with her mouth *agape*.

[猜一猜]A 颤抖的　　B 大开的
　　C 紧闭的　　D 满含东西的

[翻　译]她目瞪口呆地注视着我。

[大头巧记] a gap e(nlarged),一个扩大了的裂口,大开的。

[词义扩展] *adj./ adv.* 目瞪口呆 *She left me agape and alone.* 她把我一个人目瞪口呆的晾在那里。*n.* 神对世人的爱

aggrieved *adj.* /ə'griːvd/

He felt *aggrieved* at his father's blame.

[猜一猜]A 合理的　　B 有力的
　　C 委屈的　　D 记恨的

[翻　译]对于父亲的责备,他感到很委屈。

[分　析]ag　+ griev　+ ed
朝向 + (使)伤心 + 形容词词尾 → 悲痛的,委屈的

[词义扩展] *adj.* ①受虐待的,权利受到不法侵害的,②抱不平的

[大头例句] Nick felt himself much aggrieved that his teacher said he hadn't concentrated on the class. 尼克因为老师说他没有集中注意力听讲而愤愤不平。

agony *n.* /'ægəni/

He was in an *agony* of guilt.

[猜一猜]A 痛苦　B 激动　C 沮丧　D 缠绕

[翻　译]他正处于内疚的极端痛苦之中。

[词义扩展] *n.* ①任何精神上极度的激动(悲喜)②临死的挣扎(痛苦)③斗争 *His last agony was over.* 他临死的挣扎已经过去了。

[大头例句] The adoption of that policy would only prolong the political stalemate and the silent agony of Iraq and its people. 这个方针的采用只会带来政治僵局的延长和伊拉克及其人民无声痛苦的延续。

ail *vt.* /eil/

His poor wife has been *ailing* for months.

[猜一猜]A 工作　B 生病　C 外出　D 失眠

[翻　译]他可怜的妻子已经病了了好几个月了。

[词义扩展] *vt.* ①(使)苦恼,(使)烦恼 ②干扰
What ails you? 你怎么了?

[大头例句] My mom will not concede when anything ails my study. 我妈妈不允许任何事情来干扰我的学习。

appreciable *adj.* /ə'priːʃəbl/

The changes in Beijing will be *appreciable* in the coming several years.

[猜一猜]A 可观的　　B 令人惊奇的
　　C 可以预见的　　D 充满信心的

[翻　译]北京的变化在以下的几年中将会是很可观的。

[分　析]ap + preci + able

[大头巧记] to + price + 可…的 → 可感知,可评估的
可通过同根词 **appreciate** (赏识,感激)来记

[词义扩展] *adj.* ①看得出的 ②有一点儿的

[大头例句] There was just an appreciable quantity of sadness in his heart when he heard the bad news about his ex-girlfriend. 当他听到他前任女友的坏消息时,心里只是有一点淡淡的悲伤。

apprehension *n.* /æpri'henʃən/

He has some *apprehensions* about his career in the USA.

[猜一猜]A 野心　B 计划　C 失望　D 担心

[翻　译]他对自己在美国的事业有些担心。

[分　析]ap + prehens + ion
to + to seize + 名词词尾 → 抓住某物 → 察知,意识到危险,担心,忧惧

[词义扩展] *n.* ①理解,理解力 ②意见;观念 ③逮捕

[大头例句] His teacher said he is a boy of strong apprehension, which made him very proud. 他的老师说他理解力很强,这让他很自豪。

condemn *vt.* /kən'dem/

Most people are willing to *condemn* violence of any sort as evil.

[猜一猜] A 想象 B 恢复 C 谴责 D 宣传
[翻 译] 大多数人都愿意把任何暴力行为视作恶行加以谴责。
[大头巧记] con,加强;demn 可联想到 **damn**(诅咒)→强烈的诅咒,谴责,判刑。
[大头例句] The statement was roundly condemned by members of the teacher's union. 这个声明遭到了老师联合会会员们的完全反对。

cherish *vt.* /ˈtʃeriʃ/

We never *cherish* any unrealistic fancies about those cold-blooded criminals.

[猜一猜] A 理解 B 关心 C 抱希望 D 传讯
[翻 译] 我们从不对那些冷血的罪犯抱有不切实际的幻想。
[分 析] cher + ish
珍爱的 + 动词词尾 → 珍爱…,对…抱有希望
[词义扩展] *vt.* ①抚育 ②爱护,珍爱 ③怀有,抱有(希望等)
[大头例句] I cherish a deep love for my family. 我珍爱我的家庭。

cemetery *n.* /ˈsemitri/

A *cemetery* is a place for burying the dead.

[猜一猜] A 墓地 B 天堂 C 圣歌 D 葬礼
[翻 译] 墓地是埋葬死者的地方。
[分 析] cemet + ery
睡觉 + …地方 → 人死以后睡觉的地方 → 墓地,公墓
[大头例句] The public begins to doubt the safety of the radioactive cemetery. 公众开始对放射性废物场的安全设备表示怀疑。

dismay *v.* /disˈmei/

She was *dismayed* to learn that her favorite dancer used drugs.

[猜一猜] A 激怒 B 吃惊 C 沮丧 D 绝望
[翻 译] 获悉她喜爱的舞蹈演员吸毒,她感到很沮丧.
[分 析] dis + may
去掉 + 希望 → 沮丧,惊慌
[词义扩展] *n.* 灰心,沮丧,惊愕 *The enemy retreated in perfect dismay.* 敌人沮丧地退去。
[大头例句] I was dismayed when I recognized the voice of Mrs. Bates. 当我听出是贝司太太的声音时,我很惊慌。

fanatic *n.* /fəˈnætik/

A *fanatic* is one who can't change his mind and won't change the subject.

[猜一猜] A 入迷者 B 革命者 C 爱国者 D 领袖
[翻 译] 一个专心致志的人不会改变决心,也不会改变自己的追求。
[大头巧记] fan,…迷,…爱好者;**fanatic,狂热者,盲信者**。
[词义扩展] *adj.* 狂热的;盲信的(亦作:fanatical)
My friend, Crawley, has always been a fanatical opponent of Mr. Lane's Radical Progressive Party. 我的朋友克劳莱一向是莱恩先生激进党的狂热反对者。
[大头例句] The attacks by religious fanatics caused the deaths of thousands of people in the past few years. 宗教狂热分子发动的袭击在过去的几年里造成了几千人死亡。

frantic *adj.* /ˈfræntik/

There was a *frantic* rush to get everything ready for the unexpected inspection from the superiors.

[猜一猜] A 坦诚的 B 巨大的 C 疯狂的 D 持续的
[翻 译] 为了准备迎接上级的突然检查,出现了一片疯狂的忙乱。
[大头巧记] **frank,坦诚的,坦白的**,如果人的所有的潜意识都坦白的话,就 **frantic(狂乱)**了。
[词义扩展] *adj.* 急忙的
be in a frantic hurry 急如星火
[大头例句] Her parents are absolutely frantic with worry. 她的父母完全急疯了。

fume *n./v.* /fjuːm/

Petrol *fumes* from car engines poison the atmosphere.

[猜一猜] A 处理　　B 未净化的
C 检查　　D 冒出

[翻　译] 汽车引擎冒出的汽油尾气毒化着大气。

[词义扩展] *n.* 烟,气体
n./v. 发怒

[大头例句] Motorists are fuming over the latest petrol shortages. 驾车者对最近汽油的短缺非常愤怒。

hilarious *adj.* /hiˈlɛəriəs/

He thought his jokes were ***hilarious***, but no one laughed.

[猜一猜] A 欢闹的　　B 讽刺的
C 睿智的　　D 怪异的

[翻　译] 他觉得自己的笑话很欢闹,可是没有人笑。

[分　析] hilar + ious
高兴 + 形容词尾 → 欢闹的,愉快的,热闹的

[大头例句] For some reason, she finds his jokes hilarious. 不知道为什么,她觉得他的笑话好笑极了。

indigenous *adj.* /inˈdidʒinəs/

Indians were the ***indigenous*** inhabitants of America.

[猜一猜] A 侨居的　　B 少数的
C 本土的　　D 无辜的

[翻　译] 印第安人是美洲的土著居民。

[分　析] indi + gen + ous
内部 + 产生 + 形容词尾 → 内部产生的,本土的,土生土长的

[词义扩展] *adj.* 天生的,固有的 *feelings indigenous to human beings* 人类固有的感情

[大头例句] The indigenous method costs less money. 土办法少花钱。

mourn *v.* /mɔːn/

We are ***mourning*** the loss of our close friend.

[猜一猜] A 宣布　B 哀悼　C 调查　D 混乱

[翻　译] 我们正在哀悼痛失一位密友。

[大头例句] Some cultures, to mourn for their dead, dress completely in black during the burial ceremony; others, by contrast, wear all white. 在一些文化中,为了表示对死者的哀悼,在葬礼中全着黑服;其他的,与之相反,全穿白服。

languish *vi.* /ˈlæŋgwiʃ/

The flowers ***languished*** from lack of water.

[猜一猜] A 绽放　B 凋萎　C 延迟　D 变色

[翻　译] 花因缺水而凋萎。

[分　析] langu + ish
疲倦 + 动词词尾 → 衰弱,憔悴,凋萎

[大头巧记] language(语言)脱离了(age),它的时代气息,就失去了活力,凋萎了。

[词义扩展] *v.* 渴望,苦思 *languish for home and family* 苦苦思念家和家人

[大头例句] Oil prices continue to languish at $10.50 a barrel. 石油价格继续跌到每桶10.50美元。

pathetic *adj.* /pəˈθetik/

Everything human is ***pathetic***. (Mark Twain).

[猜一猜] A 可怜的　　B 迷惑的
C 失常的　　D 旁观的

[翻　译] 人类具有同情心。(马克·吐温)

[分　析] pathe + tic
感情 + 形容词尾 → 感情用事的,可怜的,可悲的,不足的

[大头例句] The media considers the act of killing her own kids proof of her pathetic moral fiber; her family, however, cites it as proof that she was simply insane. 媒体认为杀害自己孩子的行为证明她可怜的道德素质,但她的家人却以此证明她是精神病患者。

passion *n.* /ˈpæʃən/

The union of the mathematician with the poet, fervor with measure, ***passion*** with correctness, is surely the ideal.

[猜一猜] A 资历　B 热情　C 训练　D 记忆

[翻　译] 兼备数学家和诗人的气质,热烈而有限度,热情而有节制,这的确是最理想的。

[分　析] pass + ion
感情 + 名词词尾 → 热情,激情

[词义扩展] *n.* 激怒，情欲，耶稣在十字架上的受难
Passion music【宗】耶稣受难曲

[习语记忆] **fly into a passion** 大发雷霆

[大头例句] In order to succeed in many careers in the arts, you must have not only great talent, but also a passion that pushes you to work long hours and high intensity. 为了取得艺术领域事业的成功，你不仅必须具有极大的天赋，同时还要有驱使你长期高强度工作的激情。

zeal *n.* /ziːl/

I am surprised at his *zeal* in politics.

[猜一猜] A 热情 B 智慧 C 天赋 D 冷淡

[翻译] 他对政治的热情让我吃惊。

[大头巧记] 和 **torpor**(无感觉)对比记忆。

[习语记忆] **Zeal without knowledge is a runaway horse.** 无知的狂热犹如脱缰的野马。

[大头例句] In their zeal to industrialize, they got rid of too many farms. 在工业化热情的驱动下，他们取消了太多的农场。

习题：在下面的空格中填写本单元出现的单词。

1. I am surprised at his __________ in politics.
1. The flowers __________ from lack of water.
3. Some cultures, to mourn for their dead, dress completely in black during the burial ceremony; others, by contrast, wear all white.
4. In order to succeed in many careers in the arts, you must have not only great talent, but also a __________ that pushes you to work long hours and high intensity.
5. The media considers the act of killing her own kids proof of her __________ moral fiber; her family, however, cites it as proof that she was simply insane.
6. Manager Bower __________ sin.
7. Nick felt himself much __________ that his teacher said he hadn't concentrated on the class.
8. She was staring at me with her mouth __________.
9. My mom will not concede when anything __________ my study.
10. His teacher said he is a boy of strong __________, which made him very proud.
11. We never __________ any unrealistic fancies about those cold-blooded criminals.
12. She was __________ to learn that her favorite dancer used drugs.
13. Petrol __________ from car engines poison the atmosphere.
14. I __________ your adoring look and adorable smile.
15. Although he had already compensated the child for the loss of his boat, he was still __________ with a conscience.
16. The adoption of that policy would only prolong the political stalemate and the silent __________ of Iraq and its people.
17. The changes in Beijing will be __________ in the coming several years.
18. A __________ is a place for burying the dead.

19. My friend, Crawley, has always been a __________ opponent of Mr. Lane's Radical Progressive Party.
20. Her parents are absolutely __________ with worry.
21. Indians were the __________ inhabitants of America.
22. He thought his jokes were __________, but no one laughed.
23. Donald Duck is on __________ terms with Mickey Mouse.
24. Most people are willing to __________ violence of any sort as evil.

Note 前事不忘后事之师 *Remember the past and it will guide your future.*

Day 20

auction n. /ˈɔːkʃən/

Tens of thousands of members of that community donated time, items, and resources to raising millions of dollars during the *auction*.

[猜一猜] A 慰问会　B 演唱会　C 拍卖会　D 经贸会

[翻　译] 在拍卖过程中，那个社团的成千上万的成员贡献了他们的时间、物力和财力来筹集数百万美元的资金。

[分　析] auct + ion
增加 + 动词词尾 → 给商品一个价格，然后逐渐加价 → 拍卖

[大头巧记] action 中间加一个"u"(you)，需要你的积极行动的活动 → 拍卖。

[词义扩展] *vt.* 拍卖 *The collector has auctioned all his collections.* 这位收藏家已经拍卖光了他所有的藏品。

[大头例句] This is the auction your friend was trying to tell you about! 这就是你的朋友想要告诉你的拍卖会。

asset n. /ˈæset/

An agreeable personality is a great *asset* in the political arena.

[猜一猜] A 优点　B 障碍　C 特点　D 牺牲

[翻　译] 宜人的性格在政治舞台上是一个很大的优点。

[分　析] as + set
to + 足够的 → 充足的 → 资源，资本，优点

[大头巧记] 反过来看：set…as，把某物作为资本放置。

[大头例句] Floating assets in our company have already reached 5 million dollars. 我们公司的流动资金已达5百万美元。

boom n./v. /buːm/

This *boom* in studying abroad, in turn, helps to raise the technological standard of the whole country.

[猜一猜] A 爆炸　B 规范　C 兴隆　D 投资

[翻　译] 反过来，留学热又促进了整个国家科技水平的提高。

[大头巧记] 这个词是拟声词，隆隆声，就像汉语中的"隆隆"，引申为"兴隆"。

[词义扩展] *v.* ①隆隆响 ②迅速增长，趋于繁荣

[大头例句] In a city with booming industry, land is precious and cannot be extravagantly used for traffic. 在一个工业飞速发展的城市里，土地资源非常宝贵，不能任意地用于交通。

commodity n. /kəˈmɔditi/

The prices of the *commodities* are quite acceptable. It thanks to the efforts the government made on light industry this year.

[猜一猜] A 旅游　B 家电　C 服装　D 日用品

[翻　译] 由于政府在轻工业上的努力，今年日用品的价格让人很容易接受。

[分　析] com + modity
together + 式样 → 各种各样的东西 → 日用品。

[词义扩展] *n.* ①[常用复]商品，农(矿)产品，出口产品 ②有用的东西 ③【会】款项用途 ④便利，利益

[习语记忆] **a commodity of brown paper** 廉价货

[大头例句] Time is our most valuable commodity. 时间是我们最具价值的物品。

commute v. /kəˈmjuːt/

He, as a supervisor in an international compa ny, *commutes* from London to his house in Cambridge everyday.

[猜一猜]A 来往于　B 调解　C 管理　D 视察

[翻　译]作为一家国际公司的主管，他们每天乘车来往于伦敦和他在剑桥的家之间。

[分　析]com + mute
和，与 + 改变 → 与…互换，替换，往返

[词义扩展]*vt.* ①兑换，变换 ②改变（付款）方式，偿付 ③减轻（刑罚等）

[大头例句]The governor commuted the prisoner's sentence of death to one of life imprisonment. 州长将这名囚犯的死刑减为无期徒刑。

compensate *v.* /ˈkɔmpənseit/

The coal miners struck to demand that the management *compensate* them for the time they worked over time.

[猜一猜]A 承认　B 减轻劳动负担　C 报酬　D 伙食

[翻　译]煤矿工人们罢工要求资方按时支付他们工作时间的报酬。

[分　析]com + pens + ate
一起 + 挂 + 动词词尾 → 一起悬挂起来 → 用称称东西的样子 → 衡量工作，支付报酬

[大头巧记]拆：com(e) pens ate.来用笔吃掉…，用笔把错别字"吃"掉，校正。

[词义扩展]*v.* ①补偿，偿还 ②酬报（for）③均（平）衡；校正

[习语记忆]**Nothing can compensate for the loss of time.** 虚度光阴是无法补偿的（光阴一去不复还）。

[大头例句]They were unlikely to be compensated for the damage to the house. 他们不太可能向对房子的损坏做出补偿。

consumption *n.* /kənˈsʌmpʃən/

The nation's *consumption* of coal decreased continuously last year.

[猜一猜]A 鼓励　B 赢利　C 投资　D 消费

[翻　译]去年全国耗煤量继续下降。

[分　析]con + sump + tion
全部 + 拿去 + 名词词尾 → 消费，消费量

[大头例句]Most people need to increase their daily consumption of fruit and vegetables. 大多数人都需要提高水果和蔬菜的日消费量。

deputy *n.* /ˈdepjuti/

Matt will be my *deputy* to deal with all the business while I am away.

[猜一猜]A 信任　B 代理　C 秘书　D 合作伙伴

[翻　译]我不在的时候，马特将代理我处理所有的生意。

[分　析]de + put(e) + y
向下 + 思考 + 名词词尾 → 将想法置于其下 → 代理人，委托人

[词义扩展]*n.* ①（某些国家的）国会议员 ②副警长，副职 *deputy mayor* 副市长，代理市长

[大头例句]When the head master was away, the deputy head did his job. 当头领不在时，副手掌管他的权利。

dividend *n.* /ˈdividend/

I don't know when my *dividend* will be paid.

[猜一猜]A 工资　B 股息　C 奖金　D 定金

[翻　译]我不知道什么时候我能拿到我的股息。

[大头巧记]**divide** 分，将赢利分开 → 股分红利，**dividend** 股息。

[词义扩展]*n.* 被除数 *In 8 ÷ 2, 8 is the dividend.* 在 8 除以 2 这个式子中，8 是被除数。

[大头例句]All my hard work eventually paid dividends. 我所有的努力工作终于收益了。

enterprise *n.* /ˈentəpraiz/

Through want of *enterprise* and faith men are where they are, buying and selling, and spending their lives like serfs.

[猜一猜]A 勇气　B 智慧　C 文明　D 进取心

[翻　译]由于缺乏进取心和信仰，人类始终驻足不前，或买或卖，过着奴隶般的生活。

[分　析]enter + prise
in + 取，拿 → 进取心，事业心，干事业

[大头巧记]拆：enter prise，进入奖赏，获奖，对获奖的渴望，进取心。

[词义扩展]*n.* 事业，企业，计划
manage an enterprise 经营一个企业

[大头例句] The country needs a government that works to encourage enterprise. 这个国家需要一个鼓励企业行为的政府。

exploit *v.* /iks'plɔit/

The government plans to ***exploit*** the oil under the sea.

[猜一猜] A 控制 B 争夺 C 出口 D 开发

[翻 译] 政府计划开发海底石油。

[分 析] ex + ploit

出去 + 折叠 → 打开,开发,开采,开拓,剥削,利用

[大头巧记] **explore,探究,勘测;explo(re) it,探究它,是要开发它。**

[词义扩展] *n.* 英雄行为,辉煌业绩 *Their heroic exploits will go down in history.* 他们的英雄业绩将被载入史册。

[大头例句] Children are being exploited in many of these factories. 这些工厂中有许多剥削童工。

guarantee *n./vt.* /ˌgærən'tiː/

Blue skies are not always a ***guarantee*** of fine weather.

[猜一猜] A 保证 B 预示 C 限制 D 吸引

[翻 译] 蔚蓝的天空并不总是保证晴朗的天气。

[分 析] guarant + ee

担保 + 承担…者 → 接受担保的人,担保物,担保,保证。

[词义扩展] *vt.* 对…提出担保,约定,许诺 *Many shopkeepers guarantee satisfaction to customers.* 许多店主对顾客保证满意。

[大头例句] The government provides help for small businesses, but it cannot guarantee their success. 政府对小型企业提供帮助,但是不能保证他们的成功。

incorporate *v.* /in'kɔːpəreit/

We will ***incorporate*** your suggestion into the new plan.

[猜一猜] A 同意 B 并入 C 欣赏 D 发展

[翻 译] 我们将把你的建议编到新计划中去。

[分 析] in + corpor + ate

里面 + 身体 + 动词词尾 → 尽到身体里面去 → 并入,合并,组成公司

[词义扩展] *adj.* 合并的,一体化的

[大头例句] The Government incorporated this principle into the 1977 law. 政府把这个法则并入了1977年的法律。

inventory *n.* /'invəntri/

When the police eventually arrived, we made an ***inventory*** of the missing items.

[猜一猜] A 价值 B 详细目录 C 线索 D 告发

[翻 译] 警察来时,我们列了一个所丢物品的清单。

[大头巧记] invent,发明,想到,让人一看就可以想到货物情况的东西 → 详细目录。

[词义扩展] *n.* 存货清单

n./v. 盘存,盘点

[大头例句] Some stores inventory their stock once a month. 有些商店每月盘货一次。

inflation *n.* /in'fleiʃən/

Inflation erodes the purchasing power of families with lower income.

[猜一猜] A 生产过剩 B 宏观调控 C 倾销政策 D 通货膨胀

[翻 译] 通货膨胀使低收入家庭的购买力不断下降。

[大头巧记] **flat,平的;flation,物价稳定;inflation,通货膨胀,deflation,通货紧缩。**

[词义扩展] *n.* 膨胀,充气,夸大

inflation of language 夸大其词

[大头例句] We had expected a pay raise in line with inflation. 我们曾经期待薪水会随通货膨胀一起上升。

impulse *n./vt.* /'impʌls/

Respect for the liberty of others is not a natural ***impulse*** in most men.

[猜一猜] A 本能 B 反映 C 意识 D 品德

[翻 译] 对大多数人来说,尊重他人的自由并不是一种自然的本能。

[分 析] im + pulse

内部 + 推 → 内在的推动 → 冲动，本能

[大头巧记] **impel** *vt.* **推动，impulse 为其名词形式。**

[词义扩展] *n.* ①刺激，鼓舞 ②【物】冲量 ③【医】搏动

[大头例句] I saw her get into the car, and on an impulse I followed her. 我看到她进了汽车，由于一种冲动，我也跟了进去。

mechanism *n.* /ˈmekənizəm/

In many Western societies, there still is no established *mechanism* for the care of the elderly within the family system.

[猜一猜] A 机器　B 药物　C 机制　D 法制

[翻 译] 在很多西方国家，仍然没有确定的家庭系统内照顾长者的机制。

[分 析] mechan + ism

机器 + 名词词尾 → 机械装置 → 机构，机制

[词义扩展] *n.* ①方法 ②【哲】机械论 ③【生】机能 ④【心理】作用机理 *a defense mechanism.* 戒备心理状态

[大头例句] Because of the complicating language barrier, it was almost impossible to find a mechanism for diplomatic negotiations. 由于复杂的语言障碍，几乎不可能找到进行外交商谈的方法。

习题：在下面的空格中填写本单元出现的单词。

1. Most people need to increase their daily ________ of fruit and vegetables.
2. The country needs a government that works to encourage ________.
3. The government provides help for small businesses, but it cannot ________ their success.
4. In many Western societies, there still is no established ________ for the care of the elderly within the family system.
5. ________ erodes the purchasing power of the families with lower income.
6. Tens of thousands of members of that community donated time, items and resources to raising millions of dollars during the ________.
7. An agreeable personality is a great ________ in the political arena.
8. The prices of the ________ are quite acceptable thanks to the efforts the government made on light industry this year.
9. He, as a supervisor in an international company, ________ from London to his house in Cambridge everyday.
10. This ________ in studying abroad, in turn, helps to raise the technological standard of the whole country.
11. When the headmaster was away, the ________ head did his job.
12. The government plans to ________ the oil under the sea.
13. All my hard work eventually paid ________.
14. When the police eventually arrived, we made an ________ of the missing items.
15. I saw her get into the car, and on an ________ I followed her.
16. The Government ________ this principle into the 1977 law.
17. The coal miners struck to demand that the management ________ them for the time they worked over time.

Day 21

stoneware n.粗陶器
porcelain n.瓷 adj.瓷的,精致的

ceramic adj. /si'ræmik/

The income from the *ceramic* industry accounts for about one third of the GDP in this country.

[猜一猜] A 陶瓷业的　B 冶金业的　C 轻工业的　D 重工业的

[翻　译] 陶瓷业的收入大约占了这个国家国民生产总值的三分之一。

[大头巧记] 去尾法：ic 为词尾，ceram 可独立成词，意为：陶器，陶瓷。将 cream 中的 re 颠倒可得。

[词义扩展] *n.* (*pl*) 陶瓷制品，制陶术

[大头例句] China is world-famous for its ceramic manufactures. 中国以她的陶瓷产品而享誉世界。

brittle adj. /'britl/

The *brittle* friendship between them didn't work out.

[猜一猜] A 脆弱的　B 短暂的　C 病态的　D 模糊的

[翻　译] 他们之间脆弱的友谊最终还是没有结果。

[大头巧记] br (ing) little，只给你带来一点点温馨的关系是脆弱的。

[词义扩展] *adj.* ①硬而易碎的 ②冷淡的；浅薄的 *n.* 酥糖

[大头例句] The duchess, though well-known as a society hostess, conveyed an unmistakably brittle air. 公爵夫人虽然是有名的社交界女主人，却明显流露出冷冰冰的表情。

chip n. /tʃip/

n.碎片,薄片 v.碎裂

He is drinking from the cup with a *chip* out of it.

[猜一猜] A 缺口　B 花纹　C 商标　D 茶叶

[翻　译] 他正在用一个有缺口的杯子喝水。

[分　析] 拟声词，东西碎裂的声音，碎片，缺口。

[词义扩展] *n.* (赌注用)筹码 *The chips are down.* 赌注已下，情况危急 *vt.*，形成缺口，使成碎片 *chip the cup* 打碎杯子

[习语记忆] **chip off the old block** 和父亲/母亲像是一个模子刻出来的

[大头例句] We all chipped in for champagne. 我们凑钱买香槟。(chip in 凑份子)

collapse n. /kə'læps/

The *collapse* of popular respect for the integrity of the president finally led to his abdication.

[猜一猜] A 崩溃　B 下降　C 斗争　D 揭露

[翻　译] 大众对该总统的廉正不再有信心，此种信心的崩溃最终导致了总统的辞职。

[分　析] col + lapse
一起 + 落下→崩塌，崩溃，瓦解

[词义扩展] *vi.* ①暴跌，失败 ②(健康、精神等)衰退，垮下 ③(椅子等)折叠

[大头例句] If you go on working as hard as this, your health may collapse. 如果你继续和现在一样拼命工作的话，你的健康可能会崩溃。

breeze vi. /briːz/

You intelligent boys can *breeze* through the examination without any difficulty.

[猜一猜] A 轻易通过　B 很难通过　C 免考　D 缓考

[翻　译] 你们这些聪明的孩子能没有任何困难地轻松通过这个考试。

[词义扩展] *n.* ①微风，柔风 ②争吵 ③轻而易举地工作 ④煤渣 *v.* 轻快地走

[大头例句] She breezed in and gave me a kiss. 她悄悄地进来吻了我一下。

chaos n. /'keiɔs/

His room became a *chaos* of wine bottles and wasted food after the party.

[猜一猜] A 混乱　B 打翻　C 充满　D 败坏

[翻　译]聚会结束以后他的房间里面酒瓶和剩饭乱成了一团。

[词义扩展] *n.* ①[常用 Chaos]（天地未出现前的）混沌世界

[大头例句] There have been severe floods, bringing chaos to the region. 发生了几场洪水，给这个地区带来了混乱。

dash *n./v.* /dæʃ/

He knocked the books to the floor with an impatient *dash* of his hand while his wife was explaining why she does not want a baby.

[猜一猜]A 猛击　B 吼叫　C 脾气　D 握紧

[翻　译]当她的妻子在解释她为什么不想要孩子的时候，他不耐烦地用手将书猛推到地上。

[词义扩展] *vt.&vi.* ①突进；飞跑 *The dog dashed into our house, which scared us.* 那只狗忽然跑进了我们的房子，让我们大吃一惊。②猛撞；冲撞 *The car was dashed against the baluster.* 那辆车猛地撞到栏杆上。③粉碎；使灰心；使受挫折④咒骂（相当于 damn）*Dash it all!* 可恶！
n. 破折号

[习语记忆] **cut a dash** 大出风头，摆阔

[大头例句] The economic crisis dashed his hopes. 经济危机使他的希望破灭了。

derelict *n.* /ˈderilikt/

The ragged old *derelict* and his poor dog were finally saved by a peasant and settled down there.

[猜一猜]A 直爽的人　B 和蔼的人　C 被遗弃的人　D 受伤的人

[翻　译]那位衣衫褴褛被遗弃的老人和他可怜的狗最终被一个农民所救，并在那里安居下来。

[分　析] de + relict
使…转移 + 把…留在后面→被遗弃的（人）

[词义扩展] *adj.* ①衰退的，陈旧的；破败的 ②玩忽职守的，疏忽的

[大头例句] He was living in a derelict house. 他住在一个废弃的房子里。

demolish *vt.* /diˈmɔliʃ/

All these old houses are going to be *demolished* to make space for the new ones.

[猜一猜]A 拆除　B 搬迁　C 重建　D 保留

[翻　译]所有这些旧房屋都快要拆除了，为盖新楼让出空间。

[分　析] de + molish
去除 + 混乱 → 搞乱后去除掉 →毁坏，粉碎，拆除

[大头例句] All these old houses are going to be demolished. 所有这些旧房屋都将被拆掉。

devastate *v.* /ˈdevəsteit/

The whole of Europe was *devastated* by the long war.

[猜一猜]A 卷入　B 波及　C 改变　D 破坏

[翻　译]长期的战争破坏了整个欧洲。

[分　析] de + vastate
完全的 + 荒芜 → 完全变成荒地 → 使荒芜，毁灭

[词义扩展] *v.* 压倒，征服，击败

[大头例句] He was devastated by the rude remark from his colleagues in the meeting. 在会上他被同事们的粗鲁言语搅得昏了头。

dismiss *v.* /disˈmis/

The boss threatened to *dismiss* all the employees who had expressed their sympathy for the strike, but it was all a bluff.

[猜一猜]A 控告　B 惩罚　C 解雇　D 伤害

[翻　译]老板威胁说要解雇所有同情罢工的员工，但是这不过是恐吓而已。

[大头巧记] dis，否定前缀，**miss，想念**，不再想念 → 让某人离去，解雇。

[词义扩展] *v.* ①解散，遣散 *to dismiss a class* 下课 ②不考虑，摒弃 ③【律】驳回，拒绝受理。

[大头例句] A few good people dismiss the idea as sheer nonsense. 不少人认为这种想法完全是胡说八道。

dissolve *v.* /diˈzɔlv/

Dissolve the sugar in one tablespoon of water over a low heat.

[猜一猜] A 提取 B 溶解 C 加热 D 供应

[翻 译] 在稍微加热的情况下用一大汤匙的水溶解糖。

[分 析] dis + solve

离开 + 放松 → 放松使其成为个体 → 溶解，液化

[词义扩展] ①解散 ②【律】解除 ③感动，软化 ④摧毁，消灭 ⑤弄明白

dissolve parliament before a general election 大选前解散议会

encounter *v.* /inˈkauntə/

Mr. Wilson *encountered* an old friend on the street.

[猜一猜] A 遇到 B 结交 C 邂逅 D 羞辱

[翻 译] 韦尔逊先生在街上遇到一个老朋友。

[分 析] en + counter

在…里面 + 对抗 → 进入对抗状态 → 相遇，遭遇。

[词义扩展] *v.* 遭遇 *n.* ①遭遇战，会战 ②偶然的相见 *It was a bloody encounter between the two armies.* 这是那两军之间的一次激烈的遭遇战。

[大头例句] We had a frighteningly close encounter with a black bear. 我们和一只黑熊有过一次恐怖的近距离遭遇。

extract *vt.* /iksˈtrækt/

She managed to *extract* a promise of support from her employers.

[猜一猜] A 榨得 B 得到 C 完成 D 兑现

[翻 译] 他设法从他的雇主那里"榨"得了支持的承诺。

[分 析] ex + tract

out + 汲取 → 榨取，拔出，吸取

[词义扩展] *vt.* 求根，开方，摘录 *n.* 精华，摘录 *extract the square root of 16* 开16的平方根

[大头例句] He went to the dentist's to have his tooth extracted. 他去牙医处拔牙。

fraction *n.* /ˈfrækʃən/

Mother's careful with her money, and spends only a *fraction* of her earnings.

[猜一猜] A 储蓄 B 开支 C 小部分 D 实用

[翻 译] 母亲用钱很审慎，只花自己收入很小的一部分。

[分 析] fract + ion

打破 + 名词词尾 → 打破的碎片，片断，小部分

[词义扩展] *n.* 分数 *1/3 and 5/8 are fractions.* 三分之一和八分之五是分数。

[大头例句] Unions recruit only a small fraction of the workers. 工会仅仅吸收了工人中的很小的一部分。

fragile *adj.* /ˈfrædʒail/

Most of the exhibits are too *fragile* to be sent abroad.

[猜一猜] A 珍贵的 B 奇形怪状的 C 巨大的 D 易碎的

[翻 译] 大多数的展品由于太易碎而不能寄往国外。

[分 析] frag + ile

使破碎 + 易于…的 → 易碎的，易坏的，脆的。

[词义扩展] *adj.* 脆弱的，虚弱的，易逝的，短暂的 *fragile happiness* 易逝的幸福

[大头例句] I'm feeling a bit fragile this morning. 我今天早晨感到很虚弱。

fierce *adj.* /fiəs/

There is a vivid description of a *fierce* bayonet charge in the novel.

[猜一猜] A 突然的 B 大规模的 C 激烈的 D 灵活的

[翻 译] 这本小说中有一段激烈的白刃战的生动描写。

[分 析] fier + ce

野 + 形容词尾 → 强烈的，猛烈的，激烈的。

[大头巧记] **fear（恐怖，害怕）和fier同音** → 可怕的，凶恶的。

【词义扩展】*adj.* 残忍的；凶猛的 *a fierce dog* 凶猛的狗

【大头例句】We face fierce competition from overseas competitors. 我们面临着来自于国外竞争对手的激烈的竞争。

junk *n.* /dʒʌŋk/

You can find nothing but ***junk*** in the annual report.

【猜一猜】A 废话 B 数字 C 批评 D 表扬

【翻 译】在年度报告中除了废话你什么也找不到。

【词义扩展】*n.* 旧货，假货，*v.* 把…丢掉

【大头例句】He junked all his old furniture before moving into his new home. 他在搬入新居之前把所有的旧家具都当废物丢掉了。

litter *v.* /ˈlitə/

Selfish picnickers ***litter*** the beach with food wrappers.

【猜一猜】A 弄乱 B 污染 C 厌恶 D 覆盖

【翻 译】自私的野餐者乱扔包装纸使海滩杂乱不堪。

liter，升，好多升的垃圾——**litter** 使路面杂乱不堪。

【词义扩展】*n.* 杂乱物，担架，一胎生的小崽 *a litter of puppies* 一窝狗崽

【大头例句】The park and river are full of litter. 公园和小河里满是垃圾。

kernel *n.* /ˈkəːnl/

An almond is a kind of ***kernel***.

【猜一猜】A 果仁的 B 工具 C 小吃 D 药物

【翻 译】杏仁是果仁的一种。

【分 析】kern + el

种子 + 词尾 → 果仁，果核，谷粒

【大头巧记】注意不要和 kennel(狗窝)相混。

【词义扩展】*n.* 核心，中心，要点 *the kernel of the whole plan* 整个计划的要点

【习语记忆】**He that will eat the kernel must crack the nut.** [谚]不劳不获

【大头例句】This paragraph contains the kernel of the argument. 这段文章涵盖了该论点的核心。

precipitate *n./v./adj.* /priˈsipiteit/

His carelessness ***precipitates*** his failure.

【猜一猜】A 造成 B 预示 C 注定 D 加速

【翻 译】他的粗心加速了他的失败。

【分 析】pre + cipt + ate

提前 + 头 + 动词词尾 → 头朝下，向下抛 → 加速，鲁莽的

portion *n.* /ˈpɔːʃən/

She only eats a small ***portion*** of food.

【猜一猜】A 运输 B 部分 C 搜寻 D 纷争

【翻 译】她只吃分得的一小部分食物。

【分 析】port + ion

部分 + 词尾 → 部分。

【词义扩展】*n.* 嫁妆，命运 *v.* 使分开，命运决定 *portion a bride* 给新娘准备嫁妆

【大头例句】In making donations to organizations that claim to help people in need, make sure to pay attention to what portion of your donation goes to the actual needy, and what portion simply goes to the organization's administration. 在对那些声称要帮助他人的组织给与捐助时，我们一定要注意有多少份额是真正所需的，又有多少份额是这些组织用来经营的。

习题：在下面的空格中填写本单元出现的单词。

1. In making donations to organizations that claim to help people in need, make sure to pay attention to what __________ of your donation goes to the actual needy, and what __________ simply goes to the organization's administration.
2. He is drinking from the cup with a __________ out of it.
3. The ragged old __________ and his poor dog were finally saved by a peasant and settled down there.
4. All these old houses are going to be __________ to make the space for the new ones.
5. We had a frighteningly close __________ with a black bear.
6. __________ the sugar in one tablespoon of water over a low heat.
7. There is a vivid description of a __________ bayonet charge in the novel.
8. You can find nothing but __________ in the annual report.
9. This paragraph contains the __________ of the argument.
10. His carelessness__________ his failure.
11. He went to the dentist's to have his tooth __________.
12. Selfish picnickers __________ the beach with food wrappers.
13. Most of the exhibits are too __________ to be sent abroad.
14. Mother's careful with her money, and spends only a __________ of her earnings.
15. The boss threatened to __________ all the employees who had expressed their sympathy for the strike, but it's all a bluff.
16. China is world-famous for its __________ manufactures.
17. He knocked the books to the floor with an impatient __________ of his hand while his wife was explaining why she does not want a baby.
18. You intelligent boys can __________ through the examination without any difficulty.
19. The__________ friendship between them didn't work out.
20. He was __________ by the rude remark from his colleagues in the meeting.
21. If you go on working as hard as this, your health may __________.
22. His room became a __________ of wine bottles and waste food after the party.

complexity n. 复杂(性)

complex adj. 复杂的 n. 复合体

Day 22

blink v. /bliŋk/

As the mayor of this city you should never ***blink*** at the corruption in the city government.

[猜一猜] A 熟视无睹　B 参与　C 导致　D 注意

[翻　译] 作为这个城市的市长，你绝不应该对市政府的腐败熟视无睹。

[词义扩展] *vt.&vi.* ①眨眼 ②（常与 back 连用），止住（眼泪）③（远处灯光）闪动

[大头例句] The room is rather quiet; they just found a dog blinking lazily at the fire. 房间里特别静，他们只找到了一只在火边懒洋洋眨眼睛的狗。

blush v. /blʌʃ/

The first time I saw her, she ***blushed*** with shame.

[猜一猜] A 口吃　B 沉默　C 紧张　D 脸红

[翻　译] 我第一次见到她的时候，她羞红了脸。

[大头巧记] 形近词记忆，**brush，刷子**，把刷子上的 r(ed)颜料换成了 **liquor(烈性酒)**，你应该为这个恶作剧感到脸红。

[词义扩展] *v.* ①呈现红色 ②把…弄成红色
n. ①脸红，红晕 ②红色，红光 ③一瞥
His lyric poetry brought a blush into the girl's cheeks. 他的抒情诗使这姑娘两颊红晕。

[习语记忆] **blush like a black / blue dog** 厚脸皮

[大头例句] At first blush I knew I had found the girl for me. 第一眼看去，我就知道我已经找到了我的女孩。

complexion n. /kəmˈplekʃən/

Her rosy ***complexion*** indicates her hearty vitality of youth.

[猜一猜] A 肤色　B 精神　C 体形　D 感觉

[翻　译] 玫瑰般红润的肤色显示出她年轻旺盛的生命力。

[分　析] com ＋plex ＋ion
一起 ＋ 重叠 ＋名词词尾 → 各种事物符合在一块 → 情况，局面，肤色

[大头巧记] 古代与中世纪生理学家们认为冷、热、湿、干四种体液的特定比例的组合控制着身体的温度和体质，所以用 **complexion(复合物)**来表示体质和肤色。

[词义扩展] *n.* 思想，态度，趋向
put a false complexion on 曲解…

[大头例句] The influx of foreign players has changed the whole complexion of British soccer. 外籍球员的流入改变了英国足球的整个局面。

clash v. /klæʃ/

What the eyewitness accounted ***clashed*** with published reports.

[猜一猜] A 呼应　B 冲突　C 递交　D 欣赏

[翻　译] 那个目击证人所作的报告与公开报告相冲突。

[大头巧记] c-lash（冲击）→ 冲突

[词义扩展] *n.* ①撞击声 ②冲突；战斗 ③（颜色）抵触，不调和 *a clash of views* 见解的冲突 *v.* 撞击，相撞。

[大头例句] It is broadcast that the two armies clashed near the borderline again before dawn. 据电台广播，今天凌晨在边界线附近两国军队又发生了冲突。

combat v. /ˈkɔmbæt/

He devoted his whole life to ***combating*** feudalism.

[猜一猜] A 揭露　B 斗争　C 废除　D 描写

[翻　译] 他把他的一生献给了反对封建主义的斗争。

[分　析] com + bat

与 + 打 → 与…打斗,战斗,斗争

[大头巧记] 拆 comb at,战斗中在某地像梳子般仔细搜查

[词义扩展] *adj./n.* 战斗,格斗

single combat 一对一的打斗

[大头例句] These enzymes are important in the combat against bacteria. 这些酶在对抗细菌时很重要。

dazzle *v.* /ˈdæzl/

The figure skater *dazzled* the audience with virtuosic jumps in the finals.

[猜一猜] A 征服　　B 激动　　C 目眩　　D 转移注意力

[翻 译] 那位花样滑冰健将在决赛中以名家风度的弹跳使观众眼花缭乱。

[大头巧记] 同源词记忆:daze,迷惑,使眩晕。

[词义扩展] *n.* 令人目眩的光 *vi.* ①闪耀,受强光而目眩 ②激起赞美 *The diamond ring dazzled with brilliancy.* 这只钻石戒指闪耀夺目。

[大头例句] Such brilliant prospects almost dazzled the young girl. 这么绚丽的景色让小女孩眼花缭乱。

equilibrium *n.* /ˌiːkwiˈlibriəm/

The purpose of the new policy is to achieve the *equilibrium* of supply and demand.

[猜一猜] A 平衡　　B 平等　　C 结合　　D 质量提高

[翻 译] 这个新政策的目的是实现供需平衡。

[分 析] equi + librium

相等 + 平衡 → 平衡,平静,均衡,平衡能力

[词义扩展] *n.* 沉着,安静 *He tried hard to maintain his equilibrium.* 他努力使自己保持沉着。

[大头例句] A new arms race in the region would upset the delicate equilibrium between the opposing factions. 这一地区新的军备竞赛将会搅乱对立派系间的微妙平衡。

evade *v.* /iˈveid/

The released criminal always tries to *evade* the police.

[猜一猜] A 包袱　　B 避开　　C 遭遇　　D 交谈

[翻 译] 释放犯总想避开警察。

[分 析] e + vade

向外 + 走 → 避开,逃避。

[词义扩展] *v.* 回避,规避 *You needn't evade your responsibility.* 你不必回避你的责任。

[大头例句] She was found guilty of evading taxes amounting to nearly 100,000 pounds. 她被发现犯有偷税近一百万英镑的罪行。

excavate *v.* /ˈekskəveit/

The workmen *excavated* a hole in the wall to let the sewage pipe pass through.

[猜一猜] A 发现　　B 设计　　C 挖出　　D 留出

[翻 译] 工人们在墙上掘了个洞让污水管通过。

[分 析] ex + cav + ate

出来 + 洞 + 动词词尾 → 挖出洞来 → 挖掘,挖出

[词义扩展] *vt.* 开凿,发掘 *excavate an archaeological site* 挖掘考古现场

expenditure *n.* /iksˈpenditʃə/

The government wants to cut down on administrative *expenditure.*

[猜一猜] A 支出　　B 投资　　C 通货膨胀　　D 财政赤字

[翻 译] 政府想要削减行政支出。

[分 析] ex + pend + iture

出来 + 衡量 + 名词词尾 → 计算出来的东西 → 支出,花费

[大头巧记] 记住其特征部分:(s)pend,花费。ex,词头,出去,花出去的钱 → 支出。

[大头例句] The whole project was a wasteful expenditure of time and effort. 整个工程是一种对时间和努力支出的浪费。

grip *v./n.* /grip/

The drowning swimmer now is safely in the *grip* of a lifeguard.

[猜一猜] A 拉力　　B 紧握　　C 视野　　D 救生艇

[翻 译] 那个溺水的游泳者现已被救生员牢牢抓住。

[词义扩展] *v./n.* 握力，抓紧，柄，吸引，掌握，能力。*The pictures gripped my imagination.* 这些图画引起了我的想像。

[大头例句] Britain was still gripped by recession. 英国仍然受着工业衰败的很大影响。

grind *v.* /graind/

Laws *grind* the poor, and rich men rule the law.

[猜一猜] A 保护　B 引导　C 压榨　D 放弃

[翻　译] 法律压榨穷人，而富人统治着法律。

[词义扩展] *n.* 磨碎，折磨，磨光，咬牙，苦差事 *Do you find learning English a grind?* 你觉得学英语是一件苦事吗？

[大头例句] She ground a half-smoked cigarette into the ashtray. 她把抽了一半的烟碾灭在烟灰缸里。

ignite *v.* /igˈnait/

His speech *ignited* the crowd greatly.

[猜一猜] A 使激动　B 使愤怒　C 使开心　D 使哭笑不得

[翻　译] 他的演说使群众激动万分。

[分　析] igni + te
火 + 动词词尾 → 点火，点燃，激起，使激动

[大头例句] The fire was ignited by a spark from an electrical fault. 这场火是由一个错误导致的电火花引起的。

hover *v.* /ˈhɔvə/

Some birds *hover* when they look for animals to kill on the ground.

[猜一猜] A 俯冲　B 盘旋　C 兴奋　D 迷失

[翻　译] 有些鸟在寻杀地上的动物时，它们在空中盘旋。

[大头巧记] h(igh) over, 高高地在…的上空盘旋。

[词义扩展] *n.* 盘旋，翱翔，顶棚 *vi.* 徘徊，踌躇，犹豫 *vt.* 孵化 *A hen hovers her chicks.* 一只母鸡在孵小鸡。

[大头例句] His girlfriend is hovering between life and death. 她的女友正在生与死之间徘徊。

launch *n./vt.* /lɔːntʃ/

Our company planned to *launch* the new perfume with prime-time commercials on the major networks.

[猜一猜] A 销售　B 开发　C 推出　D 试验

[翻　译] 我们公司计划依靠在主要电视台播出黄金时段的广告来推出这种新型香水。

[分　析] laun + ch
长矛 + 动词词尾 → 挥舞长矛 → 投射，发射（火箭），使（船）下水，开发。

[大头巧记] *n.* 下水，汽艇，投放市场

[大头例句] The agency will launch a new weather satellite next month. 该机构将于下月发射一颗新的人造气象卫星。

linger *v.* /ˈliŋgə/

I was *lingering* after the concert, hoping to meet the star.

[猜一猜] A 闲荡　B 四处寻找　C 注意　D 呼唤

[翻　译] 我在演唱会后徘徊不去，希望能见到那位明星。

[大头巧记] **long，长，linger，拖长，拖延，徘徊。**

[大头例句] We lingered away the whole summer at the beach. 我们在海滩上消磨掉整个夏天。

meticulous *adj.* /miˈtikjuləs/

With *meticulous* accuracy, the surgeon carefully sewed together the severed pieces of her patient's artery.

[猜一猜] A 即时的　B 暂时的　C 小心翼翼的　D 有计划的

[翻　译] 这位外科医生非常小心而谨慎地缝合了她病人严重受伤的动脉。

[分　析] metic + ulous
害怕 + 多…的 → 很多担心的，小心的，细心的

[大头巧记] 联系记忆：ridi，嘲笑；culous，多…的 → **ridiculous，可笑的；meticulous，多担心的，小心翼翼的。**

[大头例句] Caroline was always very meticulous when doing her chinese homework. 苛瑞兰在做汉语作业时总是非常小心。

momentum *n.* /məuˈmentəm/

Interest in human rights issues has gained ***momentum.***

[猜一猜] A 势头 B 回报 C 离析 D 关注

[翻 译] 对于人权问题的兴趣势头正猛。

[分 析] moment + um

运动 + 名词词尾 → 动力,势头

[大头巧记] **moment,瞬间;momentum,**瞬间爆发的动力,**势头。**

[词义扩展] *n.* 动量 *As the rock rolled down, it gathered momentum.* 岩石滚下山坡时,动量愈来愈大。

[大头例句] With the great momentum achieved by the tractor-trailer moving at a very fast speed, it was impossible to reach a complete stop before reaching the end of the bridge. 由于运动速度很快的拖车具有的很大的冲力,在到达桥的终点之前它不可能停下来。

motivate *v.* /ˈməutiveit/

More and more scholars doubt that examinations can ***motivate*** a student to seek more knowledge.

[猜一猜] A 督促 B 激发 C 帮助 D 影响

[翻 译] 越来越多的学者质疑考试可以激发学生去追求更多的知识。

[分 析] motiv + ate

动机 + 动词词尾 → 给人以动机 → 激发

[大头例句] The crime appears to have been motivated by hatred. 这起犯罪表面看起来是由于仇恨激发的。

nibble *n./v.* /ˈnibl/

The parrot was ***nibbling*** her ear.

[猜一猜] A 晃动 B 轻咬 C 卷起 D 放下

[翻 译] 鹦鹉正在轻咬她的耳朵。

[分 析] nib + ble

小 + 动词词尾 → 一点点地啃,轻咬

[大头巧记] 声音记忆:nibble,像是轻咬东西时的声音。另:注意它和**"nipple,乳头"**的区别。

[大头例句] I'm not so hungry that I need to eat a full meal, but if I could nibble on some raw vegetables, I would be very content. 我不是太饿,不需要吃整顿饭,但是如果能够嚼一些生蔬菜,我就会非常满足了。

mobilize *v.* /ˈməubilaiz/

Our country's in great danger; we must ***mobilize*** the whole nation.

[猜一猜] A 拯救 B 逃难 C 征服 D 动员

[翻 译] 我们国家正处于严重的危险之中,我们必须把全国人民动员起来。

[分 析] mob + ilize

动 + 动此词尾 → 动员,集合

[大头巧记] mobile phone; 移动电话,手机; **mobile,可移动的;mobilize,使…动,动员。**

[大头例句] With only twenty minutes of notice before the attack, the commander did not have sufficient time to mobilize his soldiers for defense. 只是在袭击前二十分钟才得到通知,指挥官没有足够的时间去集合他的士兵进行防御。

resolve *n./v.* /riˈzɔlv/

The circumstances ***resolved*** him to go.

[猜一猜] A 说服 B 注意 C 打击 D 决定

[翻 译] 情况使他决定去。

[分 析] re + solve

再 + 解决 → 解决,(使)分解,决心。

[词义扩展] *n.* 决心 *keep one's resolve* 坚持

hatred n. 憎恨. 与 affection n. 友爱. admiration

hate v. 恨 n. 恨.

习题：在下面的空格里填写本单元的单词。

1. She __________ a half-smoked cigarette into the ashtray.
2. Some birds __________ when they look for animals to kill on the ground.
3. As the mayor of this city you should never __________ at the corruption in the city government.
4. The circumstances __________ him to go.
5. With the great __________ achieved by the tractor-trailer moving at a very fast speed, it was impossible to reach a complete stop before reaching the end of the bridge.
6. Our country's in great danger; we must __________ the whole nation.
7. The influx of foreign players has changed the whole __________ of British soccer.
8. It is broadcast that the two armies __________ near the borderline again before dawn.
9. The figure skater __________ the audience with virtuosic jumps in the finals.
10. The workmen __________ a hole in the wall to let the sewage pipe pass through.
11. She was found guilty of __________ taxes amounting to nearly 100,000 pounds.
12. His lyric poetry brought a __________ into the girl's cheeks.
13. These enzymes are important in the __________ against bacteria.
14. The fire was __________ by a spark from an electrical fault.
15. The drowning swimmer now is safely in the __________ of a lifeguard.
16. Our company planned to __________ the new perfume with prime-time commercials on the major networks.
17. I was __________ after the concert, hoping to meet the star.
18. More and more scholars doubt that examinations can __________ a student to seek more knowledge.
19. I'm not so hungry that I need to eat a full meal, but if I could __________ on some raw vegetables, I would be very content.
20. With __________ accuracy, the surgeon carefully sewed together the severed pieces of her patient's artery.
21. The government wants to cut down on administrative __________.
22. The purpose of the new policy is to achieve the __________ of supply and demand.

Nothing content her, she is alway compling..

Day 23

ascertain *vt.* /ˌæsəˈtein/

We must *ascertain* the usual customs of the local people and what exactly happened there before we make a decision.

[猜一猜] A 观察 B 查明 C 根据 D 遵从

[翻 译] 在我们做出决定前必须得查明当地的习俗和那里究竟发生了什么。

[分 析] as + certain
to + 确定 → 确定,查明

[大例 头句] Chinese scientists have ascertained that the earliest feather appeared on dinosaurs. 中国科学家已经探明,最早的羽毛是出现在恐龙的身上的。

assess *vt.* /əˈses/

The good news is that teachers have options that give them the opportunity to *assess* their students in their classrooms.

[猜一猜] A 教育 B 鼓励 C 评定 D 引导

[翻 译] 好消息是,老师们拥有选择的自由,这个自由给了他们在教室里面评定学生的机会。

[分 析] as + sess
to + to sit → 作为法官冷眼旁观 → 评定,估计

[词扩 义展] *vt.* ①征(税);分摊(费用);处以(罚款)②估计;估算

[大例 头句] They assessed the damages in the incident at 6 million pounds. 他们把这个事件中的损失估算为6百万英镑。

bibliography *n.* /ˌbibliˈɔgrəfi/

The *Bibliography* is a very important part of the paper here I am asking you to write.

[猜一猜] A 目录 B 注释 C 参考书目 D 人物生平

[翻 译] 参考书目是我要你们写的这篇论文的非常重要的一部分。

[分 析] biblio + graphy
书 + 写 → 写书使用的书,参考书目

[大巧 头记] 与 **biography**(传记)联合记忆,在bi的后面插入bli-books listed in,传记中列入的书 → 参考书目。

[大例 头句] This bibliography presents selected English-language articles, books, and other printed and electronic sources that are very useful in understanding British culture. 这个书目提供精选的英语文章、书籍和其他印刷的或电子的资源,在了解英国文化方面非常有用。

bewilder *vt.* /biˈwildə/

The first time I got there I was *bewildered* by the twists and turns in the forest.

[猜一猜] A 迷惑 B 陶醉 C 吃惊 D 控制

[翻 译] 我第一次到那里的时候,我被森林里的迂回曲折完全搞糊涂了。

[分 析] be + wilder
完全的 + 使迷路 → 使迷惑,使混乱

[词扩 义展] *vi.* 使人迷惑 *His statements at meetings always bewilder and confuse.* 他在会上的讲话总是使人糊涂而混淆。

[大例 头句] Often you have been bewildered and you bewilder your fellowmen at times too. 你接二连三地被迷惑,你也不时地使你的伙伴们迷惑。

browse *v./n.* /brauz/

I spent my last weekend *browsing* the record shops for items of interest.

[猜一猜] A 寻找 B 忙碌 C 漫步 D 检查

[翻 译] 我把上个周末花在了逛唱片店上,想找些我感兴趣的东西。

[大巧 头记] 形近同音词记忆:brows,眉毛的复数形式,中国人形容眉毛用"柳叶"眉,可联想到browse的另外一个意思,"*n.* 牲畜吃的嫩枝,

嫩叶”,可引申出吃草,放牧之意,放牧的迁移又进一步引申为浏览。

[词义扩展] v. ①随意观看:browsed the evening paper 浏览晚报 ②细咬:吃去尖端

[大头例句] The goats are browsing on shrubs. 山羊在灌木丛中吃草。

censor n. /ˈsensə/

The *censor* is authorized to examine books, films, or other material and to remove or suppress what is considered morally, politically, or otherwise objectionable.

[猜一猜] A 剪辑员　B 检查员　C 剧评家　D 制片人

[翻　译] 检查员有权审查书籍、电影或其他材料并删去或削减其中被认为在道德上、政治上或其他方面有不宜的内容。

[分　析] cens + or
评估 + …的人 → 检查员

[词义扩展] vt. 检查,审查

[大头巧记] 联系 **census**(人口普查)记忆。

[大头例句] The book had been heavily censored. 这本书经受了大量的审查。

checkup n. /ˈtʃekʌp/

Old people should have medical *checkups* often.

[猜一猜] A 身体检查　B 咨询　C 保障　D 付款

[翻　译] 老年人应该经常接受身体检查。

[大头巧记] check up 词组意为“核对,检查”。

[词义扩展] n. 审查,检查,鉴定

commentary n. /ˈkɔməntəri/

Your *commentary* on current affairs really hit the bull's-eye: it was exactly right.

[猜一猜] A 策略　B 讽刺　C 疏忽　D 评论

[翻　译] 你的时事评论十分中肯,一点都不错。

[分　析] com + ment + ary
完全地 + 想 + 名词词尾 → 评论,注解,纪事

[大头巧记] 同源词记忆:**comment** *v.* 评论

[词义扩展] n. (编者的)按语;评论;解说词

[习语记忆] **a running commentary** 现场实况转播

[大头例句] The broadcast commentary on that football match was perfectly made. 那场足球的广播报道很精彩。

considerable adj. /kənˈsidərəbl/

The economy was a *considerable* issue in the campaign.

[猜一猜] A 贬低的　B 含蓄的　C 根本的　D 相当大的

[翻　译] 在竞选运动中经济是一个重要问题。

[大头巧记] **consider**,考虑 → **considerable**,值得考虑的,相当大的,相当可观的。另:**inconsiderable**,不足取得,琐屑的。

consult v. /kənˈsʌlt/

Consult the checkbook before making a major purchase.

[猜一猜] A 开具　B 考虑　C 出示　D 改动

[翻　译] 在进行大的购买行动之前先看看支票簿。

[分　析] con + sult
一起 + 坐 → 坐在一起,商量,商议,考虑,参考

[大头例句] Mr. Bell said he had consulted his attorney about the matter. 贝尔先生说就此事,他已经和他的委托人商量过了。

critical adj. /ˈkritikəl/

He was asked to give some *critical* opinions on this latest play.

[猜一猜] A 中肯的　B 奇异的　C 评论的　D 实际的

[翻　译] 请他对这出最新剧作做出评论意见。

[大头巧记] critic *n.* 批评者；criticism *n.* 批评；criticize *v.* 挑剔，批评，非难

deliberate *v.* /di'libəreit/

You'd better *deliberate* the question before you make an answer.

[猜一猜] A 寄出 B 仔细考虑 C 分析 D 接受

[翻 译] 在你回答一个问题之前你最好要仔细考虑一下(三思而后行)。

[分 析] de + liberate

由…产生的 + 权衡 → 由权衡而产生出 → 仔细考虑

[大头巧记] liberate(解放)本身是独立的单词，解放一个地方需要谨慎，而深思熟虑的计划。

[词义扩展] *adj.* ①周密计划的 *taking deliberate action* 采取谨慎的行动 ②故意的 *He told us a deliberate lie.* 他存心说谎。③从容而谨慎的 *They were asked to move at a deliberate pace.* 要求他们小心谨慎地移动。

[大头例句] I mistook the oversight for a deliberate insult. 我错把疏忽当成了蓄意的侮辱。

envisage *v.* /in'vizidʒ/

When do you *envisage* being able to finish writing your new novel?

[猜一猜] A 确信 B 设想 C 变得 D 最早

[翻 译] 你设想什么时候完成你的新小说？

[分 析] en + vis + age

in + 看 + 动词词尾 → 进入看的状态 → 正视，设想

[大头巧记] 拆：env(y) sage 羡慕圣人，设想自己可成为圣人。

[词义扩展] *v.* 想像，设想，期望 *It is difficult to envisage living without the telephone.* 很难想像没有电话的生活。

[大头例句] The plan envisaged the creation of regional councils. 这个计划期望创立地方上的委员会。

lucrative *adj.* /'lu:krətiv/

All recent college graduates hope for a *lucrative* job which has both a high salary and good benefits.

[猜一猜] A 重要的 B 庄严的 C 有利的 D 有意义的

[翻 译] 所有当今的大学毕业生都希望找到一份有利的工作，既有高薪又能从中受益。

[分 析] lucr + ative

钱财 + 形容词尾 → 赚钱的，有利的

[大头例句] That is a lucrative marketing strategy. 这是一套赢利的市场策略。

meditate *v.* /'mediteit/

Before making a major life decision, sometimes it is helpful to take the time to *meditate* and reflect on the circumstances surrounding the decision.

[猜一猜] A 观察 B 研究 C 沉思 D 宣传

[翻 译] 在做出生命中主要的决定之前，有时花时间去沉思和反省一下关于这个决定的一切情形是有帮助的。

[分 析] medi + tate

中间 + 动词词尾 → 把思想进入某物中间 → 沉思

[大头例句] He spent hours meditating on his future. 他花好几个小时思考自己的未来。

nobility *n.* /nəu'biliti/

Their ideas gradually became accepted among the *nobility*.

[猜一猜] A 民众 B 知识阶层 C 贵族 D 实力派

[翻 译] 他们的观点逐渐地被贵族所接受。

[大头巧记] noble，贵族的 → nobility，贵族，高贵

[大头例句] Most of England's nobility, like its monarch, hold little real power, but they are greatly respected in society. 大多数的英国贵族，像他们的君主一样，拥有的实权很少，但是在社会上他们却受到很大的尊敬。

negative *adj.* /'negətiv/

You've already gotten too much *negative* advice that only tells you what not to do.

[猜一猜] A 外来的 B 错误的 C 正面的 D 消极的

[翻　译] 你已经听到太多消极的建议，只是告诉你不要做某事。

[分　析] neg + ative

否认 + 形容词尾 → 否定的，消极的，负的

[大头巧记] 联系它的反义词 **positive** 记忆。

[词义扩展] *n.* 否定，负数，底片 *I can't see any negative in this deal.* 我看不出这买卖有什么坏处。*vt.*

[大头例句] Lightning is created as a result of the narrowing of the gap between the mostly positive charged earth and the mostly negative charged rain clouds. 闪电是由于通常带正电的土地和带负电的雨云间的间隙缩小的结果。

习题：在下面的空格里填写本单元的单词。

1. We must ＿＿＿＿＿ the usual customs of the local people and what exactly happened there before we make a decision.
2. You'd better ＿＿＿＿＿ the question before you make an answer.
3. You've already gotten too much ＿＿＿＿＿ advice that only tells you what not to do.
4. The good news is that teachers have options that give them the opportunity to ＿＿＿＿＿ their students in their classrooms.
5. This ＿＿＿＿＿ presents selected English-language articles, books, and other printed and electronic sources that are very useful in understanding British culture.
6. The first time I got there I was ＿＿＿＿＿ by the twists and turns in the forest.
7. Your ＿＿＿＿＿ on current affairs really hit the bull's-eye: it was exactly right.
8. He was asked to give some ＿＿＿＿＿ opinions on this latest play.
9. Most of England's ＿＿＿＿, like its monarch, hold little real power, but they are greatly respected in society.
10. Before making a major life decision, sometimes it is helpful to take the time to ＿＿＿＿ and reflect on the circumstances surrounding the decision.
11. The ＿＿＿＿＿ is authorized to examine books, films, or other material and to remove or suppress what is considered morally, politically, or otherwise objectionable.
12. Old people should have medical ＿＿＿＿＿ often.
13. I spent my last weekend ＿＿＿＿＿ the record shops for items of interest.
14. The economy was a ＿＿＿＿＿ issue in the campaign.
15. Mr. Bell said he had ＿＿＿＿＿ his attorney about the matter.
16. The plan ＿＿＿＿＿ the creation of regional councils.
17. All recent college graduates hope for a ＿＿＿＿＿ job which has both a high salary and good benefits.

Day 24

avalanche *n.* /ˈævəˌlɑːnʃ/

The *avalanche* that happened three days ago killed two skiers from Switzerland and a local guide.

[猜一猜] A 泥石流　　B 龙卷风　　C 暴风雪　　D 雪崩

[翻　译] 三天前的雪崩杀死了两名瑞士滑雪者和一名当地的向导。

[分　析] ava + lanche

滑 + 峡谷 → 顺着峡谷滑下 → 雪崩

[大头巧记] 词形联想法：三个a，像三个滚滚落下的雪球，先后淹没了我的v, l, n —— vehicle, legs, neck (车子，腿和脖子)。

[词义扩展] *n.* 巨大的或极大的量；洪水 *received an avalanche of mail* 收到大量的信件 *vi.* 雪崩；*vt.* 大量投入(市场等)，大量涌进

[大头例句] The allied forces pounced on the enemies with the momentum of an avalanche. 盟军以排山倒海之势向敌人发起袭击。

blast *n./vt.* /blɑːst/

A *blast* of wind blew the window and the door agape.

[猜一猜] A 阵　　B 缕　　C 连续不断之物　　D 烦恼

[翻　译] 一阵风把窗户和门都吹开了。

[词义扩展] *n./v.* 爆炸 *They've blasted away the rock to build the new road.* 他们已炸掉这块岩石以便修一条新的路。

[大头例句] I was working at full blast in order to complete my work on time. 我正在全力以赴以按时完成我的工作。

calamity *n.* /kəˈlæmiti/

Last year more than 500 people were killed in the natural *calamities* caused by the hurricanes in this region.

[猜一猜] A 灾难　B 风光　C 瘟疫　D 洪水

[翻　译] 去年在这个地区死于由台风引起的自然灾害的人就有500多人。

[分　析] calam + ity

破坏 + 名词词尾 → 造成很大破坏的事情 → 灾难

[大头巧记] 去尾法，只要记住calam，就可以了，lam：潜逃，ca谐"客"，客人碰到灾难时都潜逃了。

[词义扩展] *n.* 祸患，不幸的事

[习语记忆] **Calamity is man's true touchstone.** [谚]患难是人真正的试金石，患难见人心。

[大头例句] He said marriage is a frightful calamity to him. 他说婚姻对于他是一个可怕灾难。

casualty *n.* /ˈkæʒuəlti/

It was three days after the bomb incident for the *casualty* lists to be published.

[猜一猜] A 嫌疑犯　　B 肇事者　　C 赔偿　　D 伤亡

[翻　译] 伤亡名单是在那个爆炸事件后三天公布的。

[分　析] casual + ty

偶然的 + 名词词尾 → 偶然事件中的受害者 → 伤亡

[词义扩展] *n.* ①临时救治所；急诊室 (= casualty department) ②受害者

[大头例句] The handicraft industry was a casualty of the expanding factories. 手工工业是日益扩大的工厂的受害者。

catastrophe *n.* /kəˈtæstrəfi/

If the Third World War were to begin, it would be a *catastrophe* for every country on earth.

[猜一猜] A 机遇　B 大灾难　C 考验　D 壮丽

[翻　译] 如果第三次世界大战爆发的话，对地球上的所有国家来说都是一场大灾难。

[分　析] cata + strophe

下面的 + 翻转 → 翻天覆地之祸 → 大灾难

[词义扩展] *n.* 彻底的失败；惨败 *The whole party was a catastrophe.* 整个宴会是一个失败。

[大头例句] It would be a catastrophe if we didn't make the play-offs. 如果我们不参加决赛的话，就太惨了。

casual *adj.* /ˈkæʒuəl/

His *casual* correspondence with a former girlfriend makes his wife worried.

[猜一猜] A 不定期的　B 经常的　C 秘密的　D 不正常的

[翻　译] 他和前女友的不定期的通信让他的妻子很担心。

[分　析] cas + ual

落下 + 形容词尾 → 忽然落下的 → 偶然的，随意的，不定期的

[词义扩展] *adj.* ①偶然的，不意的 *a casual meeting* 巧遇 ②疏忽的 ③非正式的，不拘礼节的 *casual clothes* 便装 ④疏远的，不可靠的 *a casual relationship* 不可靠的友谊 ⑤临时的；不定的 *a casual labourer* 临时工人 *n.* ①临时工人 ②(常用 *pl*)便服；便鞋

[大头例句] The interview took place around the kitchen table and was very casual. 这次接见发生在厨房的餐桌边，是很随意的。

famine *n.* /ˈfæmin/

Many people die of *famine* every year.

[猜一猜] A 疟疾　B 战争　C 风暴　D 饥荒

[翻　译] 每年有很多人死于饥荒。

[大头巧记] fa 谐“乏”，mine，我的东西，缺乏属于我的东西 → 饥荒。

[词义扩展] *adj.* 因缺乏而致的 *famine prices* 因缺货而造成的高价

[大头例句] My grandfather still has a clear memory of the famine in the 1960s. 我的祖父对 20 世纪 60 年代的灾荒仍记忆犹新。

hijack *vt.* /ˈhaidʒæk/

Terrorists *hijacked* the plane, ordering the pilot to fly to Tripoli.

[猜一猜] A 炸毁　B 劫持　C 开动　D 偷运

[翻　译] 恐怖分子劫持了飞机，命令飞行员飞往黎波里。

[大头巧记] Hi Jack，嗨，杰克！把你的钱拿出来！抢劫！

[词义扩展] *vt.* 挟持，把持(某组织等)

[大头例句] Environmentalists were accused of hijacking the rally to promote their own aims. 这些环保论者被控告通过把持大会来谋求自己的目标。

holocaust *n.* /ˈhɔləkɔːst/

In East Africa five years of drought have brought about a *holocaust* in which millions have died.

[猜一猜] A 大毁灭　B 斗争　C 缺乏　D 造反

[翻　译] 东非地区五年的干旱引起上百万人死亡。

[分　析] holo + caust

完全的 + 燃烧 → 最初表示在祭坛上完整焚烧公兽以示对上帝的虔诚，后来完全的毁坏成为它的中心意思 → 大毁灭，大屠杀。

[大头例句] If we let the situation go uncontrolled, a nuclear holocaust is inevitable. 如果我们坐视事态发展的话，核毁灭是不可避免的。

hostage *n.* /ˈhɔstidʒ/

The President is making every effort to obtain the release of the *hostages*.

[猜一猜] A 俘虏　B 政治犯　C 专家　D 人质

[翻　译] 总统正在尽一切努力来实现人质的获释。

[大头巧记] host，主人，hostage，被主人向留下的 → 人质。

[词义扩展] *n.* 抵押品 *v.* 做人质 *be hostaged to the enemies* 给敌人做人质

[习语记忆] **give hostages to fortune** 听天由命

[大头例句] National policies cannot be held hostage by another country. 一个国家的政策不能被另一个国家所操纵。

hurricane *n.* /ˈhʌrikən/

The *hurricane* flung their motorboat upon the rocks.

[猜一猜] A 洪水 B 海啸 C 火山 D 飓风
[翻　译] 飓风把他们的摩托艇抛到岩石上。
[大头巧记] hurry，快，急速；急速的风暴，飓风
[大头例句] This weekend's hurricane left a total damage of $7 million for the coastal city of Galveston to bear. 这个周末的飓风给海岸城市加尔维斯顿带来了共计7百万美元的损失。

infringe v. /in'frindʒ/

The increased workload *infringed* on his personal life.

[猜一猜] A 改善 B 侵犯 C 补偿 D 限制
[翻　译] 增加了的工作量侵犯了他的私生活。
[分　析] in + fringe
不 + 界限 → 不再界限内 → 违反，侵犯，破坏
[大头例句] Making an unauthorized copy of the article infringes the copyright. 制作未经授权的文章拷贝侵犯了著作权。

jeopardise v. /'dʒepədaiz/

The soldier *jeopardised* his life to save his comrade.

[猜一猜] A 牺牲 B 冒险 C 尽力 D 保护
[翻　译] 这个士兵冒生命的危险救他的同伴。
[分　析] jeo + pard + ise
游戏 + 离开 + 动词词尾 → 离开游戏，进入危险之中 → 使受危害，危及
[大头例句] Cuts in funding could jeopardise this vital research work. 削减资金会危及这个重要的调查研究工作。

lapse v. /læps/

He realized that his attention had *lapsed* and he hadn't heard the assignment.

[猜一猜] A 分散 B 自由 C 薄弱 D 终止
[翻　译] 他意识到自己当时走神了且没听到分派的任务。
[大头巧记] lap，跑道的一圈，**lapse**，跑道的终点 → 终止。
[词义扩展] *n.* 小错，差错；时间流逝，推移 *after a lapse of several years* 事隔几年之后

[大头例句] The man admitted driving over the speed limit and apologized for the lapse. 这位男士承认自己超速行驶并为自己的差错道歉。

massacre n. /'mæsəkə/

Before my first trip to Nanjing, I was not aware of the magnitude of the *massacre* Japanese soldiers carried out there.

[猜一猜] A 灾难 B 恐惧 C 屠杀 D 统治
[翻　译] 在我去南京之前，我并不知道日本在该地区进行的大屠杀规模如此之大。
[大头巧记] 拆：mass-acre：一大群人-英亩 → 把一大群人放在以英亩为单位的地方杀掉 → 大屠杀。
[词义扩展] *v./n.* 裁员，击败，残杀
[大头例句] He is collecting evidence to massacre his opponents. 他正在收集证据，要彻底击败他的对手。

mischief n. /'mistʃif/

He really is not an evil child; he only causes *mischief* with good intentions.

[猜一猜] A 损害 B 误导 C 小错 D 不及格
[翻　译] 他其实并不是个坏孩子，只是好心做坏事而已。
[分　析] mis + chief
坏的 + 首领 → 坏的首领，恶作剧，损害
[大头例句] The mischief of the matter is that you didn't keep your promise to keep it secret. 这件事坏就坏在你没有遵守诺言保守秘密上。

misfortune n. /mis'fɔːtʃən/

You are an extremely hardworking person; despite this bit of *misfortune*, you will certainly be able to improve your situation.

[猜一猜] A 不幸 B 运气 C 热情 D 消沉
[翻　译] 你非常用功，尽管现在稍有困厄，但你一定能够改善自己的处境。
[分　析] mis + fortune
不 + 运气 → 不幸，灾祸

[大头例句] He failed in business not because of misfortune, but because of his own error. 他业务上的失败不是由于遇到了厄运,而是由于他自己的过错。

mishap *n.* /ˈmishæp/

Over the course of history, what seems to one country to be merely a small ***mishap*** can be viewed as a complete tragedy by another.

[猜一猜] A 改革 B 进步 C 灾祸 D 失落

[翻　译] 在历史的进程中,对于一个国家来说只是很小的一个灾祸,对于另外一个国家来说可能是完全的悲剧。

[分　析] mis + hap

不 + 运气 → 运气不好,灾祸

[大头例句] A mishap prevented him from attending a routine meeting of the company. 他遇到一件不幸的事,使他不能来参加公司的例会。

lag *v.* /læg/

The elderly people and children always ***lag*** behind when we go for a walk.

[猜一猜] A 落后 B 躲闪 C 潜伏 D 散步

[翻　译] 我们出门散步时,年纪大的人和孩子们总是落在后头。

[大头巧记] leg,腿;**lag 拖后腿**,落后,走得慢。

[词义扩展] *n.* 落后,迟延,落后的人,相隔的时间

cultural lag 文明迟滞(指精神文明落后于物质文明)

[大头例句] There is always a lag between the policy being announced and its implementation. 在政策的发布和执行之间总是有一个差距。

latent *adj.* /ˈleitənt/

His critical remark immediately awakened all her ***latent*** hostility.

[猜一猜] A 恶意的 B 悲哀的

C 潜在的 D 错误的

[翻　译] 他的批评立刻引起了她潜在的敌意。

[分　析] lat + ent

隐藏 + 形容词尾 → 隐藏的,潜在的,潜伏的

[大头巧记] late,迟的,迟来危险通常都是隐藏着的。

[大头例句] He is in charge of a study on a kind of latent infection. 他正在负责一种潜伏性传染病的研究。

overthrow *vt.* /ˌəuvəˈθrəu/

They were arrested for attempting to ***overthrow*** the present regime.

[猜一猜] A 反对 B 诬陷 C 改革 D 推翻

[翻　译] 他们因企图推翻政府而被捕。

[大头巧记] throw over,推翻

[词义扩展] *n.* 推翻,打倒,扔得过远的球

[大头例句] The organization was dedicated to the overthrow of capitalism. 该组织致力于推翻资本主义。

plague *vt.* /pleig/

Runaway inflation further ***plagued*** the wage — or salary — earner.

[猜一猜] A 折磨 B 惊醒 C 搅乱 D 激怒

[翻　译] 失控的通货膨胀加深了工薪阶层的痛苦。

[词义扩展] *n.* 瘟疫,灾难 *black plague* 黑死病

[习语记忆] **What a plague!** 怎么啦!

slaughter *n.* /ˈslɔːtə/

I could not give my name to aid the ***slaughter*** in this war, which was fought by both sides for grossly material ends.

[猜一猜] A 罪恶 B 矫饰 C 残酷 D 屠杀

[翻　译] 我不能支持该战争中的屠杀行为,战争双方只是为了谋取巨额的物质利益。

[大头巧记] 谐音法:死 loooooot,很多人死了,大屠杀。

习题：在下面的空格里填写本单元的单词。

1. The man admitted driving over the speed limit and apologized for the __________.
2. I was working at full __________ in order to complete my work on time.
3. The __________ that happened three days ago killed two skiers from Switzerland and a local guide.
4. The handicraft industry was a __________ of the expanding factories.
5. Environmentalists were accused of __________ the rally to promote their own aims.
6. This weekend's __________ left a total damage of $7 million for the coastal city of Galveston to bear.
7. I could not give my name to aid the __________ in this war, which was fought by both sides for grossly material ends.
8. Runaway inflation further __________ the wage — or salary — earner.
9. His critical remark immediately awakened all her __________ hostility.
10. Over the course of history, what seems to one country to be merely a small __________ can be viewed as a complete tragedy by another.
11. The organization was dedicated to the __________ of capitalism.
12. The elderly people and children always __________ behind when we go for a walk.
14. He really is not an evil child; he only causes __________ with good intentions.
14. Last year more than 500 people were killed in the natural __________ caused by the hurricanes in this region.
15. If the Third World War were to begin, it would be a __________ for every country on earth.
16. His __________ correspondence with a former girlfriend makes his wife worried.
17. If we let the situation go uncontrolled, a nuclear __________ is inevitable.
18. The President is making every effort to obtain the release of the __________.
19. My grandfather still has a clear memory of the __________ in the 1960s.
20. Making an unauthorized copy of the article __________ the copyright.
21. Before my first trip to Nanjing, I was not aware of the magnitude of the __________ Japanese soldiers carried out there.
22. Cuts in funding could __________ this vital research work.
23. You are an extremely hardworking person; despite this bit of __________, you will certainly be able to improve your situation.

Day 25

aggravate *vt.* /ˈægrəveit/

Health conditions ***aggravate*** the South African famine.

[猜一猜]A 使恶化　　B 使停止
C 使扩大　　D 使经常发生

[翻　译]健康状况使得南非的饥荒进一步恶化。

[分　析]ag + gravate
朝向 + 重的 → 向重的方向发展 → 使恶化

[大巧　头记]ag=agriculture 农业，grav(e)，坟墓，ate，吃的过去时 → 坟墓占用(ate)土地，恶化了农业状况。

[词扩　义展]*vt.* 激怒 *If he aggravates me any more I shall leave immediately.* 如果他再惹我的话，我就马上离开。

[大例　头句]The American President's statement aggravated the crisis in the Middle East. 美国总统的陈述使中东危机进一步恶化。

alleviate *vt.* /əˈliːvieit/

The doctor gave him some pills to ***alleviate*** cold symptoms.

[猜一猜]A 消除　B 减轻　C 杀死　D 抵抗

[翻　译]医生给他一些药来减轻感冒的症状。

[分　析]al + lev + iate
to + 轻的 + 动词词尾 → 减轻

[大巧　头记]掐头去尾法，记住 lev 即可，与 leave 同音，使痛苦或压力离开 → 减轻。

[大例　头句]A lot of people believe that alcohol can alleviate grief. 很多人认为酒可以减轻忧伤。

almighty *adj.* /ɔːlˈmaiti/

No one is ***almighty*** except God.

[猜一猜]A 神秘的　　B 神圣的
C 全能的　　D 伟大的

[翻　译]没有人是全能的，除了上帝。

[分　析]al + mighty
all 全的 + 能力 → 全能的

[大巧　头记]might 可能，力量，引出 all mighty 全能的。

[词扩　义展]*adv.* 极端地；非常地 *I am almighty scared.* 我非常害怕。
adj. 伟大的；极度的 *an almigaty din* 极大的噪声

[大巧　头记]Money is not almighty. 金钱不是万能的。

amplify *v.* /ˈæmplifai/

The delegate ***amplified*** his nation's standpoint in the press conference.

[猜一猜]A 驳斥　B 同义　C 阐明　D 提出

[翻　译]在新闻发布会上，这位代表阐明了他所代表的国家的立场。

[分　析]ampli + fy
large + 动词词尾 → 使变大，详细阐明

[大巧　头记]谐音法，“俺不理发”，头发的量增加，扩大。

[大例　头句]Large G-forces amplify crash injuries. 巨大的地球引力加重了坠落的伤害程度。

annihilate *vt.* /əˈnaiəleit/

The enemy's air force was ***annihilated*** in three days.

[猜一猜]A 打击　B 投降　C 误导　D 消灭

[翻　译]敌人的空军在三天内被消灭了。

[分　析]an + nihil + ate
to + 虚无 + 动词词尾 → 使变成什么都没有 → 消灭

[大巧　头记]nihil 本身也是一个词，*n.* 虚无。

[大例　头句]The tenet of this organization is annihilating the apartheid. 这个组织的宗旨就是要消灭种族隔离制度。

boost *v.* /buːst/

They are making efforts to *boost* participation in the program.

[猜一猜]A 吸引 B 创造 C 提高 D 调查

[翻 译]他们正在努力提高这个节目的收视率。

[大头巧记]把 **boots**（靴子）的根儿颠倒一下，得到boost，靴子的根儿坏了，就要提高了脚走路。

[词义扩展]*vt.* ①往上推 ②增加；提高 ③增进；改善 *n.* ①上推 ②增加，提高 ③帮助；鼓舞 *We need to boost our spirits.* 我们需要鼓舞士气。

[大头例句]The boss promised a big boost in our salary. 老板承诺要给我们大幅度增加工资。

colossal *adj.* /kəˈlɔsl/

In his *colossal* ignorance of the law Bob brought huge trouble to his company.

[猜一猜]A 巨大的 B 愚蠢的
C 可笑的 D 无可奈何的

[翻 译]由于对法律极大的无知，鲍勃给他的公司带来了非常大的麻烦。

[大头巧记]词源：公元前292年罗得岛人打败了马其顿人，他们将战争中缴获的所有兵器都溶化了，铸成太阳神巨像，名字就叫colossal，成为世界七大奇观之一，后英语引入之巨形雕像，现在只取巨大之意。

[大头例句]It was a colossal waste of money. 这太浪费钱了！

eradicate *v.* /iˈrædikeit/

Their goal was to *eradicate* poverty.

[猜一猜]A 帮助 B 消灭 C 救济 D 改变

[翻 译]他们的目标是消灭贫困。

[分 析]er + radic + ate
去除 + 根部 + 动词词尾 → 根除，消灭

[大头例句]Inflation will never be completely eradicated from the economy. 通货膨胀将永远无法从经济中根除。

essence *n.* /ˈesns/

The *essence* of his religious teaching is love for all men.

[猜一猜]A 目的 B 理想 C 精髓 D 口号

[翻 译]他宣扬的宗教教义的精髓是爱天下人。

[分 析]esse + nce
存在 + 名词词尾 → 存在，本质，精髓

[词义扩展]*n.* 香精，香料，香油 *essence of mint* 薄荷油

[大头例句]The essence of their argument is that life cannot be explained by science. 他们的论点的本质是科学不能解释人生。

excess *n.* /ikˈses/

Profit is the *excess* of sales over costs.

[猜一猜]A 成功 B 过程 C 行为 D 超过

[翻 译]利润就是价格超出成本的部分。

[分 析]ex + cess
出来 + 走 → 走出，超出，超额

[词义扩展]*n./v.* 过量，过分，无节制
an excess of enthusiasm 过分热心

[大头例句]Both sides should try to avoid engaging in emotional excesses such as hysteria and fits of temper. 双方都应该尽量避免陷于像歇斯底里和大发脾气这样的感情过度冲动之中。

exorbitant *adj.* /igˈzɔːbitənt/

The man asked an *exorbitant* price for his second-hand car.

[猜一猜]A 合适的 B 过低的
C 双倍的 D 过高的

[翻 译]那个人的二手车要价太高了。

[分 析]ex + orbit + ant
出去 + 轨迹 + 形容词尾 → 出轨的，过度的，过高的

[大头例句]He didn't want to borrow money at an exorbitant rate of interest. 他并不想借高利贷。

expire *v.* /iksˈpaiə/

Our trade agreement with Britain will *expire* at the end of this year.

[猜一猜] A 生效 B 签署 C 期满 D 修改
[翻 译] 我国同英国的贸易协定今年年底期满。
[分 析] ex + (s)pire
出去 + 呼吸 → 呼吸结束，死亡，期满，中止
[大头巧记] 形近词：**empire**，帝国，帝国被打了叉(x)，宣告其死亡。
[大头例句] My passport expires in a month. 我的护照一个月以后到期。

facilitate *vt.* /fəˈsiliteit/

The new underground railway will *facilitate* travel to all parts of the city.

[猜一猜] A 打通 B 连接 C 使容易 D 使复杂
[翻 译] 新的地下铁路将为去城市各处提供方便。
[分 析] facili + tate
容易做 + 动词词尾 → 使容易，使便利
[大头巧记] **facility 设备**，是使事情变得容易的东西。
[词义扩展] *vt.* 推动，帮助，促进 *The counsellor may be able to facilitate communication between the couple.* 这个顾问也许可帮助促进这对夫妻间的交流。
[大头例句] It would facilitate matters if you were more cooperative. 如果你再合作些，事情会变得更容易。

fascinate *v.* /ˈfæsineit/

The changing vivid colours of the sunset *fascinated* the eye.

[猜一猜] A 刺伤 B 改变 C 使着迷 D 照亮
[翻 译] 日落时变化多端的色彩使人看得入迷。
[分 析] fascin + ate
符咒，魔力 + 动词词尾 → 迷住；使神魂颠倒
[大头巧记] 记住"fascin"即可，音近似 **fashion，时尚**，时尚使人着迷。
[大头例句] It's a subject that has always fascinated me. 这一直是令我心醉神迷的一个对象。

initial *adj.* /iˈniʃəl/

They took the *initial* step toward reconciliation.

[猜一猜] A 关键的 B 蹒跚的 C 最初的 D 公正的
[翻 译] 他们迈出了走向和解的第一步。
[分 析] in + iti + al
向内 + 走 + 形容词尾 → 刚入门，最初的，固有的，字首的，原始的
[词义扩展] *n.* 姓名起首的大写字母，草签 *Steven Lane's initials are S.L.* Steven Lane 这姓名的首字母是 S.L.。
[大头例句] At the initial stage of the project not everyone had access to a computer. 在工程最初阶段的时候并不是所有的人都有权使用电脑。

lethal *adj.* /ˈliːθəl/

These accusations are *lethal* to the candidate's image.

[猜一猜] A 致命的 B 有助的 C 温和的 D 清楚的
[翻 译] 这些指控对候选人的形象极其有害。
[分 析] leth + al
死 + 词尾 → 致死的，致命的，致命因子
[大头例句] The closure of that factory dealt a lethal blow to the town. 那家工厂的关闭是对该镇致命的打击。

mitigate *v.* /ˈmitigeit/

In an effort to *mitigate* the pain of childbirth, many women elect to take certain kinds of drugs that make the process more comfortable.

[猜一猜] A 避免 B 转移 C 减少 D 控制
[翻 译] 为了努力减少分娩时的痛苦，很多妇女选择使用某些麻药让这个过程更舒服些。
[分 析] miti + gate
轻 + 做 → 弄轻，减轻，减少
[大头例句] The judge said that nothing could mitigate the cruelty with which the stepmother had treated the girl. 法官说没有任何理由可以把那个残忍虐待女孩的继母的罪责减轻。

plight *n.* /plait/

His business in Europe is in a sad *plight*.

[猜一猜] A 情绪 B 困境 C 事实 D 尴尬
[翻 译] 他在欧洲的生意境况十分恶劣。

[大头巧记] 拆:p(oor) light,惨淡的光景,困境

[词义扩展] *vt.* 保证,约定 *plight* (*one's*) *troth* 订婚

[大头例句] The plight of the single mother is greatly underappreciated in today's society: how many people are capable of bearing the responsibility for being the sole financial and emotional provider for children, while maintaining a life of one's own? 在今天的社会,单身母亲的处境远没有得到足够的重视;试想:有多少人能够承受独身一人在金钱和感情两方面提供孩子们所需的责任,同时还要维持自己的生活。

rejoice *v.* /ri'dʒɔis/

She *rejoiced* in her friend's good fortune.

[猜一猜] A 羡慕　　B (使)高兴
C 祝福　　D 重复

[翻　译] 她为她朋友的好运而充满喜悦。

[分　析] re + joice
一再 + 高兴 → 使欣喜,高兴

[习语记忆] **rejoice in the name of...** [谑]名叫…

stimulate *v.* /'stimjuleit/

Exercise *stimulates* the flow of blood.

[猜一猜] A 堆积　B 松弛　C 宣泄　D 刺激

[翻　译] 体操促进血液流动。

[分　析] stimu + late
刺激 + 动词词尾 → 刺激,激励

[大头例句] An inspiring teacher can stimulate students to succeed. 启发性的老师可以激励学生获得成功。

striking *adj.* /'straikiŋ/

There is a *striking* constract between the two brothers.

[猜一猜] A 鲜明的　　B 讨厌的
C 成功的　　D 发光的

[翻　译] 两兄弟形成鲜明的对照。

[大头巧记] **strike,打,撞击;striking,打击的,显著的,鲜明的**

[大头例句] Her eye make-up was very striking. 她眼上的化妆品非常吸引人。

习题:在下面的空格里填写本单元的单词。

1. Inflation will never be completely __________ from the economy.
2. No one is __________ except God.
3. The tenet of this organization is __________ the apartheid.
4. Her eye make-up was very __________.
5. The __________ of their argument is that life cannot be explained by science.
6. At the __________ stage of the project not everyone had access to a computer.
7. Our trade agreement with Britain will __________ at the end of this year.
8. The counsellor may be able to __________ communication between the couple.
9. The __________ of the single mother is greatly underappreciated in today's society.
10. She __________ in her friend's good fortune.
11. The American President's statement __________ the crisis in the Middle East.
12. In his __________ ignorance of the law Bob brought huge trouble to his company.
13. The delegate __________ his nation's standpoint in the press conference.
14. They are making efforts to __________ participation in the program.

15. The doctor gave him some pills to __________ cold symptoms.
16. Both sides should try to avoid engaging in emotional __________ such as hysteria and fits of temper.
17. The closure of that factory dealt a __________ blow to the town.
18. In an effort to __________ the pain of childbirth, many women elect to take certain kinds of drugs that make the process more comfortable.
19. An inspiring teacher can __________ students to succeed.
20. The man asked an __________ price for his second-hand car.
21. The changing vivid colours of the sunset __________ the eye.

Note 前事不忘后事之师 *Remember the past and it will guide your future.*

algae n. /ˈældʒiː/ n.海藻

Day 26

algebra n. /ˈældʒibrə/

It is really difficult for me to manage *algebra* well.

[猜一猜]A 代数 B 几何 C 积分 D 生物

[翻 译]对于我来说很好地掌握代数确实很困难。

[分 析]al + gebra
the + 重新组合 → 重新组合的科学 → 代数

algorithm n. /ˈælgəriðəm/

I cannot completely understand that *algorithm*.

[猜一猜]A 理论 B 运算法则 C 化学式 D 现象

[翻 译]我不能完全理解这个运算法则。

[大头巧记]algo，由 **algebra** （代数） 而来，**rithm** 和 **rhythm**（节奏）同音，代数学的节奏 → 数学运算法则。

circumference n. /səˈkʌmfərəns/

səː conference 会议

The earth's *circumference* is more than 40,000 kilometers.

[猜一猜]A 直径 B 半径 C 周长 D 回归线长度

[翻 译]地球的周长超过 40000 公里。

[分 析]circum + fer + ence
环绕 + 带来 + 名词词尾 → 带来一圈的距离，周长

[词义扩展]*n.* 圆周，周线，外围，周围

[大头例句]The lamps threw deep shadows beyond the circumference of the pit. 灯在坑道的周围投下深深的阴影。

curve n. /kəːv/

From high above I saw the gentle *curve* of the bay.

[猜一猜]A 河流 B 氛围 C 温柔 D 曲线

[翻 译]从高处，我看到海湾温柔的曲线。

[词义扩展]*v.* 使弯曲，成曲形，弯曲的 *He curved the piece of wood.* 他将木条弄弯曲了。

[大头例句]The path curves around the lake. 这条道路沿着湖延伸。

database n. /ˈdeitəbeis/

He spent the whole night putting the new customers in the *database*.

[猜一猜]A 档案 B 文件 C 检查 D 数据库

[翻 译]他花了整晚的时间把新的用户存入数据库。

[大头巧记]拆：data base，数据的基地，数据库

[词义扩展]*v.* 把(数据)存入数据库

[大头例句]Our computer's database is not large enough. 我们的计算机的数据库不够大。

decimal adj./n. /ˈdesiməl/

The *decimal* system is widely used in every corner of the globe.

[猜一猜]A 选举 B 数字化 C 十进制 D 儿童教育

[翻 译]十进位法被广泛地应用于世界的每一个角落。

[分 析]decim + al
十分之一 + 形容词尾 → 十进制的

[词义扩展]小数的 *decimal point* 小数点

[大头例句]0.5, 36.8 and 872.56 are all decimals. n. 0.5，36.8 和 872.56 都是小数。

diameter n. /daiˈæmitə/

My uncle used to own a fish pond with a *diameter* of three hundred metres.

[猜一猜]A 周长 B 面积 C 深度 D 直径

[翻 译]我的叔叔曾经拥有一个直径 300 米的鱼塘。

[分　析] dia + meter

完全地 + 测量 → 有始有终的测量 → 直径

[词义扩展] n. 倍，放大倍数

[大头例句] Our magnifier has two lenses magnifying 2,000 diameters. 我们的放大镜有两个能放大2000倍的透镜。

dimension n. /diˈmenʃən/

A line has one *dimension*, a square has two, and time is sometimes called the fourth *dimension*.

[猜一猜] A 方向　B 维　C 向量　D 确定

[翻　译] 线是一维空间，平面是二维空间，时间有时候被称为第四维空间。

[分　析] di + mension

分开 + 测量 → 进行分析测量，尺寸，尺度，【数】元，维

[词义扩展] (*pl.*)容积，面积，大小，范围，规模 *What are the dimensions of this theater?* 这个剧院的容积是多少？

[大头例句] There is another dimension to this problem which you haven't mentioned. 这个问题还有一个方面你没提到。

equation n. /iˈkweiʃən/

I can hardly understand the chemical *equation*.

[猜一猜] A 定理　B 成分　C 结构　D 方程式

[翻　译] 我理解不了这个化学方程式。

[分　析] equa + tion

相等 + 名词词尾 → 相等，等式，方程式。

[词义扩展] n. 平衡，均衡，综合体

[大头例句] The world is full of equations; there must be an answer for everything, if only you know how to set forth the questions. 世界充满了复杂的事物；假使你知道如何提出问题的话，那么也许事事就会有答案了。

facet vt. /ˈfæsit/

The skill with which Mr. Smith *faceted* the diamond is remarkable.

[猜一猜] A 刻画平面　B 装饰

C 提取　D 鉴别

[翻　译] 史密斯先生在钻石上雕刻小平面的精湛技巧真是了不起。

[大头巧记] face，脸，面 facet，小平面，刻面，在…上雕琢小平面。

[词义扩展] n. （事物的）方面 *There are several facets to this question.* 这个问题有几个方面。

[大头例句] The most important facet of the President's plan is a balanced budget. 总统计划的一个重要方面就是平衡预算。

geometry n. /dʒiˈɔmitri/

Geometry is a big headache for me.

[猜一猜] A 生物学　B 天文学

C 几何学　D 遗传学

[翻　译] 几何学让我很头痛。

[分　析] geo + metry

土地 + 丈量 → 丈量土地的学问，几何学

[词义扩展] n. 几何图形［形状，结构，条件］，几何学论著

[大头例句] The room had a pleasing geometry about it. 这个房间的几何布置让人很愉快。

graphic adj. /ˈgræfik/

He described the accident in *graphic* detail.

[猜一猜] A 详尽的　B 生动的

C 秘密的　D 公共的

[翻　译] 他以生动的细节描述了那起事故。

[大头巧记] **photograph，照片；graph，图画；graphic，图画似的，生动的。**

[词义扩展] *adj.* 书写的，书法的，绘画的

[大头例句] They are all interested in graphic arts. 他们都对平面造型艺术感兴趣。

knot n./v. /nɔt/

Can you tie a *knot* in the end of my thread?

[猜一猜] A 小球　B 铜钱　C 硬币　D 结

[翻　译] 你能在我的线的末端打个结吗？

[词义扩展] n. 群，簇，一小群人；节（海里/小时）*at a rate of knots* 非常快 v. 打结，系 *knot a parcel safely* 把小包扎紧

[习语记忆] tie a knot with one's tongue that can not be untied with one's teeth 结婚

seek a knot in a ring 无事生非

[大头例句] A knot of people stood talking outside the door. 一群人站在门外聊天。

linear adj. /ˈliniə/

He bought his mother a scarf with a *linear* design.

[猜一猜] A 清晰地　B 线状的

C 简单的　D 别致的

[翻　译] 他给母亲买了一条有线条图案的围巾。

[分　析] line + ar

线 + 形容词尾 → 线状的，直线的，长度的

[大头例句] Our reading does not always progress in a linear fashion. 我们的阅读水平并不总是线性进步的。

meagre adj. /ˈmiːɡə(r)/

The report that first reached us through the newspapers was *meagre* and contradictory.

[猜一猜] A 不足的　B 有趣的

C 令人愉悦的　D 令人不快的

[翻　译] 最初通过报纸传到我们这里的报道既不全面又互相矛盾。

[大头巧记] 拆：m（没）-eager，→ meagre 没有热情的生活是贫乏不足的。

[词义扩展] *adj.* 瘦的，贫乏的 *the meagre soil of an eroded plain.* 被侵蚀的贫瘠平原

[大头例句] The appeal for help was met with a meagre response. 请求帮助的呼吁只收到了很少的回复。

numerical adj. /nju(ː)ˈmerikəl/

We are asked to keep the files in *numerical* order.

[猜一猜] A 时间的　B 科目的

C 兴趣的　D 数字的

[翻　译] 要求我们按编号顺序排列文件。

[分　析] numer + ical

数字 + 形容词尾 → 数字的

[大头例句] There are no numerical estimates for the number of people in the world living with AIDS today, but most people admit it is an epidemic of proportions that modern man has not previously seen. 并没有关于世界上艾滋病携带者人数的数字估计，但是大多数人都承认这种传染病的传染率是现代人以前从来未见到过。

precise adj./n. /priˈsais/

There is no *precise* definition of a storm.

[猜一猜] A 即成的　B 固定的

C 准确的　D 模糊的

[翻　译] 对于风暴没有准确的定义。

[分　析] pre + cise

提前 + 剪切 → 提前剪切好的，精确的，谨慎的

[大头例句] For this stew recipe, your measurements need not be so precise; for the soufflé, however, you must be as precise as possible, or it is likely to turn out incorrectly. 对于这道炖菜，你的用料量就没有必要如此精确；但是对奶油冻你就要尽可能的精确，否则出来的味道可能就不对了。

proportion n. /prəˈpɔːʃən/

We do not always find visible happiness in *proportion* to visible virtue.

[猜一猜] A 比例　B 联系

C 在…之下　D 赢得

[翻　译] 我们会发现可见的幸福不一定与可见的美德成比例。

[分　析] pro + portion

根据 + 部分 → 比率，比例，面积

[词义扩展] *vt.* 使成比例，使均衡 *proportion the expenses to the receipts* 量入为出

[大头例句] Many say Britney Spears' fame is not at all in proportion to her talent, as she is known to lip sync and rely on professional dancers in many of her performances. 很多人说小甜甜的盛名和她的才能不相符，因为他们认为她假唱并且在她的很多演出中依赖于专业舞蹈家。

previous /'priːvjəs/

partial *adj.* /'pɑːʃəl/

The police have only a *partial* description of the suspect.

[猜一猜] A 暗指的　　B 拙劣的　　C 部分的　　D 分析性的

[翻　译] 警察只对嫌疑犯进行了不完全的描述。

[分　析] part + ial

部分 + 形容词尾 → 部分的,不完全的

[词义扩展] *adj.* 偏爱的,偏袒的　*He is partial to sports.* 他特别喜欢运动。

[大头例句] My grandmother, who was my mother's own first-grade teacher, jokes that not only was she not partial to my mother, in fact, she treated my mother more strictly than anyone else in the class! 我的祖母是我妈妈一年级时的老师,她开玩笑说她不仅没有偏袒我妈妈,事实上,她对我妈妈比对班上的任何其他人都严格。

perimeter *n.* /pə'rimitə/

The *perimeter* of our university is farmland.

[猜一猜] A 背后　B 前面　C 里面　D 周边

[翻　译] 我们大学的周边是田野。

[分　析] peri + meter

周围 + 测量 → 周围的测量,周长,周边

[大头例句] Even at the perimeter of Beijing, kilometres away from the city lights and a lot of pollution, it is still nearly impossible to see stars in the night sky. 即使在北京的外围,远离好几公里外城市的灯光和很多的污染,仍然是几乎不可能看到夜空的星星。

习题:在下面的空格里填写本单元的单词。

1. Even at the ________ of Beijing, kilometres away from the city lights and a lot of pollution, it is still nearly impossible to see stars in the night sky.
2. From high above I saw the gentle ________ of the bay.
3. The ________ system is widely used in every corner of the globe.
4. The world is full of ________; there must be an answer for everything, if only you know how to set forth the questions.
5. The most important ________ of the President's plan is a balanced budget.
6. There are no ________ estimates for the number of people in the world living with AIDS today, but most people admit it is an epidemic of proportions that modern man has not previously seen.
7. It is really difficult for me to manage ________ well.
8. I cannot completely understand that ________.
9. The room had a pleasing ________ about it.
10. He described the accident in ________ detail.
11. A ________ of people stood talking outside the door.
12. For this stew ________, your measurements need not be so precise; for the soufflé, however, you must be as precise as possible, or it is likely to turn out incorrectly.
13. Many say Britney Spears' fame is not at all in ________ to her talent, as she is known to lip sync and rely on professional dancers in many of her performances.
14. My grandmother, who was my mother's own first-grade teacher, jokes that not only was she not________ to my mother, in fact, she treated my mother more strictly than anyone

else in the class!

15. The earth's __________ is more than 40,000 kilometers.
16. He spent the whole night putting the new customers in the __________.
17. My uncle used to own a fish pond with a __________ of three hundred metres.
18. There is another __________ to this problem which you haven't mentioned.
19. Our reading does not always progress in a __________ fashion.
20. The report that first reached us through the newspapers was __________ and contradictory.

Note 前事不忘后事之师 Remember the past and it will guide your future.

Day 27

alliteration *n.* /əˌlitəˈreiʃən/

"On scrolls of silver snowy sentences" is in *alliteration*.

[猜一猜]A 尾韵 B 比喻 C 象征 D 头韵

[翻 译]"On scrolls of silver snowy sentences"这个句子押头韵。

[分 析]al + liter + rat(e) + ion

to + 字母 + 动词词尾 + 名词词尾 → 根据字母的用法 → 压头韵

anthology *n.* /ænˈθɔlədʒi/

I bought an *anthology* of Lu Xun's novels on my way to school yesterday.

[猜一猜]A 评论 B 选集 C 赏析 D 导读

[翻 译]昨天在上学的路上我买了一本鲁迅小说选集。

[分 析]antho + logy

花 + 集合 → 花的集合 → 喻选集;文选

[大头例句]The Irish love their constitution for what it is: an anthology of the clerical-nationalist ideas of 1936, when it was drawn up (*Economist*). 爱尔兰人热爱他们的宪法:当它在1936年被制定出来时就是宗教民族主义思想的杂集(《经济学家》)。

antonym *n.* /ˈæntəunim/

The word "old" is an *antonym* of the word "new".

[猜一猜]A 同源词 B 同性词 C 异根词 D 反义词

[翻 译]"old"是"new"的反义词。

[分 析]anti + onym

反 + 名字 → 名字反的 → 反义

brochure *n.* /brəuˈʃjuə/

Just fill out this form to tell us what you want and we will send you a holiday *brochure*.

[猜一猜]A 礼物 B 指南 C 服务 D 兼职

[翻 译]填写这个表格告诉我们你想要的,我们会寄给你一个假日指南。

[分 析]broch + ure

缝,织 + 名词词尾 → 过去的线装书,缝起来的小书 → 小册子,指南

[大头例句]He hired a lot of college students to distribute the sales brochures. 他雇了很多大学生为他分发宣传小册子。

caption *n.* /ˈkæpʃən/

I like watching foreign films with Chinese *captions*.

[猜一猜]A 演员 B 字幕 C 配音 D 审美习惯

[翻 译]我喜欢看有中文字幕的外国电影。

[分 析]cap + tion

抓住 + 名词词尾 → 提纲挈领之物,标题,说明,字幕

[大头巧记]cap,帽子文章的帽子,标题。

[词义扩展]*vt.* 在(文件等)上加标题;在(图片等)上加说明;在(电影)上加字幕 *n.* 逮捕

[大头例句]A caption is often printed with a photograph or illustration.照片和插图常附有说明文字。

clause *n.* /klɔːz/

There is a *clause* in the contract requiring a fee to be paid if the holiday is canceled.

[猜一猜]A 附录 B 说明 C 条款 D 协议

[翻 译]在合同中有一条规定,如果假期被取消的话要付一定的补偿费用。

[词义扩展]【语】从句 principal [subordinate] clause 主[从]句

compile *vt.* /kəmˈpail/

We are *compiling* an English dictionary for the students who are preparing for the IELTS test.

[猜一猜]A 研究 B 编写 C 校订 D 设计

[翻 译]我们正在为准备雅思考试的大学生编写一本英语辞典。

[分 析]com + pile

汇 + 堆 → 堆放在一起，把各种材料汇总 → 编写

[词义扩展] *vt.* 汇集，编辑，编制，搜集（资料）；【计】编码，编译（程序）

[大头例句] The database was compiled from statistics published by *Science Daily*. 这个数据库是由《科学日报》上公布的统计数字汇编而成的。

dissertation *n.* /ˌdisəˈteiʃən/

A *dissertation* is a long piece of writing on a particular subject that you do as part of a university degree.

[猜一猜]A 申请信 B 考试

C 学术论文 D 写作

[翻 译]学术论文作为大学学位的一部分，它是关于一个具体科目的长作品。

[分 析]dissert + ation

讨论 + 名词词尾 → 论述 → 学位论文

[大头例句] I have to write my academic dissertation. 我得写我的学术论文。

formulate *v.* /ˈfɔːmjuleit/

The government is *formulating* a new strategy to combat crime.

[猜一猜]A 发布 B 推行 C 征求 D 制订

[翻 译]政府正在制订一个打击犯罪的新策略。

[大头巧记] **form** 形式；**formula** 公式，规则。formulate，-ate 为动词词尾，**formulate**，用公式表示，精确的阐明，制订。

[大头例句] The Bush team is formulating its response to the global warming treaty. 布什小组正在制订他对全球变暖条约的回应。

inspiration *n.* /ˌinspəˈreiʃən/

Poets and artists often draw their *inspiration* from nature.

[猜一猜]A 艺术 B 绘画 C 灵感 D 素材

[翻 译]诗人与艺术家往往从自然中得到灵感。

[分 析] in + spira + tion

向内 + 呼吸 + 名词词尾 → 吸气，鼓舞，神的启示，灵感

[大头例句] He has been an inspiration to other young athletes from a similar background. 对于和他有类似背景的那些年轻运动员，他已经成为了一种鼓舞力量。

literacy *n.* /ˈlitərəsi/

Teachers have been asked to concentrate on *literacy* and numeracy.

[猜一猜]A 创造力 B 推理能力

C 读写能力 D 归纳能力

[翻 译]要求老师们将注意力集中在读写和计算能力上。

[分 析]liter + acy

文字 + 词尾 → 识字，有文化，读写能力

margin *n./vt.* /ˈmɑːdʒin/

For the results of this survey, there is a very small *margin* of error, as the sample size was enormous.

[猜一猜]A 程度 B 显示 C 理由 D 幅度

[翻 译]调查结果显示，在选样量很大的情况下，误差幅度却非常小。

[词义扩展] *n.* 书页的空白处，边缘

[习语记忆] **by a wide margin** 广泛的回旋余地

[大头例句] In the margins of her book, you can see all the notes she took from her teacher's lectures. 在书的空白处，你能看到她从老师的讲课中记录的所有笔记。

marginal *adj.* /ˈmɑːdʒinəl/

In many societies, minority populations are often considered *marginal* populations because they often do not share the same rights and privileges as the majority.

[猜一猜]A 特殊的 B 有危险的

C 边缘的 D 举足轻重的

[翻 译]在很多社会中，少数民族人口经常被认为是边缘人口，因为他们经常不能和多数人口分

享相同的权利和特权。

[大头巧记] **margin**,书页的空白处,边缘;**marginal**,边缘的。

[词义扩展] *adj.* 不重要的,微小的,收益不大的 *marginal subsistence* 起码的生活

[大头例句] Eating olives during pregnancy has only a marginal effect on your baby's health. 在怀孕期间吃橄榄只对婴儿的健康有很小的影响。

modify *vt.* /ˈmɔdifai/

The equipment may be *modified* to produce VCD sets.

[猜一猜] A 示范 B 遥控 C 改装 D 做模具

[翻 译] 这设备可以经过改装用来生产光碟机。

[分 析] mod + ify

方法,模式 + 动词词尾 → 改变方式,修改,改装

[词义扩展] *vt.* 缓和,使易接受 *to modify one's demands* 使达成协议

[大头例句] The expression "it's hard to teach an old dog new tricks" means it can be difficult to modify the well established behavior of people, particularly if the habit has existed for a long time. 有句话叫 "it's hard to teach an old dog new tricks",意思是说更改已经根深蒂固的行为举止会很困难,特别是那些已经存在了很长一段时间的习惯。

monologue *n.* /ˈmɔnəlɔg/

He kept up a steady *monologue* during the whole journey.

[猜一猜] A 意向 B 领导 C 个人长篇大论 D 怨天尤人

[翻 译] 在整个旅程中他不停地独自长篇大论。

[分 析] mono + logue

独自 + 说话 → 独白,独角戏,一个人发表长篇大论

[大头例句] Romeo's first monologue in Shakespeare's tragic classic, "Romeo and Juliet", is often revered as one of the most romantic soliloquies in Western dramatic literature. 在莎士比亚经典悲剧《罗米欧和朱丽叶》中,罗米欧的第一段独白被尊为西方戏剧文学中最浪漫的独白之一。

narrative *adj./n.* /ˈnærətiv/

The *narrative* makes up most of the book.

[猜一猜] A 抒情 B 记叙 C 议论 D 实录

[翻 译] 这本书大部分是由记叙文组成。

[大头巧记] **narrate**, *v.* 叙述,讲述;**narrative**, *n./adj.* 叙述(的),记叙文(的)

[大头例句] In an attempt to give the classmates an opportunity to know each other better, the teacher asked that each student deliver a brief narrative regarding his hobbies, family, and favorite foods. 为了试着给同学们一个互相认识的机会,老师要求每位同学做一个简短的关于自己爱好、家庭,和最喜欢的食品的叙述。

nautical *adj.* /ˈnɔːtikəl/

A *nautical* almanac gives information about the sun, moon, tides, etc.

[猜一猜] A 气象的 B 航海的 C 年度的 D 综合的

[翻 译] 航海年历中提供关于日、月、潮汐等信息。

[分 析] naut + ical

船 + 形容词尾 → 船员的,航海的

[大头例句] Thanks to his nautical training as a young sailor, in his older years, the man enjoyed sailing as one of his favorite hobbies. 由于年轻做海员时受过航海训练,在稍长的时候,航海成了这个人的爱好之一。

portray *vt.* /pɔːˈtrei/

In his letter, he *portrayed* his girlfriend as a fairy.

[猜一猜] A 描绘 B 想象 C 赞扬 D 误导

[翻 译] 在他的信中,他把女朋友描绘成了仙女。

[分 析] por + tray

向前 + 画 → 描绘,描写

[大头例句] Princess Diana's most recent biography, published in 2001, portrayed her as a widely misunderstood free spirit, content in her own skin as a mature woman. 戴安娜王妃最近于2001年出版的传记,描绘了在她成熟女性外

表下被大大误解了的自由灵魂。

postscript *n.* /ˈpəustskript/

She mentioned in a *postscript* in her letter that the parcel had arrived.

[猜一猜]A 邮递的 B 印刷品 C 附言 D 说明

[翻 译]他在信末附笔中说包裹已到了。

[分 析]post + script

后 + 写 → 写在后面的,附言,后记

preface *n.* /ˈprefis/

Our defeat may be the *preface* to our successor's victory.

[猜一猜]A 开端 B 条件 C 催化剂 D 指导

[翻 译]我们的失败可能是后继者获胜的开端。

[分 析]pre + face

提前 + 说 → 提前说的,序言,开端,写序言。

[大头巧记]pre face,朝向前面的 → 开端。

[大头例句]I realize my being vegetarian may make some meat-eaters uncomfortable, so I would like to preface my reasoning behind this choice by saying I do not have any ill feelings towards those who do not share my opinions. 我意识到我作为一个素食主义者可能会引起一些吃肉的人的不舒服,所以在我讲述我这个选择的原因之时,很喜欢先说明我对于那些不同意我观点的人没有任何不好的感觉。

refrain *v.* /riˈfrein/

I was told to *refrain* from smoking by my fiancée.

[猜一猜]A 避免 B 渔利 C 控制 D 释放

[翻 译]我的未婚妻要我戒烟。

[分 析]re + frain

一再的 + 笼头 → 一再的上笼头,抑制,避免

[词义扩展]*n.* 重复,叠句

plot *v.* /plɔt/

They are *plotting* to rob a bank.

[猜一猜]A 监视 B 跟踪 C 控制 D 密谋

[翻 译]他们正在密谋打劫银行。

[大头巧记]拆:plan lot 计划很多事 → 密谋

[词义扩展]*n.* 情节,设计情节;小块地区,地图 *an exciting plot* 吸引人的情节

[习语记忆]**The plot thickens.** [口]事情愈来愈复杂了。

[大头例句]The plot of the recent blockbuster "Spiderman" is very familiar to most people; what made it worthwhile was its clever usage of special effects. 最近引起轰动的《蜘蛛侠》情节对大多数人来说很熟悉;它的价值在于其对特技的聪明运用。

习题:在下面的空格里填写本单元的单词。

1. The Bush team is __________ its response to the global warming treaty.
2. Poets and artists often draw their __________ from nature.
3. In many societies, minority populations are often considered __________ populations because they often do not share the same rights and privileges as the majority.
4. The equipment may be __________ to produce VCD sets.
5. Romeo's first __________ in Shakespeare's tragic classic, "Romeo and Juliet", is often revered as one of the most romantic soliloquies in Western dramatic literature.
6. In an attempt to give the classmates an opportunity to know each other better, the teacher asked that each student deliver a brief __________ regarding his hobbies, family, and fa-

vorite foods.

7. Princess Diana's most recent biography, published in 2001, __________ her as a widely misunderstood free spirit, content in her own skin as a mature woman.
8. The __________ of the recent blockbuster "Spiderman" is very familiar to most people; what made it worthwhile was its clever usage of special effects.
9. "On scrolls of silver snowy sentences" is an __________.
10. We are __________ an English dictionary for the students who are preparing for the IELTS test.
11. I like watching foreign films with Chinese __________.
12. There is a __________ in the contract requiring a fee to be paid if the holiday is canceled.
13. I bought an __________ of Lu Xun's novels on my way to school yesterday.
14. Just fill out this form to tell us what you want and we will send you a holiday__________.
15. The word "old" is an __________ of the word "new".
16. A __________ is a long piece of writing on a particular subject that you do as part of a university degree.
17. For the results of this survey, there is a very small __________ of error, as the sample size was enormous.
18. Thanks to his __________ training as a young sailor, in his older years, the man enjoyed sailing as one of his favorite hobbies.
19. She mentioned in a __________ in her letter that the parcel had arrived.
20. I was told to __________ from smoking by my fiancée.
21. Teachers have been asked to concentrate on __________ and numeracy.
22. Our defeat may be the __________ to our successor's victory.

Note 前事不忘后事之师 *Remember the past and it will guide your future.*

Day 28

affable adj. /ˈæfəbl/

When she is smiling, she looks fairly *affable*.

[猜一猜] A 优美的　B 和蔼的　C 迷人的　D 矫情的

[翻 译] 当她微笑的时候,她看起来非常和蔼。

[分 析] af + fable
af-=ad-,朝向,+交谈 → 易于交谈的,和蔼的,友好的

[大例 头句] An affable weasel is saying "happy new year" to the hen. 一个和蔼的黄鼠狼正在给鸡拜年。

apologetic adj. /əˌpɔləˈdʒetik/

He came into her room with an *apologetic* smile on her face.

[猜一猜] A 虚伪的　B 暧昧的　C 尴尬的　D 歉意的

[翻 译] 他带着满脸歉意的笑走进她的房间。

[分 析] apologe + tic
道歉 + 形容词尾 → 歉意的

[大巧 头记] 与 **apologize** 同源

[词扩 义展] *adj.* 自贬的;谦卑的 *an apologetic manner* 谦卑的举止 *n.* 正式辩解,正式辩护

[大例 头句] I've just quarreled with my girl. I want to leave an apologetic note on her desk. 我刚刚和女友吵了架,我想在她的书桌上留个便条道歉。

compromise n. /ˈkɔmprəmaiz/

The incongruous design is a *compromise* between high tech and antique Chinese.

[猜一猜] A 折中　B 承诺　C 结合　D 融合

[翻 译] 这个不协调的设计是高科技和古代中国风格的折中。

[分 析] com + prise
相互 + 保证 → 相互妥协,危害

[词扩 义展] *n.* ①妥协,和解 ②妥协方案 ③危害,损害(名誉) *a compromise of morality* 道德的沦丧
v. ①和解,对…妥协 ②危及,连累 ③放弃,泄露(秘密) *compromise a lawsuit* 和解诉讼

[习记 语忆] **A bad compromise is better than a good lawsuit.** [谚] 吃亏的和解强似胜利的诉讼。

[大例 头句] Traditional supporters are accusing the party of compromising its principles. 传统的拥护者们正在责难那个妥协原则的政党。

elastic adj. /iˈlæstik/

The swimming costume is made of *elastic* material.

[猜一猜] A 隔水的　B 有弹力的　C 塑料的　D 特殊的

[翻 译] 这件泳衣是用弹性材料制成的。

[大巧 头记] 形近词记忆:**plastic**(塑料),塑料具有弹性 → **elastic**(有弹力的)。或:tic,为形容词词尾;elas,谐音:易拉丝,容易被拉成丝的 → **elastic: 有弹性的,有韧性的**。

[词扩 义展] *adj.* ①灵活的 *elastic rules* 灵活的规则
adj. ②能迅速恢复的 *an elastic spirit* 开朗的精神

[大例 头句] The man of rather elastic morals was not very popular among us. 那个道德标准很灵活的人不是很受我们欢迎。

etiquette n. /ˈetiket/

He learned a lot about diplomatic *etiquette* in college.

[猜一猜] A 政策　B 传统　C 关系　D 礼节

[翻 译] 他在上大学时学了很多关于外交礼节的东西。

[分 析] e + tiguette
无实意 + 票 → 凭票出入,是一种礼节

[词义扩展] *n.* 规矩，成规 *etiquette of game* 比赛规矩

[大头例句] Man is a slave to etiquette.人是规矩的奴隶。

explicit *adj.* /iksˈplisit/

I appreciate generalizations that are powerful, precise, and ***explicit***.

[猜一猜] A 清楚的　B 中肯的　C 简短的　D 丰富的

[翻　译] 我欣赏有力、准确而又清楚的概括。

[分　析] ex + plicit
出去 + 折叠 → 向外折叠，外在的，清楚的，直率的

[大头巧记] **implicit，含蓄的，暗含的** im(向内的)，和 ex(向外的)相对 → **explicit，外在的**。

[词义扩展] *adj.* (租金等)需直接付款的

[大头例句] Possible side effects should be made explicit. 可能的副作用应该清楚表明。

farewell *n./int.* /fεəˈwel/

We've decided to have a ***farewell*** party before we leave the school.

[猜一猜] A 最后　B 告别　C 自助　D 庆祝

[翻　译] 我们决定在离开学校前举行一次告别晚会。

[分　析] fare + well
祈使语气 + 好，美满 → 告别时说再见，一路平安

[词义扩展] *adj.* 告别的，惜别的；送行的

[大头例句] Let's say our farewells. 让我们说再见吧。

flatter *vt.* /ˈflætə/

Most superiors are ***flattered*** by their inferiors with the exception of Mr. Park.

[猜一猜] A 贿赂　B 奉承　C 害怕　D 服从

[翻　译] 大多数上级都会受到下级的奉承，惟有派克先生例外。

[大头巧记] flat，平坦的；flatter，说奉承的话，让人平静下来。

[词义扩展] *vt.* (画像等)比真人美，使高兴 *I feel flattered by your invitation.* 受到你的邀请，我觉得非常荣幸。

[大头例句] We flattered ourselves that we could do without their help, but things ran counter to our wishes. 我们自以为不需要他们帮忙也能办到，但是事与愿违。

frugal *adj.* /ˈfruːgəl/

She is a ***frugal*** housekeeper.

[猜一猜] A 勤劳的　B 细心的　C 简朴的　D 严厉的

[翻　译] 她是一位简朴的主妇。

[分　析] frugt + al
道德 + 形容词缀 → 道德的，简朴的，花钱少的

[大头例句] We are having frugal lunches these days. 这些天来我们的午餐很节省。

gracious *adj.* /ˈgreiʃəs/

Mr. Bower responded to the insult with ***gracious*** humor.

[猜一猜] A 有礼的　B 尖刻的　C 美妙的　D 傲慢的

[翻　译] 鲍尔先生以礼貌的幽默回应侮辱。

[分　析] graci + ous
好意 + 形容词尾 → 好意的，亲切的，和善的，有礼的

[大头例句] He was gracious enough to invite us to his home. 他真是亲切，邀请我们到他家里去。

hail *v.* /heil/

The crowds ***hailed*** the boxing champion.

[猜一猜] A 欢呼　B 观看　C 合影　D 给…危险

[翻　译] 群众向这位拳击冠军喝彩。

[词义扩展] *n./v.* 雹子，冰雹，一阵，落下 *v.* 叫出租车，打招呼，来自于 *My father hails from Yorkshire.* 我的爸爸来自于约克郡。

[大头例句] The crowd hailed stones upon the thief. 群众对小偷大扔石头。

hospitality *n.* /ˌhɔspiˈtæliti/

The people of your village showed me great ***hospitality***.

[猜一猜] A 诚信　B 力量　C 教育　D 好客

[翻　译] 你们村里的人很好客，对我非常殷勤。

[大头巧记] **hostpital，医院，慈善机构**，字源意为"客人的"；**hospitality，好客，宜人，盛情**

[习语记忆] **Dutch hospitality.** 由参加者负担费用的聚餐。

[大头例句] Here is just a note to thank you for your hospitality. 这里只能用一张便条来表达我对您盛情款待的谢意。

humble *adj.* /ˈhʌmbl/

The doctor was ***humble*** about his work, although he cured many people.

[猜一猜] A 讨厌的　B 谦逊的　C 所知甚少的　D 狂热的

[翻　译] 这位医生虽然治好了许多人的病，但他对自己的工作仍很谦逊。

[分　析] hum + ble
低，小 + 词尾 → 卑下的，谦逊的，粗陋的

[词义扩展] *vt.* 挫锐气等，贬低，使卑下 *humble sb's pride* 使某人丢脸

[大头例句] We feel humbled by our local community's generosity and support. 地方社区的慷慨和支持让我们感到相形见绌。

innocent *adj.* /ˈinəsnt/

Can you provide any evidence that he was ***innocent*** of the crime?

[猜一猜] A 有罪的　B 清白的　C 受害的　D 指使的

[翻　译] 你能提供证据证明他没有犯这罪吗？

[分　析] in + nocent
无 + 做错事 → 没有做错事的，清白的，无害的，单纯的

[词义扩展] *n.* 无罪的人，天真无邪的人 *do the innocent* 装糊涂

[大头例句] Under the law, everyone is considered innocent until proven guilty. 根据法律，直到证明有罪之前，每个人都被先认定为是无罪的。

mediocre *adj.* /ˌmiːdiˈəukə/

Food served on many airplanes is rarely delicious; most often it is ***mediocre*** at best!

[猜一猜] A 可恶的　B 一般的　C 没有营养的　D 昂贵的

[翻　译] 飞机上提供的食品很少好吃，大多时候最好也就是一般。

[分　析] medi + ocre
中间 + 山脉 → 中等的山脉，中间状态的，一般的，普普通通的

[大头例句] The critics condemned the play as mediocre. 评论家谴责那出戏是低劣的。

moderate *v.* /ˈmɔdərit/

The pace of economic expansion has ***moderated***.

[猜一猜] A 缓和　B 控制　C 加速　D 举步维艰

[翻　译] 经济发展的步伐已经缓和下来。

[分　析] mode + rate
方法，模式 + 动词词尾 → 合模式的，适度的，中等的，缓和。

[大头巧记] **model，模特儿**，模特儿的步伐是 **moderate 适度的**。

[大头例句] Due to his moderate stance on abortion and gun control, the prime minister candidate is well received in most districts. 由于其在堕胎和枪支控制上的适中态度，这位总理候选人在绝大多数地区反映很好。

negotiable *adj.* /niˈgəuʃiəbl/

Terms and conditions are ***negotiable***.

[猜一猜] A 双方互利的　B 复杂的　C 模糊不清的　D 可通过谈判解决的

[翻　译] 条款和条件是可以通过谈判解决的。

[分　析] neg + oti + able
不 + 空闲 + 可…的 → 不空闲的，谈判的，可通过谈判解决的

[词义扩展] *adj.* 可通行的，可应付的，可兑现的（支票等）

[大例头句] As far as I am concerned, my feeling that taking an exam for someone else is wrong is completely non-negotiable, and I will not discuss it any further. 就像我说到的，替别人考试是错误的，我的这个感觉是毫无妥协余地的，并且我不会再进一步讨论它。

presentation *n.* /ˌprezenˈteiʃən/

Using a computer helped with the spelling and *presentation* of his school work.

[猜一猜] A 阅读 B 表达 C 成绩 D 记忆

[翻 译] 使用电脑可帮助学生提高其拼写和表达能力。

[分 析] present + ation

介绍 + 名词词尾 → 介绍，陈诉，表达

[大例头句] For the final presentation in this class, each student will need to prepare a twenty-minute talk with visual aids and be prepared to answer questions from his classmates. 在本课程的期末陈述中，每一个学生都需要准备一个20分钟的使用直观教具的讲话，并且要准备回答来自同学的问题。

prestige *n.* /presˈtiːʒ/

prestigious /presˈtiːdʒəs/ adj. 享有声望的

The old universities of Oxford and Cambridge still have a lot of *prestige*.

[猜一猜] A 权力 B 影响 C 福利 D 威望

[翻 译] 历史悠久的牛津大学和剑桥大学仍然享有很高的声望。

[分 析] pre + stige

前面 + 拉近 → 把人拉到前面的力量，威望

volunteer *n.* /ˌvɔlenˈtiə/

The organization is appealing for *volunteers*.

[猜一猜] A 员工 B 经理 C 志愿者 D 合作伙伴

[翻 译] 该组织正在吸引志愿者。

[分 析] volunt + eer

志愿的 + …者 → 志愿者，志愿兵

[词义扩展] *adj.* 志愿的，义务的；*v.* 自愿 *volunteer to give blood.* 自愿献血

[大例头句] Can I have a volunteer to erase the chalkboard, please? 请问有人自愿把黑板擦了吗？

chalk /tʃɔːk/ n. 粉笔；白垩 vt. 用粉笔写

习题：在下面的空格里填写本单元的单词。

1. Can I have a __________ to erase the chalkboard, please?
2. For the final __________ in this class, each student will need to prepare a twenty-minute talk with visual aids and be prepared to answer questions from his classmates.
3. The old universities of Oxford and Cambridge still have a lot of __________.
4. When she is smiling, she looks fairly __________.
5. The swimming costume is made of __________ material.
6. As far as I am concerned, my feeling that taking an exam for someone else is wrong is completely non-__________, and I will not discuss it any further.
7. Due to his __________ stance on abortion and gun control, the prime minister candidate is well received in most districts.
8. Under the law, everyone is considered __________ until proven guilty.
9. We've decided to have a __________ party before we leave the school.
10. We __________ ourselves that we could do without their help, but things ran counter to our wishes.

11. We are having __________ lunches these days.
12. Mr. Bower responded to the insult with __________ humor.
13. Here is just a note to thank you for your __________.
14. We feel __________ by our local community's generosity and support.
15. Food served on many airplanes is rarely delicious; most often it is __________ at best!
16. The crowds __________ the boxing champion.
17. I appreciate generalizations that are powerful, precise, and __________.
18. He learned a lot about diplomatic __________ in college.
19. The incongruous design is a __________ between high tech and antique Chinese.
20. I've just quarreled with my girl. I want to leave an __________ note on her desk.

Note 前事不忘后事之师 *Remember the past and it will guide your future.*

Day 29

blur v. /bləː/

Tears *blurred* my eyes when I saw her coming out of customs.

[猜一猜]A 冲出 B 模糊 C 掉下 D 充满

[翻 译]当我看到她从海关走出来的时候，泪水模糊了我的双眼。

[大头巧记]形近且意近词：**blot**，污点

[词义扩展]*v.* ①弄脏，玷污 ②使感觉不清；模糊 *n.* ①模糊；模糊不清的事物 *My memory of her stories is only a blur.* 我对关于她的事情的记忆模糊不清。② 污点 *He can not bear even a little blur on his good name.* 他不能忍受甚至一个名声上的小小的污点。

[大头例句]For street children, drugs offer the chance to blur their hopeless poverty. 对于那些流浪街头的孩子，毒品提供了一个机会，使他们对毫无希望的贫穷感到麻木。

charter n. /ˈtʃɑːtə/

The *Charter* of the United Nations outlines the principles, functions, and organization of the UN.

[猜一猜]A 蓝图 B 铭文 C 宗旨 D 宪章

[翻 译]联合国宪章略述联合国的原则、职能和组织。

[大头巧记]**chart**，海图，图表。-er，…的人，的物。为一个团体划出图表的东西 → 宪章。

[词义扩展]*vt.* 包租(飞机、汽车等)
a chartered plane 一架包租的飞机

[大头例句]The Olympic Charter forbids sex discrimination. 奥运宪章禁止性别歧视。

clamp vt. /klæmp/

Try to *clamp* these two blocks of wood together.

[猜一猜]A 粘 B 钉 C 夹 D 摞

[翻 译]试着把两块木头夹在一起。

[大头巧记]c-lamp，灯，用夹子把灯夹在床上。

[词义扩展]*n.* 夹子，夹钳，卡钉 *vt.* ①(用夹钳等)夹紧，夹住，固定 ②压制，强加

[大头例句]The police are going to clamp down on illegal stock exchange activities in the streets. 警察即将取缔街道上的非法证券交易。

clasp v. /klɑːsp/

She *clasped* my arm with fear when we were walking in the dark street.

[猜一猜]A 依靠 B 栖息 C 扶持 D 紧握

[翻 译]当我们走过那个黑暗的小巷的时候，她因为害怕握紧了我的手臂。

[同义词]**grasp** 抓紧

[词义扩展]*n.* ①钩；扣 ②紧握；拥抱；紧抱

[大头例句]The principal gave my hand a warm clasp. 校长热切地紧握我的手。

clutch v. /klʌtʃ/

The falling man *clutched* the rope.

[猜一猜]A 发现 B 紧抓 C 挂住 D 扯断

[翻 译]正在降落的人紧紧抓住了绳子。

[大头巧记]**catch**，抓住；把其中的 a 变成 lu(ck)，碰到好运时，当然要紧紧抓住机会。

[词义扩展]*v.* (与 at 连用)试图抓住 *n.* ①紧握；抓紧 ②(汽车的)离合器 ③(*pl.*)控制；掌握；权力
in the clutches of the enemy 落入敌手

[大头例句]They fled the country to escape the clutches of the secret police. 他们使这个国家脱离了秘密警察的掌握。

compress vt. /kəmˈpres/

He *compressed* two months' work into one in order that he could get a stock of money before Christmas.

[猜一猜]A 联合 B 解决 C 压缩 D 放弃

[翻 译]为了在圣诞节前拿到一笔钱他把两个月的工作并到一个月做。

[分 析]com + press

共同 + 压 → 压在一起，压缩

[词义扩展]vt. ①扼要叙述 ②镇压 vi. (受压力而)缩小 *Please compress the cotton into bales.* 请将棉花压紧打包。n.【医】敷布，绷带

[大头例句]Wood blocks may compress a great deal under pressure. 木块受压时可缩小很多。

constitution n./ˌkɔnstiˈtjuːʃən/

According to the American *Constitution*, presidential elections are held every four years.

[猜一猜]A 系统 B 宪法 C 国会 D 系统

[翻 译]按照美国宪法，总统每四年选举一次。

[分 析]con + stitut + ion

一起 + 建立，放 + 名词词尾 → 放到一起，构造，体质，宪法

Constitute vt. 制定(法律) 建立(政府) 组成 構成

[习语记忆]**suit sb.'s constitution** 适合某人体质[性格]

[大头例句]Some members were proposing changes to the club's constitution. 一些会员正在计划改变俱乐部的章程。

chapel n./ˈtʃæpəl/

He almost always attends *chapel* each morning by reason that he feels closer to God there.

[猜一猜]A 小教堂 B 墓地 C 圣坛 D 神庙

[翻 译]他几乎每天早晨都去教堂做礼拜，因为在那儿他觉得离上帝更近。

[大头巧记]词源记忆：公元4世纪时，法国有一位著名的主教，名叫St. Martain，为纪念他，基督教将11月11日定为圣马丁节。他曾被征入伍，一个严寒的冬天，他在城门边看到一个乞丐，身无分文的他挥剑将自己的披风一分为二，把一半给了乞丐，他死后披风被奉为圣物，收藏圣物的圣所也常以披风chappella（拉丁语）称之，后演变为今天的chapel表小教堂。

[词义扩展]n. ①(医院，学校，营房，大建筑物内的)附属教堂 ②教堂内的私人祈祷处 ③[英]国教以外的教堂 ④(学校的)礼拜仪式

[大头例句]The hospital has its own chapel. 该医院拥有自己的小礼拜堂。

discipline n./v./ˈdisiplin/

The soldiers showed perfect *discipline* under the fire of the enemy.

[猜一猜]A 勇气 B 技术 C 纪律 D 心理素质

[翻 译]在敌人的炮火下，那些士兵表现出良好的纪律性。

[大头巧记]**disciple，基督教中的门徒，谨遵戒律 discipline，纪律**

[词义扩展]n. ①身心的锻炼，训练 ②学科；科目 ③方法

[大头例句]In learning a foreign language, question and answer drills are good disciplines. 学外语时，问答练习是很好的训练方法。

v.n. 钻孔 训练 = train exercise

decree n./diˈkriː/

We are living in a country ruled by *decree*

[猜一猜]A 等级 B 法令 C 规则 D 君主

[翻 译]我们生活在法制国家中。

[分 析]de + cree

除掉 + 详审 → 详审后除掉不合理的东西，剩下的公布为法令

[大头巧记]形近词 **degree，学位**；"C" → create；获得学位，才有资格发布政令。

[词义扩展]n. ①命令，政令 ②天命，天意【律】司法判决 v. ①颁布(法令)，判决 ②(命运)注定 ③宣告 *They have decreed an end to all this fighting.* 他们已经宣告，这场争斗完全结束。

[大头例句]Fate decreed that we are meant to be together. 命运决定我们注定在一起。

domain n./dəuˈmein/

This is out of my *domain*

[猜一猜]A 能力 B 所有 C 原则 D 范围

[翻 译]这不属于我的范围。

[分 析]dom + ain

统治 + 名词词尾 → 统治的范围

[词义扩展] n. ①领土，版图 ②田地，产业，房地产 the domain of the People's Republic of China 中华人民共和国的领土

[大头例句] This is a subject that has now moved into the political domain. 这是一个现已转移到政治领域内的问题。

eligible adj. /ˈelidʒəbl/

He is the most *eligible* candidate for the vacancy.

[猜一猜] A 有实力　B 聪明　C 可能的　D 合适的

[翻　译] 他是这个空缺的最合适的候选人。

[分　析] elig + ible
选择 + 可…的 → 符合条件的，合适的

[词义扩展] n. 合适的人，人选

[大头例句] She is looking for an eligible bachelor. 她正在寻找一个合意的单身汉。

enclose vt. /inˈkləuz/

The football field is *enclosed* by a wall.

[猜一猜] A 关闭　B 开放　C 隔断　D 围绕

[翻　译] 足球场被一道墙围了起来。

[大头巧记] enclose= to close in，把…关在里面，围绕

[词义扩展] v. 附上，封入 I enclose lettle with a cheque for 1000 pounds. 随信附上1000英镑支票一张。

[大头例句] I enclosec my complete application form. 我附上我的完整的申请表。

entitle v. /inˈtaitl/

Every citizen is *entitled* to equal protection under the law.

[猜一猜] A 授权　B 需要　C 承担　D 争取

[翻　译] 每个公民都有权依法受同等保护

[分　析] en + title
使…具有 + 称号 → 给…题名，给…称号，授权

[大头例句] After reading an article entitled 'Cigarette Smoking and Your Health', I lit a cigarette to calm my nerves. 读完一篇题为《吸烟与您的健康》的文章后，我点燃了一支香烟，以便使我紧张的神经平静下来。

divine adj. /diˈvain/

The calm on their faces seemed almost *divine*.

[猜一猜] A 死去　B 投入　C 神圣　D 美德

[翻　译] 他们脸上宁静的表情看上去几乎是神圣的。

[大头巧记] vine，藤，向上探索攀援 → 非凡的 → devine，神圣的。

[词义扩展] vt.&vi. 占卜，预言，察觉 divine a person's intention 识破某人企图

[大头例句] He must have divined from my expression that I was angry. 她一定从我的表情看出我发怒了。

finite adj. /ˈfainait/

Human understanding is *finite*.

[猜一猜] A 奇妙的　B 有限的　C 神授的　D 进化的

[翻　译] 人类的理解力是有限的。

[大头巧记] finish，结束 → finite，有结束的，有限的

[大头例句] The world's finite resources must be used wisely. 世界上的有限资源应该被合理利用。

inhibit v. /inˈhibit/

Economic growth has been *inhibited* by the lack of investment.

[猜一猜] A 抑制　B 取消　C 承认　D 摧毁

[翻　译] 经济增长由于缺乏资金而受阻。

[分　析] in + hibit
在…里面 + 拿住 → 抓在手里面，限制，抑制，禁止，阻止

[大头例句] Students may be inhibited from coming to him with their problems. 学生们可能会怯于找他解决问题。

legislate v. /ˈledʒisˌleit/

The government could *legislate* to deal with such disturbances.

[猜一猜] A 强制　B 调整　C 立法　D 投资

[翻 译]政府可以通过立法来处理这类的干扰因素。

[分 析]legis + late

法律 + 动词词尾 → 制定法律,用法律来约束人的行为

[大头例句]It is difficult to legislate the behavior of people within their homes. 用法律来约束家庭内行为是件困难的事情。

legitimate *adj.* /liˈdʒitimit/

It is perfectly *legitimate* to ask questions about a politician's personal life.

[猜一猜]A 合理的 B 困难的 C 粗心的 D 有义务的

[翻 译]询问一个政客的个人生活情况是完全合理的。

[分 析]legitim + ate

合法 + 形容词尾 → 合法的,合理的,符合社会道德的

[词义扩展]*vt.* 使合法,证明…有理

[大头例句]Are the premises being used for legitimate business purposes? 这些事务所是被用于合法的商业目的吗?

optional *adj.* /ˈɔpʃənəl/

The price includes hotels and meals. Entertainment is *optional*.

[猜一猜]A 可选择的 B 较低的 C 无理的 D 模棱两可的

[翻 译]包括旅店和餐饮娱乐在内的价格是可自由选择的。

[分 析]option + al

机会 + 词尾 → 有机会的,可选择的,随意的

[大头巧记]联系记忆:**optional**,选修的;**compulsory**,必修的

[大头例句]Evening dress is optional. 穿不穿晚礼服没有规定。

possession *n.* /pəˈzeʃən/

He gave up *possession* of the house.

[猜一猜]A 所有 B 收购 C 装修 D 让出

[翻 译]他放弃了这房子的所有权。

[分 析]possess + ion

拥有 + 名词词尾 → 拥有,占有,所有权

[谚语记忆]**Possession in nine points of the law.** 现实占有,败一胜九。

[大头例句]Without a car in my possession, it is nearly impossible to get around in this city! 由于没有车,我几乎不能在这个城里四处行动。

prohibit *vt.* /prəˈhibit/

Smoking is strictly *prohibited* in the process of handling explosive materials.

[猜一猜]A 排斥 B 禁止 C 警惕 D 加重

[翻 译]在处理易爆物时,严格禁止吸烟。

[分 析]pro + hibit

之前 + 拿住 → 在某事发生前,将其拿住,禁止,阻止

[大头巧记]词形联想:Prof habit,教授的坏习惯是应该被阻止的。

[大头例句]Smoking is prohibited inside the building, but there is a terrace on the roof where guests are invited to smoke at their leisure. 在大楼内部吸烟是被禁止的,但是在楼顶有个楼台,客人们在闲暇时被请到这里来吸烟。

restrain *vt.* /risˈtrein/

I can't *restrain* my anger when I hear of people being cruel to animals.

[猜一猜]A 爆发 B 消除 C 抑制 D 清醒

[翻 译]当我听到人们残酷地对待动物时,我怒不可遏。

[分 析]re + strain

再次 + 拉紧 → 抑制,制止

[大头巧记]与其反义词 **impel(推动,驱使)**联系记忆。

习题：在下面的空格里填写本单元的单词。

1. I __________ my complete application form.
2. I can't __________ my anger when I hear of people being cruel to animals.
3. After reading an article __________ 'Cigarette Smoking and Your Health', I lit a cigarette to calm my nerves.
4. Smoking is strictly __________ in the process of handling explosive materials.
5. The price includes hotels and meals. Entertainment is __________.
6. Without a car in my __________, it is nearly impossible to get around in this city!
7. Tears __________ my eyes when I saw her coming out of customs.
8. Try to __________ these two blocks of wood together.
9. The __________ of the United Nations outlines the principles, functions, and organization of the UN.
10. He __________ two months' work into one in order that he could get a stock of money before Christmas.
11. He almost always attends __________ each morning by reason that he feels closer to God there.
12. The principal gave my hand a warm __________.
13. Some members were proposing changes to the club's __________.
14. They fled the country to escape the __________ of the secret police.
15. He is the most __________ candidate for the vacancy.
16. In learning a foreign language, question and answer drills are good __________.
17. This is a subject that has now moved into the political __________.
18. He must have __________ from my expression that I was angry.
19. We are living in a country ruled by __________.
20. Economic growth has been __________ by the lack of investment.
21. The world's __________ resources must be used wisely.
22. It is perfectly __________ to ask questions about a politician's personal life.
23. It is difficult to __________ the behavior of people within their homes.

Day 30

alkali *n./adj.* /ˈælkəlai/

Alkali is very useful in the chemical industry.

[猜一猜]A 酸 B 碱 C 塑料 D 盐

[翻 译]碱在化学工业中很重要。

[分 析]al + kali

the + 灰烬 → 灰烬中含有碱性物质 → 碱

[大头巧记]记住其主体部分,kali,谐音法,"客来",客人来了要蒸馒头,蒸馒头要用碱。

alloy *n.* /ˈælɔi/

Television news has always been an *alloy* of journalism and show business.

[猜一猜]A 怪胎 B 结合体 C 竞争 D 更迭

[翻 译]电视新闻一直是新闻和娱乐的结合体.

[分 析]al + loy

to + 结合 → 使…结合,此处活用为名词 → 结合体

[词义扩展]*n.* ①合金 *Brass is an alloy of copper and zinc.* 黄铜是铜和锌的合金。②成色,品位 ③[喻]掺杂品 *It's not pure silver; there is some alloy in it.* 这不是纯银,里面混有杂质。

v. 融合…,使减弱,使减轻 *Pain alloyed with hope.* 痛苦因希望而减轻

[大头例句]The external economic assistance is alloyed with political aims. 外来的经济援助是掺杂着政治目的的。

aluminum *n.* /əˈluːminəm/

Aluminum used to be precious.

[猜一猜]A 铜 B 锌 C 铝 D 银

[翻 译]铝过去曾一度很珍贵。

[分 析]alumin + um

铝 + 名词词尾 → 铝(化)

[大头巧记]注意化学上铝的元素符号是Al,即此单词的前两个字母,在记住um词尾多用于元素名称后,此单词当可很容易识别。

ajar *adj.* /əˈdʒɑː/

Keeping your door *ajar* is good for your health while sleeping.

[猜一猜]A 紧闭的 B 半开的 C 大开的 D 靠近脚边的

[翻 译]睡觉时保持门半开着对健康有利。

[大头巧记]a jar,一个瓶子 → 半开着的瓶子。

[词义扩展]*adj./adv.* 不协调,不一致 *He is ajar with the world.* 他与人处事总是格格不入。

[大头例句]In military training, Matt's pace is always ajar with his comrades. 军事训练时,迈特的步调总是和他的战友不一致。

bleach *v.* /bliːtʃ/

Have you *bleached* those clothes as I told you to?

[猜一猜]A 浆洗 B 漂白 C 熨烫 D 销售

[翻 译]你已经按照我的要求把这些衣服漂白了吗?

[词义扩展]*n.* 漂白剂

[大头例句]In the chemical industry, the two most useful kinds of bleaches are chlorine bleaches and peroxide bleaches. 在化学工业中最常用的两种漂白剂是含氯漂白剂和过氧化物漂白剂。

catalyst *n.* /ˈkætəlist/

The husband's serious breach of trust was the *catalyst* for the divorce.

[猜一猜]A 借口 B 催化剂 C 趋势 D 破裂

[翻 译]丈夫的严重背信行为是离婚的催化剂。

[分 析]cata + lyst

下面的 + to free → 溶解,起催化作用,催化剂

[大头例句] The new development will act as a catalyst for growth in business and tourism. 新的发展将对商业和旅游业的增长产生催化剂般的作用。

compound *n.* /ˈkɔmpaund/

Water is a ***compound*** of hydrogen and oxygen.

[猜一猜] A 化合物　B 液体　C 来源　D 中和

[翻　译] 水是氢和氧的化合物。

[分　析] com　+ pound

一起，合成 + 放 → 合成后的产物，化合物

[词义扩展] *n.* ①复合词，复合句　②围场，围地（场内有建筑物），商业或贸易中心

adj. ①混合而成的，能化合的，复合的　*vt.&vi.* ①使合成，把…配成 *The pharmacist is compounding a special prescription for her.* 药剂师正在为她调配一种特殊的处方。②增加，使更复杂

[大头例句] The shortage of petrol supply compounded the venture in our business. 石油供应短缺增加了我们生意的风险。

crystal *adj./n.* /ˈkristl/

The dining table shone with silver and ***crystal***.

[猜一猜] A 水晶　B 宝石　C 玻璃　D 铝

[翻　译] 餐桌上银器皿和水晶玻璃器皿闪光锃亮。

[大头巧记] **cry，哭；crystal，像泪水般的 → 水晶。**

[习语记忆] **(as) clear as crystal** 像水晶一样明澈；（文章、讲话等）极为清晰明白。

combustible *adj.* /kəmˈbʌstəbl/

Petrol is highly ***combustible***, so smoking is strictly forbidden while handling it.

[猜一猜] A 易爆的　B 有毒的　C 易燃的　D 腐蚀性的

[翻　译] 汽油极易燃烧，处理时严格禁止吸烟。

[分　析] comb　+ ust　+ ible

完全的 + 燃烧 + 形容词尾 → 可完全燃烧的，易燃的

[词义扩展] *adj.* 冲动的，容易冲动或激动的

[大头例句] Nationalism and religion are a combustible mix. 爱国主义和宗教的结合是很容易导致狂热的。

distill *v.* /diˈstil/

We were asked to ***distill*** the crucial points of the book.

[猜一猜] A 提炼　B 表现　C 叙述　D 理解

[翻　译] 要求我们从书中提炼出关键点。

[分　析] di　+ still

向下 + 滴下 → 向下滴 → 蒸馏，提炼

[词义扩展] *v.* 蒸馏，用蒸馏的办法提取。*Gasoline is distilled from crude oil.* 汽油是由原油蒸馏而得的。

[大头例句] The children ingest alimentation from breast milk as well as we distill the knowledge from books. 孩子们像我们从书中汲取知识一样从母乳中摄取营养。

electrician *n.* /ilekˈtriʃ(ə)n/

Her father is an ***electrician*** by trade.

[猜一猜] A 电工　B 电子操纵员　C 技工　D 发报员

[翻　译] 她的爸爸是一个电工。

[分　析] eletric + ian

电　+ 与…相关的人 → 电工，电学家

[大头例句] His dream is to become an electrician one day. 他的梦想是有一天成为一名电学家。

erase *vt.* /iˈreiz/

He tried to ***erase*** from his memory the terrible accident.

[猜一猜] A 记起　B 整理　C 写出　D 抹掉

[翻　译] 他试图抹掉对那个可怕事件的记忆。

[大头巧记] **eraser 橡皮擦；erase，擦，抹掉**

[词义扩展] *vt.* ①消磁　②杀死。*erase a file from the diskette* 从磁盘上清除掉一个文件

[大头例句] The virus erases all the files stored on your hard drive. 这个病毒可以清除你硬盘上的所

有文件。

flask *n.* /flɑːsk/

A vacuum *flask* keeps cool drinks cool and hot drinks hot.

[猜一猜] A 杯子 B 设备 C 燃烧 D 瓶子
[翻 译] 保温瓶使冷饮保冷，使热饮保温。
[大头巧记] 拆：fl(y) ask，苍蝇问瓶子："我怎么才能吃到你里面的东西？"
[词义扩展] *n.* 长颈瓶【化】烧瓶

fuse *v.* /fjuːz/

There was no separation between joy and sorrow; they *fused* into one.

[猜一猜] A 回合 B 连接 C 融合 D 混合
[翻 译] 痛苦与欢乐之间没有界限：它们融为了一体。
[词义扩展] *v.* 熔合，融化
n. 导火线，保险丝
[大头例句] All the lights downstairs have fused. 楼下所有灯的电路都烧断了。

hydrogen *n.* /ˈhaidrədʒən/

Hydrogen has no colour or smell and is lighter than air.

[猜一猜] A 氧气 B 氢气 C 氯气 D 氮气
[翻 译] 氢气无色无味且比空气轻。
[分 析] hydro + gen
水 + 产生 → 水分解产生的气体之一：氢气
[大头巧记] 谐音 high dragon，飞得高高的龙形气球里面充的是氢气。
[大头例句] The hydrogen bomb is very powerful. 氢弹的威力很大。

insulate *v.* /ˈinsjuleit/

Many houses in the north are warm in winter because they are *insulated* so that the heat is not lost.

[猜一猜] A 隔热 B 暖气 C 交错 D 密集
[翻 译] 北方的许多房子在冬天很暖和，因为它们都作了隔热处理，使热量不致散失。
[分 析] insul + ate
岛 + 动词词尾 → 使像岛一样 → 隔绝，隔热，绝缘
[大头例句] The president was insulated from the pressure of public opinion. 总统与民意隔绝起来。

intrinsic *adj.* /inˈtrinsik/

The *intrinsic* value of a coin is the value of the metal it is made of.

[猜一猜] A 发行的 B 内在的 C 超值的 D 直接的
[翻 译] 一枚钱币的内在价值是造这枚钱币的金属的价值。
[大头巧记] intri，词缀：向内的；insic- inside，内部的；和在一起 → 内在的，固有的，本质的。
[大头例句] Providing service to the customer is intrinsic to a successful business. 给顾客的服务根本关系到经营的成功。

fahrenheit *adj.* /ˈfærənhait/

Water freezes at 32 degrees *Fahrenheit*.

[猜一猜] A 摄氏的 B 华氏的
C 标准的 D 热力学的
[翻 译] 水在32华氏度结冰。
[大头巧记] 词源记忆：Fahrenheit 华伦海特，德国物理学家，华氏温度计的设计者。
[词义扩展] *n.* 华氏温度(计)
the Fahrenheit scale 华氏温标

lubricate *v.* /ˈluːbrikeit/

Many British view politeness as a way to *lubricate* social situations.

[猜一猜] A 润滑 B 创立 C 丰富 D 解决
[翻 译] 很多英国人认为礼貌是一种改善社会环境的方法。
[分 析] lubric + ate
滑的 + 动词词尾 → 使…润滑，加润滑剂
[大头例句] My throat needs lubricating. 我需要润润嗓子。

nucleus *n.* /ˈnjuːkliəs/

These two groups formed the *nucleus* of a new political party.

amino acide 氨基酸

[猜一猜]A 纲领　　B 先遣队
C 智囊团　　D 核心
[翻　译]这两个团体构成了一个新政党的核心。
[大头巧记]我们较熟悉短语:nuclear weapons，核武器。**nuclear，核子的，中心的 → nucleus，核子，核心。**
[大头例句]Many say Beijing is the nucleus of Chinese cultural life. 很多人说北京是中国文化生活的中心。

protein *n./adj.* /ˈprəutiːn/

They were weakened by a diet that was low in ***protein***.

[猜一猜]A 营养　　B 维生素
C 脂肪　　D 蛋白质
[翻　译]由于饮食中蛋白质含量不足，他们的身体很虚弱。
[分　析]pro　+ tein
第一 + 质量 → 质量第一的物质 → 蛋白质
[大头例句]Vegetarians must look beyond traditional protein sources to things like peanuts and tofu in order to reach their recommended daily allowance. 素食主义者必须超越原有的蛋白质来源，而去食用像花生、豆腐这样的东西来达到建议达到的每日摄入量。

习题：在下面的空格里填写本单元的单词。

1. The new development will act as a __________ for growth in business and tourism.
2. The children ingest alimentation from breast milk as well as we __________ the knowledge from books.
3. Water freezes at 32 degrees __________.
4. __________ is very useful in the chemical industry.
5. __________ used to be precious.
6. The dining table shone with silver and __________.
7. The shortage of petrol supply __________ the venture in our business.
8. He tried to __________ from his memory the terrible accident.
9. __________ has no colour or smell and is lighter than air.
10. Many houses in the north are warm in winter because they are __________ so that the heat is not lost.
11. Television news has always been an __________ of journalism and show business.
12. In the chemical industry the two most useful kinds of __________ are chlorine bleaches and peroxide bleaches.
13. Petrol is highly __________, so smoking is strictly forbidden while handling it.
14. In military training, Matt's pace is always __________ with his comrades.
15. His dream is to become a __________ one day.
16. There was no separation between joy and sorrow: they __________ into one.
17. A vacuum __________ keeps cool drinks cool and hot drinks hot.
18. Providing service to the customer is __________ to a successful business.
19. Vegetarians must look beyond traditional __________ sources to things like peanuts and tofu in order to reach their recommended daily allowance.
20. Many British view politeness as a way to __________ social situations.
21. Many say Beijing is the __________ of Chinese cultural life.

We travel from A to B via C.

Day 31

berry n. 浆果

barren adj. 不毛的，贫瘠的；空洞的

aberrant adj. /æˈberənt/

The missile is on an *aberrant* course and flying towards a wrong aim.

[猜一猜] A 精确的 B 预定的 C 异常的 D 偏僻的

[分 析] ab + errant

from + 错误的 → 从错处开始 → 异常的

[翻 译] 导弹偏离了轨道并向着错误的目标飞去。

[联 想] errant *adj.* ①错误的，犯错误的 *God brings back the errant sheep.* 上帝把迷途羔羊带回。②对配偶不忠的 *The errant husband found himself guilty.* 走邪路的丈夫感到很内疚。③漫游的，漂泊的 *an errant knight* 游侠骑士

[大头例句] I have a dream that one day I can move the earth onto an aberrant way, so we can go further and see more stars. 我有一个梦想，有一天我能把地球送上一个异常的轨道，这样我们就可以走得更远，看到更多的星星。

basement n. /ˈbeismənt/

The evenings in summer time here are always rather humid in the *basement*.

[猜一猜] A 网球场 B 运动场 C 地下室 D 游泳池

[翻 译] 夏天这里的地下室通常很湿热。

[分 析] base + ment

底部 + 名词词尾 → 根基，底层，底座，地下室

[词义扩展] *n.* 中学中的公厕

[大头例句] The old man took out some wine that had been stored in the basement for over 10 years. 这位老人拿出一些酒来，这些酒在地窖里已经藏了十年了。

bizarre adj. /biˈzɑː/

Bizarre clothing is forbidden in my former high school.

[猜一猜] A 奇怪的 B 暴露的 C 多样的 D 破旧的

[翻 译] 我以前的高中禁止穿奇装异服。

[大头巧记] 音近词：**bazaar** /bəˈzɑː/ **集市**，如果把集市说成**bizarre 就很奇怪**。

[大头例句] And now grab a candle and follow me into my bizarre bazaar! 现在抓起一个蜡烛，随我进入我的怪异市场！

via. prep. 通过，经由

deviate v. /ˈdiːvieit/

The theories you mentioned in that book *deviate* from the truth.

[猜一猜] A 符合 B 解释 C 论证 D 背离

[翻 译] 你在书中所提到的理论和事实相违背。

[分 析] de + viate

偏离 + 路 → 偏离，背离

[大头巧记] devil ate，魔鬼吃的东西，都是脱离社会常轨的。

[词义扩展] *adj.* 脱离社会常轨的

n. 脱离常轨的人，性变态者

[大头例句] The plane has to deviate from its normal flight path. 飞机被迫偏离正常的飞行轨道。

eccentric adj. /ikˈsentrik/

adj. 古怪的 n. 古怪的人

The old lady has some *eccentric* habits.

[猜一猜] A 受欢迎的 B 有名的 C 疯狂的 D 古怪的

[翻 译] 这位老妇人有一些古怪习惯。

[分 析] ec + centric

向外的 + 中心 → 偏离中心的，古怪的

[词义扩展] *n.* 行为古怪的人

[大头例句] The audience was puzzled by the eccentric decision of the referee. 所有的观众都对裁判所作的这个奇怪的决定感到迷惑。

dwarf v. /dwɔːf/

Together these two big men *dwarfed* the tiny Broadway office.

midget n. 侏儒 adj. 小型的

[猜一猜]A 拥挤　B 厌恶　C 显得矮小　D 轻松

[翻　译]两位彪形大汉挤得这百老汇街的办公室更显矮小。

[词义扩展]n. 侏儒,矮小的植物/动物,童话中的小矮人
vt. 使矮小

[大头例句]He dwarfs other dramatists. 他使其他剧作家相形见绌。

exceptional *adj.* /ikˈsepʃənl/

This school offers special educational provisions for *exceptional* children.

[猜一猜]A 外籍的　B 低龄的　C 独生的　D 特殊的

[翻　译]这所学校提供为特殊儿童而进行的特种教育。

[分　析]ex + cep + tion + al
出去 + 拿 + 名词词尾 + 形容词尾 → 拿出去的,例外的,特殊的,异常的

[大头巧记]**accept,拿进来,接受;except,拿出去,除了;exceptional,特殊的**

[词义扩展]adj. 优越的,稀有的 *an exceptional pupil* 一个杰出的小学生

[大头例句]Financial assistance may be made available in exceptional circumstances. 财政援助在特殊情况下是可能的。

exotic *adj.* /igˈzɔtik/

He was fascinated by the *exotic* buildings.

[猜一猜]A 新型的　B 外国情调的　C 惊险的　D 金璧辉煌

[翻　译]异国情调的建筑使他着迷。

[分　析]exo + tic
外面 + 形容词尾 → 外面的,外国的

[词义扩展]adj. 异乎寻常的;奇异的 *exotic costumes from the Far East* 同远东不同的奇异服饰
n. 外来品,外来词[语]

[大头例句]They're always flying off to film in exotic locations. 他们经常飞往一些奇异的外景地拍摄影片。

eclipse *n.* /iˈklips/

A composer often goes into *eclipse* after his death and never regains popularity.

[猜一猜]A 黯然失色　B 流芳千古　C 价值　D 精华

[翻　译]一个作曲家经常在死后名声衰退,不再受欢迎。

[分　析]ec + lipse
出去 + 离开 → 不能出现,失去,丧失(名声、威望等)

[词义扩展]n. 〈天〉蚀 lunar eclipse 月食
v. 使…黯然失色;超过 *She is quite eclipsed by her clever younger sister.* 在聪明的妹妹相形之下,她变得黯然失色。

[大头例句]The rise of one aristocratic family usually meant the eclipse of another. 一个贵族家庭的崛起通常意味着另一个的衰落。

hysterical *adj.* /hisˈterikəl/

Media coverage of the issue has been *hysterical*.

[猜一猜]A 明晰的　B 有害的　C 狂热的　D 虚假的

[翻　译]媒体对这个问题的报道已经过火了。

[大头巧记]音译:歇斯底里,狂热的,非常好笑的。

[大头例句]He didn't have a clue what was going on, and we all thought it was hysterica. 他不知道究竟是怎么回事,而我们都觉得非常好笑。

indignant *adj.* /inˈdignənt/

I was *indignant* because I felt that I had been punished unfairly.

[猜一猜]A 冤屈的　B 愤慨的　C 鲁莽的　D 可疑的

[翻　译]我非常愤慨,因为我觉得对我的惩罚是不公平的。

[分　析]in + dign + ant
不 + 礼貌 + 形容词尾 → 不礼貌的,愤慨的

[大头巧记]in dig → dig in,坚持自己的意见 → **indignant,愤愤不平地固执己见**。

[大头例句]She was quite indignant with my advice. 她对我的建议很恼火。

irritate v. /ˈiriteit/

The principal's loud bossy voice *irritated* the listeners.

[猜一猜]A 提醒 B 激怒 C 感染 D 放弃

[翻 译]该校长大而专横的声音让听众很恼火。

[词义扩展] v. 刺激，使兴奋，使疼痛，使过敏

[大头例句] The more intrusive advertisements become, the more they irritate Web users. 插入的广告越多，越让网民们恼火。

jerk v. /dʒəːk/

She *jerked* out the knife that was stuck in the wood.

[猜一猜]A 猛拉 B 撬 C 抛弃 D 守护

[翻 译]她把戳在木头里的刀猛地拔了出来。

[词义扩展] v. 颠簸地行进，结结巴巴地说话
n. 性情古怪的人 *What a jerk you are*! 你真傻！

[习语记忆] **clean and jerk**【体】(举重)挺举

[大头例句] Jerking her head towards the valley, she said, "What's down there?" 她猛然把头转向山谷，说："下面那是什么？"

madden v. /ˈmædn/

It *maddens* me that he was chosen to be sent abroad instead of me.

[猜一猜]A 使恼火 B 使吃惊
C 使不懂 D 使清楚

[翻 译]选中他派送出国，而不是我，让我很恼火。

[大头巧记] **mad，疯狂的，恼火的；madden，使疯狂，使恼火，= drive mad。**

[词义扩展] vi. 发狂，发怒，发疯

[大头例句] He maddened at the thought of how he had been betrayed by his friend. 他一想起自己被朋友出卖时就感到恼火。

malnutrition n. /ˌmælnjuːˈtriʃən/

Many are aware of the *malnutrition* of people in deeply impoverished countries, but college students in the developed world often subsist on similar levels of malnutrition, consuming only beer and coffee.

[猜一猜]A 挑食 B 饥饿
C 营养失调 D 浪费事物

[翻 译]对于深度贫困国家人口的营养失调我们知之甚详，可是发达世界大学生们却也生活在类似的失调之中，他们只是消费啤酒和咖啡。

[分 析] mal + nutrition
坏的 + 营养 → 营养不良，营养失调

[大头例句] In the past, a lot of poor people suffered from severe malnutrition. 过去很多穷人有严重的营养不良。

marvelous adj. /ˈmɑːvələs/

The sight of snow falling on the Grand Canyon at sunset was the most *marvelous* sight of my life.

[猜一猜]A 不可思议的 B 滑稽的
C 可怕的 D 著名的

[翻 译]大峡谷落日时的雪景是我一生中所见的最不可思议的景观。

[分 析]marvel + ous
奇迹 + 形容词尾 → 惊奇的，不可思议的，绝妙的

[大头例句] China's literary accomplishments during the Tang Dynasty are a marvelous feat indeed. 中国唐代文学的造诣确实是一大壮举。

monstrous adj. /ˈmɔnstrəs/

They complain that the *monstrous* edifices interfere with television reception.

[猜一猜]A 讨厌的 B 密集的
C 巨大的 D 混凝土的

[翻 译]他们抱怨说，那些怪物般的庞大建筑，干扰了电视接收。

[大头巧记] **monster，怪物；monstrous，畸形的，恐怖的，凶暴的，巨大的。**

[词义扩展] adj. 难以置信的，令人极厌恶的
A monstrous attack 无耻的袭击

[大头例句] The morning after I hosted my high school graduation party, my living room hosted the most monstrous mess my eyes have ever seen. 在我主办完我们高中的毕业宴会之后的那个早晨,我的起居室是我有史以来见到的最乱的情形。

mania *n.* /ˈmeinjə/

The intensely popular reaction the *Beatles* received in America is often referred to as "*Beatle Mania*."

[猜一猜]A 狂热　B 影响　C 打击　D 方式

[翻　译]甲壳虫乐队在美国受到的强烈反响经常被称为"甲壳虫狂"。

[分　析]man + nia
疯狂 + 病 →【医】狂躁,狂热,癖好

[大头例句] Strictly, mania is a kind of madness which makes people violent. 严格地说,狂热是一种使人极端的精神病。

placid *adj.* /ˈplæsid/

There is no wind and the lake is *placid*.

[猜一猜]A 清澈的　B 迷人的　C 平静的　D 混浊的

[翻　译]没有风,湖面很平静。

[分　析]plac + id
平静 + 形容词尾 → 平静的,安静的

[大头巧记] **acid,蒙汗药;placid,平静的。**

quaint *adj.* /kweint/

There is something almost *quaint* in the image of Irish organized crime, something that calls to mind old movies with Jimmy Cagney.

[猜一猜]A 离奇的　B 残酷的　C 晦涩的　D 死板的

[翻　译]在爱尔兰有组织犯罪的影像中,有一些离奇古怪的东西,这让人想起吉米·卡格尼的老式电影。

[大头巧记]拆:qu(estion)(p)aint,有很多问题的画 → 很离奇。

queer *v.* /kwiə/

His cheating on the final *queered* his chances of graduation.

[猜一猜]A 弄糟　B 减少　C 嘲弄　D 受罚

[翻　译]他在大考中作弊影响了他的毕业。

[大头巧记]联系**weird(怪异的)**记忆。另:拆:qu(aint)(b)eer,奇异的啤酒,奇怪的。

[词义扩展] *adj.* 可疑的,搞同性恋的
n. 怪人,同性恋者

[习语记忆] **in queer street** 陷入困境,负债

[大头例句] He is a queer character. 他是个可疑的人。

rage *n.* /reidʒ/

My father was in a *rage* last night.

[猜一猜]A 糊涂　B 骗局　C 吃惊　D 激愤

[翻　译]我父亲昨天晚上十分生气。

[词义扩展] *n.* 激烈,热望; *v.* 发怒,发狂　*have a rage for* 对…具有狂热爱好

[习语记忆] **burst into a rage of tears** 号啕大哭
fly into a rage 勃然大怒

习题:在下面的空格里填写本单元的单词。

1. The plane has to __________ from its normal flight path.
2. Together these two big men __________ the tiny Broadway office.
3. __________ her head towards the valley, she said, "What's down there? "
4. The sight of snow falling on the Grand Canyon at sunset was the most __________ sight of my life.

/ˈkænjən/

5. My father was in a __________ last night.
6. The missile is on an __________ course and flying towards a wrong aim.
7. The audience was puzzled by the __________ decision of the referee.
8. __________ clothing is forbidden in my former high school.
9. The old man took out some wine that had been stored in the __________ for over 10 years.
10. They're always flying off to film in __________ locations.
11. This school offers special educational provisions for __________ children.
12. The more intrusive advertisements become, the more they __________ Web users.
13. The rise of one aristocratic family usually meant the__________ of another.
14. He didn't have a clue what was going on, and we all thought it was __________.
15. I was __________ because I felt that I had been punished unfairly.
16. He __________ at the thought of how he had been betrayed by his friend.
17. Many are aware of the __________ of people in deeply impoverished countries, but college students in the developed world often subsist on similar levels, consuming only beer and coffee.
18. They complain that the __________ edifices interfere with television reception.
19. His cheating on the final __________his chances of graduation.
20. There is something almost __________ in the image of Irish organized crime, something that calls to mind old movies with Jimmy Cagney.
21. There is no wind and the lake is __________.
22. The intensely popular reaction the *Beatles* received in America is often referred to as "*Beatle* __________."

Note 前事不忘后事之师 *Remember the past and it will guide your future.*

Day 32

defect *n.* /diˈfekt/

There exist in our present educational system many *defects*.

[猜一猜] A 缺陷　B 方面　C 成绩　D 落后

[翻　译] 我们目前的教育制度中存在着很多的缺陷。

[分　析] de　+ fect

否定 + 做 → 反面的做法 → 缺陷,过失

[词义扩展] *n.* ①不足,缺乏,亏损 ②故障　*vi.* 变节,背叛,开小差 *He defected from the party over the issue of land settlement policy.* 他在移民政策的问题上背叛了自己的政党。

[大头例句] These years the government paid more attention to the defects in the education system. 这些年来政府更多地注意到了教育系统中的缺陷。

delinquency *n.* /diˈliŋkwənsi/

These years the problem of juvenile *delinquency* is getting more and more serious.

[猜一猜] A 犯罪　B 吸毒　C 失学　D 失业

[翻　译] 近几年来,青少年犯罪问题变得越来越严重。

[分　析] de + linqu + ency

从 + 离开 + 名词词尾 → 从职务离开,失职,怠工,犯罪

[词义扩展] *n.* ①失约,毁约 ②拖欠的债务

tax delinquency 税收滞纳

[大头例句] Most of the people didn't notice the juvenile delinquency problems until the 1950s. 大多数人直到20世纪50年代才注意到青少年犯罪的问题。

feeble *adj.* /ˈfiːbl/

Grandmother has been getting more *feeble* lately.

[猜一猜] A 年老　B 虚弱　C 糊涂　D 严厉

[翻　译] 近来祖母愈加衰弱了。

[分　析] feeb　+ le

流泪 + 形容词尾 → 爱流泪的,意志薄弱的,虚弱的

[词义扩展] *adj.* 微弱的,(声、光等)轻微的,无效的

a feeble attempt 无益的尝试

[大头例句] Don't be so feeble. Stand up to her for once. 别这么怯懦,勇敢地面对她一次。

flaw *n.* /flɔː/

What you've just said is the fatal *flaw* in your argument.

[猜一猜] A 证据　B 观点　C 缺点　D 特色

[翻　译] 你刚刚所说的是你的论点旦的重大缺陷。

[大头巧记] f(ool) law,愚蠢的法律,是有缺陷的。

[词义扩展] *n.* 裂纹,瑕疵,一阵风 *v.* 破裂,有缺陷,无效 *It's a pity that the scar flawed her skin.* 很遗憾,这块疤痕在她皮肤上造成了缺陷。

[大头例句] There are serious flaws in the way we train our teachers. 我们训练老师的方法上有很严重的缺陷。

ignorance *n.* /ˈignərəns/

We are in complete *ignorance* of his plans.

[猜一猜] A 明白　B 控制　C 反对　D 不知

[翻　译] 我们完全不知道他的计划。

[分　析] ignor　+ ance

不顾,不理 + 名词词尾 → 无知,不知,愚昧

[习语记忆] **Where ignorance is bliss, it is folly to be wise.** 难得糊涂。

Ignorance of the law excuses no man. [谚] 不知法不能作为免罪的借口。

[大头例句] There is a lot of public ignorance about how the disease is spread. 对于这种疾病的传播方式很多公众一无所知。

illiterate *n./adj.* /iˈlitərit/

About half of the population in the country is still *illiterate*.

[猜一猜]A 贫困 B 文盲 C 生病 D 悲伤

[翻 译]这个国家大约有一半人口仍是文盲。

[分 析]il + literate

不 + 有文化的 → 没有文化的，不识字的，没受教育的，文盲

[大头例句] She is musically illiterate. 她缺乏音乐方面的知识。

indulge *v.* /inˈdʌldʒ/

Many people feel that the holidays are the time to *indulge*.

[猜一猜]A 接近自然 B 团聚 C 充电 D 放纵

[翻 译]很多人觉得假日是放纵自我的时候。

[分 析]in + dulge

向 + 亲切的 → 对…很亲切 → 使满足，纵容，迁就，放纵，沉迷

[大头例句] He indulges his children too much. 他对他的孩子太放任了。

inert *adj.* /iˈnəːt/

Helium and neon are *inert* gases.

[猜一猜]A 有毒的 B 重的 C 惰性的 D 易燃的

[翻 译]氦和氖为惰性气体。

[分 析]in + ert

不 + 技巧 → 没有技巧的，无活动能力的，惰性的

[大头例句] To avoid tragedies like the Hindenburg explosion, modern blimp operators use inert gases like helium to keep their vessels flying high. 为了避免像兴登堡爆炸那样的悲剧，现代飞艇的操作员们用像氦这样的惰性气体来使他们的船高高飞起。

insolent *n./adj.* /ˈinsələnt/

The salesman was *insolent* to the customers.

[猜一猜]A 热情的 B 真诚的 C 粗鲁的 D 欺骗的

[翻 译]这位售货员对顾客很粗鲁。

[分 析]in + sol + ent

不 + 感情 + 形容词尾 → 没有感情的 → 蛮横的，粗鲁的，侮慢的

[大头巧记] **sole**，鞋底儿；**insole**，放在鞋里面的东西，鞋垫。**insolent**，把人当鞋垫对待的，**粗鲁的**。

invalid *n./adj.* /inˈvælid/

The vote has been declared *invalid* and another election scheduled.

[猜一猜]A 无效的 B 结束的 C 非法的 D 可行的

[翻 译]这次选举被宣布无效，另外一个选举被提上日程。

[分 析]in + valid

不 + 有效的 → 无效的，作废的，病弱的

[词义扩展] *n.* 病人，残废者 *vt.* 使病弱；使伤残 *vt.&vi.* 因病或伤残而退职［役］*She had been an invalid for many years.* 她病了好多年了。

[大头例句] I was not quite sick enough to be invalidated, even though I was of no more use. 即使我不再有用处，还不至病得严重到可以免除义务。

hostile *adj./n.* /ˈhɔstail/

Ever since I got better marks than Parker, he has been *hostile* to me.

[猜一猜]A 重视 B 友好 C 敌视 D 歧视

[翻 译]自从我比派克得分高以后，他就对我不友好了。

[分 析]hosti + le

敌人 + 形容词尾 → 敌对的，敌方的

[大头例句] The southern half of the island was controlled by hostile forces. 南面半岛被敌军所控制。

grudge *v.* /grʌdʒ/

He does not *grudge* him for his good ways with the children.

[猜一猜]A 同意 B 嫉妒 C 理解 D 合作

[翻 译]他不妒忌他那善待孩子的方式。

[词义扩展] *v.* 吝惜 *n.* 恶意，怨恨，妒忌 *I always feel she has a grudge against me.* 我总觉得她对我怀恨在心。

[大头例句] There's a whole list of people who might bear a grudge against him. 这儿有个名单记载了所有有可能对他产生怨恨情绪的人。

lame *adj./v.* /leim/

Lame from the accident, he walked with a cane.

[猜一猜] A 伤害　B 经受　C 跛足　D 逃避

[翻　译] 在一次事故中变跛了后，他只能拄着拐杖走路。

[词义扩展] *adj.* 站不住脚的；*vt.&vi.* 使跛，跛行 *The accident lamed the boy for life.* 事故使这个孩子终身残废。

[习语记忆] **lame as a tree** 像树一样跛，极跛的

[大头例句] It sounds like a lame excuse, but I never seem to have time to visit. 这听起来理由并不充分，但是我确实好像从来都没有时间造访。

leak *n./v.* /liːk/

The damaged reactor was *leaking* radioactive material into the atmosphere.

[猜一猜] A 泄露　B 挥发　C 升华　D 混合

[翻　译] 那座损坏的反应堆正向大气中泄露出放射性物质。

[词义扩展] *n.* 漏洞，走漏的消息；撒尿
take a leak 撒尿

[大头例句] Sometimes we can't respond to stories based on leaks. 有时候我们不能对泄露的消息做出反应。

merit *n./v.* /ˈmerit/

Indeed, he has made several mistakes, but you must not overlook his significant *merits*: he is honest, and he cares deeply for you.

[猜一猜] A 贡献　B 优点　C 甜蜜　D 婚姻

[翻　译] 他确实犯了几个错误，但是你也的确不能忽视他的优点：诚实，并且很关心你。

[大头巧记] mer(ry) (i)t 它让人很愉快，是它的长处之一。

[词义扩展] *vt.* 值得，应得 *The suggestion merits serious consideration.* 该建议值得认真考虑。

[习语记忆] **on its merits** 按事情的是非曲直，按实质说
stand on one's own merits 靠实力

[大头例句] We should judge her on her own merits rather than on her father's position in the company. 我们应该按照她自身的条件来评价她，而不应根据她父亲在公司的职位。

nuisance /ˈnjuːsəns/

Setting off firecrackers is seen not merely as a *nuisance*, but also as a big threat to man's life and property.

[猜一猜] A 违法的事　B 不道德的事
C 讨厌的事　D 刺激的事

[翻　译] 燃放鞭炮不仅仅被看做讨厌的事，而且还被认为是对人的生命财产的严重威胁。

[习语记忆] **nuisance analysis** 公害分析
nuisance taxs 小额税收，零星税收

[大头例句] Though adorable while still small, this grown dog has developed bad habits that make house cleaning a giant nuisance! 这只狗小的时候很可爱，可是它长大以后养成的坏习惯却使房子的清扫成为一个大难题。

obsolete *adj./n.* /ˈɔbsəliːt/

Most computer hardware rapidly becomes *obsolete*.

[猜一猜] A 消耗　B 过时　C 销售　D 完备

[翻　译] 大多数的电脑硬件过时得很快。

[分　析] ob + solete
不 + 使用 → 不再使用，过时的，陈旧的，陈腐的

[大头例句] Current production methods will soon be rendered obsolete. 当前的生产方法很快就会陈旧。

poverty *n.* /ˈpɔvəti/

She has lived in *poverty* all her life.

[猜一猜] A 实力　B 贫困　C 幸福　D 偏见

[翻　译] 她一生都过着贫困的生活。

[分　析] pover + ty
贫穷 + 名词词尾 → 贫穷，缺乏，虚弱

[习语记忆] **Poverty is not a shame, but being ashamed of it is.** [谚]贫不足耻，耻贫乃耻。**Poverty makes strange bedfellows.** [谚]同病相怜。

[大头例句] Many are surprised to learn that Bill Clinton, one of the most well-educated of the American presidents, actually grew up in deep poverty. 比尔·克林顿——美国受教育程度最好的总统之一——居然是在极度贫困的环境中长大的，这让很多人吃惊不已。

precarious *adj.* /priˈkɛəriəs/

The refugees' life was always *precarious*.

[猜一猜] A 贫苦　B 困厄　C 不稳定　D 多病

[翻　译] 难民们的生活总是不稳定的。

[分　析] pre + car + ious
在…之前 + 关心 + 形容词尾 → 提前就要很小心 → 不稳定的

potential *adj./n.* /pəˈtenʃəl/

Our common goal is to maximize our *potential* for economic growth.

[猜一猜] A 潜能　B 杰出　C 经验　D 成果

[翻　译] 我们共同的目标是最大限度地增大我们经济增长的潜能。

[分　析] potent + ial
力量 + 词尾 → 潜力，潜能。

[词义扩展] *adj.* 可能的，潜在的
a potential problem 潜在的问题

[大头例句] During their teen years, many girls make it a rule to only date boys they see as potential husbands; boys, however, seem to date only those girls with whom there is no chance of lasting commitment. 十几岁的时候，很多女孩子规定自己只和那些有可能成为自己丈夫的男孩约会；而男孩子却似乎只要和那些没有长久承诺机会的女孩约会。

scar *n.* /skɑː/

The cut left a *scar* on his face.

[猜一猜] A 血印　B 伤口　C 疤痕　D 恐吓

[翻　译] 刀口在他脸上留下了疤痕。

[大头巧记] s(uffer) car，车祸后的承受 → 疤痕。

[词义扩展] *v.* 结疤，创伤 *Delicate skin that scars easily.* 娇嫩的皮肤很容易留下疤痕。

[习语记忆] **He jests at scars that never felt a wound.** [谚]没有受过伤的人总爱嘲笑别人的伤疤。

[大头例句] She is likely to be scarred for life by the attack. 这次攻击可能会造成她终生残疾。

jest: n. vt. vi. 笑话

习题：在下面的空格里填写本单元的单词。

1. There is a lot of public __________ about how the disease is spread.
2. These years the government paid more attention to the __________ in the education system.
3. Many are surprised to learn that Bill Clinton, one of the most well-educated of the American presidents, actually grew up in deep __________.
4. About half of the population in the country is still __________.
5. The salesman was __________ to the customers.
6. She is likely to be __________ for life by the attack.
7. What you've just said is the fatal __________ in your argument.
8. Most of the people didn't notice the juvenile __________ problems until the 1950s.
9. Don't be so __________. Stand up to her for once.
10. During their teen years, many girls make it a rule to only date boys they see as ________ husbands; boys, however, seem to date only those girls with whom there is no chance of

lasting commitment.

11. The refugees' life was always __________.
12. Many people feel that the holidays are the time to __________.
13. To avoid tragedies like the Hindenburg explosion, modern blimp operators use __________ gases like helium to keep their vessels flying high.
14. I was not quite sick enough to be __________, even though I was of no more use.
15. Ever since I got better marks than Parker, he has been __________ to me.
16. Indeed, he has made several mistakes, but you must not overlook his significant ______: he is honest, and he cares deeply for you.
17. Current production methods will soon be rendered __________.
18. Though adorable while still small, this grown dog has developed bad habits that make house cleaning a giant __________!
19. It sounds like a __________ excuse, but I never seem to have time to visit.
20. There's a whole list of people who might bear a __________ against him.
21. Sometimes we can't respond to stories based on __________.

Note 前事不忘后事之师 *Remember the past and it will guide your future.*

Day 33

assume *vt.* /əˈsjuːm/

I'm not the fool you *assumed* me to be.

[猜一猜] A 假定 B 希望 C 迫使 D 担心

[翻 译] 我并不是你认为的那种笨蛋。

[分 析] as + sume

to + 拿 → 采用，假定，设想

[词义扩展] ①承担 *assume a leading position* 担任领导职务 ②装出，假装 *assume great airs* 神气活现，装作要人的模样，摆架子

[大头例句] Do you assume too much about other people? 你对别人期望的是不是太多了。

aftermath *n.* /ˈɑːftəmæθ/

The youth who are born in peaceful environments can't imagine the *aftermath* of the war.

[猜一猜] A 残酷 B 情景 C 价值 D 后果

[翻 译] 出生在和平环境中的年轻人不能想象战争的后果。

[大头巧记] math 在现代英语中意为数学，超难度数学考试以后，对于"大头"当然是个不幸的后果。

[大头例句] The people on the banks of the Yangtze River were suffering the pestilence as an aftermath of the flood. 长江两岸的人们正承受着洪水过后瘟疫的苦难。

conceive *v.* /kənˈsiːv/

Half a century ago it was difficult to *conceive* of traveling to the moon.

[猜一猜] A 设想 B 实现 C 证实 D 发动

[翻 译] 半个世纪前去月球旅行是难以想象的。

[分 析] con + ceive

with + 拿 → 拿着…，怀(胎)，构思，设想。

[大头巧记] **receive**，收到 → **conceive**，收到孩子 → 怀孕 → 孕育，构思。

[大头例句] The exhibit was originally conceived as a tribute to Scott's family. 这个展品最早被认为是给斯克特家族的礼品。

consequence *n.* /ˈkɔnsikwəns/

As a *consequence* of being in the hospital, Shelly decided that she wanted to become a nurse.

[猜一猜] A 欺骗 B 请求 C 结果 D 目的

[翻 译] 由于在医院的缘故，谢莉决定当一名护士。

[分 析] con + sequ + ence

和 + 跟随 + 名词词尾 → 跟随而来的事物 → 结果，推论，因果关系

[大头巧记] 注意同根词：**sequence**（顺序），**obsequious**（拍马屁）。

[词义扩展] *n.* 重要性，重大意义 *a person of consequence* 举足轻重的人

[习语记忆] **face the consequences of one's action** 自食其果

[大头例句] She said exactly what she felt, without fear of the consequences. 不担心结果，她说了她真正想说的话。

deadlock *n.* /ˈdedlɔk/

Negotiations are finally due to begin after months of political *deadlock*.

[猜一猜] A 敌对 B 死亡 C 谈判 D 僵局

[翻 译] 在数月的政治僵局之后谈判终于启动了。

[大头巧记] 拆：dead lock，死锁，死结，僵局。

[词义扩展] *vi.&vt.* 相持不下，停顿 *The meeting deadlocked over the wage issue.* 会议因工资问题而停顿下来。

[大头例句] The meeting deadlocked over the wage issue. 会议在工资问题上陷入了僵局。

deduce *vt.* /diˈdjuːs/

If you see a doctor leaving a house, you may *deduce* that someone in the house is ill.

[猜一猜] A 猜想 B 推论 C 暗示 D 调查

[翻　译]如果你看见一个医生从某一家出来，你就可以推知这家有人病了。

[分　析]de　+ duce

向下 + 引导 → 向下引导出，推论，推导

[词义扩展] *vt.* 追溯根源

[大头例句] Finding fossils far inland, he deduced that the area had once been covered by water. 在内陆深处发现了化石，他推断这个地区曾经被水所覆盖。

elicit *vt.* /iˈlisit/

After much questioning among the people concerned, the headmaster at last *elicited* the truth about the incident.

[猜一猜]A 引出　B 推理出　C 证明　D 理解

[翻　译]经在有关人员中反复询问，校长终于问出了那件事的真相。

[分　析]e　+ licit

出来 + 诱使 → 诱出，得出，探出

[大头例句] Their research had elicited very little so far. 迄今为止，他们的研究收效甚微。

exterior *adj.* /eksˈtiəriə/

In the meeting he criticized the *exterior* influences on the negotiations.

[猜一猜]A 不正当的　　B 敌意的

C 外部的　　D 内部的

[翻　译]在会上他批评了外界对谈判的影响。

[分　析]exter + ior

外面 + 词尾 → 外部的，外在的，表面的

[词义扩展] *n.* 外部，外面，外观 *Underneath that gruff exterior is a very kind person.* 在粗暴的外表之下他其实是一个亲切的人。

[大头例句] A murderous heart under a smiling exterior. 笑里藏刀。

hence *adv.* /hens/

They grew up in the Sudan; *hence* their interest in Nubian art.

[猜一猜]A 因为　B 说明　C 业余　D 因此

[翻　译]他们在苏丹长大，因此产生了对努比亚艺术的兴趣。

[分　析]hen　+ ce

离开此处 + 副词词缀 → 由此，因此，从此

[大头巧记] hen，母鸡；是有鸡，由此有蛋；还是有蛋，由此有鸡？

[大头例句] We must await the result of the election two weeks hence. 我们必须等候两周以后的选举结果。

inference *n.* /ˈinfərəns/

From his manner, we drew the *inference* that he was satisfied with the exam.

[猜一猜]A 会议　B 推论　C 效果　D 画面

[翻　译]我们从他的态度来推断，他对这次测验很满意。

[分　析]infer　+ ence

推断 + 名词词尾 → 推断，推论，含义，意味

[大头巧记] **conference**，会议，在讨论会里面(in)得到推论 **inference**。

[大头例句] The editorial contained an inference of foul play in the awarding of the contract. 社论暗示在合同案的判决过程中有肮脏交易。

interpret *v.* /inˈtəːprit/

Political apathy can be *interpreted* as a sign of satisfaction with the current government.

[猜一猜]A 解释　B 塑造　C 推动　D 突出

[翻　译]政治上的冷漠可以被认为对现行政府满意的标志。

[分　析]inter　+ pret

在…之间 + 价格 → 在价格之间调停 → 解释，说明，口译，了解，表演

[大头例句] I interpret his answer as a refusal. 我把他的回答理解为拒绝。

minute *adj.* /maiˈnjuːt/

With such a *minute* amount of money, you will not even be able to afford one stick of gum!

[猜一猜]A 短暂的　B 奇怪的　C 迟来的　D 微小的

[翻　译]这么一点点钱，你连块口香糖也买不起。

[大头巧记] 此单词的另一个意思"分钟"为我们所熟知，只是发音不同，为/ˈminit/。分钟，很微小的

时间。

[词义扩展] *adj.* 详细的 *vt.* 纪录

[大头例句] Our lawyer went over the contract in minute detail. 我们的律师对合同的细节进行了仔细的检查。

nominate *vt.* /ˈnɔmineit/

He has been *nominated* to represent his country at the negotiations.

[猜一猜] A 选举 B 内定 C 暂定 D 提名

[翻 译] 他已经被提名代表其国家进行谈判。

[分 析] nomin + ate

名字 + 动词词尾 → 提名,任命

[大头例句] For many young actresses, to even receive an Oscar nomination is a tremendous honor. 对许多年轻的女演员们来说,即使受到奥斯卡提名也是一件极大的荣誉。

omit *vt.* /əuˈmit/

Important details had been *omitted* from the article.

[猜一猜] A 刊发 B 证实 C 遗漏 D 寻找

[翻 译] 这篇文章遗漏了重要的细节。

[大头例句] Oliver omitted mention of his marriage. 奥利弗没有提到他已婚的事。

premise *n.* /ˈpremis/

We started from the *premise* that the situation could get no worse.

[猜一猜] A 背景 B 前提 C 过程 D 誓言

[翻 译] 我们是在情况不会更坏的前提下开始的。

[分 析] pre + mise

先于 + 发送 → 设在前面 → 前提

[词义扩展] *v.* 提论,做出前提,假定

[习语记忆] **see sb. off the premise** 下逐客令

[大头例句] The basic premise of the classic movie "Roman Holiday" involves a bored princess who steps out of her life for a day to live her life as a more ordinary person would. 经典电影"罗马假日"的基本前提背景包括了一个觉得无聊的公主,一天走出了她的现有生活,去过一个更普通人的生活。

presumption *n.* /priˈzʌmpʃən/

The *presumption* is that he had lost his way.

[猜一猜] A 推想 B 想像 C 事实 D 娱乐

[翻 译] 推想起来,他当时是迷了路。

[分 析] pre + sump + tion

预先 + 拿 + 名词词尾 → 先拿 → 假定,推测

[大巧头记] **presume**, *vt.* 假定,假设

presumption, *n.* 假定

[词义扩展] *n.* 专横,自大

[大头例句] If you are under the presumption that our relationship consists of anything more than mere friendship, you are badly mistaken, and my real boyfriend would be more than willing to help prove that to you. 如果你认为我们的关系包含任何超出普通朋友关系的成分,那你就大大地错了,并且我真正的男朋友会非常愿意向你证明这一点。

psychology *n.* /saiˈkɔlədʒi/

The professor is a specialist of studying a criminal's *psychology*.

[猜一猜] A 目的 B 倾向 C 量刑 D 心理学

[翻 译] 这位教授是位研究罪犯心理学的专家。

[分 析] psych + ology

心的 + …学 → 心理学,心理状态

[习语记忆] **social science psychology** 社会科学心理学 **pedagogical psychology** 教育心理学 **criminal psychology** 犯罪心理学

[大头例句] Modern-day psychology students devote little time to the theories of German psychologist Sigmund Freud, as most of his theories are no longer widely accepted. 当代的心理学学生很少注意德国心理学家西格蒙德·弗洛伊德的理论,因为他大多数的理论已经不再被广泛接受。

quest *n.* /kwest/

Some people really enjoy the *quest* for knowledge.

[猜一猜]A 提问　B 置疑　C 寻求　D 积累

[翻　译]有些人求知欲很强。

[大头巧记]**question**，问题；反推得到：**quest** *vt./n.* 寻求，探索

[习语记忆]**in quest of** 为了寻求…

rational *adj./n.* /ˈræʃənl/

There didn't seem to be any *rational* explanation for his actions.

[猜一猜]A 有说服力的　B 具体的　C 合理的　D 虚张声势的

[翻　译]对于他的行为似乎没有任何合理的解释。

[分　析]ration ＋al

原因 ＋词尾 → 合理的，理性的，推理的

[大头巧记]**rational number**，有理数；**irrational number**，无理数。另：联系**perceptual**(感性的)记忆。

[大头例句]I know it seems strange that I am wearing my pants backwards, but there is a rational explanation: they are much easier to put on quickly this way! 我知道我把裤子穿倒了看起来很奇怪，但我是有合理解释的：这样穿更容易穿得快！

speculate *vi.* /ˈspekjuˌleit/

I've been *speculating* on my future.

[猜一猜]A 忧虑　B 思索　C 怀疑　D 徘徊

[翻　译]我一直在思索我的未来。

[分　析]spec ＋ulate

看 ＋做的多 → 看得太多 → 引起思索。

[词义扩展]*v.* 推测，做投机买卖

speculate in stocks 做股票投机

[大头例句]Nick had speculated in gold and lost heavily. 尼克曾投机倒卖黄金，损失惨重。

习题：在下面的空格里填写本单元的单词。

1. I'm not the fool you ________ me to be.
2. Negotiations are finally due to begin after months of political ________.
3. If you see a doctor leaving a house, you may ________ that someone in the house is ill.
4. The basic ________ of the classic movie "Roman Holiday" involves a bored princess who steps out of her life for a day to live her life as a more ordinary person would.
5. Nick had ________ in gold and lost heavily.
6. I know it seems strange that I am wearing my pants backwards, but there is a ________ explanation: they are much easier to put on quickly this way!
7. Important details had been ________ from the article.
8. Some people really enjoy the ________ for knowledge.
9. If you are under the ________ that our relationship consists of anything more than mere friendship, you are badly mistaken, and my real boyfriend would be more than willing to help prove that to you.
10. After much questioning among the people concerned, the headmaster at last ________ the truth about the incident.
11. In the meeting he criticized the ________ influences on the negotiations.
12. They grew up in the Sudan; ________ their interest in Nubian art.
13. With such a ________ amount of money, you will not even be able to afford one stick

of gum!

14. Modern-day __________ students devote little time to the theories of German psychologist Sigmund Freud, as most of his theories are no longer widely accepted.
15. From his manner, we drew the __________ that he was satisfied with the exam.
16. The people on the banks of the Yangtze River were suffering the pestilence as an ______ of the flood.
17. The exhibit was originally __________ as a tribute to Scott's family.
18. As a __________ of being in the hospital, Shelly decided that she wanted to become a nurse.
19. Political apathy can be __________ as a sign of satisfaction with the current government.
20. For many young actresses, to even receive an Oscar __________ is a tremendous honor.

Note 前事不忘后事之师 *Remember the past and it will guide your future.*

Day 34

adjure *vt.* /ə'dʒuə/

"*Adjuring* her in the name of God to declare the truth."(Increase Mather)

[猜一猜] A 认识 B 命令 C 陪伴 D 劝阻

[翻 译] "命令她以上帝的名义讲出事实"。(因克瑞斯·马瑟)

[分 析] ad + jure
朝向 + 起誓 → 使…起誓，严肃地命令或责令

[大头巧记] 记住他的另一个意思，恳求。谐音法：饿，助我。饥饿是渴求帮助的。

[词义扩展] *vt.* 恳求 *He adjured me to speak the truth.* 他恳求我说实话。

[大头例句] I adjured my wife to give me some beer money. 我恳求妻子给我一点零花钱。

alibi *n.* /'ælibai/

He is trying to offer an *alibi* to the charge of murder.

[猜一猜] A 不在场证明 B 无犯罪证明 C 身份证明 D 贿赂

[翻 译] 他正在试着提供一个谋杀时不在现场的证明。

[分 析] ali + bi
other + 地方 → 在别的地方 → 不在场的证明

[词义扩展] *n.* [美口]托辞，辩解
vi. 辩解；找托辞开脱 *alibi for being late* 为迟到找到一个借口
vt. 为(某人)作不在场的证词 *He alibied his neighbour out of a fix.* 他为他的邻居作了不在现场的证词，帮他解脱了困境。

bid *v.* /bid/

I *bid* 200 dollars for that antique clock that you found in Switzerland.

[猜一猜] A 净赚 B 赔本 C 出价 D 砍价

[翻 译] 我出价200美金买你在瑞士发现的古董时钟。

[词义扩展] *vt.&vi.* ①出价，投标 ②(打牌时)叫牌 *I bid 2 spades.* 我叫两个黑桃。③致意 ④吩咐 *Do as you are bidden.* 按吩咐你的去做。
n. 出价，投标，招标

[大头例句] Wilson wants to sell his stock in that company, and he has already had several large bids for it. 威尔逊想要卖掉他在那家公司中的股份，他已经有好几个大买家了。

coerce *vt.* /kəu'ə:s/

The chamber of commerce was making efforts to *coerce* the strikers into compliance.

[猜一猜] A 引导 B 谈判 C 迫使 D 欺诈

[翻 译] 商会正在努力迫使罢工者妥协。

[分 析] co + erce
一起 + 限制 → 一起约束 → 强迫，压迫

[大头例句] Superpowers are known to coerce others to get what they want. 超级强权国家通过高压政治获得他们想要的东西。

commission *n.* /kə'miʃən/

The ministry of education puts the investigation of fraud as one of their most important *commissions* this year.

[猜一猜] A 目标 B 研究 C 任务 D 法规

[翻 译] 教育部把对欺诈行为的调查作为今年最重要的任务之一。

[分 析] com + miss + ion
with + 送，放出 + 名词词尾 → 送出之物 → 委托，任务

[词义扩展] *n.*①委员会；调查团 ②犯法 ③佣金；酬劳金 *vt.* 委任，授权，命令

[大头例句] I have commissioned the bank to pay my taxes. 我授权银行代我缴税。

compel *vt.* /kəmˈpel/

The energy crisis related to the war would ***compel*** a block of companies to raise the prices of their products.

[猜一猜]A 造成 B 迫使 C 劝说 D 导致

[翻 译]由战争引起的能源危机将迫使一大批公司提高他们产品的价格。

[分 析]com + pel

和，与 + 驾驭 → 迫使，强迫

[词义扩展]*vt.* 获得；强取 *vi.* 驱策；驱使

[大头例句]The emperor had a voice that inspired and compelled. 国王的声音权威，令人不得不遵从。

denote *vt.* /diˈnəut/

A flashing yellow light ***denotes*** caution in the traffic lights.

[猜一猜]A 表示 B 注定 C 奉献 D 图解

[翻 译]交通灯中闪烁的黄灯表示警告。

[分 析]de + note

自…导出 + 标记 → 表示

[词义扩展]*vt.* 作标志，指明 *The mark '∧' denotes a place of omission.* "∧"记号指示有脱漏的地方。

[大头例句]Her frown denoted increasing impatience. 她紧皱眉头，表示她越来越不耐烦。

dictate *v.* /dikˈteit/

The union leaders are trying to ***dictate*** their demands to the employer.

[猜一猜]A 说服 B 诱使 C 强迫 D 离间

[翻 译]工会领导人正设法迫使雇主接受他们的要求。

[分 析]dict + ate

说 + 动词词尾 → 反复地说 → 命令，要求

[词义扩展]*v.* 听写，口述 *to dictate a letter to a secretary* 向秘书口授信稿 *n.* 指示，命令

[大头例句]I refuse to be dictated to by some mindless bureaucrat! 我不要让某些没头脑的官僚主义者指使。

execute *vt.* /ˈeksikjuːt/

The manager's assistant came here to ***execute*** a few small commissions for the manager.

[猜一猜]A 实行 B 宣布 C 解释 D 加强

[翻 译]经理助理到这里来是代替经理办几件小事的。

[分 析]ex + ecute

出去 + 跟随 → 跟出去，继续往外走 → 实行，执行，完成

[词义扩展]*vt.* 处死，履行执行或实行命令 *execute the terms of a will* 执行遗嘱

[大头例句]Sidney and Russell were both executed for their part in the plot. 希德尼和罗素都因参与这个阴谋而被处死。

exile *n.* /ˈeksail/

He had spent six years in ***exile***.

[猜一猜]A 留学 B 监狱 C 流放 D 婚姻

[翻 译]他过流放生活已经六年了。

[分 析]e + xile

外面 + 坐着 → 使坐在外面 → 流放，放逐

[词义扩展]*vt.* 放逐，使充军，使背井离乡

[大头例句]Napoleon was first exiled in 1814. 1814年的时候，拿破仑被第一次流放。

guarantee *n.* /ˌgærənˈtiː/

Blue skies are not always a ***guarantee*** of fine weather.

[猜一猜]A 保证 B 预示 C 限制 D 吸引

[翻 译]蔚蓝的天空并不永远保证是晴朗的天气。

[分 析]guarant + ee

担保 + 承担…者 → 接受担保的人 → 担保物，担保，保证

[词义扩展]*vt.* 对…提出担保，约定，许诺 *Many shopkeepers guarantee satisfaction to customers.* 许多店主对顾客保证满意。

[大头例句]The government provides help for small businesses, but it cannot guarantee their success. 政府对小型企业提供帮助，但是不能保证他们的成功。

imperative *adj.* /imˈperətiv/

It is ***imperative*** that every one of us remould his world outlook.

[猜一猜]A 有力的　B 长期的　C 多变的　D 必须的

[翻　译]我们每个人都必须改造自己的世界观。

[分　析]imper　+ ative

命令　+ 形容词尾 → 命令的，强制的，必要的，紧急的

[词义扩展]*n.*〈语法〉祈使语气（的）；命令，规则，需要

imperatives in education 教育规则

[大头例句]Solidarity between rich and poor nations is a moral imperative. 穷国和富国间的团结是道德上的必须。

implement *n./v.* /ˈimplimənt/

The agreement was signed but its recommendations were never ***implemented***.

[猜一猜]A 通过　B 提出　C 实现　D 废除

[翻　译]协议签订了，但是它的建议却从未履行过。

[分　析]im　+ plement

里面 + 充满 → 把…的里面充满东西 → 使…实现，履行

[大头巧记]**complement,**(com-表强调) 补足（使…满）；**implement**，也有补充的意思，另一词意：履行。

[词义扩展]*n.*［常用复数］工具，器具 *flint and bronze implements* 石器和铜器

[大头例句]The committee's decisions will be implemented immediately. 委员会的决定将立即执行。

intimidate *v.* /inˈtimideit/

Atomic energy may ***intimidate*** the human race into bringing order into its international affairs, which, without the pressure of fear, it would not do.

[猜一猜]A 帮助　B 引起　C 胁迫　D 变更

[翻　译]原子能可能胁迫人类有秩序地处理国际事务，而这在没有恐惧的压力下，是不可能实现的。

[分　析]in　+ timid　+ ate

使 + 胆小的 + 动词词尾 → 使人害怕 → 恐吓，胁迫。

[大头例句]We should never be intimidated by big names and authorities. 我们决不应被名人、权威所吓倒。

impact *vt.* /ˈimpækt/

The war has ***impacted*** the area with military and defense workers.

[猜一猜]A 挤满　B 供给　C 打击　D 导致

[翻　译]战争使那个地区挤满了军队和防御工程人员。

[分　析]im　+ pact

里面 + 打，击 → 向里面打 → 挤满，压紧，打击，撞击，影响

[词义扩展]*n.* 冲击（力），碰撞，冲突，效果，影响 *the impact of automation on the lives of factory workers* 自动化对工厂工人生活的影响

[大头例句]The missile does not explode or impact. 这个导弹在冲击时没有爆炸。

mandate *n.* /ˈmændeit/

Many emperors of eras gone by were said to possess a "***mandate*** of heaven," that is, they believed it was God who directed them to rule.

[猜一猜]A 命令　B 财富　C 爱心　D 热情

[翻　译]过去时代的很多皇帝都宣扬自己是"君权神授"，这是因为他们相信是上帝指导他们来统治的。

[分　析]mand　+ ate

命令　+ 词尾 → 命令，委托管理，授权

[大头巧记]man date，真正男人的约会，命令自己决不准失约背信。

[词义扩展]*vt.* 委托统治，托管，颁布

mandate a policy 批准一项政策

[大头例句]These proposals hope to reduce traffic and mandate lower speed limits. 这些建议希望减少交通量并批准更低的速度限制。

mandatory *adj.* /ˈmændətəri/

In most primary schools, physical education courses are ***mandatory***; few, however, require the study of ancient Chinese.

[猜一猜]A 选修的　B 多样的　C 强制的　D 足够的

[翻 译]在大多数的小学里，体育课是强制性的，可是却很少有要求学习古代汉语的。

[分 析]mand + atory

命令 + 形容词尾 → 命令的，强制的，受委托的

[大 例 头 句]A new accounting system will soon become mandatory for all departments. 新的会计系统不久将在所有的部门强制实行。

mission *n.* /ˈmiʃən/

As teachers, your ***mission*** is not only to educate your students, but to motivate them and inspire them as well.

[猜一猜]A 行为 B 表现 C 成果 D 使命

[翻 译]作为老师，你们的使命不仅仅是教育学生，也要激励和鼓舞他们。

[分 析]miss + ion

发送 + 动词词尾 → 奉命送往 → 使命，使团。

[大 巧 头 记]**missile，导弹**，导弹带有的使命—**mission**。

[大 例 头 句]She believed that her mission in life was helping the old and the sick. 她认为她一生的天职就是帮助老人和病人。

nevertheless *conj./adv.* /ˌnevəðəˈles/

She was very tired, ***nevertheless*** she kept on working.

[猜一猜]A 然而 B 同时 C 另外 D 除非

[翻 译]她虽然很疲倦，可仍在继续工作。

[大 巧 头 记]拆：never the less，少点可以，但是绝对不能更少。

[大 例 头 句]Of course I love my country and its people, nevertheless, I can see its problems clearly, and I recognize the need for improvement. 我当然爱我的祖国和人民，但是，我也能清楚看到她的问题，并能认识到进步的需要。

oppress *vt.* /əˈpres/

A sense of trouble ahead ***oppressed*** my spirits.

[猜一猜]A 激励 B 警告 C 压抑 D 敦促

[翻 译]对今后困难的预感使我情绪低落。

[分 析]op + press

向下 + 压 → 压下去 → 压迫，压抑

[大 巧 头 记]联系**depress（降低，抑制）**和**impress（留下印象）**记忆。

[大 例 头 句]Native tribes had been oppressed by the government and police for years. 当地的部族被政府和警察压迫过很多年。

prescribe *v.* /prisˈkraib/

What punishment does the law ***prescribe*** for corruption?

[猜一猜]A 建议 B 意味 C 争论 D 规定

[翻 译]法律规定对贪污行贿该处以什么刑罚？

[分 析]pre + scribe

在先 + 写 → 指示，规定，开处方

[词 扩 义 展]*v.* 开药方，命令，规定

[大 例 头 句]Though this infection is quite common, you will need to find a doctor to prescribe the appropriate antibiotics; they are not available over-the-counter in pharmacies. 虽然该传染病很平常，但你还是需要让医生给你开些合适的抗生素；在药店的柜台上这些抗生素是不卖的。

stern *adj.* /stəːn/

She was ***stern*** with her students.

[猜一猜]A 严格的 B 滑稽的 C 冷酷的 D 卑躬屈膝的

[翻 译]她对自己的学生很严格。

[词 扩 义 展]*n.* 船尾，臀部，后部。

[大 巧 头 记]和**stem（船首）**联系记忆：from stem to stern 从船头到船尾，从头到尾。

[习 记 语 忆]**sit at the stern** 执政

[大 例 头 句]These groups are calling for sterner penalties for drug offences. 这些群体要求对毒品犯罪实施更严厉的处罚。

penalty
n. 处罚，罚款
反：reward

习题：在下面的空格里填写本单元的单词。

1. "__________ her in the name of God to declare the truth." (Increase Mather)
2. The energy crisis related to the war would __________ a block of companies to raise the prices of their products.
3. Napoleon was first __________ in 1814.
4. In most primary schools, physical education courses are __________; few, however, require the study of ancient Chinese.
5. The union leaders are trying to __________ their demands to the employer.
6. He is trying to offer an __________ to the charge of murder.
7. I __________ 200 dollars for that antique clock that you found in Switzerland.
8. The ministry of education puts the investigation of fraud as one of their most important __________ this year.
9. A flashing yellow light __________ caution in the traffic lights.
10. The chamber of commerce was making efforts to __________ the strikers into compliance.
11. The manager's assistant came here to __________ a few small commissions for the manager.
12. It is __________ that every one of us remould his world outlook.
13. The government provides help for small businesses, but it cannot __________ their success.
14. Many emperors of eras gone by were said to possess a "__________ of heaven," that is, they believed it was God who directed them to rule.
15. Atomic energy may __________ the human race into bringing order into its international affairs, which, without the pressure of fear, it would not do.
16. The agreement was signed but its recommendations were never __________.
17. The war has __________ the area with military and defense workers.
18. These groups are calling for __________ penalties for drug offences.
19. As teachers, your __________ is not only to educate your students, but to motivate them and inspire them as well.
20. What punishment does the law __________ for corruption?
21. Of course I love my country and its people, __________, I can see its problems clearly, and I recognize the need for improvement.
22. Native tribes had been __________ by the government and police for years.

Day 35

advent *n.* /ˈædvənt/

> Now, with the *advent* of the new president, the reforms in many fields have been a subject of discussion.

【猜一猜】A 离开 B 成功 C 提议 D 到来

【翻 译】现在,随着新总统的到来,很多领域的改革问题成为大家讨论的话题。

【分 析】ad + vent
朝向 + 来 → 到来

【大头巧记】我们知道adventure意思为冒险,经历不同寻常的事情,它是由本词变化而来的。advent就有不同寻常的事物到来之意。

【联 想】**adventitious** *adj.* 偶发的,偶然的 *This is an adventitious meet.* 这是一次邂逅。

【词义扩展】Advent *n.* 基督降临,降临节
second Advent【宗】基督复临

【大头例句】The advent of spring revives the lives which hibernated in winter. 春天的到来唤醒了冬眠的生命。

conceal *v.* /kənˈsiːl/

> After completing their scheme, the two criminals *concealed* the evidence that they had been in the building.

【猜一猜】A 说明 B 隐藏 C 带走 D 铺展

【翻 译】完成他们的阴谋后,这两个罪犯隐藏了他们曾经来过这个楼的痕迹。

【分 析】con + ceal
加强语气 + 藏 → 隐藏,对…保密

【大头例句】Don't try to conceal anything from me! 不要试图对我隐瞒任何事情。

disclose *vt.* /disˈkləuz/

> The president *disclosed* the fact that he was put into prison wrongly twenty years before.

【猜一猜】A 透露 B 否认 C 提出 D 决定

【翻 译】董事长透露说他自己在20年前曾被冤枉地送进监牢。

【大头巧记】close,关,dis,否定前缀,放弃对某个消息的关闭 → 透露,揭发,泄露。

【大头例句】The curtains rose, disclosing a stage bathed in red light. 幕升上去了,露出浴在红光中的舞台。

emerge *vi.* /iˈməːdʒ/

> Sea mammals must *emerge* periodically to breathe.

【猜一猜】A 浮现 B 移动 C 回游 D 进食

【翻 译】海生哺乳动物必须不断地浮出海面呼吸。

【分 析】e + merge
出来 + 水中 → 由水中出来,浮现,出现,显露

【形近词】**emergence**,突发事件,突然的显露

【词义扩展】*vi.* ①形成,发生 ②脱颖而出 ③排出,冒出
The ship emerged from behind the fog. 船从雾里露了出来。

【大头例句】Leeds is emerging as an important financial centre. 利兹正脱颖而出成为一个重要的金融中心。

emit *vt.* /iˈmit/

> The tail exhaust pipe of the motor vehicle *emitted* poisonous smoke.

【猜一猜】A 发出 B 处理 C 净化 D 控制

【翻 译】摩托车的排气管排放出有毒的烟雾。

【分 析】e + mit
出去 + 让走 → 发出,散发(光、热、气味等)

【词义扩展】*vt.* 发表,颁布,发行
emit an opinion 表达一个观点

【大头例句】She emitted her small, strange laugh. 她发出了她那小而奇怪的笑声。

engage *v.* /inˈgeidʒ/

> Can you *engage* that he can pay back the money in due time?

[猜一猜]A 担保 B 攻击 C 鼓励 D 难堪
[翻 译]你能担保他能如期还清欠款吗？
[分 析]en + dow
在…里 + 担保 → 担保，保证，允诺
[词义扩展]v. 雇用，从事，订婚，吸引，啮合
We've engaged a new secretary. 我们已经聘请了新秘书。
[大头例句]He is currently engaged in a dispute with his former business partner. 他经常参与到和以前的生意伙伴的争执中去。

flare v. /flɛə/

The candle *flared*, then flickered and went out.

[猜一猜]A 突然变亮 B 点燃 C 倒落 D 流泪
[翻 译]蜡烛忽然亮了一下，晃了晃又灭了。
[词义扩展]n./v. ①闪光，闪耀，熊熊燃烧 ②(衣裙等)张开 *The skirt flares at the knees.* 这裙子从膝部向外展开。
[大头例句]Tempers flared during the debates. 在争论中忽然发怒。

flicker v. /ˈflikə/

The candle *flickered* in the wind.

[猜一猜]A 闪烁 B 熄灭 C 照明 D 夸耀
[翻 译]蜡烛在风中闪烁不定。
[分 析]flick + er
摇晃 + 指动作的反复 → 闪烁不定
[词义扩展]vt. 使闪烁；使颤动 *flicker a warning with a lifted brow* 皱眉头以示警告
[大头例句]A little smile flickered around the corners of his mouth. 一丝微笑在他的嘴角边一现而逝。

gleam n. /gliːm/

We saw *gleams* of daylight through the cracks.

[猜一猜]A 微光 B 象征 C 征兆 D 火花
[翻 译]我们从缝隙中看到黎明的曙光。
[大头巧记]区别联系：glean(收集)，囊萤照读，车胤收集萤火虫，发出微光来读书。
[习语记忆]**not a gleam of hope** 毫无希望
[词义扩展]v. 闪烁，发光 n. 闪光，短暂的闪现
[大头例句]Courage gleamed in his eyes. 他的眼睛中闪现勇气。

glimmer vi. /ˈglimə/

A faint light *glimmered* at the end of the corridor.

[猜一猜]A 闪烁 B 熄灭 C 照耀 D 出现
[翻 译]走廊的尽头闪着一星微光。
[大头巧记]根据 **gleam** 来记，两者基本同义。
[词义扩展]n. 少许，微量
a glimmer of intelligence 很少一点情报
[大头例句]There was a glimmer of amusement in his eyes. 他的眼中有少许快乐。

haphazard n./adj./adv. /hæpˈhæzəd/

He can never forget that *haphazard* vacation.

[猜一猜]A 遭透的 B 远程的 C 任意的 D 浪漫的
[翻 译]他永远忘不了那次随意的旅行。
[分 析]hap + hazard
运气 + 游戏 → 游戏时仅凭运气 → 偶然的(地)，任意的(地)，随意的(地)
[大头例句]I got a sum of money by haphazard means. 我偶然得到一笔钱。

inflict v. /inˈflikt/

Such a policy would *inflict* severe hardship and suffering.

[猜一猜]A 违反 B 愚弄 C 扩大 D 造成
[翻 译]这样的政策会造成很严重的困难和痛苦。
[分 析]in + flict
在…上 + 打击 → 给予(打击等)，使遭受，处罚，造成
[大头例句]We should stop the environmental damage we are inflicting on the Earth. 我们应该停止正在强加给地球的环境破坏。

manifest n./adj./v. /ˈmænifest/

Sometimes a mother's love *manifests* itself in subtle ways, such as making sure the bathwater is warm before her son gets in.

radical adj. 根本的，基本的，激进的
n. 激进分子
radicalism n. 激进主义

[猜一猜] A 温暖 B 挑剔 C 关怀 D 表明

[翻 译] 有时候母爱通过一些细小的方面表现，例如在孩子沐浴之前确定水是否温暖。

[分 析] mani + fest
手 + 打 → 用手公开打 → 公开的，明了的，表明

[大头巧记] man(i) fest(ival)，男人的节日，向努力工作的男士们表明关爱的日子

[词义扩展] n. 载货单，旅客名单 outward manifest【经贸】出口货舱单

[大头例句] Three years of dedicated research finally was manifested in a successful project designed to help teenagers know more about health issues. 三年的专心研究终于在一个帮助青少年了解更多健康问题的成功设计项目中表现出来。

novelty n. /ˈnɔvəlti/

Computers were a *novelty* in the 1980s in China.

[猜一猜] A 新鲜事物 B 珍贵物品
C 滞后之物 D 摆设

[翻 译] 20世纪80年代电脑在中国是个新鲜事物。

[分 析] novel + ty
新鲜的 + 名词词尾 → 新鲜事物，新颖

[大头巧记] **novel**，小说，**novelty**，小说中的新鲜事儿。

[大头例句] She purchased the old war helmet not for its objective aesthetic beauty, but for its inherent novelty factor. 她买这个旧的军盔，并不是为它客观上的美学价值，而是为它新鲜的内在因素。

landscape n. /ˈlændskeip/

Local residents describe the power station as a blot on the *landscape*.

[猜一猜] A 地域经济 B 区域政治
C 风景 D 地理

[翻 译] 当地居民把这所发电站描述为风景上的一个污点。

[分 析] land + scape
土地 + 情况 → 描绘风景的绘画，风景，地形

[词义扩展] vt. 美化 n. 情况，前景 *The 1990s saw the political landscape radically reshaped.* 20世纪90年代时，政治景况风云突变。

[大头例句] They occupy the whole landscape of my thought. 他们占据了我的整个心田。

lens n. /lenz/

When viewing through the *lens*, we can see things clearer, larger or smaller.

[猜一猜] A 仪器 B 透镜 C 介质 D 惰性气体

[翻 译] 通过透镜我们可以把物体看得更大、更小或更清晰。

[词义扩展] n. 眼睛的晶状体，镜头
vt. 摄影

telescope n. 望远镜

[大头例句] I bought a camera with a telescopic lens. 我买了一个带可伸缩性镜头的相机。

telescopic adj. 远视的，伸缩的

lucid adj. /ˈluːsid/

He does have occasional *lucid* moments.

[猜一猜] A 糊涂的 B 清醒的
C 草率的 D 失去理智的

[翻 译] 他确实偶然会清醒。

[分 析] luc + id
光 + 形容词词尾 → 明晰的，清醒的，易懂的

[大头巧记] lucy，露西，很明智的女孩 → **lucid**，明智，清醒。另：lily，莉莉，女孩名，也指百合花。

[大头例句] In the era in which Shakespeare lived, his style was considered straightforward and clear; to modern students, however, his works are anything but lucid. 在莎士比亚生活的时代，他的风格被认为是直接和清楚的，对于现代的学生则绝不易懂。

presence n. /ˈprezns/

These famous film stars' *presence* greatly brightened up the evening party.

[猜一猜] A 在场 B 表演 C 评论 D 傲慢

[翻 译] 这些电影明星在场使晚会大为活跃。

[大头巧记] **present**, *adj.* 出席的，在场的
presence, *n.* 出席，到场，风度

[习语记忆] **lose one's presence of mind** 心慌意乱
saving your presence 恕我冒昧

obvious *adj.* /ˈɔbviəs/

The most *obvious* explanation is not always the correct one.

[猜一猜] A 客观的 B 主观的 C 简单的 D 明显的

[翻 译] 最明显的解释往往不是正确的。

[分 析] ob + vious

相对 + 路 → 和路对着的 → 明显的，显而易见的。与**obscure(模糊的)**对比记忆。

[大头例句] The obvious thing would have been to travel with her husband, but she couldn't. 最好的选择本应该是和丈夫一起旅行，可是她做不到。

overt *adj.* /ˈəuvəːt/

It will not solve your problem with *overt* hostility.

[猜一猜] A 危险的 B 背叛的 C 激烈的 D 公然的

[翻 译] 公开的敌对解决不了你的问题。

[大头巧记] 拆：over (i)t，在其上面的 → 公然的，明显的。另：与**covert(偷偷摸摸地)**对比记忆。

[大头例句] He made an overt attempt to silence their political opponents. 他公然试图让其政治对手沉默。

symptom *n.* /ˈsimptəm/

The affair is a *symptom* of a global marital disturbance; it is not the disturbance itself.

[猜一猜] A 征兆 B 结果 C 悲剧 D 表演

[翻 译] 这一事件是全球婚姻混乱的征兆；它并不是混乱本身。

[分 析] sym + ptom

一起 + 降落 → (随病)一起降落的东西 → 病症，征兆

[大头例句] Symptoms include headaches and vomiting. 病症包括头疼和呕吐。

transparent *adj.* /trænsˈpεərənt/

Citizens are asking for a more *transparent* democratic government.

[猜一猜] A 传统的 B 透明的 C 特色的 D 精细的

[翻 译] 民众们要求透明度更高的民主。

[分 析] trans + par + ent

穿过 + 一样 + 形容词尾 → 穿过以后看起来还一样 → 透明的，明晰的

[大头巧记] 拆：trans parent，通过双亲，可以很明晰地了解学生。另：联系**opaque(不透明)**记忆。

visible *adj./n.* /ˈvizəbl/

At night the planet is clearly *visible* to the naked eye.

[猜一猜] A 可视的 B 无邪的 C 鲜既的 D 可喜的

[翻 译] 晚间，肉眼也可以清晰地看到这颗行星。

[分 析] visi + ble

看 + 可…的 → 可视的，明显的，可见物

[大头例句] There is a visible change in attitudes to working women. 对工作妇女的观念有了显著地改变。

习题：在下面的空格里填写本单元的单词。

1. A little smile __________ around the corners of his mouth.
2. After completing their scheme, the two criminals __________ the evidence that they had been in the building.
3. There is a __________ change in attitudes to working women.
4. The affair is a __________ of a global marital disturbance; it is not the disturbance itself.
5. Local residents describe the power station as a blot on the __________.
6. There was a __________ of amusement in his eyes.
7. The president __________ the fact that he was put into prison wrongly twenty years before.
8. The tail exhaust pipe of the motor vehicle __________ poisonous smoke.
9. He can never forget that __________ vocation.

10. Such a policy would __________ severe hardship and suffering.
11. She purchased the old war helmet not for its objective aesthetic beauty, but for its inherent __________ factor.
12. Sometimes a mother's love __________ itself in subtle ways, such as making sure the bathwater is warm before her son gets in.
13. When viewing through the __________, we can see things clearer, larger or smaller.
14. In the era in which Shakespeare lived, his style was considered straightforward and clear; to modern students, however, his works are anything but __________.
15. He made an __________ attempt to silence their political opponents.
16. The __________ thing would have been to travel with her husband, but she couldn't.
17. These famous film stars' __________ greatly brightened up the evening party.
18. Citizens are asking for a more __________ democratic government.
19. We saw __________ of daylight through the cracks.
20. The candle __________, then flickered and went out.
21. He is currently __________ in a dispute with his former business partner.
22. Sea mammals must __________ periodically to breathe.
23. Now, with the __________ of the new president, the reforms in many fields have been a subject of discussion.

Note 前事不忘后事之师 *Remember the past and it will guide your future.*

Day 36

bucket *n.* /ˈbʌkit/

Two ***buckets*** of water will be enough for the roses in the garden.

[猜一猜]A 盆　B 桶　C 碗　D 品脱

[翻　译]两桶水来浇花园里的玫瑰就够了。

[大头巧记]词形记忆basket是篮子，是一种容器，bucket，是形状像U的一种容器，桶。而C是桶的柄。

[词义扩展]*v.* 倾泻；颠簸 *The car bucketed over the unpaved lane.* 车子在没有铺石子的小巷里颠簸而行。*vt.*用桶装，用桶运；[英口]催(马)猛奔；(横冲直撞地)驾驶(汽车)

[习语记忆]**rain buckets** [口]下倾盆大雨

drop a bucket into an empty well 空井打水，(竹篮打水一场空)

a drop in the bucket 沧海一粟

[大头例句]The rain was coming down in buckets. 天上下着倾盆大雨。

hinge *n./v.* /hindʒ/

The lid of the suitcase had a broken ***hinge***, so it wouldn't open easily.

[猜一猜]A 锁　B 提环　C 棱角　D 合页

[翻　译]小提箱箱盖的合页坏了，因此不容易打开。

[词义扩展]*n.* 铰链，枢纽，关键。*vt.* 装铰链，随…而定

[大头例句]A lot hinges on the result of tomorrow's match. 很多事都随明天的考试结果而定。

installment *n.* /inˈstɔːlmənt/

We're paying for the "colour telly" by monthly ***installments***.

[猜一猜]A 分期付款　B 工资　C 租金　D 行情

[翻　译]我们按月分期付款购买电视机。

[大头巧记]**install**，安装，安置，**installment**，按照安排付款→分期付款/分期收款。

[词义扩展]*n.* 连载，连续剧 *Do you want to hear the latest installment of my love life?* 你想听听我爱情生活的最新剧目吗？

integrate *v.* /ˈintigreit/

The teachers are trying to ***integrate*** all the children into society.

[猜一猜]A 介绍　B 使成为一体　C 建议　D 教导

[翻　译]教师们正设法使所有的孩子都能与社会融为一体。

[分　析]integr + ate

完整 + 名词词尾→使完整，使一体化

[词义扩展]【数】求…的积分；*vi.*与…结合起来 (with) *Care will also be taken to integrate the buildings with surrounding architecture.* 还要注意使这些建筑和周围的建筑融为一体。

implicit *adj.* /imˈplisit/

Frustration is ***implicit*** in any attempt to express the deepest self.

[猜一猜]A 内含的　B 强制性的　C 粗鲁的　D 专横的

[翻　译]表达最深沉的自我的任何企图都内含着挫折感。

[分　析]im + plic + it

进入 + 重叠 + 意义 → 意义叠在里面 → 含蓄的，内含的，暗示的

[词义扩展]*adj.* 无疑的，绝对的，盲从的

implicit trust 绝对信任

[大头例句]His suggestions may be seen as an implicit criticism of government policy. 他的建议也许可以被看做是对政府政策的一种含蓄的批评。

pompous *adj.* /ˈpɔmpəs/

He bowed to the lady in a *pompous* manner.

[猜一猜] A 装模作样的　B 彬彬有礼的
C 滑稽的　D 无礼的

[翻　译] 他装模作样的向这位女士鞠了一躬。

[分　析] pomp + ous
炫耀 + 形容词尾 → 自负的,装模作样的

[词义扩展] *adj.* 豪华的,盛大的
a pompous feast 盛筵

radical *adj./n.* /ˈrædikəl/

A *radical* is a man with both feet firmly planted in the air.

[猜一猜] A 雷达兵　B 激进分子
C 恐怖分子　D 罪犯

[翻　译] 激进分子就是不讲实际的人。

[分　析] rad + ical
根 + 形容词尾 → 根本的, 完全的, 激进的,激进分子

[词义扩展] 【数】根的
a radical expression 根式

[大头例句] I don't see how anything short of the most radical of changes can give this economy the jolt it needs to start growing. 我看缺乏最根本变化的事物是无法产生经济增长所需的震撼的。

radius *n.* /ˈreidjəs/

They searched within a *radius* of one mile from the school.

[猜一猜] A 仔细　B 雷达　C 半径　D 影响

[翻　译] 他们在学校周围1英里内寻找。

[大头巧记] 和**diameter**(直径),**perimeter**(周长)联系记忆。

remnant *n.* /ˈremnənt/

The *remnants* of last night's meal were still on the table.

[猜一猜] A 杯子　B 账单　C 请柬　D 残余

[翻　译] 昨天晚饭的剩饭还在桌子上。

[大头巧记] 和**remain**(残余)联系记忆。

[词义扩展] *adj.* 剩余的, 残留的。*some remnant feeling of disgrace* 某种残留的耻辱感。

[大头例句] Whereas only faint remnants of most of China's ancient city walls remain, the Great Wall has been thoroughly restored in many places. 尽管只有很少的一部分的中国古城墙遗址保存了下来,可是长城在很多地方已经被完全修复了。

simplify *vt.* /ˈsimplifai/

The English in this story has been *simplified* to make it easier to understand.

[猜一猜] A 简单化　B 统一　C 比喻　D 塑造

[翻　译] 这个故事里的英语被简写了,更容易理解。

[大头巧记] **simple**,简单 → **simplify**,简单化,单一化。

sponsor *n./v.* /ˈspɔnsə/

The exhibition was *sponsored* by the Society of Culture.

[猜一猜] A 赞助　B 领导　C 主办　D 协调

[翻　译] 这个展览会是由文化学会主办的。

[分　析] spons + or
约定 + …的人 → 主持约定的人, 主办(者),保证人

[大头巧记] 同根词:**responsor**,回答。re-回,**sponsor**,保证。

[大头例句] I asked my uncle to stand sponsor for me. 我请求叔父做我的保证人。

succinct *adj.* /səkˈsiŋkt/

Please give me a *succinct* summary of your points.

[猜一猜] A 准确的　B 标准的
C 成功地　D 简明的

[翻　译] 请简要总结你的观点。

[分　析] suc + cinct
下面 + 束起 → 把衣服束起来,利落地干活 → 紧身的,简明的

/si'metrical/ same meter
symmetrical adj 对称的,匀称的

symmetry *n.* /ˈsimitri/ Same metre

The *symmetry* of her features is striking.

[猜一猜] A 爱好 B 典型 C 匀称 D 敏锐
[翻 译] 她五官端正,给人留下深刻的印象。
[分 析] sym + metry
相同的 + 尺寸 → 对称,匀称

systematic *adj.* /sistiˈmætik/

She is very *systematic* in everything she does.

[猜一猜] A 严格的 B 吹毛求疵的
C 系统化的 D 偏见的
[翻 译] 她做任何事都井井有条。
[分 析] system + atic
系统 + …化 → 系统化的,体系的
[大头例句] The way they've collected their data is not very systematic. 他们收集数据的方法不是很系统化。

习题:在下面的空格中填写本单元的单词。

1. He bowed to the lady in a ________ manner.
2. Two ________ of water will be enough for the roses in the garden.
3. Care will also be taken to ________ the buildings with surrounding architecture.
4. The way they've collected their data is not very ________.
5. The ________ of her features are striking.
6. Whereas only faint ________ of most of China's ancient city walls remain, the Great Wall has been thoroughly restored in many places.
7. The English in this story has been ________ to make it easier to understand.
8. The exhibition was ________ by the Society of Culture.
9. I don't see how anything short of the most ________ of changes can give this economy the jolt it needs to start growing.
10. They searched within a ________ of one mile from the school.
11. Please give me a ________ summary of your points.
12. His suggestions may be seen as an ________ criticism of government policy.
13. We're paying for the "colour telly" by monthly ________.
14. The lid of the suitcase had a broken ________, so it wouldn't open easily.

Day 37

arduous *adj.* /ˈɑːdjuəs/

The work there is ***arduous*** and the hours are long.

[猜一猜]A 费力的 B 枯燥的 C 闲适的 D 有趣的

[翻 译]那里的工作很费力,工作时间也很长。

[分 析]ard + uous
燃烧 + 多…的 → 很多热,流汗的 → 费力的

[词义扩展]*adj.* ①辛勤的,努力的 *an arduous student* 勤奋的学生 ②险峻的

[大头例句]Preparing for overseas study is arduous work. 为出国学习做准备是一件艰苦的工作。

buckle *n./v.* /ˈbʌkl/

Wells finally ***buckled*** under the excessive pressure from the job.

[猜一猜]A 通过 B 任职 C 发展 D 屈服

[翻 译]韦尔斯最终还是被工作的过度压力压垮了。

[大头巧记]用**bucket(桶)**使某物弯曲,屈服。

[词义扩展]*vt.&vi.* 用扣扣住;弯曲,变形;专心做事 *n.* 带扣,扣形装饰物;弯曲,皱纹

[大头例句]I found it hard to buckle down to write with such a cute girl opposite me. 有这样一个可爱的女孩在我的对面,我发现很难专心写作。

dilemma *n.* /diˈlemə/

The ideas of how to help their company get out of their ***dilemma*** occupied the proscenium of his mind.

[猜一猜]A 官司 B 困境 C 误解 D 毁誉

[翻 译]他首先想的是怎样帮助他们的公司走出困境。

[分 析]di + lemma
两个 + 命题 → 在两个命题之间徘徊 → 陷入两难的境地,困境,进退维谷

[词义扩展]【逻】双关论法,两端论法
energy dilemma 能源危机

endeavour *n.* /inˈdevə/

We have ***endeavoured*** to make the vehicle environmentally friendly.

[猜一猜]A 尽力 B 设法 C 不考虑 D 永久

[翻 译]我们已尽力使这辆车不污染环境。

[分 析]en + deavour
在…里面 + 职责 → 负担某职责 → 尽力,竭力

[大头巧记]词形记忆:词头是end,词尾是our,end our,结束了我们的精力(v-vigour),竭力,尽力。

[词义扩展]*n.* 努力
The business was built up largely through the endeavours of his mother. 他生意的建立很大程度上是由于他母亲的努力。

dim *adj.* /dim/

We have no reason to take a ***dim*** view of our prospects in our careers.

[猜一猜]A 彷徨 B 光明 C 愤怒 D 悲观

[翻 译]我们没有理由对我们事业的前景持悲观态度。

[词义扩展]*adj.* 昏暗的;模糊的 *a dim light* 昏暗的光线
v. 使模糊,使昏暗 *n.* 停车灯

[大头例句]The theatre lights dimmed and the show began. 剧院的灯光变暗,演出开始了。

fatigue *n./v.* /fəˈtiːg/

A child's sleep problems cause parents ***fatigue*** and unnecessary guilt.

[猜一猜]A 担心 B 疲惫 C 恼火 D 无助

[翻 译]孩子睡眠的问题让父母感到疲惫和不必要的内疚。

[大头巧记]fat,胖人很容易**劳累(fatigue)**。

[词义扩展]*vt.* 使疲劳 *vi.* 疲劳 *n.* 疲劳,困乏
suffer from fatigue 感到疲劳

[大头例句] Too many requests for aid can cause compassion fatigue. 总是要求帮助，就会让人产生对同情心的疲惫感。

formidable *adj.* /ˈfɔːmidəbl/

They faced *formidable* difficulties in their attempt to reach the mountain summit.

[猜一猜] A 难以应付的　B 各种各样的　C 预计中的　D 计划外的

[翻　译] 他们在试图登上山顶时遇到了难以克服的困难。

[大头巧记] **formic(蚂蚁的)**，成群结队的蚂蚁来袭 → 可怕的，令人敬畏的，难以应付的。

[词义扩展] *adj.* 不可思议的，丰富的，强有力的

[大头例句] Though a true hero, he was also a thorough-going bureaucrat and politician: a formidable combination. 虽然他是一个真正的英雄，但他也是一个十足的官僚和政治家，一个不可思议的混合体。

harsh *adj.* /hɑːʃ/

I can hardly endure this *harsh* voice.

[猜一猜] A 甜蜜的　B 恐怖的　C 刺耳的　D 庸俗的

[翻　译] 我简直忍耐不了这种刺耳的声音。

[词义扩展] *adj.* 粗糙的，荒芜的，苛刻的，刺目的 *the harsh environment of the desert* 沙漠地与荒芜的环境

[大头例句] Harsh words were spoken in the dressing room after the match. 比赛后的更衣室里有人说了很苛刻的话。

misery *n.* /ˈmizəri/

It truly is a wonderful use of time to attempt to alleviate the *misery* of others.

[猜一猜] A 负担　B 痛苦　C 迷惑　D 要求

[翻　译] 尝试去减轻别人的痛苦确实是对时间的极好利用。

[大头巧记] **miser(吝啬鬼)**，吝啬鬼的生活很痛苦(**misery**)。

[大头例句] Children are living in misery, without housing, school, or clinics. 孩子们生活在痛苦之中，没有住处，没有学校，也没有诊所。

moist *adj.* /mɔist/

These plants do best in fertile, *moist* soil.

[猜一猜] A 肥沃的　B 热带的　C 温带的　D 潮湿的

[翻　译] 这种植物最适合在肥沃而潮湿的土壤中生长。

[大头巧记] most中间插入"i"-ice，大多数的冰都潮湿(**moist**)。

[大头例句] These clothes are still too moist to fold; I don't want them to develop mildew before they have fully dried. 这些衣服由于太湿还不能折叠，在他们完全干透之前我不想他们发霉。

muscular *adj.* /ˈmʌskjulə/

The player's big and *muscular*.

[猜一猜] A 灵活的　B 肌肉发达的　C 经验丰富的　D 谦虚的

[翻　译] 这个运动员长得魁梧强壮。

[大头巧记] **muscle**，肌肉；**muscular**，肌肉发达的。

[大头例句] A body with a high degree of muscular tone may be heavier but appear slimmer than another body with a higher concentration of fat. 肌肉高度发达的身体可能比脂肪度高的身体重点儿，但看上去更瘦点儿。

nautical *adj.* /ˈnɔːtikəl/

A *nautical* almanac gives information about the sun, moon, tides, etc.

[猜一猜] A 气象的　B 航海的　C 年度的　D 综合的

[翻　译] 航海年历中提供关于日、月、潮汐等信息。

[分　析] naut + ical
船 + 形容词尾 → 船员的，航海的

[大头例句] Thanks to his nautical training as a young sailor, in his older years, the man enjoyed sailing as one of his favorite hobbies. 由于年轻做海员时受过航海训练，在年龄稍长的时候，航海成了这个人的爱好之一。

plateau *n.* /ˈplætəu/

The recent boom in mobile phone sales seems to have reached a *plateau*.

[猜一猜]A 高潮 B 低谷 C 危机 D 平稳

[翻 译]最近在手机销售方面的繁荣似乎开始进入平稳时期。

[分 析]plat + eau

平的 + 词尾 → 高地,高原,平稳状态。

[大头巧记]**plate,盘子 → plateau**,像盘子一样平的状态,**平稳状态**。

plea *n.* /pliː/

The boy's parents have made an emotional *plea* for him to come home.

[猜一猜]A 错误 B 协调 C 帮助 D 恳求

[翻 译]这个男孩的父母充满感激地恳求他到家里来。

[大头巧记]**please,请;plea,恳求**。

[词义扩展]*n.* 托词,借口,【律】辩解。

[习语记忆]**the Court of Common Pleas** (英国的)高等民事法庭。

[大头例句]By entering a plea of guilty as opposed to innocent, some defendants can significantly lessen the sentence they receive. 一些被告者,通过递交服罪书,而不是抗辩无罪,其受到的判罚可能被大大减少。

relief *n.* /riˈliːf/

I felt great *relief* when I heard I had passed the examination.

[猜一猜]A 轻松 B 悲伤 C 好笑 D 情绪低沉

[翻 译]听说自己已经通过了考试,我感到轻松多了。

[大头巧记]**relieve *vt.* 减轻;relief *n.* 减轻,免除,救济,放松**。

[大头例句]The United Nations recently gave over $10 million to help bring relief to the people of Brazil in the wake of their devastating earthquake. 联合国最近拨出一千万美金用来帮助救济刚刚遭受毁灭性地震袭击的巴西人民。

stiff *adj.* /stif/

It was a *stiff* climb to the top of the hill.

[猜一猜]A 危险的 B 费劲的 C 丰富的 D 漫长的

[翻 译]爬到山顶上去是很费劲的。

[词义扩展]*adj.* 硬的,僵直的,拘谨的

stiff muscles 僵直的肌肉

[大头例句]He replied in a stiff, ironic voice. 他用僵硬而充满讽刺的声音回答了问题。

suicide *n.* /ˈsjuːisaid/

Suicide attempts by young men in this age group have tripled.

[猜一猜]A 犯罪 B 自杀 C 暴力 D 痛苦

[翻 译]这个年龄段的年轻人企图自杀的增加了三倍。

[分 析]sui + cide

自己 + 切 → 切自己 → 自杀,自毁

[大头例句]Gill committed suicide last year after losing her job. 去年,吉尔在失业后自杀了。

toil *n./v.* /tɔil/

A bit of the blackest and coarsest bread is the sole recompense and the sole profit attaching to so arduous a *toil*.

[猜一猜]A 辛苦 B 投入 C 土地 D 训诫

[翻 译]一小块黑得不能再黑,粗糙得不能再粗糙的面包是这样一种艰苦的工作的惟一的补偿和惟一的收益。

[大头巧记]t(oss) oil,搅拌油是一件辛苦的活。另:**foil,阻挠;coil,卷绕;roil,搅拌**。

[词义扩展]*vt.* 苦干,跋涉

toil at a task 辛勤工作

[大头例句]I've been toiling away at this essay all weekend. 我整个周末都在忙这篇文章。

torment *n./v.* /ˈtɔːment/

He suffered *torments* from his aching teeth.

[猜一猜]A 失业 B 休假 C 责备 D 疼痛

[翻 译]他牙痛得难受。

[分　析]tor　+ ment
扭曲 + …的状态 → 痛苦,苦恼,疼痛
[大头巧记]和torture联合记忆。torment指精神上处于较长期的痛苦或烦恼的状态下,torture指精神上或身体上所受到的撕裂般的巨大痛苦。
[大头例句]The older boys would torment him whenever they had the chance. 那些大点的孩子一有机会就折磨他。

torture n./vt. /ˈtɔːtʃə/

I couldn't bear the *torture* of waiting in suspense any more.

[猜一猜]A 无聊　B 闷热　C 模糊　D 煎熬
[翻　译]我再也忍受不了在不知结果中等待的痛苦了。
[分　析]tor　+ ture
扭打 + 词尾 → 折磨,扭打
[大头例句]Political opponents of the regime may be tortured. 政府的政治对手可能会被摧残。

shelter n./v. /ˈʃeltə/

We built a temporary *shelter* out of branches.

[猜一猜]A 居住　B 架子　C 掩蔽　D 凉亭
[翻　译]我们用树枝建了一个临时掩体。
[大头巧记]shelf,架子;shelter,架子构成的掩体。
[词义扩展]v. 掩蔽,躲避
to shelter under a tree 避在树下
[习语记忆]**fly to sb. for shelter**
逃进某人家里避难
[大头例句]Make sure to shelter your eyes from the sun during the solar eclipse this weekend: the rays will be so intense that they could potentially damage your eyes. 在本周末的日食时,一定要保护好你的眼睛:届时太阳的光线会很强,可能对你的眼睛造成伤害。

superstition n. /ˌsjuːpəˈstiʃən/

A common *superstition* considers it bad luck to sleep in a room numbered 13.

[猜一猜]A 超能力　B 迷信　C 默契　D 神秘
[翻　译](西方)一种普遍的迷信认为在13号房间睡觉是不吉利的。
[分　析]super + stition
超　+ 站→超过人能理解的东西→迷信。
[大头例句]He believes the old superstition that walking under a ladder is unlucky. 他相信在梯子下走路会不幸的老迷信。

习题:在下面的空格中填写本单元的单词。

1. Children are living in __________, without housing, school, or clinics.
2. A common __________ considers it bad luck to sleep in a room numbered 13.
3. The work there is __________ and the hours are long.
4. We have no reason to take a __________ view of our prospects in our career.
5. A child's sleep problems cause parents __________ and unnecessary guilt.
6. A body with a high degree of __________ tone may be heavier but appear slimmer than another body with a higher concentration of fat.
7. The United Nations recently gave over $10 million to help bring __________ to the people of Brazil in the wake of their devastating earthquake.
8. It was a __________ climb to the top of the hill.
9. Gill committed __________ last year after losing her job.
10. A bit of the blackest and coarsest bread is the sole recompense and the sole profit attaching to so arduous a __________.

11. Make sure to __________ your eyes from the sun during the solar eclipse this weekend: the rays will be so intense that they could potentially damage your eyes.
12. The older boys would __________ him whenever they had the chance.
13. I found it hard to __________ down to write with such a cute girl opposite me.
14. We have __________ to make the vehicle environmentally friendly.
15. The ideas of how to help their company get out of their __________ occupied the proscenium of his mind.
16. Though a true hero, he was also a thoroughgoing bureaucrat and politician: a __________ combination.
17. These clothes are still too __________ to fold; I don't want them to develop mildew before they have fully dried.
18. __________ words were spoken in the dressing room after the match.
19. Thanks to his __________ training as a young sailor, in his older years, the man enjoyed sailing as one of his favorite hobbies.
20. The recent boom in mobile phone sales seems to have reached a __________.
21. The boy's parents have made an emotional __________ for him to come home.
22. I couldn't bear the __________ of waiting in suspense any more.

Note 前事不忘后事之师 *Remember the past and it will guide your future.*

Day 38

accede *v.* /ækˈsiːd/

The prince *acceded* to the throne when the king died.

[猜一猜]A 理解 B 继承 C 调解 D 加强

[翻 译]国王死后,王子继承了王位。

[分 析] ac + cede

ac-=ad-,to 朝,向 + to go → 走向…,就职,继承

[词义扩展] *v.* ①同意;应允 *We acceded to his request.* 我们同意他的请求。②就职 *accede to the throne* 就任国王 ③参加,加入 *Our government acceded to the treaty.* 我国政府加入了该条约。

[联 想] **accession** *n.* 就任,就职,加入 *vt.* 把(新书等)编入目录

accession to an estate 继承产业

accession to a party 加入一个党派

The librarian had these new books promptly accessioned. 图书馆员迅速地把这些新书登记于图书目录。

accessional *adj.* 附加的

accessory *adj./n.* 附件

[大头例句] China has already acceded to the WTO. 中国已经加入了世贸组织。

acclaim *n.* /əˈkleim/

He was *acclaimed* as the champion.

[猜一猜]A 欢呼 B 诅咒 C 侮辱 D 降临

[翻 译]他在欢呼声中被承认获得了冠军。

[分 析]ac + claim

to 朝,向 + to shout → 向…喊叫,引申为欢呼,承认

[大头巧记] **claim** *n.* 要求,主张 acc(ept) (the) claim,接受主张,表示承认。

[联 想] **applaud**,鼓掌接受;**approve**,赞成,通过;**acclamation** *n.* 欢呼,喝彩

[词义扩展] *v.* ①欢呼着拥戴;欢呼着同意 *Penicillin was acclaimed as the most important discovery during the 1940's.* 青霉素曾被公认是20世纪40年代最重大的发现。②向…欢呼,喝彩,称赞

n. [诗]喝彩,欢呼,称赞 *He deserves the acclaim he has received.* 他得到的称赞是受之无愧的。

[大头例句] The fairy is dancing in the acclaim. 仙女般美丽的姑娘在称赞声中跳舞。

accolade *n.* /ˌækəˈleid/

"His works are invariably *accoladed* as definitive even as they sparkle and spark"—(Malcolm S. Forbes)

[猜一猜]A 荣誉 B 倡导 C 合作 D 习惯

[翻 译]"当他的作品大放光彩时,一直被放在举足轻重的地位"(马尔科姆·S·福布斯)

[分 析] ac + colade

在…上边 + collum, collar 颈 → 在脖子上面,表示拥抱。原来是指骑士授予时所给予的拥抱,这事实可解释 accolace 一词带"授予骑士称号的典礼"的意义。此处引申为给某物美誉。

[词义扩展] *n.* 表扬;推崇 *The play received accolades from the press.* 这部戏受到报纸的称赞。

[大头例句] We are immensely proud of this latest accolade. 对这最近的赞美我们无比的自豪。

acquiesce *vi.* /ˌækwiˈes/

The president *acquiesced* in his resignation.

[猜一猜]A 拒绝 B 公认 C 批评 D 默许

[翻 译]总统默许了他的辞职。

[分 析]ac + quiesce

to + to rest,休息 → 去休息,平息某事,默许,勉强同意

[大头巧记] 谐音:ac(cept), qui(亏), esce(yes)接受一点亏,仍然要说yes,勉强同意。

[近义词] **assent**; **comply**; **concur**; **consent**;

submit; succumb

[大头例句] She is begging her parents to acquiesce in their marriage. 她正在乞求她的父母答应他们的婚事。

acknowledge *vt.* /əkˈnɔlidʒ/

I *acknowledge* the truth of your statement.

[猜一猜] A 反对 B 揭露 C 附和 D 承认

[翻 译] 我承认你说的都是事实。

[分 析] ac + know + ledge

to + to know 确信 + 名词词尾 → 对…的确认，此处活用为动词 → 承认

[大头巧记] ac(cept the) knowledge，接受某一知识，认识 → 承认。

[近义词] **accept; admit; answer; concede; grant; recognize**

[反义词] **deny; disregard; ignore**

[词义扩展] *v.* ①公认为；认为 *He was acknowledged to be the best player.* 他被公认为是最佳选手。②对…表示感谢，答谢，致谢 *to acknowledge a help* 答谢所受到的帮助 ③表明已收到 *to acknowledge his gift* 表明已收到他的礼物

[大头例句] It is universally acknowledged that you are hen-hearted before your wife. 地球人都知道，你在老婆面前胆小如鼠。

affirmative *adj.* /əˈfəːmətiv/

Different from the other people, she has an *affirmative* outlook for the football team's future.

[猜一猜] A 乐观的 B 悲观的 C 具体的 D 总体的

[翻 译] 和别人不同的是，她对球队的未来展望还是乐观的。

[分 析] affirm + ative

断言，肯定 + 形容词词尾 → 肯定的，乐观的

[词义扩展] *adj.* 表示同意或赞成的 *an affirmative vote.* 赞成票 *n.* 辩论中的正方 *Her team will speak for the affirmative.* 她所在的队伍将作为正方辩护。

[大头例句] Two negatives make an affirmative. 负负得正。

adverse *adj.* /ˈædvəːs/

Adverse working conditions compelled him finally to leave that company.

[猜一猜] A 悠闲 B 多变 C 不良 D 朴素

[翻 译] 不良的工作环境迫使他最终离开了那家公司。

[分 析] ad + verse

朝向 + to turn → 转向，相反面 → 引申为不利的，不良的

[联 想] **adversary** ***n.*** **敌手，对手 adversely** ***adv.*** **不利地，相反地 adversity** ***n.*** **逆境，不幸**

[词义扩展] *adj.* 方向相反的，敌对的；不利的，有害的 *adverse wind* 逆风；*adverse fortune* 恶运；*an adverse decision* 相反的决定

[大头例句] When adverse fortune is coming, strong will is the weapon you can use to struggle. 当恶运到来的时候，坚强的意志是你斗争的武器。

comply *vi.* /kəmˈplai/

All citizens must *comply* with the law.

[猜一猜] A 学习 B 尊重 C 遵守 D 使用

[翻 译] 所有的市民都必须遵守法律。

[分 析] com + ply

加强语气 + 满足 → 满足对方的要求 → 顺从，答应，遵守

[大头例句] If you don't comply you could face a penalty of 100 pounds. 如果你不服从的话，你将面临100英镑的罚款。

compliment *n.* /ˈkɔmplimənt/

The new government received many *compliments* on its new immigration policy.

[猜一猜] A 指责 B 赞扬 C 困难 D 反馈

[翻 译] 新政府的新移民政策收到一片赞扬之声。

[分 析] com + pli + ment

加强语气 + 满足 + 名词词尾 → 使对方很满足的东西 → 称赞，问候

[词义扩展] *vt.* 恭维，称赞 *David complimented Bob on the birth of his son.* 大卫祝贺鲍勃儿子的出生。

consensus *n.* /kən'sensəs/

The voters' *consensus* was that the measure should be adopted.

[猜一猜]A 兴奋 B 意志 C 大多数意见 D 理智

[翻 译]大多数选民的意见是采取这个措施。

[分 析]con + sens + us
共同 + 感觉 + 词尾 → 感觉一致 → 一致同意,多数人意见,舆论

[大头例句]It will be difficult to reach any sort of consensus on this issue. 在这个问题上将很难达成任何一种共识。

coincide *vi.* /kəuin'said/

My birthday *coincides* with hers.

[猜一猜]A 接近 B 庆祝 C 甜蜜 D 一致

[翻 译]我的生日和她的恰好一样。

[分 析]co + incide
相同,一起 + 发生 → 一起发生的

[大头巧记]拆:coin-cide → coin side, 硬币一面,都是一致的。

[大头例句]The members of the committee do not coincide in opinion. 委员们的意见不一致。

contradict *vt.* /kɔntrə'dikt/

Your actions *contradict* your declared moral principles.

[猜一猜]A 符合 B 规定 C 阐明 D 同…抵触

[翻 译]你的行为违背了你宣称的道德准则。

[分 析]contra + dict
反 + 说话 → 反说,反驳,同…矛盾,同…抵触

[大头巧记]和**contradiction(反驳,矛盾),contradictory(互相矛盾的)**联合记忆。

[大头例句]Her account of the accident contradicts that of the other driver. 他对于这次事故的说明和另一名司机相抵触。

controversy *n.* /'kɔntrəvəːsi/

The election ended in *controversy*, with allegations of widespread vote-rigging.

[猜一猜]A 丑闻 B 矛盾 C 辨别 D 争论

[翻 译]选举最终以争论告终,托词是广泛分布的选举设备。

[分 析]contro + vers + y
反 + 转 + 名词词尾 → 反驳,争论,辩论。

[习语记忆]**beyond/out of controversy** 无可争议

[大头例句]This contract has given rise to much controversy. 这个合同引起了很多争议。

conversely *adv.* /kən'vəːsli/

Some wrong answers were marked right and, *conversely*, some right answers had been rejected.

[猜一猜]A 同时 B 相反地
C 本质对立 D 特别地

[翻 译]一些错误的答案被评为对,相反,一些正确的答案却被判为错误。

[分 析]con + verse + ly
完全 + 转 + 副词词尾 → 倒,逆,相反地

[大头例句]Fourth graders in the school are not allowed to climb trees outside during recess; conversely, fifth graders can be seen hanging by the limbs like monkeys. 四年级的学生不可以在课间休息的时候爬外面的树,与之相反,却可以看到五年级的学生像猴子似地挂在树枝上。

endorse *v.* /in'dɔːs/

The application was *endorsed* by the governers' board.

[猜一猜]A 拒绝 B 通过 C 审查 D寄往

[翻 译]申请书已由董事会批准。

[分 析]en + dorse
在…上 + 背面 → 在(支票)背面签字,批准,通过。

[大头巧记]谐音:in doors,在门里面,放行通过,批准。

[词义扩展]*v.* [英]在(驾驶员执照)上注明违章录

[大头例句]All endorsed the treaty is critically important to achieve peace. 所有方面都认可这个协议对于和平的获得起到很重要的作用。

deem *v.* /diːm/

He *deemed* it his duty to help the women who were suffering from abuse.

[猜一猜]A 认为　　B 承担
　　C 完成　　D 致力于

[翻　译]他认为去帮助那些受虐待女性是他的责任。

[大头巧记]**seem**，看起来;d, 谐"定" → **deem**，看起来决心已定：主张，断定，认为。

[词义扩展]*vi.* 想，相信

[大头例句]The institute senate deemed his academic level high. 大学评议会对他的学术水平给予高度的评价。

dispute *v./n.* /disˈpjuːt/

The members of the town coucil *disputed* for hours about whether to build a new museum.

[猜一猜]A 准备　B 研究　C 争论　D 比较

[翻　译]市议会的议员们就是否要新建一所博物馆辩论了好几个小时。

[分　析]dis + pute
相反的 + 考虑，计划 → 争论，辩论，竞争

[词义扩展]*v.* 反驳，驳斥；怀疑，阻止 *n.* 争论，辩论 *The lawyer disputed the truth of the witness's statement.* 律师对证人的话的真实性提出了怀疑。

[大头例句]Monroe's behaviour eventually led to a dispute with the referee. 门罗的行为最终引起了裁判的反对。

denial *n.* /diˈnaiəl/

The *denial* of human rights to the mass of the population is the essence of his speech.

[猜一猜]A 呼唤　B 维护　C 不给　D 启动

[翻　译]他的讲话的实质就是不给群众以人权。

[大头巧记]它源于**deny**，否定，拒绝，不给。

[大头例句]Her denial of my passion hurt my feelings. 她对我的热情的拒绝伤害了我的感情。

discrepancy *n.* /disˈkrepənsi/

There was a *discrepancy* in the two reports of the accident.

[猜一猜]A 疏忽　　B 不一致的地方
　　C 错误　　D 共同点

[翻　译]该事件的两个报告有不一致之处。

[分　析]dis + crep + ancy
分开 + 破裂 + 名词词尾 → 有破裂，差异，矛盾，不同

[词义扩展]*n.* 偏差，误差，失调，亏损 *a discrepancy between estimated and actual spending* 预算和实际花销间的误差

[大头例句]How do you explain these discrepancies in the accounts? 你怎样解释这些账目上的不符？

grant *vt.* /grɑːnt/

I *grant* the genius of your plan, but you still will not find backers.

[猜一猜]A 赞赏　B 明白　C 承认　D 不同意

[翻　译]我承认你的计划有创意，但你还是不会找到支持者。

[大头巧记]**grand**，盛大的，重要的，对于重要的事实我们要承认(**grant**)。

[词义扩展]*vt.* 准予，准许 *n.* 补助金，赠款，津贴 *n./v.* 赠与，给予

[大头例句]The UK embassy urged the government to grant amnesty to all political prisoners. 英国大使馆力劝政府给予所有政治犯以特赦。

feud *n./vi.* /fjuːd/

The *feud* between these two families has lasted for generations.

[猜一猜]A 联姻　B 合作　C 交往　D 不和

[翻　译]这两家的不和已经持续了好几代了。

[词义扩展]*vi./n.* 仇视，争执，争斗

[大头例句]He feuds with most of his neighbours. 他和大多数的邻居经常发生争吵。

opponent *adj./n.* /ə'pəunənt/

The president's former adviser is now one of his most outspoken *opponents*.

[猜一猜] A 军事　B 逃兵　C 组织者　D 对手

[翻　译] 该总统以前的顾问现在是他最直言不讳的对手。

[分　析] op + pon + ent

对 + 放 + …人 → 对手，对立的

[大头例句] She beat her opponent by three sets to zero. 她以三比零击败对手。

oppose *v.* /ə'pəuz/

We are firmly *opposed* to the practice of power politics between nations.

[猜一猜] A 支持　B 反对　C 委婉　D 赞扬

[翻　译] 我们坚决反对在国与国之间实行强权政治。

[分　析] op + pose

对 + 放 → 对着放，放对，抗争。

[习语记忆] **oppose M against N** 把M与N相对照

[大头例句] Congress is continuing to oppose the President's healthcare budget. 议会不断反对总统的医疗预算。

prejudice *n.* /'predʒudis/

Jackson apologized, saying the song was supposed to illustrate the evils of *prejudice*.

[猜一猜] A 傲慢　B 贫困　C 痛苦　D 偏见

[翻　译] 杰克逊道歉说道，这首歌本来是用来阐明偏见的罪恶的。

[分　析] pre + judice

先于 + 判断 → 见到之前先行判断 → 偏见

[词义扩展] *n.* 损害，伤害　*without prejudice* 无害于，不影响　*v.* 使有成见

[大头例句] This teacher's prejudice against non-white students is completely unacceptable, and must result in her termination from this university's faculty. 该老师对于有色人种学生的偏见是不能接受的，她必须离开这所大学。

recommendation *n.* /ˌrekəmen'deiʃən/

We went to that Indian restaurant on their *recommendation*.

[猜一猜] A 例子　B 邀请　C 接触　D 推荐

[翻　译] 在他们的推荐下，我们去了那家印度餐馆。

[分　析] re + commend + ation

一再 + 称赞 + 名词词尾 → 一再称赞 → 推荐，推荐信

[大头例句] I've been to every Chinese restaurant in this city and cannot find a single one that serves delicious tofu; could you give me your recommendation for one? 这个城市里的所有中国餐馆我都去过了，可就是找不到一家豆腐做得好吃的，你能给我推荐一个吗？

sympathetic *adj.* /simpə'θetik/

When I told her why I was worried she was very *sympathetic*.

[猜一猜] A 担心的　B 紧张的　C 平静的　D 同情的

[翻　译] 当我告诉她我着急的原因时，她很同情。

[分　析] sym + pathe + tic

相同 + 感情 + 形容词尾 → 共同感情的 → 同情的

[词义扩展] *adj.* 交感的，共鸣的
sympathetic vibrations 共振

[大头例句] Paul's great if you need a sympathetic ear or advice. 如果你需要一个人去倾诉或者给你建议，保罗是个非常好的选择。

unanimous *adj.* /juː'næniməs/

The whole school was *unanimous* in its approval of the headmaster's plan.

[猜一猜] A 不可思议的　B 接近的　C 意见一致的　D 费力的

[翻　译] 全校一致通过了校长的计划。

[分　析] un(i) + anim + ous

一 + 思想 + 形容词尾 → 思想一致的，无异议的

[大头例句] All 15 member states were unanimous in approving the deal. 全部15个成员国一致同意通过该决议。

uphold *vt.* /ʌpˈhəuld/

The kid *upheld* the banner proudly.

[猜一猜] A 举起 B 举行 C 弄污 D 卖弄

[翻 译] 这个孩子骄傲地把条幅高高举起。

[大头巧记] up hold → hold up 举起，支持，赞成。另：联系**abrogate**(废除)，**subvert**(推翻)记忆。

[大头例句] They want to uphold traditional family values. 他们决定支撑起传统的价值观念。

习题：在下面的空格中填写本单元的单词。

1. When __________ fortune coming, strong will is the weapon you can use to struggle.
2. Her account of the accident __________ that of the other driver.
3. They want to __________ traditional family values.
4. The prince __________ to the throne when the king died.
5. The members of the committee do not __________ in opinion.
6. If you don't __________ you could face a penalty of 100 pounds.
7. The new government received many __________ on its new immigration policy.
8. It will be difficult to reach any sort of ______on this issue.
9. All __________ the treaty is critically important to achieve peace.
10. Some wrong answers were marked right and, __________, some right answers had been rejected.
11. How do you explain these __________ in the accounts?
12. The __________ between these two families has lasted for generations.
13. When I told her why I was worried, she was very __________.
14. I've been to every Chinese restaurant in this city and cannot find a single one that serves delicious tofu; could you give me your __________for one?
15. This teacher's __________ against non-white students is completely unacceptable, and must result in her termination from this university's faculty.
16. Congress is continuing to __________ the President's healthcare budget.
17. The members of the town coucil __________ for hours about whether to build a new museum.
18. The __________ of human rights to the mass of the population is the essence of his speech.
19. He __________ it his duty to help the women who were suffering from abuse.
20. The UK embassy urged the government to __________ amnesty to all political prisoners.
21. The election ended in __________, with allegations of widespread vote-rigging.
22. Penicillin was __________ as the most important discovery during the 1940's.
23. Different from the other people, she has an __________outlook for the football team's future.
24. She is begging her parents to __________ in their marriage.

25. It is universally ________ that you are hen-hearted before your wife.
26. "His works are invariably ________ as definitive even as they sparkle and spark". (Malcolm S. Forbes)
27. The president's former adviser is now one of his most outspoken ________.
28. The whole school was ________ in its approval of the head-master's plan.

Note 前事不忘后事之师 *Remember the past and it will guide your future.*

Day 39

aforementioned

adj. /əˈfɔːˌmenʃənd/

The *aforementioned* problems are very urgent to be solved.

[猜一猜] A 以下的　B 以上的　C 外事的　D 历史上的

[翻　译] 以上提到的问题是急需解决的。

[分　析] afore + mentioned
=before，在…前方 + 提及，说起 → 前面提到的

relevant *adj.* /ˈrelivənt/

The scientist corresponds with colleagues in order to learn about matters *relevant* to her own research.

[猜一猜] A 决定　B 影响　C 相关　D 献身

[翻　译] 那个科学家和同事们相互通信，以了解和她自己的研究有关的事。

[分　析] re + lev + ant
重新 + 举出 + 词尾 → 相关的，中肯的

[大头例句] It annoys me when my classmates ask questions that are not even a little bit relevant to the professor's topic, thus distracting the professor's train of thought and making her task of teaching much more difficult. 我很讨厌那些学生问及与教授的主题风马牛不相及的问题，因为他们打乱了老师的思路，让老师的教学任务变得更难。

regarding *prep.* /riˈɡɑːdiŋ/

I wrote a letter *regarding* my daughter's school examinations.

[猜一猜] A 称赞　B 咨询　C 关于　D 减少

[翻　译] 我写了一封关于我女儿学校考试的信。

[大头巧记] **regard**，关心 → **regarding** *prep.* 关于

[大头例句] Political leaders usually prefer to refrain from comments regarding the ideology issue as it is so politically charged. 很多政客通常更喜欢避免对有关意识形态的问题发表评论，因为它政治争论性很强。

resemblance *n.* /riˈzembləns/

= similarity

The *resemblance* between the twins is striking.

[猜一猜] A 相同之处　B 心灵感应　C 友情　D 关怀

[翻　译] 双胞胎间的相同之处是很明显的。

[分　析] re + sembl + ance
再次 + 相同 + 名词词尾 → 相似之处

[大头巧记] 注意他的动词形态：**resemble**。

[习语记忆] **bear a resemblance to** 与…相像

[大头例句] Though the baby's father is Chinese and his mother is British, he bears little resemblance to his father, having light hair and big blue eyes. 虽然孩子的父亲是中国人，母亲是英国人；但是孩子和父亲的相同点很少，有着浅色的头发和蓝色的眼睛。

resort *vi.* /riˈzɔːt/

The government *resorted* to censorship of the press.

[猜一猜] A 诉诸　B 倾向　C 徘徊　D 轻视

[翻　译] 政府以新闻审查制度为手段。

[分　析] re + sort
一再 + 出现 → 常去，求助，诉诸

[词义扩展] *n.* 胜地，常去之地，手段，凭借 *a health resort* 休养胜地；*to pass without resort to cheating* 不靠作弊获得通过

[习语记忆] **in the last resort** 作为最后的手段

scatter *v.* /ˈskætə/

The crowd *scattered* when the police came.

[猜一猜]A 散开 B 骚动 C 混乱 D 井井有条

[翻 译]警察一来人群就散开了。

[大头巧记]和**nucleate(集结)**联系记忆。

[大头例句]Our hopes and plans are scattered to the four winds. 我们的希望和计划全落空了。

segregate *v.* /ˈsegrigeit/

The army has decided not to *segregate* men and women during training.

[猜一猜]A 隔离 B 顾忌 C 比较 D 鼓励

[翻 译]军方决定在训练时不将男兵和女兵隔离开来。

[分 析]se + greg + ate

分开 + 团体 + 动词词尾 → 和团体分开 → 隔离

[大头巧记]词形记忆：两个"g"把三个"e"给隔离开了。另，联系**aggregate(集合)**记忆。

sequence *n.* /ˈsiːkwəns/

Could you describe the exact *sequence* of events that evening?

[猜一猜]A 情形 B 影响 C 顺序 D 处理方式

[翻 译]你能清楚地描述一下那天晚上事情发生的顺序吗？

[分 析]sequ + ence

跟随 + 名词词尾 → 顺序，序列

[大头例句]In order to complete this university's requirements, students must complete a sequence of math courses that includes algebra, geometry, and advanced calculus. 为了完成该大学的要求，学生们必须完成一系列的数学课程，包括代数，几何和高等微积分学。

solidarity *n.* /ˌsɔliˈdæriti/

The perennial conflict between national egoism and international *solidarity* becomes more and more visible.

[猜一猜]A 冲突 B 走私 C 互相怀疑 D 团结

[翻 译]国家利己主义和国际联合之间的长期冲突变得越来越明显。

[分 析]solid + arity

固体的 + 名词词尾 → 固体状态，团结

[大头例句]Without the solidarity of the British people behind him, Prime Minister Tony Blair will have a difficult time convincing the government to prepare for war. 没有背后英国人民的团结支持，汤尼·布莱尔首相将很难说服政府备战。

specific *adj.* /spiˈsifik/

The leaders met for the *specific* purpose of preserving the ceasefire.

[猜一猜]A 神圣的 B 遥不可及的 C 兴奋的 D 明确的

[翻 译]领导们会面的目的明确，就是要保持停火。

[分 析]speci + fic

看 + 使…得 → 让人看的 → 特殊的，明确的

[词义扩展]*n.* 特效药，细节 *I can't go into specifics at this time, but I can tell you that we have an agreement.* 现在我不能谈及细节，但是我能够告诉你们的是，我们已经达成了协议。

staff *n.* /stɑːf/

The department has a *staff* of 30.

[猜一猜]A 电脑 B 领导 C 全体员工 D 灯具

[翻 译]本部门有30名员工。

[词义扩展]*n.* 棒，支柱 *vt.* 充当职员

[习语记忆]**A staff is quickly found to beat a dog with.** 欲加之罪，何患无辞（打狗不愁找不到棍子）。

the staff of life 面包

Never lean on a broken staff. 破杖不可倚。

[大头例句]The refuge is staffed mainly by volunteers. 这个避难所里的大部分员工是志愿者。

subjective *adj.* /sʌbˈdʒektiv/

Subjective judgements are often wrong.

[猜一猜]A 偏激的 B 藻饰的 C 笨拙的 D 主观的

[翻 译]主观判断常常是错的。

[大头巧记] **subject**,主语;**subjective**,主观的,个人的。和**objective**(客观的)对比记忆。

[大头例句] The assessment of a student's work is often subjective.对于学生学习的评估经常比较主观。

super face

superficial *adj.* /sjuːpəˈfiʃəl/

The house suffered *superficial* damage from the flood.

[猜一猜] A 过分的 B 瞬间的 C 单侧的 D 表面的

[翻　译] 这栋房屋在洪水中表面受到了损害。

[分　析] super + fic + ial

在上面 + 做 + 形容词尾 → 只在上面做 → 表面的,肤浅的

[大头例句] She felt so sad to have such a weak-minded and superficial husband who seemed only interested in football. 她为自己有这样一个意志软弱而肤浅的丈夫伤心,他似乎只对足球感兴趣。

surpass *vt.* /səːˈpɑːs/

The latecomers *surpass* the early starters.

[猜一猜] A 逼近 B 超过 C 占领 D 反感

[翻　译] 后来者居上。

[分　析] sur + pass

超 + 路过 → 超过,胜过

[大头例句] You've really surpassed yourself this time! 这次你真是超常发挥了!

tactic *n.* /ˈtæktik/

The governor's *tactics* involved accusing his opponent of being to resign.

[猜一猜] A 危害 B 序幕 C 战略 D 心意

[翻　译] 该领导的战略包括谴责对手而让其辞职。

[分　析] tact + ci

机智 + 词尾 → 手段,战略

[词义扩展] *adj.* 依次排列的,规则的

[大头例句] Salesmen employ all sorts of clever tactics to try and persuade you. 销售者使用各种聪明的办法来试图说服你购买。

strategy
n.策略

tension *n./vt.* /ˈtenʃən/

The *tension* in the Middle East is building up again.

[猜一猜] A 紧张 B 恢复 C 衰退 D 震撼

[翻　译] 中东的形势又逐步紧张起来。

[大头巧记] **tense** ***adj.*** 紧张的
tension ***n.*** 紧张,拉近,压力; ***vt.*** 拉紧

[大头例句] In business there's always a tension between the needs of customers and shareholders. 在生意上,顾客和股东的需求之间经常有一种强烈对立的平衡关系。

tragedy *n.* /ˈtrædʒidi/

Their holiday ended in *tragedy* when their hotel caught fire.

[猜一猜] A 间断 B 悲剧 C 奋斗 D 逃跑

[翻　译] 他们住的旅馆着了火,他们的假日就以不幸而告终。

[大头巧记] 和**comedy**(喜剧)联系记忆。

[大头例句] It's a tragedy to see so much talent going to waste. 看到这么多的天赋被浪费真让人痛心。

uniform *n.* /ˈjuːnifɔːm/

The company asks all its employees to wear *uniforms*.

[猜一猜] A 徽章 B 证件 C 制服 D 化妆品

[翻　译] 公司要求所有雇员统一着装。

[分　析] uni + form

一 + 形式 → 统一的,均衡的,制服

[词义扩展] *v.* 使一样,提供制服
adj. 相同的

[大头例句] Most of the kids were wearing the standard student uniform of jeans and black T-shirts. 大多数孩子都穿着标准的校服——牛仔裤和黑色的体恤衫。

unify *vt.* /ˈjuːnifai/

They are trying to find a candidate who will *unify* all factions.

[猜一猜] A 抵消　　B 解释
C 负担　　D 统一

[翻　译] 他们在寻找一个可以统一所有势力的候选人。

[分　析] uni + fy
一 + 使…→ 统一,使成一体

[大头巧记] 与**partition**(分割,划分)联系记忆。

[大头例句] Spain was unified in the 16th century.16世纪时西班牙获得了统一。

习题:在下面的空格中填写本单元的单词。

1. The government __________ to censorship of the press.
2. Our hopes and plans are __________ to the four winds.
3. In order to complete this university's requirements, students must complete a __________ of math courses that included algebra, geometry, and advanced calculus.
4. The perennial conflict between national egoism and international __________ becomes more and more visible.
5. I can't go into __________ at this time, but I can tell you that we have an agreement.
6. They are trying to find a candidate who will __________ all factions.
7. In business there's always a __________ between the needs of customers and shareholders.
8. She felt so sad to have such a weak-minded and __________ husband who seemed only interested in football.
9. Most of the kids were wearing the standard student __________ of jeans and black T-shirts.
10. It's a __________ to see so much talent going to waste.
11. The __________ problems are very urgent to be solved.
12. Political leaders usually prefer to refrain from comments __________ the ideology issue as it is so politically charged.
13. The scientist corresponds with colleagues in order to learn about matters __________ to her own research.
14. Though the baby's father is Chinese and his mother is British, he bears little __________ to his father, having light hair and big blue eyes.
15. The army has decided not to __________ men and women during training.
16. The assessment of a student's work is often __________.
17. The department has a __________ of 30.
18. You've really __________ yourself this time!
19. Salesmen employ all sorts of clever __________ to try and persuade you.

Day 40

allegory n. 寓言

adamant adj. /ˈædəmənt/

He's so *adamant* that however hard I tried to persuade him to give in, he did not change his mind.

[猜一猜] A 呆板 B 固执 C 苦恼 D 平静

[翻 译] 不管我怎样劝他屈服，他就是固执己见。

[分 析] a + damant

at + 硬石头 → 像硬石头一样的坚硬，固执

[大头巧记] Adam，人名，ant，蚂蚁，无论别人怎么说，Adam都要和蚂蚁一起生活，当然很固执。（要注意adamant 的发音不等于Adam + ant）

[词义扩展] n.坚硬无比的东西；硬石 *will of adamant* 坚强的意志 *She became as rigid as adamant.* 她变得如顽石般的固执。

adj. 坚硬的；不可动摇的，坚决的

[大头例句] He is as adamant as a donkey. 他像驴一样倔。

agitate v. /ˈædʒiteit/

His fiery speech *agitated* the crowd at the party.

[猜一猜] A 激动 B 冒犯 C 征的同情 D 平息了

[翻 译] 他在聚会上热情洋溢的讲话让群众激动。

[词义扩展] *v.* 使不安；使焦虑 *He was agitated by the alarming news.* 他因为那令人吃惊的消息而焦虑不安。

vi. 煽动，鼓动 *agitate for a strike* 鼓动罢工

[大头例句] The flowers that my wife constantly received agitated me. 我的妻子不断地收到鲜花，这让我很不安。

allege vt. /əˈledʒ/

声称

The police *allege* that the man was murdered but they have given no proof.

[猜一猜] A 指控 B 声称 C 承认 D 回避

[翻 译] 警方声称这男子是被人谋杀的，但未提出任何证据。

[分 析] al + lege

朝向 + 证明 → 向…证明，宣称，托辞

Legend /ledʒənd/ n. 传说

legendary n. 传奇文学

[联 想] **allegation** *n.* ①主张；辩解 *This is a serious allegation.* 这是一个严肃的主张。

②推诿，托词

allegedly *adv.* 依其申述，据说 *This antique was allegedly made 5000 years ago.* 这个古董据说是5000年前制造的。

[词义扩展] *vt.* ①断言 *He alleged his innocence of the charge.* 他声称自己无罪 ②辩解，声称在没有证据或得到证据之前宣称

The indictment alleges that the principal took bribes. 控告称校长收受贿赂。

③推诿 *allege sth. as a reason* 提出某事作为理由

[习语记忆] **It is alleged that** …据说

assert v. /əˈsəːt/

I had to *assert* myself in the meeting in order to ensure acquisition of the support from the directorate.

[猜一猜] A 坚持 B 控制 C 展示 D 欺骗

n. 董事会

[翻 译] 在会上我必须坚持我的看法以保证得到董事会的支持。

[分 析] as + sert

to + 参加 → 一再参加讨论…，坚持…

[词义扩展] *vt.* 宣称，断言，声明

[大头例句] For example, if you write a method that calculates the speed of a particle, you might assert that the calculated speed is less than the speed of light. 例如，如果你写下一个计算离子速度的方法，你可以断言计算出来的速度是小于光速的。

constant n./adj. /ˈkɔnstənt/

The distortion of form is a *constant* in his painting.

[猜一猜] A 关荣 B 常有特点 C 渲染 D 毁坏

[翻 译] 曲线型是他绘画的一贯特点。

[分　析]con　+ stant
一直 + 站立 → 一直站着，不变的，持续的

[词义扩展]*n.* 常数，恒量
adj. 不断的，不变的

[大头例句]His health has been a constant source of concern for us. 他的健康一直都是我们关心的对象。

durable *adj.* /ˈdjuərəbl/

Finding a *durable* solution will not be easy.

[猜一猜]A 彻底的　　B 长久的
C 可行的　　D 公正的

[翻　译]找到一个长久的解决办法不是件容易的事情。

[大头巧记]dur(ing) -able，能够持续一段时间的。

[词义扩展]*n.* (*pl.*) 耐久物品　*adj.* 耐久的，持久的
durable cloth 耐用的布

[大头例句]Plastic window frames are more durable than wood. 塑料的窗框比木头的耐用。

inhabit *vt.* /inˈhæbit/

The islands are *inhabited* by 150,000 people.

[猜一猜]A 创造　B 建设　C 开发　D 居住

[翻　译]这个岛上居住着15万人。

[分　析]in　+ habit
进入 + 有 → 存在于，占据，居住

[大头巧记]in habit，在某一个地方养成习惯了，居住在某地。

[大头例句]Thoughts inhabit his mind. 各种思想占据了他的心灵。

inherent *adj.* /inˈhiərənt/

Weight is an *inherent* property of matter.

[猜一猜]A 重要的　B 主要的　C 固有的　D 必要的

[翻　译]重量是物质固有的特性。

[大头巧记]inhere (in here)，在这儿，存在，**inherent**，内在的，固有的，与生俱来的。

[大头例句]What are the long-term risks and dangers inherent in this kind of work? 什么是这种工作所固有的且长期的风险和危险。

immerse *vt.* /iˈməːs/

I *immersed* myself in work so as to stop thinking about her.

[猜一猜]A 屈身　B 沉浸　C 发展　D 模拟

[翻　译]我埋头于工作以便不再思念她。

[分　析]im　+ merse
在…里面 + 浸 → 浸入，使陷于，沉浸于，沉溺于

[大头巧记]谐音，merse，没死，把…淹没死 → 把…浸入水中。

[大头例句]Loosen the contents by immersing the bowl in warm water. 把碗放在热水中使其中的东西松开。

pursuit *n.* /pəˈsjuːt/

They did all this for the *pursuit* of profit.

[猜一猜]A 提高　B 扩大　C 平衡　D 追求

[翻　译]他们做这一切都是为了追求利润。

[分　析]pur　+ suit
向前 + 跟随 → 追求，追击
其动词形态为pursue.

[习语记忆]**in hot pursuit** 穷追

[大头例句]In the pursuit of physical perfection, some people spend several hours every day exercising and consuming only the very healthiest food. 为了追求体质上的完美，很多人每天花好几个小时锻炼，只吃非常健康的食品。

positive *adj.* /ˈpɔzətiv/

I am *positive* that I gave you his address.

[猜一猜]A 怀疑　B 阻挡　C 欺骗　D 肯定

[翻　译]我肯定把他的地址给你了。

[大头巧记]**position**，位置，**posit**，安置，**positive**，(位置)肯定的。另：联系**negative**(否定的)记忆。

[词义扩展]*adj.* 正面的，积极的，正的，阳极的
a positive refusal 当面拒绝

[大头例句]Make sure to prepare yourself mentally for receiving the results of the pregnancy test: if they are positive, your entire life will change forever. 你要确定做好接受怀孕试验结果的

心理准备:如果是阳性的话,你的整个生活都会永远改变。

steadfast *adj.* /ˈstedfəst/

He is *steadfast* in his beliefs.

[猜一猜] A 坚定的 B 明智的 C 崩溃的 D 消瘦的

[翻 译] 他坚信自己的信仰。

[分 析] stead + fast

站立 + 稳固的 → 坚定的

[大头例句] She remained steadfast in her Christian faith throughout her life. 她终生保持对基督教的信仰。

stereotype *n.* /ˈstiəriəutaip/

Caroline was tired of the old *stereotype* that Americans only liked to eat McDonald's and only drank Coca-Cola.

[猜一猜] A 讽刺 B 公式化 C 赞美 D 糊涂

[翻 译] 卡罗琳很讨厌一些人对于美国人的公式化的陈旧看法,他们认为美国人只喜欢吃麦当劳,喝可口可乐。

[大头巧记] 拆:stereo type,立体声类型音乐很老套。

[词义扩展] v. 使用铅版,套用老套

[大头例句] Homeless people are often stereotyped as a bunch of alcoholics. 无家可归者常常被看做是一群酒鬼。

strengthen *v.* /ˈstreŋθən/

Our enemy has greatly *strengthened* during the truce talks.

[猜一猜] A 改变 B 分解 C 增强 D 休息

[翻 译] 和谈期间,敌人力量已大为增强。

[分 析] stength + en

力量 + 动词词尾 → 增加力量,增强,巩固

[大头巧记] 与其反义词**weaken**(削弱)联合记忆。

[大头例句] Her objections only strengthened my resolve to open my own business. 她的反对只会加强我开辟属于自己生意的决心。

substantial *adj.* /səbˈstænʃəl/

The study reveals very *substantial* defferences between population groups.

[猜一猜] A 很多的 B 恶毒的 C 可变的 D 革新的

[翻 译] 该研究揭示了人类群体间大量的差异。

[分 析] substant + ial

物质 + 形容词尾 → 坚固的,结实的,实质的,很多的

[大头例句] We have the support of a substantial number of parents. 我们拥有大量为人父母者的支持。

taxation *n.* /tækˈseiʃən/

Reducing *taxation* further could have disastrous economic consequences.

[猜一猜] A 税收 B 质量 C 意义 D 腐败

[翻 译] 进一步减少税收有可能会产生惨重的经济后果。

[分 析] tax + ation

税收 + 名词词尾 → 征税,税款

[大头例句] We'll have to consider even higher taxation in the next year or two. 我们必须考虑到下一两年内的税收会更高。

trustworthy *adj.* /ˈtrʌstˌwəːði/

He looks a bit strange but is really *trustworthy*.

[猜一猜] A 怀疑的 B 有用的 C 可信的 D 成功的

[翻 译] 他看起来有点怪,但确实值得信赖。

[大头巧记] 此词为合成词,trust worthy,值得信赖的。另:与**deceitful(欺诈的,不诚实的)**联系记忆。

uneasy *adj./adv.* /ʌnˈiːzi/

I had an *uneasy* feeling that sb. was watching me.

[猜一猜] A 过敏的 B 残忍的 C 不自在的 D 浑浑噩噩的

[翻 译] 有人在盯着我看,我感到挺不自在。

[分 析] un + easy

不 + 舒适的 → 不舒服的,心神不安的

[大头例句] There has always been an uneasy relationship between workers and management. 在工人

和管理者之间常常会有一种不舒服的关系。

variable *n./adj.* /ˈveəriəbl/

All these *variables* can affect a student's performance.

[猜一猜]A 猜测　　B 压力
C 大吹大擂　　D 可变因素

[翻　译]所有这些的可变因素都会影响学生的表现。
[分　析]vari + able
改变 + 可…的 → 可变的，易变的，变量
[大头巧记]联系**immutable**(不可变的)记忆。
[大头例句]Her husband is a man of variable character.
她的丈夫是个性格多变的人。

immovable

习题：在下面的空格中填写本单元的单词。

1. His health has been a __________ source of concern for us.
2. I __________ myself in work so as to stop thinking about her.
3. There has always been an __________ relationship between workers and management.
4. All these __________ can affect a student's performance.
5. He's so __________ that however hard I tried to persuade him to give in he did not change his mind.
6. In the __________ of physical perfection, some people spend several hours every day exercising and consuming only the very healthiest food.
7. Make sure to prepare yourself mentally for receiving the results of the pregnancy test: if they are __________, your entire life will change forever.
8. He looks a bit strange but is really __________.
9. Her objections only __________ my resolve to open my own business.
10. The flowers that my wife constantly received __________ me.
11. For example, if you write a method that calculates the speed of a particle, you might __________ that the calculated speed is less than the speed of light.
12. Plastic window frames are more __________ than wood.
13. The islands are __________ by 150,000 people.
14. The police __________ that the man was murdered but they have given no proof.
15. What are the long-term risks and dangers __________ in this kind of work?
16. She remained __________ in her Christian faith throughout her life.
17. Homeless people are often __________ as a bunch of alcoholics.
18. The study reveals very __________ defferences between population groups.
19. We'll have to consider even higher __________ in the next year or two.

Day 41

accumulate *v.* /ə'kjuːmjuleit/

Soot quickly ***accumulates*** if we don't sweep our chimney.

[猜一猜]A 积聚 B 生成 C 脱落 D 变质

[翻 译]如果我们不清扫烟囱的话，煤灰就会很快地积聚起来。

[分 析]ac + cumulate
to + 积聚 → 慢慢积累起来

[大头巧记]acc（ept）一个"u,"再要m（ore）"u", late（晚），在很晚的时候就积累了很多的u。

[近义词]**amass; assemble; collect; compile; gather; increase; store; up**

[辨 析]**accumulate, amass**这两个词都可解释为"积累"，区别如下：

①**accumulate** 强调"经过一段比较长的时间由少积多的积累"，使用范围较广，似乎凡是数量方面的增长都可以表示。*However, as the evidence began to accumulate, experts from the zoo felt obliged to investigate.* 然而，随着证据开始积聚，动物园的专家们感到有必要进行调查了。

②**amass** 强调"大量的聚集"，常用于财富、信息、所有物等的聚集，这种积累可能一下子完成，也可能在短期内完成，也可能在比较长的时间内完成，但是数量总是很大的。*People tend to amass possessions, sometimes without being aware of doing so.* 人们倾向于积攒东西，有时并未意识到这样做。

[词义扩展]*vi.* 堆积；积聚
His debts accumulated. 他债台高筑。

[大头例句]The fat in my belly accumulates as my capacity for liquor does. 我肚子上的脂肪量随我的酒量一同积累。

affluent *adj.* /'æfluənt/

Our motherland is ***affluent*** in natural resources.

[猜一猜]A 紧张的 B 丰富的
C 著名的 D 光荣的

[翻 译]我们国家具有丰富的自然资源。

[分 析]af + fluent
朝向 + 流动 → 流入的，滔滔不绝的，引申为丰富的

[词义扩展]*adj.* 富裕的 *With the leading of the Party, we can built China to be an affluent and democratic country.* 在党的领导下，我们能把中国建设成为富强而民主的国家。
n. 支流；富人

[大头例句]I don't like hanging around in the affluent circle; on the contrary, I like talking with the common people. 我不喜欢在富人圈子里闲逛，恰恰相反，我喜欢和平民聊天。

anecdote *n.* /'ænikdəut/

He knows a lot of ***anecdotes*** about the emperors in Chinese history.

[猜一猜]A 礼仪 B 轶事 C 戏曲 D 史书

[翻 译]他知道关于中国历史上皇帝的好多轶事。

[分 析]an + ecdote
未 + 出版 → 没有出版的 → 流传于民间的故事，轶事

[大头巧记]拆：an e(mperor) (of) C(hina) dote(s)，一个中国皇帝昏聩的轶事。

[大头例句]There are many anecdotes about the president's extra-marital affairs. 有很多关于总统婚外恋的轶事。

appliance *n.* /ə'plaiəns/

He bought some household ***appliances*** for his new apartment.

[猜一猜]A 食品 B 睡衣 C 用品 D 宠物

[翻 译]他为他的新公寓买了一些家用电器。

[分 析]appli + ance
使用 + 名词词尾 → 使用的东西，用品，设备

[大头巧记] 通过同根词**apply**记忆。

[词义扩展] *n.* 使用

[大头例句] The appliance of your principle to practical diplomatic affairs is not that easy. 把你的原则应用到实际的外交事务中并不是那么简单。

barren *adj.* /ˈbærən/

That remote *barren* land has blossomed into rich granaries.

[猜一猜] A 富饶的　B 贫瘠的　C 光秃秃的　D 历史悠久的

[翻　译] 过去的穷乡僻壤变成了富饶的谷仓。

[分　析] bar + ren

bare（光光的）+ 词尾 → 一无所有的 → 贫瘠的

[大头巧记] 拆：bar(e) ren(人)，赤裸的人，一无所有。

[词义扩展] *adj.* ①不生育的；不孕的 ②无益的；无效果的 *a barren argument* 无益的争论

n. [常用复]不毛之地，荒地，瘠地

[大头例句] What I have done to her has finally proved to be a barren effort. 我对她所做的一切最终被证明是无效的努力。

canvas *v./n.* /ˈkænvəs/

In his new novel, Tomas gave us a grim portrait of despair from the heart against the bright *canvas* of the postwar economy.

[猜一猜] A 希望　B 背景　C 前景　D 失落

[翻　译] 在托马斯的新小说里，他给我们描绘了战后经济发展亮丽背景下衬托出的内心深处绝望的冷酷肖像。

[大头巧记] 倒过来看，vas can → 血管能够作为生命活动的背景。

[词义扩展] *n.* ①帆布 ②一套风帆，一套帐篷 ③一块画布，一幅油画 *vt.* 盖上帆布，装上帆布 *adj.* 帆布制的

[习语记忆] **get the canvas** 被解雇；被驱逐；被拒婚

[大头例句] The young artist showed me his recent canvas. 这位年轻画家给我看了他近来的油画。

culminate *v.* /ˈkʌlmineit/

Years of waiting *culminated* in a tearful reunion.

[猜一猜] A 激动　B 谢意　C 深情　D 结局

[翻　译] 多年的等待最终以含泪团聚而结局。

[分　析] culmin + ate

顶点 + 动词词尾 → 达到顶点，结局

[大头例句] A series of financial disasters culminated in the collapse of the country's largest bank. 随着该国最大银行的破产，一系列的金融灾难达到了顶点。

cumulative *adj.* /ˈkjuːmjulətiv/

The team is currently carrying out research on the *cumulative* effect on the body of repeated doses of the medicine.

[猜一猜] A 累积的　B 生理的　C 心理的　D 明显的

[翻　译] 这个组目前正在研究重复使用该药物对身体的累积影响。

[分　析] cumul + ative

堆积 + 词尾 → 积累的

[大头巧记] 联系**cumulus**(积云)记忆。

filter *v.* /ˈfiltə/

Sunlight *filtered* through the chinks of the shutters.

[猜一猜] A 过滤　B 加热　C 晃动　D 变化

[翻　译] 阳光从百叶窗的缝隙中透过来。

[词义扩展] *n.* 过滤器，过滤嘴；渐为人知，慢慢传开 *News of the decision filtered out to reporters.* 关于这个决定的消息慢慢地传到了记者那里。

[大头例句] Everything we download from the Internet is automatically filtered through our virus software. 我们通过国际互联网下载的每一件东西都要经过杀毒软件的过滤。

fundamental *adj.* /ˌfʌndəˈmentl/

We need to know some knowledge about the *fundamental* laws of the universe.

[猜一猜]A 神奇的　B 深奥的　C 基本的　D 客观的

[翻　译]我们需要知道一些关于宇宙的基本规律的知识。

[分　析]funda + mental

基础 + 精神的 → 基础的，基本的，原始的

[词义扩展]n. 基本原则，基本原理 *A fundamental of good behavior is consideration for others.* 良好行为的一个基本原则是体谅他人。

[大头例句]We shall have to make some fundamental changes in the way we do business. 在营业方式上我们必须做出一些根本的变化。

fruition *n.* /fruːˈiʃən/

After years of hard work, his hopes came to *fruition*.

[猜一猜]A 实现　B 出现　C 理解　D 绚丽

[翻　译]几年辛勤工作之后，他的希望实现了。

[大头巧记]**fruit，果实，有结果**
fruition，结果实，实现，成就

[大头例句]Nobody was sure whether the deal would ever come to fruition. 没有人知道这个交易是否会实现。

massive *adj.* /ˈmæsiv/

I'm sorry, I will not be able to attend your birthday party due to the *massive* amount of homework I have this evening.

[猜一猜]A 大量的　B 困难的　C 紧急的　D 重要的

[翻　译]很抱歉，由于今晚有大量的家庭作业，我不能去参加你的生日宴会了。

[分　析]mass + ive

大块，大量 + 形容词尾 → 大量的，厚重的

[词义扩展]adj. 坚定的，胸襟宽广的，雄伟的

[大头例句]We must make massive efforts to improve things. 我们必须做出极大的努力去改善一切。

monologe 独白

monopoly *n.* /məˈnɔpəli/

A university education shouldn't be the *monopoly* of the minority whose parents are rich.

[猜一猜]A 垄断　B 游戏　C 狂热　D 抛弃物

[翻　译]大学教育不应是少数富家子弟的专利。

[分　析]mono + poly

独自 + 运用 → 一个人使用，垄断，专利

[大头例句]In most markets, the Microsoft software company has a monopoly over production, as only their products can meet the needs of consumers. 微软公司的产品在大多数市场上形成了垄断，这是因为只有他们的产品能够满足顾客的要求。

nutrition n.营养，营养学

nourishment *n.* /ˈnʌriʃmənt/

A young baby can obtain all the *nourishment* it needs from its mother's milk.

[猜一猜]A 热量　B 维生素　C 营养　D 水分

[翻　译]婴儿能够摄取来自母乳的所有营养。

[分　析]nourish + ment

滋养 + 名词词尾 → 营养，营养品

[大头例句]Food and nourishment are not necessarily the same thing: potato chips and soda have so little nutritional value that the body is no better off for having consumed them. 食物并不等同于营养品：薯条和苏打水中的营养物质非常少，大吃大喝它们并不会对身体有什么好处。

sufficiency n.充足　efficiency n.效率

proficiency *n.* /prəˈfiʃənsi/

He achieved *proficiency* in English in just six months.

[猜一猜]A 努力　B 文学　C 赞扬　D 进步

[翻　译]他仅用了六个月就掌握了熟练的英语。

[分　析]pro + ficien + cy

…之前 + 做 + 名词词尾 → 向前进步的，进步，精通

rally *v.* /ˈræli/

They paused to refresh themselves and *rally* their strength.

[猜一猜]A 重振 B 证实 C 保养 D 源泉
[翻 译]他们暂停了一下，以恢复体力。
[大头巧记]拆：r(e) ally → 再次结盟，以图东山再起
[词义扩展]*n./v.* 召集，集会，反弹 *a mass rally* 群众大会
[习语记忆]**rallying cry** 呐喊 **rally round** *v.* 聚集在…周围，齐心协力

spore n.孢子 /spɔː/

sporadic *adj.* /spəˈrædik/

The explosions are only *sporadic* now.

[猜一猜]A 拘束的 B 在监视下的
C 控制的 D 零星的
[翻 译]爆炸现在只是零星地发生。
[分 析]spora + dic
分散 + 形容词尾 → 零星的，不时发生的

storage *n.* /ˈstɔːridʒ/

My house always lacks *storage* space.

[猜一猜]A 娱乐 B 储存 C 比较 D 理想
[翻 译]我家里总是缺少存储空间。
[分 析]stor(e) + age
储存 + 名词词尾 → 储存，贮藏室
[大头例句]The table can be folded flat for easy storage. 该桌子可以折叠，以便于储存。

thesis *n.* /ˈθiːsis/

I don't agree with the central *thesis* of the article.

[猜一猜]A 理论 B 破坏 C 系数 D 论点
[翻 译]我不同意这篇论文的中心论点。
[分 析]thes + is
放置 + 名词词尾 → 把想法放进去，论文，论题，论点
[大头巧记]拆：the sis(ter) → 我把自己的论点，当成妹妹一样来呵护。
[大头例句]Writing a thesis on dance cubs is not as strange as it seems. 写一篇关于舞蹈俱乐部的论文并不像看起来那么奇怪。

triple *n./adj./v.* /ˈtripl/

The money they were asking for was *triple* the amount we expected.

[猜一猜]A 无礼 B 降低 C 三倍 D 超出
[翻 译]他们要的钱数是我们料想的三倍。
[分 析]tri + ple
三 + 重(词尾) → 三倍于，增至三倍，三倍数
[大头巧记]二倍**double**，三倍**triple**，四倍**fourfold**，五倍……
[大头例句]We should triple our profits next year. 下年我们要将利润增至三倍。

tumour *n.* /ˈtjuːmə/

He has a big *tumour* in his back.

[猜一猜]A 疤痕 B 标志 C 吃惊 D 肿块
[翻 译]他背上有个大肿块。
[大头巧记]拆：t(oo) (h)umour → 太幽默了，笑得我脸都肿了。

veteran *n.* /ˈvetərən/

The privilege, a token income, was allowed for *veterans* of both world wars.

[猜一猜]A 纪念 B 理念 C 老兵 D 习惯
[翻 译]这种特权，一种象征性收入，是参加过两次世界大战的老兵所拥有的。
[分 析]veter + an
老 + …的人 → 老兵，老手
[词义扩展]*adj.* 老兵的，经验丰富的
veteran workers 老工人

习题：在下面的空格中填入本单元的单词。

1. Everything we download from the Internet is automatically __________ through our virus software.
2. The team is currently carrying out research on the __________ effect on the body of repeated doses of the medicine.

3. A university education shouldn't be the __________ of the minority whose parents are rich.
4. Food and __________ are not necessarily the same thing: potato chips and soda have so little nutritional value that the body is no better off for having consumed them.
5. They paused to refresh themselves and __________ their strength.
6. The privilege, a token income, was allowed for __________ of both world wars.
7. However, as the evidence began to __________, experts from the zoo felt obliged to investigate.
8. The __________ of your principle to practical diplomatic affairs is not that easy.
9. I don't like hanging around in the __________ circle; on the contrary, I like talking with the common people.
10. A series of financial disasters __________ in the collapse of the country's largest bank.
11. In his new novel, Tomas gave us a grim portrait of despair from the heart against the bright __________ of the postwar economy.
12. What I have done to her is finally proved to be a __________ effort.
13. He knows a lot of __________ about the emperors in Chinese history.
14. Nobody was sure whether the deal would ever come to __________.
15. I'm sorry, I will not be able to attend your birthday party due to the __________ amount of homework I have this evening.
16. In most markets, the Microsoft software company has a __________ over production, as only their products can meet the needs of consumers.
17. He achieved __________ in English in just six months.
18. He has a big __________ in his back.
19. The explosions are only __________ now.
20. Writing a __________ on dance clubs is not as strange as it seems.
21. The table can be folded flat for easy __________.
22. The money they were asking for was __________ the amount we expected.
23. We shall have to make some __________ changes in the way we do business.

Day 42

defendant *n.* /diˈfendənt/

There are two sides in a case: the prosecutor and the *defendant*.

[猜一猜]A 原告　　B 被告
C 辩护人　　D 公诉人

[翻　译]一个案件中有原告和被告两方。

[大头巧记]**defend,防护**,-ant(词尾),…的人,防护自己的人,被告。

[词义扩展]*adj.* 被告人的,辩护的
defendant company 被告方面

[大头例句]You are not the defendant. 你不是被告。

deprive *vt.* /diˈpraiv/

They were *deprived* of a normal life by heart disease.

[猜一猜]A 期望　B 蹂躏　C 诊断　D 剥夺

[翻　译]心脏病使他们失去了正常的生活。

[分　析]de　+ prive
离开 + 抢 → 抢走，夺去，剥夺；使丧失(of)

[词义扩展]*vt.* 撤职，免去…的职务，使失去 *As a child he had been deprived of love and attention.* 当他还是个孩子的时候,他就失去了爱和关注。

[大头例句]The court ruling deprived us of any share in the inheritance. 法院裁决我们分不到任何遗产。

discern *v.* /diˈsəːn/

It was so dark outside that he was just able to *discern* the road in the dark.

[猜一猜]A 辨明　B 关心　C 低估　D 指明

[翻　译]外面一片漆黑,他在黑暗中勉强能分辨出道路。

[分　析]dis　+ cern
离开 + 察觉 → 分辨出,辨明,识别,了解

[大头例句]It was difficult to discern which of them was telling the truth. 很难分清他们中的哪一个在说实话。

priority *n.* /praiˈɔriti/

Japan has got *priority* over other countries in the field of microelectronics.

[猜一猜]A 垄断　B 停滞　C 优先　D 力量

[翻　译]日本在微电子学领域领先于其他国家。

[分　析]prior　+ ity
在前的 + 名词词尾 → 优先,优先权

[大头例句]In an effort to make its students more competitive in the evermore technologically advanced world, Oxford University has made technology education its highest priority. 为了让自己的学生在前所未有的科技发展的世界上具有更强的竞争力,牛津大学把科技教育放在最优先发展的位置。

probation *n.* /prəˈbeiʃən/

She received a fine and was placed on *probation* for four years.

[猜一猜]A 察看　B 监禁　C 放逐　D 更正

[翻　译]她被罚款并被监外察看四年。

[分　析]prob(e)　+ ation
探测　+ 名词词尾 → 探索时期,试用期,察看

[词义扩展]*n.* 见习，考验 *educational probation* 教育见习

[大头例句]After being charged with possession of marijuana, the young man was placed on probation for five years, during which time if he was found with any sort of illegal substance, he would be eligible for up to fifteen years in prison. 因为被证明携有大麻,这个年轻人被判了五年的监外察看,在此期间如果他被发现有任何实质性的违法行为的话,他将有可能被判最长15年的监禁。

procedure *n.* /prəˈsiːdʒə/

The new work *procedure* is a great improvement on / over the old one.

[猜一猜] A 计划 B 工序 C 宣传 D 潜力
[翻 译] 新工序比起老工序来是一个巨大的改善。
[分 析] proce(e)d + ure
进行 + 名词词尾 → 程序,工序,过程
[大头例句] Organ donation is becoming a more and more common procedure as society's ideas about body parts become more liberalized. 随着关于身体各部位的社会观点更加自由化,器官捐献的手续变得越来越简单。

prone *adj.* /prəun/

Children of poor health are very *prone* to colds in winter.

[猜一猜] A 避开 B 倾向于 C 凌驾 D 固执
[翻 译] 体弱的孩子在冬天易患感冒。
[词义扩展] *adj.* 俯卧的 lie prone on the bed病人俯卧在床上
[大头例句] With such a low intake of vitamin C, you are much more prone to minor sicknesses such as the common cold. 由于你对维生素C的摄入量如此低,你会更易患像普通感冒那样的小病。

prosecute *v.* /ˈprɔsikjuːt/

He was *prosecuted* for murder.

[猜一猜] A 诬陷 B 谣传 C 起诉 D 认为
[翻 译] 他被指控犯有谋杀罪。
[分 析] pro + secute
向前 + 跟随 → 实行,从事,起诉
[大头巧记] 拆:p(屁) rose cute → 玫瑰可爱个屁,我要告发它!
[大头例句] In many cases of statutory rape, it is up to the victim's family to prosecute, as the victim rarely finds fault in the accused. 在很多的幼女强奸案中,都依靠受害者的家人起诉,因为受害者很难指认被告的罪行。

revelation *n.* /ˌreviˈleiʃən/

The *revelation* of his identity caused him to be watched.

[猜一猜] A 疑点 B 复杂 C 丢失 D 暴露
[翻 译] 由于身份暴露,他被监视了。
[大头巧记] **reveal** *vt.* **暴露,展示;revelation** *n.* **暴露,启示**
[大头例句] The solution to my problem seemed to come as a brilliant revelation in my dream last night. 我昨天晚上在梦中灵光一闪,问题的解决办法似乎来了。

revise *vt.* /riˈvaiz/

Don't interrupt her: she is *revising* for her final test.

[猜一猜] A 冲突 B 列提纲 C 复习 D 咨询
[翻 译] 别打搅她:她在为期末考试复习呢。
[分 析] re + vise
再 + 看 → 再看一遍,复习
[词义扩展] *vt.* 修订,修改,校订 *revise one's ideas about sb.* 修正自己对某人的看法
[大头例句] The basic premise of this paper is strong, but you will need to revise it carefully before turning in the final draft because there are numerous grammatical errors. 这篇论文的基本前提是坚实的,但是在你定稿之前需要很细致地修改它,因为其中有很多语法错误。

objection *n.* /əbˈdʒekʃən/

He has a strong *objection* to getting up early.

[猜一猜] A 异议 B 物质 C 客观 D 对象
[翻 译] 他强烈反对早起。
[分 析] ob + ject + ion
against + throw + 名词词尾 → 投向反对者 → 反对,异议
[大头巧记] 与 **object(物体,目标)**联合记忆。两者是同根词;object,被掷于眼前的东西。
[词义扩展] 反对的理由 *What is your objection to my plan?* 你反对我计划的理由是什么?
[大头例句] I think I'll move on to the next point, if you have no objection. 如果你们没有异议的话,我就要讲下一点了。

sanction *v.* /ˈsæŋkʃən/

The president, we are told, has *sanctioned* greed at the cost of compassion.

[猜一猜] A 公布　B 提交　C 批准　D 抛弃

[翻　译] 据说董事长已批示放弃同情心，选择贪婪方针。

[分　析] sanct + ion

神圣 + 名词词尾 → 圣物，宗教的法令，批准，赞许

[大头巧记] section(部门) → 部门给出的回答(answer)把an(awer)插入section → **sanction(批准)**

[词义扩展] *n./v.* 批准，支持，认可，约束 *moral sanction* 道德制裁

[习语记忆] **suffer the last sanction of the law** 被处死刑

scrutiny *n.* /ˈskruːtini/

All the documents are subjected to close *scrutiny*.

[猜一猜] A 分类　B 保密　C 详细审查　D 纯洁

[翻　译] 所有文件都需要认真审查。

[分　析] scrutin + y

检查 + 名词词尾 → 详细审查，监视

[大头例句] For his famous annual State of the Union Address, in which he discusses all the major issues America is facing at the moment, the President is under intense national scrutiny and can scarcely afford mistakes. 在每年一度的著名国情咨文中，总统都讨论美国正面对的所有主要问题，国家对其审查认真细致，几乎不允许出现任何错误。

session *n.* /ˈseʃən/

A question-and-answer *session* will be held after the lecture.

[猜一猜] A 会议　B 赠礼　C 闭幕　D 安排

[翻　译] 讲座后还有提问题的时间。

[分　析] sess + ion

坐 + 名词词尾 → 座谈会，会议，讨论，治安法庭

species *n.* /ˈspiːʃiz/

No *species* of performing artist is as self-critical as a dancer.

[猜一猜] A 特色　B 出色　C 类型　D 荣誉

[翻　译] 在所有类型的艺术家中，没有像舞蹈家那样严格地自我要求的。

[分　析] spec + ies

看 + 名词词尾 → 看起来相似的一类事物，类型，种类

[大头例句] This type of rattlesnake has been declared an endangered species. 这种响尾蛇已被宣布为濒临灭绝种类。

spokesman *n.* /ˈspəuksmən/

He works as a foreign affairs *spokesman*.

[猜一猜] A 讲师　B 发言人　C 咨询处　D 指导

[翻　译] 他是外交发言人。

[大头巧记] 此词为合成词：spokes man 发言人

[大头例句] Through his spokesman the president expressed his condolences to the victims of the accident. 通过发言人，总统表达了自己对那次事故受害者的哀悼之意。

suspect *n./adj./v.* /səsˈpekt/

I *suspect* they are very disappointed.

[猜一猜] A 不相信　B 炫耀　C 装饰　D 猜想

[翻　译] 我猜想他们很失望。

[分　析] sus + pect

下面 + 看 → 在下面偷着看 → 怀疑，猜想

[词义扩展] *adj.* 令人怀疑的(人) *suspect motives* 令人怀疑的动机

[大头例句] Two suspects were arrested today in connection with the robbery. 两名与该劫案有联系的嫌疑犯今天被捕了。

territory *n.* /ˈteritəri/

Wild animals will not allow other animals to enter their *territory*.

[猜一猜] A 仓库　B 妨碍　C 竞争　D 领地

[翻 译]野生动物不许其他动物进入它们的领地。
[分 析]terr + itory
土地 + 范围 → 领地,领土,版图
[习语记忆]**take in too much territory** 走极端
[大头例句]The company is moving into unfamiliar territory with this new software. 用这种新软件,该公司正转向一个不熟悉的领域。

treaty *n.* /ˈtriːti/

He had no difficulty in persuading parliament to approve the *treaty*.

[猜一猜]A 法案 B 合同 C 契约 D 条约
[翻 译]他可以轻而易举地说服国会通过这个条约。
[大头巧记]**treat:处理;treaty:**用来处理问题的协约→**条约**。
[大头例句]A peace treaty was signed between the US and Vietnam. 美国和越南间签署了和平协议。

verdict *n.* /ˈvəːdikt/

We would like to know your *verdict* in this matter.

[猜一猜]A 判断 B 处置 C 标准 D 形象
[翻 译]我们愿意知道你对此事的判断。
[分 析]ver + dict
真实 + 说 → 认真地说,判断,裁决,定论
[大头例句]The coroner recorded a verdict of accidental death. 验尸官记录了下事故死亡的结论。

vital *adj.* /ˈvaitl/

Skillful employees are *vital* to the success of any company.

[猜一猜]A 细节的 B 至关重要的
C 清楚的 D 有条理的
[翻 译]训练有素的雇员是任何一个公司成功至关重要的因素。
[分 析]vit + al
生命 + 词尾 → 生命的,生死攸关的,重大的,充满活力的
[大头巧记]联系反义词**moribund(垂死的)**记忆。
[大头例句]It is vital that schools teach students to use computer technology. 学校教学生使用电脑技术是至关重要的。

submit *v.* /səbˈmit/

I was not prepared to *submit* to the painful course of treatment.

[猜一猜]A 承认 B 形成 C 逃避 D 接受
[翻 译]我还没有准备好接受痛苦的疗程。
[分 析]sub + mit
下面 + 使离开 → 使服从 → 服从 → 接受
[词义扩展]*v.* 提交,主张,建议,指出 *submit a plan* 提出一项计划
[大头例句]I submit that the jury has been influenced by the publicity in this case. 我指出在本案中陪审团受到了宣传的影响。

stipulate *v.* /ˈstipjuleit/

It was *stipulated* that the goods should be delivered within two days.

[猜一猜]A 预计 B 错误 C 规定 D 最初
[翻 译]按规定,货物应在二日内送达。
[分 析]stip + ulate
点 + 动词词尾 → 点明,规定,保证
[大头例句]We clearly stipulated payment in advance. 我们事先明白地规定了报酬。

习题:在下面的空格中填入本单元的单词。

1. In many cases of statutory rape, it is up to the victim's family to __________, as the victim rarely finds fault in the accused.
2. The solution to my problem seemed to come as a brilliant __________ in my dream last night.
3. It was __________ that the goods should be delivered within two days.

4. There are two sides in a case: the prosecutor and the __________.
5. She received a fine and was placed on __________ for four years.
6. It was so dark outside that he was just able to __________ the road in the dark.
7. The basic premise of this paper is strong, but you will need to __________ it carefully before turning in the final draft because there are numerous grammatical errors.
8. I think I'll move on to the next point, if you have no __________.
9. A question-and-answer __________ will be held after the lecture.
10. The company is moving into unfamiliar __________ with this new software.
11. I __________ that the jury has been influenced by the publicity in this case.
12. We would like to know your __________ in this matter.
13. He had no difficulty in persuading parliament to approve the__________.
14. Skillful employees are __________ to the success of any company.
15. As a child he had been __________ of love and attention.
16. In an effort to make its students more competitive in the evermore technologically advanced world, Oxford University has made technology education its highest __________.
17. Organ donation is becoming a more and more common __________ as society's ideas about body parts become more liberalized.
18. With such a low intake of vitamin C, you are much more __________ to minor sicknesses such as the common cold.
19. For his famous annual State of the Union Address, in which he discusses all the major issues America is facing at the moment, the President is under intense national __________ and can scarcely afford mistakes
20. The president, we are told, has __________ greed at the cost of compassion.
21. This type of rattlesnake has been declared an endangered __________.
22. Through his __________ the president expressed his condolences to the victims of the accident.
23. Two __________ were arrested today in connection with the robbery.

Day 43

automate *v.* /ˈɔːtəmeit/

All of the assembly process needs to be fully *automated*.

[猜一猜] A 机械化　　B 近代化
C 自动化　　D 规模化

[翻　译] 所有的装配过程都需要自动化。

[分　析] auto + mate
self + 动 → 使自动化,自动操作

[大头巧记] auto本身是一个词,表汽车,mate(伙伴)→汽车的伙伴 → 自动化系统。

[大头例句] To automate a factory we have to deal with the problem that there will be a loss of many jobs. 要使一个工厂自动化,我们必须处理减少很多工作职位的问题。

carton *n.* /ˈkɑːtən/

My uncle ate a *carton* of 20 cans every week while he was studying in Britain.

[猜一猜] A 大批　B 大堆　C 纸箱　D 小车

[翻　译] 我叔叔在英国读书的时候，每星期吃一箱20听的罐头。

[大头巧记] 形近词记忆cartoon，卡通，漫画，是由许多画在纸上的图像组成的，很多"carton"纸(箱)组成"cartoon"。

detergent *n.* /diˈtəːdʒənt/

Detergent is a kind of liquid or powder used for washing clothes or dishes.

[猜一猜] A 药水　　B 整洁的
C 去污剂　　D 威慑性武器

[翻　译] 去污剂是一种液体或粉末状的物质，用于清洗衣服或盘子。

[分　析] de + terg + gent
掉 + 擦 + 名词词尾 → 清洁剂,去污剂

[大头例句] We don't have to use detergent to clean everything in the world. 我们不必用清洁剂去清洗世界上所有的东西。

hardware *n.* /ˈhɑːdwɛə/

Military *hardware* alone is not sufficient to ensure victory.

[猜一猜] A 硬件　B 士气　C 人数　D 战略

[翻　译] 仅有军事的硬件设备还不足以保证胜利。

[分　析] hard + ware
硬的 + 器皿 → 硬件,部件,五金器具

[大头例句] We have to get used to the ever-changing nature of computing hardware and software. 我们必须适应电脑硬件和软件那不断变化的特性。

harness *vt.* /ˈhɑːnis/

Some scientists are working hard at how tides can be *harnessed* to produce electricity.

[猜一猜] A 减弱　B 伤害　C 利用　D 有利于

[翻　译] 有些科学家正在努力研究怎样利用潮汐发电。

[大头巧记] 此词为马具,horse gear,马具用来驾驭马,所以引申为驾驭一种天然力为人类所用。

[词义扩展] *n.* 摩托驾驶员的全套衣帽装备，降落伞背带，安全带

[大头例句] Although we've harnessed the force of electricity, we still know very little about its effects on us. 虽然我们已经驾驭了电力,但是我们对于它对我们的影响仍然所知甚少。

granary *n.* /ˈgrænəri/

The Mid-West is the *granary* of the US.

[猜一猜] A 标志　　B 粮仓
C 油田　　D 科技中心

[翻　译] 美国的中西部等于是全国的粮仓

[分　析] gran + ary
谷物 + 聚集…的地方 → 谷仓,粮仓

[大头例句] Our granaries are filled with corn. 我们的谷仓里装满了粮食。

junction *n.* /ˈdʒʌŋkʃən/

The hydraulic power station stands at the *junction* of two rivers.

[猜一猜]A 之间　B 河畔　C 交叉点　D 合力
[翻　译]那个水力发电站在两条河流的汇合处。
[分　析]junct + ion
连接 + 名词词尾 → 连接处,交叉点,结合点
[大头例句] Leave the motorway at Junction 3.在第三个出口下高速公路。

lever *n./v.* /ˈliːvə/

Friendship should never be used as a *lever* to obtain advancement.

[猜一猜]A 代价　B 借口　C 夸口　D 工具
[翻　译]友谊绝不应该被当作晋升的工具。
[分　析]lev + er
轻 + …的东西 → 把某物弄轻的东西 → 杠杆,工具,手段
[词义扩展] *v.* 使用杠杆,撬　*lever up* 把…撬起来
[大头例句] Move this lever to change gears. 搬动这根操作杆换挡。

platform *n.* /ˈplætfɔːm/

The train at *Platform* 6 goes to London.

[猜一猜]A 出口　B 入口　C 售货点　D 站台
[翻　译]六号站台的火车开往伦敦。
[分　析]plat + form
平的 + 形式 → 平台,站台,讲台
[词义扩展] *n.* 演讲,纲领　*the platform of the new political party* 新政党的纲领
[习语记忆] **be at home on the platform** 善于演说

portable *adj.* /ˈpɔːtəbl/

Computers become lighter, smaller, and more *portable* every year.

[猜一猜]A 智能的　B 便携的　C 多能的　D 强劲的
[翻　译]电脑一年年地变得更轻、更小、更加便携。
[分　析]port + able
拿 + 可…的 → 轻便的,便携的
[大头巧记] 联系记忆:**portage** 运费。
[大头例句] On Super Bowl Sunday, the culmination of an entire season's worth of competitive aspirations, the back row of the church service was lined with men carrying portable televisions, all seeming to pay attention to the minister, but in fact studying their true love. 在周日超级杯橄榄球赛的当天,积累了整整一个赛季的竞争激情达到了顶点,在教堂的后排站满了带着便携电视来做礼拜的人,看起来他们的注意力都在牧师身上,而实际上却是在研究他们真正所爱好的东西。

register *n.* /ˈredʒistə/

The teacher kept a *register* of the names of the children.

[猜一猜]A 申请　B 分析　C 比较　D 记录
[翻　译]这个老师保留了一份孩子们的名册。
[分　析]re + gister
一再 + 运载 → 要进行记录,登记
[词义扩展] *v.* 记录,登记,注册　*register sth. in one's memory* 把某事记在心里
[大头例句] Before one can be considered an official student at this school, he must choose a set of classes and formally register for them with the administration. 在成为该校的正式学生之前,他必须先选择课程并且在教务处正式为之登记。

shield *v.* /ʃiːld/

He *shielded* his eyes from the sun.

[猜一猜]A 遮护　B 连接　C 敏感　D 明亮
[翻　译]他把手放在眼前遮住太阳光。
[词义扩展] *n.* 护罩,盾　*both sides of the shield* 事物的表里
[习语记忆] **be the shield and buckler** 做靠山,做后盾

symbolize *v.* /ˈsimbəlaiz/

Munich, the site of the 1938 Hitler-Chamberlain meeting, now *symbolizes* the idea of appeasement.

[猜一猜]A 恐慌　B 象征　C 纳粹　D 揭露

[翻　译]慕尼黑，1938年希特勒与张伯伦的会晤现已成为绥靖主义的象征。

[分　析]symbol + ize

符号 + 动词词尾 → 成为…符号，象征

[大头例句]In Europe, the colour white symbolizes purity. 在欧洲，白色象征纯洁。

tissue *n.* /ˈtisjuː/

She used paper *tissues* to blow her nose.

[猜一猜]A 袋子　B 纸巾　C 毛巾　D 餐具

[翻　译]她用纸巾擤鼻子。

[词义扩展]*n.*〈生〉组织，一整套，一系列 *a tissue of lies* 一整套谎话

towel *n./v.* /ˈtauəl/

Joey accused his players of throwing in the *towel*.

[猜一猜]A 毛巾　B 惩罚　C 肠子　D 旗帜

[翻　译]乔伊责备他的队员不应该认输。

[习语记忆]**throw in the towel** 认输

ultraviolet *adj./n.* /ˈʌltrəˈvaiəlit/

The sun gives out *ultraviolet* rays.

[猜一猜]A 辐射的　B 紫外的　C 有害的　D 永恒的

[翻　译]太阳释放紫外线。

[分　析]ultra + violet

超过 + 紫罗兰 → 紫色以外的 → 紫外的，紫外线

utility *n.* /juːˈtiliti/

I have always doubted the *utility* of these conferences on disarmament.

[猜一猜]A 目的　B 迷乱　C 诚意　D 效用

[翻　译]我一直怀疑这些裁军会议的效用。

[分　析]ut + ility

用 + 名词词尾 → 效用，有用，【计】应用程序，【哲】功利主义

[大头巧记]特征记忆：其中间部分“tilit”前后对称，结构特殊的应用程序。

[大头例句]Tests have proved the utility of this material. 测试已证明了该材料的效用。

validity *n.* /vəˈliditi/

The *validity* of our contract spans two years.

[猜一猜]A 历史　B 有效　C 红利　D 恩惠

[翻　译]合同的有效期是两年。

[分　析]valid + ity

有效的 + 名词词尾 → 有效性，合法性，正确性

ventilate *vt.* /ˈventileit/

The matter should not be hushed up, but freely *ventilated*.

[猜一猜]A 幽默　B 自助　C 公开讨论　D 振作精神

[翻　译]这事不该掩盖起来，而应公开自由讨论。

[大头巧记]**vent**，通风口 → **ventilate**，使通风，公开讨论。

[大头例句]Cold sea breezes ventilated the house. 冷冷的海风使房子的空气更清新。

versatile *adj.* /ˈvəːsətail/

The most *versatile* of vegetables is the tomato.

[猜一猜]A 通用的　B 醒目的　C 漂亮的　D 流行的

[翻　译]蔬菜中用途最广的是西红柿。

[分　析]vers + atile

转 + 形容词词尾 → 对什么都运转自如的 → 通用的，多才多艺的

[大头例句]This versatile summer jacket is a great buy. 这件多用的夏装夹克太合算了。

习题：在下面的空格中填入本单元的单词。

1. My uncle ate a __________ of 20 cans every week while he was studying in Britain.
2. To __________ a factory we have to deal with the problem that there will be a loss of many jobs.
3. We don't have to use the __________ to clear everything in the world.
4. Munich, the site of the 1938 Hitler-Chamberlain meeting, now __________ the idea of appeasement.
5. This __________ summer jacket is a great buy.
6. I have always doubted the __________ of these conferences on disarmament.
7. We have to get used to the ever-changing nature of computing __________ and software.
8. Before one can be considered an official student at this school, he must choose a set of classes and formally __________ for them with the administration.
9. Friendship should never be used as a __________ to obtain advancement.
10. Computers become lighter, smaller, and more __________ every year.
11. Although we've __________ the force of electricity, we still know very little about its effects on us.
12. The matter should not be hushed up, but freely __________.
13. The __________ of our contract spans two years.
14. The sun gives out __________ rays.
15. He __________ his eyes from the sun.
16. She used paper __________ to blow her nose.
17. The Mid-West is the __________ of the US.
18. The train at __________ 6 goes to London.
19. The hydraulic power station stands at the __________ of two rivers.
20. Joey accused his players of throwing in the __________.

Day 44

airborne *adj.* /ˈɛəbɔːn/

You can see the Yellow River through the window beside you when this plane is *airborne*.

[猜一猜] A 起飞时　B 降落时　C 飞行中　D 空降时

[翻　译] 在飞机飞行过程中,你可以通过身旁的窗口看到黄河。

[分　析] air　+ borne
空气 + 被负担 → 被空气负担的 → 空运的,飞行的

[词义扩展] *adj.* ①空气传播的 *airborne pollen* 空气传播的花粉 ②空运的,机载的 *airborne troops* 空降部队 ③在空中的;在飞行中的 *The plane is airborne* 飞行中的飞机

airlock *n.* /ˈɛəlɔk/

The *airlock* of the machine is so old that we have to replace it .

[猜一猜] A 点火器　B 气塞　C 汽缸　D 排气管道

[翻　译] 这个机器的气塞旧了,我们必须更换。

[分　析] air　+ lock
空气 + 锁 → 锁住空气的装置 → 气塞

[联　想] **airtight** *adj.* ①不透气的,密封的 ②无懈可击的 *an airtight excuse.* 无懈可击的借口
airway *n.* 航线,航空公司 *the British Airways* 英国航空公司

circuit *n.* /ˈsəːkit/

These days the popular singer is on his concert *circuit* in Britain.

[猜一猜] A 旅行　B 招待会　C 筹款会　D 巡回

[翻　译] 这些天这位流行歌手正在进行他在英国的巡回演出。

[分　析] circu　+ it
aroud　+ to go → 一圈,电路,周游,巡回

[大头巧记] 形近词: **circle 一圈,圆形物**

[词义扩展] *n.* ①同行业联合组织 ②事物变化的顺序 ③工序,流程 *the ski jumping circuit* 跳高滑雪协会
vt., *vi.* 绕…环行,接(成电路),巡回

[大头例句] We did a quick circuit of the park and then went home.我们飞快地绕着公园转了一圈,然后回家了。

circulate *v.* /ˈsəːkjuleit/

The blood *circulates* through the body.

[猜一猜] A 代谢　B 运输　C 流动　D 循环

[翻　译] 血液在体内循环。

[分　析] circul + ate
aroud + 动词词尾 → 循环

[词义扩展] *v.* ①散布;流传;扩散 *Rumors circulated rapidly.* 谣言迅速散布开来。②随意地到处走动 ③流通,周转

[大头例句] The premier circulated from group to group in the hall. 总理在宴会中穿梭于大厅的人群之间。

code *n./v.* /kəud/

The note was written in *code* and the police could not understand it.

[猜一猜] A 密码　B 表格　C 俗语　D 术语

[翻　译] 笔记是用密码写成的,警方看不懂。

[词义扩展] *n.* ①代号,代码,编码 ②规范,礼法 ③法典;法规 *the civil code* 民法

[大头例句] They coded each sample and sent them to the lab for analysis.他们把每个样本编了号,然后送到实验室做分析。

analysis. n.分析
analytic, adj.分析的 / cal
analyze. v.
analyst n.分析家(者)

convey *vt.* /kən'vei/

The ambassador personally ***conveyed*** the president's message to the premier.

[猜一猜]A 转达　B 敬献　C 解释　D 纷争

[翻　译]大使亲自向总理转达了总统的问候。

[分　析]con　+ vey

相同 + 路 → 使归于同道 → 传达，运输，转让

[大头例句]These results will enable us at least to convey a sense of progress. 这些结果至少可以使我们表达一些有进展的感觉。

currency *n.* /'kʌrənsi/

You can use credit cards but it's best to take some ***currency*** as well.

[猜一猜]A 优惠券　B 发票　C 货币　D 身份证明

[翻　译]你可以使用信用卡，但你最好还是带些钱。

[大头巧记]**current** 流通的，当前的；**currency** 流通，流通之物，通货，货币。

entail *vt./n.* /in'teil/

Producing a TV series ***entails*** a lot of work.

[猜一猜]A 包括　B 产生　C 需要　D 接触

[翻　译]拍摄一部电视连续剧需要做大量的工作。

[分　析]en　+ tail

[大头巧记]into + 切开 → 使负责切割 → 使承担，使需要

in tail，在…的尾巴里，使它承担你的重量。

[大头例句]Building the airport entails reclaiming huge areas of land from the sea. 建设这个机场需要将很大的海洋区域还为陆地。

excerpt *n./vt.* /'eksə:pt/

An ***Excerpt*** is a short piece of writing or music that is taken from a longer piece.

[猜一猜]A 摘录　B 提纲　C 目录　D 附录

[翻　译]摘录就是从一个长的文字或音乐作品中取出来的一小段。

[分　析]ex　+ cerpt

出来 + 选，拔 → 选出之物 → 摘录，摘要，剪辑

[大头例句]He is reading the excerpts from that novel. 他正在读那部小说的摘录。

expose *v.* /iks'pəuz/

He ***exposed*** the plan to the newspapers.

[猜一猜]A 透露　B 反对　C 启动　D 执行

[翻　译]他向几家报纸透露了这个计划。

[分　析]ex　+ pose

在外 + 放 → 放在外面 → 暴露，揭露，揭示，透露，揭发

[词义扩展]*v.* 使受影响，使受到，遗弃（婴儿）*exposed their children to classical music* 使他们的孩子们受到古典音乐的影响

[大头例句]Why do we still sunbathe when we know the dangers of exposing our skin to the sun? 为什么知道了在阳光下暴露我们皮肤的危险以后我们仍然进行日光浴呢？

drift *n./v.* /drift/

He worked as a day laborer, ***drifting*** from town to town.

[猜一猜]A 服务　B 务工　C 漂流　D 兜售

[翻　译]他作为临时工，从一个城镇漂泊到另一个城镇。

[词义扩展]*n.* ①吹积物 *Drifts of snow blocked the way.* 大雪积堆，阻塞了交通。②主旨，意向 *vi.&vt.* 漂浮，漂流 *We drifted down the stream.* 我们顺流而下。

[大头例句]Thick smoke from a forest fire drifted across the town. 森林大火的浓烟飘过城市。

infectious *adj.* /in'fekʃəs/

Colds are ***infectious***, and so are some eye diseases.

[猜一猜]A 危险的　B 无足轻重的　C 遗传的　D 传染的

[翻　译]感冒可传染，有些眼病也可以传染。

[分　析]infect　+ ious

传染　+ 形容词尾 → 传染的 → 有影响的，

有感染力的

[大头例句] Her enthusiasm was infectious. 她的热心很有感染力。

journal *n.* /ˈdʒəːnl/

The doctor reads the British Medical *Journal.*

[猜一猜] A 手册 B 注解 C 词典 D 杂志

[翻 译] 这位医生读英国医学杂志。

[大头巧记] **journalist**（记者）→ 记者工作的对象：**journal杂志，定期刊物，日报**。

[词义扩展] *n.* 日记，航海日志，分类账 *classroom journal* 教室日志

[大头例句] I went back home for my journal. 我回家拿我的日记。

monsoon *n.* /mɔnˈsuːn/

The *monsoon* brings rain to us.

[猜一猜] A 蘑菇 B 季风 C 风暴 D 气压带

[翻 译] 季风给我们带来雨水。

[分 析] mono + ton + ous

单一 + 声音 + 形容词尾 → 单一声音的 → 单调的，令人厌倦的

[大头巧记] 拆：Mon. 星期一 → Mon. soon 不久的星期一将会开始季风。

[大头例句] The southwest typically has an extremely arid climate, with the notable exception of early March, which locals refer to as the "Monsoon" because the rainfall of a single day in that period can sometimes surpass the sum of the rainfall for the entire rest of the year. 西南部是典型的极端干旱气候，三月份是个明显的特例，当地人称之为"雨季"，因为在此期间，一天的降雨量可能比这一年中其余所有时间的降雨总量还要多。

prevalent *adj.* /ˈprevələnt/

The *prevalent* opinion is in favour of election.

[猜一猜] A 得体的 B 普遍的 C 对立的 D 中肯的

[翻 译] 舆论普遍支持选举。

[分 析] pre + val + ent

前面 + 力量 + 形容词尾 → 盛行的，普遍的

[联 想] **prevail** *v.* 盛行

[大头例句] In most parts of Western Europe, AIDS is not a prevalent condition; that does not mean, however, that there are not isolated cases in nearly every city. 在西欧的大多地方，艾滋病不是一种普遍的现象，但是几乎在每一个城市都有个别的病例存在。

telecommunication *n.* /ˈtelikəˌmjuːniˈkeiʃən/

Telecommunications were disrupted by the brownout.

[猜一猜] A 困惑 B 内部交流 C 恐惧 D 电信通讯

[翻 译] 电信通讯因灯火管制而不能进行。

[分 析] tele + communication

电子 + 传达 → 电讯，远程通讯，电信学

[大头例句] Telecommunications is an important area of professional growth. 电信学是增加专业知识的重要领域。

transmission *n.* /trænzˈmiʃən/

New telephone lines allow faster data *transmission* by fax or modem.

[猜一猜] A 传送 B 竞争 C 信息 D 聚集

[翻 译] 新的电话线路使得通过传真或调试解调器进行更快的数据传送成为可能。

[分 析] trans + misstion

横过 + 送 + 名词词尾 → 送过去 → 传送，播送，转播

[大头巧记] 它来自：**transmit** *v.* 传送。

[大头例句] My car has automatic transmission. 我的汽车有自动传动系统。

习题：在下面的空格中填入本单元的单词。

1. The blood __________ through the body.
2. Building the airport __________ reclaiming huge areas of land from the sea.
3. The southwest typically has an extremely arid climate, with the notable exception of early March, which locals refer to as the "__________" because the rainfall of a single day in that period can sometimes surpass the sum of the rainfall for the entire rest of the year.
4. They __________ each sample and sent them to the lab for analysis.
5. You can see the Yellow River through the window beside you when this plane is __________.
6. Colds are __________, and so are some eye diseases.
7. __________ is an important area of professional growth.
8. New telephone lines allow faster data __________ by fax or modem.
9. I went back home for my __________.
10. In most parts of Western Europe, AIDS is not a __________ condition; that does not mean, however, that there are not isolated cases in nearly every city.
11. Thick smoke from a forest fire __________ across the town.
12. __________ is a short piece of writing or music that is taken from a longer piece.
13. Why do we still sunbathe when we know the dangers of __________ our skin to the sun?
14. You can use credit cards but it's best to take some __________ as well.
15. The __________ of the machine is so old that we have to replace it.
16. These days the popular singer is on his concert __________ in Britain.
17. The ambassador personally __________ the president's message to the premier.

Day 45

anthropology *n.* /ˌænθrəˈpɔlədʒi/

Anthropology is the study of the origin, the behavior, and the physical, social, and cultural development of human beings.

[猜一猜]A 社会学　B 种族学　C 进化论　D 人类学

[翻　译]人类学是研究人类的起源、行为及其本质、社会和文化发展的学科。

[分　析]anthropo + logy
人类　+…学 → 人类学

[大头巧记]an thro' p(e)o(ple)，一个透视人的行为的学科 → 人类学。

aquarium *n.* /əˈkweəriəm/

An *aquarium* is a place for the public exhibition of live aquatic animals and plants.

[猜一猜]A 动物园　B 森林公园　C 水族馆　D 纪念堂

[翻　译]水族馆是一个公开展出活的水族动植物的地方。

[分　析]aquari + um
水　+ 名词词尾 → 水生动物的栖息地 → 水族馆，鱼缸

[大头巧记]掐头去尾法：quar(rel)(争吵，嘈杂) → 水族馆里的鱼很多，所以很嘈杂。

dwell *vi.* /dwel/

He *dwelled* on the need to trim the budget.

[猜一猜]A 解释　B 详述　C 坚持　D 修正

[翻　译]他娓娓道出修正预算的必要。

[大头巧记]拆：d(escribe) well，很好地叙述，详述。

[词义扩展]*vi.* 居住，踌躇 *n.* 延长，停止 *I used to dwell in the country.* 我过去住在乡下。

[大头例句]Don't dwell on the past-try and be more positive! 别在过去徘徊，试着积极点儿！

garment *n.* /ˈgɑːmənt/

You shouldn't leave these *garments* on the floor.

[猜一猜]A 杂志　B 衣服　C 小食品　D 枕头

[翻　译]你不应该把衣服放在地板上。

[分　析]garm　+ ent
装备，装饰 + 名词后缀 → 装饰身体的东西 → 衣服，外衣

[词义扩展]*n.* 外表，外观

[大头例句]The garment workers were being paid very low wages. 那些制衣工人的报酬很低。

residence *n.* /ˈrezidəns/

I met an artist in *residence* at Beijing University.

[猜一猜]A 教学　B 居住　C 工作　D 混

[翻　译]我碰到一位住在北京大学的艺术家。

[分　析]re　+ sid + ence
加强语气 + 坐 + 名词词尾 → 居住，住处

routine *n.* /ruːˈtiːn/

I arrive at nine o'clock, teach until twelve thirty and then have a meal — that is my morning *routine.*

[猜一猜]A 计划　B 形态　C 工作　D 例行做法

[翻　译]我九点钟到，教课教到十二点半，然后吃饭——这是我上午的例行做法。

[分　析]rout(e) + ine
路线　+ 词尾 → 事情的脉络，程序，常规，例行做法

[习语记忆]**go into one's routine** 说自己照例要说的话，做自己照例要做的事

pamper *v.* /ˈpæmpə/

He had a whole evening in which to *pamper* himself.

[猜一猜]A 反省　B 放纵　C 折磨　D 武装

[翻　译]他整个晚上都在放纵自己。

[大头巧记]形近词:**camper** 宿营者;**hamper** 妨碍,牵制;**tamper** 干预,篡改。另:paper 里面加入 m(oney) → 把钱当纸用 → 放纵,纸醉金迷。

[大头例句]After taking on the difficult job, the young manager promised herself she would pamper herself with a weekly manicure as a way of releasing stress. 承担了这份艰难的工作以后,这位年轻的经理承诺自己要每个星期做一次指甲美容,以此作为释放压力的方法。

pharmacy *n.* /ˈfɑːməsi/

There should be more all-night ***pharmacies*** in this area.

[猜一猜]A 工厂　　B 培训学校　　C 药房　　D 农场

[翻　译]这一地区本应有更多夜间售药的药房。

[分　析]pharma + cy
药物 + 名词词尾 → 药学,药房,制药业

[大头例句]As a pharmacy that serves such a diverse population, this store not only needs pharmacists who are fluent in several languages, but also specialists who are familiar with the hesitations and habits of these distinct cultures with regard to medicine. 这家药店面对的顾客很复杂,所以他们不仅需要熟练掌握几种语言的药剂师,同时也需要对各种独特文化的用药习惯和忌讳熟悉的专门人才。

pessimism *n.* /ˈpesimizəm/

We have seen too much defeatism, too much ***pessimism***, too much of a negative approach.

[猜一猜]A 乐观主义　　B 悲观主义　　C 矛盾　　D 愤怒

[翻　译]我们看到太多的失败主义、太多的悲观主义和太多的负面倾向。

[分　析]pessim + ism
最坏的 + …主义 → 悲观主义,悲观,悲观者

[大头巧记]与 **optimism**(乐观主义)对应记忆。

[大头例句]Don't let his pessimism dissuade you: if you know your idea has potential, pursue it with all your energy. 不要因他的悲观主义而停滞不前,如果知道你的想法有潜力的话,就尽力去追求。

sanitary *adj./n.* /ˈsænitəri/

Hospital operating instruments must be ***sanitary***.

[猜一猜]A 进口的　　B 隔离的　　C 一次性的　　D 卫生的

[翻　译]医院的手术器械必须是消过毒的。

[分　析]sanit + ary
健康 + 形容词尾 → 健康的,卫生的

[大头巧记]和 **noxious**(有毒的)联合记忆。

signature *n.* /ˈsignitʃə/

A surprise ending is the ***signature*** of an O. Henry short story.

[猜一猜]A 平庸　B 奢侈　C 特征　D 本质

[翻　译]一种带有欧·亨利短篇小说特征的出人意料的结尾。

[大头巧记]**sign** *v.* 标记,符号,签名 → **signal** 信号 → **signature** *n.* 签名,特征。

[习语记忆]**over sb.'s signature** 经某人签名

[大头例句]The software company is currently working on new technology that will enable shoppers to give an electronic signature that involves neither pen nor paper, but allows the computer to verify a person's identity. 该软件公司现正在开发一项新技术,它可以让购买者签署电子签名,不需笔和纸,但电脑却能查证人的身份。

sociology *n.* /ˌsəusiˈɔlədʒi/

He got a degree in ***sociology*** and politics.

[猜一猜]A 社会学　　B 组织学　　C 人类学　　D 动物学

[翻　译]他拿到了社会学和政治学的学位。

[分　析]soci + ology
社会 + …学 → 社会学

spouse *n.* /spauz/

The insurance policy covers the named driver and ***spouse***.

[猜一猜] A 配偶 B 亲属 C 监护人 D 师傅

[翻　译] 本保险适用于驾车人及其配偶。

[大头巧记] **spout** 滔滔不绝地讲；→ 有时我们抱怨配偶(**spouse**)总滔滔不绝地说个没完。

starve *vt.* /stɑːv/

I'm lonely, and *starving* for companionship.

[猜一猜] A 号召 B 渴望 C 发怒 D 头脑发热

[翻　译] 她很寂寞，渴望友谊。

[大头巧记] 和 **sate**(使饱足)，**surfeit**(使过饱)联系记忆。

[大头例句] Thousands of people will starve if food dosen't reach the stricken city. 如果食品送不到受灾城市的话，成千上万的人将受到饥饿的威胁。

statesman *n.* /ˈsteitsmən/

As a leading *statesman* he has to deal with many international affairs.

[猜一猜] A 发言人 B 代表 C 政治家 D 才子

[翻　译] 作为一名领袖，他要处理很多国际事务。

[大头巧记] 合成词：states man，国家的人，政治家。另：和 **statement**(陈述)对比记忆。

[大头例句] As always, the Minister tried to be statesman-like. 大多数情况下，该部长试图表现出政治家的风度。

survival *n.* /səˈvaivəl/

The man's *survival* was surprising, as the doctors thought he would die.

[猜一猜] A 坚定 B 运气 C 生存 D 僵化

[翻　译] 这个人能活下来真是出人意外，因为医生们认为他必死无疑。

[大头巧记] **survive** *v.* 幸存；引申出 **survival** *n.* 生存，幸存者。

[大头例句] Our disregard for the environment threatens the long-term survival of the planet. 我们对环境的漠视威胁着我们星球的长久生存。

sustenance *n.* /ˈsʌstinəns/

He gave money for the *sustenance* of a poor family.

[猜一猜] A 支持 B 帮助 C 交友 D 全貌

[翻　译] 他把钱给了一个穷人家维持生活。

[分　析] susten + ance

谋生 + 名词词尾 → 事务，生计，支持

[大头巧记] 由 **sustain**(*v.* 支撑，维持)引申而来。

[大头例句] The children were thin and badly in need of sustenance. 这些孩子身体消瘦，急需食物。

tourism *n.* /ˈtuərizəm/

Space *tourism* may be a reality by the year 2010.

[猜一猜] A 开放 B 重组 C 旅行 D 灾难

[翻　译] 空间旅游在2010年可能变为现实。

[分　析] tour + ism

旅行 + 词尾 → 观光事业，游览

[大头例句] The country depends on tourism for most of its income. 这个国家的主要收入靠旅游业。

tournament *n.* /ˈtuənəmənt/

We are preparing for the tennis *tournament*.

[猜一猜] A 表演赛 B 锦标赛 C 交流 D 颁奖

[翻　译] 我们在为网球锦标赛做准备。

[分　析] torna + ment

马上比武 + 名词词尾 → 原指中世纪武士马上比赛，现在表示锦标赛，联赛

[大头巧记] 拆：tour name nt，巡回参加比赛，使自己的名字荣登榜首，锦标赛。

viable *adj.* /ˈvaiəbl/

The economy of the country is not *viable*.

[猜一猜] A 能维持的 B 灾难性的 C 成功的 D 可笑的

[翻　译] 这个国家的经济是难以维持的。

[大头巧记] via，通过 → **viable，可通过的，能养活的，能生育的**

[大头例句] Hospitals plan to stop services that are not financially viable. 医院计划中止那些费用上不具可行性的医疗服务。

wander *vi.* /ˈwɔndə/

I *wandered* around for hours before I found your house.

[猜一猜]A 精力充沛　　B 想知道
　　C 徘徊　　D 压缩

[翻　译]我转了半天才找到你的房子。

[大头巧记]wonder(想知道)路怎么走,所以漫游,徘徊(wander)。

[大头例句]Jim wandered into the kitchen to make breakfast. 吉姆晃荡进厨房,想做点早餐。

wrinkle *n./v.* /ˈriŋkl/

She is beginning to get *wrinkles* around her eyes.

[猜一猜]A 龟裂　B 皱纹　C 雀斑　D 妨碍

[翻　译]他的眼角开始出现鱼尾纹了。

[大头巧记]wring,绞,扭,折磨;产生了 wrinkle(皱纹)。

[大头例句]The trouble with linen is that it wrinkles so easily. 亚麻布的问题是它太容易起皱了。

sprawl *n./v.* /sprɔːl/

He *sprawled* his signature over the paper.

[猜一猜]A 签署　　B 潦草地写
　　C 展示　　D 卖弄

[翻　译]他在纸上潦草地签了名。

[大头巧记]同意形近词:scrawl 潦草地写。

[词义扩展]*n./v.* 四肢展开地坐卧,爬行,蔓生

[大头例句]He just sprawled out in his chair and expected me to bring his dinner. 他伸展四肢坐在椅子里,指望我给他拿来晚餐。

习题:在下面的空格中填写本单元的单词。

1. I met an artist in __________ at Beijing University.
2. Hospital operating instruments must be __________.
3. Don't let his __________ dissuade you: if you know your idea has potential, pursue it with all your energy.
4. __________ is the study of the origin, the behavior, and the physical, social, and cultural development of human beings.
5. __________ is a place for the public exhibition of live aquatic animals and plants.
6. As a __________ that serves such a diverse population, this store not only needs pharmacists who are fluent in several languages, but also specialists who are familiar with the hesitations and habits of these distinct cultures with regard to medicine.
7. The software company is currently working on new technology that will enable shoppers to give an electronic __________ that involves neither pen nor paper, but allows the computer to verify a person's identity.
8. He got a degree in __________ and politics.
9. The insurance policy covers the named driver and __________.
10. He just __________ out in his chair and expected me to bring his dinner.
11. We are preparing for the tennis __________.
12. As a leading __________ he has to deal with many international affairs.
13. The children were thin and badly in need of __________.
14. The trouble with linen is that it __________ so easily.

15. Hospitals plan to stop services that are not financially __________.
16. I __________ around for hours before I found your house.
17. The country depends on __________ for most of its income.
18. Thousands of people will __________ if food dosen't reach the stricken city.
19. Our disregard for the environment threatens the long-term __________ of the planet.
20. After taking on the difficult job, the young manager promised herself she would __________ herself with a weekly manicure as a way of releasing stress.
21. I arrive at nine o'clock, teach until twelve thirty and then have a meal; that is my morning __________.
22. The __________ workers were being paid very low wages.
23. Don't __________ on the past-try and be more positive!

Note 前事不忘后事之师 *Remember the past and it will guide your future.*

Day 46

abrade *v.* /ə'breid/

Your shoes have been ***abraded*** so much that you can't use them any more.

[猜一猜]A 磨损　B 积聚　C 经历　D 承受

[分　析]ab　+ rade

去掉 + 擦 → 被慢慢地擦掉 → 磨损

[翻　译]你的鞋已经磨损太严重了,不能再穿了。

[大头巧记] a bread,因为磨损,把它的一个 e 掉在了旁边,有 abrade。

[大头例句] I hate learning English: it is so boring and is kind of abrading to me. 我很讨厌学英文,它很枯燥,对我来说简直是一种精神上的折磨。

array *v.* /ə'rei/

The captain ***arrayed*** his soldiers for battle.

[猜一猜]A 列队　B 召集　C 武装　D 检阅

[翻　译]上尉命令士兵列队准备战斗。

[分　析]ar + ray

to + 线,射线 → 使成线 → 列队

[词义扩展] *n.* 展示,盛装

[大头例句] An array of heavily armed troops suddenly appeared on the border, which caused a stir among the residents. 大批全副武装的部队突然出现在边境线上,引起了当地居民的不安。

blunt *adj.* /blʌnt/

Too much alcohol and smoking made his senses ***blunt***.

[猜一猜]A 偏激的　　B 神经质的

C 单纯的　　D 迟钝的

[翻　译]过多的喝酒和抽烟使他的感觉变得迟钝。

[大头巧记]音近词:**blond *n.* 金发女郎**。在西方文化中,金发女郎常成为被开玩笑的对象,说她们反应迟钝,可联想到 blunt。

[词义扩展] *adj.* ①钝的,不尖的②直言的,不转弯抹角的

On screen, the conscript father was a blunt talker and straight shooter. 在荧屏上,那位参议员是一个直言不讳、一针见血的人。

v. 使迟钝;使减弱 *She blunted the somber atmosphere with her lovable smile.* 她用她可爱的微笑减缓了阴郁的气氛。

[大头例句] His infatuation with antiques has made him blunt about the feelings of his wife. 对于古董的痴迷使得他对妻子感觉麻木。

coarse *adj.* /kɔːs/

The soldiers were watching a stand-up comedian performing a ***coarse*** imitation of the enemy's President.

[猜一猜]A 滑稽的　　B 拙劣的

C 讽刺的　　D 激烈的

[翻　译]士兵们在观看一个滑稽可笑的喜剧演员拙劣地模仿敌方总统。

[大头巧记]音同形近词:**course 课程**,把 u 变成 a,从 useful 课变成了 ass(屁股)似的很拙劣的课程。

[词义扩展] *adj.* 粗(糙)的,劣等的,不精确的,低级的,粗鲁(暴,俗)的 *coarse words* 粗俗的话

[大头例句] Her skin was coarse from years of working outdoors. 由于多年的户外工作,她的皮肤很粗糙。

blaze *n.* /bleiz/

Until now the firemen still haven't figured out an effective method to control the ***blaze***.

[猜一猜]A 洪水　B 浓雾　C 浓烟　D 大火

[翻　译]到现在消防员仍未想出有效的办法控制这场大火。

[词义扩展] *n.*①光辉;明亮 *The girl likes flowers that are a blaze of color.* 那个女孩喜欢色彩鲜艳的花朵。

②突然发怒 *In a blaze of anger he was shivering then.* 他勃然大怒，那时他浑身发抖。

③(*pl.*)邪恶的地方 *Go to blazes!* 该死！

vi./vt. 发光，燃烧 *The fire blazed all night.* 火整夜都燃烧着。

[大头例句] The supermarket has blazed a trail in new methods of selling by using the internet. 这家超市利用国际互联网已经开拓了新的销售方法。

beneficial *adj.* /ˌbeniˈfiʃəl/

The temperate climate in this area is ***beneficial*** to health.

[猜一猜]A 有益的 B 有害的 C 特殊的 D 相反的

[翻　译]这个区域温和的气候对健康有好处。

[分　析]benefi(t) + cial

有利 + 形容词词尾 → 有益的

[大头例句] The arms limitation agreement we are working on should be beneficial to all countries. 我们正在为之操劳的这个武器限制协议将对所有的国家都有益。

dread *n.* /dred/

When he was young he lived in constant ***dread*** of poverty.

[猜一猜]A 恐惧 B 威胁 C 破落 D 折磨

[翻　译]年轻的时候他经常担忧贫穷。

[大头巧记]和 **dead**(死亡)形似，对死亡的恐惧。

[词义扩展]*vt./vi.* 害怕，担心 *adj.*令人畏惧的，使人敬畏的，可怕的 *a dreadly disease* 可怕的疾病

[大头例句] I dread a visit to the dentist. 我害怕去看牙医。

evacuate *v.* /iˈvækjueit/

The village was ***evacuated*** because of the danger of a flood.

[猜一猜]A 惊恐 B 失踪 C 撤离 D 愤慨

[翻　译]由于洪水的威胁，村里人都已撤走了。

[分　析]e. + vacu + ate

使 + 空 + 动词词尾 → 使…空出去 → 撤离，疏散

[词义扩展]*v.* 剥夺，抽空，排泄 *Fear evacuated their minds of reasons.* 恐惧使他们失去了理智。

[大头例句] Over 10,000 refugees have now been evacuated to neighbouring countries. 一万多难民已经被疏散到邻国去了。

friction *n.* /ˈfrikʃən/

In designing a machine, it is necessary to reduce ***friction*** as much as possible.

[猜一猜]A 消耗 B 成本 C 摩擦 D 错误

[翻　译]在设计一种机器时，必须尽可能减少摩擦。

[分　析]fric + tion

摩擦 + 名词词尾 → 摩擦，摩擦力，倾轧，冲突

[大头巧记]**fiction** ***n.*** 小说，加进去一个 r(ole)，角色，也就加了一份冲突。

[大头例句] The decision is likely to lead to friction with neighbouring countries. 这个决定有可能导致与周边国家的冲突。

huddle *v.* /ˈhʌdl/

During the crisis, the President's national security advisers ***huddled***.

[猜一猜]A 争吵 B 下台 C 会商 D 窘迫

[翻　译]危机时期，总统的国家安全顾问们聚到了一起。

[词义扩展]*v.* 挤作一团，乱堆 *n.*一堆，一团

[大头例句] A huddle of photographers were waiting outside the courtroom. 一大堆摄影记者等在法庭外面。

polish *v./adj.* /ˈpɔliʃ/

He is ***polishing*** his shoes with a brush.

[猜一猜]A 修补 B 浆洗 C 擦亮 D 上蜡

[翻　译]他正在用刷子把鞋擦亮。

[大头巧记]谐音：polish"抛"光，擦亮。另：Polish 意为荷兰人，皮鞋擦亮的荷兰人。

[词义扩展]*v.*润饰，使优雅 *n.*光滑，擦亮，优雅 *a man of polish* 文雅的人

[习语记忆] **polish the apple** 拍马屁

[大头例句] Your writing has potential, but it lacks polish. 你的写作有潜力，但还缺乏润色。

reciprocal *adj.* /riˈsiprəkəl/

The two nations signed a ***reciprocal*** trade agreement.

[猜一猜] A 公正的　B 长期的　C 互惠的　D 对立的

[翻　译] 两国间签订了一项互惠贸易协定。

[分　析] re + ciproc + al
再次 + 向前放下 → 互相给予，互惠的

[词义扩展] *adj.* 彼此相反的 *n.* 倒数 *The reciprocal of 8 is 1/8.* 八的倒数为八分之一。

reconcile *vt.* /ˈrekənsail/

He is looking to ***reconcile*** with his girlfriend.

[猜一猜] A 和解　B 结婚　C 订婚　D 接触

[翻　译] 他正在想着和女朋友和解。

[分　析] re + concile
一再 + 安抚 → 和解，和谐，使顺从

[大头巧记] 和 **harmonize** (协调) 联系记忆。

[大头例句] It is rare for divorced couples to reconcile after finalizing their separation, though sometimes people remember the reasons they fell in love the first time, and are actually able to resolve their disagreements. 即使有的时候离婚夫妇间还记得他们第一次坠入爱河时的原因，并且实际上还能够解决他们之间的争执，但是在他们分开确定以后，他们很少会和好。

revenge *n./v.* /riˈvendʒ/

I broke Mary's pen by accident, and in ***revenge*** she tore up my school work.

[猜一猜] A 报复　B 意外　C 相反　D 以德报怨

[翻　译] 我不留心弄坏了玛丽的钢笔，出于报复，她撕掉了我的作业。

[分　析] re + venge
回 + 惩罚 → 回以惩罚 → 报复，复仇

[词义扩展] *v.* 给…报仇，复仇 *I'll revenge that insult.* 我要报复那侮辱。

[习语记忆] **give sb. his revenge** 给某人雪耻的机会。**seek one's revenge on** 找机会向…报仇。

[大头例句] Some critics of capital punishment see the practice as a misplaced attempt at revenge. 一些对于死刑的批评家把这种行为看做是一种错位的报复企图。

paralyse *v.* /ˈpærəlaiz/

The old lady was ***paralysed*** from the waist down.

[猜一猜] A 手术　B 衣衫褴褛　C 疼痛　D 瘫痪

[翻　译] 这位老太太从腰以下都瘫痪了。

[分　析] para + lyse
旁边 + 分开 → 使身体的一边分开 → 使瘫痪，使麻痹

[大头例句] Following a tragic bus accident, famed Mexican artist Frida Kahlo was paralysed from her neck down, and spent many weeks strictly confined to her bed. 由于悲惨的车祸，著名的墨西哥画家弗黎达。卡洛颈部以下瘫痪，卧床很长时间。

peel *v.* /piːl/

Caroline enjoyed eating apples, however, she knew it was necessary to ***peel*** the fruit to avoid getting sick.

[猜一猜] A 清洗　B 出售　C 削皮　D 榨汁

[翻　译] 苛瑞兰喜欢吃苹果，但是她知道吃水果有必要削皮，这样可以避免疾病的发生。

[大头巧记] peel，谐 "皮"，得到该词的另一个义项：*n.* 果皮，蔬菜皮。

[词义扩展] *vt./vi.* 脱皮，剥落，脱(衣服) *The skin is peeling off his sunburnt face.* 他晒黑的脸正在脱皮。

[习语记忆] **Keep your eyes peeled!** 睁大眼睛看着，留神监视。

[大头例句] Though hardly delicious, the peel of a common orange is believed to contain many agents that can prevent and reverse the course of some cancers. 虽然并不好吃，但是大家相信普通的桔子皮含有很多可以预防和反转癌症进程的物质。

parallel *v.* /ˈpærəlel/

The river enters the town from the east and flows *parallel* with the main street.

[猜一猜] A 平行 B 临近 C 交叉 D 偏离

[翻 译] 这条河从东头进入城镇，与主街平行流淌。

[分 析] par(a) + allel
旁边的 + 互相 → 在彼此的旁边 → 平行，类似

[词义扩展] *adj.* 平行的，类似的 *n.* 平行线，类似，纬线
without (a) parallel 无与伦比之事

[大头例句] In earlier years, our lives were quite parallel, thus allowing our friendship to be strong; when I went to college, however, and he joined the military, our paths diverged and our communications grew thin. 早几年的时候，我们的生活很类似，因而友谊也很牢固，但我上了大学，而他参了军以后，我们也就分道而驰，通信渐少了。

pinch *n./v.* /pintʃ/

I had to *pinch* myself to make sure I wasn't dreaming.

[猜一猜] A 掐捏 B 呼喊 C 惩罚 D 废弃

[翻 译] 我掐自己来确定我不是在做梦。

[大头巧记] **pin,** **大头针** → pinch, 像大头针大小的，一小撮(pinch 的另一个义项)。

[习语记忆] **at a pinch** 在紧要关头
drop a pinch of salt on the tail of 捉住某人
with a pinch of salt 有保留地，不全信地
pinch and save 节衣缩食地攒钱

[大头例句] As a student with little or no income, it is often necessary to "pinch pennies," that is to say, be mindful of every single thing one purchases, and save as much money as possible. 对于没有收入或只有很少一点收入的学生来说，经常需要"节衣缩食"，就是说对每一件买的东西都要很小心，尽可能省钱。

slippery *adj.* /ˈslipəri/

The road is *slippery* after snow.

[猜一猜] A 冰冻的 B 滑的
C 泥泞的 D 肮脏的

[翻 译] 下雪后路很滑。

[大头巧记] **slip** 滑动 → **slipper** 拖鞋 → **slippery** 滑的，光滑的

[习语记忆] **as slippery as an eel** 难于应付的，滑头的

[大头例句] It is too dangerous to drive on this bridge in the winter because it freezes and the ice becomes very slippery, causing many cars to crash. 冬天在这个桥上开车很危险，因为它上冻了，冰变得很滑，造成了很多汽车坠桥事件。

temperament *n.* /ˈtempərəmənt/

He's a radical by *temperament*.

[猜一猜] A 温度 B 集会 C 评价 D 性情

[翻 译] 他性情激进。

[分 析] temper + ament
脾气 + 名词词尾 → 气质，性情，急躁

turmoil *n.* /ˈtəːmɔil/

The demonstration turned into a *turmoil*.

[猜一猜] A 骚乱 B 狂热 C 命令 D 战争

[翻 译] 示威演变成骚乱。

[大头巧记] turm oil → term oil 一个学期的时间都在学石油，学生受不了了，发生骚乱。

velocity *n.* /viˈlɔsiti/

There will be strong winds tonight with *velocities* of 60 miles an hour and more.

[猜一猜] A 规模 B 沉重 C 力量 D 速度

[翻 译] 今晚将有大风，时速达 60 英里以上。

[分 析] veloc + ity
速度 + 词尾 → 速度，速率，周转率

[习语记忆] **accelerated velocity** 加速度
angular velocity 角速度

versus *prep.* /ˈvəːsəs/

We feel we have some advantages *versus* the competition.

[猜一猜]A 排除 B 胜出 C 投入 D 相对于

[翻 译]我们觉得相对于竞争我们有自己的优势。

[大头巧记]vers us→我们相对于对方转变自己。玩游戏时的对战符号"vs"即是它的简写。

[大头例句]The Finance Minister must weigh the benefits of a tax cut versus those of increased public spending. 财政部长必须掂量一下减少税收相对于增加公共消费哪一个好处更多。

scratch *v.* /skrætʃ/

The cat is *scratching* the table again.

[猜一猜]A 抓 B 跳 C 玩弄 D 认识

[翻 译]猫又在抓桌子了。

[大头巧记]**catch 抓住;scratch 抓**

[词义扩展]*n./v.* 乱写，擦；*adj.* 打草稿的 *scratch a match* 擦火柴

[习语记忆]**If you'll scratch my back, I'll scratch yours.** 投桃报李。

a scratch of the pen 大笔一挥,签字

[大头例句]Scratches in the enamel of cars can greatly lower the value of a car and be quite costly to repair. 汽车表面瓷漆的刮痕会大大降低汽车的价值,修起来花费也很高。

习题：在下面的空格中填写本单元的单词。

1. An __________ of heavily armed troops suddenly appeared on the border, which caused a stir among the residents.
2. Until now the firemen still haven't figured out an effective method to control the________.
3. The soldiers were watching a stand-up comedian performing a __________ imitation of the enemy's president.
4. Your shoes have been __________ so much that you can't use any more.
5. She __________ the somber atmosphere with her lovable smile.
6. As a student with little or no income, it is often necessary to "__________ pennies," that is to say, be mindful of every single thing one purchases, and save as much money as possible.
7. It is too dangerous to drive on this bridge in the winter because it freezes and the ice becomes very __________, causing many cars to crash.
8. He's a radical by __________.
9. __________ in the enamel of cars can greatly lower the value of a car and be quite costly to repair.
10. The Finance Minister must weigh the benefits of a tax cut __________ those of increased public spending.
11. The temperate climate in this area is __________ to health.
12. The two nations signed a __________ trade agreement.
13. Following a tragic bus accident, famed Mexican artist Frida Kahlo was __________ from her neck down, and spent many weeks strictly confined to her bed.

14. In earlier years, our lives were quite ________, thus allowing our friendship to be strong; when I went to college, however, and he joined the military, our paths diverged and our communications grew thin.
15. Though hardly delicious, the ________ of a common orange is believed to contain many agents that can prevent and reverse the course of some cancers.
16. When he was young he lived in constant ________ of poverty.
17. During the crisis the President's national security advisers ________.
18. Over 10,000 refugees have now been ________to neighbouring countries.
19. It is rare for divorced couples to ________ after finalizing their separation, though sometimes people remember the reasons they fell in love the first time, and are actually able to resolve their disagreements.
20. I broke Mary's pen by accident, and in ________ she tore up my school work.
21. In designing a machine it is necessary to reduce ________ as much as possible.
22. Your writing has potential, but it lacks ________.
23. The demonstration turned into a ________.
24. There will be strong winds tonight with ________ of 60 miles an hour and more.

Note 前事不忘后事之师 *Remember the past and it will guide your future.*

Day 47

aborigine *n.* /ˌæbəˈridʒini/

They are the ***aborigines*** in America, which means they are the indigenous or earliest known population there.

[猜一猜] A 主人　B 领袖　C 骄傲　D 土著

[翻　译] 他们是美洲大陆的土著居民，也就是说他们是那里最原始最早的居民。

[分　析] ab + origine

from + 起源，最初 → 从最初（就在一个地方），土著

authentic *adj.* /ɔːˈθentik/

They buy and sell ***authentic*** antique hardware from 1650 to 1925.

[猜一猜] A 真正的　B 悠久的　C 微型的　D 雕花的

[翻　译] 他们买卖真正的从1650年到1925年间的古董五金器皿。

[分　析] aut + hent + ic

self + 著作 + 形容词尾 → 作者亲笔所作，真品，真正的

[词义扩展] *adj.* ①可信的，可靠的，权威性的 ②【律】认证了的，正式的

[大头例句] Is that an authentic account by an eye-witness, or just your imagination? 那是一份目击者的真实证言，还是只是你的想象？

autonomy *n.* /ɔːˈtɔnəmi/

Many indigenous peoples of the region are struggling for reestablishment of full cultural and political ***autonomy***.

[猜一猜] A 自治　B 权威　C 环境　D 交流

[翻　译] 这个地区的很多本土人士正在为完全的文化和政治自主的重建而奋斗。

[分　析] auto + nomy

self + 治理 → 自我治理，自治

[词义扩展] *n.* ①自治团体，有自主权的国家 ②人身自由 ③【哲】自律，意志自由

[大头例句] The overall objective of this project is to advance the state of the art in ground operations and onboard autonomy for flight rovers. 这个工程全部的目标是提高飞行探测器的地面控制和随机自控的技术发展水平。

berth *n.* /bəːθ/

Our barque took up a ***berth*** at a small pier on the coast of the Aegean Sea.

[猜一猜] A 故障　B 交易　C 比赛　D 停泊

[翻　译] 我们的帆船在爱琴海岸的一个小码头停泊了下来。

[大头巧记] 其同音词 **birth**（出生），出生就是在这个世界占有一席之地，停泊。

[词义扩展] *n.* ①（船与灯塔，沙滩等之间留出的）安全距离 ②卧铺 ③停泊地，船台 ④职位 ⑤名次，席次 *vt./vi.* 停泊

[大头例句] He gave his wife a wide berth when she got angry and unreasonable. 当他的妻子发火并变得蛮不讲理时，他就对她敬而远之。

derive *v.* /diˈraiv/

The knowledge ***derived*** from real life is as important as that derived from books.

[猜一猜] A 学习　B 掌握　C 总结　D 来自于

[翻　译] 来自于现实生活中的知识和来自于书本的知识同样重要。

[分　析] de + rive

自…转移 + 水流 → 水流的源头，来自，源自，出自

[大头巧记] 拆：de-rive(r)，河流，源自于，或 drive（开车），中间插入一个E(ve)，夏娃开车是所有开车者的源头。

[词义扩展] *v.* ①推论，推究(from) ②溯源 ③【化】衍生 *derive a conclusion from facts* 从事实推出结论

[大头例句] It is not such an easy thing to derive a conclusion from facts. 从事实中得出一个结论并不是这么简单的一件事。

default *n./v.* /diˈfɔːlt/

He won the championship by ***default*** in the badminton tournament.

[猜一猜] A 作弊　　B 对方弃权　　C 高素质　　D 歪打正着

[翻　译] 由于对方弃权，他赢得了羽毛球锦标赛的冠军。

[分　析] de + fault

下去 + 错误 → 错误下去，拖债，不履行责任，弃权

[大头例句] They defaulted in the badminton tournament. 他们在羽毛球比赛中缺席。

duplicate *v.* /ˈdjuːplikeit/

He ***duplicated*** his former mistakes.

[猜一猜] A 重复　B 纠正　C 憎恨　D 理解

[翻　译] 他又犯了和以前一样的错误。

[分　析] du + pli + cate

两个 + 折 + 词尾 → 复制，加倍，重复

[词义扩展] *adj.* 复制的，成双的，二重的，抄存的，做底子的 *n.* 复制品，副本 *type the document in duplicate* 把这份文件打成一式两份

[大头例句] Digital images can be duplicated in seconds. 数字信息能在几秒钟之内被复制。

linen *n.* /ˈlinin/

In Europe household articles were formerly made of ***linen***.

[猜一猜] A 丝绸　B 花边　C 毛线　D 亚麻

[翻　译] 在欧洲，家用织品在过去是用亚麻做的。

[词义扩展] *adj.* 亚麻做的，像亚麻布的

[习语记忆] **wash one's dirty linen at home** 家丑不可外扬

manuscript *n.* /ˈmænjuskript/

The first version of the ***manuscript*** is too long for use in this journal.

[猜一猜] A 原稿　　B 通俗小说　　C 论文　　D 报告文学

[翻　译] 该稿件的第一个版本太长而无法在这个杂志中使用。

[分　析] manu + script

手 + 写 → 手稿，原稿，手抄本

[大头例句] Does Lu Xun's original manuscript include any mention of the main character's mother? 鲁迅最初的手稿里面提到主角的母亲了吗？

notion *n.* /ˈnəuʃən/

He has no ***notion*** of what I mean.

[猜一猜] A 注意　B 观点　C 通知　D 感觉

[翻　译] 他不明白我的意思。

[分　析] not + ion

记住 + 名词词尾 → 应该记住的想法，概念，意见

[大头巧记] 形近词记忆：**notation**，符号，注释 → **notion**，符号所反映的内涵：概念

[大头例句] When I first had the notion of studying English, I did not realize I might spend a whole lifetime trying to master it! 当我第一次想到学习英语的时候，我并没有认识到我可能会花整整一生的时间试着去掌握它。

predecessor *n.* /ˈpriːdisesə/

Linda seems to have learned nothing from the faults of her ***predecessors***.

[猜一猜] A 教授　B 卖国贼　C 学者　D 前任

[翻　译] 琳达似乎没有从她前任的错误中吸取任何教训。

[分　析] pre + decess + or

以前 + 离开 + …的人 → 前任，前辈，原先之物

[大头例句] Life in my new job has been challenging, as my boss expects me to have the knowledge and speed of my predecessor. 我的新工作充满挑战，因为我的老板希望我有像我前任一样的知识和速度。

qualitative *adj.* /ˈkwɔlitətiv/

There is no ***qualitative*** difference between them.

[猜一猜]A 明显的　　B 合理的
C 性质上的　　D 不可调和的

[翻　译]他们之间没有性质上的区别。

[分　析]qualita + tive
性质 + 形容词尾 → 性质上的，定性的

[大头巧记]注意和 **quantitative(数量的)** 的区别记忆。

[大头例句]In analyzing historical social movements for which we have no statistics or other numbers, we must take a qualitative approach to understanding the forces behind the events that took place. 在对于没有统计数据或任何其他数据可依靠的历史社会运动分析中，我们必须采取定性分析的方法来理解所发生事件背后的力量。

repent *v.* /ri'pent/

I *repented* for my intemperate behavior.

[猜一猜]A 道歉　　B 后悔
C 重蹈覆辙　　D 警告

[翻　译]我对我过激的举止感到懊悔。

[分　析]re + pend
一再 + 后悔 → 懊悔，悔改，忏悔

[大头巧记]re (s)pend，多花一次钱，后悔

perpetual *adj.* /pə'petjuəl/

These two countries signed a treaty of *perpetual* friendship.

[猜一猜]A 双方的　　B 永久的
C 有条件的　　D 暂时的

[翻　译]这两国签订了永久友好条约。

[分　析]per + pet + ual
全部 + 追求 + 形容词尾 → 永远追求的，永久的，一再重复的

[大头巧记]去尾：ual，典型形容词尾。只需记住其特征部分：perpet，拆：per pet，每一个宠物，都是他主人永远的朋友。另：联系其反义词 **temporary(暂时的)** 记忆。

[大头例句]Following the attacks of September 11, 2001, it seemed the debilitating wounds on the spirits of Americans would be perpetual; over a year later, however, there are significant signs of hope that indicate Americans are not only healing, but looking for ways to prevent future acts of terrorism. 2001年"9·11"袭击后，那令美国人民精神上消沉的伤口似乎是永久性的；但一年后，很多迹象表明，美国人民不仅仅是在恢复，同时也在积极寻找预防未来恐怖袭击的方法。

persist *vi.* /pə:'sist/

On the top of very high mountains, snow *persists* throughout the year.

[猜一猜]A 持续　B 很难　C 呆滞　D 屈从

[翻　译]高山顶上，积雪终年不化。

[分　析]per + sist
完全 + 不变 → 持续，坚持，耐久

[大头巧记]与 **desist**(常与 from 连用，**停止**)联合记忆。

[大头例句]The doctor advised his patient to first take two pills, and if the pain persisted after two hours, to follow-up by taking two more. 这位医生建议他的病人先吃两粒药，如果两个小时后疼痛继续的话，再吃两粒。

persevere *v.* /pə:si'viə/

Police negotiators will *persevere* with their efforts to free the hostages.

[猜一猜]A 提议　B 迫使　C 坚持　D 罪犯

[翻　译]警方代表将坚持努力，给人质以自由。

[分　析]per + severe
全部 + 严重 → 情况严重时仍始终坚持

[大头例句]Foreign language study is not only a test of intelligence, but of endurance: only those who persevere will become fluent in the finer aspects of the language of choice. 对外语学习不仅仅是对智力的测验，也是对耐力的考验：只有那些坚持不懈者才会在所选语言的微妙领域中得心应手。

transcript *n.* /'træskript/

The singer published a *transcript* of the tapes.

[猜一猜]A 说明　B 总结　C 评价　D 抄本

[翻　译] 该歌星出版了这些磁带的原文。

[分　析] tran + script

互相 + 写 → 照着写，抄本 副本

[大头巧记] 它来自于 transribe，抄写。

[词义扩展] *n.* 成绩单

school transcript 学生成绩单

[大头例句] A transcript of the tapes was presented in court as evidence. 录音带的一个副本在法庭上作为证据被提出。

typical *adj.* /ˈtipikəl/

It is *typical* of him to take hard jobs.

[猜一猜] A 规矩的　B 典型的

C 愚蠢的　D 聪慧的

[翻　译] 抢挑重担是他的特点。

[大头巧记] tye，类型；**typical**，**典型的**，**象征性的**。

[大头例句] This painting is fairly typical of his early work. 这幅画在他的早期作品中很典型。

utterly *adv.* /ˈʌtəli/

I was at an *utter* loss for what to do.

[猜一猜] A 奇异地　B 完全地

C 忽视地　D 祸根地

[翻　译] 我完全不知道该怎样做才好。

[分　析] utter + ly

完全的 + 词尾 → 完全地，彻底地

[大头巧记] **butter**，**黄油**，**utter**，用黄油彻底地把锅底涂一遍。

[大头例句] Young children are utterly dependent on their parents. 小孩子们完全依靠他们的父母。

习题：在下面的空格中填写本单元的单词。

1. Our barque took up a __________ at a small pier on the coast of the Aegean Sea.
2. I __________ of my intemperate behavior.
3. Linda seems to have learned nothing from the faults of her __________.
4. They are the __________ in America, which means they are the indigenous or earliest known population there.
5. Young children are __________ dependent on their parents.
6. These two countries signed a treaty of __________ friendship.
7. Foreign language study is not only a test of intelligence, but of endurance: only those who __________ will become fluent in the finer aspects of the language of choice.
8. A __________ of the tapes was presented in court as evidence.
9. The doctor advised his patient to first take two pills, and if the pain __________ after two hours, to follow-up by taking two more.
10. This painting is fairly __________ of his early work.
11. Is that an __________ account by an eyewitness, or just your imagination?
12. The knowledge __________ from real life is as important as that derived from books.
13. In Europe household articles were formerly made of __________.
14. When I first had the __________ of studying English, I did not realize I might spend a whole lifetime trying to master it!
15. In analyzing historical social movements for which we have no statistics or other numbers, we must take a __________ approach to understanding the forces behind the events that took place.

16. Many indigenous peoples of the region are struggling for reestablishment of full cultural and political __________.
17. He won the championship by __________ in the badminton tournament.
18. Digital images can be __________ in seconds.
19. Does Lu Xun's original __________ include any mention of the main character's mother?

Note 前事不忘后事之师 *Remember the past and it will guide your future.*

Day 48

arbitrary *adj.* /ˈɑːbitrəri/

At that time the Germans were under the *arbitrary* rule of the dictator, Hitler.

[猜一猜] A 独裁的　B 血腥的
C 紧张的　D 可悲的

[翻　译] 那个时候德国人处于独裁者希特勒的专制统治之下。

[分　析] arbitr + ary
判断 + 形容词尾 → 自己做出判断，任意的，随意的，武断的，独裁的

[大头巧记] arbi，谐音 RB 风格，蓝调，忧伤的，(con)trary，相反的，忧伤的反面：任意的，独断的

[大头例句] My choice of that laptop was quite arbitrary. 我选择那台笔记本电脑相当随意。

absolve *v.* /əbˈzɔlv/

They agree to *absolve* us of our obligation.

[猜一猜] A 免除　B 解决　C 惩罚　D 警告

[翻　译] 他们同意免除我们的责任。

[分　析] ab + solve
away + to loosen 解开 → 解开，让其离开，宣布赦免

[近义词] **acquit; cleanse; discharge; excuse; forgive; pardon**

[反义词] **accuse; blame**

[大头例句] Law shouldn't absolve adults who hit kids. 法律不应免除殴打孩子的成人的责任。

avert *v.* /əˈvəːt/

Many highway accidents can be *averted* by careful driving.

[猜一猜] A 查明　B 避免　C 改善　D 逃避

[翻　译] 很多高速公路上的交通事故，小心驾驶的话是可以避免的。

[分　析] a + vert
to + turn → 避开，避免

[词义扩展] *vt.* 转移(目光、思想等)(from)

[大头例句] Don't avert my gaze and tell me the truth! 别避开我的眼睛，告诉我真相！

clarity *n.* /ˈklæriti/

He is seeking for *clarity* of the difficult problem by giving a full explanation.

[猜一猜] A 明了　B 解决
C 实现　D 引起关注

[翻　译] 他通过充分的说明来寻求澄清这个问题。

[大头巧记] 同源词：clear → cl(e)arity 清晰，明了

[大头例句] He is expected to clarify his position today. 大家期待他今天能阐明自己的立场。

discard *v.* /disˈkɑːd/

What we should do is *discard* the dross and select the essential.

[猜一猜] A 吸收　B 运输　C 抛弃　D 取代

[翻　译] 我们应该做的是去粗存精。

[分　析] dis + card
离开 + 纸片 → 扔掉无用的纸牌，抛弃

[词义扩展] *n.* 被抛弃的人[物]，废品(物) → *the discards of society* 被社会抛弃者

[大头例句] The gang discarded their weapons after the attack. 这群人在袭击后把他们的武器丢弃了。

discharge *v./n.* /disˈtʃɑːdʒ/

Many cities *discharge* their sewage into the sea without treating it at all.

[猜一猜] A 处理　B 排出　C 试验　D 增加

[翻　译] 很多城市未对污水进行处理就将其排入了大海。

[分　析] dis + charge
去除 + 装载 → 卸载，卸货，排出，放出

[大头巧记] 同源词：**charge，主管**，dis 否定前缀，不再主管某物 → 卸载。

[词义扩展] *v.* ①开除，解雇 ②履行，偿清 ③发射 → *He died owing the bank 3,000 dollars, and his widow was unable to discharge the debt.* 他死的时候欠银行3000美金，他的遗孀无力偿还这个债务。

[大头例句] After it discharged its cargo of coal, the ship left for Tokyo. 轮船在卸掉装载的煤炭以后离开了东京。

eliminate *v.* /iˈlimineit/

They are making an effort to ***eliminate*** capital punishment in this state.

[猜一猜] A 减少　B 取消　C 实行　D 加强

[翻　译] 他们正努力在这个州取消死刑。

[分　析] e + limin + ate
出去 + 门槛 + 动词词尾 → 扫地出门，除去，淘汰，取消

[大头例句] He has had to eliminate dairy products from his diet. 他必须除去他日常饮食中的乳制品。

exempt *v./adj.* /igˈzempt/

His identity as a foreign official ***exempted*** him from the customs duties for these basic necessities.

[猜一猜] A 禁止　B 免除　C 牵涉　D 愚蠢

[翻　译] 他是个外交官，因而这些日用品免除关税。

[分　析] ex + empt
外 + 买，拿 → 拿出去，免除，被豁免的

[词义扩展] *n.* 被免除(义务，责任)的人，免税人

[大头例句] Currently, developing nations are exempt from certain restrictions on carbon emissions. 通常，发展中国家可以免除某些关于炭的排放限制。

neglect *vt./n.* /niˈglekt/

If you ***neglect*** this property, it will depreciate.

[猜一猜] A 忽视　B 取得　C 卖出　D 觊觎

[翻　译] 如果你忽视这份资产，它无形中就贬值了。

[分　析] neg + lect
不 + 紧密 → 不紧密，松懈，忽视。

[词义扩展] *n.* 忽视，松懈 *neglect of duty* 疏于职守

[大头例句] For parents to neglect their responsibilities of feeding, clothing, and otherwise providing for their children is illegal in most places. 在大多数地方，父母负有给他们的孩子吃、穿及其他供给的责任，如果忽视的话，就会违反法律。

permit *n./v.* /pəːˈmit/

Travel in Tibet still requires a special ***permit*** for foreign visitors.

[猜一猜] A 证明　B 资历　C 调查　D 通行证

[翻　译] 对于外国游客来说去西藏旅行还需有一个通行证。

[分　析] per + mit
通过 + 走 → 放行，允许，许可证，通行证，执照

[大头巧记] 和 **prohibit(禁止，阻止)** 对应记忆。

[大头例句] The British government, like many others, does not permit the practice of polygamy. 和其他很多政府一样，英国政府不允许一夫多妻的行为。

paramount *adj.* /ˈpærəmaunt/

This duty is ***paramount*** to all the others.

[猜一猜] A 神圣的　B 无理的　C 最重要的　D 困难的

[翻　译] 没有比这更重要的义务了。

[分　析] par(a) + amount
超过 + 数量 → 量上超过其他，最高的，最重要的

[大头例句] It is of paramount importance that you remember to bring these documents to the trial; otherwise, we will have no evidence of the defendant's innocence. 记着把这些文件带到审判庭极为重要，否则我们将没有证据给被告以清白。

parliament *n.* /ˈpɑːləmənt/

The president dissolved ***parliament*** and called for new elections.

[猜一猜] A 内阁 B 国防部 C 议会 D 政府

[翻 译] 总统解散了议会，要求进行新的选举。

[分 析] parlia + ment

谈话 + 名词词尾 → 商讨国家法律的地方，议会，国会

[大头例句] The British Parliament is famous the world over for its playful, often rude exchanges between members in debate. 英国议会以其议员在辩论时十分幽默，并经常行为粗鲁而闻名于世。

patriotism *n.* /ˈpætriətizəm/

Some scholars claim that greater importance should be attached to the education of ***patriotism***.

[猜一猜] A 革新 B 爱国主义 C 技术素质 D 智慧

[翻 译] 一些学者主张应该加强爱国主义教育。

[分 析] patriot + ism

爱国者 + 名词词尾 → 爱国主义，爱国精神

[大头例句] Among many modern young people, the notion of blind patriotism is outdated and dangerous, as it promotes a mindset that ignores the mistakes governments make. 在很多现代的年轻人当中，盲目的爱国主义是危险且不合潮流的，因为它会鼓励一种倾向：对政府所犯的错误毫不在乎。

peculiar *adj./n.* /piˈkjuːljə/

Each person's handwriting has its own ***peculiar*** characteristics.

[猜一猜] A 艺术的 B 外形的 C 内在的 D 特殊的

[翻 译] 每个人的笔记都有它自己独特的特点。

[分 析] pecu + liar

钱财 + 词尾 → 专有财产，专有特权，特权的，独特的

[大头例句] It is peculiar indeed that so few people chose to attend the free concert: it was well-advertised, and the performer is loved for miles around. 事实上，这么少的人来参加这个免费的演唱会是很罕见的：广告做得很，表演者也是数英里内为人们所喜爱的。

petty *adj.* /ˈpeti/

I am not interested in your ***petty*** squabbles.

[猜一猜] A 美丽的 B 无理的 C 呆滞的 D 琐碎的

[翻 译] 我对你们无聊的争论没有兴趣。

[大头巧记] **Pet，宠物 → petty，小的，琐碎的。**

[词义扩展] *adj.* 小的，地位低下的，心胸狭窄的 → *petty minds* 小心眼儿 *petty bourgeois* 小资产阶级分子

[大头例句] It is such a shame that their entire friendship ended over such a petty disagreement as whose wife was more attractive. 让人脸红的是，他们整个友谊结束的原因只是为了谁的妻子更有魅力这样的一个无关紧要的争执。

trivial *adj.* /ˈtriviəl/

What to eat is always a ***trivial*** matter to me.

[猜一猜] A 重要的 B 不诚实的 C 热情的 D 微不足道的

[翻 译] 对我来说吃什么是微不足道的。

[分 析] tri + via + (a)l

三 + 路 + 词尾 → 三条路交汇的地方，三岔路口，公众常去的地方，通俗的，微不足道的

[习语记忆] **put the trivial above important** 轻重倒置

[大头例句] I'm sorry to bother you with what must seem a trivial problem. 很抱歉麻烦你，这个问题看起来一定是太微不足道了。

undo *v.* /ˌʌnˈduː/

She ***undid*** the string around the parcel.

[猜一猜] A 毁坏 B 解开 C 负担 D 点燃

[翻 译] 她解开了绕在包裹上的绳子。

[大头巧记] do，做；**undo**，不做，解开，松开，取消，毁坏。

[习语记忆]**What is done cannot be undone.** [谚]覆水难收。

[大头例句]She warned that one mistake could undo all their achievements. 她警告说一个错误就可能把所有他们获得的成就搞砸了。

withdraw *v.* /wiðˈdrɔː/

He *withdrew* all his savings from the bank.

[猜一猜]A 存储　B 收回　C 保护　D 增加

[翻　译]他把存在银行里的钱都取出来了。

[大头巧记]draw with，把钱从银行里拉回来，收回，撤销，退出。

[大头例句]The right to withdraw work is a basic principle of union membership. 退出合作的权利是联盟关系的一个基本原则。

习题：在下面的空格中填写本单元的单词。

1. What we should do is to ________ the dross and select the essential.
2. They are making an effort to ________ capital punishment in this state.
3. For parents to ________ their responsibilities of feeding, clothing, and otherwise providing for their children is illegal in most places.
4. It is of ________ importance that you remember to bring these documents to the trial; otherwise, we will have no evidence of the defendant's innocence.
5. The right to ________ work is a basic principle of union membership.
6. At that time the Germans were under the ________ rule of the dictator, Hitler.
7. Many cities ________ their sewage into the sea without treating it at all.
8. Currently, developing nations are ________ from certain restrictions on carbon emissions.
9. The British government, like many others, does not ________ the practice of polygamy.
10. Among many modern young people, the notion of blind ________ is outdated and dangerous, as it promotes a mindset that ignores the mistakes governments make.
11. It is such a shame that their entire friendship ended over such a ________ disagreement as whose wife was more attractive. 18. I'm sorry to bother you with what must seem a ________ problem.
12. She warned that one mistake could ________ all their achievements.
13. They agree to ________ us from our obligation.
14. He is seeking for the ________ of the difficult problem by giving a full explanation.
15. Many highway accidents can be ________ by careful driving.
16. The British ________ is famous the world over for its playful, often rude exchanges between members in debate.
17. It is ________ indeed that so few people chose to attend the free concert: it was well-advertised, and the performer is loved for miles around.

Day 49

a la carte *adj.* /ɑː lɑː ˈkɑːt/

We only have an *a la carte* menu.

[猜一猜] A 贴报式的 B 照单点菜式的 C 套餐的 D 网上预定的

[翻 译] 我们只有照单点菜式的分类菜单。

[分 析] a la + carte
按照…方式的 + 菜单 → 按照菜单的

[词义扩展] *adj./adv.* 照单点菜的(地)

[大头例句] When you book a holiday to the Greek islands with Travel a la carte, you can be sure you are in good hands. 当你照单点菜似的预定在希腊群岛上的假日时,你肯定会觉得心里很不踏实。(in good hands 在不中用/不可靠的人手里)

abstemious *adj.* /æbˈstiːmjəs/

He has an *abstemious* way of life: he never drinks or eats too much.

[猜一猜] A 节制的 B 奢侈的 C 丰富的 D 有趣的

[翻 译] 他生活节制,从来不喝太多的酒,吃饭也不太多。

[分 析] abs + temi + ous
away + 酒 + 形容词词尾 → 不沾酒,节制的

[词义扩展] *adj.* ①饮食适度的,有节制的 *an abstemious person* 一个饮食有度的人
②节省的,节俭的节俭地使用或消费的 *abstemious meals* 节俭的餐饭
③朴素的只有最基本的需要的 → *an abstemious way of life* 朴素的生活

[大头例句] An abstemious man refuses to have even a sip of champagne. 节制的人一点儿香槟都不沾。

ale *n.* /eil/

His business mends like sour *ale* in summer.

[猜一猜] A 淡啤酒 B 牛奶 C 果酱 D 黄油

[翻 译] 他的生意每况愈下。(像夏天的酸啤酒一样发展)

[词义扩展] ale, *n.* (淡色)浓啤酒(约含百分之六的酒精),爱尔啤酒
ale wife 啤酒店老板娘
ginger ale 姜汁啤酒,姜汁汽水

alcoholism *n.* /ˈælkəhɔlizəm/

Alcoholism is a serious problem among the youth.

[猜一猜] A 酒精 B 酗酒 C 近视 D 犯罪

[翻 译] 酗酒是当今青年人一个很严重的问题。

[分 析] alcohol + ism
酒精 +…主义 → 酒精主义,酗酒,酒精中毒

appetite *n.* /ˈæpitait/

I lost my *appetite* for meat.

[猜一猜] A 胃口 B 厌恶 C 偏见 D 辨别力

[翻 译] 我失去了吃肉的胃口。

[分 析] ap + pet + ite
to + to seek + 名词词尾 → 寻求,对某物欲望

[大头巧记] 掐尾法:ite 为名词词根可略去不记,appet,拆:ap(ple) pet 宠物对苹果有很好的胃口。

[大头例句] He has a huge sexual appetite now. → 他现在性欲很强。

calcium *n.* /ˈkælsiəm/

Calcium is one of the most important factors essential to life.

[猜一猜] A 锌 B 钙 C 铁 D 铝

[翻 译] 钙是生命必需的最重要元素之一。

[分 析] calc + ium
lime, 石灰 + 表元素的名词词尾 → 石灰中富含的元素:钙

[大头巧记] 很多元素单词都是以"ium"结尾的,化学中钙的代号是Ca,即是此单词的首字母,看到

这两个特征，这个单词就很容易识别了。

cereal *n.* /ˈsiəriəl/

It is good for your health to eat more food prepared from *cereals*.

[猜一猜] A 高蛋白　　B 液体
C 谷类　　D 无污染食品

[翻　译] 吃更多谷类调制的食物对你的健康有益。

[大头巧记] 记住它的特征部分 real，真正的好食品是谷类食品。

[大头例句] A bowl of cereal could save a family in the famine. 在闹饥荒时，一碗谷子可以救一家人。

champagne *n.* /ʃæmˈpein/

Most people believe that France produces the best *champagne* in the world.

[猜一猜] A 香波　B 香水　C 香槟　D 时装

[翻　译] 很多人相信法国出产世界上最好的香槟。

[大头巧记] Champagne 原为法国的一个省，起泡沫的葡萄香槟酒于1700年首次在这里酿造，后以此名之，中文音译为香槟。

[词义扩展] *n.* 香槟色

[大头例句] The champagne cider suddenly became really popular among my friends. 苹果香槟酒忽然在我的朋友中间变得很受欢迎。

beverage *n.* /ˈbevəridʒ/

I want to see the supervisor of the *beverage* department.

[猜一猜] A 食品　B 住宿　C 人士　D 饮料

[翻　译] 我要见饮料部的主管。

[分　析] bever + age
饮　+ 名词词尾 → 饮料，任一种饮用的液体，通常不包括水在内

[词义扩展] *n.* [英方]餐费，酒费

[大头例句] The ready-to-drink beverages are more and more popular among college students. 现成可饮的即时饮料在大学生中间越来越流行。

contaminate *v.* /kəmˈtæmineit/

Industrial sewage continues to *contaminate* our beaches.

[猜一猜] A 流入　B 阻挡　C 污染　D 分割

[翻　译] 工业污水不断污染我们的海滩。

[分　析] con + tamin + ate
一起 + 接触　+ 动词词尾 → 接触到一起，沾染，污染

[大头例句] Don't be contaminated by bureaucratism. 不要沾染官僚主义作风。

dairy *n.* /ˈdɛəri/

We bought milk in the *dairy* section at the grocery store.

[猜一猜] A 食品　　B 日常用品
C 乳品　　D 新鲜食物

[翻　译] 我们在杂货店的乳品部买乳品。

[分　析] dai　+ ry
挤奶女工 + 表地方的词尾 → 挤奶女工工作的地方，牛奶场，引申为奶制品

[词义扩展] *n.* 牛奶场，奶制品厂，奶品店 *dairy cattle* 奶牛(总称) *dairy products* 乳制品

[大头例句] The dairy section at the grocery store is really welcome among the local residents. 杂货店里的奶制品区很受当地居民的欢迎。

edible *adj.* /ˈedibl/

Are these berries and mushrooms *edible*, or are they poisonous?

[猜一猜] A 免费的　　B 无毒的
C 可食用的　　D 深加工的

[翻　译] 这些草莓和蘑菇可以吃，还是有毒？

[分　析] edi + ble
吃 + 可…的 → 可食用的

[词义扩展] *n.*(*pl.*) 食品；可吃的东西

[大头例句] The food in the cafeteria is barely edible. 自助餐厅的食物难以下咽。

endow *v.* /inˈdau/

Nature *endowed* her with a beautiful singing voice.

[猜一猜]A 锻炼 B 沉迷 C 赋予 D 赎回

[翻 译]大自然赋予她一副美妙的歌喉。

[分 析]en + dow

on + 给予 → 赋予,天赋

[词义扩展]*v.* 捐助,捐赠 → *endow a hospital* 捐助一所医院

[大头例句]Our great motherland is favorably endowed climate-wise. 我们祖国的气候真是得天独厚。

graze *v./n.* /greiz/

Cattle were *grazing* in the field.

[猜一猜]A 耕作 B 吃草 C 慢跑 D 溜达

[翻 译]牛在地里吃草。

[大头巧记]grass,草 → graze,吃草

[词义扩展]*vt.&vi.* 擦过,擦伤,放牧 *She grazed her knee.* 她擦伤了膝盖。

[大头例句]She let her fingers graze lightly against his skin. 她用手指轻轻地在他的皮肤上擦过。

hitherto *adv.* /ˌhiðəˈtuː/

The weather, which had *hitherto* been sunny and mild, suddenly turned cold.

[猜一猜]A 一般 B 迄今 C 过去 D 误认为

[翻 译]迄今一直晴朗温暖的天气突然变冷了。

[分 析]hither + to

到此 + 到 → 迄今,到目前为止

[大头例句]Wight's book includes hitherto unpublished material. 怀特的书中包括迄今还未发表过的材料。

manure *n./v.* /məˈnjuə/

On my farm, we reuse cow *manure* as fertilizer for our plants.

[猜一猜]A 粪肥 B 食物 C 抛弃物 D 废料

[翻 译]在我的农场上,我们再利用牛粪作为庄稼的肥料。

[分 析]man + ure

手 + 词尾 → 用手劳作,给…施肥,粪肥

[大头例句]Flies flock to manure like children flock to playgrounds. 苍蝇聚结在粪上,就像孩子们聚集在操场上。

respiration *n.* /ˌrespəˈreiʃən/

Artificial *respiration* is very important in first aid.

[猜一猜]A 量血压 B 呼吸 C 止血 D 降温

[翻 译]人工呼吸在急救时非常重要。

[分 析]re + spir + ation

来回 + 呼吸 + 名词词尾 → 呼吸,呼吸作用

perishable *adj.* /ˈperiʃəbl/

Bananas are *perishable*, especially in hot weather.

[猜一猜]A 畅销的 B 易腐烂的 C 防水的 D 清爽的

[翻 译]香蕉易坏,特别是天热的时候。

[分 析]perish + able

腐烂 + 可…的 → 易腐烂的,脆弱的

[大头例句]Perishable fruits and vegetables are strictly forbidden through most customs gates because of the hazard they pose to local agriculture. 易腐烂的水果和蔬菜被大多数的海关严格禁止,因为它们可能危及当地的农业。

random *n./adj./adv.* /ˈrændəm/

The *random* drug testing of Olympic athletes is very common today.

[猜一猜]A 严格的 B 随意的 C 复杂的 D 有偏见的

[翻 译]对奥运会运动员的随意药物抽查,现今是很普通的事。

[大头巧记]**ran**,跑;**freedom**,自由 → **random**,自由的跑,随意的。

[词义扩展]*n.* 随意,任意

hit out at random 无的放矢

[大头例句]To determine the opinions of a large group of people, sometimes it is useful to choose a small representative number of people at random and allow their opinions to stand for the whole group's. 为了统一一大群人的思想,有时任意选择几个典型出来,让他们的思想代表所有的人是有用的。

toxic *adj.* /ˈtɔksik/

Food preservatives are *toxic* in concentrated amounts.

[猜一猜]A 有毒的　　B 乱哄哄的

C 没营养的　　D 公正的

[翻　译]食物防腐剂浓缩后有毒。

[分　析]tox + ic

毒 + 形容词尾 → 有毒的，中毒的

[大头巧记]联系 **sanitary**(卫生的，消毒的)记忆。

yield *v.* /jiːld/

We were forced to *yield* in contract.

[猜一猜]A 中止　B 承认　C 表现　D 让步

[翻　译]我们被迫在合同中做出让步。

[大头巧记]y(ell) (f)ield，有人在地里喊叫，我们当然要向她让步了。

[词义扩展]*v.* 出产，生长；*n.* 产量，收益

That tree yields fruits. 这种树结果。

[大头例句]Knowing about our past does not automatically yield solutions to our current problems.

了解我们的过去不会自动地就得出我们当前问题的解决办法。

习题：在下面的空格中填写本单元的单词。

1. Nature __________ her with a beautiful singing voice.
2. Knowing about our past does not automatically _________ solutions to our current problems.
3. To determine the opinions of a large group of people, sometimes it is useful to choose a small representative number of people at __________ and allow their opinions to stand for the whole group's.
4. Food preservatives are __________ in concentrated amounts.
5. The __________ section in the grocery store is really welcome among the local residents.
6. When you book a holiday to the Greek islands with Travel __________, you can be sure you are in good hands.
7. Industrial sewage continues to __________ our beaches.
8. It is good for your health to eat more food prepared from __________.
9. He has an __________ way of life, he never drinks or eats too much.
10. __________ is a serious problem among the youth.
11. The ready-to-drink __________ are more and more popular among college students.
12. The __________ cider suddenly became really popular among my friends.
13. His business mends like sour __________ in summer.
14. I lost my __________ for meat.
15. __________ is one of the most important factors essential to life.
16. Are these berries and mushrooms __________, or are they poisonous?
17. __________ fruits and vegetables are strictly forbidden through most customs gates because of the hazard they pose to local agriculture.
18. She let her fingers __________ lightly against his skin.
19. Artificial __________ is very important in first aid.
20. On my farm, we reuse cow __________ as fertilizer for our plants.
21. The weather, which had __________ been sunny and mild, suddenly turned cold.

Day 50

almanac *n.* /ˈɔːlmənæk/

I spent my whole day in the library reading the *almanac* of British politics for my papers.

[猜一猜] A 年鉴 B 历史 C 词典 D 报告

[翻 译] 为了写论文，我花了一整天的时间在图书馆里读英国政治年鉴。

[大头巧记] al(l) man ac(ting) (included)，包括了一年中某领域所有人的活动东西，年鉴。

[词义扩展] *n.* 历书

[大头例句] The antique almanac found in Xi'an is a very historic finding. 在西安发现的古历书是一个很有历史意义的发现。

alumnus *n.* /əˈlʌmnəs/

The *alumni* are going to party together after 10 o'clock.

[猜一猜] A 男校友 B 女校友 C 男老师 D 女老师

[翻 译] 十点后男校友将会去聚会狂欢。

[联 想] **alumna *pl.* alumnae 女校友，女毕业生**

antique *n./adj.* /ænˈtiːk/

This is the best online source where you can find *antique* shops.

[猜一猜] A 丝绸的 B 古董的 C 瓷器的 D 珠宝的

[翻 译] 这是你找寻古董店在线信息的最好来源。

[分 析] ant + ique
before 以前 + 风格的 → 过去风格的，古董的

[大头巧记] an tea(谐) que(stion)，关于茶的话题，是个古老的话题。

[词义扩展] *adj.* 古代的；老式的 *a suit of rather antique appearance.* 一套相当过时的衣服 *vt.* 使显得古色古香 *antique the vase* 把这个花瓶做旧

[大头例句] The antique dealer is a trickster; most of his antique potteries are fake. 那个古董商是个骗子，他的古陶器大多都是赝品。

archive *vt./n.* /ˈɑːkaiv/

The earliest file I've found in the *archive* is dated July 15, 1992.

[猜一猜] A 科目 B 获得 C 档案 D 图书馆

[翻 译] 我在档案中找到最早的文件日期是1992年7月15日的。

[分 析] archi + ve
政府 + 名词词尾 → 政府，官方所留的档案

[大头巧记] 形近词 **achieve 获得**，把所获得之物去掉e(mpty)-空洞之物，加上r(eason)-理性的选择，就成为了正式的档案。

[词义扩展] *vt.* 存档

[大头例句] I found proof that they have a blood relationship in the family archives. 在家谱中我找到了他们两个有血缘关系的证据。

centenary *n./adj.* /senˈtiːnəri/

The university is planning to hold a celebration to mark the *centenary* to its library's birth.

[猜一猜] A 翻新 B 落成 C 祝贺 D 百年

[翻 译] 这所大学正在计划为纪念图书馆诞生100周年而举行庆典。

[分 析] cent + en + ary
一百 + 年 + 词尾 → 一百年的，一百年

chronological *adj.* /ˌkrɔnəˈlɔdʒikəl/

It is less difficult to learn the *chronological* table of the European battles in *chronological* order.

[猜一猜] A 按时间顺序的 B 按地点顺序的 C 帝王年号顺序 D 历史人物顺序

[翻 译] 按照时间先后的顺序来记忆欧洲战争年表

就不是那么难了。

[分　析] chron　+ ologi　+ cal
时间　+…学的 + 形容词尾 → 与年代学有关的，按年代顺序的

conform *v./adj.* /kən'fɔːm/

On the first day when a pupil enters school, he is asked to *conform* to the school rules.

[猜一猜] A 牢记　B 组合　C 冲掉　D 遵守

[翻　译] 从进校的第一天起，学校就要求学生遵守校规。

[分　析] con　+ form
共同 + 形式 → 形式共同，使一致，使遵守，符合

[大头例句] Products are always tested to make sure that they conform to standard specifications. 产品经常要通过检测来确定他们是否符合标准规格。

decay *v./n.* /di'kei/

Stone does not *decay*, and so the tools of long ago have remained when even the bones of the men who made them have disappeared without a trace.

[猜一猜] A 消失　B 移动　C 死亡　D 腐烂

[翻　译] 石头是不腐烂的，因此远古年代的工具至今尚存，即使制造这些工具的人的骨头已经毫无痕迹地消失了。

[分　析] de　+ cay
向下 + 变弱 → 衰退，衰败，腐烂

[大头巧记] 形近词记忆：**delay**，延迟，c(orpse)(尸体)，延迟了以后会腐败。

[词义扩展] *n.* 衰退，腐朽，腐烂 *Radioactive decay* 放射性的衰变

[大头例句] Dentists advise their patients to brush and floss regularly to prevent their teeth from decaying. 牙医们让他们的病人，按时刷牙和剔牙以防止他们蛀牙。

geology *n.* /dʒi'ɔlədʒi/

Geology is the scientific study of the origin, history, and structure of the Earth.

[猜一猜] A 社会学　B 生物学
C 人类学　D 地质学

[翻　译] 地质学是关于地球起源、历史和结构的科学研究。

[分　析] geo　+ logy
地球 + …学 → 研究地球的学科，地质学

[词义扩展] *n.* (某一地区的)地质概况，地质学的著作

[大头例句] He made a brilliant achievement in the study of geology of oil fields. 他在油田地质的研究方面获得了辉煌的成就。

memento *n.* /me'mentəu/

As a *memento* from my trip to Xi'an, I asked politely if I could take a Terracotta Warrior home with me; alas, the security guard seemed to regard me as a malicious thief!

[猜一猜] A 回报　B 纪念品　C 研究　D 汇报

[翻　译] 作为西安之行的纪念品，我有礼貌地问讯是否我可以带走一个兵马俑；唉，那个保安看起来好像把我当成了心怀不轨的小偷。

[大头巧记] **remember**，记忆；**memento**，勾起人回忆的事物：纪念品

[大头例句] Crockett kept the cross as a memento of his trip. 克罗吉特把这个十字架作为他旅行的纪念品。

millennium *n.* /mi'leniəm/

In the coming *millennium*, man can expect unimaginable advances in health, technology, and overall human capacity.

[猜一猜] A 世纪　B 发展　C 前景　D 千年

[翻　译] 在接下来的千年里，人们期待着在健康、科技和人类全面能力有不可思议的发展。

[分　析] millen　+ nium
一千　+ 年 → 千年，千禧年，太平盛世

[大头例句] People celebrating the millennium filled the streets. 庆祝千禧年的人们充满了街道。

orthodox *adj.* /'ɔːθədɔks/

His opinions are very *orthodox*.

[猜一猜] A 诡异的　B 合理的
C 灵活的　D 正统的

[翻 译]他的想法非常正统。

[分 析]ortho + dox

正 + 观点 → 正统的，传统的，保守的

[大头巧记]与 **heathen**(异教的，野蛮的)对比记忆。

productivity *n.* /ˌprɔdʌkˈtiviti/

The factory is looking for ways of improving *productivity*.

[猜一猜]A 知名度　B 占有率　C 生产率　D 待遇

[翻 译]工厂正设法提高生产率。

[分 析]productiv(e) + ity

多产的 + 名词词尾 → 生产率，生产力

recall *vt.* /riˈkɔːl/

Twenty years later he could still clearly *recall* the event.

[猜一猜]A 回应　B 支撑　C 号召　D 回忆

[翻 译]二十年后他仍然可以清楚地记得这个事件。

[大头巧记]拆：re call，再次唤起，回忆。

[词义扩展]*n./v.* 召回，取回

recall one's words 收回前言

[大头例句]For today's quiz, you will be asked to simply recall as many of the words we have studied this semester and write them on a sheet of paper. 今天的考试很简单，要求你们回忆尽可能多的本学期学过的单词，并把他们写到一张纸上。

retrospect *n.* /ˈretrəuspekt/

It was, in *retrospect*, the happiest day of her life.

[猜一猜]A 理论上　B 感情上　C 回顾　D 总体

[翻 译]回想起来，那是她一生最幸福的日子。

[分 析]retro + spect

向后 + 看 → 向后看一下，回顾

[词义扩展]*v.* 回顾，追溯 *retrospect to an early period* 追溯到早期。

sovereign *adj.* /ˈsɔvrin/

The people are considered a source of *sovereign* power.

[猜一猜]A 神圣的　B 最高的　C 无敌的　D 感激的

[翻 译]人民被认为是最高权力之源。

[分 析]sove + reign

超过 + 统治 → 以超过一切的地位统治，君主的，至高无上的，独立自主的。

[词义扩展]*n.* 独立自主的，君主，最高统治者。

[大头例句]The UN was designed as an association of sovereign states. 联合国被设计为独立主权国家的联盟。

undergo *vt.* /ˌʌndəˈgəu/

My house is *undergoing* renovations.

[猜一猜]A 下流　B 争论　C 部署　D 经历

[翻 译]我的房子正在装修。

[大头巧记]拆：under go，在…下面走，忍受，遭受，经历。

[大头例句]The bridge has undergone a series of modifications and will be re-opened in two weeks. 该桥正经受一系列的改造，将于两周后重新开放。

vacant *adj.* /ˈveikənt/

Are there any rooms *vacant* in this hotel?

[猜一猜]A 高档的　B 空闲的　C 顽皮的　D 巨大的

[翻 译]这家旅馆有空房吗？

[分 析]vaca + nt

空 + 形容词尾 → 空的，空闲的，头脑空虚的

[大头巧记]**vacation**，假期 → **vacancy** *n.* 空闲 → **vacant**，空闲的。

[大头例句]This house has been vacant since early spring. 从早春时这个屋子就空闲下来了。

wretched *adj.* /ˈretʃid/

The *wretched* prisoners were huddling in the stinking cages.

[猜一猜] A 恐怖的　　B 秘密的
C 控制的　　D 可怜的

[翻　译] 那些不幸的囚犯全挤在恶臭的牢笼里。

[分　析] wretch　+ ed
不幸的人 + 词尾 → 可怜的,悲惨的,恶劣的

[大头例句] I looked everywhere and eventually found the wretched letter. 我到处都找了,终于找到了这封讨厌的信。

thereby /ˌðɛəˈbai/

I asked him to stop smoking in my house, *thereby* indicating that he was being rude.

[猜一猜] A 因为　B 但是　C 既然　D 从而

[翻　译] 我要求他不要在我的房子里抽烟,从而暗示他这样做很粗鲁。

[大头巧记] 拆:there by,通过那儿,从而,因此。

[习语记忆] **Thereby hangs a tale.** 其中有点蹊跷。

[大头例句] He became a citizen in 1978, thereby gaining the right to vote. 1978年的时候我成为一名公民,因此获得了选举的权利。

习题:在下面的空格中填写本单元的单词。

1. The university is planning to hold a celebration to mark the __________ of its library's birth.
2. Stone does not __________, and so the tools of long ago have remained when even the bones of the men who made them have disappeared without a trace.
3. __________ is the scientific study of the origin, history, and structure of the Earth.
4. The bridge has __________ a series of modifications and will be re-opened in two weeks.
5. It was, in __________, the happiest day of her life.
6. For today's quiz, you will be asked to simply __________ as many of the words we have studied this semester and write them on a sheet of paper.
7. As a __________ from my trip to Xi'an, I asked politely if I could take a Terracotta Warrior home with me; alas, the security guard seemed to regard me as a malicious thief!
8. I spent my whole day in the library reading the __________ of British politics for my papers.
9. In the coming __________, man can expect unimaginable advances in health, technology, and overall human capacity.
10. This is the best online source where you can find __________ shops.
11. He became a citizen in 1978, __________ gaining the right to vote.
12. Are there any rooms __________ in this hotel?
13. The __________ prisoners were huddling in the stinking cages.
14. The __________ are going to party together after 10 o'clock.
15. It is less difficult to learn the __________ table of the European battles in chronological order.
16. His opinions are very __________.
17. The factory is looking for ways of improving __________.
18. The UN was designed as an association of __________ states.
19. Products are always tested to make sure that they __________ to standard specifications.
20. I found the proof that they have a blood relationship in the family __________.

Day 51

appropriate *adj.* /əˈprəupriət/

Your casual clothes were not *appropriate* for such a formal occasion in the embassy.

[猜一猜]A 影响的　　　　B 适合的
　　　　C 要求的　　　　D 休闲的

[翻　译]你的便服不适合在大使馆这样的正式场合穿。

[分　析]ap + propri + ate
to + 适合的(proper) + 形容词词尾 → 适合的

[词义扩展]*vt.* ①拨给，拨出 *The government appropriated a large sum of money for improving the teachers' housing situation.* 政府拨出一大笔钱改善老师的住房情况。②挪用；盗用 *to appropriate public funds* 挪用公款

[大头例句]I'm looking for an appropriate occasion to tell her my feelings.我在寻找一个合适的时机告诉她我的感觉。

acoustics *n.* /əˈkuːstiks/

The hall has good *acoustics*.

[猜一猜]A 声响效果　B 视觉效果
　　　　C 防火装置　D 监视系统

[翻　译]这个大厅的音响效果很好。

[联　想]acoustic *adj.* 声学的，声响效果好的

[词义扩展]*n.* 声学

analogous *adj.* /əˈnæləgəs/

This proposal was *analogous* to/ with the one we discussed at the last meeting.

[猜一猜]A 类似的　　　　B 抵触的
　　　　C 补充的　　　　D 阐释的

[翻　译]这项提案与上次会议上我们讨论过的那份提案相似。

[分　析]ana + logous
根据 + 比例 → 成比例的，类似的

[大头例句]His opinions are always analogous to his wife's, so his friends think him henpecked.他的观点总是和他妻子的看法类似，所以他的朋友都觉得他是个妻管严。

dialect *n.* /ˈdaiəlekt/

Cockney is a *dialect* of English.

[猜一猜]A 因素　B 语法　C 精神　D 方言

[翻　译]伦敦话是英语的一种方言。

[分　析]dia + lect
在…之间 + 说话 → 在一定的区域内使用的语言，方言

[词义扩展]*n.* ①【语】同语系的语支 ②(某人的)惯用语 ③某行业用语

[大头例句]English is an Indo-European dialect.英语是印欧语的一个分支。

eloquent *adj.* /ˈeləkwənt/

His speech is touchingly *eloquent*.

[猜一猜]A 雄辩的　　　　B 缜密的
　　　　C 极端的　　　　D 内容丰富的

[翻　译]他的演说雄辩而感人。

[分　析]e + logu + ent
出去 + 说 + 形容词尾 → 说出的

[词义扩展]*adj.* ①雄辩地，有说服力的 ②动人的，意味深长的，眉飞色舞的

[大头例句]His eloquent look with compassion impressed me deeply. 他充满同情的眼色给我留下很深的印象。

degenerate *v.* /diˈdʒenəreit/

His health *degenerated* rapidly as he continued to drink.

[猜一猜]A 恶化　B 糊涂　C 好转　D 成熟

[翻　译]他的健康随着他的酗酒而很快恶化。

[分　析]de + generate

降低 + 种类 → 从自己所属的种类中降低，退化，恶化

[词义扩展] *adj.*, *n.* ①腐化的[者]，颓废的[者]，退化的（动物）②变质的（东西），【遗传学】简并 *doubly degenerate* 二度简并

[大头例句] The old water pipes are degenerating with age. 水管随时间而老化。

giggle *v./n.* /ˈɡiɡl/

The girls were *giggling* in class.

[猜一猜] A 小声说话 B 讨论问题 C 吵架 D 咯咯地笑

[翻 译] 女孩们在课堂上格格地笑。

[大头巧记] **giggle**，谐音为咯咯，咯咯地笑。

[词义扩展] *n.* 傻笑，痴笑

[大头例句] During his speech, I got the giggles and had to leave. 在他讲话的时候，我忍不住咯咯地笑，不得不离开。

gossip *n.* /ˈɡɔsip/

She likes *gossiping* about the neighbors' domestic problems.

[猜一猜] A 评价 B 参与 C 闲谈 D 打听

[翻 译] 她喜欢闲谈邻居们的家务事。

[分 析] gos + sip

god + …的亲属 → 神的亲戚 → 教父、教母 → 亲密的朋友 → 酒肉朋友 → 边喝边聊 → 闲聊，闲话 → 长舌妇

[大头例句] He liked a good gossip when he arrived at the office. 当他到办公室的时候，他喜欢快乐的闲谈。

groan *v.* /ɡrəun/

The wounded man lay there *groaning*, with no one to help him.

[猜一猜] A 挣扎 B 呼救 C 发火 D 呻吟

[翻 译] 受伤者躺在那里呻吟着，无人救助。

[词义扩展] *n.* 呻吟声，抱怨声 *n./v.* 吱吱声 *They've got the usual moans and groans like everybody else.* 像所有其他人一样，他们也经常抱怨和叹息。

[大头例句] The chair gave a groan when the fat woman sat down. 当胖女人坐在椅子上时，椅子发出吱吱声。

grumble *adj./v.* /ˈɡrʌmbl/

He *grumbled* at the low pay offered to him.

[猜一猜] A 改变 B 满足 C 抱怨 D 废弃

[翻 译] 他抱怨给他的工资低。

[词义扩展] *v./n.* 埋怨，发牢骚，咕哝 *grumbling subway trains* 隆隆地响着的地铁

[大头例句] My only grumble is that the system is a bit slow. 我惟一的牢骚就是这个系统有点慢。

hubbub *n.* /ˈhʌbʌb/

Her voice was barely audible in the growing *hubbub*.

[猜一猜] A 乐音 B 广告 C 吵闹声 D 距离

[翻 译] 她的声音在增长的吵闹声中几乎听不见。

[大头巧记] 声音特征，嘴唇不断张合 → 喧哗，吵闹声不断。

[大头例句] I can hardly endure the hubbub upstairs. 我无法忍受楼上的吵闹声。

gear *n.* /ɡiə/

Always use a low *gear* when driving down a steep hill.

[猜一猜] A 油门 B 挡位 C 声调 D 要求

[翻 译] 当你在开车下陡坡的时候，要总是用低挡位。

[大头巧记] g(ather) ear(s). 聚在一起的耳状物，齿轮，汽车排挡，传动装置。

[词义扩展] *n.* 设备，装置，机构 *vt./vi.* 齿轮连接，机器开动，使适合(to) *adj.* 极好的，极棒的

[大头例句] Is the program geared to a fixed salary increase schedule? 这一方案是同一个固定的工资增长日程配套的吗？

incentive *n.* /inˈsentiv/

Money is still a major *incentive* in most occupations.

[猜一猜]A 手段　B 目的　C 基础　D 激励

[翻　译]在许多职业中，钱仍是主要的鼓励因素。

[分　析]in　+ cent　+ ive

里面 + 说，唱 + 词尾 → 用歌声激励，刺激，鼓励

[大头巧记]拆：in cent(er)，在中心的东西，刺激，激励大家的东西。

[词义扩展]v./ n./ adj. 刺激（的），鼓励（的）；n. 动机 incentive to work hard. 努力工作的动机

[大头例句]They want to stimulate growth in the region by offering incentives to foreign investors. 他们想要通过给予外国投资者鼓励条件来刺激其地域经济的增长。

melodious *adj.* /mi'ləudjəs/

I will never forget the *melodious* ring of my mother's voice as she called out for me to come home for dinner.

[猜一猜]A 高高的　B 长长的　C 音调优美的　D 嘹亮的

[翻　译]我永远无法忘怀妈妈唤我回家吃晚饭时那优美的嗓音。

[分　析]melodi　+ ous

悦耳音调 + 形容词尾 → 音调优美的

[大头例句]They are enjoying the melodious cello. 他们正在欣赏优美的大提琴演奏。

metaphor *n.* /'metəfə/

As a *metaphor* for the two countries' relative positions on the globe, the young man held up his clenched fist and used his other hand to point to different places on it.

[猜一猜]A 比喻　B 说明　C 发展趋势　D 历史

[翻　译]作为两国之间在国际上所处位置的比喻，这个年轻人举起了他紧握的拳头，用另一只手指点着上面不同的地方。

[分　析]meta + phor

改变 + 传达 → 用变化了的方式表达，隐喻，暗语，比喻

[词义扩展]n. 象征 *The high-rise garbage repository is a metaphor for both accomplishment and failure*，堆积如山的垃圾场既是人类成就的象征，也是人类失败的象征。

[大头例句]He often uses the metaphor of the family to describe the role of the state. 他经常用家庭的比喻来形容国家的作用。

represent *v.* /repri'zent/

The museum had several paintings *representing* the artist's early style.

[猜一猜]A 出现　B 执行　C 代表　D 消退

[翻　译]博物馆藏有几幅代表这个艺术家早期风格的油画。

[分　析]re　+ present

加强语气 + 表现 → 表现，象征，代表

[词义扩展]v. 再次上演　*represent a play* 再上演某剧

[大头例句]In the Western poetic tradition, water is often used to represent life and vitality. 在西方诗歌传统中，水经常被用来描写生活和生命力。

resilience *n.* /ri'ziliəns/

This is an alloy combining strength and *resilience*.

[猜一猜]A 硬度　B 色泽　C 弹力　D 锤炼

[翻　译]这是一块既有强度又有弹力的合金。

[分　析]re　+ silie + nce

再次 + 跳 + 名词词尾 → 再次跳起的性质，弹性，弹力

[词义扩展]n. 恢复力，愉快的心情

slight *adj.* /slait/

A *slight* prick, and the injection was over.

[猜一猜]A 轻轻的　B 疼痛的　C 震撼的　D 升高的

[翻　译]轻轻的一扎，针就打好了。

[大头巧记]**light，轻；slight，轻微的，微小的**

[习语记忆]**not in the slightest** 一点不，完全不

[大头例句]I looked at the homework earlier this afternoon, but I don't have the slightest clue of how I'm supposed to do it; I think I will call my classmate and ask for her help. 今天下午早些时候我看了一下家庭作业，可是我对于应该怎么做一点头绪都没有；我想我会给我的同学打电话来寻求帮助。

tranquility *n.* /træŋˈkwiliti/

The *tranquility* seemed really strange.

[猜一猜] A 风格　B 气氛　C 宁静　D 和睦

[翻　译] 那种平静看起来很奇怪。

[分　析] tran + quil + ity

上 + 静止 + 名词词尾 → 宁静

vivid *adj.* /ˈvivid/

I have a *vivid* memory of the first time we met.

[猜一猜] A 稳定的　B 凝结的　C 清晰的　D 秘密的

[翻　译] 我清晰地记得我们的第一次相见。

[大头巧记] 词性记忆：vivid，两个“vi”形似两棵努力生长的小草(v)和两株可爱的小花(i)，清晰生动的。

[词义扩展] *adj.* 亮色的 *The lake was a vivid blue.* 那个湖亮蓝亮蓝的。

[大头例句] The incident is a vivid illustration of the hysteria currently gripping the nation. 这个事件清楚地表明最近该国已为狂热所支配。

shrink *v.* /ʃriŋk/

The dress *shrank* when I washed it.

[猜一猜] A 退色　B 缩水　C 起皱　D 破损

[翻　译] 这件衣服洗后缩水了。

[习语记忆] **shrink into oneself** 踌躇

[大头例句] The Prime Minister is unlikely to shrink from making tough decisions. 该总理不太可能收回自己强硬的决定。

习题：在下面的空格中填写本单元的单词。

1. The government __________ a large sum of money for improving the teachers' housing situation.
2. English is an Indo-European __________.
3. His opinions are always __________ to his wife's, so his friends think him henpecked.
4. The hall has good __________.
5. Always use a low __________ when driving down a steep hill.
6. The Prime Minister is unlikely to __________ from making tough decisions.
7. His __________ look with compassion impressed me a lot.
8. I looked at the homework earlier this afternoon, but I don't have the __________ clue of how I'm supposed to do it; I think I will call my classmate and ask for her help.
9. Money is still a major __________ in most occupations.
10. During his speech, I got the __________ and had to leave.
11. His health __________ rapidly as he continued to drink.
12. Her voice was barely audible in the growing __________.
13. The wounded man lay there __________, with no one to help him.
14. She likes __________ about the neighbors' domestic problems.
15. I will never forget the __________ ring of my mother's voice as she called out for me to come home for dinner.
16. In the Western poetic tradition, water is often used to __________ life and vitality.
17. This is an alloy combining strength and __________.

18. The __________ seemed really strange.
19. The incident is a __________ illustration of the hysteria currently gripping the nation.
20. As a __________ for the two countries' relative positions on the globe, the young man held up his clenched fist and used his other hand to point to different places on it.
21. He __________ at the low pay offered to him.

Note 前事不忘后事之师 *Remember the past and it will guide your future.*

Day 52

acute *adj.* /əˈkjuːt/

"a raw, chilling and psychologically *acute* novel of human passions reduced to their deadliest essence." (Literary Guild Magazine)

[猜一猜] A 呆板的　B 激动的　C 冷漠的　D 敏锐的

[翻　译] "一部不加雕琢，令人不寒而栗并且心理敏锐的小说，反应了人类激情减至其最致命本质"(文学协会杂志)。

[大头巧记] a cute (girl)，见到一个可爱的女孩，感觉就敏锐起来。

另，本词源于 acus，针，引申为尖锐，敏锐。

[联　想] **acuity** ***n.*** 尖锐，锐利，(病况的) 急剧，(才智等的)敏锐 *acuity of wit* 才思敏捷

acumen ***n.*** 敏锐，聪明 *political acumen* 政治才干

activate ***vt.*** ①使…活动，对…起作用 ②开 [起] 动，触发 *His mistake activated a snowslide.* 他的错误诱发了雪崩。 ③创设，成立 (机构等) *activated by selfish motives* 在自私动机的驱使下

[大头例句] Although he had a cold, he still had a very acute sense of smell to wards meat. 虽然感冒了，可是对于肉他还是有着非常敏锐的嗅觉。

adroit *adj.* /əˈdrɔit/

He is *adroit* in playing the piano because his long fingers.

[猜一猜] A 忙碌的　B 熟练的　C 热衷的　D 沉迷的

[翻　译] 由于他有修长的手指，所以钢琴弹得很好。

[分　析] ad + droit

向 + 正确的 → 总是正确的，熟练的，机巧的

[大头例句] The president is an adroit crisis handler. 总统是一位处理危机的能手。

allergy *n.* /ˈælədʒi/

I have an *allergy* to penicillin.

[猜一猜] A 过敏　B 依赖　C 感情　D 感染

[翻　译] 我对青霉素过敏。

[分　析] all + ergy

其他的 + 行为 → 对…有其他的行为反应，过敏

[联　想] **allergic** 过敏的 *allergic to*

[词义扩展] *n.* 厌恶，讨厌 *He has an allergy to cocktail parties.* 他对对鸡尾酒会很厌恶。

[大头例句] More than 50 million Americans are afflicted with asthma, seasonal hay fever, or other allergy-related conditions each year. 每年有超过 5 千万的美国人在受着哮喘，周期性黑河热和其它过敏症相关症状的折磨。

admonish *vt.* /ədˈmɔniʃ/

The derbies and wards *admonished* the criminals the fate that awaited them.

[猜一猜] A 预示　B 命令　C 告诫　D 暗示

[翻　译] 手铐和牢房告诫着那些犯罪分子等待他们的命运。

[分　析] ad + monish

朝向 + 警告 → 向…发出警告，告诫

[大头巧记] 只要记住 monish 这个字根就可以了，monitor 是班长的意思，去掉 tor，加上 sh，使它动词化，班长的行为是告诫学生们日常事务中要注意的事情。

[词义扩展] *vt.* 劝告，警告，提醒

He admonished those frantic soccer fans to change their wicked ways. 他告诫那些疯狂的足球迷改变那种捣蛋的做法。

[大头例句] My stomach admonished me to change my drinking habit. 我的胃警告我要改变我喝酒的习惯。

caution n. /ˈkɔːʃən/

The car proceeded over the rickety bridge with *caution*.

[猜一猜]A 小心 B 摇晃 C 紧张 D 危险

[翻 译]汽车小心地在摇晃的桥上前进。

[分 析]cau + tion
小心谨慎 + 名词词尾 → 小心

[词义扩展]n. ①警告，告诫 give sb. a caution 告诫某人 ② 预防 vt. 警告，劝…使小心，告诫

[习语记忆]**Caution is the mother of security.**[谚]谨慎为安全之母。

[大头例句]The policeman cautioned the prisoners not to play any tricks. 警察正式告诫罪犯不要耍花招。

delicate adj. /ˈdelikit/

The amphibolous attitude of the British government over this issue makes the international situation very *delicate* at present.

[猜一猜]A 危险的 B 冲突的
C 稳定的 D 微妙的

[翻 译]英国政府在这个问题上的暧昧姿态使得当今的国际局势很微妙。

[分 析]de + lic + ate
一再 + 诱引 + 动词词尾 → 一再的诱引人的，精美的，微妙的，棘手的

[词义扩展]adj. ①易损的，纤细的 *The glasswork is delicate.* 玻璃制品容易碎。②易病的，体质差的 *a delicate looking child* 看起来瘦弱的小孩 ③精美的，优美的，奢华的，关心的 *delicate feeling* 温情

[大头例句]Delicate plants must be protected from cold wind and frost. 柔弱的植物必须被保护不受冷风和霜冻的侵害。

elaborate v. /iˈlæbərət/

The chairman just wanted the facts; you don't need to *elaborate* on them.

[猜一猜]A 评论 B 曲解
C 掩饰 D 详细阐述

[翻 译]主席只想了解事实；你不必作详细说明。

[分 析]e + labor + ate
强调 + 工作 + 动词词尾 → 在某方面加强工作，精心制作，详细阐述

[词义扩展]adj. 精致的，精巧的 *an elaborate machine* 精致的机器

[大头例句]There are times when you need a more elaborate flower arrangement. 有些时候你需要更精美的插花。

hazard vt. /ˈhæzəd/

He *hazarded* all his money to save the business.

[猜一猜]A 冒险 B 投资 C 取出 D 带走

[翻 译]他孤注一掷，拿出了所有的钱来挽救企业。

[大头巧记]hazard，本义是投骰游戏，赌博性的行为，冒险，孤注一掷。

[词义扩展]n. 危险，冒险，公害

[大头例句]One of the most widespread natural hazards is flooding. 洪水是分布最广泛的自然灾害之一。

induce vt. /inˈdjuːs/

Both treatments were effective in *inducing* remission of the disease.

[猜一猜]A 引起 B 灌输 C 反作用 D 缺乏

[翻 译]两种治疗方式都对诱导疾病消退有功效。

[分 析]in + duce
进入 + 引导 → 诱导，导致，引起

[大头巧记]**introduce**，引起，引进，介绍。**induce**，与此近义：引起。

[词义扩展]【逻】归纳，【电】感应，感生

[大头例句]Too much food induces sleepiness. 吃得过饱会产生睡意。

lump n. /lʌmp/

A *lump* of coal the size of a man's fist is all that is required to power this highly efficient machine for twelve hours.

[猜一猜]A 堆 B 块 C 车 D 铁斗

[翻 译]一块拳头大小的煤就完全能够满足这台高效机器运转 12 小时所需能量。

lump sum 一次性付款
lump sugar 块糖

[大头巧记] lamp(灯)里的"a"变成了"u",灯就不亮了,变成了一块废铁。

[词义扩展] *n.* 肿块,大块头的人;*v.* 形成块状,和在一起,忍耐 *lump the expense of their food* 把伙食费用混在一起

[习语记忆] **a lump in one's throat** 如骨鲠在喉,喻情感被压抑的状态。

[大头例句] You can like it or lump it, but I've got to work. 你要么喜欢,要么忍着,但我必须得去工作了。

mentality *n.* /menˈtæliti/

An optimistic ***mentality*** and approach to life is the most important factor in overall happiness.

[猜一猜] A 精神　B 行为　C 理论　D 意思形态

[翻　译] 一个乐观的精神和生活态度是所有快乐中最重要的因素。

[分　析] mental + ity

精神的 + 名词词尾 → 精神,智力,心理,意识

[习语记忆] **self-contradictory mentality** 矛盾心理 **single-child mentality** 独生子女心理 **juvenile mentality** 少年心理

[大头例句] I can't understand the mentality of these people who say such things. 我不能理解讲这些话的人的心理状态。

neurosis *n.* /njuəˈrəusis/

Adam can't finish his study because of his ***neurosis***.

[猜一猜] A 心脏病　B 散漫　C 精神衰弱症　D 灾难

[翻　译] 由于精神衰弱症,亚当不能完成他的学业。

[分　析] neur + osis

神经 + 病 → 神经病,神经衰弱症

[大头例句] It is a fine line between problematic neurosis and commonplace characteristics that create problems and limit one's happiness. 在问题性精神病和一般的造成问题并限制人的快乐的性格特征之间有很清楚的界线。

neuro- 表神经之义
neurology n. 神经学
neuron n. 神经细胞 神经元
neurotic n. 神经病患者 adj. 神经质的

menace *n./ v.* /ˈmenəs/

Mosquitoes have been the perpetual ***menace*** of many a summer picnic; to frogs, however, they are a delicious snack!

[猜一猜] A 打闹　B 担心　C 事故　D 危险物

[翻　译] 蚊子对于夏天的野餐来说成了一个永远的威胁,但是对于青蛙们来说,他们却是一顿可口的小吃。

[分　析] mena + ce

威胁 + 名词词尾 → 威胁,危险物,令人困扰的人或事物

[大头巧记] 拆:men-(f)ace,人的脸缺了一块(f),很危险,令人困扰。

[大头例句] The escaped prisoners are considered a menace to society. 逃亡的犯人被认为是对社会的一种威胁。

precaution *n.* /priˈkɔːʃən/

He took the ***precaution*** of locking his door when he went out.

[猜一猜] A 警惕　B 愚蠢　C 喜悦　D 责任

[翻　译] 当他外出的时候谨慎地锁上了门。

[分　析] pre + cau + tion

提前 + 意识 + 名词词尾 → 提前意识到危险,预防,警惕

[大头例句] Wearing a helmet while riding motorcycles is not merely a wise precaution; in this county, it is required by law. 骑摩托时戴上头盔不仅仅是一种聪明的预防措施;在这个国家,它还是个法律规定。

panic *n.* /ˈpænik/

When the theater caught fire, there was a ***panic***.

[猜一猜] A 浓烟　B 悲剧　C 恐慌　D 大死亡

[翻　译] 当剧场着火的时候,出现了恐慌。

[大头巧记] Pan 是希腊神话中的畜牧之神,panic,指 Pan 出现时产生的恐慌。另:pan,平底锅,平底锅着火时造成恐慌-panic。

[大头例句] The panic induced by the stock market crash was indeed understandable; millions of people faced unemployment, poverty, and decreased security. 股市危机所诱发的恐慌确实是可以理解的：好几百万人面临着失业、贫困和减少的保障。

passport *n.* /ˈpɑːspɔːt/

In those days a university degree was a ***passport*** to a secure job.

[猜一猜]A 通行证 B 文凭 C 助手 D 清晰

[翻 译]那个时候大学学位是得到一份有保障工作的敲门砖。

[大头巧记]pass port，通过港口，需要护照

[大头例句]Without a passport, the Chinese-American businessman had no proof of his citizenship, and was consequently detained for 48 hours before the embassy was able to assist him. 由于没有护照，该美籍华裔商人无法证明自己的公民身份，在使馆帮助他之前被拘留了 48 小时。

pavement *n.* /ˈpeivmənt/

I set it down on the ***pavement*** by the door of the shop.

[猜一猜]A 人行道 B 高速公路 C 花园 D 观景台

[翻 译]我把它放在店门边的人行道上。

[大头巧记]注意这个词在美式英语和英式英语中的语义区别，英文中意思是人行道，表示此义的美语用 sideway。美语中 pavement 的意思是铺筑过的路面，公路。

[习语记忆]**on the pavement** 徘徊街头

[大头例句]Many doctors say that jogging on grass or other softer surfaces is much less damaging to the knees and other leg joints than running on pavement. 很多医生说，在草地或其他柔软的表面上慢跑对膝盖的损伤要比在公路上跑步少的多。

recipient *n.* /riˈsipiənt/

The ***recipients*** of prizes had their names printed in the paper.

[猜一猜]A 参与者 B 接受者 C 竞争对手 D 同事

[翻 译]获奖者名单登在报上。

[分 析]re + cip + ient

再 + 拿 + …的人 → 下一个拿的人，接受者，容器

[词义扩展]*adj.* 容易接受的

[大头例句]In 2002, Halle Berry became the first African-American recipient of the most highly-coveted of Oscars: the award for Best Actress. 2002 年，Halle Berry，成为第一个赢得最具价值的奥斯卡奖项——最佳女主角的非裔美国人。

sensible *adj.* /ˈsensəbl/

This seems to be a ***sensible*** way of dealing with the problem.

[猜一猜]A 糊涂的 B 明智的 C 间接的 D 简单的

[翻 译]这似乎是解决问题的一个明智的办法。

[分 析]sens(e) + ible

感觉 + 形容词尾 → 有判断力的，明智的，有感觉的

[大头例句]By making sensible purchases of only items you need which are on sale, you should be able to trim off roughly one third of your monthly budget. 只明智地购买那些你需要而又有打折的东西，你就大约可以降低你月开支的三分之一。

sentiment *n.* /ˈsentimənt/

I had considerable sympathy with the ***sentiments*** expressed in his letter.

[猜一猜]A 悲剧 B 敏感 C 同感 D 感情

[翻 译]我对他信中表达的感情产生了相当大的共鸣。

[分 析]senti + ment

感觉 + 名词词尾 → 感情，多愁善感，情操

[习语记忆]**run to sentiments** 感情用事。

[大头巧记]sen(t) time 把时间寄给感情。

[大头例句]There's no space for sentiment in business!商场如战场!

subtle adj. /ˈsʌtl/

She was being so *subtle*, I didn't realize she liked me.

[猜一猜]A 真挚的　B 微妙的
C 慎重的　D 情绪化的

[翻　译]她的感情是如此的微妙,我没有意识到她喜欢我。

[大头巧记]**sub**,下面;**subtle**,下面的,隐藏着的,**微妙的**,**狡猾的**。

[词义扩展]*adj.* 精细的,敏锐的　*a subtle observer* 敏锐的观察者

[大头例句]The pictures are similar, but there are subtle differences between them.这两张画虽然相似,但是有些微妙的区别。

vengeance n. /ˈvendʒəns/

Something of *vengeance* I had tasted for the first time. An aromatic wine it seemed.

[猜一猜]A 成功　B 幸福　C 报复　D 宽容

[翻　译]我第一次尝到报复的滋味。它似乎是一种芳香的醇酒。

[大头巧记]**revenge**,报仇 → **vengeance** *n.* **报复**,**复仇**

[习语记忆]**Heaven's vengeance is slow but sure.**[谚]天网恢恢,疏而不漏。
with a vengeance [口]猛烈地

[大头例句]He was desperate to take vengeance on Marie's killer.他不顾一切的要对杀死玛丽的人报复。

violate vt. /ˈvaiəleit/

The soldiers *violated* the church by using it as a stable.

[猜一猜]A 征服　B 超越　C 亵渎　D 摧毁

[翻　译]士兵们把教堂当马厩,亵渎了它。

[分　析]viol + ate
力量 + 动词词尾 → 用暴力侵犯,强暴,亵渎,违反

[大头例句]Companies that violate environmental laws will be heavily fined.违反环境法的公司将受到严惩。

virus n. /ˈvaiərəs/

Malaria is caused by a *virus* carried by mosquitos.

[猜一猜]A 信息　B 病毒
C 毒液　D 遗传基因

[翻　译]疟疾是由蚊子携带的病毒引发的。

[大头例句]Most viruses are spread over the Internet.大多数的病毒是通过互联网传播的。

习题:在下面的空格中填写本单元的单词。

1. The derbies and wards __________ the criminals the fate that awaited them.
2. Adam can't finish his study because of his __________.
3. Wearing a helmet while riding motorcycles is not merely a wise __________: in this county, it is required by law.
4. In 2002, Halle Berry became the first African-American __________ of the most highly-coveted of Oscars: the award for Best Actress.
5. "a raw, chilling and psychologically __________ novel of human passions reduced to their deadliest essence."(Literary Guild Magazine)
6. More than 50 million Americans are afflicted with asthma, seasonal hay fever, or other __________-related conditions each year.
7. The policeman __________ the prisoners not to play any tricks.
8. One of the most widespread natural __________ is flooding.

9. A __________ of coal the size of a man's fist is all that is required to power this highly efficient machine for twelve hours.
10. An optimistic __________ and approach to life is the most important factor in overall happiness.
11. Both treatments were effective in __________ remission of the disease.
12. The amphibolous attitude of the British government over this issue makes the international situation very __________ at present.
13. He is __________ in playing the piano because of his long fingers.
14. The chairman just wanted the facts; you don't need to __________ on them.
15. Mosquitoes have been the perpetual __________ of many a summer picnic; to frogs, however, they are a delicious snack!
16. The __________ induced by the stock market crash was indeed understandable: millions of people faced unemployment, poverty, and decreased security.
17. Without a __________, the Chinese-American businessman had no proof of his citizenship, and was consequently detained for 48 hours before the embassy was able to assist him.
18. Many doctors say that jogging on grass or other softer surfaces is much less damaging to the knees and other leg joints than running on __________.
19. Most __________ are spread over the Internet.
20. Companies that __________ environmental laws will be heavily fined.
21. By making __________ purchases of only items you need which are on sale, you should be able to trim off roughly one third of your monthly budget.
22. I had considerable sympathy with the __________ expressed in his letter.
23. Something of __________ I had tasted for the first time. An aromatic wine it seemed.
24. She was being so __________, I didn't realize she liked me.

Day 53

adjacent *adj.* /əˈdʒeisənt/ =near.

Beijing and its *adjacent* suburbs, like Huairou, Miyun and so on, are very beautiful.

[猜一猜] A 附近的　B 较远的　C 可爱的　D 迷人的

[翻　译] 北京和它邻近的郊区，像怀柔、密云等地，是非常漂亮的。

[分　析] ad + jacent
临近 + 位于 → 位于邻近的地方，附近

[大头巧记] adj. 表示形容词，a cent，一分，相差只有一分的形容词，语义上是邻近的。

[联　想] **adjoin** *v.* 邻接，毗邻 *Mongolia adjoins to PRC.* 蒙古和中国毗邻。

[词义扩展] *adj.* 前后紧接着的；对面的 *a picture on an adjacent page* 对面一页上的图画

[习惯用语] **be adjacent to** 接近…

alienate *v.* /ˈeiljəneit/

Any attempt to *alienate* us will be doomed to failure because we have complete faith.

[猜一猜] A 攻击　B 离间　C 说服　D 误导

[翻　译] 任何离间我们的企图都注定失败，因为我们有完全的信任。

[分　析] alien + ate
不同的 + 动词词尾 → 使…不同，离间

[词义扩展] *vt.* ①使疏远 *You should not alienate yourselves from your classmates.* 你不应该疏远你的同学。
②使孤立，迟钝或不合群 *The numbing labor tended to alienate workers.* 枯燥的工作可以使工人变得麻木。

[大头例句] Due to his extreme position, the president alienated potential supporters. 由于总统极端的立场，他失去了其潜在的支持者。

cluster *n./ vi.* /ˈklʌstə/

He sent his girlfriend a *cluster* of flowers on Valentine's Day.

[猜一猜] A 包　B 支　C 礼品盒　D 束

[翻　译] 情人节的时候他给女朋友寄了一束鲜花。

[词义扩展] *vt.* 使成群；把…集成一束(或一簇、一组)
vi. 群集；丛生

[大头例句] People stood in clusters around the noticeboards. 人们成群地站在告示栏前。

coil *v.* /kɔil/

The cobra *coiled* itself up around the branch.

[猜一猜] A 盘绕　B 游动　C 觅食　D 恐惧

[翻　译] 眼镜蛇盘绕在树枝上。

[词义扩展] *n.* 卷；圈；盘卷；圈形物 *long coils of hair* 一长卷头发

context *n.* /ˈkɔntekst/

Can you tell the meaning of this word from its *context*?

[猜一猜] A 上下文　B 记录　C 供词　D 目击

[翻　译] 你能根据它的上下文说出这个词的意思吗？

[分　析] con + text
共同 + 编织 → 共同编织在一起的，上下文

[大头巧记] **text**，文章；**context**，上下文

[大头例句] The decline in the stock market, though dramatic, has to be seen in context. 股市的下降，虽然极具戏剧性，但也必须放在一定背景中理解。

damp *adj.* /dæmp/

None of us likes to sleep between *damp* sheets in damp weather.

[猜一猜] A 肮脏的　B 多沙的　C 潮湿的　D 干燥的

damp humid moist. wet

[翻 译]我们没有人愿意在潮湿的天气睡在潮湿的被单里。

[大头巧记]dam,水坝,dam p(lace),水坝边的地方,很潮湿。

[词义扩展]n. ①潮湿,湿度 ②沮丧,消沉,失望 ③令人消沉的东西 vt. 弄潮湿,阻止,妨碍,使沮丧 vi. 变湿,(振幅)衰减 *The rain dampened our spirits.* 雨使我们很扫兴。

[大头例句]Their mother's illness cast a damp over the Christmas holidays. 他们妈妈的病使圣诞假期失去了乐趣。

interact *vi.* /ˌintərˈækt/

More than a dozen variable factors could ***interact***, with their permutations running into the thousands.

[猜一猜]A 表现 B 活动 C 互相影响 D 侵犯

[翻 译]十二个以上的可变因素可以相互作用,它们的排列以千万计。

[分 析]inter + act

在中间 + 作用 → 相互作用,相互影响

[大头巧记]注意词根 inter,表示中间的,在内部的,例如:**interior** (内部的);**intermediate** (inter + mediater,中间 + 媒介 → **中间物,中间的**);**interim** (中间的 + 名词词尾 → 中间时期,过渡时期);**intermittent** (间歇的);**interval** (间隔的时间,间隔,间歇);**intervene**(中间的 + 来 → 来到中间,干涉);**interrogate** (inter + rog + ate,中间 + 问 + 动词词尾 → 在中间问,**审问**)。

[大头例句]In large classes, children feel that they cannot interact with the teacher properly. 在大教室里面,孩子们觉得他们和老师不能真正地互相影响。

isolate *vt./ n.* /ˈaisəleit/

Important witnesses are ***isolated*** from the media for their own safety.

[猜一猜]A 介绍 B 征召 C 涉及 D 隔绝

[翻 译]为了安全起见,重要的目击证人与媒体隔绝了。

[大头巧记]**island**,岛 → isle,岛 → **isolate**,使成为岛,隔绝,孤立。

[大头例句]We should never isolate ourselves from the masses. 我们永远不能脱离群众。

hitchhike *v.* /ˈhitʃhaik/

They ***hitchhiked*** around the coast of Ireland.

[猜一猜]A 漫步 B 考察 C 观光 D 搭便车

[翻 译]他们在爱尔兰海岸上搭便车旅行。

[大头巧记]**hitch**:钩住,**hike**:远足旅行,挂住别人旅行,**搭便车旅行**。

[大头例句]You should never go hitchhiking alone. 你永远不应该独自搭便车旅行。

incidence *n.* /ˈinsidəns/

The drug has been shown to reduce the ***incidence*** of thrombosis after surgery.

[猜一猜]A 影响 B 发生率 C 疼痛 D 崩溃

[翻 译]这种药品被用来减少手术后血栓症的发生率。

[分 析]in + ciden + ce

上面 + 落下 + 名词词尾 → 发生,发生率,影响,【物】入射(角)

[大头例句]What is the incidence of the tax? 这税会落在谁的身上?

liaison *n.* /liːˈeizən/

He served as the President's ***liaison*** with Congress in the 1970s.

[猜一猜]A 顾问 B 特使 C 发言人 D 联络人

[翻 译]20世纪70年代的时候他担任总统与议会的联系员。

[分 析]lia + ison

结合 + 名词词尾 → 联系,联系人,合作

[大头例句]We had an excellent liaison between our two companies. 我们两个公司间曾有过很好的合作。

mutual *adj.* /ˈmjuːtjuəl/

The scheme would be to our ***mutual*** benefit.

[猜一猜]A 共同的 B 纯粹的 C 最合理的 D 期货的

[翻 译]这个方案对我们都有利。

[分 析]mut + ual

改变 + 形容词尾 → 彼此调和的，共同的，互相的

[大头巧记] 注意它和"**mature,成熟的**"的区别。

[大头例句] My parents, who have been married for over 50 years, say the secret to their happiness has been mutual respect and willingness to compromise. 我父母已经结婚50年了，他们说他们幸福的秘诀是相互的尊重和积极地去让步和解。

locality *n.* /ləuˈkæliti/

Localities, even individual villages, developed their own languages.

[猜一猜] A 民族 B 地区 C 国家 D 乡村

[翻　译] 每一地区，甚至小村子都有他们自己的语言。

[分　析] local + ity

地方的 + 名词词尾 → 地方，地区，位置

[大头例句] Many people had moved to different localities. 很多人都已搬到别处去了。

polar *adj.* /ˈpəulə/

Kids like the *polar* bear very much.

[猜一猜] A 极地的 B 雨林地 C 温带地 D 棕色的

[翻　译] 孩子们很喜欢北极熊。

[大头巧记] **pole,极点,polar,极点的**。

[词义扩展] *adj.* 正好相反的；南辕北辙的 *polar personalities* 相反的个性

revolve *v.* /riˈvɔlv/

The Earth *revolves* around the sun.

[猜一猜] A 运动 B 变化 C 受力 D 旋转

[翻　译] 地球围绕太阳旋转。

[分　析] re + volve

一再 + 翻转 → 旋转，考虑，循环出现

[大头巧记] 同根词：**involve,卷进来**

pillar *n.* /ˈpilə/

The roof of the church was supported by stone *pillars*.

[猜一猜] A 大厅 B 枕头 C 力量 D 柱子

[翻　译] 这座教堂的屋顶由石柱支撑着。

[词义扩展] *n.* 栋梁，成为栋梁，支撑 *a pillar of the state* 国家的栋梁

[习语记忆] **from pillar to post** 东奔西跑，到处碰壁

[大头例句] Throughout the difficult trials she faced during her cancer treatments, her loyal husband was an invaluable pillar of support. 在她接受癌症治疗期间，她忠实的丈夫是她巨大的支持，伴随她面对那些困难考验。

throughout *prep./adv.* /θruːˈaut/

Though unsure how her speech would be received, she remained calm and professional *throughout*.

[猜一猜] A 一直 B 秘密 C 透彻 D 宁静

[翻　译] 尽管她不能确信演讲是否会被接受，但她一直保持镇静且职业化。

[大头巧记] through out，穿过，直到出去，始终，全部

[词义扩展] *prep.* 遍及，贯穿 *throughout one's life* 毕生

[大头例句] He had misled the court throughout the trial. 在审判中，他从头至尾都在误导法庭。

unilateral *adj.* /ˈjuːnilætərəl/

At first it was just a *unilateral* declaration.

[猜一猜] A 非官方的 B 官方的 C 联合的 D 单方面的

[翻　译] 开始的时候那只是一个单方面的宣言。

[分　析] uni + later+ al

一 + 面 + 形容词尾 → 单方面的，片面的

[大头巧记] 拆：Uni. later，大学后来做出了单方决定。

[大头例句] Such unilateral action violates international trade rules. 这种单方行为违反了国际贸易规则。

unique *adj.* /juː'niːk/

That building is *unique* because all the others like it were destroyed.

[猜一猜]A 持久的 B 独特的 C 幸运的 D 迷人的

[翻 译]那座建筑很独特，因为所有像它那样的其他建筑都毁坏了。

[分 析]uni + que

一 + 形容词尾 → 单一的，独特的

[大头巧记]和 **eunuch(太监)**声音相似，注意区别；太监是很独特的。另：联系 **ubiquitous(普通的)**记忆。

[大头例句]You will be given the unique opportunity to study with one of Europe's top chefs. 你将会得到跟着欧洲一位顶级厨师学习的极难得的机会。

universal *adj.* /juːni'vəːsəl/

This discovery of literature has as yet only partially penetrated the *universal* consciousness.

[猜一猜]A 影视的 B 遗产的 C 世界的 D 回绕的

[翻 译]此文学发现到目前为止仅是部分地为世人所认知。

[分 析]univers(e) + al

宇宙 + 形容词尾 → 宇宙的，世界的，通用的，普遍的

[大头巧记]和 **individual(个体的，个体)**对比记忆。

[大头例句]The proposal has not met with universal agreement. 该决议还没有得到普遍的认同。

verge *n.* /vəːdʒ/

I was on the *verge* of accepting.

[猜一猜]A 边缘 B 挣扎 C 徘徊 D 盘算

[翻 译]我差点儿接受。

[词义扩展]*v.* 将近，接近，向…倾斜 *dusk verging into night* 天色渐渐地暗了下来

[大头例句]The test was so difficult it was verging on ridiculous. 这个考试太难了，几乎近于荒谬。

vicinity *n.* /vi'siniti/

He is in the *vicinity* of fifty.

[猜一猜]A 开端 B 中间 C 末尾 D 附近

[翻 译]他在五十岁左右。

[分 析]vicin + ity

邻近 + 词尾 → 邻近，附近

[大头例句]The present value is in the vicinity of $120,000. 当前的价值在 12 万左右。

width *n.* /widθ/

What is the *width* of this material?

[猜一猜]A 长度 B 宽度 C 高度 D 重力

[翻 译]这种材料的宽度是多少？

[分 析]wid(e) + th

宽的 + …度 → 宽度，广博

[大头巧记]联系：**length(长度)**，**depth(深度)**记忆。

[大头例句]Swimming a width is their first major achievement in water. 能够游完泳池的一个宽度，是他们在水中取得的第一个重大成绩。

stagger *v.* /'stægə/

She *staggered* and fell to the ground.

[猜一猜]A 颤抖 B 受伤 C 厌烦 D 蹒跚

[翻 译]他蹒跚走了几步，摔倒在地上。

[大头巧记]**stage**，舞台，**stagger**，在很多台子上摇摇晃晃地走。

[词义扩展]*adj.* 交错的

[大头例句]What staggered us was the sheer size of that teacher's salary. 让我们吃惊的是那位老师单薄的工资。

习题：在下面的空格中填写本单元的单词。

1. More than a dozen variable factors could ________ with their permutations running into

the thousands.

2. The Earth __________ around the sun.
3. Beijing and its __________ suburbs, like Huairou, Miyun and so on, are very beautiful.
4. Due to his extreme position, the president __________ potential supporters.
5. The decline in the stock market, though dramatic, has to be seen in __________.
6. My parents, who have been married for over 50 years, say the secret to their happiness has been __________ respect and willingness to compromise.
7. __________, even individual villages, developed their own languages.
8. Kids like the __________ bear very much.
9. What __________ us was the sheer size of that teacher's salary.
10. Throughout the difficult trials she faced during her cancer treatments, her loyal husband was an invaluable __________ of support.
11. Though unsure how her speech would be received, she remained calm and professional __________.
12. You will be given the __________ opportunity to study with one of Europe's top chefs.
13. Swimming a __________ is their first major achievement in water.
14. Such __________ action violates international trade rules.
15. He sent his girlfriend a __________ of flowers on Valentine's Day.
16. The cobra __________ itself up around the branch.
17. Important witnesses are __________ from the media for their own safety.
18. None of us likes to sleep between __________ sheets in damp weather.
19. The drug has been shown to reduce the __________ of thrombosis after surgery.
20. They __________ around the coast of Ireland.
21. We had an excellent __________ between our two companies.
22. This discovery of literature has as yet only partially penetrated the __________ consciousness.
23. The present value is in the __________ of $120,000.
24. The test was so difficult it was __________ on ridiculous.

a→plenty. 一个数量的…

Day 54

apprenticeship n.学徒期;学徒的身份

apprentice *n.* /əˈprentis/

When he was fifteen years old, his mother sent him to be an *apprentice* to a tailor.

[猜一猜]A 学徒 B 助手 C 仆人 D 朋友

[翻　译]他十五岁的时候,妈妈送他去做了一名裁缝学徒。

[分　析]ap + prentice
to + to seize → 捉来做学徒

[大头巧记]记住其主体部分,拆:apprent → app(liance)(设备) rent 出租设备给学徒。

[词义扩展]v. (常与 to 连用)使做学徒 *to be apprenticed to a craftsman* 跟一名手艺人当学徒

addendum *n.* /əˈdendəm/

This is an *addendum* to my book.

[猜一猜]A 目录 B 说明 C 附录 D 翻译

[翻　译]这个是我的书的附录。

[分　析]此词是 add 的一个变化,附加上的部分,附录。

[联　想]**additive** ①*adj.* **附加的;增加的;累积的** *additive information* 补充报告 *additive samples* 附加样本 ②*n.* **添加剂;添加物** *It is known that most food additives are bad for the health.* 我们都知道,大多数的食品添加剂都是对人体有害的。

affiliate *v.* /əˈfilieit/

Our company is *affiliated* with an international organization of similar companies.

[猜一猜]A 联合 B 加入 C 竞争 D 适合

[翻　译]我们公司加入了同类公司的国际组织。

[分　析]af + filiate
朝向 + 儿子 → 成为…的儿子,成为某机构的子机构

[大头巧记]掐头去尾法,去掉词头 af-,去掉动词词尾 ate,于是只要记住词中 fili 即可,fili,意为(古代爱尔兰的)诗人,地位高于吟游诗人而可法学家、历史学家等属于的 阶层。

[联　想]**affiliation** *n.*;**联盟,亲密关系** → **Affinity** *n.* **亲密关系,吸引力**

[词义扩展]*vt.* ①使联合,接纳…为分支机构 ②[常接 oneself 或用被动态]使加入,使隶属 ③把…收为养子 ④追溯,寻根(to),来自(upon)

She affiliated the orphan into her own. 她收养那个孤儿为养子。

Mike affiliates with the drama society. 麦克是话剧团的成员。

This school is affiliated with that university. 这个学校是那所大学的附属机构。

n. 成员 *network affiliates* 网络成员

[大头例句]China gradually affiliated herself into the international market after the Reform and Opening to the outside in 1978.
在 1978 年改革开放之后,中国逐渐加入了世界市场。

aide *n.* /eid/

助手,副官

She found a job in China to work as a teacher's *aide* in a high school.

[猜一猜]A 助手 B 督学 C 主任 D 次长

[翻　译]她在中国找到了在高中作教师助手的一个工作。

[大头巧记]记住他的同音近义词:**aid** 帮助。 /eid/

[大头例句]He has worked as an aide-de-camp. 他曾经作过侍从武官。

alias *n.* /ˈeiliæs/

His real name was William Johnson, but he often went by the *alias* of Steven.

[猜一猜]A 爵位 B 职能 C 名义 D 化名

[翻　译]他的真名叫威廉·约翰逊,但是他经常用化名史蒂文。

alien. n.外侨
adj.外国的,不同的,相异的

[大头巧记] a sail，将 sail 翻转，alias 经过乔装作为 a sail 的假名。

[词义扩展] *adv.* 化名

[大头例句] The spy worked under various aliases when he was in Shanghai. 在上海的时候，那个特工用好多的化名工作。

appendix *n.* /əˈpendiks/

This dictionary has several *appendices*, including one on names and abbreviations of China's provinces.

[猜一猜] A 部分　B 线索　C 附录　D 简表

[翻　译] 这本辞典有几个附录，其中包括中国各省名称和简称附录。

[分　析] ap + pend + ix

to + to hung + 名词词尾 → 挂上去的东西，附录

[词义扩展] *n.* 阑尾

anonymous *adj.* /əˈnɔniməs/

He received an *anonymous* letter which made him nervous.

[猜一猜] A 恐吓的　B 言情的　C 控告的　D 匿名的

[翻　译] 他收到一封匿名信，这让他感到不安。

[分　析] an + onym + ous

无 + 名字 + 形容词尾 → 没有名字的，匿名

[大头巧记] 记住 onym 这个词根，on y(our) m(ail)，当然要写上名字。

[词义扩展] *adj.* 无特色的

[大头例句] It is the anonymous people who create history. 是那些无名的百姓创造了历史。

complement *n.* /ˈkɔmplimənt/

Love is the *complement* of the law.

[猜一猜] A 核心　B 精神　C 表现　D 补充

[翻　译] 爱的精神是对法律的补充。

[分　析] comple + ment

使…满 + 名词词尾 → 使…完满（的东西），补充

[词义扩展] *n.* ①补（足）语 ②（船员的）定员，全数，足额 *vt.* 补足，补充，使完备

[大头例句] The diamond brooch complemented her suit perfectly that night. 那晚这个钻石胸针使得她的套装成为盛装。

concise *adj.* /kənˈsais/

This *concise* dictionary is good to use

[猜一猜] A 综合的　B 简明的　C 传统的　D 英明的

[翻　译] 这本简明辞典很好用。

[分　析] con + cise

加强语气 + 切 → 把不必要的全部切掉，简明的，简练的

[大头巧记] 联系 **prolix（冗长的）**记忆

infringe v. 侵犯，破坏；违反

fringe *n.*/ *adj.*/ *v.* /frindʒ/

They like to hang out on the geographical *fringes*; the seedy outposts.

[猜一猜] A 边缘　B 奇观　C 考察　D 村落

[翻　译] 他们喜欢去偏僻地区和肮脏的偏远村落。

[大头巧记] 联合记忆：**flange**，突出的边缘。

[词义扩展] *n.* 穗，缘饰，（与政治有关的）小圈子 *v.* 成为边缘 *The road was fringed with willows.* 道路两旁柳树成行。

[大头例句] Vegetarianism is no longer considered the preserve of the lunatic fringe. 素食主义不再被认为是极端主义者的行为。

lunatic adj. 疯狂的 n. 疯子

memorandum *n.* /ˌmeməˈrændəm/

In a brief *memorandum* to all of his colleagues, the manager reminded everyone of the afternoon meeting.

[猜一猜] A 便笺　B 奖励　C 报告　D 建议

[翻　译] 在给全体同事的备忘录摘要中，这位经理提醒每个人记住下午的会。

[大头巧记] **remembrance**，回想，记忆，**memorandum**，备忘录，便笺。在应用中我们经常使用它的简略形式"memo"。

ˈmemory n. 记忆(力)

ˈmemorize v. 记住，记忆

[大头例句] I need you to write me a memorandum for this meeting. 我需要你为我写一份关于这个会议的备忘录。

namely *adv.* /ˈneimli/

Some groups, *namely* students and pensioners, will benefit from the new tax.

[猜一猜] A 命名为　B 只是　C 也就是　D 除了

[翻　译] 一些团体，也就是学生和领养老金者，会受益于新的税收。

[大头巧记] namely，name 的副词形式-名字也是，也就是。

[大头例句] I enjoy vegetable dumplings, namely ones containing spinach. 我喜欢蔬菜馅的饺子，即包菠菜的。

nourishment *n.* /ˈnʌriʃmənt/

A young baby can obtain all the necessary *nourishment* from its mother's milk.

[猜一猜] A 热量　B 维生素　C 营养　D 水分

[翻　译] 婴儿能够摄取来自母乳的所有营养。

[分　析] nourish + ment
滋养 + 名词词尾 → 营养，营养品

[大头例句] Food and nourishment are not necessarily the same thing: potato chips and soda have so little nutritional value that the body is no better off for having consumed them. 食物并不等同于营养品：薯条和苏打水中的营养物资非常少，大吃大喝它们并不会对身体有什么好处。

nutrition *n.* /njuːˈtriʃən/

Our product contains all the *nutrition* you need.

[猜一猜] A 脂肪　B 钙质　C 锌　D 营养

[翻　译] 我们的产品提供您需要的所有营养。

[分　析] nutri + tion
滋养 + 名词词尾 → 营养

[大头巧记] 注意和 **nourishment**，联合记忆。**nutrition**，还有营养学的意思。

[大头例句] Maintaining good nutrition is one of the surest ways to defend oneself from minor health problems ranging from the common cold to headaches. 保持好的营养是预防像一般感冒和头痛这样的各种小病的最可靠方法之一。

reference *n.* /ˈrefərəns/

She made frequent *references* to her promotion.

[猜一猜] A 催促　B 建议　C 提及　D 自信

[翻　译] 她时常提到她的升迁。

[大头巧记] **refer，提及 → reference *n.* 提及，涉及**。另，**conference，会议**，大家做到一起提到某事。

[词义扩展] *n.* 证明，鉴定，介绍信 *banker's reference* 银行资信证明书

[大头例句] Many say the captain in the famous poem — "Captain, My Captain" — is actually a respectful reference to Civil War-era president, Abraham Lincoln. 很多人说著名诗篇《船长，我的船长》实际上是对南北战争期间总统亚伯拉罕·林肯充满敬意的纪念。

saturate *v.* /ˈsætʃəreit/

The recollection was *saturated* with sunshine.

[猜一猜] A 模糊　B 充满　C 宣誓　D 罕有

[翻　译] 回忆中充满阳光。

[分　析] satur + ate
足够 + 动词词尾 → 使足够，充满

[大头例句] Water poured through the hole, saturating the carpet. 水流过洞口，地毯湿透了。

substitute *n./ v.* /ˈsʌbstitjuːt/

The objective is to *substitute* conflict and violence with real democratic policies.

[猜一猜] A 代替　B 发扬　C 反对　D 计划

[翻　译] 目的是用真正的民主来取代矛盾和暴力。

[分　析] sub + stitute
下面 + 站 → 代替品，代替

[大头例句] The lead singer was ill and her substitute wasn't nearly as good. 主唱生病了，其替代者的演唱与其相差甚远。

supplement n.补充.附录.增刊 v.补充
// complement

supplementary

n./ adj. /ˌsʌpliˈmentəri/

The new students received *supplementary* instruction.

[猜一猜]A 废除的　B 挑剔的　C 有联系的　D 增补的

[翻　译]新生接受补课。

[分　析]supple + mentary
提供 + 词尾 → 提供补充，补充的，辅助的

[大头例句]There is a supplementary water supply in case the main supply fails. 万一主供应失败的话，还有一个辅助的供水途径。

vice versa

adv. /ˈvaisi ˈvəːsə/

We gossip about them and *vice versa*.

[猜一猜]A 副长官　B 低迷的　C 混乱　D 反之亦然

[翻　译]我们谈论他们，他们也谈论我们。

[大头巧记]vice versa，外来词汇：vice，位置；versa，转换→转换位置，反之亦然。

[大头例句]Should I come to your house or vice versa? 是我去你家还是你来我家？

whereas

conj. /(h)wεərˈæz/

John is a big man, *whereas* his girlfriend is nice and small.

[猜一猜]A 同时　B 希望　C 相对　D 然而

[翻　译]约翰身材高大，而他的女朋友却相当娇小。

[大头巧记]拆：where as(s)，屁股的地方，背面：然而，但是。

[大头例句]Whereas knowledge can be acquired from books, skills must be learned through practice. 尽管知识可以从书本中获得，但是技术必须从实践中学得。

习题：在下面的空格中填写本单元的单词。

1. He received an __________ letter which made him nervous.
2. Whereas __________ can be acquired from books, skills must be learned through practice.
3. The objective is to __________ real democratic policies for conflict and violence.
4. When he was fifteen years old, his mother sent him to be an __________ to a tailor.
5. She found a job in China to work as a teacher's __________ in a high school.
6. This __________ dictionary is good to use.
7. Some groups, __________ students and pensioners, will benefit from the new tax.
8. Maintaining good __________ is one of the surest ways to defend oneself from minor health problems ranging from the common cold to headaches.
9. His real name was William Johnson, but he often went by the __________ of Steven.
10. This is an __________ to my book.
11. Our company is __________ with an international organization of similar companies.
12. The diamond brooch __________ her suit perfectly that night.
13. Should I come to your house or __________?
14. There is a __________ water supply in case the main supply fails.
15. This dictionary has several __________, including one on names and abbreviations of China's provinces.
16. The recollection was __________ with sunshine.
17. Many say the captain in the famous poem — "Captain, My Captain" — is actually a respectful __________ to Civil War-era president, Abraham Lincoln.

18. Food and __________ are not necessarily the same thing: potato chips and soda have so little nutritional value that the body is no better off for having consumed them.
19. In a brief __________ to all of his colleagues, the manager reminded everyone of the afternoon meeting.
20. They like to hang out on the geographical __________; the seedy outposts.

Note 前事不忘后事之师 *Remember the past and it will guide your future.*

Day 55

chunk *n.* /tʃʌŋk/

I won quite a *chunk* of money in Las Vegas last night.

[猜一猜] A 大量　B 筹码　C 好运　D 冒险

[翻　译] 昨天我在拉斯维加斯赢了一大笔钱。

[词义扩展] *n.* ①厚块或大片：*a chunk of ice* 一块厚冰 ②矮胖的人或物

[大头例句] In the old days having meat and milk every day often meant a big chunk of the family income. 过去，每天吃肉，喝牛奶意味着要花费掉家庭收入的大部分。

embrace *v.* /imˈbreis/

Kate and Lena *em braced* and kissed each other when they met again after ten years.

[猜一猜] A 使尴尬　B 理解了　C 谅解了　D 拥抱

[翻　译] 凯特和李娜十年后重逢时相互拥抱亲吻。

[分　析] em + brace
在…里面 + 胳膊 → 在胳膊里面，拥抱，搂抱

[词义扩展] *v.* ①包括，包含 The article embraces many important points of the government reconstruction plan. 文章中包括着政府重建计划的许多要点。②利用 *n.* 拥抱 a loving embrace 一个深情的拥抱

[大头例句] I only regret, in my chilled age, certain occasions and possibilities I didn't embrace. 我只是遗憾，在我失意的时候没有利用某些情况和某些可能。

hereditary *adj.* /hiˈreditəri/

A *hereditary* disease or quality is passed from a parent to a child in their genes.

[猜一猜] A 慢性的　B 遗传的　C 天生的　D 急性的

[翻　译] 遗传疾病或品性是通过基因由父母传给孩子的。

[分　析] here + ditary
heir 继承 + 形容词为 → 继承的，遗传的

[词义扩展] *adj.* 世袭的，祖传的 *a hereditary prejudice* 祖传的偏见

[大头例句] His disease is hereditary. 她的病是遗传的。

intimate *adj.*/ *vt.*/ *n.* /ˈintimit/

Island communities commonly feel an *intimate* connection with the sea and with seafarers.

[猜一猜] A 强烈的　B 神奇的　C 恐惧的　D 亲近的

[翻　译] 岛屿上的居民一般对海洋和船员们有种亲近感。

[大头巧记] 记住它的另一个义项：暗示，宣布，通知，in tim(e) + 动词词尾，及时地告知，暗示。

[大头例句] He intimated that he intends to leave. 他暗示他想要离开。

kin *n.* /kin/

What *kin* is he to you?

[猜一猜] A 亲戚　B 种类　C 作用　D 王国

[翻　译] 他和你是什么亲戚关系？

[词义扩展] *n.* 家族，门第，亲属，性质相似的东西 *adj.* 有亲属关系的 *near of kin* 近亲

[习语记忆] **more kin than kind** 亲戚不亲

[大头例句] His good kin helped him a lot in his career. 他良好的出身对他的事业帮助很大。

maternal *adj.* /məˈtəːnl/

Though not yet a mother herself, the young girl has a strong *maternal* instincts, and you will often see her taking care of small animals and dolls.

[猜一猜] A 爱心的　B 母性的

C 勤奋的 D 控制的

[翻 译]但是,不仅母亲本身,年轻的女孩身上也具有很强的母性,你会经常看到她照料小动物和洋娃娃。

[分 析]mater + nal

母亲 + 形容词尾 → 母亲的,母性的

[大头例句]Because they are my maternal cousins, we don't share the same last name. 因为他们是我母系的表亲,所以我们的姓不同。

matrimony n. /ˈmætrimәni/

Couples should not engage in the ponderous commitment of *matrimony* without careful planning and exceedingly high dedication to each other.

[猜一猜]A 生意 B 方案 C 婚姻 D 争吵

[翻 译]在没有对生活做好仔细的计划且没有非常强烈的愿望将自己献给对方的情形下,男女双方不应该草率地做出沉重的婚姻承诺。

[分 析]matri + mony

母亲 + 名词词尾 → 成为母亲的关系,婚姻,婚姻关系

[大头巧记]通过音近同义词 **marriage**,联系记忆。

[大头例句]Matrimony may technically be a sterile legal status, but in practice it involves the much more human emotions of happiness, care, patience, and compromise. 婚姻可能被看成一种没有感情色彩的法律关系,但是在实际生活中,它却涵盖了更多人性因素:快乐、关怀、耐心和互让。

migrate v. /maiˈgreit/

With the cold weather coming earlier in the fall this year, I wonder if the birds will have time to *migrate* south before the temperature falls too low.

[猜一猜]A 储粮 B 长出新毛 C 迁徙 D 煽动

[翻 译]由于今年秋天冷天气的提前来临,我想知道在温度太低之前这些鸟是否有时间迁移到南方。

[分 析]migr + ate

移动 + 动词词尾 → 移动,迁徙,移植

[大头巧记]**migrant**,移民,候鸟;**migrate**,移居,迁徙。另:与my great同音,我伟大的梦想:移民成功。

nostalgia n. /nɔsˈtældʒiә/

When people get old they are easier to fall into the mood of *nostalgia*.

[猜一猜]A 压抑 B 思乡 C 悲伤 D 糊涂

[翻 译]人老的时候就更容易陷入怀旧的情绪中。

[分 析]nost + alg + ia

家乡 + 痛 + 名词词尾 → 思家病,乡愁,怀旧

[大头巧记]同根词还有:**nostrum,秘方**(家里不外传的万用良药)。另:feel homesick = in the mood of nostalgia。

[大头例句]The nostalgia of hearing the first song they heard while dancing together reminded the old married couple why they had fallen in love in the first place. 一起跳舞时听到的第一首乐曲的怀旧情绪唤起了这对老夫妇对当初一见钟情的追忆。

nurture n./ vt. /ˈnә:tʃә/

The magazine had a reputation for *nurturing* young writers.

[猜一猜]A 培养 B 锻炼 C 轻视 D 考虑

[翻 译]在培养年轻作家方面,这家杂志拥有声誉。

[分 析]nurt + ure

营养 + 词尾 → 给…营养,教养,训练

[词义扩展]n. 教养,训练

[大头例句]A comprehensive education nurtures not only the student's mind, but also his body and spirit. 全面的教育不仅要培养学生的思想,还要培养他的身体和精神。

offspring n. /ˈɔfspriŋ/

The birds will see you as a threat to their *offspring*.

[猜一猜]A 后代 B 领域 C 付出 D 秘密

[翻 译]这些鸟会把你视为对它们幼仔的威胁。

[大头巧记]off spring,离开春天以后,动物开始繁育后代。

[大头例句] Sometimes success is the offspring of curiosity. 有时成功是好奇的结果。

posterity *n.* /pɔsˈteriti/

Dealing with pollution is for the benefit of *posterity*.

[猜一猜] A 民众　B 国家　C 后代　D 报应

[翻　译] 治理污染是在为子孙后代造福。

[分　析] post + erity

后 + 名词词尾 → 后代

[大头巧记] **poster，海报**，贴海报，是为了让后代知道，流芳百世。

[习语记忆] **go down to posterity** 载入史册

proximity *n.* /prɔkˈsimiti/

All of my family live in close *proximity*.

[猜一猜] A 关系　B 生活　C 接近　D 混合

[翻　译] 我所有的家人都住得很近。

[分　析] proxim + ity

接近 + 名词词尾 → 接近，亲近

paternity *n.* /pəˈtəːniti/

The boxer finally acknowledged *paternity* of the child following a bitter court case.

[猜一猜] A 虐待　B 欺骗　C 父子关系　D 统治

[翻　译] 经过一场激烈的官司以后，该拳击手最终承认了和这个孩子的父子关系。

[分　析] patrern + ity

父亲的 + 词尾 → 父权，父子关系

[词义扩展] *adj.* 父权的；*n.* [喻]渊[来]源，出处

[大头例句] In modern cases of unwed pregnancy, some men require proof of paternity, as shown through DNA testing, before agreeing to help support a child financially. 在现代的未婚怀孕的案件中，一些男士要求通过 DNA 测试来证明父子关系，然后才同意给孩子经济支持。

personality *n.* /ˌpəːsəˈnæliti/

Though their *personalities* differed, they got along as friends.

[猜一猜] A 身份　B 国籍　C 个性　D 隐私

[翻　译] 虽然他们性格迥异，但却相处友好。

[大头巧记] person，人 → **personality**，个人的秉性，个性

[词义扩展] *n.* 名人，[常用复] 人物批评 *Personalities are not in good taste in general conversation.* 在一般的谈话中诽谤他人是不高尚的。

[大头例句] Few people find his personality easy to accomodate: he is quick to anger, prone to blame other people for his own mistakes, and rarely optimistic or encouraging of others' ideas. 很少有人能适应他的个性，他易怒，经常用为自己的错误而指责别人，并且很少夸奖或对别人的观点保持乐观。

picturesque *adj.* /piktʃəˈresk/

I was attracted by the *picturesque* scene on Lake Windermere.

[猜一猜] A 如画的　B 冷清的　C 经济的　D 热情的

[翻　译] 我被温德米尔湖上如画的风景迷住了。

[大头巧记] picture，画 → **picturesque**，如画的，生动的，栩栩如生的。

[词义扩展] *adj.* 别致的，独创的 *a picturesque French café* 一个别具风格的法国咖啡店

[大头例句] Few photographers have captured the beauty of mountain scenes consistently featured in the picturesque black-and-white's of Ansel Adams. 几乎没有几个摄影师能够抓拍到像安瑟尔·亚当斯在他的黑白照片中一直表现的那种山地景观独特的神韵。

partition *n.* /pɑːˈtiʃən/

Mary hung a calendar on her *partition* at work.

[猜一猜] A 办公桌　B 隔墙　C 房间　D 娱乐

[翻　译] 玛丽把一个日历挂在她工作地方的隔墙上。

[分　析] part + ition

部分 + 名词词尾 → 分开，隔离物，隔墙

[词义扩展] *n./v.* 分开，分割，隔开 *the partition of former Yugoslavia* 对原南斯拉夫的分割

[大头例句] Following the war, Shanghai was partitioned into several different districts, each controlled by different foreign powers. 战后，上海被分割成了几个区，不同的外国势力各占一块。

spoil *vt.* /spɔil/

Our holidays were *spoiled* by bad weather.

[猜一猜]A 搞糟 B 拖延 C 懒惰 D 限制

[翻 译]我们假日的乐趣被恶劣天气所破坏。

[大头巧记]拆：sp(ill) oil，撒出的油会损坏事物

[词义扩展]v. 宠坏，搅乱

[大头例句]Spare the rod and spoil the child. 棒打出孝子。

succession *n.* /sək'seʃən/

The story brought an endless *succession* of journalists to the city.

[猜一猜]A 表演 B 喧闹 C 一连串的人或事 D 代谢

[翻 译]这个故事为该城带来了一连串的新闻记者。

[大头巧记]success，成功；succession，成功带来的一连串的记者。

[词义扩展]n. 继续，连续，继任。*be first in succession to the throne* 是王位的第一继承人

[大头例句]She won the championship four times in succession. 她连续获得了四次锦标赛冠军。

习题：在下面的空格中填写本单元的单词。

1. In the old days having meat and milk every day often meant a big __________ of the family income.
2. With the cold weather coming earlier in the fall this year, I wonder if the birds will have time to __________ south before the temperature falls too low.
3. __________ may technically be a sterile legal status, but in practice it involves the much more human emotions of happiness, care, patience, and compromise.
4. Though not yet a mother herself, the young girl has a strong __________ instincts, and you will often see her taking care of small animals and dolls.
5. I only regret, in my chilled age, certain occasions and possibilities I didn't__________.
6. A __________ disease or quality is passed from a parent to a child in their genes.
7. Island communities commonly feel an__________ connection with the sea and with seafarers.
8. His good __________ helped him a lot in his career.
9. The story brought an endless __________ of journalists to the city.
10. When people get old they are easier to fall into the mood of __________.
11. A comprehensive education __________ not only the student's mind, but also his body and spirit.
12. In modern cases of unwed pregnancy, some men require proof of __________, as shown through DNA testing, before agreeing to help support a child financially.
13. Few people find his __________ easy to accomodate: he is quick to anger, prone to blame other people for his own mistakes, and rarely optimistic or encouraging of others' ideas.
14. I was attracted by the __________ scene on Lake Windermere.
15. Our holidays were __________ by bad weather.
16. The birds will see you as a threat to their __________.

17. Dealing with pollution is for the benefit of _________.
18. Following the war, Shanghai was _________ into several different districts, each controlled by different foreign powers.
19. All of my family live in close _________.

Note 前事不忘后事之师 *Remember the past and it will guide your future.*

Day 56

acerbic *adj.* /əˈsəːbik/

"At times, the playwright allows an *acerbic* tone to pierce through otherwise arid or flowery prose", (Alvin Klein)

[猜一猜] A 美丽的　B 刻薄的　C 风趣地　D 深刻的

[翻　译] "有时，剧作家在枯燥或华丽的散文中插入刻薄的语调"(阿尔文·克莱因)。

[大头巧记] ace，王牌飞行员，要他把 Arabic(阿拉伯)的两个(a)ims，都给完全毁掉，这个要求很刻薄。

[近义词] **acidulous** *His acidulous remark made us very upset.* **他尖酸的话让我们很不舒服。**

[大头例句] You are correct to point out a difficulty. But you are wrong to do so in such an acerbic fashion. 指出一个困难是对的，但是你这种尖酸的方式是错误的。

acrid *adj.* /ˈækrid/

The dish you cooked has an *acrid* smell.

[猜一猜] A 呛人的　B 甜蜜的　C 酸的　D 奇怪的

[翻　译] 你炒的菜很呛人。

[联　想] ①近义词 **biting; bitter; harsh; nasty sharp; stinging**

②**acrimony** *n.* (态度、语言等的)毒辣，激烈，刻毒 *speak with acrimony* 说刻薄的话

acrimonious *adj.* **acrimoniously** *adv.*

[词义扩展] *adj.* 尖刻的，刻毒的；泼辣的 *an acrid speech* 言语尖刻的演说

[大头例句] Forest fires blanket Honduras with acrid haze. 森林大火发出的辛辣的雾气覆盖了洪都拉斯。

affront *n.* /əˈfrʌnt/

The boss put an *affront* to him with the remark.

[猜一猜] A 奖赏　B 任命　C 侮辱　D 信任

[翻　译] 老板的话使他深受侮辱。

[分　析] af　+ front

朝向 + 脸 → 直向某人的脸，冒犯，当众侮辱，此处活用为名词

[词义扩展] *vt.* ①侮辱，冒犯 *He was affront in the meeting.* 在会上他被当众侮辱。

②泰然面对，毅然对抗 *affront death* 临死不惧

[大头例句] Affronting the danger that awaits us, we are intent on the democracy in this society. 泰然面对前方的危险，我们致力于这个社会的民主事业。

betray *vt.* /biˈtrei/

Don't *betray* the people's trust in you.

[猜一猜] A 沾沾自喜　B 辜负　C 失去　D 蔑视

[翻　译] 不要辜负人民对你的信任。

[分　析] be　+ tray

全面地 + 背叛 → 背叛，不忠于，辜负

[词义扩展] *vt.* ①背叛，告密，陷害 ②把....引入歧途 ③泄漏(秘密) ④不自觉地露出

She was betrayed into a snare. 她被诱入陷阱。

[大头例句] His confusion and nervousness betrayed his guilt. 他的慌乱和紧张显出他心里有鬼。

conscience *n.* /ˈkɔnʃəns/

Let your *conscience* be your guide.

[猜一猜] A 良心　B 理性　C 感情　D 自信

[翻　译] 让你的良心指引你。

[分　析] con　+ sci　+ ence

全部 + 知道 + 词尾 → 全部都知道，有良知，良心，道德心

[大头巧记] science，科学，和科学打交道的人要有良知。

[习语记忆] **A clear conscience is a sure card.** [谚] 只要问心无愧，旁人的指责可一笑置之

A quiet conscience sleeps in thunder.[谚]
没做亏心事，不怕鬼叫门。
A guilty conscience needs no accuser.[谚]
做贼心虚。

[大头例句] Discrimination is a problem that's been troubling America's social conscience for years. 歧视是很多年来一直在困扰美国社会良心的问题。

despise vt. /dis'paiz/

Despising any thought of their own safety, the firefighters went into that burning building again in search of possible survivors.

[猜一猜] A 蔑视 B 通向 C 向上延伸 D 展示

[翻 译] 蔑视任何关于他们自身安全性的考虑，那些消防员再次走进了那座燃烧着的大楼去搜寻可能的幸存者。

[分 析] de + spise
向下 + 看 → 向下看，蔑视，轻视，鄙视

[大头巧记] 形近词 **despite，不管，不论，动词化得到 despise，蔑视**。

[大头例句] She despises cheap clothes and will only wear the best. 她看不起便宜的衣服并且只穿最好的。

disdain vt. /dis'dein/

disdainful adj. 轻蔑的，不屑的

Mrs. Grey *disdained* to answer her husband's rude remarks.

[猜一猜] A 不屑 B 紧张 C 愤怒 D 亟待

[翻 译] 对于她丈夫的那些无礼的话，格雷太太不屑回答。

[分 析] dis + dain
不 + 值得 → 不屑，轻视，蔑视

stain n. 污点 瑕疵 v. 染污 沾污

[词义扩展] *n.* 轻蔑，蔑视

[大头例句] Disdain is the feeling that someone or something is not important and does not deserve any respect. 轻蔑是觉得某人或某物不重要或不值得尊敬。

decent adj. /'diːsnt/

Her *decent* language and behavior made her distinguished at the party.

[猜一猜] A 出众的 B 高雅的 C 过激的 D 奇怪的

[翻 译] 她高雅的谈吐和行为使得她在宴会上卓然不群。

[大头巧记] 形近词记忆：**recent，最近的**，recent d(esign)，最近的设计很**高雅(decent)**。

[词义扩展] *adj.* ①合适的，得体的 ②过得去的，像样的
He made a decent record. 他成绩尚佳。

[大头例句] The director of my factory was very decent about my being away when my wife was ill. 工厂的主管对于我由于妻子生病而没能到场反应得很有分寸。

exaggerate v. /ig'zædʒəreit/

All these new gadgets are indeed ingenious inventions, but he's *exaggerating* when he calls them the greatest inventions ever made!

[猜一猜] A 阐述 B 批评 C 夸大 D 否定

[翻 译] 这些新玩意儿确实是天才的发明，但他把它们称做是有史以来最伟大的发明是言过其实了。

exact /ig'zækt/ adj. 精确的 vt. 强索 索要

[分 析] ex + ag + ger + ate
出 + 一再 + 带 + 动词词尾 → 一再带出去，夸大，夸张

[词义扩展] *v.* 使过大，使增大 *Her hairstyle exaggerates the roundness of her face.* 她的发式使她的脸形显得更圆。

[大头例句] The paper's political influence has been greatly exaggerated. 这份报纸的政治影响力被大大地夸大了。

insult vt. /'insʌlt/

His absurd speech *insulted* the intelligence of the audience.

[猜一猜] A 符合 B 侮辱 C 唤醒 D 超越

[翻 译] 他的荒唐演说侮辱了听众们的智力。

[分 析] in + sult
在…上 + 跳跃 → 对…无礼，侮辱，凌辱

[词义扩展] *n.* 侮辱，无礼，危害，刺激，攻击 *radiation insult* 辐射伤害

[大头例句] Such low wages are an insult to hard-working employees. 如此低的工资是对雇工们辛勤劳动的一种侮辱。

irony *n.* /ˈaiərəni/

"You've been so kind," she said, her voice heavy with *irony*.

[猜一猜] A 讽刺　B 热情　C 感激　D 歉意

[翻　译] "你太友好了",她说道,她的声音里充满着讽刺。

[大头巧记] iron,铁;irony,钢铁的,伤人的,讽刺的,反语的。

[词义扩展] *n.* 出人意料的事情或情况

[大头例句] Hyde noted the irony of Ireland's copying the nation she most hated. 海德注意到了爱尔兰模仿它最憎恨的国家这其中所包含的讽刺意味。

ludicrous *adj.* /ˈluːdikrəs/

To say that the AIDS virus is not a worldwide epidemic sounds *ludicrous* to most people.

[猜一猜] A 荒谬的　B 熟悉的　C 担心的　D 侮辱性的

[翻　译] 说艾滋病不是一种世界范围的传染病,对大多数人来说听起来很荒谬。

[分　析] ludicr + ous
玩 + 形容词尾 → 闹着玩的,可笑的,荒谬的

[大头巧记] **ludic,顽皮的,游戏的。ludicrous,**在他的基础上进一步游戏化,**荒唐可笑的**。

[大头例句] It is ludicrous to suggest that she was a government agent. 建议让她做政府官员真是荒唐。

mock *v.* /mɔk/

Although he failed the math test, it was wrong to *mock* his efforts.

[猜一猜] A 掩盖　B 否定　C 嘲笑　D 宣扬

[翻　译] 虽然他的数学没有考及格,但是嘲笑他的努力是不对的。

[大头巧记] 谐音:"帽壳",成为嘲笑的对象。

[词义扩展] *adj.* 假的,模拟的 *n.* 模拟考试 → *Each year they stage a mock battle to entertain tourists.* 每年他们都上演一出模拟战斗来娱乐游客。

[大头例句] Because of his frequent public verbal blunders, President Bush is often mocked by American comedians. 由于在公共场合频繁说错话,布什总统经常被美国媒体嘲笑。

mature *adj.* /məˈtjuə/

This apple is not *mature* enough yet: its peel is still very green, and it will be far too sour to taste good!

[猜一猜] A 发酵的　B 腐烂的　C 成熟的　D 美味的

[翻　译] 这个苹果还没有熟,皮还是青的,他的酸味远远大于可口。

[词义扩展] *adj.* 成熟的,理智的,深思熟虑的,酿成的;使成熟 *a mature plan of action.* 经过深思熟虑的行动计划

[习语记忆] **Wine and judgement mature with age.** [谚]酒老味醇,人老识深。

[大头例句] Childhood hardships matured in him a precocious sense of responsibility. 童年的艰苦生活使他提早形成了一种超前的责任感。

provoke *vt.* /prəˈvəuk/

He couldn't *provoke* her into arguing.

[猜一猜] A 说服　B 挑拨　C 欺骗　D 驱使

[翻　译] 他无法挑拨她进行争吵。

[分　析] pro + vote
向前 + 召唤 → 激发,挑拨,驱使

passive *adj.* /ˈpæsiv/

And the rest of us, we *passives* of the world, proceeded as if nothing untoward had happened.

[猜一猜] A 消极分子　B 积极分子　C 平常人　D 旁观者

[翻　译] 而我们其余的人,这个世界的屈服者、继续生活者,就好像没有任何不幸的事发生。

[分　析] pass + ive
感情 + 词尾 → 感情用事的,被动的(人),消极的(人)

[大头巧记] 与 **active(主动的)**联合记忆。

[大头例句] Some experts in the field of educational psychology claim that students who take a passive approach to their educations retain far less information than their active peers who question the instructor and texts and participate regularly in class discussions. 一些教育心理学领域的专家称那些用被动方式对待自己学习的人所记住的信息，比那些主动者，那些向老师提问题，就课文提问，经常参与课堂讨论的学生要少的多。

perverse *adj.* /pəːˈvəːs/

It is simply *perverse* to refuse a perfectly safe treatment.

[猜一猜] A 反常的　B 无礼的　C 暴躁的　D 敏慧的

[翻　译] 拒绝这一完全安全的疗法真是反常。

[分　析] per　+ verse

完全 + 转 → 完全和别人对着干，反常的

[大头巧记] **pervert，性变态者，堕落的人 → perverse，adj. 反常的**。另：与同根词 **adverse**，(向 + 转移 → 相反的)联合记忆。

[词义扩展] *adj.* 刚愎自用的，人性的，乖张的

[大头例句] It takes a perverse sense of humor to find laughter in such dark, biting, sarcasm. 要具有很荒谬的幽默感才会觉得如此黑色的、尖锐的讽刺好笑。

persecute *v.* /ˈpəːsikjuːt/

Lots of Jews were *persecuted* in the Second World War.

[猜一猜] A 引渡　B 驱逐　C 征集　D 迫害

[翻　译] 二战期间，很多犹太人受到了迫害。

[分　析] per　+ secute

完全 + 跟随 → 总是跟着你，麻烦，困扰，迫害

[大头巧记] 拆：**perse(深灰色) cute**，受迫害时能保持可爱的本色是深灰色的可爱。

[大头例句] Persecution of civilians is one of the most severe and punishable war crimes. 迫害平民是最严重也是最应受到惩罚的战争犯罪行为。

parody *n./ vt.* /ˈpærədi/

The trial was a *parody* of justice.

[猜一猜] A 昭示　B 攻击　C 鼓励　D 拙劣的模仿

[翻　译] 这次审判是对公正的一次拙劣的模拟。

[分　析] par　+ ody

平等 + 唱 → 一样唱，模拟诗文，借模拟以嘲弄

[大头巧记] **parrot，鹦鹉，parody，鹦鹉拙劣模仿**别人说话的行为。

[大头例句] For their final project, the two beginning Chinese students created a parody of the well-loved Chinese classic, "Crouching Tiger, Hidden Dragon," inserting comedy and references to material covered in their class. 作为期末设计，这两个初学汉语的学生创作了一个广受喜爱的中国经典"卧虎藏龙"的模拟剧，加入了戏剧成分并和他们课堂上所学的材料相关。

qualification *n.* /ˌkwɔlifiˈkeiʃən/

He hadn't fulfilled the *qualifications* for registering to vote in the presidential election then.

[猜一猜] A 表格　B 资格　C 成就　D 成熟

[翻　译] 那个时候他还没有达到能在总统大选中报名投票的资格。

[大头巧记] 来源于动词 **qualify(具有资格)**。鉴定，执照，限制，条件。

[词义扩展] admission qualification 入学资格

[大头例句] As a mere sixteen-year-old high school student, I'm afraid you don't have the necessary qualifications for this position. 一个仅仅十六岁的高中生，做这个职务在我看来恐怕资历不够吧。

sarcasm *n.* /ˈsɑːkæzəm/

"Fascinating," she said, her voice heavy with *sarcasm*.

[猜一猜] A 讽刺　B 惊奇　C 激动　D 悲伤

[翻　译] "迷人，"她说，声音里充满的讽刺。

[分　析] sarc　+ asm

肌肉 + 痉挛 → 讽刺使人肌肉痉挛

[大头例句] Dripping with sarcasm, the students said to their teacher, "Please give us more tests; we feel so sad when we don't have stressful exams to prepare for!"满含着反语的意味,学生们对老师说:"给我们更多的测验吧,没有机会准备充满压力的考试使我们太伤心了!"

vulnerable *adj.* /ˈvʌlnərəbl/

The government must help the most *vulnerable* groups in our society.

[猜一猜] A 易受攻击的　B 有实力的　C 得意的　D 顺从的

[翻　译] 政府必须帮助社会中最易受攻击的团体。

[分　析] vulner + able

伤　+ 可…的 → 易受伤的,易受攻击的

[大头例句] Their constant arguments left her feeling increasingly vulnerable and insecure. 他们无休止的争论让她愈加觉得脆弱和不安全。

习题:在下面的空格中填写本单元的单词。

1. Don't __________ the people's trust in you.
2. All these new gadgets are indeed ingenious inventions, but he's __________ when he calls them the greatest inventions ever made!
3. Because of his frequent public verbal blunders, President Bush is often __________ by American comedians.
4. The government must help the most __________ groups in our society.
5. You are correct to point out a difficulty. But you are wrong to do so in such an ________ fashion.
6. His absurd speech __________ the intelligence of the audience.
7. This apple is not __________ enough yet: its peel is still very green, and it will taste far too sour to taste good!
8. It takes a __________ sense of humor to find laughter in such dark, biting, sarcasm.
9. Some experts in the field of educational psychology claim that students who take a __________ approach to their educations retain far less information than their active peers who question the instructor and texts and participate regularly in class discussions.
10. He couldn't __________ her into arguing.
11. Dripping with __________, the students said to their teacher, "Please give us more tests; we feel so sad when we don't have stressful exams to prepare for!"
12. Discrimination is a problem that's been troubling America's social __________ for years.
13. __________ any thought of their own safety, the firefighters went into that burning building again in search of the possible survivors.
14. As a mere sixteen-year-old high school student, I'm afraid you don't have the necessary __________ for this position.
15. Forest fires blanket Honduras with __________ haze.
16. __________ the danger that awaits us, we are intent on the democracy in this society.

17. The director of my factory was very __________ about my being away when my wife was ill.
18. Hyde noted the __________ of Ireland's copying the nation she most hated.
19. To say that the AIDS virus is not a worldwide epidemic sounds __________ to most people.
20. __________ of civilians is one of the most severe and punishable war crimes.
21. For their final project, the two beginning Chinese students created a __________ cf the well-loved Chinese classic, "Crouching Tiger, Hidden Dragon," inserting comedy and references to material covered in their class.
22. Mrs. Grey __________ to answer her husband's rude remarks.

Note 前事不忘后事之师 *Remember the past and it will guide your future.*

Day 57

allegiance *n.* /ə'liːdʒəns/

He swore *allegiance* to his native land.

[猜一猜]A 责任　B 贡献　C 忠贞　D 理想

[翻　译]他宣誓忠于自己的祖国。

[分　析]al　+　legi　+　ance

朝向 + 有臣服义务的 + 名词词尾 → 效忠

[大头巧记]掐头去尾法，记住 legi 即可，leg i（ron）铁镣，用铁镣使人诚服。

[大头例句]I pledge allegiance to the flag of the United States of America and to the republic for which it stands, one nation under God, indivisible, with liberty and justice for all. 我宣誓效忠美利坚合众国国旗和其所代表的共和国，这上帝麾下的国度，这不可分割的，给所有人平等和自由的国家。(美国效忠宣誓时的誓言)

conspiracy *n.* /kən'spirəsi/

The *conspiracy* of the assassination of the president was brought to light in time.

[猜一猜]A 阴谋　B 结局　C 献身　D 恐怖

[翻　译]一个刺杀总统的阴谋被及时揭露了。

[分　析]con　+ sprira + cy

共同　+ 呼吸 + 名词词尾 → 一个鼻孔出气，搞阴谋，共谋

[大头例句]The charges against them include conspiracy to smuggle heroin. 对他们的指控包括合谋走私海洛因。

evoke *vt.* /i'vəuk/

We sang a lot of songs that *evoked* old memories at the party.

[猜一猜]A 涉及　B 唤起　C 表现　D 激情

[翻　译]在聚会上我们唱了很多唤起往日回忆的歌曲。

[分　析]e　+ voke

向外 + 呼唤 → 唤起，引起

[词义扩展]*vt.* 使再现 *a novel that evokes the Depression in accurate detail.* 以精确的细节再现大萧条的小说

[大头例句]The recent flood evoked memories of the great flood of 1972. 最近的一次洪水唤起了人们对于 1972 年大洪灾的记忆。

delegate *n./ vt.* /'deligeit/

With the leadership of the Chinese Communist Party, the people *delegate* their power to the People's Congress.

[猜一猜]A 努力　B 拥戴　C 授权　D 掌权

[翻　译]在中国共产党的领导下，人民授权给人民代表大会。

[分　析]de　+ legate

出去 + 发送，派遣 → 派遣出去，委派，委托，代表

[大头巧记]拆：dele gate 消除门第，用代表制度来实现权利。

[词义扩展]*n.* 代表，委员，特派员

[大头例句]He was selected to be the delegate to the conference on trade and development. 他被选定为参加贸易与发展会议的代表。

foster *vt./ n.* /'fɔstə/

Frequent cultural exchange will certainly help *foster* friendly relations between our two universities.

[猜一猜]A 建立　B 交流　C 结合　D 培养

[翻　译]经常的文化交流肯定有助于发展我们两校之间的友好关系。

[词义扩展]*n.* 养育，抚养，怀抱(希望)foster hopes for success 抱有成功的希望

[大头例句]She had a good relationship with her foster mother. 她和养母之间的关系很好。

inspection *n.* /inˈspekʃən/

On closer *inspection*, it was found to be false.

[猜一猜] A 接触　B 检查　C 碰撞　D 证实

[翻　译] 经过更仔细的检查，发现那是假的。

[分　析] in　+ spect + ion

向内 + 看　+ 名词词尾 → 检查，视察，验收

[大头例句] The organization is responsible for the maintenance and inspection of offshore structures. 这个组织对维护和检查海面上的建筑物负有职责。

fidelity *n.* /fiˈdeliti/

Fidelity to one's spouse is widely respected.

[猜一猜] A 忠实　B 尊敬　C 帮助的　D 理解

[翻　译] 对配偶的忠实得到广泛的尊敬。

[分　析] fedel　+ ity

忠实的 + 名词词尾 → 忠实，忠贞，忠诚

[词义扩展] *n.* 尽职，逼真度 *reproduce with complete fidelity* 原样复制

[大头例句] His fidelity and industry brought him speedy promotion. 他的尽职及勤奋使他很快地得到晋升。

liability *n.* /ˌlaiəˈbiliti/

Nobody admitted *liability* for the damages in this accident.

[猜一猜] A 赔偿　B 价值　C 责任　D 收益

[翻　译] 没有人承认对该事故中产生的损坏负责。

[大头巧记] li(e) ability，别人依赖你的能力 → 你的义务，责任。

[词义扩展] *n.* 负债，不利条件，倾向

[大头例句] The business failed because its assets were not as great as its liabilities. 这家商行因资不抵债而倒闭。

moreover *adv.* /mɔːˈrəuvə/

There is opposition to capital punishment. *Moreover*, there is now evidence that many executed prisoners were innocent.

[猜一猜] A 但是　B 因为　C 所以　D 此外

[翻　译] 有人反对死刑，此外，现在有证据表明很多被执行死刑的犯人是无辜的。

[大头巧记] 合成词：more over，更多的关于此方面的信息：此外(*adv.*)。

[大头例句] I have no interest in watching that television program; moreover, I have so much important work to complete tonight that I really don't have the time. 我对那种电视节目没有兴趣，此外，我今天还要完成这么多的重要工作，我真的是没有时间。

levy *n./ v.* /ˈlevi/

There is a departure tax *levied* on all travelers.

[猜一猜] A 征集　B 联系　C 限制　D 保护

[翻　译] 向所有的旅客征收离境税。

[分　析] lev　+ y

升起 + 动词词尾 → 把税收起来，征集，征税

[词义扩展] *v.* 仰赖，依赖

[大头例句] I have levied on many wrters for my essential conception of British culture. 我从许多作家的作品中获得有关英国文化的基本概念。

lure *v.* /ljuə/

The *lure* of ten million dollars and a beautiful home proved enough to convince the woman of thirty to marry a stranger of eighty-five.

[猜一猜] A 渴求　B 意义　C 诱惑　D 悲哀

[翻　译] 千万美金和美丽家居的诱惑被证明足以说服一个三十岁的女人嫁给一个85岁的陌生人。

[大头巧记] **lure**，谐音"诱饵"，**诱惑**，**吸引**。可以和 **allure** (**v.** 吸引)一起记忆。

[词义扩展] *v.* 引诱，吸引

[大头例句] Industry often seeks to lure scientists from universities by offering them huge salaries. 企业经常以高额薪金诱引科学家们离开大学。

magistrate *n.* /ˈmædʒistrit/

You had to come up before the *magistrate* at first.

[猜一猜]A 师傅　　B 专家

C 地方法官　　D 宗教领袖

[翻　译]你们必须先在地方法院出庭。

[分　析]magistr + ate

主人 + 表人的名词词尾 → 做一方之主的人，地方官，文职官员，地方法官

[大头例句]The chief magistrate court is the final destination of those who commit "petty crimes": that is, crimes that are less serious than most felonies. 地方最高法院对轻度罪犯进行最终审判，所谓轻度犯罪，是指比大多数犯罪行为轻的犯罪。

monarchy *n.* /ˈmɔnəki/

They supported the idea of *monarchy* as the natural state of things.

[猜一猜]A 民主政体　　B 君主政体

C 官僚制度　　D 等级制度

[翻　译]他们把君主政体思想作为万物的自然状态来维护。

[分　析]mon + archy

单个 + 统治 → 一个人独裁统治的政体，君主政体

[大头例句]In political terms, the British monarchy has little power; only prestige. 在政治方面，英国君主权力很少，只是拥有威望。

mortgage *n.* /ˈmɔːgidʒ/

On my present salary I can't get a *mortgage*.

[猜一猜]A 汽车　　B 信用卡

C 会员证　　D 抵押贷款

[翻　译]以我当前的工资，我还拿不到购房贷款。

[分　析]mort + gage

死亡 + 抵押品 → 抵押贷款

[词义扩展]*v.* 抵押 *He will have to mortgage his land for a loan.* 他必须抵押土地来贷款。

[大头例句]For many newlywed couples, the mortgage payment is the largest of any of their debts. 对于很多新婚夫妇，购房贷款是他们债务中最大的款项。

petition *n.* /piˈtiʃən/

Students put forward a *petition* against the closing of the library.

[猜一猜]A 讨论　B 报告　C 请愿书　D 回报

[翻　译]学生们提交了反对关闭图书馆的请愿书。

[分　析]pet + tion

寻求 + 名词词尾 → 请愿，恳求，诉状。

[大头巧记]**pet**，宠物 → **petition**，请求获得养宠物的许可。

[词义扩展]*vt.* 向…请愿，祈求 *petition the government for the release of the political prisoners* 请求释放政治犯

[大头例句]In most cases, superiors don't offer their workers pay raises; instead, the employees have to petition for more money. 很多情况下，上级不主动给工人涨工资；相反，雇工们必须请求获得更多的报酬。

observance *n.* /əbˈzəːvəns/

The market will be closed in *observance* of Easter and Passover.

[猜一猜]A 庆祝　B 稳定　C 避开　D 破坏

[翻　译]为了庆祝复活节和逾越节，这个市场将会关闭。

[分　析]ob + serv + ance

强调 + 服务 + 名词词尾 → 必须服务，遵守，惯例，仪式，庆祝

[大头巧记]本词来自于 **observe** 观察，遵守。

[大头例句]Strict observance of the law is asked in modern marketing. 在现代交易中，要求严格遵守法律。

reliable *adj.* /riˈlaiəbl/

It's not *reliable* to judge a man only by his looks.

[猜一猜]A 流行的　　B 准确

C 协调的　　D 可靠的

[翻　译]单凭容貌来判断一个人是不可靠的。

[大头巧记]**rely** 依赖 → 可依赖的，可信赖的（**reliable**）。

[大头例句] Most people do not think this newspaper is very reliable: it often fabricates juicy stories in an attempt to sell copies. 大多数人认为这家报纸不是十分可信，他们经常捏造一些绘声绘色的小道消息，试图提高销量。

righteous adj. /ˈraitʃəs/

The *righteous* indignation from those freespeech campaigners impressed a lot of students.

[猜一猜] A 巨大的　　B 正义的　　C 感人的　　D 勇敢的

[翻　译] 那些言论自由推动者的正义愤慨给学生们很深的印象。

[分　析] right + eous
正确 + 方法的 → 非常正确的；正义的，正直的

[大头巧记] 与 **iniquitous**（不公正的）相对记忆。

peril n. /ˈperil/

We soon discovered that you disobeyed Eve at your *peril*.

[猜一猜] A 疲惫　　B 伤心　　C 危险　　D 考验

[翻　译] 我们不久发现，你没有服从伊夫，这让你处境危险。

[习语记忆] **All is not lost that's in peril.** [谚]危险不等于完蛋。
Keep off at your peril! 走开点，否则危险自负。

[大头例句] Most of Asia's local economies were in grave peril through the end of the 1990's. 20世纪90年代末的时候大多数的亚洲地方处于严重的经济危机中。

piety n. /ˈpaiəti/

We go to church with *piety* every Sunday.

[猜一猜] A 平静　　B 虔诚　　C 希望　　D 祭品

[翻　译] 我们每个星期天都虔诚地去教堂。

[词义扩展] *n.* 孝顺，孝敬　*filial piety* 孝道

[大头例句] Many say both the piety and the respectability of the Roman Catholic Church have been severely diminished in light of the recent pedophilia scandals. 很多人说罗马天主教堂的虔诚和名望由于最近淫亵儿童丑闻的曝光而严重降低了。

perfume vt. /ˈpəːfjuːm/

Jasmine flowers *perfumed* the air.

[猜一猜] A 飘散　　B 使…香　　C 陶醉　　D 弥漫

[翻　译] 茉莉花使空气飘香。

[分　析] per + fume
遍布 + 气味 → 使气味遍布，使发香，发香味

[词义扩展] *n.* 香味，香水，香精

[大头例句] Perfume has only become preferable to man in recent years; in man's most primitive form, the more unchanged man's natural odor, the more capable one is of attracting the opposite sex. 只是近几年来香水才受到男士的钟爱，根据男士最早的方式，男人的气味越是保持不变，越能够吸引异性。

perplexed adj. /pəˈplekst/

"What's the matter?" Bob said, looking totally *perplexed*.

[猜一猜] A 困惑的　　B 气氛的　　C 迷人的　　D 友好的

[翻　译] "怎么回事？"鲍勃说道，满脸的困惑。

[分　析] per + plex + ed
全部 + 重叠 + 形容词尾 → 全部交错在一起的

[大头例句] It was not until she saw the perplexed look on her students' faces that the teacher realized she had misspelled the word "physics" on the syllabus, instead printing "psychics"! 直到看到学生脸上困惑的表情，这位老师才意识到他把课程表上的"physics（物理学）"拼错了，印出来的是"psychics（心理学）"。

undertake v. /ʌndəˈteik/

I *undertook* the task of teaching the children English.

[猜一猜] A 归功于　B 许诺　C 禁止　D 渴望
[翻　译] 我答应教孩子们英语。
[分　析] under + take
下面 + 带 → 把…带在手下,承担,担任,许诺

[大头例句] State senators undertook to use federal funds for improving schools.国家参议员们许诺要用联邦资金来改善学校教育。

习题：在下面的空格中填写本单元的单词。

1. It was not until she saw the __________ look on her students' faces that the teacher realized she had misspelled the word "physics" on the syllabus, instead printing "psychics"!
2. State senators __________ to use federal funds for improving schools.
3. The organization is responsible for the maintenance and __________ of offshore structures.
4. I have __________ on many writers for my essential conception of British culture.
5. The chief __________ court is the final destination of those who commit "petty crimes": that is, crimes that are less serious than most felonies.
6. In most cases, superiors don't offer their workers pay raises; instead, the employees have to __________ for more money.
7. Strict __________ of the law is asked in modern marketing.
8. Most of Asia's local economies were in grave __________ through the end of the 1990's.
9. __________ has only become preferable to man in recent years: in man's most primitive form, the more unchanged man's natural odor, the more capable one is of attracting the opposite sex.
10. The business failed because its assets were not as great as its __________.
11. His __________ and industry brought him speedy promotion.
12. I have no interest in watching that television program; __________, I have so much important work to complete tonight that I really don't have the time.
13. The __________ of ten million dollars and a beautiful home proved enough to convince the woman of thirty to marry a stranger of eighty-five.
14. In political terms, the British monarchy has little power; only __________.
15. For many newlywed couples, the __________ payment is the largest of any of their debts.
16. Most people do not think this newspaper is very __________: they often fabricate juicy stories in an attempt to sell copies.
17. Many say both the __________ and the respectability of the Roman Catholic Church have been severely diminished in light of the recent pedophilia scandals.
18. The __________ indignation from those free-speech campaigners impressed a lot of students.
19. The __________ of the assassination of the president was brought to light in time.
20. Frequent cultural exchange will certainly help __________ friendly relations between our two universities.
21. With the lead of the Chinese Communist Party the people __________ their power to the People's Congress.
22. He swore __________ to his native land.
23. The recent flood __________ memories of the great flood of 1972.

Day 58

adduce *vt.* /əˈdjuːs/

I could *adduce* many reasons for your rudeness.

[猜一猜] A 争辩　B 命名　C 责骂　D 指出

[翻　译] 我能指出你粗鲁的很多原因。

[分　析] ad + duce

to + lead → 带领至…，把证据或原因带出来，举证，指出

[词义扩展] *v.* 举出证据 *He could not adduce any proof to persuade the judge.* 他举不出任何证据来说服审判员。

attorney *n.* /əˈtəːni/

The supervisor of our department employed a private *attorney* to get legal advice.

[猜一猜] A 秘书　B 顾问　C 律师　D 助理

[翻　译] 我们部的主管请了一位私人律师来获得法律咨询。

[分　析] at + torn + ey

to + 指派，委派 + 名词词尾 → 委派人，代理人，律师

[词义扩展] *vt.* 获得，得到

[大头例句] The organization granted the power of attorney to me. 这个组织把其代理权委托给我。

ascribe *vt.* /əsˈkraib/

He *ascribed* his failure to the new government's economic policy.

[猜一猜] A 描述　B 抱怨　C 归因于　D 躲开

[翻　译] 他把他的失败归因于新政府的经济政策。

[分　析] as + cribe

to + to write → 把…写上去，归因于

[大头巧记] 根据同根词 describe 来记。Describe 第二次世界大战的时候，把德国的失败（词头的 de 去掉）归因于美国的加入［在词头加上 A(merica)］。

[词义扩展] *vt.* 认为…属于

[大头例句] The novel Dream of Red Mansions is usually ascribed to Cao Xueqin. 人们一般认为《红楼梦》这部小说是曹雪芹所著。

attribute *n.* /əˈtribjuːt/

Ross *attributed* his success to his persevering hard work and team spirit.

[猜一猜] A 分析　B 回顾　C 理解　D 归因于

[翻　译] 罗斯把他的成功归因于他不懈的努力工作和团队精神。

[分　析] at + tribu + te

to + 分配，拨给 + 动词词尾 → 把…给与，把…归于

[词义扩展] *v.* 被认为是…写的 *n.* 性质，属性，标志，象征

This tune is usually attributed to Chopin. 这个曲子通常认为是萧邦写的。

The scale is the attribute of justice. 天平是公正的象征。

abstruse *adj.* /æbˈstruːs/

Your statement is too *abstruse* to be understood.

[猜一猜] A 深奥的　B 正确的　C 佳妙的　D 风趣地

[分　析] abs + truse

away + to thrust → 推开，被推开的，很深奥的，一般人无法理解的

[翻　译] 你的话太深奥了，我理解不了。

[大头巧记] abs(olutely) truth(se) 绝对的真理当然很深奥。

[大头例句] The intellectual, who is working on some abstruse problem, should have everything coordinated and organized for the matter at hand. 在攻克深奥问题的智者要把身边所有的事都做得有条有理。

altar n. /ˈɔːltə/

I want to find the basics of setting up a proper *altar* and what the specific items on the altar represent.

[猜一猜]A 祭坛　B 点将台　C 城堡　D 墓碑

[翻　译]我想知道设立一个正规的祭坛的基本要素并搞明白祭坛上特殊的祭品代表着什么意思。

[联　想]**altarage** *n.* **祭品，香火钱**

[习语记忆]**lead (a woman) to the altar** 与(某女)结婚

[大头例句]I am going to offer my life on the altar of freedom. 我将把我的生命献给自由。

certify v. /ˈsəːtifai/

All the accounts of our firm were *certified* as correct.

[猜一猜]A 评价　B 证明　C 造假　D 决定

[翻　译]我们公司所有的账目经证明是正确无误的。

[分　析]certi + fy

肯定 + 使…化 → 使…肯定化，证明

[词义扩展]*v.* ①宣称 ②授予合格证书 ③(医生)诊断(某人)是疯子

[大头例句]He was certified insane. 他已由医生出具证书证明为精神错乱。

cite vt. /sait/

The judicial minister *cited* the latest crime figures as proof of the need for strengthening of the comprehensive administration of social public order.

[猜一猜]A 引用　B 做出　C 固定　D 规划

[翻　译]司法部长引用最新的犯罪统计数字来证明需要加强社会治安的综合治理。

[大头巧记]同音词：**site 地点**，web site 网站上有很多可引用的证据。

[词义扩展]*vt.* ①引用，引证；列举；说到 ②【律】传讯 ③召集，发动

[大头例句]Bates pulled out of the competition, citing personal reasons. 由于个人问题，贝茨退出了竞赛。

client n. /ˈklaiənt/

He was in charge of a famous hotel with lots of *clients* from all over the world.

[猜一猜]A 投资者　B 业务　C 风格　D 顾客

[翻　译]他曾经在一个拥有来自世界各地顾客的著名旅馆作主管工作。

[词义扩展]*n.* ①委托人；(律师的)当事人 ②接受社会照顾的人 *a client state* 附庸国

[大头例句]Sometimes a social worker has to act against a client's wishes. 有时社会工作者要违背顾客的意愿行事。

confirm v. /kənˈfəːm/

Please *confirm* your telephone message by writing to me.

[猜一猜]A 记起　B 降格　C 发送　D 证实

[翻　译]请给我来封信，好进一步证实你在电话中传达的消息。

[分　析]con + firm

加强语气 + 坚定 → 完全的坚定，确证，使巩固，批准

[大头例句]The new results confirm what most of us knew already.新的结果坚定了我们已知的东西。

exemplify vt. /igˈzemplifai/

The recent oil price rise *exemplifies* the difficulties which the motor industry is now facing.

[猜一猜]A 导致　B 解释　C 是由于　D 例证

[翻　译]最近的石油涨价是汽车工业正面临困难的一个例子。

[分　析]exempl + ify

例子 + …化 → 举例说明，作为…的例证

[大头例句]The bank's collapse exemplifies the risks of large-scale currency dealing. 这家银行的失败是大数额流通交易风险的一个例子。

demonstrate vt. /ˈdemənstreit/

The salesman *demonstrated* how to use the new air drying machine.

[猜一猜] A 注意　B 演示　C 介绍　D 学习
[翻　译] 售货员演示怎样使用新型的空气干燥机。
[分　析] de　+ monstr + ate
加强 + 演示　+ 动词词尾 → 示范，证明，示威
[大头巧记] 掐头去尾法，抓住起特征部分 monst(er)，怪物示威。
[词义扩展] v. ①证实，证明 ②图解；插图 ③显示，表明 *demonstrate a proposition.* 证明一个命题
[大头例句] He demonstrated affection by hugging me. 他拥抱我以示亲热。

embody *vt.* /im'bɔdi/

The new edition of the encyclopedia ***embodies*** many improvements.

[猜一猜] A 添加　B 包含　C 引起　D 介绍
[翻　译] 百科全书的新版本有许多改进之处。
[大头巧记] em=in，body，把事情具体到每个人身上。
[词义扩展] vt. ①使具体化，使形象化，体现 ②使（精神）肉体化
[大头例句] The spirit of hope is embodied in the character Anna. 人物安娜身上被赋予了自由的精神。

hypothesis *n.* /hai'pɔθisis/

This is only a sort of scientific ***hypothesis*** which has not been proven by experiments.

[猜一猜] A 假说　B 定理　C 理想　D 研究
[翻　译] 这仅仅是一个尚未被实验证明的科学假说。
[分　析] hypo　+ thesis
在…下面 + 论点 → 还未达到真正地位的论点，假说，前提
[大头例句] Darwin offered a working hypothesis for the mechanism of evolution. 达尔文为进化机制提供了一个可行的假说。

illustrate *v.* /'iləstreit/

The speaker said he would endeavor to ***illustrate***.

[猜一猜] A 出席　B 含蓄　C 明了　D 举例说明
[翻　译] 演讲人说他将设法举例说明。
[分　析] il　+ lustrate
在…上 + 照耀 → 照在…上面，使…明晰，阐明，举例说明，图解
[大头巧记] 和 **illuminate** 有相同的意项，照明。可联系记忆。
[大头例句] The cookbook is beautifully illustrated with colour photographs. 这本食谱里面插入了漂亮的彩色照片。

jury *n./ adj.* /'dʒuəri/

The ***jury*** found him guilty of murdering three people.

[猜一猜] A 法官　B 审判长　C 警察　D 陪审团
[翻　译] 陪审团认为他犯有杀害三人的罪行。
[分　析] jur　+　y
发誓 + 名词词尾 → 发誓的人，陪审团，评委会，评委
[大头例句] He served on the jury of the Miss World competition. 他是世界小姐选美大赛评判小组成员之一。

justify *v.* /'dʒʌstifai/

The course of events fully ***justifies*** our views.

[猜一猜] A 公正　B 证明　C 推翻　D 使…扬名
[翻　译] 事情的发展完全证明我们的意见是正确的。
[分　析] just　+ ify
正当 + 动词词尾 → 证明…为正当的或有理的，为…辩护
[大头例句] I don't see why I should justify myself to you. 我似乎不需向你辩白。

numb *adj./ v.* /nʌm/

The heavy blow had ***numbed*** his arm.

[猜一猜] A 伤害　B 使疼痛　C 使折断　D 使麻木
[翻　译] 那一记重击使他的胳膊麻木了。
[大头巧记] 不停的读数字 number 我都麻木了，后来干脆读成了 numb。
[大头例句] I have heard that for the first few seconds after receiving a non-life-threatening gunshot

wound, the body is completely numb and victims sometimes don't even realize what has taken place. 我听说人在受到致命枪击的最初几秒钟里，身体完全麻木，有时受害人甚至意识不到发生了什么。

precedent *n.* /priˈsiːdənt/

The President followed historical *precedent* in forming the Cabinet.

[猜一猜] A 宪法 B 先例 C 契约 D 民意

[翻 译] 总统遵循历史惯例来组建内阁。

[分 析] pre + cede + nt

前 + 走 + 词尾 → 过去人走过的，前例，在前的

[大头例句] Forgiving her cheating husband's first extramarital affair proved a dangerous precedent for the woman to set. 原谅丈夫第一次婚外关系的不忠证明是女性为自己设置的危险先例。

overall *adj.* /ˈəuvərɔːl/

The *overall* cost of the trip was about 2,000 pounds.

[猜一猜] A 最低的 B 全部的 C 延展的 D 奢侈的

[翻 译] 旅行的全部费用大约是两千磅。

[大头巧记] all over，遍布的：**overall 全部的，全面的**

[大头例句] My overall impression of her personality is good. 我对她的性格总体印象不错。

testimony *n.* /ˈtestiməni/

The latest trade figures are *testimony* to the failure of government policies.

[猜一猜] A 造成 B 损害 C 回旋 D 证明

[翻 译] 最新的贸易数字证明了政府政策的失败。

[大头巧记] 拆：test i(t) mon(e)y，为了钱测试它，以获得证明。

[词义扩展] *n.* 证词，宣言，陈述

[大头例句] Christina's testimony is crucial to the prosecution's case. 克里斯蒂娜的证词对诉方的案子至关重要。

witness *n./ v.* /ˈwitnis/

These facts are a *witness* to his carelessness.

[猜一猜] A 后果 B 前奏 C 证明 D 膨胀

[翻 译] 这些事实证明了他的粗心。

[分 析] wit + ness

才智 + 词尾 → 用才智证明 → 作证，证词，证人 → 目击者 → 目击

[大头例句] We were witness to the worst period in the team's history. 我们是该队历史上最困难时期的见证者。

习题：在下面的空格中填写本单元的单词。

1. The intellectual, who is working on some __________ problem, should have everything coordinated and organized for the matter at hand.
2. I am going to offer my life on the __________ of freedom.
3. We were __________ to the worst period in the team's history.
4. I have heard that for the first few seconds after receiving a non-life-threatening gunshot wound, the body is completely __________ and victims sometimes don't even realize what has taken place.
5. Forgiving her cheating husband's first extramarital affair proved a dangerous __________ for the woman to set.
6. The __________ cost of the trip was about 2,000 pounds.
7. The latest trade figures are __________ to the failure of government policies.

8. I could __________ many reasons for your rudeness.
9. The novel *Dream of Red Mansions* is usually __________ to Cao Xueqin.
10. The supervisor of our department employed a private __________ to get legal advice.
11. All the accounts of our firm were __________ as correct.
12. The judicial minister __________ the latest crime figures as proof of the need for strengthening of the comprehensive administration of social public order.
13. He was in charge of a famous hotel with lots of __________ from all over the world.
14. The salesman __________ how to use the new air drying machine.
15. The __________ found him guilty of murdering three people.
16. Ross __________ his success to his persevering hard work and team spirit.
17. The new results __________ what most of us knew already.
18. The cookbook is beautifully __________ with colour photographs.
19. The recent oil price rise __________ the difficulties which the motor industry is now facing.
20. The new edition of the encyclopedia __________ many improvements.
21. This is only a sort of scientific __________ which has not been proven by experiments.
22. The course of events fully __________ our views.

Day 59

adumbrate *vt.* /ˈædʌmˌbreit/

His invention *adumbrated* a world-wide revolution in computer technology.

[猜一猜] A 影响　B 相关　C 预示　D 引发

[翻　译] 他的发明预示着计算机技术的一次世界性大革命。

[分　析] ad　+ umbrate

朝向 + 阴影 → 给…蒙上阴影，此处引申为预示

[大头巧记] 只要我们记住 umbrate 这个词根就行了，umbrella 是雨伞的意思，把 ate 看成动词词尾，就很容易记住了。

[联　想] **adumbration n. 暗示，预示** *Her red face is an adumbration that she is in drunk.* 她脸红表示她喝了很多酒。

[词义扩展] *v.* ①勾画出轮廓 ②隐约显示，预示 → ③给…蒙上阴影

[大头例句] His pride and prejudice adumbrated our meeting. 他的傲慢和偏见给我们的会谈蒙上了一层阴影。

anticipate *v.* /ænˈtisipeit/

He *anticipates* great pleasure from his visit to his friend in Luoyang.

[猜一猜] A 拥有　B 感激　C 带着　D 期望

[翻　译] 他期待洛阳的访友之行带给他很大的快乐。

[分　析] anti　+ cipate

在…之前 + 采取 → 抢先，期望

[词义扩展] *v.* ①占先；抢先 *We anticipated our competitors by getting our products into the market first.*

我们赶在竞争对手之前，先把产品推向市场。

②预支；提前使用 *Anticipating income is allowed in this company.* 在这家公司你可以预支收入。

③预先考虑；预先准备 *He had already anticipated all I needed before I came.* 我来以前他已经准备好了我所有需要的东西。

allegory *n.* /ˈæligəri/

The blindfolded figure with scales is an *allegory* of justice.

[猜一猜] A 图标　B 象征　C 商标　D 形象

[翻　译] 蒙着眼睛手执天平的形象象征着正义。

[大头巧记] 析：alle(y) gory (血腥的)，血腥的小。巷是恐怖的象征。

[词义扩展] *n.* 比喻，预言

[大头例句] The allegory of the story about the tortoise and the rabbit is that pride results in failure. 龟和兔的故事的寓意是说骄傲导致失败。

alchemy *n.* /ˈælkimi/

He wondered by what *alchemy* it was changed, so that what sickened him one hour, maddened him with hunger the next. (Marjorie K. Rawlings)

[猜一猜] A 原因　B 工具　C 魔力　D 药物

[翻　译] "他想知道是什么样的魔力导致了这样的变化，一小时前使他厌恶的东西，现在却发疯似的想得到它"(玛乔丽 K.罗林斯)

[分　析] al　+ chemy

the + 化学 → 指点金术，炼丹术，此处引申为魔力

[大头例句] We believe that alchemy is the beginning of modern chemistry. 我们相信炼丹术是现代化学的起始。

destiny *n.* /ˈdestini/

Destiny brought us together.

[猜一猜] A 利益　B 兴趣　C 命运　D 文化背景

[翻　译] 命运将我们带到一起。

[分　析] de　　+ stin +　　y
向下 + 站 + 名词词尾 → 我们都站立在命运之下

[大头例句] Bob accepts his destiny without complaint. 鲍勃毫无怨言地接受了自己的命运。

ensue *v.* /inˈsjuː/

A hand grenade exploded by accident and I got lost in the *ensuing* confusion.

[猜一猜] A 混乱的　B 接下来的　C 令人昏厥的　D 逃跑的

[翻　译] 一枚手榴弹意外地发生了爆炸，接着是一片混乱，使我不知所措。

[分　析] en　　+ sue
加强前缀 + 跟随 → 紧紧跟随，紧跟着的，接着发生的

[大头巧记] **sue**,独立的单词,追求 → **ensue**,追随,紧跟着。

[词义扩展] *vt.* 追求［随］*Let him seek peace and ensue it!* 让他去追求和平并为和平而奔波吧!

forecast *n.* /ˈfɔːkɑːst/

The newspaper's *forecast* that the Democrats would be totally beaten in the general election came true.

[猜一猜] A 预测　B 报道　C 消息　D 情报

[翻　译] 报纸预测民主党人在这次大选中将被彻底击败，后来果然如此。

[分　析] fore　　+ cast
…之前 + 估算 → 超前的估算，预测，预见

[大头巧记] 类似的词还有：**foremost** ***adj./ adv.*** **最重要的，第一流的。forerunner，跑在前面的人—先驱。foresee，*v.* 预见，预知。**

[词义扩展] *vt.* 预想，预测，预兆 *He forecast that the economy's downturn would be short-lived.* 他预言说经济的低迷是短期的。

[大头例句] The UN has revised its forecast of global grain production. 联合国修正了它对世界粮食产量的预测。

incur *v.* /inˈkəː/

He *incurred* substantial losses during the stock market crash.

[猜一猜] A 遭受　B 造成了　C 避免了　D 预测了

[翻　译] 他在股票市场剧跌时蒙受了巨大的物质损失。

[分　析] in　　+ cur
在…上 + 跑 → 跑到…上，遭致，惹起，遭受

[大头巧记] **occur，发生，出现。**in (oc)cur 惹起…发生，遭受。

[大头例句] Each stage of the process incurs an additional risk. 进程的每一步都招致了一个额外的风险。

indicative *adj.* /inˈdikətiv/

His presence is *indicative* of his interest in our plan.

[猜一猜] A 创造的　B 建议的　C 调解的　D 表示的

[翻　译] 他的到来表示他对我们的计划有兴趣。

[分　析] indicate + ive
指出 + 形容词尾 → 指示的，表示的，预示的

[词义扩展] *adj.*【语】陈述的，直述的 *the indicative mood* 陈述语气，陈述式

[大头例句] These latest figures are indicative of a slowing economy. 这些最新的数字表示经济发展缓慢。

inevitable *adj.* /inˈevitəbl/

Such a difficult operation may not succeed; it's an *inevitable* gamble.

[猜一猜] A 不可避免的　B 重要的　C 值得一试的　D 效果好的

[翻　译] 这种难度很大的手术可能不成功，但这是一次非做不可的冒险。

[分　析] in + evitable
不 + 可避免地 → 不可避免的，必然的，逼真的

[大头巧记] **evitable = avoidable，inevitable =** not avoidable **不可避免的**

[大头例句] It is perhaps inevitable that advanced technology will increase the pressure on employees. 先进的技术会增长雇工们的压力，这也许是必然的。

intuition *n.* /ˌintjuːˈiʃən/

Archaeologists often use their *intuition* to decide where to dig.

[猜一猜]A 仪器 B 知识 C 直觉 D 图片

[翻 译]考古学家们经常用他们的直觉来决定在哪里挖掘。

[分 析] in + tui + tion
在…里 + 看 + 名词词尾 → 洞察力，直觉，直觉到的事物/知识

[大头例句] Sometimes you just have to rely on your intuitions. 有时你只需依靠你的直觉。

fabulous *adj.* /ˈfæbjuləs/

A marathon runner needs *fabulous* endurance to finish the race.

[猜一猜]A 有趣的 B 坚定的
C 难以置信的 D 能持久的

[翻 译]马拉松运动员需要令人难以置信的耐力来完成比赛。

[分 析] fabul + ous
寓言，神话 + 形容词尾 → 神话般的，难以置信的，惊人的，巨大的

[词义扩展] *adj.* 寓言中的，传说中的 *fabulous heroes* 神话中的英雄

[大头例句] You look fabulous! 你看起来好极了！

forthcoming *adj./n.*/fɔːθˈkʌmiŋ/

Forthcoming events include a concert and a trip to the mountains.

[猜一猜]A 即将来临的 B 重要的
C 已付费的 D 额外的

[翻 译]即将来临的事情包括一场音乐会和一次山中旅行。

[分 析]forth + coming
前方的 + 到来了 → 即将来临的，随手可得的

[词义扩展] *adj.* 现有的，愿意帮助的，可亲的 *n.* 来临，出现

[大头例句] We asked several villagers the way to the mine, but none of them were very forthcoming. 我们向好几个村民询问通往矿山的路，但他们都不愿回答。

imminent *adj.* /ˈiminənt/

According to the weather report a rainstorm is *imminent.*

[猜一猜]A 迫近的 B 可能的
C 发生的 D 消失的

[翻 译]据天气预报说暴风雨即将来临。

[分 析] im + min + ent
在…里面 + 威胁 + 形容词尾 → 在威胁之中的，逼近的，迫近的，紧迫的

[大头巧记] **eminent，突出的，闻名的**，当危险很突出时，它是**迫近的，紧迫的(imminent)**。

[大头例句] Many species of animals are in imminent danger of extinction.很多的动物种类处在灭绝危险的边缘。

ominous *adj.* /ˈɔminəs/

The present trade war is far more *ominous*.

[猜一猜]A 有利的 B 不吉利的 C 困惑的 D 缓和的

[翻 译]目前的贸易战的兆头非常不妙。

[大头巧记] **omen，预兆，征兆；→ ominous，预兆的，不吉利的。**

[大头例句] **This wind is ominous. I think a typhoon is coming.**这阵风兆头不妙，我想是台风要来了。

predictable *adj.* /priˈdiktəbl/

Most of the films we've reviewed this summer have had one thing in common — *predictable* plots.

[猜一猜]A 无聊的 B 诡异的
C 可预见的 D 谨慎的

[翻 译]今年夏天我们看到的大多数电影都有一个共同点——可以预见的情节。

[分 析]pre + dict + able
提前 + 说 + 可…的 → 可提前说出的，可预见的

[大头例句] When will Hollywood movies stop being so painfully predictable and start taking risks that challenge their audiences? 好莱坞电影何时才能脱出令人讨厌的可预见的老套，开

始冒险挑战观众？

prophecy *n.* /ˈprɔfisi/

He is said to have the born gift of *prophecy*.

[猜一猜] A 特异功能　　B 通灵　　C 第六感　　D 预言

[翻　译] 据说他有预言的天赋。

[分　析] pro + phe + cy

预先 + 说 + 名词词尾 → 预言，预言的能力

paraphrase *v./ n.* /ˈpærəfreiz/

Our teacher always asks us to *paraphrase* the long sentences in texts.

[猜一猜] A 意译　B 翻译　C 抄写　D 模仿

[翻　译] 我们的老师总是让我们意译课文里的长句子。

[分　析] para + phrase

旁边 + 说 → 用另外一种方法说，意译，释义

[大头例句] The young suitor, failing to remember Shakespeare's exact romantic words, paraphrased Romeo's famous monologue in an effort to woo his sweetheart. 这位年轻的求婚者记不起莎翁浪漫台词的原话了，他演绎了罗米欧的独白尽力向爱人求爱。

posthumous *adj.* /ˈpɔstjuməs/

For his family, his *posthumous* awards for bravery are a kind of comfort.

[猜一猜] A 丰富的　　B 怜悯的　　C 最终的　　D 死后的

[翻　译] 对他的家庭来说，死后对其勇敢的奖励是一种安慰。

[分　析] post + hum + ous

后 + 土 + 形容词尾 → 入土后的，死后的

[大头例句] The Catholic Church is still in deliberations over whether or not to grant Mother Theresa posthumous sainthood. 天主教会还在考虑是否承认女修道院长特里沙死后圣徒的身份。

习题：在下面的空格中填写本单元的单词。

1. His presence is __________ of his interest in our plan.
2. A marathon runner needs __________ endurance to finish the race.
3. The Catholic Church is still in deliberations over whether or not to grant Mother Theresa __________ sainthood.
4. __________ brought us together.
5. He __________ substantial losses during the stock market crash.
6. Archaeologists often use their __________ to decide where to dig.
7. This wind is __________. I think a typhoon is coming.
8. The young suitor, failing to remember Shakespeare's exact romantic words, __________ Romeo's famous monologue in an effort to woo his sweetheart.
9. When will Hollywood movies stop being so painfully __________ and start taking risks that challenge their audiences?
10. He is said to have the born gift of __________.
11. Many species of animals are in __________ danger of extinction.
12. We asked several villagers the way to the mine, but none of them were very __________.
13. It is perhaps __________ that advanced technology will increase the pressure on employees.
14. We __________ our competitors by getting our products into the market first.

15. The blindfolded figure with scales is an __________ of justice.
16. His invention __________ a world-wide revolution in computer technology.
17. He wondered by what __________ it was changed, so that what sickened him one hour, maddened him with hunger the next.(Marjorie K. Rawlings)
18. A hand grenade exploded by accident and I got lost in the __________ confusion.
19. The newspaper's __________ that the Democrats would be totally beaten in the general election came true.

Note 前事不忘后事之师 *Remember the past and it will guide your future.*

Day 60

acclimate *v.* /əˈklaimit/

It took him several months to *acclimate* to life in the countryside.

[猜一猜]A 出现　B 发现　C 提高　D 适应

[翻　译]他花了几个月的时间才适应了乡村的生活。

[分　析] ac　+ climate
to 朝,向 + 气候 → 向着气候(生活) → 适应

[大头巧记] ac(cept) climate,接受气候,适应。

[词义扩展] *vi.*, *vt.*([美]=acclimatize)(使)适应,驯化
The rice has been acclimated in this area. 水稻已能适应这一地区的环境。

[大头例句] Like African Americans, we Asians should acclimate to the community in a positive way. 我们亚洲人应该像非裔美国人一样积极地去适应社会。

correspond *vi.* /ˌkɔriˈspɔnd/

The American Congress *corresponds* to the British Parliament.

[猜一猜]A 相当　B 抵制　C 联合　D 谈判

[翻　译]美国国会相当于英国议会。

[分　析] cor　+ respond
共同 + 响应 → 相当,协调,符合,通信

[大头例句] The statistics do not correspond with our own experience. 统计数字和我们自己的经验不相符。

emigrate *v.* /ˈemigreit/

After the Nazis came to power in Germany, many scientists *emigrated*.

[猜一猜]A 开发　B 奋斗　C 迁出　D 思考

[翻　译]纳粹夺取了德国的政权之后,许多科学家都迁走了。

[分　析] e　+ migrate
出去 + 移动 → 移出,迁出,移民外国

[词义扩展] *vt.* (使)移民

[大头例句] We are thinking of emigrating to New Zealand. 我们正想着移民去新西兰。

navigable *adj.* /ˈnævigəbl/

The lake can be deep and wide enough to be *navigable* if it rains.

[猜一猜]A 形成潮水的　B 危险的
C 可灌溉的　D 可航行的

[翻　译]如果下雨的话,这个湖是可以有足够的深度和宽度适于航行的。

[分　析]nav + ig + able
船 + 走 + 可…的 → 可通航的,适于航行的。

[大头例句] After the hard rains, the dirt roads became muddy and barely navigable. 大雨过后,土路变得泥泞不堪而几乎不能通行。

necessitate *v.* /niˈsesiteit/

New laws will *necessitate* rethinking our retirement policy.

[猜一猜]A 迫使　B 涉及
C 成为必要　D 消除必要

[翻　译]新的法律将会使重新思考退休政策成为必要。

[分　析]necessi + tate
需要 + 动词词尾 → 成为必要,使需要

[大头巧记] 联系"**necessary,必要的**"记忆。

[大头例句] Entering into a crowded classroom does not necessitate singing and dancing; on the contrary it is inappropriate and disruptive. 进入一个拥挤的教室,并不需要载歌载舞,相反这是不相称,的并会引起混乱。

overcome *v.* /ˌəuvəˈkʌm/

She tried her best to *overcome* her weakness.

[猜一猜] A 理解 B 克服 C 抢夺 D 掩饰

[翻 译] 她努力克服自己的弱点。

[大头巧记] come over 过来；**overcome** 得胜，克服。另：与 **submit**(顺从)联合记忆。

[大头例句] Those who died in the fire were overcome by the gas fumes.那些死在火灾中的人是被浓烟熏死的。

promote *vt.* /prəˈməut/

The company is *promoting* their new products on television.

[猜一猜] A 宣传 B 辟谣 C 展示 D 交换

[翻 译] 这家公司在电视上宣传他们的新产品。

[分 析] pro + mote

向前 + 运动 → 向前动 → 促进，发扬，提升，宣传

[大头例句] As part of an effort to promote his movie "Hero," director Zhang Yimou agreed to countless interviews with the international press in the early months of 2003. 作为宣传其电影《英雄》的一部分，导演张艺谋在2003年的头几个月里接受了很多国际媒体的采访。

reluctant *adj.* /riˈlʌktənt/

He was very *reluctant* to go away.

[猜一猜] A 焦急的 B 不愿意的

C 忙碌的 D 激动的

[翻 译] 他很不愿意离去。

[分 析] re + luct + ant

一再 + 斗争 + 形容词词尾 → 一再反对 → 不愿意的，难处理的

[大头例句] I am reluctant to lend money to him again because he still hasn't paid me back from the time I let him borrow a huge amount two years ago. 我不愿意再借给他钱了，他两年前向我借的一大笔钱还没还呢。

physiological *adj.* /ˌfiziəˈlɔdʒikəl/

The drug produced no obvious *physiological* response.

[猜一猜] A 物理学的 B 生理的

C 心理的 D 敏感的

[翻 译] 该药不会产生明显的生理反应。

[分 析] physi + ologi + cal

自然 + …学 + 形容词词尾 → 生理学的，生理的

[大头例句] Many people confuse eating disorders such as bulimia and anorexia as a mere physiological condition in which a person refuses to eat enough food; in fact, the conditions are complex and multilayered, encompassing psychological factors as well. 很多人将饮食失调，如食欲过剩和厌食误以为只是一种生理状态，病人拒绝吃足够的食品；实际上情形是复杂的和多层面的，还包含有心理方面的因素。

perceive *v.* /pəˈsiːv/

Computers were often *perceived* as a threat.

[猜一猜] A 认为 B 误解 C 习惯 D 保险

[翻 译] 电脑过去常常被认为是一种威胁。

[分 析] per + ceive

全部 + 拿住 → 全部拿住 → 发觉，认为

[词义扩展] 感觉，察觉，理解

perceive by the nose 用鼻嗅出

[大头例句] Humans are only capable of visually perceiving a tiny percentage of the entire range of radiation present in the atmosphere. 人类视觉只能感觉到大气中射线的极小的部分。

permanent *adj.* /ˈpəːmənənt/

The universal human yearning is for something *permanent*, enduring, without shadow of change.

[猜一猜] A 永久的 B 有价值的

C 丰富的 D 可行的

[翻 译] 全人类渴望没有变化、永恒且持久的东西。

[分 析] per + man + ent

自始至终 + 拿住 + 形容词词尾 → 永久的，持久的

[大头例句] Though highway construction has created a huge problem for commuters in recent weeks, residents should be thankful that at least it will not be a permanent headache. 虽然近几周来高速公路的施工给经常来往的人造成了极大的问题，但是居民们应该庆幸的是，这至少不是个永久的麻烦。

phenomenal *adj.* /fiˈnɔminəl/

The *phenomenal* success of this movie proved his talent in directing.

[猜一猜] A 生气勃勃的　B 戏剧性的　C 非凡的；惊人的　D 失败的

[翻　译] 该影片惊人的成功证明了他在导演方面的天才。

[分　析] phenome + nal

现象 + 形容词词尾 → 现象的，能知觉的，显著的

[大头巧记] 拆：pheno → **phenix**，凤凰 phenix + men + al 凤凰人的，即非凡的。

[大头例句] Yao Ming's performance up to this point has been nothing short of phenomenal: it is a rare person indeed who could be placed in a foreign country with unfamiliar traditions and receive such a welcoming response. 姚明能取得这样的成绩确实杰出：在身处传统迥异的异国他乡能获得如此热情的回应确实是凤毛麟角。

tendency *n.* /ˈtendənsi/

His *tendency* to utter acrimonious remarks alienated his roommates.

[猜一猜] A 答辩　B 倾向　C 规律性　D 活力

[翻　译] 他老是说话尖刻，使同寝室的人和他疏远了。

[分　析] tend + ency

趋向 + 名词词尾 → 趋向，倾向

[大头例句] We've noticed a growing tendency for people to work at home instead of in offices. 我们注意到人们在家里工作而不是在办公室工作的倾向在增长。

tolerance *n.* /ˈtɔlərəns/

We need to show greater *tolerance* foward each other.

[猜一猜] A 兴趣　B 信任　C 宽容　D 善良

[翻　译] 我们应该更宽容地对待对方。

[分　析] toler + ance

宽容 + 名词词尾 → 宽容，容忍

[大头例句] Many old people have a very limited tolerance to cold. 很多老人抗拒寒冷的能力很有限。

transfer *n./ v.* /trænsˈfəː/

Wait until the cakes cool before *transferring* them to a plate.

[猜一猜] A 合并　B 吞咽　C 转移　D 争夺

[翻　译] 等到蛋糕凉了以后再把它们移到盘子里去。

[分　析] trans + fer

转移 + 带 → 转移过去，转移

[大头例句] Penny has applied for a transfer to another part of the company. 彭妮已申请调到公司的其他部门。

turbulent *adj.* /ˈtəːbjulənt/

The river becomes *turbulent* in summer.

[猜一猜] A 恶臭的　B 汹涌的　C 过分的　D 单调的

[翻　译] 夏天河水很汹涌。

[分　析] turb + ulent

搅拌 + 形容词词尾 → 搅得厉害 → 狂暴的，骚乱的，汹涌的

[大头例句] The Reformation was one of the most turbulent periods in English history. 宗教改革时期是英国历史上最动荡的时期之一。

utmost *n.* /ˈʌtməust/

I worked every day to the *utmost* of my abilities during that period.

[猜一猜] A 最大可能　B 最少　C 生命　D 超人

[翻　译] 在那段时间里我每天尽全力工作。

[分　析] ut + most

外面 + 最 → 最外面 → 最大可能,极限

[大头巧记] 协:at most,最多的,最大可能的

[词义扩展] *adj.* 极度的,最远的

a matter of the utmost importance 最重要的事情

[习语记忆] **to the utmost of one's power**

竭尽全力

[大头例句] All equipment should be handled with the utmost care.所有的设备在操作时都要极度小心。

vocational *adj.* /vəuˈkeiʃənəl/

The teacher will give us *vocational* guidance before we graduate.

[猜一猜] A 职业的　　B 有用的

C 指导性的　　D 压制的

[翻　译] 毕业前教师会给我们就业指导。

[分　析] voc + ational

叫喊 + 形容词词尾 → 受到召唤的 → 有职业的,职业的

[大头巧记] 将 **vacation**(假期)中的"a"变成了"o",就不能休假了,被召唤,有职业。

习题:在下面的空格中填写本单元的单词。

1. The teacher will give us __________ guidance before we graduate.
2. The universal human yearning is for something __________, enduring, without shadow of change.
3. We've noticed a growing __________ for people to work at home instead of in offices.
4. Like African-Americans, we Asians should __________ to the community in a positive way.
5. Entering into a crowded classroom does not __________ singing and dancing; on the contrary, it is inappropriate and disruptive.
6. Humans are only capable of visually __________ a tiny percentage of the entire range of radiation present in the atmosphere.
7. I am __________ to lend money to him again because he still hasn't paid me back from the time I let him borrow a huge amount two years ago.
8. After the hard rains, the dirt roads became muddy and barely __________.
9. She tried her best to __________ her weakness.
10. As part of an effort to __________ his movie "Hero," director Zhang Yimou agreed to countless interviews with the international press in the early months of 2003.
11. The drug produced no obvious __________ response.
12. After the Nazis came to power in Germany, many scientists __________.
13. The American Congress __________ to the British Parliament.
14. Yao Ming's performance up to this point has been nothing short of __________.
15. We need to show greater __________ foward each other.
16. The Reformation was one of the most __________ periods in English history.
17. I worked every day to the __________ of my abilities during that period.
18. Penny has applied for a __________ to another part of the company.

Day 61

barter *v.* /ˈbɑːtə/

Whether you're new to ***bartering*** or you have been ***bartering*** goods and services for years, our company is here to help you to get all the useful market information.

[猜一猜] A 实物交易　　B 投资
C 讨价还价　　D 市场开发

[翻　译] 无论你是刚刚介入还是已经从事实物交换好多年，我们公司在这里会帮助你了解所有有用的市场信息。

[词义扩展] *n.* 易货，易货贸易 *vi.* 进行易货贸易 *vt.* 出卖，丧失(权利，荣誉等)
We bartered for furs with pearls and wine. 我们用珍珠和葡萄酒换取毛皮。

[大头例句] No matter what happens, we will never barter away principles. 不管发生什么事，我们都不会出卖我们的原则。

diligence *n.* /ˈdilidʒəns/

Diligence is just one of his many outstanding attributes which led to his success.

[猜一猜] A 诚信　B 交际能力　C 智慧　D 勤奋

[翻　译] 勤奋只是使他成功的许多优秀品质之一。

[分　析] di + lig + ence
分开 + 选择 + 名词词尾 → 快速选择区别，勤勉

[习语记忆] **Diligence is the parent of success.** [谚]勤奋为成功之母。

foil *n.* /fɔil/

I am resolved that my husband shall not be a rival, but a ***foil*** to me.

[猜一猜] A 敌人　B 陪衬　C 朋友　D 同伴

[翻　译] 我决定不把我丈夫当成敌手而把他当成我的衬托。

[词义扩展] *n.* 箔，金属薄片 *vt.* 铺箔于，衬托，阻挠 *The escape attempt was foiled by wardens firing in the air.* 看守人对天放枪阻止了犯人逃跑的企图。

[大头例句] Wrap the cheese in foil to keep it moist. 把奶酪包在金箔里面来保持潮湿。

indifferent *adj.* /inˈdifrənt/

The universe is not hostile, nor yet is it friendly. It is simply ***indifferent***.

[猜一猜] A 冷淡的　　B 伟大的
C 神秘的　　D 启示的

[翻　译] 宇宙没有敌意，但也不是友好的，它只是冷淡的。

[分　析] in + different
不 + 不同的 → 任何不同的事均与己无关 → 冷淡的，不感兴趣的，不关心的

[词义扩展] *adj.* 不重要的，不积极的，平凡的，质量不高的，中立的
remain indifferent in a dispute 在争论中保持中立

[大头例句] It's easy to be indifferent to money when you've never been poor. 如果你从来都未曾贫困，就很容易对钱漠不在乎。

premium *n.* /ˈpriːmiəm/

Work paid according to the amount done puts a ***premium*** on speed and not on quality.

[猜一猜] A 偷懒　B 诱使　C 鼓励　D 幻想

[翻　译] 按件付酬是导致重速度、轻质量的原因。

[分　析] pr(e) + em + ium
在先 + 买 + 名词词尾 → 事先买的 → 保险金，奖金，鼓励

[大头例句] As a child, my parents placed a high premium on educational opportunities, and to this day I enjoy the habits of reading and exploring that I established while still heavily under their influence. 还是孩子的时候，我父母在

对我的教育机会上煞费苦心，直到今天，他们仍深深地影响着我，我很喜欢我建立起的阅读和探索的习惯。

quota *n.* /ˈkwəutə/

No boat is allowed to catch more than its *quota* of fish.

[猜一猜] A 选择　B 分类　C 特长　D 限额

[翻　译] 任何船都不允许捕获超过限量的鱼。

[大头巧记] 区别 **quote**（引用）和 **quota**，巧记：写作时引用别人作品的量有限制。

[词义扩展] 定额，配额，分得的量

the quota system 定额分配制

redeem *vt.* /riˈdiːm/

He *redeemed* his watch from the pawn shop.

[猜一猜] A 典当　B 赎回　C 购买　D 抢得

[翻　译] 他把他的手表从当铺赎回。

[分　析] re　+ deem

重新 + 买 → 买回，赎回，挽回，赎罪

[大头例句] If you shop at this store between the hours of 10 am and noon, you can redeem this coupon for a 20% discount of your total purchase. 如果你在上午10点到正午之间在该店购物的话，你就可以兑换这张优惠券而享受8折优惠。

refund *v./ n.* /riˈfʌnd/

We will *refund* your money in full if you are not completely satisfied.

[猜一猜] A 建立　B 归还　C 补偿　D 分离

[翻　译] 如果你不是完全满意的话，我们将退还你所有的钱。

[分　析] re　+ fund

再 + 资金 → 再次给你资金 → 归还，退款

[词义扩展] *n./ v.* 偿还，退款

appropriation refund 拨款退回

remedy *n./ vt.* /ˈremidi/

Your only *remedy* is to go to the law.

[猜一猜] A 机会　B 环境　C 治疗法　D 私心

[翻　译] 你惟一的补救法是诉诸法律。

[分　析] re　+ medy

再次 + 治愈 → 治疗法，药物

[大头巧记] 区别 **comedy**（喜剧）和 **remedy**，巧记：喜剧是伤心者的治疗方法。

[词义扩展] *v.* 治疗，补救，修补

remedy a mistake 纠正一个错误

[习语记忆] **There is a remedy for all things but death.** 除死亡外，一切都有补救方法。

[大头例句] I was surprised to learn that my grandmother used cucumbers on her eyes as a remedy for headaches. 我很惊奇地听说我奶奶把黄瓜放在眼睛上来治头痛。

penalty *n.* /ˈpenəlti/

We were given a *penalty* kick after one of our players was hit.

[猜一猜] A 机会　B 处罚　C 退出　D 突袭

[翻　译] 我们的一名队员被对方撞倒后，我们队得到一次罚点球的机会。

[分　析] penal + ty

惩罚 + 名词词尾 → 处罚，罚款，报应

[大头例句] There is a stiff penalty for paying one's taxes late; the penalty is infinitely stiffer, however, if one consistently fails to pay them at all. 迟付税款会有一个棘手的罚款，但是如果你总是一点税都不交的话，罚款就更加棘手了。

patron *n.* /ˈpeitrən/

He was an enthusiastic *patron* of the arts.

[猜一猜] A 赞助人　B 偏见　C 隐士　D 老手

[翻　译] 他是一个艺术的热心支持者。

[分　析] patr　+ on

父亲的 + 人 → 父亲般的人 → 赞助人

[大头例句] Many public arts organizations such as museums and dance troupes have a handful of patrons and donors to thank for the majority of their annual budgets. 很多的公共艺术团体，例如博物馆和舞蹈团，都有一些赞助者和捐赠者来提供他们年度预算的主要部分。

deem v. 认为，相信 = believe

恢复，补偿，兑换

purchase /ˈpɜːtʃəs/ 买 n. v.

pater n. 父亲

paterfamilias n. 家长

n. 预算

patronage n. 保护人身份，保护，赞助，光顾

patronize v. 资助

phase n. /feiz/

The American occupation of Japan fell into three successive *phases*.

[猜一猜] A 阶段　B 秘决　C 成就　D 平庸

[翻　译] 美国占领日本的过程可以划分为三个连续的阶段。

[大头巧记] 区别 **phrase(习语，短语)** 和 **phase**，去掉"r(ule)"，短语发展的第一个**阶段**，就是把束缚的一些条条框框开始去掉。

[词义扩展] *n.* 侧面，状态，相位 *vt.* 使分阶段 *phase down* 逐步减少；*one phase of the problem* 该问题的一个方面

[大头例句] In this early phase of Beijing's bullet train construction, it is difficult to know for sure how much traffic woes will be eased. 在北京高速火车初建阶段，还很难确定它在减轻交通忧患方面能够起多大作用。

participate vi. /pɑːˈtisipeit/

If only I could *participate* in your good fortune.

[猜一猜] A 分享　B 获得　C 分离　D 集中

[翻　译] 要是我能分享你的好运就好了。

[分　析] part + cip + ate
部分 + 进入 + 动词词尾 → 作为一个部分进入 → 参与，分享，分担

[大头例句] You are not required to participate in today's class debate, though practicing the vocabulary we've just learned will surely increase your chances of doing well on the next exam. 并不要求你参加今天的课堂辩论，但是对我们刚学词汇的练习一定会对你下次考试取得好成绩有帮助。

patent n. /ˈpeitənt/

In 1878, Edison received a *patent* for his phonograph.

[猜一猜] A 奖赏　B 满足　C 独特　D 专利

[翻　译] 1878年，爱迪生获得了留声机的专利。

[分　析] pat + ent
公开 + 形容词词尾 → 公开的，被公认的 → 专利

[词义扩展] *adj.* 专利的，公开的，显而易见的 *vt.* 获得专利 *patent right* 专利权

[大头例句] Having failed to patent his life-saving invention, the genius inventor remains poor today while his device has revolutionized modern medicine. 由于没能取得其所发明的救生设备的专利，这位天才的发明家至今仍然贫困，而他的设计却彻底革新了现代医学。

preserve v./ n. /priˈzəːv/

Our goal is to *preserve* the dignity and independence of our patients.

[猜一猜] A 说服　B 尊重　C 保护　D 提高

[翻　译] 我们的目标是要保护我们病人的尊严和独立。

[分　析] pre + serve
预先 + 保存 → 保护，保持，保存

[大头巧记] 拆：pre serve，在做服务之前要做的事情是要保护自己。

[词义扩展] *v.* 做蜜饯，腌制 *n.* 蜜饯 *preserve eggs in salt* 腌蛋

scholarship n. /ˈskɔləʃip/

For a few, *scholarships* were sources of support.

[猜一猜] A 工资　B 福利　C 家庭　D 奖学金

[翻　译] 有少数人，奖学金是他们接受教育的学费来源。

[大头巧记] 拆：scholar ship，载你驶向成为学者的船 → 奖学金。

[词义扩展] *n.* 学术成就，学识。

[大头例句] Without a scholarship, it would be impossible for many low-income children to attend college. 没有奖学金的话，很多低收入家庭的孩子将不可能上大学。

subscribe v. /səbˈskraib/

We *subscribe* to all the main medical journals.

[猜一猜] A 改变　B 投稿　C 预订　D 通知

[翻　译] 我们预订了所有的医学杂志。

[分　析] sub + scribe
下面 + 写 → 写下订单 → 预订，签署，捐款

[大头例句] We did not subscribe to the view that Dan's authority had diminished.我们不支持认为丹的权威已经降低了的观点。

tuition n. /tjuːˈiʃən/

Foreigners pay a much higher *tuition* than the locals.

[猜一猜] A 餐费 B 保险金 C 税款 D 学费

[翻　译] 外国人付的学费比本国人高得多。

[分　析] tuit + ion

保护 + 名词词尾 → 教诲,教学,学费

[大头例句] I have to have extra tuition in maths. 在数学上你要补补课。

= adventure v. n. 冒险

venture v. /ˈventʃə/

Nobody *ventured* to interrupt him.

[猜一猜] A 保险 B 承认 C 斗胆 D 经历

[翻　译] 没有人敢打断他的话。

venturesome adj. 冒险的

[分　析] vent + ure

来到 + 动词词尾 → 来到危险 → 冒险,冒昧,斗胆

[词义扩展] n. 冒险,投机,风险

[习语记忆] **Nothing ventured, nothing gained.** [谚]不入虎穴,焉得虎仔。

[大头例句] I would venture to guess that Anon., who wrote so many poems without signing them, was a woman.我冒昧地猜测,那个写下如此多诗歌的无名氏多半是个女人。

wage n. /weidʒ/

She got a weekly *wage* of 300 pounds.

[猜一猜] A 外汇 B 工资 C 消费 D 小费

[翻　译] 他每周有300英镑的工资。

[词义扩展] v. 开始,进行(战争等)

[大头例句] Wage levels in manufacturing and mining dropped again last month. 制造业和矿业的工资水平上月再次下滑。

welfare n./adj. /ˈwelfeə/

We should be concerned about the national *welfare* and the people's livelihood.

[猜一猜] A 调控 B 法制 C 政策 D 福利

[翻　译] 我们应该关心国计民生。

[分　析] wel + fare

好 + 相处 → 有了福利,可以很好地相处

[大头巧记] 注意与 **farewell**(再见)的区别。

"*Farewell to Arms*"《永别了,武器》(海明威作品)。

[大头例句] Police are concerned for the welfare of the child's mother.警方很关心孩子母亲的幸福。

wholesale n./adj. /ˈhəulseil/

The prices at that *wholesale* shop are lower.

[猜一猜] A 杂货的 B 服务好的 C 批发的 D 零售的

[翻　译] 那家批发店的价格比较便宜。

[大头巧记] 拆:whole sale,整批的卖,批发的,批发。

[大头例句] Wholesale prices fell last month.上个月批发价格下降了。

worthwhile adj. /wəːðˈ(h)wail/

It is not *worthwhile* to change jobs.

[猜一猜] A 值得的 B 必要的 C 纷争的 D 满意的

[翻　译] 换个工作不值得。

[大头巧记] 拆:worth while,当有价值的时候,值得。

[大头例句] I'd rather the money went to a worthwhile cause.我更想让钱用到值得的事业上。

souvenir n. /ˌsuːvəˈniə/

When Uncle Bill went abroad to live, he left me his watch as a *souvenir*.

[猜一猜] A 纪念品 B 财产 C 嗜好 D 礼貌

[翻　译] 比尔叔叔出国时把表留给我作为纪念品。

[大头巧记] 拆:sou(1) veneer(ir)(装饰),有精神价值的装饰物 → 纪念品。 /vəˈniə/ n. 胶合板、饰面 v. 胶合、镶饰

[大头例句] As a souvenir of his trip to Africa, my uncle brought me a small purse that had been hand-made by one of the local tribes he visited.作为去非洲旅行的纪念品,我的叔叔给我买了一个提包,是他访问过的一个部落手工制作的。

习题：在下面的空格中填写本单元的单词。

1. We were given a __________ kick after one of our players was hit.
2. As a __________ of his trip to Africa, my uncle brought me a small purse that had been handmade by one of the local tribes he visited.
3. No boat is allowed to catch more than its __________ of fish.
4. Many public arts organizations such as museums and dance troupes have a handful of __________ and donors to thank for the majority of their annual budgets.
5. You are not required to __________ in today's class debate, though practicing the vocabulary we've just learned will surely increase your chances of doing well on the next exam.
6. In this early __________ of Beijing's bullet train construction, it is difficult to know for sure how much traffic woes will be eased.
7. Having failed to __________ his life-saving invention, the genius inventor remains poor today while his device has revolutionized modern medicine.
8. I would __________ to guess that Anon., who wrote so many poems without signing them, was a woman.
9. I'd rather the money went to a __________ cause.
10. __________ levels in manufacturing and mining dropped again last month.
11. We should be concerned about the national __________ and the people's livelihood
12. The prices at that __________ shop are lower.
13. If you shop at this store between the hours of 10 am and noon, you can __________ this coupon for a 20% discount of your total purchase.
14. I was surprised to learn that my grandmother used cucumbers on her eyes as a __________ for headaches.
15. We will __________ your money in full if you are not completely satisfied.
16. Our goal is to __________ the dignity and independence of our patients.
17. Without a __________, it would be impossible for many low-income children to attend college.
18. Foreigners pay a much higher __________ than the locals.
19. We did not __________ to the view that Dan's authority had diminished.
20. Work paid according to the amount done puts a __________ on speed and not on quality.
21. Whether you're new to __________ or you have been bartering goods and services for years, our company is here to help you to get all the useful market information.
22. I am resolved my husband shall not be a rival, but a __________ to me.
23. __________ is just one of his many outstanding attributes which led to his success.
24. It's easy to be __________ to money when you've never been poor.

Day 62

archaic *adj.* /ɑːˈkeiik/

"Thou art" is an *archaic* form of "you are."

[猜一猜]A 拉丁语的　B 音标的　C 古体的　D 变体的
[翻　译]"Thou art"是"you are"的古体。
[分　析]archa + ic
古 + 形容词词尾 → 古代的，古体的(语言)
[联　想]archaeology *n.* 考古学 archaeological *adj.* 考古学的 archaeologist *n.* 考古学家
[大头例句]In the mausoleum he found an archaic bronze statuette which is very valuable. 在这个陵墓中他发现了一个相当古老的小青铜像，它非常有价值。

amid *prep.* /əˈmid/

He always looks confident and cultivated *amid* his supporters.

[猜一猜]A 面前　B 当中　C 接待　D 会谈
[翻　译]在支持者当中，他总是表现得自信而有修养。
[分　析]a + mid
在 + middle 当中 → 在…当中
[大头例句]He is like a Triton amid the minnows. 他鹤立鸡群，卓然不同。

curriculum *n.* /kəˈrikjuləm/

Our mathematics *curriculum* is much broader now.

[猜一猜]A 思维　B 方法　C 测试　D 课程
[翻　译]我们的数学课程现在丰富多了。
[分　析]curr + iculum
跑，发生 + 词尾 → 按发生的顺序排列的课程
[习语记忆]place…on its curriculum 把…列入课程之内

bustle *v.* /ˈbʌsl/

She was *bustling* about washing clothes when the earthquake happened.

[猜一猜]A 抱怨　B 忙着　C 就要结束　D 规避
[翻　译]地震发生时她正在忙着洗衣服。
[大头巧记]形近词记忆：buster 精力特别旺盛的孩子，动词化，er 变 le，成天忙来忙去。
[词义扩展]*n./ v.* 喧闹；熙攘　*vt.* 催促他人赶快，使忙乱，使活跃
[大头例句]Tell her to bustle up. 让她快点。

crucial *adj.* /ˈkruːʃəl/

Experience is, of course, a *crucial* factor in deciding who would be the best person for the job.

[猜一猜]A 惟一的　B 至关重要的　C 参考的　D 控制的
[翻　译]当然，经验是决定谁将是这个工作的最佳人选的关键因素。
[分　析]cruc + ial
十字形 + 形容词词尾 → 十字路口的 → 关键的，至关紧要的
[大头例句]We believe the question being investigated by the Commission is one of crucial importance to the country. 我们认为调查团对这个问题进行调查是这个国家最重要的事情之一。

empirical *adj.* /emˈpirikəl/

They are hoping to find *empirical* evidence to confirm their theories.

[猜一猜]A 权威的　B 经验的　C 理性的　D 皇族的
[翻　译]他们想找到基于经验的证据来验证他们的理论。
[分　析]em + piri + cal
在…里面 + 经验 + 形容词词尾 → 基于经

验的

[词义扩展] *adj.* 经验主义的，经验证明的

empirical formula【化】实验式

[大头例句] He finally found the empirical results that supported his hypothesis. 他最终找到了证明他的假设成立的经验性结论。

elapse *vi.* /iˈlæps/

> Several weeks were to *elapse* before the actress's case was brought to trial.

[猜一猜] A 准备　B 通知　C 调查　D 流逝

[翻　译] 等了好几个星期的时间，这个演员的案件才开始审理。

[分　析] e + lapse

向外 + 滑，溜 → 悄然溜走，流逝

[词义扩展] *n.* 过去，逝去

met again after an elapse of many years 多年后又相逢

[大头例句] Another hour elapsed and still the wind continued to howl. 又是一小时过去了，风怒吼依旧。

fortnight *n.* /ˈfɔːtnait/

> My aunt's coming in a *fortnight's* time.

[猜一猜] A 后天　B 明天晚上　C 下周　D 两星期后

[翻　译] 我的姨妈将在两周后到这儿来。

[大头巧记] fo(u)rt(een) night，十四个夜晚，十四天，两个星期。

[大头例句] I see her once a fortnight. 我每两周见她一面。

improvise *v.* /ˈimprəvaiz/

> We *improvised* a tent out of two blankets and some long poles.

[猜一猜] A 进口　B 临时准备　C 参考　D 居住

[翻　译] 我们用两条毛毯和几根长竿搭成一个临时帐篷。

[分　析] im + provise

不 + 准备 → 没有准备 → 临时准备(制作)

[词义扩展] *v.* 即席创作，即席演奏

improvise a new verse 临时作一首新词

[大头例句] I'd forgotten my carefully written speech, but knew I could easily improvise. 我忘记了我精心写成的发言稿，但是我知道我可以轻松地即席演说。

postpone *vt.* /pəustˈpəun/

> Bad weather forced us to *postpone* Friday's game.

[猜一猜] A 推迟　B 取消　C 耽误　D 迟到

[翻　译] 恶劣的天气迫使我们推迟了周五的比赛。

[分　析] post + pone

后 + 放 → 向后放 → 使延期，推迟

[大头例句] When our professor suddenly went into labor with her first child, she was forced to postpone our final exam until she could invigilate it herself almost two weeks later. 由于我们的教授突然临产她的第一个孩子，她被迫推迟了我们的期末考试，直到两个星期后她才能自己监考。

preliminary *adj./n.* /priˈliminəri/

> There are a lot of *preliminaries* to go through before you can visit Italy.

[猜一猜] A 预备　B 公益　C 热闹　D 应酬

[翻　译] 在你得以访问意大利之前，你有很多的准备工作要做。

[分　析] pre + liminary

…之前 + 开始 → 开始做事情前，做准备，预备 → 预备的，初步的

[大头例句] Before going to trial, there needs to be a preliminary investigation of this case to determine the amount of evidence and the potential witnesses for this case. 在审判之前，需要对本案进行预备调查，来决定证物和可能的目击者的数量。

prolong *vt.* /prəˈlɔŋ/

> The delegation decided to *prolong* their visit by one week.

[猜一猜] A 提前　B 退后　C 延长　D 缩短

[翻　译] 代表团决定把访问延长一个星期。

[分　析] pro + long

向前 + 长的 → 向前拉长 → 延长，拖延

[大头例句] One of the most common arguments in support of euthanasia is that once a person is comatose, artificially prolonging life undermines the dignity of life itself. 支持安乐死的最普通的论点之一就是，一旦一个人进入了昏睡状态，人工的延长他的生命是对生命本身尊严的破坏。

coma
n. 昏迷
comatose
adj. 昏迷的

propel *vt.* /prə'pel/

She was ***propelled*** by a desire to prove everyone else wrong.

[猜一猜] A 迷惑 B 兴奋 C 驱使 D 统治

[翻 译] 她被一种愿望驱使，想要去证明别人都是错的。

[分 析] pro + pel
向前 + 驱使 → 驱使，推进

recede *v.* /ri'siːd/

The mountain peaks ***recede*** into the distance as one leaves the shore.

[猜一猜] A 后退 B 美丽 C 缓和 D 离心

[翻 译] 人离岸时，山峰向后退去。

[分 析] re + cede
反向 + 走 → 后退

[大头巧记] 联合 **proceed**(进行)记忆。

[大头例句] For genetic reasons, some men are predisposed to have a receding hairline as they get older, meaning they slowly lose their hair starting from the front. 由于遗传因素，一些人随着年龄的增长头发容易退化，也就是说他们从前额开始慢慢失去头发。

pastime *n.* /'pɑːstaim/

Skateboarding is the favourite ***pastime*** of many teenagers.

[猜一猜] A 体育项目 B 系统 C 娱乐 D 歌谣

[翻 译] 溜冰板是很多年轻人最喜爱的运动。

[大头巧记] past time，度过时间 → 进行娱乐

[大头例句] British people tend to favor cricket as a national pastime, whereas most Americans not only prefer baseball, but do not even know the rules of cricket. 英国人趋向于赞成板球作为他们的国家性娱乐活动，美国人则更喜欢棒球，甚至不知道板球的规则。

simultaneous *adj.* /ˌsiməl'teiniəs/

The two ***simultaneous*** shots sounded like one.

[猜一猜] A 恐怖的 B 疯狂的 C 同时的 D 深邃的

[翻 译] 同时发出的两声枪响听起来像一声。

[分 析] simul + taneous
相同 + 形容词词尾 → 同时的，同时发生的

subsequent *adj.* /'sʌbsikwənt/

In ***subsequent*** interviews, Daniel has contradicted his original story.

[猜一猜] A 证实的 B 后来的 C 现场的 D 规范的的

[翻 译] 在后来的采访中，丹尼尔所说的话和开始时相矛盾。

[分 析] sub + sequent
后 + 跟着 → 紧跟其后，后来的，并发的

[大头例句] These skills were then passed on to subsequent generations. 然后，这些技术被传给了下一代。

temporary *adj.* /'tempərəri/

These policies are only ***temporary***.

[猜一猜] A 雏形的 B 暂时的 C 实际的 D 和解的

[翻 译] 这些政策只是暂时性的。

[分 析] temo + rary
事件 + 形容词词尾 → 暂时的，临时的

[大头巧记] 和 **permanent**(永久的，持久的)联合记忆。

[大头例句] The council has placed us in temporary accommodation. 委员会把我们放在了一个临时住宿的地方。

ultimately *adv.* /'ʌltimətli/

We hope ***ultimately*** to be able to buy a house of our own.

[猜一猜] A 最后 B 现实中 C 想象中 D 有关方面

ultimate /'ʌltimit/
adj. 最终的
n. 最终

[翻　译]我们希望最终能够自己买一所房子。

[分　析]　ultim　　+ ately
最远，最后 + 词尾 → 最后地，终于，基本上

[大头巧记]同根词：**ultimatum**，最后通牒

[大头例句]Technological advances could ultimately lead to even more job losses. 科技上的进步最后可能会造成更多的失业现象。

underlying *adj.* /ˌʌndəˈlaiiŋ/

Her *underlying* reason of examination failure was laziness.

[猜一猜]A 根本的　　B 公开的
C 明显的　　D 愚弄的

[翻　译]他没考好的根本原因是懒。

[大头巧记]拆：under lying，位于下面的 → 根本的，潜在的。

[大头例句]While superficially similar, the two films have very different underlying messages. 虽然表面类似，但这两部影片有着非常不同的内在信息。

superficial adj 表面

习题：在下面的空格中填写本单元的单词。

1. When our professor suddenly went into labor with her first child, she was forced to __________ our final exam until she could invigilate it herself almost two weeks later.
2. They are hoping to find __________ evidence to confirm their theories.
3. While superficially similar, the two films have very different __________ messages.
4. She was __________ by a desire to prove everyone else wrong.
5. For genetic reasons, some men are predisposed to have a __________ hairline as they get older, meaning they slowly lose their hair starting from the front.
6. Before going to trial, there needs to be a __________ investigation of this case to determine the amount of evidence and the potential witnesses for this case.
7. One of the most common arguments in support of euthanasia is that once a person is comatose, artificially __________ life undermines the dignity of life itself.
8. Several weeks were to __________ before the actress's case was brought to trial.
9. I'd forgotten my carefully written speech, but knew I could easily __________.
10. My aunt's coming in a __________'s time.
11. British people tend to favor cricket as a national __________, whereas most Americans not only prefer baseball, but do not even know the rules of cricket.
12. The two __________ shots sounded like one.
13. We hope __________ to be able to buy a house of our own.
14. The council has placed us in __________ accommodation.
15. In __________ interviews, Daniel has contradicted his original story.
16. In the mausoleum he found an __________ bronze statuette which is very valuable.
17. Experience is, of course, a __________ factor in deciding who would be the best person for the job.
18. She was __________ about washing clothes when the earthquake happened.
19. He always looks confident and cultivated __________ his supporters.
20. Our mathematics __________ is much broader now.

Day 63

arc n. /ɑːk/

The vivid *arc* of the rainbow attracted a lot of people.

[猜一猜] A 色彩　B 弧线　C 形象　D 传说

[翻　译] 彩虹那鲜明的弧线吸引了很多人。

[大头巧记] car 将它弧线形的"C"拿到后面展示。

[词义扩展] *vi.* 沿曲线前进

[大头例句] That a comet arced across the sky, they said, was an ill omen. 一颗彗星在空中划过一条曲线，他们说这是凶兆。

arch n. /ɑːtʃ/

The bridge has three *arches*.

[猜一猜] A 桥头堡　B 拱　C 桥墩　D 辅桥

[翻　译] 这座桥有三个拱。

[大头巧记] 谐音联想，听起来像打喷嚏，打喷嚏时背部拱起。

[词义扩展] *adj.* ①主要的；首要的
their arch foe 他们主要的对手
②调皮的；嬉戏的：
an arch glance 调皮的一瞥
vt./ vi. 成为弓形

[大头例句] A bright rainbow arched above after the rain. 雨后彩虹在天上形成弓状。

astronomy n. /əˈstrɔnəmi/

He is studying *astronomy* in Beijing University, which is why he knows such a lot about the Big Bang.

[猜一猜] A 物理学　B 天文学
C 地质学　D 电子学

[翻　译] 他正在北京大学攻读天文学，这是他之所以知道很多关于宇宙大爆炸知识的原因。

[分　析] astro + nomy
宇宙 + 后缀，表学科 → 研究宇宙的学科 →

[大头例句] A&A is a European Journal that publishes papers on all aspects of astronomy and astrophysics. A&A 是欧洲的一个全面发表关于天文学和天体物理学论文的杂志。

aerodynamic adj. /ˌeərəudaiˈnæmik/

We have already developed the *aerodynamic* missile.

[猜一猜] A 核动力的　B 高精确的
C 空对空的　D 空气动力的

[翻　译] 我们已经研制了空气动力导弹（飞航式导弹）。

[分　析] aero + dynamic
航空的 + 动力学的 → 空气动力学的

[大头巧记] **dynam** 力学
dynamic，动力学的

[联　想] **aerodynamics** *n.* 空气动力学
aeronautics *n.* 航空学

axis n. /ˈæksis/

The earth's *axis* is the line between the North and South Poles.

[猜一猜] A 经线　B 纬线　C 轴心　D 磁力线

[翻　译] 地轴是连接南北极的线。

[词义扩展] ①轴，轴线 ②中心线，中枢 ③轴心(国家或集团之间的联盟)

[大头例句] The overall concern is that calling those three countries the axis of evil is way too simplistic. 其大体上的观点是，把那三个国家称作为邪恶联盟是过于单纯化的。

comet n. /ˈkɔmit/

Comets are thought to consist chiefly of ammonia, methane, carbon dioxide, and water.

[猜一猜]A 木星　B 火星　C 水星　D 彗星

[翻　译]人们认为彗星主要由氨、甲烷、二氧化碳和水构成。

[大头巧记]词源记忆：在亚里士多德的著作中，他使用的 kome(希腊语中意为"头发")表示"彗星明亮的尾巴"，导出单词 kometes(戴长发)作为名词意义的"comet"来表示名词彗星。

[大头例句]Comets move around the sun in an eccentric orbit.彗星沿离心轨道绕太阳旋转。

dense *adj.* /dens/

The *dense* population caused a series of social problems in this area.

[猜一猜]A 大量的　B 稠密的　C 太少的　D 分散的

[翻　译]稠密的人口在这个地区造成了一系列的社会问题。

[词义扩展]*adj.* ①密度大的，密实的 ②愚钝的 ③强烈的 ④半透明的 ⑤极度的

[大头例句]He is so dense that he'll never understand why what he did is a huge mistake. 他愚蠢到极点以致永远也不明白为什么他所做的是一个巨大的错误。

eject *vt.* /iˈdʒekt/

The patron of the bar was *ejected* for creating a disturbance.

[猜一猜]A 警告　B 强制离开　C 禁止　D 起诉

[翻　译]酒吧里的客人因为制造骚乱被强制离开。

[分　析] e　+ ject

向外 + 扔 → 逐出，撵出，驱逐，喷射

[词义扩展]*n.* 推断的事物

[大头例句]It's annoying that the chimneys of those plants in the city eject a lot of smoke every day. 城里工厂的烟囱每天都吐出大量的烟尘，很是讨厌。

doctrine *n.* /ˈdɔktrin/

The *doctrine* of evolution influenced this world a lot.

[猜一猜]A 学说　B 政策　C 系统　D 精神

[翻　译]进化论的思想对这个世界影响很大。

[大头巧记]拆：doct(o)r (l)ine 教授的条条框框 → 教条 → 学说，主义。

[词义扩展]*n.* 法律的原理、规则 *the legal doctrine of due process* 法律程序原则

gravel *n.* /ˈgrævəl/

The country road was paved with *gravel*.

[猜一猜]A 压路机　B 细沙　C 沙砾　D 石板

[翻　译]这条乡村公路是使用沙砾铺成的。

[大头巧记]**grave，坟墓 → gravel，沙砾**砌成的坟墓。

[大头例句]The company decided to fill the parking lot with gravel because it was a cheap alternative to concrete. 这家公司决定在停车场里灌注沙砾，因为这是一种便宜的混凝材料。

hemisphere *n.* /ˈhemiˌsfiə/

The Northern *Hemisphere* is the part of the world north of the equator, and the Southern Hemisphere is south of the equator.

[猜一猜]A 回归线　B 美洲　C 半球　D 热带

[翻　译]北半球是地球赤道以北的部分，南半球是赤道以南的部分。

[分　析]hemi　+ sphere

一半 + 球 → 半球，(地球或天体) 半球，半球上所有的国家和人民

[词义扩展]*n.* 领域，范围 *a hemisphere of science and technology* 科技领域

[大头例句]If you cut a round fruit into two, each half is a hemisphere. 如果你把一个圆的水果切成两半，每一半就是一个半球。

galaxy *n.* /ˈgæləksi/

Edwin Hubble discovered that distant *galaxies* are moving away from us.

[猜一猜]A 行星　B 恒星　C 星系　D 星云

[翻　译]埃德温·哈勃发现远距离的星系正在做远离我们的运动。

[分　析]gala　+ xy

牛奶 + 后缀 → 牛奶色的东西 → 银河，星系

[词义扩展] 一群著名的或出色的人(或物)
a galaxy of beauties 一群美女

[大头例句] This city has produced a galaxy of soccer talent. 这个城市产生了一群足球天才。

gauge *v.* /geidʒ/

I *gauge* the distance to the office building to be about 200 metres.

[猜一猜] A 测量 B 设计 C 标明 D 判定

[翻 译] 我估量到办公楼大约有200米的距离。

[大头巧记] 注意它与gouge的区别，**gouge /gaudʒ/** 意为：**圆凿，欺骗，敲竹杠**。

[词义扩展] *n.* 标准尺寸，(铁道)轨距，测量仪器，(电线)直径 *v.* 估计，评价

[大头例句] New orders are a gauge of how well manufacturers are doing. 新规则是制造商经营情况的衡量标准。

meteorology *n.* /ˌmiːtiəˈrɔlədʒi/

Without deeper knowledge of *meteorology* and climate patterns, it would be impossible for you to successfully predict the amount of rainfall this area will receive next spring.

[猜一猜] A 测绘学 B 研究 C 第六感 D 气象学

[翻 译] 没有较深的气象学和气候模式方面的知识，你不可能成功地预测这个地区来年春天的降雨量。

[分 析] meteor + ology
流星，大气现象 + …学 → 关于大气现象的学科 → 气象学。

[大头例句] Many people view meteorology as a pseudo-science because it is impossible to predict the weather with 100% accuracy. 由于不可能100%精确地预测天气，很多人把气象学看成是伪科学。

magnitude *n.* /ˈmægnitjuːd/

The *magnitude* of the flood was impossible to comprehend.

[猜一猜] A 大小 B 原因 C 无奈 D 辉煌

[翻 译] 这场水灾的危害性是无法了解的。

[分 析] magni + tude
大 + …的度 → 大的程度，大小，数量，巨大

[大头巧记] 联系记忆：**longitude 经度(长的度)，latitude 纬度(宽的度)，magnitude 大小(大的度)**

[词义扩展] 【数】量值，绝对值；等级
earth-quake magnitude 地震等级

[大头例句] They hadn't grasped the magnitude of the task we were facing. 他们还没有领会到我们所面对的任务的艰巨性。

perpendicular *adj.* /ˌpəːpənˈdikjulə/

Line A is *perpendicular* to line B.

[猜一猜] A 平行的 B 相接的 C 重合的 D 垂直的

[翻 译] 线A和线B垂直。

[分 析] per + pend + icular
全部 + 悬挂 + 词尾 → 悬挂着的 → 垂直的 → 陡峭的

[大头巧记] 与 **parallel /ˈpærəlel/(平行的)** 对应记忆。

[词义扩展] *n.* 垂直，垂线
The wall is out of the perpendicular. 这墙有些倾斜。

[大头例句] My partner on this last project seemed to have goals and ideas exactly perpendicular to my own, thus making him a very difficult person to work with. 我上个项目的合作者在目标和观点上和我格格不入，因此和他共事也变得很难。

scale *n.* /skeil/

This ruler has one *scale* in centimetres and another in inches.

[猜一猜] A 标准 B 不同 C 图表 D 刻度

[翻 译] 这把尺子上有厘米和英寸两种刻度。

[词义扩展] *n.* 鳞片，天平 *v.* 衡量，攀登
scale new heights of science and technology 攀登科学技术新高峰

[习语记忆] **the scales fell from my eyes** 我茅塞顿开
turn the scales 改变为有利局势

[大头例句]On a scale of 1 to 10, how do you rate his performance? 十分制,你给他的表演打几分?

spectrum n. /ˈspektrəm/

This book reviews the whole *spectrum* of 20th-century thought.

[猜一猜]A 范围　B 特点　C 成功　D 失误

[翻　译]该书回顾了20世纪所有不同的思潮。

[分　析]spectr + um

看 + 名词词尾 → 看到颜色 → 光,光谱,范围

[大头例句]Our speakers tonight come from both ends of the political spectrum. 我们今晚的讲演者来自政坛的两个不同方面。

statistics n. /stəˈtistiks/

Statistics show that there's been a sharp increase of cars.

[猜一猜]A 媒体　B 民众　C 市场　D 统计数字

[翻　译]统计数字表明,汽车数量迅速增加。

[分　析]statis + tics

国家 + 名词词尾 → 描述国家所处状况的事物 → 统计数字

[大头例句]Are you aware of the statistics that women make up 40% of the work force? 你注意到这样一个数字了吗? 女性占劳动力的40%。

tornado n. /tɔːˈneidəu/

A *tornado* is a very strong wind.

[猜一猜]A 台风　B 龙卷风　C 积雨云　D 风暴

[翻　译]龙卷风是一种非常强烈的风。

[分　析]torna + do

旋转 + 词尾 → 旋风,龙卷风

tremendous adj. /triˈmendəs/

We have a *tremendous* amount of work to get through.

[猜一猜]A 伪造的　B 紧急的　C 外围的　D 巨大的

[翻　译]我们有非常多的工作要做。

[分　析]trem(ble) + endous

颤抖 + 形容词词尾 → 吃惊的发抖 → 巨大的,极大的

[大头巧记]tre(e) mend us,用树来修理我们,实在是太大了。

[大头例句]She's got a tremendous voice, hasn't she? 她的嗓子美极了,不是吗?

volcano n. /vɔlˈkeinəu/

The *volcano* last erupted over fifty years ago.

[猜一猜]A 市场　B 火山　C 海啸　D 竞争

[翻　译]该火山的上次爆发是在50多年以前。

[习语记忆]**dance on a volcano** 大难将至,犹自取乐 **sit on a volcano** 处境危险

[大头例句]Pompeii was destroyed when the volcano erupted in 79AD. 庞贝城在公元79年的火山爆发中被毁灭了。

solar adj. /ˈsəulə/

This apartment is equipped with a *solar* heating system.

[猜一猜]A 全自动的　B 太阳的　C 节能的　D 环保的

[翻　译]这个公寓装配了太阳能加热系统。

[大头巧记]sun,太阳 → **solar**,太阳的,日光的 另:和 **lunar**(月的)对比记忆。

[大头例句]Some scientists say solar energy will be the panacea of the future as it is in limitless supply, most everywhere has at least partial access to it, and it does not create any pollution. 一些科学家说太阳能将成为未来社会的万能药,它供应无限,几乎每个地方都最少能部分地使用它,它还不会造成任何污染。

vertical adj. /ˈvəːtikəl/

The pilots were being trained in *vertical* take-off.

[猜一猜]A 活动的　B 垂直的　C 水上的　D 模拟的

[翻　译]飞行员们正在训练垂直起飞。

[大头巧记]**vertex**,顶点 **vertical**,从顶点向下的,垂直的,顶点的。

[词义扩展]*n.* 垂直线,垂直面,竖向

[大头例句] It is very important to build a vertical power relationship between top decision makers and the rest of the organization. 在高层决策者和组织的其他部分之间建立起一个纵向的联合关系是非常重要的。

习题：在下面的空格中填写本单元的单词。

1. The company decided to fill the parking lot with ________ because it was a cheap alternative to concrete.
2. Many people view ________ as a pseudoscience because it is impossible to predict the weather with 100% accuracy.
3. It is very important to build a ________ power relationship between top decision makers and the rest of the organization.
4. That a comet ________ across the sky, they said, was an ill omen.
5. A bright rainbow ________ above after the rain.
6. He is so ________ that he'll never understand why what he did is a huge mistake.
7. Edwin Hubble discovered that distant ________ are moving away from us.
8. My partner on this last project seemed to have goals and ideas exactly ________ to my own, thus making him a very difficult person to work with.
9. This ruler has one ________ in centimetres and another in inches.
10. Pompeii was destroyed when the ________ erupted in 79AD.
11. He is studying ________ in Beijing University, which is why he knows such a lot about the Big Bang.
12. The Northern ________ is the part of the world north of the equator, and the Southern Hemisphere is south of the equator.
13. The ________ of evolution influenced this world a lot.
14. The overall concern is that calling those three countries the ________ of evil is way too simplistic.
15. ________ are thought to consist chiefly of ammonia, methane, carbon dioxide, and water.
16. It's annoying that the chimneys of those plants in the city ________ a lot of smoke every day.
17. We have already developed the ________ missile.
18. New orders are a ________ of how well manufacturers are doing.
19. The ________ of the flood was impossible to comprehend.
20. Our speakers tonight come from both ends of the political ________.
21. Are you aware of the ________ that women make up 40% of the work force?
22. ________ is a very strong wind.
23. Some scientists say ________ energy will be the panacea of the future as it is in limitless supply, most everywhere has at least partial access to it, and it does not create any pollution.
24. We have a ________ amount of work to get through.

Day 64

approximate *adj.* /əˈprɔksimeit/

He sketched an *approximate* likeness of the suspect according to the witnesses' descriptions.

[猜一猜] A 大概的　B 逼真的　C 素描的　D 电子的

[翻　译] 根据目击者们的描述，他已经勾画出了嫌疑犯大致的肖像。

[分　析] ap + proximate
to + 靠近 → 靠近的，近似的，大概的

[词义扩展] *vt.*, *vi.* (常与 to 连用)近似
The design approximates perfection. 这个设计几乎是完美的。

[大头例句] His docility only approximates to the requirements of his wife. 他的温顺仅仅是接近他妻子的要求。

aspire vi 热望 立志

aspiration *n.* /ˌæspəˈreiʃən/

The *aspiration* for establishing a democratic and affluent China encourages him to work hard.

[猜一猜] A 目标　B 抱负　C 号召　D 业绩

[翻　译] 建设一个民主而富裕的中国的抱负激励着他努力工作。

affluent society n 富足社会

[分　析] a + spir + ation
to + 呼吸 + 名词词尾 → 志气，抱负

[词义扩展] ① 渴望；热望 ②发送气音

[大头例句] This tutorial on explosives deals with aspiration and voicing. 这个关于爆破音的指南是处理送气和发音问题的。

aptitude *n.* /ˈæptitjuːd/

The boy shows a remarkable *aptitude* for mathematics.

[猜一猜] A 兴趣　B 资质　C 成绩　D 印象

[翻　译] 这个男孩已经展现出了数学上的相当的才华。

attitude n. 看法 态度 姿势 立场

[分　析] apt + itude
适合的 + 名词词尾 → 适合性，才能，资质

[词义扩展] *n.* 倾向

[大头例句] Overwork led to his aptitude for crime. 过度的操劳使他很容易走向犯罪。

cultivate *vt.* /ˈkʌltiveit/

Most of the world's fertile land is already being *cultivated*.

[猜一猜] A 征服　B 耕作　C 贡献　D 侵蚀

[翻　译] 世界上大多数的富饶土地都正被耕作。

[大头巧记] culture 文化，人类耕耘的结果
cultivate 培养，耕作

[大头例句] He always tries to cultivate rich and famous people. 他总是试图结交有钱有势的人。

elevate *vt.* /ˈeliveit/

He was *elevated* to the rank of major due to his wise command in the battle.

[猜一猜] A 降级　B 提升　C 邀请　D 青睐

[翻　译] 由于在战斗中英明指挥，他被提升为少校。

[分　析] e + levate
向上 + 提高 → 提升，举起，抬高

[大头巧记] elevator 电梯，提升(elevate)东西的工具。

[词义扩展] *v.* 使高尚，提高(品质)
Reading good books elevate one's mind. 阅读好书可提高人的心灵修养。

[大头例句] We need to work together to elevate the position of women in society. 我们应该并肩努力，来提高妇女在社会中的地位。

gloomy *adj.* /ˈgluːmi/

He became very *gloomy* and depressed.

[猜一猜] A 气愤的　B 悲哀的　C 忧郁的　D 开心的

[翻　译] 他变得很忧郁且沮丧。

[分 析] gloom + y
阴暗 + 形容词词尾 → 阴暗的,忧郁的,黑暗的

[大头例句] The economic news is gloomy. 经济新闻令人沮丧。

foam *n.* /fəum/

Foam **rubber is soft rubber full of small air bubbles.**

[猜一猜] A 简易 B 便宜 C 泡沫 D 回收

[翻 译] 泡沫橡胶是充满了小气泡的软橡胶。

[词义扩展] *v.*起泡沫
The mad dog was foaming at the mouth. 疯狗口吐白沫。

[大头例句] The polluted river was covered with chunks of foam. 污染的河上覆盖着大片的泡沫。

motto *n.* /ˈmɔtəu/

The school *motto* is "Never lose hope".

[猜一猜] A 格言 B 目标 C 名字 D 俗语

[翻 译] 这所学校的格言是"永不气馁"。

[大头巧记] 谐:猫头。猫头上挂"王"字,作为自己的座右铭:我要当老虎!

[大头例句] One of the most successful advertising campaigns of this generation was the Pepsi Company's 1990's motto "you got the right one baby, uh huh!"这个年代广告竞争中最成功的例子之一是百事公司1990年度的标语:"you got the right one baby, uh huh!"。

postgraduate *n./ adj.* /pəustˈgrædjuət/

He was determined to be a *postgraduate*.

[猜一猜] A 有用之才 B 研究生 C 本科生 D 博士生

[翻 译] 他决心要做一名研究生。

[分 析] post + graduate
后 + 毕业 → 毕业后的 → 研究生

[大头例句] Many people enjoy the study of sociology, but without a postgraduate degree in the field, one cannot expect to become a professor of it. 很多人喜欢社会学的学习,但是没有硕士学位的话,一个人是不能指望成为这个领域的专家的。

profound *adj.* /prəˈfaund/

We had a *profound* lesson in ideological education yesterday.

[猜一猜] A 深奥的 B 有用的 C 生动的 D 失责的

[翻 译] 昨天我们上了一堂深刻的思想教育课。

[分 析] pro + found
之前 + 底部 → 底部的前面 → 深奥的,渊博的,造诣深的

[大头巧记] 拆:Pro (f) found,只有教授才能发现的 → 深奥的

[大头例句] The profound societal implications of George Orwell's classic novel, "1984," is often lost on young readers who simply enjoy the story of farm animals who talk to each other. 年轻的读者们通常仅被对于故事中农场上的动物们互相交谈的情节所吸引,而忽略了它深刻的社会内涵。

reputation *n.* /ˌrepjuːˈteiʃən/

He did not have a good *reputation* in his company.

[猜一猜] A 职位 B 报酬 C 机遇 D 名声

[翻 译] 他在公司的名誉不好。

[分 析] re + put(e) + ation
一再 + 想 + 名词词尾 → 大家一再想起他 → 名声

[习语记忆] **live up to one's reputation** 名副其实 **stake one's reputation on** 拿名誉打赌

[大头例句] Following the scandal with Monica Lewinsky, Bill Clinton's reputation as a moral leader and upright citizen was almost completely destroyed. 由于和莫尼卡·莱温斯基的丑闻,比尔·克林顿作为一个有道德的领袖和正直的市民的名声几乎被完全毁掉了。

paradise *n.* /ˈpærədais/

Hong Kong is a *paradise* for shoppers and travelers.

[猜一猜] A 乐园 B 集中地 C 坟墓 D 混乱

[翻 译] 香港是购物旅游者的天堂。

[分　析] para　+ dise

平等 + 名词词尾 → 万物都平等的地方 → 天堂,乐园

[大头例句] After arriving at our vacation spot, we realized it was not the paradise the brochure made it out to be: the "panoramic ocean view" was, in fact, a window that overlooked a dirty sewage reservoir. 到达休假地点之后，我们注意到它并不是像小册子说的那样是一个天堂。所谓的"全景海滩"实际上只是一个窗户，可以俯瞰下面肮脏的污水池。

perspective *n.* /pəˈspektiv/

It is useful occasionally to look at the past to gain a *perspective* on the present.

[猜一猜] A 反思　B 展望　C 放弃　D 参与

[翻　译] 偶尔回顾过去有助于展望未来。

[分　析] per　+ spect + ive

全部 + 看　+ 词尾 → 从各个方面看,判断食物的角度 → 透视法,展望

[词义扩展] 洞察力,眼力,观点,看法

see thing in perspective 正确地观察事物

[大头例句] One of the great joys of being in school is having one's own carefullyformed opinions enhanced by the erudite perspectives of elder scholars. 上学最大的欢娱之一是用年长学者们博学的观点来提高你自己精心组织的意见。

significant *adj.* /sigˈnifikənt/

Davis is one of the most *signigicant* musicians of the last century.

[猜一猜] A 有个性的　B 外国的　C 虚伪的　D 重要的

[翻　译] 戴维斯是上个世纪最重要的音乐家之一。

[分　析] signifi　+ cant

表示，有重要性 + 形容词词尾 → 有意义的,重要的

[大头例句] My stomach has been hurting slightly for over a week, but in the past few days, it has become significantly more painful, so I made an appointment to see the doctor tomorrow. 我的胃有轻微的疼痛已经一个多星期了，前几天忽然明显加重；所以我做了预约明天去看病。

soar *v./ n.* /sɔː/

The mountain *soars* to heaven above all rivals.

[猜一猜] A 展示　B 骄傲　C 折射　D 高耸

[翻　译] 此山高耸于群山之上。

[词义扩展] *v.* 高飞,滑翔,剧增 *n.* 高涨程度,高飞范围

[大头例句] Health care costs continue to soar. 保健费用持续增高。

tangible *adj.* /ˈtændʒibl/

The scheme will bring *tangible* economic benefits to this area.

[猜一猜] A 非凡的　B 切实的　C 浪费的　D 杂乱的

[翻　译] 这个方案将给这个地区带来切实的经济利益。

[分　析] tang　+ ible

接触 + 可…的 → 可触摸的,切实的

[大头巧记] tang,谐音,唐人,中国人 → 中国人注重切实的利益——tangible。

[大头例句] His hostility was almost tangible. 他的敌意几乎可以触摸到。

target *n.* /ˈtɑːgit/

The hunter's *target* was a wild animal.

[猜一猜] A 愿望　B 眼界　C 资源　D 目标

[翻　译] 这个猎人的目标是一只野兽。

[大头巧记] 谐音:它 get → 需要它到的地方 → 目标

[词义扩展] *vt.* 瞄准,为…定指标

be targeted for 指标定为

[习语记忆] **be dead on the target** 正中目标

[大头例句] We want to target more welfare on the poorest groups in society. 我们想要给与社会中最穷的群体更多的福利。

tentative *n./ adj.* /ˈtentətiv/

The peace talks are ***tentatively*** planned for next week.

[猜一猜]A 取消 B 约定 C 暂定 D 宣布

[翻 译]和平会谈暂定为下周举行。

[大头巧记] **tent** 帐篷 → **tentative** 帐篷是试验性的，暂定的

[词义扩展] *n.* 试验，假设 *adj.* 试探的

[大头例句] Austin knocked tentatively and entered. 奥斯汀试探着敲了敲门，走了进来。

terminal *n./ adj.* /ˈtəːminəl/

The coal industry is now feared to be in ***terminal*** decline.

[猜一猜]A 后悔的 B 终点的 C 大型的 D 部分的

[翻 译]煤矿工业现在恐怕是最终衰败了。

[分 析]termin + al

结尾 + 词尾 → 终点站，终端，终点的

[大头巧记] **term** 学期 **terminal** 每学期的，末期的

[大头例句] Please get off at the terminal station. 请在终点站下车。

triumph *n./ v.* /ˈtraiəmf/

It was a ***triumph*** for me to enter the university.

[猜一猜]A 运气 B 必然 C 胜利 D 推延

[翻 译]考上大学对我来说是个胜利。

[大头巧记] 词源记忆：源自希腊语 thriambos，酒神狄俄尼索斯的赞歌 → 胜利

[词义扩展] *v.* 获得胜利

Our team triumphed over theirs. 我们这队胜了他们那队。

[大头例句] We know that in the end we shall triumph over evil. 我们知道我们最后会战胜邪恶。

virtually *adv.* /ˈvəːtjuəli/

Vaccines have ***virtually*** eliminated many childhood diseases.

[猜一猜]A 事实上 B 理论上 C 激励 D 挑战

[翻 译]疫苗事实上除去了很多少儿疾病。

[大头巧记] **virtue** 美德，功效 **virtually** 有效地，实质上，事实上，几乎是

[大头例句] It's virtually impossible to convince him to eat vegetables. 说服他吃蔬菜几乎不可能。

习题：在下面的空格中填写本单元的单词。

1. He was ________ to the rank of major due to his wise command in the battle.
2. One of the most successful advertising campaigns of this generation was the Pepsi Company's 1990's ________ "you got the right one baby, uh huh!"
3. We know that in the end we shall ________ over evil.
4. He sketched an ________ likeness of the suspect according to the witnesses' descriptions.
5. It's ________ impossible to convince him to eat vegetables.
6. Many people enjoy the study of sociology, but without a ________ degree in the field, one cannot expect to become a professor of it.
7. We had a ________ lesson in ideological education yesterday.
8. One of the great joys of being in school is having one's own carefully-formed opinions enhanced by the erudite ________ of elder scholars.
9. The coal industry is now feared to be in ________ decline.
10. My stomach has been hurting slightly for over a week, but in the past few days, it has become ________ more painful, so I made an appointment to see the doctor tomorrow.

11. The mountain __________ to heaven above all rivals.
12. The peace talks are __________ planned for next week.
13. The __________ for establishing a democratic and affluent China encourages him to work hard.
14. The boy shows a remarkable __________ for mathematics.
15. Most of the world's fertile land is already being __________.
16. The polluted river was covered with chunks of __________.
17. Following the scandal with Monica Lewinsky, Bill Clinton's __________ as a moral leader and upright citizen was almost completely destroyed.
18. He became very __________ and depressed.
19. After arriving at our vacation spot, we realized it was not the __________ the brochure made it out to be.
20. The scheme will bring __________ economic benefits to this area.
21. We want to __________ more welfare on the poorest groups in society.

Note 前事不忘后事之师 *Remember the past and it will guide your future.*

Day 65

aerobatics *n.* /ˌeərəuˈbætiks/

The *aerobatics* displays benefit the aeroplane manufacturers a lot, but they are very dangerous.

[猜一猜] A 杂技　B 马戏　C 特技飞行　D 低空飞行

[翻　译] 特技飞行给飞机制造商带来了很多利益，但是非常危险。

[分　析] aero + batics
航空的 + 源于 acrobatics（杂技）→ 飞行中的杂技 → 特技飞行

[大头巧记] 只要记住词根 batics 表示杂技就可以了。**Bat**（蝙蝠），ics(I can spin)，蝙蝠说："我能快速旋转"，当然是杂技了。

[大头例句] As a lot of people were watching an aerobatics display, suddenly the plane flew into the auditorium and crashed into the sea. 很多人在看飞行表演，忽然飞机向观众席冲来，并且坠毁在大海中。

amateur *n.* /ˈæmətə/

Only *amateurs* are allowed to compete in the Olympic Games.

[猜一猜] A 专职运动员　B 业余选手　C 国家队员　D 民间团体选手

[翻　译] 奥运会只允许业余运动员参加。

[分　析] am + areur
to love + …的人 → …的爱好者

[大头巧记] 源于拉丁语，原表"爱人，奉献者，对目标热情的追求者"，后发展为"对某个行业热爱但并不作为事业来做"。

[词义扩展] 外行的，缺乏经验的
He is an amateur in acting. 他是一位业余演员。

afforest *vt.* /æˈfɔrist/

It will take a long time to *afforest* the mountains, but would be much easier to destroy.

[猜一猜] A 绿化　B 灌溉　C 开采　D 修建

[翻　译] 绿化高山需要花去很长的时间，但是摧毁它却简单的多。

[分　析] af + forest
朝向 + 森林 → 使…成为森林 → 绿化

carpenter *n.* /ˈkaːpintə/

Lu Ban is one of the most famous *carpenters* in history.

[猜一猜] A 钟表匠　B 发明家　C 木匠　D 领袖

[翻　译] 鲁班是历史上最著名的木匠之一。

[分　析] capent + er
两轮马车 + …的人 → 造马车的人；木匠

[词义扩展] *vi.* 做木工 *vt.* 以木工手艺造（家具、房屋等）

[习语记忆] **Like carpenters, like chips.**
[谚]什么木匠出什么活。

chore *n.* /tʃɔː/

It's such a *chore* to do translating every day!

[猜一猜] A 繁锁　B 愚蠢　C 陈腐　D 衰弱

[翻　译] 每天做翻译真烦人！

[词义扩展] *n.* 家庭杂务；日常零星工作 *vi.* 作零星工作

[大头例句] You can go and play after you've done your chores. 你可以做完杂务后再出去玩。

chorus *v.* /ˈkɔːrəs/

The papers all *chorused* the praises of the positive suggestions of the government.

[猜一猜] A 不屑一顾　B 威胁　C 齐声　D 揭露

[翻　译] 各报齐声颂扬政府积极性的建议。

[词义扩展] *n.* 合唱，合唱队

[习语记忆] **swell the chorus** 附和别人的意见

[大头例句] Her first job was in the chorus and now she plays the leading role. 她最开始时在合唱队中工作,现在她已经是领唱了。

charity *n.* /ˈtʃæriti/

The Red Cross is an international *charity*.

[猜一猜] A 救援机构 B 慈善机构 C 医学机构 D 研究机构

[翻译] 红十字协会是国际性的慈善机构。

[大头巧记] char,英国口语"茶",中国敬茶时表现了自己的爱心 → 博爱,慈善。

[词义扩展] *n.* ①【宗】基督徒间的爱,博爱 ②施舍 ③慈善事业,慈善团体 ④宽厚,宽容

[习语记忆] **charity begins at home** 仁爱先自家中始(常作不捐款的借口)

[大头例句] Their plight is a miserable one, but they do not want charity. 他们境况悲惨,但是他们不想要施舍。

exert *v.* /igˈzəːt/

For college students to have a part-time job will *exert* a profound influence on their personality and life.

[猜一猜] A 有利于 B 使受… C 组成 D 发送

[翻译] 打工对大学生的个性培养和今后生活都具有深远的影响。

[分析] ex + ert
出来 + 连接 → 发挥(威力等),使受(影响)

[词义扩展] *vt.* 尽力,施行
exert all one's powers 尽全力

[大头例句] A well-funded national organization would be able to exert more influence in Parliament. 一个组建良好的国家机构应该能够在国会中发挥更大的影响。

expertise *n.* /ˌekspəˈtiːz/

They want to recruit university graduates with foreign language *expertise*.

[猜一猜] A 水平 B 专门知识 C 接受能力 D 进修

[翻译] 他们想要招聘有外语专业知识的大学生。

[大头巧记] **expert** 专家
expertise 专门知识

[词义扩展] 专家评价,鉴定

[大头例句] The company is keen to develop its own expertise in the area of computer programming. 这家公司热衷于发展电脑设计领域的专业技能。

faculty *n.* /ˈfækəlti/

Eve has the *faculty* to learn languages easily.

[猜一猜] A 兴趣 B 动机 C 方法 D 才能

[翻译] 伊芙有轻而易举学会语言的才能。

[分析] facul + ty
做 + 名词词尾 → 做事的能力 → 才能,资质,天赋

[词义扩展] (大学的)院;系;全体教员
Faculty of Engineering 工学院 *the medical faculty* 医界同仁

[大头例句] For the moment her critical faculties seemed to have deserted her. 在那个时候,她评论的能力好像是弃她而去了似的。

feasible *adj.* /ˈfiːzəbl/

It is financially *feasible* to use coal as an energy source.

[猜一猜] A 可行的 B 失败的 C 浪费的 D 拮据的

[翻译] 用煤来作能源在经济上是可行的。

[分析] feas + ible
做 + 可…的 → 可做的,可行的,可用的,适宜的

[大头例句] There seems to be only one feasible solution. 看起来只有一种可能的解决办法。

feat *n.* /fiːt/

The Chinese people have performed great historic *feats*.

[猜一猜] A 作用 B 戏剧 C 功绩 D 发明

[翻译] 中国人民创立了伟大的历史功绩。

[大头巧记] **feat** 与 **feet**(脚)同音,英勇的足迹 → **功绩,壮举**

[词 义扩 展] *n.* 技艺,武艺,本领
adj. 灵巧的,漂亮的,整洁的

[大 头例 句] We've remained profitable for 27 years, and that's no small feat. 我们已经保持赢利27年了,这来之不易。

ferry *n.* /ˈferi/

People used to cross the river by *ferry*, but now there is a newly built concrete bridge.

[猜一猜] A 索道　B 渡船　C 浮桥　D 大桥

[翻　译] 从前人们在这里常乘船过河,然而现在这里已经建起了一座新的混凝土大桥。

[词 义扩 展] *n.* 摆渡,渡口 *v.* 渡运,飞渡,运送
ferry across to the opposite bank 渡到对岸

[大 头例 句] Passengers were ferried to the island in a small plane. 旅客乘飞机飞渡到那个岛上。

freight *n.* /freit/

This aircraft company deals with *freight* only; it has no passenger service.

[猜一猜] A 旅游　B 运输　C 表演　D 客运

[翻　译] 这家航空公司只办理货运业务,没有客运服务。

[词 义扩 展] *vt.* 运输,装货上船

[大 头例 句] Every word the professor said was freighted with meaning. 教授的每一句话都是意味深长的。

haul *v.* /hɔːl/

Rescue workers attached the men to ropes before *hauling* them to safety.

[猜一猜] A 送　B 推　C 拖　D 保证

[翻　译] 救援人员事先把这些人系到绳子上,然后把他们拖到安全地带。

[大 头巧 记] 山东地区方言(hao)表示拖,拉,扯,音谐haul。

[词 义扩 展] *n.* 拖,拉,捕获量,拖运的距离
It was a long haul home, carrying all these bags of books up the hill. 背着这几口袋书籍上山回家,真是长途运输。

[大 头例 句] Their latest win hauled them into fourth position. 他们最近的一次胜利使得他们的排名达到了第四名。

innovation *n.* /ˌinəuˈveiʃən/

The *innovation* of air travel during the 20th century has made the world seem smaller.

[猜一猜] A 革命　B 补充　C 专长　D 新发明

[翻　译] 20世纪发明的空中飞行似乎使世界变小了。

[分　析] in　+ novat + ion
强调 + 新　+ 名词词尾 → 革新,创新,新发明

[大 头巧 记] 是 **innovate**(*vt.* 更新)的名词形式。

[大 头例 句] These companies reward creativity and innovation. 这些公司奖励创造和革新。

investigate *v.* /inˈvestigeit/

He has been *investigated* and found blameless.

[猜一猜] A 释放　B 问询　C 调查　D 平反

[翻　译] 他已被调查过,发现并无罪过。

[大 头巧 记] **invest**,投资;invest(i) gate,通往投资的门是进行调查。

[大 头例 句] She was thoroughly investigated by the FBI before being offered the job. 在给予她这个工作之前,美国联邦调查局对她进行了彻底的调查。

irrigation *n.* /ˌiriˈgeiʃən/

Only ten percent of the area was under *irrigation*.

[猜一猜] A 城市　B 开垦　C 灌溉　D 丛林

[翻　译] 该地区只有百分之十的土地得到灌溉。

[分　析] irrigat + ion
灌溉　+ 名词词尾 → 灌溉,水利,冲洗

[大 头例 句] This center plays a vital role in assisting designers, manufacturers and users of irrigation equipment to make technological advances. 这个中心在援助水利设备的设计者、制造商和用户以取得科技进步方面,扮演着重要角色。

kit *n.* /kit/

The soldiers packed their *kit* for the journey.

[猜一猜] A 食物　B 装备　C 枪弹　D 帐篷

[翻　译]士兵们整理他们的装备,准备行军。

[词义扩展] *n.* 工具,用具,配套元件 *v.* 配备

first-aid kit 急救药箱

[大头例句] Adam was wearing the new season's kit.亚当穿着新季度的服装。

layman *n.* /ˈleimən/

That is just the *layman*'s view of medicine.

[猜一猜]A 懒汉　B 门外汉　C 少数派　D 胆小鬼

[翻　译]那只是门外汉对医学的看法。

[大头巧记] lay,有"外行的"之义:**layman 门外汉,laity 信徒,门外汉。**

另,拆:lay man 躺着的男人,只能当门外汉

[大头例句] What does that mean in layman's terms? 通俗地说,这是什么意思?

layout *n.* /ˈleiˌaut/

The user gradually becomes familiar with the *layout* of the keyboard.

[猜一猜]A 行情　B 功能　C 好处　D 布局

[翻　译]使用者慢慢地对键盘的布局熟悉起来。

[大头巧记] lay out,摆开,展示 → **layout,布局,规划,设计,编排,版面设计**

[大头例句] The layout of your house and garden can deter crime. 你家房子和花园的设计可以阻止犯罪的发生。

loom *v.* /luːm/

Revolution *loomed* but the aristocrats paid no heed.

[猜一猜]A 爆发　B 失败　C 迫近　D 燎原

[翻　译]革命已迫在眉睫,但贵族们并未加以注意。

[大头巧记] 谐音法:露模,模模糊糊的显露 → 隐现,迫近。

[词义扩展] *n.* 织布机,织布,织布业

knitting loom 针织机

[大头例句] This episode finds her deep in depression as divorce looms large. 本集中,她因为离婚倾向的突出而意志消沉。

manipulate *v.* /məˈnipjuleit/

I don't want you to feel like I am *manipulating* you, but I really would love it if you would join us.

[猜一猜]A 欺骗　B 威胁　C 操纵　D 使人生气

[翻　译]我不想给你一种我在操纵你的感觉,但我真的是很想你能加入我们。

[分　析]mani + pul + ate

手　+ 拉 + 动词词尾 → 用手拉 → 操纵,操作,应付

[词义扩展] 〈计〉处理(数据等);【医】推拿

manipulate a joint 推拿关节

[大头例句] The steering wheel on this mode of car is difficult to manipulate, but with practice, it can be mastered in time. 该汽车模型的方向盘很难操纵,但通过练习,我们是能够及时掌握的。

misery *n.* /ˈmizəri/

It truly is a wonderful use of time to attempt to alleviate the *misery* of others.

[猜一猜]A 负担　B 痛苦　C 迷惑　D 要求

[翻　译]尝试去减轻别人的痛苦确实是对时间的极好利用。

[大头巧记] **miser,吝啬鬼**,吝啬鬼的生活很痛苦。

[大头例句] Children are living in misery, without housing, school, or clinics. 孩子们生活在痛苦之中,没有住处,没有学校,也没有诊所。

monotonous *adj.* /məˈnɔtənəs/

My job at the assembly line of the car factory is rather *monotonous*.

[猜一猜]A 有趣的　B 有意义的 C 热门的 D 单调的

[翻　译]我在汽车工厂装配线上的工作颇为单调乏味。

[分　析]mono + ton　+ ous

单一　+ 声音 + 形容词词尾 → 单一声音的 → 单调的,令人厌倦的

[大头巧记] 词形记忆法:本词中出现了四个"o",实在是单调。

[大头例句] Due to the lecturer's steady monotonous tone of speech, I quickly fel asleep, and slept soundly throughout the hour. 由于演讲者的讲话正经而单调,我很快就睡着了,并且整整熟睡了一个小时。

portfolio *n.* /pɔːtˈfəuliəu/

They are looking to expand their *portfolio* of customers.

[猜一猜]A 业务量 B 信任度 C 知名度 D 回报
[翻 译]他们正在打算扩大对顾客的业务量。
[分 析]port + folio

拿 + 纸张 → 文件夹，业务量，部长职务

[大头例句] Make sure to include your rendition of Romeo and Juliet in clay in your portfolio: it is, in my opinion, your greatest masterpiece to date.
一定要把你制作的罗米欧和朱丽叶的泥人剧收入到你的作品中，在我看来，它是你至今为止最好的作品。

习题：在下面的空格中填入本单元的单词。

1. The company is keen to develop its own __________ in the area of computer programming.
2. Children are living in __________, without housing, school, or clinics.
3. As a lot of people were watching an __________ display, suddenly the plane flew into the auditorium and crashed into the sea.
4. It will take a long time to __________ the mountains, but would be much easier to destroy.
5. Her first job was in the __________ and now she plays the leading role.
6. For college students to have a part-time job will__________ a profound influence on their personality and life.
7. Rescue workers attached the men to ropes before __________ them to safety.
8. The steering wheel on this model of car is difficult to __________, but with practice, it can be mastered in time.
9. The __________ of air travel during the 20th century has made the world seem smaller.
10. Adam was wearing the new season's __________.
11. Only __________ are allowed to compete in the Olympic Games.
12. Lu Ban is one of the most famous __________ in the history.
13. You can go and play after you've done your __________.
14. The Red Cross is an international __________.
15. For the moment her critical __________ seemed to have deserted her.
16. There seems to be only one __________ solution.
17. This aircraft company deals with __________ only; it has no passenger service.
18. People used to cross the river by __________, but now there is a newly built concrete bridge.
19. We've remained profitable for 27 years, and that's no small __________.
20. She was thoroughly __________ by the FBI before being offered the job.
21. This center plays a vital role in assisting designers, manufacturers and users of ________ equipment to make the technological advances.
22. The user gradually becomes familiar with the __________ of the keyboard.
23. This episode finds her deep in depression as divorce __________ large.
24. That is just the __________'s view of medicine.
25. They are looking to expand their __________ of customers.
26. Due to the lecturer's steady __________ tone of speech, I quickly fell asleep, and slept soundly throughout the hour.

Day 66~70

IELTS 核心词汇

第2阶段

进阶篇

Day 66~70 ☞ 快乐指南

大家好，我是Sof，相信大家在这65天里，跟着“大头”一定是认识了很多很好的朋友，下面是我们出去闯荡世界的时候了！

在下面的5天里，我要认识1000个单词，“天啊，这怎么可能?!”。先别急，听我说清楚：是“认识”，不是“交朋友”。这主要为雅思阅读服务，也为提高大家的词汇量。只要求大家记住词性和词意，也就是所说的“见面认识”即可。我们大家“临阵磨枪”，发动视觉(看)，听觉(读)，嘴部感觉(读)和手部感觉(写)等一切手段，最大限度地在雅思考试前期增大单词量，提高阅读能力。这5天是痛苦的，但是却是很长见识啊！加把劲，胜利属于我们！

Day 66

abbreviate /əˈbriːvieit/ *v.* 缩写

abdomen /ˈæbdəmen/ *n.* 腹部

abhor /əbˈhɔː/ *v.* 厌恶

abridge /əˈbridʒ/ *v.* 删节

abrupt /əˈbrʌpt/ *adj.* 突然的

absolutism /ˈæbsəluːˌtizəm/ *n.* 专制主义

abstract /ˈæbstrækt/ *n. v.* 抽象

abstraction /æbˈstrækʃən/ *n.* 抽取

absurd /əbˈsəːd/ *adj.* 荒谬的

accelerate /ækˈseləreit/ *v.* 加速

accessible /əkˈsesibl/ *adj.* 可接近的

baboon /bəˈbuːn/ *n.* 狒狒

badge /bædʒ/ *n.* 勋章;象征

bailiff /ˈbeilif/ *n.* 法庭监守;镇长;执行的副手

bake /beik/ *v.* 烘;烤

ballistics /bəˈlistiks/ *n.* 弹道学;发射学

bandit /ˈbændit/ *n.* 土匪;歹徒

banish /ˈbæniʃ/ *v.* 排除

banjo /ˈbændʒəu/ 班卓琴(一种类似吉他的琴)

barbecue /ˈbɑːbikjuː/ *n.* 烤肉架;烤肉

barge /bɑːdʒ/ *n.* 驳船;大型游船

baron /ˈbærən/ *n.* 男爵

baronet /ˈbærənit/ *n.* 准男爵

baroque /bəˈrɔk/ *n.* 巴罗克式的作风;艺术

barrack /ˈbærək/ *n.* 军营;兵舍

callisthenics /ˌkælisˈθeniks/ *n.* 健美运动;健力操

callous /ˈkæləs/ *adj.* 冷酷无情的

capitulate /kəˈpitjuleit/ *v.* 投降

carcinogen /kɑːˈsinədʒən/ *n.* 致癌物

cardigan /ˈkɑːdigən/ *n.* (无领、有扣、前对襟)毛衣;羊毛衫

cardinal /ˈkɑːdin(ə)l/ *adj.* 深红色的

carnage /ˈkɑːnidʒ/ *n.* 大屠杀

cavalry /ˈkævəlri/ *n.* 骑兵;装甲兵

disaffected /ˌdisəˈfektid/ *adj.* 不满的;不忠的

disavow /ˌdisəˈvau/ *v.* 否认;不承认

disciple /diˈsaipl/ *n.* 门徒;信徒

discourteous /disˈkəːtjəs/ *adj.* 粗鲁的;无礼的

discreet /disˈkriːt/ *adj.* 言行审慎的

discrete /disˈkriːt/ *adj.* 分离的;截然分开的

disenchant /ˌdisinˈtʃɑːnt/ *v.* 使不再着迷

disgruntled /disˈgrʌntld/ *adj.* 不高兴的;不满的

disingenuous /ˌdisinˈdʒenjuəs/ *adj.* 不真诚的

disobedient /ˌdisəˈbiːdjənt/ *adj.* 不顺从的

disown /disˈəun/ *v.* 脱离关系

disparity /disˈpæriti/ *n.* 不同

dispatch /disˈpætʃ/ *v.* 派遣;发送

dispensation /ˌdispenˈseiʃən/ *n.* 神的安排;天命

dispense /disˈpens/ *v.* 分配;施与

disquiet /disˈkwaiət/ *v.* 忧虑;不安

estrange /iˈstreindʒ/ *v.* 离间;使疏远

etymology /ˌetiˈmɔlədʒi/ *n.* 词源学

euthanasia /ˌjuːθəˈneiziə/ *n.* 安乐死

exclaim /ikˈskleim/ *v.* 惊叫;呼喊

exhilarate /igˈziləreit/ *v.* 使愉快(或活跃)

exquisite /ˈekskwizit/ *adj.* 优雅的;制作精良的

extort /ikˈstɔːt/ *v.* 强夺;勒索

extraneous /ekˈstreinjəs/ *adj.* 与正题无关的

extravagant /ikˈstrævəgənt/ *adj.* 挥霍的;放肆的

extrovert /ˈekstrəvəːt/ *n.* 性格外向的人

exuberant /igˈzjuːbərənt/ *adj.* 活跃的;愉快的

fabricate /ˈfæbrikeit/ *v.* 编造;伪造

facetious /fəˈsiːʃəs/ *adj.* 引人发笑的;诙谐的

fad /fæd/ *n.* 流行的时尚、爱好、狂热等

faint /feint/ *adj.* 微弱的;模糊的 *n.*失去知觉;昏倒 *v.* 昏厥;不省人事

faith /feiθ/ *n.* 信任;信仰

famished /ˈfæmiʃt/ *adj.* 挨饿的

farce /fɑːs/ *n.* 闹剧;滑稽戏

gaiety /ˈgeiəti/ *n.* 欢乐;愉快

gala /ˈgɑːlə/ *n.* 特别场合;盛会

gall /gɔːl/ *n.* 胆汁;怨恨;伤痛处 *v.* 擦痛;擦伤;烦扰;侮辱

gallant /ˈgælənt/ *adj.* 勇敢的;华丽的;雄伟的

gallop /ˈgæləp/ *n.* (马等)飞奔;飞快 *v.* 奔驰;使(马等)飞奔;飞速前进

gape /geip/ *v.* 目瞪口呆的凝视(at)

garb /gɑːb/ *n.* 服装;服装式样

garbled /ˈgɑːbld/ *adj.* 混乱的;引起误解的

garland /ˈgɑːlənd/ *n.* 花环;花冠

haywire /ˈheiwaiə/ *adj.* 失去控制的;乱糟糟的

headway /ˈhedwei/ *n.* 进步;进展

headstrong /ˈhedstrɔŋ/ *adj.* 刚愎自用的;固执任性的

heal /hiːl/ *v.* 康复;愈合;使完结

heap /hiːp/ *n.* 堆;大量 *v.* 堆积物品;给予(某人)大量的(某事物)

hearse /həːs/ *n.* 灵车

heathen /ˈhiːðən/ *n.* 不信任何宗教的人;未开化的人;行为不端的人

heave /hiːv/ *v.* 提升;举起

indoctrinate /inˈdɔktrineit/ *v.* 向(某人)灌输

infantry /ˈinfəntri/ *n.* 步兵

ingratiating /inˈgreiʃieitiŋ/ *adj.* 讨好的;奉承的

inhumane /ˌinhjuːˈmein/ *adj.* 残忍的;不人道的

iniquitous /iˈnikwitəs/ *adj.* 罪恶的;极不公正的

injunction /inˈdʒʌŋkʃən/ *n.* 命令;禁令;指令

inlet /ˈinlet/ *n.* 水湾;进口

innocuous /iˈnɔkjuəs/ *adj.* 无毒的

innuendo /ˌinjuːˈendəu/ *n.* 影射;暗射

inoculate /iˈnɔkjuleit/ *v.* 给…接种;…打预防针

inquisition /ˌinkwiˈziʃən/ *n.* 调查;盘问

inquisitive /inˈkwizitiv/ *adj.* 好打听闲事的

javelin /ˈdʒævəlin/ *n.* 标枪

jeer /dʒiə/ *v.* 嘲笑;嘲弄(at)

karate /kəˈrɑːti/ *n.* 空手道(一种徒手武术)

keel /kiːl/ *n.* (船的)龙骨

litigate /ˈlitigeit/ *v.* 诉讼

locale /ləuˈkɑːl/ *n.* (事情发生的)现场

locus /ˈləukəs/ *n.* 所在地;场所

loot /luːt/ *n.* 战利品;赃物

lopsided /ˈlɔpˈsaidid/ *adj.* 不均匀的;两侧不平衡的

lore /lɔː/ *n.* (某学科的或某部分人的)学问;传统信仰

lowbrow /ˈləubrau/ *adj.* 无文化修养的;无知识的

motley /ˈmɔtli/ *adj.* 混杂的;形形色色的

mundane /ˈmʌndein/ *adj.* 平凡的;世俗的

munificent /mjuːˈnifisənt/ *adj.* 丰厚的;慷慨的

munition /mjuːˈniʃən/ *n.* 军需品

murk /məːk/ *n.* 黑暗;昏暗

muse /mjuːz/ *v.* 沉思;冥想

mutable /ˈmjuːtəbl/ *adj.* 可变的;不定的

mutation /mjuːˈteiʃən/ *n.* 变化;转变;突变

mutiny /ˈmjuːtini/ *n.* 反叛;兵变

muzzy /ˈmʌzi/ *adj.* 糊涂的

myriad /ˈmiriəd/ *n.* 无数;极大数量

nark /nɑːk/ *n.* 提供情报者;密探

nepotism /ˈnepətizəm/ *n.* 有厚亲属的作风;裙带关系

neurology /njuəˈrɔlədʒi/ *n.* 神经学;神经病学

neuter /ˈnjuːtə/ *adj.* 中性的

neutron /ˈnjuːtrɔn/ *n.* 中子

outright /ˈautrait/ *adj.* 坦率的;诚实的

oval /ˈəuvəl/ *adj.* 椭圆形的

overdue /ˈəuvəˈdjuː/ *adj.* 到期未完成的;过期的

override /ˌəuvəˈraid/ *v.* 蔑视

oversight /ˈəuvəsait/ *n.* 疏忽

overstate /ˈəuvəˈsteit/ *v.* 夸大;言过其实

overtone /ˈəuvətəun/ *n.* 暗示;弦外之音

overwrought /ˌəuvəˈrɔːt/ *adj.* 过分劳累的;过分紧张的

pacifism /ˈpæsifizəm/ *n.* 和平主义

pacify /ˈpæsifai/ *v.* 抚慰

paediatrician /ˌpiːdiəˈtriʃən/ *n.* 儿科医师

pagan /ˈpeigən/ *n.* 异教徒(尤指非基督教、犹太教和回教教徒)
pageant /ˈpædʒənt/ *n.* 盛装的游行；壮丽的场面；丰富多彩的历史
palatable /ˈpælətəbl/ *adj.* 美味的；合意的；认同的
palette /ˈpælit/ *n.* 调色板
pamper /ˈpæmpə/ *v.* 纵容；宠
pandemonium /ˌpændiˈməunjəm/ *n.* 大混乱；喧闹
pander /ˈpændə/ *v.* 迎合；纵容
parable /ˈpærəbl/ *n.* (尤指圣经中)寓言故事
paradigm /ˈpærədaim/ *n.* 词形变化(表)；范例；样式
paragon /ˈpærəgən/ *n.* (有某品质的)典范人物；完人
paranoia /ˌpærəˈnɔiə/ *n.* 偏执狂；妄想狂
paraphernalia /ˌpærəfəˈneiliə/ *n.* 零星物品；(业余爱好或体育活动所需的)随身物品
pariah /pəˈraiə/ *n.* 贱民；社会的遗弃者
partisan /ˌpɑːtiˈzæn/ *n.* 热心的(但常为盲目的)拥护者；游击队员
quibble /ˈkwibl/ *n.* 反对(或批评)意见
quip /kwip/ *n.* 妙语；讽刺话
reprieve /riˈpriːv/ *v.* 缓期执行(或撤销惩罚)
reprimand /ˈreprimɑːnd/ *v.* 训斥；斥责
reproach /riˈprəutʃ/ *n.* 责备
repugnant /riˈpʌgnənt/ *adj.* 令人厌恶的；讨厌的
repulse /riˈpʌls/ *v.* 击退；驱逐
resurgent /riˈsəːdʒənt/ *adj.* 复苏的；恢复生机、活力的
resuscitate /riˈsʌsiteit/ *v.* (使)恢复知觉；苏醒
retentive /riˈtentiv/ *adj.* (记忆力)强的
retort /riˈtɔːt/ *v.* 反驳
retract /riˈtrækt/ *v.* 撤回(或撤销声明)等
stretcher /ˈstretʃə/ *n.* 担架
strife /straif/ *n.* 冲突；争斗
striking /ˈstraikiŋ/ *adj.* 引人注意的；显著的
stumble /ˈstʌmbl/ *n.* 绊倒；出错；
submission /səbˈmiʃən/ *n.* 投降；归顺
substantive /ˈsʌbstəntiv/ *adj.* 真实的；实际的；非临时的
subvert /səbˈvəːt/ *v.* 颠覆；破坏
suffrage /ˈsʌfridʒ/ *n.* 选举权；投票权
supple /ˈsʌpl/ *adj.* 柔软的；灵活的
suppress /səˈpres/ *v.* 镇压；平定
surf /səːf/ *n.* 冲浪
surmount /səˈmaunt/ *v.* 克服；战胜
susceptible /səˈseptəbl/ *adj.* 易受影响(或损害)的
sustenance /ˈsʌstinəns/ *n.* 食物；营养
swindle /ˈswindl/ *v.* 诈骗
syllable /ˈsiləbl/ *n.* 音节
synonym /ˈsinənim/ *n.* 同义词
synopsis /siˈnɔpsis/ *n.* 大纲；提要
syntax /ˈsintæks/ *n.* 语句结构；句法
trash /træʃ/ *n.* 拙劣的材料、作品；垃圾；没有出息的人
trauma /ˈtrɔːmə/ *n.* 创伤；痛苦
treacherous /ˈtretʃərəs/ *adj.* 不忠的；有潜在危险的
treason /ˈtriːzən/ *n.* 叛国；背叛
tremor /ˈtremə/ *n.* 颤抖；激动
tribulation /ˌtribjuˈleiʃən/ *n.* 忧患；苦难
trivia /ˈtriviə/ *n.* 无关紧要的事、细节、信息；琐事
trolley /ˈtrɔli/ *n.* 手推车
trophy /ˈtrəufi/ *n.* (尤指体育比赛的)奖品；纪念品
trot /trɔt/ *n.* 小跑
truant /ˈtruːənt/ *n.* 逃学者；游手好闲的人
truce /truːs/ *n.* 休战协定；休战期
trudge /trʌdʒ/ *v.* 缓慢或吃力地走
ulterior /ʌlˈtiəriə/ *adj.* 隐秘的；别有用心的
unabated /ˌʌnəˈbeitid/ *adj.* 仍然强烈的；并未消退的
unadulterated /ˌʌnəˈdʌltəreitid/ *adj.* 纯的；完全的
uncanny /ʌnˈkæni/ *adj.* 异乎寻常的；超常的
vehement /ˈviːimənt/ *adj.* 感情强烈的；热情的
venerable /ˈvenərəbl/ *adj.* 值得敬重的
vernacular /vəˈnækjulə/ *n.* 本地语；本国话
worn /wɔːn/ *adj.* 损坏的；破旧的；筋疲力尽的
wrath /rɔθ/ *n.* 怒气；愤怒
wrongful /ˈrɔŋful/ *adj.* 不公平的；不合法的；不正当的
xenophobia /ˌzenəˈfəubiə/ *n.* 排外；仇外；惧外者
yacht /jɔt/ *n.* 快艇
yank /jæŋk/ *v.* 猛拉

Day 67

accordion /əˈkɔːdiən/ *n.* 手风琴 *adj.* 可折叠的

accumulative /əˈkjuːmjulətiv/ *adj.* 积累的

acrobatics /ˌækrəuˈbætiks/ *n.* 杂技

adage /ˈædidʒ/ *n.* 箴言

adept /ˈædept/ *n.* 行家 *adj.* 熟练的

adolescence /ˌædəuˈlesəns/ *n.* 青春期

adolescent /ˌædəuˈlesənt/ *n.* 青少年 *adj.* 青春期的

adrift /əˈdrift/ *adj.* 漂浮的

affidavit /ˌæfiˈdeivit/ *n.* 宣誓书

aghast /əˈgɑːst/ *adj.* 吓呆的

bedraggled /biˈdrægld/ *adj.* (全身)湿透的

bedsore /ˈbedsɔː(r)/ *n.* 褥疮

beehive /ˈbiːhaiv/ *n.* 蜂窝;蜂箱

begrudge /biˈgrʌdʒ/ *v.* 羡慕;嫉妒

beguile /biˈgail/ *v.* 欺骗;消遣

behead /biˈhed/ *v.* 斩首;砍头

belabour /biˈleibə/ *v.* (过分冗长地)做;痛打

beleaguer /biˈliːgə/ *v.* 围攻

belie /biˈlai/ *v.* 掩饰

bequeath /biˈkwiːð/ *v.* 把…传给

bereft /biˈrɔft/ *adj.* 被剥夺的

bestow /biˈstəu/ *v.* 把…赠与

bewail /biˈweil/ *v.* 悲哀;哀泣

contort /kənˈtɔːt/ *v.* 扭曲

contraband /ˈkɔntrəˌbænd/ *n.* 违禁品 *adj.* 禁运的;走私的

cordial /ˈkɔːdiəl/ *n.* 兴奋剂;兴奋饮料 *adj.* 热忱的;兴奋的

corpus /ˈkɔːpəs/ *n.* 尸体;文集

court-martial /ˈkɔːtˈmɑːʃəl/ *n.* 军事法庭 *v.* 以军法审判

curfew /ˈkəːfjuː/ *n.* 宵禁

custodian /kʌsˈtəudjən/ *n.* 看管人;监护人

cyclone /ˈsaikləun/ *n.* 气旋;暴风

depreciate /diˈpriːʃieit/ *v.* 贬值;轻视

derision /diˈriʒən/ *n.* 嘲笑;笑柄

desolate /ˈdesələt/ *adj.* 荒凉的;无人烟的

despicable /ˈdespikəbl/ *adj.* 卑鄙的

despoil /disˈpɔil/ *v.* 抢劫(有价值之物)

despot /ˈdespɔt/ *n.* 暴君

detain /diˈtein/ *v.* 耽误;延误

detention /diˈtenʃən/ *n.* 拘留;滞留

dethrone /diˈθrəun/ *v.* 废黜;撵下台

deviant /ˈdiːviənt/ *adj.* 离经叛道的 *n.* 偏常者

devilish /ˈdevəliʃ/ *adj.* 邪恶的;残忍的

devious /ˈdiːviəs/ *adj.* 刁滑的;蜿蜒的

devout /diˈvaut/ *adj.* 虔诚的

dexterity /deksˈteriti/ *n.* 技巧;灵活的手法

dialysis /daiˈælisis/ *n.* 透析

dimple /ˈdimpl/ *n.* 酒窝

eavesdrop /ˈiːvzdrɔp/ *v.* 偷听(私人谈话)

echelon /ˈeʃəlɔn/ *n.* 职权的等级;梯形编队

eddy /ˈedi/ *n.* 旋涡;旋转

edgy /ˈedʒi/ *adj.* 紧张的;暴躁的

edict /ˈiːdikt/ *n.* 法令;敕令

edification /ˌedifiˈkeiʃən/ *n.* 开导;陶冶

eerie /ˈiəri/ *adj.* 可怕的;怪异的

effeminate /iˈfeminit/ *adj.* (男人或其行为)没有男子气的;好气的

egalitarian /igæliˈteəriən/ *adj.* 平等主义的

egotism /ˈiːgətizəm/ *n.* 自我为中心;自大

elated /iˈleitid/ *adj.* 情绪高昂的

fastidious /fæsˈtidiəs/ *adj.* 爱挑剔的;吹毛求疵的

felicitous /fəˈlisitəs/ *adj.* 恰当的

fervent /ˈfəːvənt/ *adj.* 强烈的;热情的

fervour /ˈfəːvə/ *n.* 热情;热烈

fetish /ˈfetiʃ/ *n.* 崇拜物;物神;盲目崇拜的对象

fiasco /fiˈæskəu/ *n.* 惨败

fickle /ˈfikl/ *adj.* 无常的；易变的

garrison /ˈgærisən/ *n./ v.* 卫戍部队；警备部队

gastric /ˈgæstrik/ *adj.* 胃部的

gaudy /ˈgɔːdi/ *adj.* 华丽而俗气的

genocide /dʒenəuˌsaid/ *n.* 种族灭绝

genre /ˈʒɑːnrə/ *n.* 种类；风格

genuine /ˈdʒenjuin/ *adj.* 真的；非伪造的；非人工的

geriatrics /ˌdʒeriˈætriks/ *n.* 老年医学；老年保健学

gesticulate /dʒeˈstikjuleit/ *v.* 做手势示意（或强调）

giddy /ˈgidi/ *v.* 偷运；眩晕 *adj.* 头晕的

haemorrhage /ˈhemәridʒ/ *n.* 失血

haggle /ˈhægl/ *n.* 争论；讨价还价 *v.* 争价

halting /ˈhɔːltiŋ/ *adj.* 迟疑不绝的；犹豫的

hammock /ˈhæmәk/ *n.* 吊床

hapless /ˈhæplis/ *adj.* 不幸的；不走运的

harass /ˈhærәs/ *v.* 不断骚扰；打扰

haughty /ˈhɔːti/ *adj.* 高傲自大的

hawk /hɔːk/ *n.* 鹰；"鹰派"人物 *v.* 猛扑(at)

idiosyncrasy /ˌidiәˈsiŋkrәsi/ *n.* （个人特有的）习性，气质，癖好

idolater /aiˈdɔlәtә/ *n.* 偶像崇拜者

ignominy /ˈignәmini/ *n.* 耻辱；丑行

illiberal /iˈlibәrәl/ *adj.* 心胸狭隘的；吝啬的

illusive /iˈluːsiv/ *adj.* 幻觉的；虚假的

imbecile /ˈimbisail/ *n.* 低能者 *adj.* 低能的

imitate /ˈimiteit/ *v.* 仿效

imminent /ˈimәnәnt/ *adj.* 即将发生的；临近的

immigrate /ˈimigreit/ *v.* （自外国）移居入境

immodest /iˈmɔdist/ *adj.* 下流的；不端庄的；自负的

immutable /iˈmjuːtәbl/ *adj.* 不可改变的；永恒不变的

impale /imˈpeil/ *vt.* 用（尖物）刺；刺穿

jest /dʒest/ *n.* 玩笑；笑话 *v.* 开玩笑；说笑话

jingle /ˈdʒiŋgl/ *n.* （金属发出的）丁当声 *v.* （使）丁当响

keepsake /ˈkiːpseik/ *n.* 纪念品

kerb /kәːb/ *n.* （马路）边栏

labyrinth /ˈlæbәrinθ/ *n.* 迷宫

laden /ˈleidәn/ *adj.* 装满的；满载的

laid-back /ˈleidˈbæk/ *adj.* 安详的；轻松的

lampoon /læmˈpuːn/ *n.* 讽刺文章 *v.* 讽刺

languor /ˈlæŋgә/ *n.* 倦怠；平静；沉闷

larceny /ˈlɑːsәni/ *n.* 盗窃；盗窃罪

largess /lɑːˈdʒes/ *n.* 慷慨的赠与；赏赐

machismo /mɑːˈtʃiːzmәu/ *n.* （贬）大男子气概

macho /ˈmɑːtʃәu/ *adj.* 大男子气概的

mackintosh /ˈmækintɔʃ/ *n.* 雨衣

macrocosm /ˈmækrәukɔzәm/ *n.* 宇宙；宏观世界

madcap /ˈmædkæp/ *adj.* 鲁莽的 *n.* 爱冲动的人

magnanimous /mægˈnænimәs/ *adj.* 宽宏大量的；慷慨的

malign /mәˈlain/ *v.* 中伤；诽谤 *adj.* 有害的；恶意的

mammoth /ˈmæmәθ/ *adj.* 庞大的；巨大的 *n.* [古生] 猛犸

manifesto /ˌmæniˈfestәu/ *n.* 宣言；声明

mannerism /ˈmænәrizәm/ *n.* （行为、言语等的）特殊习惯

mar /mɑː/ *v.* 损坏；损毁 *n.* 污点；瑕疵

nick /nik/ *n.* 监狱；警察分局；派出所

nifty /ˈnifti/ *adj.* 聪明的；伶俐的；有效的；便利的 *n.* 妙语；漂亮姑娘

niggard /ˈnigәd/ *n.* 小气鬼 *adj.* 小气的；吝啬的

ointment /ˈɔintmәnt/ *n.* 软膏

olfactory /ɔlˈfæktәri/ *adj.* 嗅觉的

oligarchy /ˈɔligɑːki/ *n.* 寡头政治；寡头统治

omen /ˈәumen/ *n.* 预兆；征兆 *v.* 预示；预告

omnipotent /ɔmˈnipәtәnt/ *adj.* 有无限权力的；全能的

onrush /ˈɔnrʌʃ/ *n.* 猛冲；急流

onslaught /ˈɔnslɔːt/ *n.* 猛攻；冲击

operetta /ˌɔpәˈretә/ *n.* 轻歌剧

pinnacle /ˈpinәkl/ *n.* 小尖塔；高峰；顶点；顶峰 *v.* 把…置于尖塔上

pitfall /pitfɔːl/ *n.* 意想不到的危险（或困难）

placard /ˈplækɑːd/ *n.* 布告；海报 *v.* 公布；张贴

plutocracy /pluːˈtɔkrәsi/ *n.* 富豪统治；财阀统治

poignant /ˈpɔinjənt/ *adj.* 痛切的；伤心的

poise /pɔiz/ *v.* 处于平衡(或悬起状态) *n.* 姿势；动作

polemic /pəˈlemik/ *n.* 慷慨陈词；辩论文章

pomp /pɔmp/ *n.* 宏伟壮观的盛况；虚荣；浮华

pore /pɔː/ *v.* 审查；审视 *n.* 毛孔；气孔

porous /ˈpɔːrəs/ *adj.* 能渗透的

potent /ˈpəutənt/ *adj.* 效力大的；说服力强的

pounce /ˈpauns/ *v.* 突然袭击；猛扑 *n.* 猛扑

pragmatic /prægˈmætik/ *adj.* 实事求是的；注重实效的

prank /præŋk/ *n.* 玩笑；恶作剧 *v.* 装饰；打扮

preamble /priːˈæmbl/ *n.* 开场白；前言

preconception /ˌpriːkənˈsepʃən/ *n.* 先人之见；事先形成的观点(或思想)

predicament /priˈdikəmənt/ *n.* 窘况

quail /kweil/ *v.* 畏缩；感到恐惧

quandary /ˈkwɔndəri/ *n.* 困惑；窘况

racket /ˈrækit/ *n.* 球拍；墙网球 *v.* 喧闹；敲诈

rake /reik/ *n.* 耙子；浪子；倾斜 *v.* 用耙子干活；扫视；仔细搜寻；倾斜

rampage /ˈræmpeidʒ/ *n.&v.* 狂暴的乱冲乱撞

rampant /ˈræmpənt/ *adj.* 猖獗的；遏制不住的

rancour /ˈræŋkə/ *n.* 积怨；深仇

ransack /ˈrænsæk/ *vt.* 彻底搜索；抢劫

ransom /ˈrænsəm/ *n.* 赎金；赎身

rapture /ˈræptʃə/ *n.* 极度的欢喜；狂喜 *v.* 使狂喜

rascal /ˈrɑːskəl/ *n.* 不诚实的人；流氓 *adj.* 无赖的

rash /ræʃ/ *n.* 皮疹 *adj.* 轻率的

scorch /skɔːtʃ/ *v.* 将(物体表面)烫焦、烫煳或烫的变色；枯萎 *n.* 烧焦；焦痕

scotch /skɔtʃ/ *v.* 遏制；阻止(尤指谣言等) *n.* 刻痕；切口

scout /skaut/ *v.* 到处寻找；物色；侦察 *n.* 侦察(者)

screwy /ˈskruːi/ *adj.* 奇怪的；疯狂的

scrimmage /ˈskrimidʒ/ *n.* 混战 *v.* 争夺

seam /siːm/ *n.* (两边缘相结合的)缝；矿层 *v.* 缝合；接合

secede /siˈsiːd/ *vi.* 退出；脱离

secrete /siˈkriːt/ *vt.* (指器官)分泌；隐藏

secretive /ˈsiːkritiv/ *adj.* 爱保密的；爱深藏不露的

sedate /siˈdeit/ *adj.* 镇静的；沉着的 *v.* (用镇静剂)使(某人)安静下来

sedentary /ˈsedəntəri/ *adj.* (指工作)坐着做的

sedition /siˈdiʃən/ *n.* 煽动叛乱的言论(或行动)

seductive /siˈdʌktiv/ *adj.* 有魅力的；诱人的

seep /siːp/ *v.* (指液体)漏出；渗漏

seismic /ˈsaizmik/ *adj.* 地震的

semantic /siˈmæntik/ *adj.* 语义的；语义学的

semblance /ˈsembləns/ *n.* 外表；外貌；与(某物)相似

senile /ˈsiːnail/ *adj.* 衰老的

sentry /ˈsentri/ *n.* 岗哨；哨兵

tint /tint/ *n.* 色度；颜色的浓淡

tiptoe /ˈtiptəu/ *vi.* 踮着脚走 *n.* 脚趾尖；脚尖

tonic /ˈtɔnik/ *n.* 滋补品；使人感到健康(或快乐)的事 *adj.* 滋补的；有兴奋作用的

topple /ˈtɔpl/ *v.* (不稳而)倒下；将…推翻

torrent /ˈtɔrənt/ *n.* 急流；湍流

tortuous /ˈtɔːtjuəs/ *adj.* 弯弯曲曲的；含混不清的

totter /ˈtɔtə/ *vi.* 踉跄 *n.* 摇晃

trance /trɑːns/ *n.* 昏睡状态；催眠状态 *vt.* 使恍惚；使出神

transcend /trænˈsend/ *vt.* 超出；超越范围

transfusion /trænsˈfjuːʒən/ *n.* 输血

transient /trænziənt/ *adj.* 短暂的 *n.* 过客；流浪者

translucent /træzˈljuːsənt/ *adj.* 半透明的

transpire /trænsˈpaiə/ *v.* 公开；为人所知

underling /ˈʌndəliŋ/ *n.* 职位低的人；下属

underrate /ˌʌndəˈreit/ *vt.* 过低评价

understudy /ˈʌndəˌstʌdi/ *n.* 候补演员；替补 *v.* 充当(演员)的替角

unfailing /ˌʌnˈfeiliŋ/ *adj.* 永恒的；可靠的

vacuous /ˈvækjuəs/ *adj.* 空洞的；无智慧的

vanquish /ˈvæŋkwiʃ/ *vt.* 征服；战胜

vapid /ˈvæpid/ *adj.* 乏味的；无趣味的

wail /weil/ *n.&v.* 哭；诉苦

waive /weiv/ *v.* 放弃

wallow /ˈwɔləu/ *v.* 打滚；放纵自己 *n.* 打滚；泥沼

warden /ˈwɔːdən/ *n.* 负责监督、监护或监管的人

wayward /ˈweiwəd/ *adj.* 不听话的；任性的；刚愎的

Day 68

ā la mode /ˌɑːlə'məud/ *adj.* <法>流行的；加冰淇淋的

ally /'ælai/ *n.* 联盟

aloe /'æləu/ *n.* 芦荟

amber /'æmbə/ *n.* 琥珀 *adj.* 琥珀制的

ambience /'æmbiəns/ *n.* 环境；气氛

ampere /'æmpɛə/ *n.* 安培

amphibious /æm'fibiəs/ *adj.* 两栖的

amulet /'æmjulit/ *n.* 护身符

animosity /ˌæni'mɔsiti/ *n.* 憎恶

annals /'ænəlz/ *n.* 编年史

annexe /'æneks/ *n.* 附属建筑

annul /ə'nʌl/ *v.* 废止

bassoon /bə'suːn/ *n.* 低音管

baste /beist/ *v.* 殴打；公开责骂

batch /bætʃ/ *n.* 批；批量

baton /'bætən/ *n.* 指挥棒；接力棒

beacon /'biːkən/ *n.* 烽火；烽火台；灯塔；指向标 *v.* 照亮；引导

bearer /'bɛərə/ *n.* 搬运者；持票者

beck /bek/ *n.* 点头示意；招手；小河

bedlam /'bedləm/ *n.* 混乱；疯人院

bewitch /bi'witʃ/ *v.* 施魔法于；迷惑

bias /'baiəs/ *n.* 偏好 *v.* 使有偏见

bibliophile /'bibliəufail/ *n.* 喜欢读书的人；藏书家

biennial /bai'eniəl/ *adj.* 两年一次的

bigamy /'bigəmi/ *n.* 重婚；重婚罪

censure /'senʃə/ *v.* 严厉批评 *n.* 责备；指责

charisma /kə'rizmə/ *n.* 号召力

chide /tʃaid/ *v.* 指责；责骂

chromatic /krə'mætik/ *adj.* 有颜色的

cinch /sintʃ/ *n.* 容易做的事情 *v.* 紧握；肯定

citation /sai'teiʃən/ *n.* 引用；引证

cleave /kliːv/ *v.* 裂开；劈开

cling /kliŋ/ *v.* 紧紧抓住(或抱住)

dabble /'dæbl/ *v.* 戏水；涉足

dainty /'deinti/ *adj.* 小巧的；精致的 *n.* 美味精致的食物

dally /'dæli/ *v.* 浪费时间；戏弄；玩弄

damnable /'dæmnəbl/ *adj.* 可恶的；恶劣的

dandruff /'dændrʌf/ *n.* 头皮屑

dandy /'dændi/ *n.* 花花公子 *adj.* 服装华丽的

dart /dɑːt/ *v.* 猛冲；突进

debar /di'bɑː/ *v.* 将(某人)排斥在外

debilitate /di'biliteit/ *v.* 使非常虚弱

debrief /di'briːf/ *v.* (军事)询问执行任务的情况

debunk /diː'bʌŋk/ *v.* 揭穿(某人、物或机构)名不副实

decipher /di'saifə/ *v.* 破译(密码)；辨认(潦草字迹)

decontaminate /ˌdiːkən'tæmineit/ *v.* 排除(尤其放射性的)污染

defiance /di'faiəns/ *n.* 违抗；藐视

deflect /di'flekt/ *v.* (使)运动转向

defrost /ˌdiː'frɔst/ *v.* 除去冰(或霜)

ellipsis /i'lipsis/ *n.* 省略

elude /i'ljuːd/ *v.* 逃避

elusive /i'ljuːsiv/ *adj.* 逃避的；难以理解的

emaciated /i'meiʃieitid/ *adj.* 瘦弱的；憔悴的

embargo /em'bɑːgəu/ *n.* 禁令；禁止贸易令 *v.* 禁止出入港口；禁运

embellish /im'beliʃ/ *v.* 美化；装饰；修饰

ember /'embə/ *n.* 余烬

embezzle /im'bezl/ *v.* 挪用；盗用

emblem /'embləm/ *n.* 象征；标志

emporium /em'pɔːriəm/ *n.* 贸易中心

emulate /'emjuleit/ *n.* 与…竞赛；努力赶上(或超出)

fiddle /'fidl/ *n.* 骗局；欺诈

fidget /'fidʒit/ *v.* 烦躁不安

figment /ˈfigmənt/ *n.* 想象中的事物

finale /fiˈnɑːli/ *n.* 终曲；结局

flagrant /ˈfleigrənt/ *adj.* 公然的；骇人听闻的

flamboyant /flæmˈbɔiənt/ *adj.* 非常自信的；爱炫耀的；奢华的

florist /ˈflɔrist/ *n.* 花商

gratuity /grəˈtjuːiti/ *n.* 报酬；小费

graven /ˈgreivən/ *adj.* 雕刻的

greed /griːd/ *n.* 贪婪

grim /grim/ *adj.* 非常严肃的；严厉的；无情的

grimace /griˈmeis/ *n.* 怪相；鬼脸 *v.* 作怪相；装鬼脸

groggy /ˈgrɔgi/ *adj.* 喝醉酒的虚弱的；不稳的

grope /grəup/ *v.&n.* 摸索；探索

groundless /ˈgraundlis/ *adj.* 无根据的

grovel /ˈgrɔvəl/ *vi.* 匍匐；爬行

gruesome /ˈgruːsəm/ *adj.* 讨厌的；令人恐怖的

heckle /ˈhekl/ *vt.&n.* 质问；责难

heed /hiːd/ *n.&v.* 注意；留心

heinous /ˈheinəs/ *adj.* 极凶恶的

heirloom /ˈeəluːm/ *n.* 传家宝

henchman /ˈhentʃmən/ *n.* (忠实的)追随者；(政治上的)支持者

heresy /ˈherəsi/ *n.* 异端；持异端学说

hermit /ˈhəːmit/ *n.* 隐士

heyday /ˈheidei/ *n.* 鼎盛时期；黄金时期

hieroglyph /ˈhaiərəglif/ *n.* 象形字

impermeable /imˈpəːmiəbl/ *adj.* 不透水的

impertinent /imˈpəːtinənt/ *adj.* 粗鲁的；没礼貌的

impetuous /imˈpetjuəs/ *adj.* 鲁莽的；冲动的

impetus /ˈimpitəs/ *n.* 推动；刺激

impiety /imˈpaiəti/ *n.* 不敬；不敬的行为

impinge /imˈpindʒ/ *v.* (对某事物)起作用；影响

implant /imˈplɑːnt/ *v.* 灌输；移植

implausible /imˈplɔːzibl/ *adj.* 难以置信的；不真实的

imposition /ˌimpəˈziʃən/ *n.* 强加；征收；施加

impostor /imˈpɔstə/ *n.* 冒名顶替的人

impotent /ˈimpətənt/ *adj.* 无能为力的

impoverish /imˈpɔvəriʃ/ *vt.* 使贫困

jinx /dʒiŋks/ *n.* 厄运；祸根

jockey /ˈdʒɔki/ *n.* 骑师 *v.* 用计谋获取

kleptomania /ˌkleptəuˈmeiniə/ *n.* 偷窃狂；盗窃癖

knack /næk/ *n.* 诀窍；(招人厌烦的)毛病(或习惯)

lash /læʃ/ *n.&v.* 鞭打；抽打

laud /lɔːd/ *v.* 称赞；赞美

lax /læks/ *adj.* 疏忽的；不严厉的

leap /liːp/ *v.* 跳跃

lectern /ˈlektəːn/ *n.* 讲台；读经台

leery /ˈliəri/ *adj.* 机警的；怀疑的

leeway /ˈliːwei/ *n.* 余地；偏航；漂移

mirage /ˈmirɑːʒ/ *n.* 海市蜃楼

misbegotten /ˈmisbiˌgɔtən/ *adj.* 考虑不周的

misgiving /misˈgiviŋ/ *n.* 疑虑；顾虑

misrule /ˌmisˈruːl/ *n.* 混乱；无政府状态

mite /mait/ *n.* 微薄的贡献(或捐助)；螨

monger /ˈmʌŋgə/ *n.* 贩子

moor /muə/ *n.* 荒野；漠泽 v. 使停泊

moot /muːt/ *adj.* 悬而未决的

morbid /ˈmɔːbid/ *adj.* 病态的；忧郁的

morose /məˈrəus/ *adj.* 闷闷不乐的

morpheme /ˈmɔːfiːm/ *n.* 词素

nitty-gritty /ˈnitiˈgriti/ *n.* 基本事实

nominal /ˈnɔminəl/ *adj.* 名义上的；不真实的

nonentity /nɔˈnentəti/ *n.* 庸才；不重要的人

obviate /ˈɔbvieit/ *vt.* 排除；消除

occident /ˈɔksidənt/ *n.* 西方国家

occult /ɔˈkʌlt/ *adj.* 神秘的；秘密的；超自然的

ocular /ˈɔkjulə/ *adj.* 眼睛的；用眼睛的

odyssey /ˈɔdisi/ *n.* 长途的冒险行程；《奥德赛》

off-beat /ˈɔːfˈbiːt/ *adj.* 非传统的

offhand /ˈɔːfˈhænd/ *adj.* 过于随便的；唐突的 *adv.* 未假思索地

officiate /əˈfiʃieit/ *v.* 执行(公务)；主持

photogenic /ˌfəutəuˈdʒenik/ *adj.* 适于拍照的；上照的

picket /ˈpikit/ *n.* 纠察队；警察(或士兵)的警戒队

pigment /ˈpigmənt/ *n.* 颜料；色素

pilfer /ˈpilfə/ *v.* 小偷小摸

preferential /ˌprefəˈrenʃəl/ *adj.* 优先的；优待的

prelim /priˈlim/ *n.* 初试；预考

premiere /ˈpremiə/ *n.* (戏剧或电影等的)首次公演

preordain /ˌpriːɔːˈdein/ *v.*注定

prepossessing /ˌpriːpəˈzesiŋ/ *adj.*给人良好印象的；有吸引力的

preposterous /priˈpɔstərəs/ *adj.*反常的；荒谬的

prerogative /priˈrɔgətiv/ *n.*权利；(尤指)特权

presumptuous /priˈzʌmptjuəs/ *adj.*专横的；胆大妄为的；放肆的

pretension /priˈtenʃən/ *n.*主张；要求；权利

pretentious /priˈtenʃəs/ *adj.*自负的；自命不凡的

prod /prɔd/ *v.*刺；戳；促使；激励

prodigal /prɔdigəl/ *adj.*挥霍的；铺张的

prodigious /prəˈdidʒəs/ *adj.*大的令人惊叹的；巨大的

quell /kwel/ *v.*镇压；压制

quench /kwentʃ/ *v.*扑灭(火焰等)；解(渴)；终止

quibble /ˈkwibl/ *n.*反对(或批评)意见

rave /reiv/ *v.*胡言乱语；说胡话 *n.*热情地赞美

raze /reiz/ *v.*彻底破坏(或摧毁)

realm /relm/ *n.*王国；领域；范围

rebate /ˈriːbeit/ *n.*可减免的款额；折扣

recant /riˈkænt/ *v.*宣布放弃（以前的意见或信仰等)；撤回；撤销

recess /riˈses/ *n.*终止(或暂停)期间；休会期

recession /riˈseʃən/ *n.*衰退；撤退

recluse /riˈkluːs/ *n.*隐士

recompense /ˈrekəmpens/ *v.*酬谢（或报答)(某人) *n.*报酬；补偿

recount /riˈkaunt/ *v.*讲述；详细叙述

shovel /ˈʃʌvəl/ *n.*铁锨 *v.*(用铲子或铁锨)铲

shred /ʃred/ *n.*细条；碎片；少量

shrewd /ʃruːd/ *adj.*精明的；敏锐的

shriek /ʃriːk/ *v.*尖叫；尖声说出

shrill /ʃril/ *adj.*尖锐的；刺耳的

shudder /ˈʃʌdə/ *vi.*发抖；战栗

shun /ʃʌn/ *vt.*避开；回避

siege /siːdʒ/ *n.&v.*围困；围攻

siesta /siˈestə/ *n*/ *vt.*（尤指在气候炎热国家中的)午睡

simile /ˈsimili/ *n.*明喻

singe /sindʒ/ *v.*烧焦(或烫焦)

singular /ˈsiŋgjulə/ *adj.*单数的；异常的；奇怪的

skew /skjuː/ *adj.*歪的；斜的

skirmish /ˈskəːmiʃ/ *n.*小冲突；小规模战斗

slander /ˈslɑːndə/ *n.*诽谤；中伤

slant /slɑːnt/ *v.&n.*倾斜

sleet /sliːt/ *n.*雨夹雪(或雹)

slit /slit/ *n.*狭长的切口；裂缝

slogan /ˈsləugən/ *n.*标语；口号

tenet /ˈtenit/ *n.*信条；教义

tenor /ˈtenə/ *n.*常规；大意

tenuous /ˈtenjuəs/ *adj.*细的

tepid /ˈtepid/ *adj.*温的

terminology /ˌtəːmiˈnɔlədʒi/ *n.*专门用语；术语

terse /təːs/ *adj.*简短的；洗练的

testy /ˈtesti/ *adj.*急躁的

theism /ˈθiːizəm/ *n.*有神论

thesaurus /θiˈsɔːrəs/ *n.*分类词语汇编；分类词典

thorn /θɔːn/ *n.*刺；荆棘

threshold /ˈθreʃəuld/ *n.*门槛；开端

throttle /ˈθrɔtl/ *v.*使窒息；勒死

thud /θʌd/ *n.*沉闷的响声

unintelligible /ˌʌninˈtelidʒibl/ *adj.*不可理解的；难懂的

unison /ˈjuːnizn/ *n.*齐唱；一致的(或协调的)行动

unkempt /ˌʌnˈkempt/ *adj.*凌乱的

unpalatable /ˌʌnˈpælətəbl/ *adj.*不可口的

vascular /ˈvæskjulə/ *adj.*血管的

vault /vɔːlt/ *n.*拱顶 *v.*(用手或竿支撑)跳跃

vicarious /vaiˈkɛəriəs/ *adj.*有同感的；设身处地的

waddle /ˈwɔdl/ *v.*摇摆的行走

waft /wɑːft/ *v.*飘浮 *n.*香味；气味

wag /wæg/ *v.*(迅速)摇摆

whim /(h)wim/ *n.*突然的念头；心血来潮

Day 69

anthem /ˈænθəm/ *n.* 圣歌;颂歌
apricot /ˈeiprikɔt/ *n.* 杏;杏树
arbiter /ˈɑːbitə/ *v.* 仲裁人
arbitrate /ˈɑːbitreit/ *v.* 仲裁
arc /ɑːk/ *n.* 弧
arcane /ɑːˈkein/ *adj.* 秘密的;神秘的
archer /ˈɑːtʃə/ *n.* 弓箭手
archetype /ˈɑːkitaip/ *n.* 原型
armour /ˈɑːmə/ *n.* 盔甲
arson /ˈɑːsən/ *n.* 纵火
asphalt /ˈæsfælt/ *n.* 沥青
boozer /ˈbuzə(r)/ *n.* 酒馆;经常酗酒的人
bounty /ˈbaunti/ *n.* 奖赏;恩惠
bouquet /buːkei/ *n.* 花束
bourgeois /ˈbuəʒwɑː/ *n.* 中产阶级 *adj.* 中产阶级的
boutique /buːˈtiːk/ *n.* 精品店
braille /breil/ *n.* 盲文
bravado /brəˈvɑːdəu/ *n.* 虚张声势
brink /briŋk/ *n.* (陡峭处的、危险事物的)边缘
bronchitis /brɔŋˈkaitis/ *n.* 支气管炎
budge /bʌdʒ/ *v.* 稍微移动;使改变态度(或意见)
buff /bʌf/ *n.* 暗黄色;软皮;爱好者,迷
buffet /ˈbʌfit/ *n.* 自助餐
bullfight /ˈbulfait/ *n.* 斗牛
colossus /kəˈlɔsəs/ *n.* 巨像
compliance /kəmˈplaiəns/ *n.* 服从;遵从
conciliate /kənˈsilieit/ *v.* 安抚;抚慰
condolence /kənˈdəuləns/ *n.* 同情;吊慰
conducive /kənˈdjuːsiv/ *n.* 有益;容许(或有助于)(某事)发生
conjecture /kənˈdʒektʃə/ *n.&v.* 猜测
connoisseur /ˌkɔniˈsəː/ *n.* 鉴赏家;行家
deft /deft/ *adj.* 熟练的;敏捷的
dejected /diˈdʒektid/ *adj.* 沮丧的;情绪低落的
delineate /diˈlinieit/ *v.* 描绘;描写
delirious /diˈliriəs/ *adj.* 神志混乱的
delude /diˈluːd/ *v.* 欺骗
demean /diˈmiːn/ *v.* 降低自己的身份
demeanour /diˈmiːnə/ *n.* 行为;举止
demented /diˈmentid/ *adj.* 疯狂的;焦虑不安的
denouement /ˌdeinuːˈmɔŋ/ *n.* 最后部分;结局
depict /diˈpikt/ *v.* 描述;描画
deplete /diˈpliːt/ *v.* 大量削减;消耗
deport /diˈpɔːt/ *v.* 将…驱逐出境
dissect /diˈsekt/ *v.* 解剖
disseminate /diˈsemineit/ *v.* 散布
dissident /ˈdisidənt/ *n.* 持不同政见者
enamour /iˈnæmə/ *v.* 倾心于
enchant /inˈtʃɑːnt/ *v.* 使喜悦
encompass /inˈkʌmpəs/ *v.* 包含;包括
engender /inˈdʒendə/ *v.* 造成;引起
enigma /iˈnigmə/ *n.* 谜;奥秘
enlist /inˈlist/ *v.* 从军
enmity /ˈenməti/ *n.* 敌意;仇恨
ensemble /ɔnˈsɔmbl/ *n.* 整体;总效果
entice /inˈtais/ *v.* 诱惑;怂恿
entreat /inˈtriːt/ *v.* 恳求;请求
enumerate /iˈnjuːməreit/ *v.* 列举;数
fondle /ˈfɔndl/ *v.* 爱抚
foolhardy /ˈfuːlˌhɑːdi/ *adj.* 鲁莽的;有勇无谋的
forebode /fɔːˈbəud/ *v.* 预示(尤指不祥之事)
forensic /fəˈrensik/ *adj.* 法庭的;用于法庭的
forestall /fɔːˈstɔːl/ *v.* 抢在(别人)之前行动
fortify /ˈfɔːtifai/ *v.* 防卫
fortuitous /fɔːˈtjuːitəs/ *adj.* 偶然发生的;巧合的
girdle /ˈgəːdl/ *n.* 腰带;围绕物
gladiator /ˈglædieitə/ *n.* 角斗士
glaze /gleiz/ *v.* 装玻璃于(某物);给…镶嵌玻璃

glimmer /ˈglimə/ *v.* 发出微弱的闪光

glint /glint/ *v.* 闪闪发光;闪现(某种神色) *n.* 光泽;反光;闪现

glittery /ˈglitəri/ *adj.* 闪闪发光的;富丽堂皇的

gloat /gləut/ *v.* 得意扬扬;沾沾自喜

glum /glʌm/ *adj.* 忧郁的

gluttonous /ˈglʌtənəs/ *adj.* 贪吃的;贪嘴的

hive /haiv/ *n.* 蜂箱 *v.* 使(蜂群)进入蜂箱

hoard /hɔːd/ *v.* 贮藏;积存

hobo /ˈhəubəu/ *n.* 无业游民

hock /hɔk/ *n.&v.* 典当;抵押

horde /hɔːd/ *n.* 群;帮;人群

horrendous /hɔˈrendəs/ *adj.* 令人吃惊的;可怕的

howl /həul/ *v.* (狼、狗等)尖利的嚎叫;高声叫喊 *n.* 尖声嚎叫;高声大笑;大声哭;吼叫着说

howling /ˈhəuliŋ/ *adj.* 极大的;极端的

hue /hjuː/ *n.* ①颜色;色彩;色调 ②呐喊

impart /imˈpɑːt/ *vt.* 将…给予(或赋予);通知;透露

impasse /æmˈpɑːs/ *n.* 绝境

impassioned /imˈpæʃənd/ *adj.* 热烈的;充满激情的

impeccable /imˈpekəbl/ *adj.* 无瑕疵的;极好的

impenetrable /imˈpenitrəbl/ *adj.* 不能通过的;透不过的

imperceptible /ˌimpəˈseptibl/ *adj.* 感觉不到的

imperil /imˈperil/ *vt.* 使陷于危险

impregnable /imˈpregnəbl/ *adj.* 坚不可摧的

impromptu /imˈprɔmptjuː/ *adj.* 即兴的;临时的

imprudent /imˈpruːdənt/ *adj.* 轻率的

impute /imˈpjuːt/ *vt.* 把(责任、原因)归咎于(某人)(to)

inadvertent /ˌinədˈvəːtənt/ *adj.* 漫不经心的;无意的

jolly /ˈdʒɔli/ *adj.* 愉快的;快乐的

kilt /kilt/ *n.* (苏格兰男子穿的)短褶裙

kimono /kiˈməunəu/ *n.* (日本的)和服;(和服式)晨服

legion /ˈliːdʒən/ *n.* 古罗马军团;外籍军团;大批的人

lesion /ˈliːʒən/ *n.* 损害;损伤

lexicon /ˈleksikən/ *n.* 词典;词汇

libel /ˈlaibəl/ *n.* 诽谤性文字;有损荣誉之事 *v.* 诽谤;中伤

ligament /ˈligəmənt/ *n.* 韧带

limelight /ˈlaimˌlait/ *n.* 众人注目的中心

lineage /liniidʒ/ *n.* 血统;宗系

marrow /ˈmærəu/ *n.* ①骨髓;精华;要点 ②西葫芦

martial /ˈmɑːʃəl/ *adj.* 战争的;军事的

martyr /ˈmɑːtə/ *n.* 烈士;(贬)为博得赞赏而受苦、自我牺牲的人

masquerade /ˌmæskəˈreid/ *n./ v.* 伪装;化装舞会

matriarch /ˈmeitriɑːk/ *n.* 女家长;女族长

matriarchy /ˈmeitriɑːki/ *n.* 母系社会;母权制

mercurial /məːˈkjuəriəl/ *adj.* ①多变的;无常的 ②水银的;汞的

meritocracy /ˌmeriˈtɔkrəsi/ *n.* 英才管理;英才;贤能

meritorious /ˌmeriˈtɔːriəs/ *adj.* 有功绩的;值得称赞(或奖励)的

mermaid /ˈməːmeid/ *n.* (传说中的)美人鱼

microbe /ˈmaikrəub/ *n.* 微生物

notary /ˈnəutəri/ *n.* 公证人

novice /ˈnɔvis/ *n.* 新手;初学者

orgiastic /ˌɔːdʒiˈæstik/ *adj.* 狂欢的;狂乱的

ornate /ɔːˈneit/ *adj.* (贬)装饰华丽的

ornithology /ˌɔːniˈθɔlədʒi/ *n.* 鸟类学

oscillate /ˈɔsileit/ *v.* 使摆动;波动;犹豫

osmosis /ɔzˈməusis/ *n.* 渗透;潜移默化

ostentatious /ˌɔstenˈteiʃəs/ *adj.* 夸耀的;卖弄的

outlandish /ˌautˈlændiʃ/ *adj.* 怪异的;奇特的

outpouring /ˈautpɔːriŋ/ *n.* 流露;洋溢

prodigy /ˈprɔdidʒi/ *n.* 天才;奇才

profess /prəˈfes/ *v.* 声称;伪称

profiteer /ˌprɔfiˈtiə/ *n.* 牟取暴利者;投机倒把者

profuse /prəˈfjuːs/ *adj.* 大量的;丰富的

propaganda /ˌprɔpəˈgændə/ *n.* 宣传;传播

propulsion /prəˈpʌlʃən/ *n.* 推进

proscribe /prəuˈskraib/ *v.* 正式宣布(某物)有危险(或被禁止)

protocol /ˈprəutəkɔl/ *n.* 外交礼节;(外交条约的)草案、议定书

proverb /ˈprɔvəːb/ *n.* 谚语；格言

providence /ˈprɔvidəns/ *n.* 天意；远见

proxy /ˈprɔksi/ *n.* 代理人；代理权

psychosomatic /ˌsaikəusəuˈmætik/ *adj.* 由精神压力引起的

psychotherapy /ˌsaikəuˈθerəpi/ *n.* 精神疗法；心理疗法

puberty /ˈpjuːbəːti/ *n.* 青春期

pulsate /pʌlˈseit/ *vi.* 脉搏；有节奏的舒张(或收缩)

punitive /ˈpjuːnitiv/ *adj.* 惩罚的；惩罚性的

puny /ˈpjuːni/ *adj.* 弱小的；发育不良的

quip /kwip/ *n.* 妙语；讽刺话

reflate /riˈfleit/ *v.* 通货再膨胀

reflex /ˈriːfleks/ *n.* 发射作用

refrain /riˈfrein/ *vi.* 克制；抑制

regress /ˈriːgres/ *v.&n.* 退步；退化

reinstate /ˌriːinˈsteit/ *v.* 使恢复职位(或地位)

rejuvenate /riˈdʒuːvineit/ *v.* 使恢复青春容貌、活力等

relegate /ˈreligeit/ *v.* 使降级(或降低地位)

relent /riˈlent/ *vi.* 决定采取较为温和、宽容的态度和做法；发慈悲

relish /ˈreliʃ/ *n.* 美味；滋味

sage /seidʒ/ *n.* 智者；贤人

salute /səˈljuːt/ *n.&v.* 敬礼；致敬；颂扬

savant /ˈsævənt/ *n.* 博学之人；学者

saviour /ˈseivjə/ *n.* 救世主；拯救者

scamper /ˈskæmpə/ *v.&n.* 奔跑；蹦蹦跳跳

scapegoat /ˈskeipgəut/ *n.* 替罪羊

scathing /ˈskeiðiŋ/ *adj.* 严厉的；刻薄的

scenario /siˈnɑːriəu/ *n.* 脚本；剧情概要

scoff /skɔf/ *n.* 嘲弄；嘲笑 *v.* 贪婪的吃；嘲笑；狼吞虎咽

serenade /ˌserəˈneid/ *n.* 小夜曲

sever /ˈsevə/ *v.* 切断；割断

shaft /ʃɑːft/ *n.* 箭杆；旨在伤人(或刺激人)的话

shaggy /ˈʃægi/ *adj.* 粗糙、浓密而不整齐的

shaky /ˈʃeiki/ *adj.* 摇晃的；颤抖的

sham /ʃæm/ *v.* 假装 *n.* 装成与自己实际情况不符的人

shear /ʃiə/ *v.* 剪(羊的)毛；使弯曲(或折断)

sheepish /ˈʃiːpiʃ/ *adj.* 羞怯的；腼腆的

shove /ʃʌv/ *v.* 乱推；挤

sloppy /ˈslɔpi/ *adj.* 衣着不整的；做事马虎的；草率的

thwart /θwɔːt/ *v.* 阻止；阻挠 *adj.* 横放的 *adv.* 横过 *n.* 横坐板

tickle /ˈtikl/ *v.* (轻触或抚摸)使发痒

tiff /tif/ *n.&v.* 拌嘴；口角

tingle /ˈtiŋgl/ *v.* (皮肤)感到轻微的刺痛

trappings /ˈtræpiŋz/ *n.* (威望、财富等的)外部标志

truism /ˈtruːizm/ *n.* 不言而喻的道理

trump /trʌmp/ *n.* 王牌 *v.* 出王牌吃掉；编造(谎言)加害

trumpet /ˈtrʌmpit/ *n.* 喇叭；小号

tweezers /ˈtwiːzəz/ *n.* 镊子

twinkle /ˈtwiŋkl/ *v.&n.* 闪烁；(人的眼睛)发亮；闪光

twitch /twitʃ/ *v.&n.* 抽搐；痉挛

tycoon /taiˈkuːn/ *n.* (企业界的)巨头；大亨

tyrant /ˈtaiərənt/ *n.* 暴君；专职君主

unsparing /ˌʌnˈspɛəriŋ/ *adj.* 慷慨的；大方的

unwitting /ˌʌnˈwitiŋ/ *adj.* 未察觉的；不知道的

upstanding /ʌpˈstændiŋ/ *adj.* 强健而有力的；正派而诚实的

upstart /ˈʌpstɑːt/ *n.* 突然发迹者；暴发户

vicious /ˈviʃəs/ *adj.* 恶毒的；堕落的；剧烈的

vigil /ˈvidʒil/ *n.* 保持清醒；不眠

vigilant /ˈvidʒilənt/ *adj.* 警觉的；警惕的

woe /wəu/ *n.* 悲哀；痛苦

wondrous /ˈwʌndrəs/ *adj.* 令人惊奇的；意想不到的

yelp /jelp/ *n.* 尖叫声

zing /ziŋ/ *n.* 活力；精力

zonked /zɔŋkt/ *adj.* 醉的；昏迷的；精疲力尽的

Day 70

asphyxia /æsˈfiksiə/ *n.* 窒息
asterisk /ˈæstərisk/ *n.* 星号(即 *)
asthma /ˈæsmə/ *n.* 哮喘
astronautics /ˌæstrəˈnɔːtiks/ *n.* 航天学
attaché /əˈtæʃei/ *v.* 使馆参赞
aura /ˈɔːrə/ *n.* 氛围
aurora /ɔːˈrɔːrə/ *n.* 曙光;极光
autocrat /ˈɔːtəkræt/ *n.* 独裁者
aviation /ˌeiviˈeiʃən/ *n.* 航空学
avid /ˈævid/ *adj.* 贪婪的;渴望的
axiom /ˈæksiəm/ *n.* 公理
bilingual /baiˈlingwəl/ *adj.* (能说)两种语言的
biomass /ˈbaiəumæs/ *n.* 生物量
bionic /baiˈɔnik/ *adj.* 仿生学的;利用仿生学的
bittersweet /ˈbitəswiːt/ *adj.* 苦乐交加的
blab /blæb/ *v.* 泄露秘密
blanch /blɑːntʃ/ *v.* 漂白;使变白
bliss /blis/ *n.* 洪福;极乐
blister /ˈblistə/ *n.* 水疱
blitz /blits/ *n.&v.* 空袭;快速攻击
body armour /ˈbɔdi ˈɑːmə/ *n.* 防弹衣
bogey /ˈbəugi/ *n.* (高尔夫球)标准杆数
bonus /ˈbəunəs/ *n.* 奖金
bungalow /ˈbʌŋgələu/ *n.* 平房
bungle /ˈbʌŋgl/ *v.* 粗制滥造;笨手笨脚地做事
buoy /bɔi/ *n.* 浮标;航标
byword /ˈbaiwəːd/ *n.* 代表某种品性的人(或事)
conservatory /kənˈsəːvətəri/ *n.* 温室
consign /kənˈsain/ *v.* 移交;交付
consonance /ˈkɔnsənəns/ *n.* 协调
conspire /kənˈspaiə/ *v.* 密谋(尤指干坏事)
contention /kənˈtenʃən/ *v.* 竞争;争夺
contingent /kənˈtindʒənt/ *n.* 小分队;代表团
dissipate /ˈdisipeit/ *v.* 消散;消失
dissonance /ˈdisənəns/ *n.* 不和谐;不一致
dissuade /diˈsweid/ *v.* 劝阻
distress /disˈtres/ *n.* 极大的痛苦;悲痛;苦痛
divulge /daiˈvʌldʒ/ *v.* 泄漏
dodge /dɔdʒ/ *v.* 闪开;躲避 *n.* 躲避;诡计
don /dɔn/ *n.* 大学教师(尤指在牛津或剑桥大学)
dope /dəup/ *n.* 毒品
dossier /ˈdɔsiei/ *n.* 材料;卷宗
drab /dræb/ *adj.* 单调的;乏味的
drape /dreip/ *v.* 悬挂
drench /drentʃ/ *v.* 使…湿透
dubious /ˈdjuːbjəs/ *adj.* 可疑的
duress /djuəˈrəs/ *n.* 威胁;逼迫
dyslexia /disˈleksiə/ *n.* 诵读困难
dystrophy /ˈdistrəfi/ *n.* 营养障碍;营养不良
enviable /ˈenviəbl/ *adj.* 引起忌妒的
epitaph /ˈepitɑːf/ *n.* 祭文;悼词
equanimity /ˌiːkwəˈniməti/ *n.* 心情平静;情绪稳定
equivocal /iˈkwivəkəl/ *adj.* 模棱两可的;意义不明的
erect /iˈrekt/ *adj.* 直立的
erratic /iˈrætik/ *adj.* 不规则的;无常的
erroneous /iˈrəunjəs/ *adj.* 错误的
escalate /ˈeskəleit/ *v.* 逐步增长(或发展)
esoteric /ˌesəuˈterik/ *adj.* 神秘的;难懂的
estimate /ˈestimeit/ *n.&v.* 估计;估价
freckle /ˈfrekl/ *n.* 雀斑
frenzy /ˈfrenzi/ *n.* 极度激动的状态
fresco /ˈfreskəu/ *n.* 壁画
frisk /frisk/ *v.* 搜查
frivolous /ˈfrivələs/ *adj.* 不明事理的;轻率的;肤浅的
frosty /ˈfrɔsti/ *adj.* 严寒的;霜冻的
gnash /næʃ/ *v.* (因情绪激动)咬或磨(牙)
go-between /ˈgəu biˌtwiːn/ *n.* 中间人;信使
goblet /ˈgɔblit/ *n.* 高脚杯

goggle /ˈgɔgl/ *v.* 瞪圆眼睛看
gourmet /ˈguəmei/ *n.* 美食家
grandiose /ˈgrændiəus/ *adj.* 浮夸的；庞大的
granule /ˈgrænjuːl/ *n.* 小颗粒
gratuitous /grəˈtjuːitəs/ *adj.* 故意的；无正当理由的
hurtle /ˈhəːtl/ *v.* 猛烈地(或飞快地)奔驰
hydroelectric /ˈhaidrəiˈlektrik/ *adj.* 水力发电的
hydroponics /ˌhaidrəˈpɔniks/ *n.* 水栽法；无土栽培
hyperbole /haiˈpəːbəli/ *n.* 夸张
hypersensitive /ˌhaipəˈsensətiv/ *adj.* 对…过敏的；有过敏反应的
hypnosis /hipˈnəusis/ *n.* 催眠状态
hysteria /hiˈstiəriə/ *n.* 歇斯底里；精神错乱
inane /iˈnein/ *adj.* 愚蠢的；无意义的
incarnation /ˌinkɑːˈneiʃən/ *n.* 典型人物；化身
incipient /inˈsipiənt/ *adj.* 早期的；刚出现的
incisive /inˈsaisiv/ *adj.* 直接的；尖锐的；清晰而准确地
incite /inˈsait/ *vt.* 煽动；鼓动
increment /ˈinkrimənt/ *n.* 增加；增长
indemnity /inˈdemnəti/ *n.* (为防伤害或损失的)保障；保险；赔偿
indignant /inˈdignənt/ *adj.* 愤慨的；恼火的
insatiate /inˈseiʃiit/ *adj.* 永不满足的
inscription /inˈskripʃən/ *n.* 题名；题字
inscrutable /inˈskruːtəbl/ *adj.* 不可理解的；神秘的
insinuate /inˈsinjueit/ *vt.* 旁敲侧击
intercede /intəˈsiːd/ *v.* 求情；调停；调解
intercept /ˌintəˈsept/ *vt.* 中途阻止(或拦截)
intern /inˈtəːn/ *v.* 将(某人)拘留、扣押 *n.* 被拘留者；住院实习医生
intersperse /ˌintəːˈspəːs/ *vt.* 散布；点缀
invoice /ˈinvɔis/ *n.* 发票；发货清单
invoke /inˈvəuk/ *v.* 援用；求助于
involuntary /inˈvɔləntəri/ *adj.* 不自觉地；无意识的
irascible /iˈræsibl/ *adj.* 性情暴躁的
irritant /ˈiritənt/ *adj.* 有刺激的 *n.* 刺激物；令人烦恼的事
iterate /ˈitəreit/ *vt.* 一再提出；反复说
jostle /ˈdʒɔsl/ *v.&n.* 推；挤
jubilant /ˈdʒuːbilənt/ *adj.* 欣喜的；欢欣的
kindred /ˈkindrid/ *n.* 亲属关系；家人和亲戚
lingo /ˈliŋgəu/ *n.* 外国语言
linguist /ˈliŋgwist/ *n.* 语言学家；通晓几国语言的人
lull /lʌl/ *v.* 使安静；抚慰；缓和
luminary /ˈluːminəri/ *n.* 鼓舞(或影响他人)的人；发光天体
lunge /lʌndʒ/ *n.&v.* 前冲；刺；戳
lurid /ˈljuərid/ *adj.* 光彩耀眼的；斑斓的
lush /lʌʃ/ *adj.* 茂盛的
lusty /ˈlʌsti/ *adj.* 健康的；充满活力的
lyrical /ˈlirikəl/ *adj.* 狂热的；奔放的
microcosm /ˈmaikrəukɔzəm/ *n.* 小宇宙；微观世界
microfiche /ˈmaikrəufiːʃ/ *n.* 缩微胶片
midget /ˈmidʒit/ *n.* 矮人；侏儒
midst /midst/ *n.* 中央；中部
midwife /ˈmidwaif/ *n.* 助产士
militant /ˈmilitənt/ *adj.* 好战的；用武力(或高压)的
militia /miˈliʃə/ *n.* 民兵队伍；国民自卫队
minion /ˈminjən/ *n.* 下属；助手
morsel /ˈmɔːsəl/ *n.* 少量；一小块
mortify /ˈmɔːtifai/ *v.* 使感到羞辱(或难堪)
noxious /ˈnɔkʃəs/ *adj.* 有害的；有毒的
null /nʌl/ *adj.* 无法律约束力的；无效的
obliterate /əˈblitəreit/ *vt.* 除去；擦掉
obtrude /əbˈtruːd/ *v.* 强加；使突出
officious /əˈfiʃəs/ *adj.* 爱发号施令的；好管闲事的
off-key /ˈɔfkiː/ *adj.* 不和谐的
off-putting /ˈɔfputiŋ/ *adj.* 令人尴尬的；令人烦恼的
opportune /ˈɔpətjuːn/ *adj.* 恰好的；适宜的
orator /ˈɔrətə/ *n.* 演说家
ordnance /ˈɔːdnəns/ *n.* 军需品和军用器材
pasty /ˈpeisti/ *adj.* 糊状的
pathological /ˌpæθəˈlɔdʒikəl/ *adj.* 病理学的；疾病的；病态的
patriarchy /ˈpeitriɑːki/ *n.* 父权制
pauper /ˈpɔːpə/ *n.* 贫民
pawn /pɔːn/ *n.* (国际象棋中的)卒；被人利用的人 *vt.* 典当；抵押

pedestal /ˈpedistəl/ *n.* 基座；柱基

peer /piə/ *n.* 同等的人；同龄人

penitent /ˈpenitənt/ *adj.* 悔过的；忏悔的

perennial /pəˈreniəl/ *adj.* 长久的；反复出现的

periscope /ˈperiskəup/ *n.* 潜望镜

perjury /ˈpəːdʒəri/ *n.* 做伪证；伪证

perquisite /ˈpəːkwizit/ *n.* （工资以外的）津贴；奖金；财务补贴

perversion /pəˈvəːʃən/ *n.* 变坏；反常；曲解；变态心理

petrify /ˈpetrifai/ *v.* 使（某人）惊呆（或吓呆）

phoney /ˈfəuni/ *adj.* 假装的；冒充的

rendezvous /ˈrɔndivuː/ *n.* 约会；约会地点

renege /riˈniːɡ/ *v.* 违背诺言；背信

renunciation /riˌnʌnsiˈeiʃən/ *n.* 放弃；断绝关系；拒绝承认

replica /ˈreplikə/ *n.* 精确的复制品

revert /riˈvəːt/ *v.* 恢复；回归

revoke /riːˈvəuk/ *vt.* 撤销（或废除）（法令等）；吊销（许可证）

roulette /ruːˈlet/ *n.* 轮盘赌

ruminate /ˈruːmineit/ *v.* 思索；沉思

rupture /ˈrʌptʃə(r)/ *v.&n.* 破裂；断裂

sabbatical /səˈbætikəl/ *adj.* （给大学教师用于旅行、研究等的）假期

sack /sæk/ *n.* 大口袋；解雇 *vt.* 掠夺；毁坏

sluggish /ˈslʌɡiʃ/ *adj.* 行动迟缓的；无精打采的

slump /slʌmp/ *n.&v.* 沉重的落下（或倒下）

slur /sləː/ *v.* 含糊不清地发出（声音）或说

smother /ˈsmʌðə/ *v.* 使窒息；闷死

smudge /smʌdʒ/ *n.* 污点；污迹

snatch /snætʃ/ *v.* 抢；迅速（或粗鲁）地抓住

sneak /sniːk/ *v.* 告状；打小报告

sneer /sniə/ *v.&n.* 嘲笑；讥笑

snitch /snitʃ/ *v.* 迅速偷走

snug /snʌɡ/ *adj.* 温暖而舒适的

sober /ˈsəubə/ *adj.* 认真的；慎重的

sojourn /ˈsɔdʒəːn/ *v.&n.* 暂住

solace /ˈsɔləs/ *v.&n.* 安慰

sophomore /ˈsɔfəmɔː/ *n.* （中学、专科学校或大学的）二年级学生

sparse /spɑːs/ *adj.* 稀少的；稀疏的

spell /spel/ *n.* 咒语；中魔；魅力；魔力；一段时间 *v.* 拼写；讲清楚；详细解释

sprint /sprint/ *v.* 短距离全速奔跑

sprout /spraut/ *v.* 出现；萌芽

spurious /ˈspjuəriəs/ *adj.* 伪造的

squander /ˈskwɔndə/ *v.* 浪费；挥霍

stale /steil/ *adj.* 不新鲜的；走味的；因陈旧而乏味的

staple /ˈsteipl/ *adj.* 基本的；主要的；标准的 *n.* 订书钉

stigma /ˈstiɡmə/ *n.* 耻辱的标记；污名

stink /stiŋk/ *v.* 发臭；有臭味

stray /strei/ *v.* 走失；迷失；闲逛

tabloid /ˈtæblɔid/ *n.* 小报

taboo /təˈbuː/ *n.* 禁忌

taciturn /ˈtæsitəːn/ *adj.* 沉默寡言的

tactile /ˈtæktail/ *adj.* 触觉的

tally /ˈtæli/ *n.* 记分；计算；标签；票据 *v.* 符合；一致

tamper /ˈtæmpə/ *v.* 干预；擅自改动

tantamount /ˈtæntəmaunt/ *adj.* 同等的；相等的

tardy /ˈtɑːdi/ *adj.* 行动缓慢的

tarnish /ˈtɑːniʃ/ *v.* 失去光泽；玷污；损害

teetotal /tiːˈtəutəl/ *adj.* 滴酒不沾的

tempest /ˈtempist/ *n.* 暴风雨；风暴

tenacious /tiˈneiʃəs/ *adj.* 粘牢的；坚决的

tenement /ˈtenimənt/ *n.* （出租的）公寓；房间

uptight /ˈʌpˈtait/ *adj.* 精神紧张的

up-to-the-minute *adj.* 最新的；包含最新信息的

upturn /ˈʌptəːn/ *n.* 好转；改进

urbane /əːˈbein/ *adj.* 有礼貌的；老于世故的

virtuoso /vəːtjuˈəuzəu/ *n.* 技艺超群的人；（尤指）演奏家、歌唱家

volatile /ˈvɔlətail/ *adj.* 易挥发的；情绪多变的；无常的

voracious /vɔˈreiʃəs/ *adj.* 贪吃的；渴求的

vouch /vautʃ/ *v.* 为…担保（或作证）

willful /ˈwilful/ *adj.* 故意的

wilt /wilt/ *n.&v.* 凋谢

withstand /wiðˈstænd/ *vt.* 承受住

wizard /ˈwizəd/ *n.* 男巫；有非凡才能的人

Note 工欲善其事，必先利其器 *You cannot make bricks without straw.*

Day 71~80

IELTS 核心词汇

第3阶段

冲刺篇

Day 71~80 ☞ 快乐指南

大家好，能够坚持到今天，真不容易啊！特别是刚刚过去的5天。但是像长跑一样，现在是到了最后一圈了，大家再加把劲，最后冲刺，胜利就在前方！

在这里我们根据雅思考试常涉及的内容，制作了十个专题，分10天记忆。每个专题提供100至200个最常用单词。对这些单词大家只要有个印象就可以了。目的是为雅思阅读再加一把火，我们还在几个相关专题后面提供了相应的阅读材料，来扩展大家的视野，巩固相关词汇，希望大家最后冲刺成功。

Drive out the inch as you have done the span!（最后的成功，就在于再努力一下！）

大家辛苦了，祝大家成功！

Day 71

食品类词汇

subsistence /səbˈsistəns/ *n.* 衣食
nutrition /njuːˈtriʃ(ə)n/ *n.* 食物
appetite /ˈæpitait/ *n.* 胃口
gluttony /ˈɡlʌtəni/ *n.* 暴食
diet /ˈdaiət/ *n.* 食谱
apricot /ˈeiprikɔt/ *n.* 杏
pineapple /ˈpəinæp(ə)l/ *n.* 菠萝
watermelon /ˈwɔːtəmelən/ *n.* 西瓜
strawberry /ˈstrɔːbəri/ *n.* 草莓
peanut /ˈpiːnʌt/ *n.* 花生
cucumber /ˈkjuːkʌmbə(r)/ *n.* 黄瓜
aubergine /ˈəubəʒiːn/ *n.* 茄子
eggplant /ˈegplɑːnt/ *n.* 茄子
garlic /ˈɡɑːlik/ *n.* 蒜
chive /ˈtʃaiv/ *n.* 葱
mushroom /ˈmʌʃrum/ *n.* 蘑菇
celery /ˈseliri/ *n.* 芹菜
hors d'oeuvre (正餐前的)开胃食品
main course 主菜
sweet /ˈswiːt/ *n.* 糖果
dessert /diˈzəːt/ *n.* 甜食
snack /snæk/ *n.* 点心,小吃
sausage /ˈsɔsidʒ/ *n.* 香肠
cold meats 冷盘(美作:cold cuts)
turkey /ˈtəːki/ *n.* 火鸡
cheese /tʃiːz/ *n.* 奶酪
butter /ˈbʌtə(r)/ *n.* 奶油
biscuit /ˈbiskit/ *n.* (英)饼干,(美)小面包
mustard /ˈmʌstəd/ *n.* 芥末
mineral water 矿泉水
cider /ˈsaidə(r)/ *n.* 苹果酒
champagne /ʃæmˈpein/ *n.* 香槟酒
cocktail /ˈkɔkteil/ *n.* 鸡尾酒
liqueur /liˈkjuə(r)/ *n.* 白酒,烧酒
vodka /ˈvɔdkə/ *n.* 伏特加
whisky /ˈwiski/ *n.* 威士忌
brandy /ˈbrændi/ *n.* 白兰地
bill of fare, menu 菜单,菜谱
tablecloth /ˈteib(ə)lklɔθ/ *n.* 桌布
napkin /næpkin/ *n.* 餐巾
serviette /səːviˈet/ *n.* 餐巾
cutlery /ˈkʌtləri/ *n.* 餐具
coffeepot /ˈkɔfipɔt/ *n.* 咖啡壶
cruet /ˈkruːit/ *n.* 调味瓶架

jasmine /ˈdʒæsmin/ n. 茉莉
chrysanthemum /kriˈsænθəməm/ n. 菊花

补充读物

COFFEE AND CAFÉS IN AMSTERDAM

A new generation of coffee establishments have taken over from the old 'Brown Cafés'

Sitting in **Gary's Muffins**, sipping a frothy cappuccino and munching a toasted onion bagel oozing with cream cheese, you might easily be in San Francisco or New York. The fact that you're in Amsterdam isn't all that surprising since the energetic duo who launched this thriving little chain are Americans — one from the East coast and the other from the West. But the open, light, friendly and relaxed ambiance at Gary's couldn't be more in contrast to the dour, dark and often dingy Brown Cafés where Amsterdamers have traditionally congregated.

Coffee has long been taken for granted in this city of infinite delights. The Dutch, of course, have an intimate connection with the bean as they were the first to actually grow the plant on European soil. And Dutch traders were quick to exploit the potential of the black brew, setting up the earliest coffee plantations and using the proceeds to fuel themselves as well as their nascent stock market. But even though Amsterdam, along with London, was one of the twin centres of the early worldwide coffee network, consumption at home was generally the quick and bitter fix that became the standard fare for caffeine starved workers. Of course there were specialty shops like **Geels** that served the more sophisticated tastes but, in the main, coffee in cafés was seen as simply a chaser for alcoholic stuff flavoured with hops or juniper. The entrepreneurial spirit of the Dutch, however, knew a good thing when they sniffed it. The mad growth of 'designer' cafes in America made coffee part of the youth culture and gave it a new kind of glamour. American imports like Gary's were successful because they were able to merge easily into the culture — it worked out of fusion rather than force. But it took the Dutch themselves to show how enterprise, coupled with an intimate knowledge of the trade and the boundless energy for business which bubbles in Amsterdam like a fired-up percolator pot, could develop new models which, unlike the Starbucks template being stamped all over England, is uniquely theirs.

An example of this new coffee enterprise is located far enough from the city centre to avoid being McDonaldised, it still has an advantageous location being a stone's throw from the Museum district, thus benefiting from the tourist trade. Brandmeester's has the feel of a neighbourhood café — friendly, open and warm. You enter into a well designed space which articulates its focus on coffee in every conceivable way — from a charmingly drawn mural of world-wide coffee production covering an entire wall to the appetising variety of beans in great see-through containers affixed behind the counter and the brilliant collection of exotic coffee paraphernalia displayed on glass-enclosed shelves like a museum exhibition. In the rear of the shop a miniature coffee roaster fills the room with a seductive fragrance that sets the tone for a smallish café in the back. The drinks are expertly made by well-trained staff and consumed by regulars who know their coffee and are delighted to find a place like this in which to drink it. But the heart of Brandmeester's operation is downstairs, which is where the packing and shipping of the coffee, equipment and supplies is consigned for their growing European mail-order business. There is a buzz about the place that is palpable. Brandmeester's is in the midst of expansion and sees the potential of their market growing by leaps and bounds — a salutary example to a good many small businesses that knowledge, energy, a good organisation and love of your trade can take you a very long way.

Note 前事不忘后事之师 *Remember the past and it will guide your future.*

Day 72

学科类词汇

news agency 新闻社
editor /ˈeditə(r)/ *n.* 编辑
feature article 特写
editor's note 编者按
copyright /ˈkɔpirait/ *n.* 版权
scientific literature 科学文献
index /ˈindeks/ *n.* 索引
semester /siˈmestə(r)/ *n.* 学期
discipline /ˈdisiplin/ *n.* 纪律
timetable /ˈtaimteib(ə)l/ *n.* 课程表
to play truant, to play hooky 逃学，旷课
headmaster /hedˈmɑːstə/ *n.* 校长（女性为：headmistress）
dean /diːn/ *n.* 教务长
private tutor 私人教师，家庭教师
matriculation /mətrikjuˈleiʃ(ə)n/ *n.* 注册
crib /krib/ *n.* 夹带（美作：trot）
project /ˈprɔdʒekt/ *n.* 毕业论文
thesis /ˈθiːsis/ *n.* 毕业论文
doctorate /dɔktərət/ *n.* 博士学位
competitive examination 答辩考试
science /ˈsaiəns/ *n.* 理科
algebra /ˈældʒibrə/ *n.* 代数
geometry /dʒiˈɔmitri/ *n.* 几何
sociology /səusiˈɔlədʒi/ *n.* 社会学
psychology /saiˈkɔlədʒi/ *n.* 心理学
philosophy /fiˈlɔsəfi/ *n.* 哲学
engineering /endʒˈniəriŋ/ *n.* 工程学
medicine /meds(ə)n/ *n.* 医学
social science 社会科学
agriculture /ægrikʌltʃə(r)/ *n.* 农学
astronomy /əˈstrɔnəmi/ *n.* 天文学
economics /iːkəˈnɔmiks/ *n.* 经济学
commercial science 商学
biochemistry /baiəuˈkemistri/ *n.* 生物化学
anthropology /ænθrəˈpɔlədʒi/ *n.* 人类学
linguistics /liŋˈɡwistiks/ *n.* 语言学
accounting /əˈkauntiŋ/ *n.* 会计学
law, jurisprdence 法学
banking /ˈbæŋkiŋ/ *n.* 银行学
metallurgy /miˈtælədʒi/ *n.* 冶金学
finance /ˈfainæns/ *n.* 财政学
mass-communication 大众传播学
journalism /ˈdʒəːnəliz(ə)m/ *n.* 新闻学
atomic energy 原子能学
civil engineering 土木工程
architecture /ˈɑːkitektʃə(r)/ *n.* 建筑学
chemical engineering 化学工程
accounting and statistics 会计统计
business administration 工商管理
library /ˈlaibrəri/ *n.* 图书馆学
diplomacy /diˈpləuməsi/ *n.* 外交
business school 商业学校
technical school 工业学校
technical college 专科学校
faculty /ˈfæk(ə)lti/ *n.* 系
lecture theatre 阅览室（美作：lecture theater）
amphitheatre /ˈæmfiθiətə(r)/ *n.* 阶梯教室（美作：amphitheater）

补充读物

More Dads Help with Home-Schooling

As the father and son stroll the aisles, Tim finds plenty of visual aids to teach 8-year-old Nicholas about subjects like health and nutrition, agriculture and economics.

No longer content to sit on the sidelines, fathers like Tim Peebles are getting more involved in what was once firmly a woman's domain: home-schooling.

Erika Karres, an education professor at the University of North Carolina at Chapel Hill, said she has seen an evolution in fathers' roles since homeschooling first caught on in the 1960s and 1970s.

"The role of dads then was nonexistent, except maybe nodding their heads and saying, 'OK, if that's what you want to do, wife,'" Karres said. "I welcome this as a great, positive change in the home-schooling movement."

Mother majority

While statistics and the stories of home-schoolers suggest mothers still tend to be the stay-at-home teachers, Karres said fathers in general are showing more interest in their children's education. Many homeschooling fathers are following that trend by sharing some of the teaching burden with their wives, she said.

Clark Aldrich, who designs computer programs from his home in Madison, Connecticut, lets 8-year-old Slater sit on his lap and listen in when he takes conference calls for work. Aldrich and his wife split teaching duties and often have science class as a family during their outdoor walks.

"We tried kindergarten at public school, but I didn't like their attitude," Aldrich said. "They were of the philosophy that we know better than you know how to raise your child."

About 850,000 students were homeschooled in the spring of 1999, according to the most recent statistics available from the U.S. Department of Education. Homeschool advocates estimate the current number is closer to 2 million this year, based on their own surveys.

In 1998, a voluntary survey of homeschooling parents whose children took one of two national standardized tests found that 23 percent of the mothers of those students were employed, while almost all the fathers — 98 percent — had jobs.

Federal figures from 1999 showed one of two parents worked in the homes of 444,000 homeschooled children; both parents worked in the homes of 237,000 homeschooled children.

Father factor

Susan Wise Bauer, co-author of "The Well-Trained Mind: A Guide to Classical Education at Home," said fathers participate in different ways depending on their reasons for homeschooling.

Conservative Christian families tend to view the father as the head of the household, so those fathers may serve as homeschool "principals," setting curricula or checking homework, Bauer said.

In other families dissatisfied with the quality of public or private schools, fathers may have less traditional jobs that allow them to work from home and share teaching duties, she said.

Whatever the reasons, Bauer said she has noticed more male faces in the crowd when she speaks at home-school conferences.

"There used to be no men at these conferences," Bauer said. "At the latest one I was at it was almost 50/50."

Peebles, a theology doctorate student in Chicago, stays home with Nicholas while his wife works. He sees nothing but benefits in his decision.

"I'm completely confident it's been a good thing. I have no second guessing at all," Peebles said. "I feel blessed that I've been able to be home with him more than most fathers have time to be with their kids."

Cultural considerations

Luis Oviles took three of his children out of private schools in the San Francisco area to teach them himself. Oviles schedules his job counseling troubled teens around his children's schoolwork.

"Many of the teachers are not well-trained to deal with multicultural children," said Oviles, who is Hispanic.

Oviles' wife helps with the basics, such as arithmetic, but leaves most of the teaching to him because she speaks limited English, he said. He also gets help from a homeschooling program run by the Laguna Salada Union School District in Pacifica, California.

"I think there's a real awakening going on," said Robert Ziegler, spokesman for the Home School Legal Defense Association. "As we continue to evaluate ourselves family by family, I think dads are saying, hey, there is a role for me."

Day 73

交通旅游类词汇

motorway /ˈməutəwei/ *n.* 高速公路
crossroad /ˈkrɔsrəud/ *n.* 立交桥
roundabout /ˈraundəbaut/ *n.* 街心转盘
traffic signs 道路标志信号
underground, tube, subway 地铁
excursion train 游览列车
platform ticket 站台票
registration /redʒiˈstreiʃ(ə)n/ *n.* 登记
yacht /jɔt/ *n.* 游船
first-class stateroom (cabin) 头等舱
tourist class 普通舱，经济舱
customs formalities 报关单
stewardess /stjuːəˈdes/ *n.* 空中小姐，女乘务员
pleasure trip 游览，漫游
business trip 商务旅行
organized tour 组团旅游
circular tour 环程旅行
excursion, outing 远足
expedition /ekspiˈdiʃ(ə)n/ *n.* 远征，探险
itinerary /aiˈtinərəri/ *n.* 旅行指南
travel agency 旅行社
traveller's cheque 旅行支票
luxury hotel 豪华饭店
residential hotel 公寓旅馆
check-out 结账
reservation /ˌrezəˈveiʃən/ *n.* 预定房间
label /leib(ə)t/ *n.* 行李标签
domestic service 国内航线
international service 国际航线

补充读物

Affordable to the Individual Space Flight

Affordable to the Private Individual Space Flight has been the dream of just about everyone who has ever wanted to travel into space. Its existence has been one of the basic assumptions of almost every major science fiction novel and movie ever produced.

The movie *2001* had a horizontal take-off, horizontal landing single stage spaceplane with Pan Am markings flying into Earth's orbit and docking with a large wheeled space station.

The *Star Wars* series of movies has both shuttlecraft and starships taking off from planetary surfaces with the ease and frequency of light planes from a local airport.

Babylon V also had many types of spacecraft built by many different species that all made that first step of getting off planet into a very common event.

Yet here we are, 30 years after the first manned landing on the Moon, struggling to launch the Space

Shuttle 6 times a year at $500 million per flight, and no one talks about making the development of Affordable to the Private Individual Space Flight a primary goal of NASA.

Why?

Sally Ride, America's first woman in space, once said, "Without a clear vision of the future we flounder in the present."

Based on the popularity of science fiction novels and movies, it is obvious that we have the dream but that we lack the vision to make it happen.

The solution to the problem appears to be twofold. As citizens of this planet, we need to make the development of Affordable to the Private Individual Space Flight a primary goal of our space program. In addition, we need a technically and economically believable concept that will give us Affordable to the Private Individual Space Flight once it is built.

This article is about one vision, based on today's technology, on how we can make Affordable to the Private Individual Space Flight a reality. It is a vision that has 10 + years of effort invested in it to determine if it is technically and economically feasible.

To date everything shows that it is.

It works due to a new concept in space transportation that makes use of a low cost reusable sub-orbital launch vehicle and an Earth Orbiting Elevator that can be built with today's materials. It is an evolutionary system that starts with a reusable first stage and expendable upper stage launch vehicle that launches satellites and astronauts into low Earth orbit. This is followed by the addition of the Earth Orbiting Elevator, which eliminates the small expendable upper stage from the system, making the launch vehicle into a Single Stage to Orbit vehicle when it flies to the bottom of the Earth Orbiting Elevator. The Earth Orbiting Elevator is the most important part of this concept. It is the heart and soul of the vision that makes all the other parts come together both technically and economically and makes space flight affordable to the private individual. Quite literally, it is our bridge to the rest of the Solar System and eventually the stars. Once it is built, the next step is how it will allow us to return to the Moon to stay and how this will further reduce the cost of living, working, and traveling in space by allowing us to start making use of Lunar resources. Once the Lunar base is in place the next step will be the building of an L-5 shipyard where Satellite Solar Power Stations, Space Colonies, and Mars Exploration/Colony ships will be built.

NASA representatives have described this concept as, "The first idea we have seen that offers a believable path to $100 per pound to low Earth orbit."

Day 74

自然科学类词汇

1 数学

theorem /ˈθiərəm/ *n.* 定理
calculation /kælkjuˈleiʃ(ə)n/ *n.* 计算
arithmetic /əˈriθmətik/ *n.* 算术,四则运算
addition /əˈdiʃ(ə)n/ *n.* 加法
subtraction /səbˈtrɔkʃ(ə)n/ *n.* 减法
multiplication /mʌltipliˈkeiʃ(ə)n/ *n.* 乘法
division /diˈviʒ(ə)n/ *n.* 除法
sum /sʌm/ *n.* 和
remainder /riˈmeində(r)/ *n.* 余
product /ˈprɔdʌkt/ *n.* 积
quotient /ˈkwəuʃənt/ *n.* 商
multiplicand /ˈmʌltipliˈkænd/ *n.* 被乘数
multiplier /ˈmʌltiplaiə(r)/ *n.* 乘数
divisor /diˈvaizə(r)/ *n.* 除数
dividend /dividend/ *n.* 被除数
decimal point 小数点
fraction /ˈfrækʃ(ə)n/ *n.* 分数
ratio /ˈreiʃiəu/ *n.* 比
proportion /prəˈpɔːʃ(ə)n/ *n.* 比例
numerator /ˈnjuːməreitə/ *n.* 分子
common denominator 公分母
exponent /eksˈpəunənt/ *n.* 指数
differential calculus 微分学
integral calculus 积分
function /ˈfʌŋkʃən/ *n.* 函数
derivative /diˈrivətiv/ *n.* 导数
power /ˈpauə/ *n.* 幂,乘方
x squared 某数的平方
square root 平方根
cube root 立方根
rule of three 比例法
logarithm /ˈlɔgəriθ(ə)m/ *n.* 对数
logarithm table 对数表
algebra /ˈældʒibrə/ *n.* 代数
equation /iˈkweiʃ(ə)n/ *n.* 等式,方程式
unknown /ʌnˈnəun/ *n.* 未知数
simple equation 一次方程
quadratic equation 二次方程
cubic equation 三次方程
plane geometry 平面几何
solid geometry 立体几何
circumference 圆周
radius /ˈreidiəs/ *n.* 半径
diameter /daiˈæmitə(r)/ *n.* 直径
parallel /ˈpærəlel/ *n.* 平行线
polygon /ˈpɔligɔn/ *n.* 多边形
equilateral triangle 等边三角形
isosceles triangle 等腰三角形
scalene triangle 不等边三角形
right-angled triangle 直角三角形
hypothenuse /haiˈpɔθinjuːz/ *n.* 斜边,弦
quadrilateral /kwɔdriˈlætər(ə)/ *n.* 四边形
rectangle /ˈrektæŋgl/ *n.* 矩形
trapezium /trəˈpiːziəm/ *n.* 斜方形
rhomb /rɔmb/ *n.* 菱形
rhombus /ˈrɔmbəs/ *n.* 菱形
ellipse /iˈlips/ *n.* 椭圆
acute angle 锐角
right angle 直角
obtuse angle 钝角
sphere /sfiə(r)/ *n.* 球体
cylinder /ˈsilində(r)/ *n.* 圆柱体
cone /kəun/ *n.* 锥体
pyramid /ˈpirəmid/ *n.* 棱锥

prism /ˈpriz(ə)m/ *n.* 棱柱
frustum /ˈfrʌstəm/ *n.* 截锥
rectangular, **right-angled** 直角的
infinity /inˈfiniti/ *n.* 无限大

2 物理学,化学

matter /ˈmætə(r)/ *n.* 物质
vacuum /ˈvækjuəm/ *n.* 真空
liquid /ˈlikwid/ *n.* 液体
mass /mæs/ *n.* 质量
density /ˈdensiti/ *n.* 密度
intensity /inˈtensiti/ *n.* 强度
friction /ˈfriction/ *n.* 摩擦力
vector /ˈvektə(r)/ *n.* 矢量,向量
conductor /kənˈdʌktə(r)/ *n.* 导体
quantum theory 量子论
dynamics /daiˈnæmiks/ *n.* 动力学
kinetics /kiˈnetiks/ *n.* 动力学
kinematics /kiniˈmætiks/ *n.* 运动学
statics /ˈstætiks/ *n.* 静力学
metalloid /ˈmetəlɔid/ *n.* 非金属
Barium(Ba) /ˈbeəriəm/ *n.* 钡
Calcium(Ca) /ˈkælsiəm/ *n.* 钙
Carbon(C) /ˈkɑːbən/ *n.* 碳
Chlorine(Cl) /ˈklɔːriːn/ *n.* 氯
Copper(Cu) /ˈkɔpə(r)/ *n.* 铜
Fluorine(F) /ˈfluəriːn/ *n.* 氟
Helium(He) /ˈhiːliəm/ *n.* 氦
Hydrogen(H) /ˈhaidrədʒ(ə)n/ *n.* 氢
Iodine(I) /ˈaiədiːn/ *n.* 碘
Lead(Pb) /liːd/ *n.* 铅
Magnesium(Mg) /mægˈniːziəm/ *n.* 镁
Manganese(Mn) /ˈmæŋgəniːz/ *n.* 锰
Mercury(Hg) /ˈmɜːkjuri/ *n.* 汞
Nitrogen(N) /ˈnaitrədʒ(ə)n/ *n.* 氮
Oxygen(O) /ˈɔksidʒ(ə)n/ *n.* 氧
Phosphorus(P) /ˈfɔsfərəs/ *n.* 磷
Potassium(K) /pəˈtæsiəm/ *n.* 钾
Selenium(Se) /siˈliːniəm/ *n.* 硒
Silicon(Si) /ˈsilikən/ *n.* 硅
Sodium(Na) /ˈsəudiəm/ *n.* 钠
Sulphur(S) /ˈsʌlfə/ *n.* 硫
Tin(Sn) /tin/ *n.* 锡
Uranium(U) /juəˈreiniəm/ *n.* 铀
organic chemistry 有机化学
inorganic chemistry 无机化学
acid /ˈæsid/ *n.* 酸
alkali /ˈælkəlai/ *n.* 碱,强碱
hydrate /ˈhaidreit/ *n.* 水合物
hydroxide /haiˈdrɔksaid/ *n.* 氢氧化物,羟化物
hydrocarbon /haidrəuˈkɑːbən/ *n.* 碳氢化合物,羟
oxide /ˈɔksaid/ *n.* 氧化物
methane /ˈmiːθein/ *n.* 甲烷,沼气
ester /ˈestə(r)/ *n.* 酯
analysis /əˈnæləsis/ *n.* 分解
endothermic reaction 吸热反应
exothermic reaction 放热反应
precipitation /prisipiˈteiʃ(ə)n/ *n.* 沉淀
to neutralize 中和
combustion /kəmˈbʌstʃ(ə)n/ *n.* 燃烧
synthesis /ˈsinθisis/ *n.* 合成
litmus paper 石蕊试纸
graduate, **graduated flask** 量筒,量杯
reagent /riːeidʒənt/ *n.* 试剂
crucible pot, **melting pot** 坩埚

其他

economic geography 经济地理
cosmology /kɔzˈmɔlədʒi/ *n.* 宇宙论
oceanography /əuʃəˈnɔgrəfi/ *n.* 海洋学
meteorology /miːtiəˈrɔlədʒi/ *n.* 气象学
vegetation /redʒiˈteiʃ(ə)n/ *n.* 植被
relief /riˈliːf/ *n.* 地形,地貌
continent /ˈkɔntinənt/ *n.* 大陆
archipelago /ɑːkiˈpeligəu/ *n.* 群岛
peninsula /pəˈninsjulə/ *n.* 半岛
marsh, **bog**, **swamp** 沼泽
oasis /əuˈeisis/ *n.* 绿洲
virgin forest 原始森林
meadow /ˈmedəu/ *n.* 草甸
prairie /ˈpreəri/ *n.* 大草原
land reform, **agrarian reform** 土地改革
mechanization of farming 农业机械化
agronomist /əˈgrɔnəmist/ *n.* 农学家
horticulture /ˈhɔːtikʌltʃə(r)/ *n.* 园艺
multistage rocket 多级火箭

Telstar /ˈtelstɑː(r)/ *n.* 通信卫星
antenna /ænˈtenə/ *n.* 天线
spacecraft /ˈspeiskrɑːft/ *n.* 航天器
lunar module 登月舱
astronaut /ˈæstənɔːt/ *n.* 航天员
cosmos /ˈkɔzmɔs/ *n.* 宇宙
cosmography /kɔzˈmɔgrəfi/ *n.* 宇宙结构学
cosmogony /kɔzˈmɔgəni/ *n.* 宇宙起源学
shooting star 流星
polestar /ˈpəulˌstɑː/ *n.* 北极星
comet /ˈkɔmit/ *n.* 彗星
constellation /kɔnstəˈleiʃ(ə)n/ *n.* 星座
galaxy /ˈgæləksi/ *n.* 星系
Milky Way 银河
equator /iˈkweitə(r)/ *n.* 赤道
solar system 太阳系

补充读物

(1)地理

Great Rivers of the Ocean

Picture the ocean and you probably imagine waves racing across the surface and tides surging around the coast. But the real action is less visible. Vast currents, like giant rivers, flow throughout the seas driven by differences in temperature and salt concentration. For instance, the Gulf Stream discharges around 30 million tonnes of water every second, compared with just one million for all the world's rivers combined.

These giant currents transport so much heat around the globe that they play a critical role in shaping the Earth's climate. Compare the freezing Labrador Coast of Canada to the south-western tip of Britain, although they are on the same latitude, in Cornwall, thanks to warm ocean currents, palm trees grow and frosts are rare.

Our urgent need to unravel the complicated mechanisms of climate and global warming makes forming a clear picture of ocean circulation vital. Although surface currents are relatively straightforward to monitor, studying the deep seas is far more problematic. At the immense depths and pressures near the ocean floor, sea water rapidly corrodes and destroys instruments making work expensive and slow.

Only now are scientists piecing together the parts of the ocean-circulation puzzle at low and intermediate depths. This means they are beginning to appreciate the sea's inextricable link with present and past climate, which, hopefully, will help them predict our planet's future.

Closing the circuit

Oceanographers call these deep-sea currents collectively the 'thermohaline circulation' — *thermo* meaning heat and *haline* meaning saltiness. Heat and salt change the density of water. Colder, saltier water plummets to the bottom of the ocean whereas warmer, fresher water rises. Areas of oceans where cold salty water predominates are called 'sinks', those dominated by warm, less salty water are dubbed 'upwellings'.

The Earth's biggest ocean sinks are in the North Atlantic: the Labrador and Greenland seas. Here, frigid polar air-cools the surface of the sea beyond freezing point, which raises its density. Sea ice grows leaving behind salt, further increasing the salinity of the remaining water. The very dense water that is left plummets into the depths — dramatically named the 'abyssal ocean'.

As polar water sinks, warmer water is drawn in from the south to take its place, creating a current flowing across the Atlantic from south to north. This flow, powered by tropical Caribbean winds, is the Gulf Stream, which adds around 20% more warmth to the heat from northern Europe's winter sun.

Meanwhile, the cold, dense water locked into the deep ocean flows along the bed of the Atlantic from north to south, balancing the surface current. It travels as far Antarctica, where it joins the 'Southern Ocean Raceway' — a complex of currents that circumnavigates the South Pole, knitting together the Atlantic, Pacific and Indian oceans.

The Pacific and Indian Oceans also play their part in the thermohaline circulation. They have little or no ice formation, and therefore no source of abyssal waters, but differences in rainfall and temperature mean that there are large flows in and out of their basins via the Southern Ocean.

What goes down must come up

Although the vast sinking of dense waters in the north and around Antarctica ought to be balanced by an upwelling, there are no large upwellings on the scale of the North Atlantic sinks. Instead the abyssal water returns to the surface by gradual mixing and turbulence.

However, like weather systems, bodies of water retain their identity when they move past each other, even when they only have tiny differences in temperature and salinity. Forcing different masses of water to combine requires a lot of energy — the puzzle is where this energy comes from.

The answer, Gary Egbert of Oregon State University announced last year, is the Moon. By scrutinizing tidal movement from satellites, Egbert found that around a third of the energy that the Moon supplies to the sea goes into the deep ocean. This propels water over the rough ocean floor, causing turbulence and mixing. Thus, water that would otherwise be locked on the seabed can return to the upper layers, completing the cycle.

Before Egbert's observation, oceanographers had always believed that the energy put into the sea by the Moon — some three terawatts, enough to illuminate 50,000 million light bulbs — is dissipated in shallow waters by the tides.

Currents past and future

However the true picture is far more complex than this simple sketch, with a web of smaller inter-dependent currents joining the main circulation. Researchers have pieced together a surprisingly intricate system of oceanic circulation that can be used in the increasingly robust computer models of the ocean-atmosphere system.

But it is the variability of ocean currents over long periods of time that holds the biggest implications for climate. Have the currents always looked like this? If they were different, then how and why were they?

Fortunately, some of the answers are lying on the seabed in the form of tiny, Dead Sea creatures called 'foraminifera'. Dig deeper to older foraminifera layers and you can build up a picture of the ocean currents over many years.

In 1999 Jean Lynch-Stieglitz of the Lamont-Doherty Earth Observatory, Palisades, New York, analysed foraminifera shells from the Caribbean and estimated the density of the water at the time the animals died from the thickness of their shells. From this, her team calculated the approximate temperature, and thence the flow, of the Gulf Stream at the time.

Lynch-Stieglitz' team uncovered a very different circulation pattern from today's. During the last Ice Age, some 12,000 years ago, the deep-water current transported far less water than it does today. Indeed the sinking of dense water at the Poles may have stopped entirely.

So there appear to be at least two stable patterns of circulation in the world's oceans, one associated with ice ages and the other similar to the present day. Unfortunately it is not yet clear is what triggers the shift from one circulation pattern to another. Changing from the current pattern to the glacial circulation mode is one of the most potentially worrying aspects of climate shifts: it could plunge the planet into another ice age.

(摘自 www.nature.com)

(2)自然

Nosy Neighbors

Nosiness isn't nice. But in the past few years, behavioral biologists have shown the trait in a more positive and intriguing light. Animals from fish to songbirds, they have found, can achieve success by keeping watch on their neighbors' social lives. Such eavesdropping may also be woven into the fabric of human societies — and might even help to explain why people often behave charitably.

Prying animals reap significant rewards. They know when to pick a fight and when to back down; who to mate with, and who to cuckold. Not surprisingly, perhaps, researchers have also found that animals behave differently depending on who is watching or listening. Animal communication, experts are coming to realize, has evolved to fit into a social network, rather than being a collection of signals intended simply to impress a particular mate or rival.

Eavesdropping shows "how incredibly subtle animal strategies are", says evolutionary biologist Lee Dugatkin of the University of Louisville in Kentucky. This subtlety explains why it went unnoticed until recently — it's tricky to design experiments to tease out the effects on one animal of watching other animals interact. Peter McGregor, a behavioural ecologist at the University of Copenhagen in Denmark, suggests that researchers may also have neglected such experiments because they underestimated animals' cunning. "For most people, fish don't rate when it comes to cognitive abilities." he observes.

Yet McGregor's team has shown that Siamese fighting fish possess considerable social nous. Males of this famously aggressive species defend their territories with displays of fin waving and gill-raising. But if this doesn't settle matters, things turn physical — sometimes fatally so.

Like human boxers, Siamese fighting fish study their opponents' previous bouts. Males pay more attention to their neighbors when they fight than at other times, McGregor and his colleagues found. And after viewing such contests, males approach the winners more warily than they do the losers, relying more on visual displays and less on biting.

Verbal abuse

Some researchers have questioned whether such experiments prove that bystanders scrutinize the interaction between opponents — they might be responding to the animals' inherent toughness or weediness. McGregor's team tackled this issue in great tits by using recordings of the birds' songs. To a male great tit, victory is a question of timing. A male threatens a rival by singing over his song, and shows deference by singing only in the gaps between the other's choruses. This allowed the researchers to use the same songs, regardless of any intrinsic property they might have, to denote attack or defense, belligerence or tact.

Setting up two loudspeakers outside a male's territory, the researchers played out duets of differing structures and outcomes. They then moved either the winning or losing speaker into the bird's territory, and noted his reaction. Males sang less to losers, perhaps because they regard them as less of a threat, or perhaps because they are more ready to escalate contests with losers to visual displays or violence. A winner got the same cautious treatment as a stranger.

Playback experiments with nightingales yield similar results — except that males intensify their singing towards winners, rather than giving losers the silent treatment. Again, it is hard to know whether the differences reflect a more, or less, aggressive response. "The interpretation can go into hand-waving," McGregor admits. But in each case, it is clear that eavesdropping influences the animals' subsequent behavior.

Watching a fight also changes physiology. Cichlid fish that see a contest experience a rush of testosterone, perhaps priming them to fight. Dugatkin believes that the next challenge is to integrate behavioral and physiological data on eavesdropping. "There are very few studies looking at the physiology and behavior of one system," he says. "I think that synthesis is going to happen soon."

Males are not the only ones noting the results of their neighbors' squabbles — females use the same information to help them to choose their mates. Again using song playback, McGregor's team escalated contests with some male great tits, while backing down against those on neighboring territories. Subsequently, the mates of defeated males were more likely to visit the adjacent territory. Seemingly disenchanted with their partner — but impressed by what they heard coming from next door — the females were presumably seeking what behavioral ecologists call 'extra-pair copulations'.

Experiments on a closely related species lend support to this idea. Daniel Mennill of Queen's University in Kingston, Ontario, and his colleagues picked playback fights with male black-capped chickadees, and then analyzed the DNA of the chicks born to their mates. The researchers found that the female partners of defeated males were about five times more likely to lay eggs fertilized by other males, compared with females who never heard their partner get beaten.

Covert struggle

With such high stakes, it is likely that eavesdroppers have shaped the evolution of animal communication. Some behaviors seem adapted to avoid prying ears. In many songbirds, says Mennill, the longest, most evenly matched song duels are the quietest. Where both males are struggling to dominate, he suggests, "they might not want to broadcast what's going on".

The effect of an audience on animals' social interactions is harder to study than eavesdropping, and this work is at an early stage. Again working with fighting fish, McGregor's team has found that males display to each other differently when a female is watching. They reduce their aggression, and switch to conspicuous displays incorporating some of the elements used in courting, such as tail waving. And in July, Michael Kidd of the University of New Hampshire in Durham told the Animal Behavior Society's annual meeting at Indiana University in Bloomington that defeated male fighting fish prefer to court females that didn't witness their humiliation.

Eavesdropping is thought to help animals to avoid fights they cannot win. But paradoxically, eavesdroppers might make contests more aggressive, according to evolutionary biologist Rufus Johnstone of the University of Cambridge, UK. He used game theory to analyse the costs and benefits of winning and losing fights, and of backing down quickly versus a prolonged tussle. Eavesdroppers, he found, increase the value of victory: an animal that wins its current contest will get the deterrent benefit of a tough-guy reputation, and so is more likely to escalate a fight.

Replace acts of violence with ones of charity, and Johnstone's model becomes similar to those used to explain apparently selfless kindness. We often help people we are unlikely to meet again. One reason might be that good deeds get their perpetrator a glowing reputation that helps them in the future. Theoretical models suggest that altruism can survive in populations where individuals trust those they have seen cooperate with others, but give nothing to those they have seen behave selfishly.

Research by Manfred Milinski, a behavioral ecologist at the Max Planck Institute for Limnology in Plön, Germany, and his colleagues supports this idea. In one experiment, volunteers were given money and told they could donate some of it to the other participants over a series of rounds. This benefited the recipients more than the donors, because the experimenters supplemented each donation. Even though participants could not donate to someone who had given to them, they were more generous towards those who they had seen give to others. In another game, Milinski found that people were more likely to contribute to a public fund if their enhanced reputation could be used to attract private donations from other players.

The behavioral science of eavesdropping might soon be tested in the human social marketplace. Milinski's research has attracted the attention of managers trying to control demands on Germany's health service. He suggests that doctors could publish lists of how many treatments they have prescribed and how much each has cost. Even without naming names, Milinski argues, people might be so concerned about gaining a bad reputation that they will be shamed out of seeking needless medical attention. "If peoples' reputation is at stake they are much more cooperative." he says.

(摘自 *www.nature.com*)

Note 前事不忘后事之师 *Remember the past and it will guide your future.*

Day 75

计算机类词汇

access time 存取时间
alphanumeric /ælfənjuːˈmerik/ *adj.* 字母数字的
analog computer 模拟计算机
analyst /ˈænəlist/ *n.* 分析员
area /ˈeəriə/ *n.* 区域
array /əˈrei/ *n.* 数组，阵列
assembler /əˈsemblə(r)/ *n.* 汇编程序
automation /ɔːtəˈmeiʃ(ə)n/ *n.* 自动化
band /bænd/ *n.* 区
binary digit 二进制位，二进制数字
buffer storage 缓冲存储器
calculator /ˈkælkjuleitə(r)/ *n.* 计算器
character /ˈkæriktə(r)/ *n.* 字符
circuit /ˈsəːkit/ *n.* 电路，线路
to clear 清除，清零
to code 编码
command /kəˈmɑːnd/ *n.* 指令，命令
compiler /kəmˈpailə(r)/ *n.* 编译程序
computer language 计算机语言
counter /ˈkautə/ *n.* 计数器
data /ˈdeitə/ *n.* 数据
data processing 数据处理
debugging /diːˈbʌgiŋ/ *n.* 调试
digital computer 数字计算机
disc, disk 磁盘
display unit 显示装置
to edit 编辑
electronics /ilekˈtrɔniks/ *n.* 电子学
to encode 编码
feedback /ˈfiːdbæk/ *n.* 反馈
file /fail/ *n.* 文件
floppy disk 软磁盘
hardware /ˈhɑːdweə/ *n.* 硬件
index /ˈindeks/ *n.* 索引
information /infəˈmeiʃ(ə)n/ *n.* 信息
inline processing 内处理
input /ˈinput/ *n.* 输入
instruction /inˈstrʌkʃ(ə)n/ *n.* 指令
integrated circuit 集成电路
keyboard /ˈkiːbɔːd/ *n.* 键盘
latency time 等待时间
library /ˈlaibrəri/ *n.* 库，程序库
linkage /ˈliŋkidʒ/ *n.* 连接
to load 装入，寄存，写入，加载
logger /ˈlɔgə(r)/ *n.* 登记器，记录器
machine language 机器语言
magnetic storage 磁存储器
matrix /ˈmeitriks/ *n.* 矩阵
memory /ˈmeməri/ *n.* 存储器
microcomputer /ˈmaikrəukəmpjuːtə(r)/ *n.* 微型计算机
module /ˈmɔdjuːl/ *n.* 组件，模块
monitor /ˈmɔnitə(r)/ *n.* 监视器，监督程序，管程
network /ˈnetwəːk/ *n.* 网络，网
operator /ˈɔpəreitə(r)/ *n.* 操作员
optical character reader 光符阅读机
optical scanner 光扫描器
output /ˈautput/ *n.* 输出
overflow /əuvəˈfləu/ *n.* 溢出，上溢
panel /ˈpæn(ə)l/ *n.* 平板
parameter /pəˈræmitə(r)/ *n.* 参数，参量
perforator /ˈpəːfəreitə/ *n.* 穿孔机

peripheral equipment 外围设备,外部设备
personal computer 个人计算机
printed circuit 印制电路
printer /ˈprintə(r)/ *n.* 打印机
printout /ˈprintˌaut/ *n.* 打印输出
to process 处理
processing unit 处理部件
program /ˈprəugræm/ *n.* 程序
pulse /pʌls/ *n.* 脉冲
punch /pʌntʃ/ *n.* 穿孔
random access 随机存取
reader /ˈriːdə(r)/ *n.* 阅读程序
real time 实时
record, register 记录
redundancy /riˈdʌndənsi/ *n.* 冗余
routine /ruːˈtiːn/ *n.* 例行程序
sentinel /ˈsentin(ə)l/ *n.* 标记
sequence /ˈsiːkwəns/ *n.* 序列,顺序
signal /ˈsignl/ *n.* 信号
simulation /simjuˈleiʃ(ə)n/ *n.* 模拟
software /ˈsɔftweə(r)/ *n.* 软件,软设备
storage /ˈstɔːridʒ/ *n.* 存储器
subroutine, subprogram 子程序
switch /switʃ/ *n.* 开关
symbolic language 符号语言
system /ˈsistəm/ *n.* 系统
teleprinter /ˈteliprintə(r)/ *n.* 电传打字机
terminal unit 终端设备
to update 更新
working storage 工作存储器

补充读物

Home networks: A couch potato's dream

Endeavoring to create the consumer entertainment system that does it all, computer companies are battling gadget makers for control of what can best be described as the home's digital nerve center.

It's where stray digital media files — music, video, family photos — are stored and catalogued for delivery anywhere we want them: the bedroom computer, the living room television, the kitchen radio.

"People want their Sony Net MD (minidisc player) to talk to their TiVo, to talk to their Nomad MP3 jukebox," said Richard Doherty of the Envisioneering Group, which evaluates technology. "It's been talked about for 10 years."

What's on the horizon?

Devices announced at the recent International Consumer Electronics Show that should hit the market this year blend the storage and networking capability of a computer server with the TV recording and time-shifting ability of a TiVo.

They add the ability to play and arrange CDs and MP3 music files alongside digital photos, DVDs and digital video files.

And they can download any of the above from the Internet, sometimes automatically, by programming them to record selections on broadcast schedules of television and radio stations.

"It's the holy grail," said Tim Bajarin, president of technology consulting firm Creative Strategies.

"The consumer electronics guys ask, 'Can you build a box that sits next to the TV that can manage the digital entertainment experience?'" Bajarin said. "And the computer guys are trying to get to the heart of the consumer entertainment experience. They all want to own the digital living room."

Sending and getting data

Wireless networking is key. Every device that can send and receive data through the air adds another node to the network, without adding to a rat's nest of cables.

As yet, no device performs all these requirements. Several are close.

Leading the pack is the PC crowd: Microsoft Corp., Gateway, Hewlett-Packard, ViewSonic and others. Their

Media Center PCs, launched in the fall, can play and record TV programs, storing them on hard drives as large as 120 gigabytes. The machines can be operated by a keyboard or a remote control and networked with a TV.

The big consumer electronics players are firing back with their own vision. Sony, Panasonic, RCA and others say the network itself should be the centerpiece, not the PC.

"For now, the PC has the edge," Bajarin said. "A full PC is extremely versatile. It can manage pictures, audio and video and can sit at the center of a network. The problem is, it doesn't interact with the TV well."

Who has an edge?

That's where the consumer electronics companies have the edge.

Sony president Kunitake Ando unveiled a Linux-based personal video recorder with a 160 GB hard drive called CoCoon at the CES show. CoCoon, released in November in Japan, uses alwayson Internet and cable connections to surf for video and music that match the owner's tastes. If CoCoon gets it wrong, it apologizes.

Sony hasn't said when the machine will arrive in North America.

Ando also displayed a Sony Vaio PC that can record and play TV programs, and, with the company's forthcoming RoomLink receiver, can stream the programs wirelessly to a TV.

Samsung said it would release by 2004 its Home AV Center system, which could handle many of the same functions. And Panasonic demonstrated its own home networking system, dubbed One, a TV-centric hard-drive server. The company hasn't said when it will be released.

Philips, SONICblue, Toshiba, Hewlett-Packard and other companies offered networking DVD player-recorders, some with hard drives as large as 80 GB, that can connect to the Internet as well as link a home TV to a PC. Some even let a couch potato dig into his computer media files by clicking a TV remote.

New players getting attention

Even makers of high-end stereo components are getting into the act. Escient's Fireball music servers can store entire collections digitally, piping everything from CD music to Internet radio to separate receivers throughout the house.

And then there's SnapStream's Personal Video Station 3.0, a clever piece of TV recording software that gives a personal computer most of the capabilities of a TiVo for just $50. The software, set to emerge in February, requires a fast computer with a big hard drive.

All such video recording capabilities are beset by yet-undefined concerns over violating copyrights, especially if the copied movies or songs are shared outside the home. Most current devices prevent such sharing. SONICblue's Replay TV is one of the few that allows it.

Even kitchen appliances are getting networked. Tonight's Menu, an appliance maker near Cleveland, displayed its $2,000 Intelligent Oven, which refrigerates food until an Internet command tells it to start cooking.

Vegetating longer on couches

For the next three to five years, the do-it-all home "gateway" will be a top goal — perhaps the top goal — of competing consumer electronics and PC manufacturers, Bajarin said.

As to whether home networks encourage folks to vegetate longer on their couches, some argue the opposite, saying they help users avoid time-wasting commercials and bland entertainment.

"A bunch of us will still be couch potatoes, but we'll be happier couch potatoes." said Rob Enderle, an analyst with Giga Information Group.

(摘自 *www.cnn.com*)

Day 76

艺术类词汇

masterpiece /ˈmɑːstəpiːs/ *n.* 杰作
plastic arts 造型艺术
graphic arts 形象艺术
salon /ˈsælɔn/ *n.* 沙龙
inspiration /inspiˈreiʃ(ə)n/ *n.* 灵感,启发
Gothic /ˈgɔθik/ *n.* 哥特式
classicism /ˈklæsisiz(ə)m/ *n.* 古典主义,古典风格
romanticism /rəuˈmæntisiz(ə)m/ *n.* 浪漫主义
realism /ˈriːəliz(ə)m/ *n.* 现实主义
symbolism /ˈsimbəliz(ə)m/ *n.* 象征主义
impressionism /imˈpreʃəniz(ə)m/ *n.* 印象主义
Art Nouveau 新艺术主义
expressionism /ikˈspreʃəniz(ə)m/ *n.* 表现主义
fauvism /ˈfəuvizəm/ *n.* 野兽派
abstract art 抽象派, 抽象主义
cubism /ˈkjuːbiz(ə)m/ *n.* 立体派, 立体主义
dadaism /ˈdɑːdəizəm/ *n.* 达达主义
surrealism /səˈriəliz(ə)m/ *n.* 超现实主义
naturalism /ˈnætʃərəliz(ə)m/ *n.* 自然主义
existentialism /egziˈstenʃəliz(ə)m/ *n.* 存在主义
contemporary literature 现代文学
reportage /repɔːˈtɑːʒ/ *n.* 报告文学
criticism /ˈkritisiz(ə)m/ *n.* 评论
composition /kɔmpəˈziʃ(ə)n/ *n.* 学术著作
criticism /ˈkritisiz(ə)m/ *n.* 批判主义
eloquence /ˈeləkwəns/ *n.* 文才
wash /wɔʃ/ *n.* 水墨画
tracing /ˈtreisiŋ/ *n.* 临摹
caricature /kærikəˈtjuə(r)/ *n.* 漫画
sculptor /ˈskʌlptə(r)/ *n.* 雕塑学
architecture /ˈɑːkitektʃə(r)/ *n.* 建筑学
monument /ˈmɔnjumənt/ *n.* 纪念碑
temple /ˈtemp(ə)/ *n.* 庙宇
basilica /bəˈzilikə/ *n.* 皇宫,教堂
cathedral /kəˈθiːdr(ə)l/ *n.* 大教堂

补充读物

Paying Attention to Youth Culture

Three provocative books challenge our concept of youth ministry and question our capacity to transmit the faith across generations. In Youth Leadership Josephine Long and Carl I. Fertman take up a topic that many churches, schools and other youth-serving organizations have ignored since the late 1960s. Long, director of the Leadership Development Network at the University of Pittsburgh, and Fertman, executive director of the Maximizing Adolescent Potentials Program at the University of Pittsburgh, explore patterns of leadership in teenagers and examine how leadership is nurtured.

The authors frame the discussion with two theoretical perspectives. The first is that of developmental psychology, an approach that dominates the literature on youth ministry. Drawing on the insights of Erik Erikson, Carol Gilligan and others, Long and Fertman note that while young people begin to engage in leadership at a very young age, their involvement intensifies rapidly as they move into the teenage years. They are busy acquiring information about leadership and forming attitudes toward leadership in these years. They learn to communicate, make decisions and manage leadership roles. The authors identify three distinctive stages in this effort: awareness, in which youth self-consciously begin to identify ways to function as leaders in various social contexts; interaction, in which they explore and test their growing knowledge and skills of leadership; and mastery, when they begin to develop a vision of themselves as leaders and take responsibility for preparing to be leaders.

Long and Fertman's second theoretical perspective is drawn from the research of E. P. Hollander, J. M. Burns and J. V. Downton, which emphasizes leadership as "transactions or exchanges" that take place between the leader and the one who is led, as well as the transformation of "self-interests for the good of the group, organization or society." The transactions are the skills and tasks associated with leadership, while the transformation of self-interests describes the act of leadership itself. From these two perspectives, the authors locate the impetus to leadership in the developing capacities of teenagers, who respond to the situations in which they find themselves and practice leadership.

The task of developing youth leaders is a matter of creating environments that will nurture capacities for leadership. This changes the role of adult leaders. Instead of *teaching* people to be leaders, they are to *nurture* their potential for leadership. Parents become partners to youth leadership efforts, while teachers and other adults "support," "empower" and "facilitate" their developing capacities.

The authors suggest ways to create these conditions and give examples of leadership-nurturing environments. They challenge the value of youth ministries that don't meet these conditions, including those that isolate teenagers from children and adults in the congregation, those that emphasize entertainment, and those that prefer charismatic adults who direct youth over adults who nurture youth capacities.

The youth in *Youth Leadership* are familiar to most church people. They are active in school and community, live at home with at least one parent and accept the basic values and perspectives of society's dominant social institutions.

We are not familiar, however, with the young people we encounter in *Cold New World*. William Finnegan introduces us to disenfranchised young people whose families seem overwhelmed. Schools do not hold these young people's attention. Their skills do not translate into success in the job market. With the exception of some rural African-American youth, these youths find the institutional church irrelevant. Yet many of the deepest issues of their lives are inherently religious, especially when they are trying to make some sense out of the violence and hostility they experience.

Finnegan presents the lives of African-American young people in a New Haven neighborhood through the eyes of a teenage drug dealer. He presents Mexican-American youth in Washington State who struggle with the experience of immigration, and white supremacist Anglo-American youth in the Los Angeles suburbs. All of these youth are experiencing the downward economic movement of their families; all of them have had repeated encounters with direct, overt and systemic violence.

Finnegan researched this book by living with these young people. He ate with them, attended their gatherings, interviewed family members and community, business and school leaders who touched their lives. He returned to visit the youths over the course of his research, and on several occasions intervened in their lives.

Despite the grimness and violence of their stories, the youth reveal their resilience and their capacity for tenderness and compassion. I found myself hoping that these young people would find a way to improve their situation, give some socially acceptable response or find enough institutional or personal support to escape the downward spiral of their lives. It does not happen. Their environments do not contain the resources to alter this tragic course. And most of our congregations are unaware of or inattentive to their quests for meaning and place.

The young people in *Virtual Faith* represent another group that has had little contact with the church — GenXers, or those middle-class, educationally successful young people born between 1961 and 1981. This book is a generational autobiography of their quest for religious meaning. According to Tom Beaudoin, a GenXer and theology student, the distinguishing feature of the GenX experience is the influence of the images and values of television and popular music.

Wade Clark Roof observes that Beaudoin "takes us on a romping, eye-opening voyage through GenX culture — its music, its fashion, its imagery, its spiritual quests." Many readers will consider that culture to be not only irreverent, but sacrilegious. It turns the authority of tradition upside down, relativizes religious imagery and symbols, and celebrates theological ambiguity. Beaudoin contends that unlike previous generations of students and young adults, who contested secular culture with critiques found in religious tradition (Beaudoin's mentor Harvey Cox would be one good example), he and his peers embrace pop culture as the primary source of and catalyst to faith. They then turn to religious traditions to confirm, support and energize symbols and myths.

Beaudoin models the "ministry imagination" he espouses by leaping back and forth between the religious themes of an MTV clip and the exegesis of a biblical passage. This, he says, is the GenXer's way of nurturing "virtual faith." By this term he means that "Xers live religiously in real ways (involving real faith, real practice and a real spiritual journey)," while simultaneously imitating "real faith and real practice, simulating what they expect institutional religion and real religiousness to be." They want both the "real thing" and an "imitation" of the real thing — the "genuine and the posture, the authentic and the artificial."

The GenXer is suspicious of institutions, especially religious institutions. He focuses on personal experience in the spiritual quest, and on a sense of suffering expressed in a psychological and spiritual crisis of meaning. The GenXer also accepts the ambiguity that may be found in the fusion of sacred and profane, spiritual and sensual, orthodox and blasphemous in popular culture. He does not reject or dismiss faith tradition or religious institutions, but they are not the only sources of spirituality. The implications are clear: If traditional Christianity is to engage the spiritual quest of the GenXer, it must attend to the ways in which these young adults draw on the church and popular culture.

Read together, the three books suggest that the range and diversity of youth and young adult experience in the U.S. is much broader and more diverse than is evident in most congregational ministries. The labels we use — "youth culture," the "silent generation" of my own college years, or "GenXer" — do not describe the experience of many youth and young adults. The teenagers in *Youth Leadership* and the GenXers in *Virtual Faith* have possibilities that are distant to the young people in *Cold New World.* While the racism and classism that weigh heavily on Finnegan's youth may represent intellectual or political issues for some of Beaudoin's GenXers, it hardly catches the attention of the youth that Long and Fertman describe. The teenagers they describe do not share the suspicion or disregard of institutions — including the church — that is found among GenXers and the disenfranchised young people in *Cold New World.* The traditional values, symbols and practices that provide the context for nurturing youth leadership for Long and Fertman function only as backdrop for the imaginative reconstructions of pop culture undertaken by Beaudoin's peers, and they may generate negative self-images for Finnegan's youth.

Our lack of attention to the range and diversity of the experience of youth and young adults inevitably limits our capacity to speak truthfully and faithfully to these people. Consequently, many simply do not find a welcoming place in the congregation.

We have left the task of defining what it means to be a youth to the youth themselves. As a result, they are picking and choosing images, symbols and values from media, religious and other social institutions, as they try to produce meaning for and give shape to their lives. In this process, the church becomes another boutique in the shopping mall of options for personal and group identity.

We have also abandoned the notion of the interdependence of the generations in congregational life. Few adults see themselves engaged in a communal effort to sponsor, nurture and mentor young people. Indeed, few pastors identify this as a central role in their ministry.

A 1984 study found that few teenagers in an affluent suburban high school had an adult — other than their parents — with whom they could discuss important matters. Another study found that 70 percent of high school students are "generally ignored and poorly served" — i.e., "unspecial" in the system. Adults are certainly present in the lives of young people. But the well-intentioned parents, grandparents, teachers and social workers in Cold New World are unable to create environments that nurture socially acceptable norms and practices; meanwhile, many of the parents described by Finnegan and Beaudoin acquiesce to the dominant role of television and media in their children's lives.

Mentoring in youth ministry tends to be individualistic rather than communal or strategic. Youth ministry literature has not yet challenged the practice of letting youth ministries be directed by adults. Long and Fertman need to emphasize the reciprocity of youth and adults — of possibility and experience, imaginative exploration and wise reflection — in the leadership development of the group or community. Youth need to be viewed as full members, and challenged accordingly

The churches need critical perspective on the influence of contemporary media and the values of consumer capitalism. The authors of these three works document the pervasiveness of consumer capitalism and media in defining the young people's experience. These forces may take diverse forms: the market economy of the "drug culture" and the appeal of the violence in the "media culture" in Finnegan's study, the MTV "pop culture" for Beaudoin's GenXer, or the middle-class values implicit in the patterns of leadership promoted by Long and Fertman. Common in each book are themes of individualism, competition, ambition and success, and consumption.

Fashion, entertainment and possessions are identity markers for the youth in all these books — although the object of consumption varies. The youth of *Cold New World* may have little vision of their participation in a democratic society, but they certainly do see themselves as full participants in a consumer culture. The "irreverent spirituality" of Beaudoin's GenXers more easily aligns itself with Newt Gingrich's anti-institutional vision of economic well-being than with the ecological visions of justice and stewardship of the earth.

（摘自 *www.edu.org*）

Day 77

医药卫生类词汇

psychiatrist /saiˈkaiətrist/ *n.* 精神病学专家
surgeon /ˈsəːdʒ(ə)n/ *n.* 外科医师
wholesome /ˈhəulsəm/ *adj.* 合乎卫生的，有益于健康的
hygiene /ˈhaidʒiːn/ *n.* 卫生
ailment, complaint 疾病
ulcer /ˈʌlsə(r)/ *n.* 溃疡
fracture /ˈfræktʃə(r)/ *n.* 骨折
symptom /ˈsimptəm/ *n.* 症状
diagnosis /daiəgˈnəusis/ *n.* 诊断
epidemic /epiˈdemik/ *n.* 流行病
contagion /kənˈteidʒ(ə)n/ *n.* 传染
treatment /ˈtriːtmənt/ *n.* 疗法
diabetes /daiəˈbiːtiz/ *n.* 糖尿病
indigestion /indiˈdʒestʃ(ə)n/ *n.* 消化不良
influenza, flu 流感
malnutrition /mælnjuːˈtriʃ(ə)n/ *n.* 营养不良
neurasthenia /njuərəsˈθiːniə/ *n.* 神经衰弱
rheumatism /ˈruːmətiz(ə)m/ *n.* 风湿病
tuberculosis /tjuːbəːkjuˈləusis/ *n.* 结核病
blood transfusion 输血
graft, transplant 移植
plastic surgery 整形手术
first-aid station 急救站
medical department 内科
surgical department 外科
dental department 牙科
ophthalmology department 眼科
otorhinolaryngological department 耳鼻喉科
X-ray department 放射科
registration office 挂号处
emergency room 急诊室
pharmacist, druggist 药剂师

补充读物

Study: Vitamin A can be harmful

The research, conducted on men, confirms three earlier studies in women showing that high intake of vitamin A raises the risk of broken hips and weak bones. The latest study is the first to measure levels of the vitamin in blood, rather than just asking about diet and supplement use.

The three-decade study and other evidence suggest that daily vitamin A consumption of more than 1.5 milligrams can be dangerous, and that most people should not take vitamin A supplements.

Current dietary recommendations call for only 0.7 mg of vitamin A for women and 0.9 mg for men a day. That is easily supplied by a healthy diet. But many popular multivitamins contain 0.75 mg to 1.5 mg of vitamin A, generally listed on labels as 2,500 international units and 5,000 IUs, respectively.

"Vitamin A is potentially harmful," said Dr. Donald Louria, chairman emeritus of preventive medicine at the University of Medicine and Dentistry of New Jersey in Newark, New Jersey. "Unless there is a known medical reason like certain diseases of the eye, people should not be taking vitamin A supplements."

The study by doctors at University Hospital in Uppsala was reported in Thursday's New England Journal of Medicine. It involved 2,322 men.

Vitamin A is known as an antioxidant. Antioxidants are believed to reduce the risk of cancer and heart disease. Government studies show one-third to one-half of Americans take vitamin A or multivitamins containing it.

Vitamin A can interfere with cells that produce new bone, stimulate cells that break down old bone and interfere with vitamin D, which helps the body maintain normal calcium levels.

In the study, about one-fifth, or roughly 465 of the men, were found to be at risk because they had the highest levels of vitamin A. The men were about 21/2 times more likely to break a hip and 65 percent more likely to suffer any fracture than those with lower levels of the vitamin in their blood.

Those in the 99th percentile were about seven times more likely to break a bone.

Louria said that people should not take fish oil supplements or eat liver more than once a week, but that multivitamins containing 0.1 mg or less of vitamin A are fine for people eating a healthy diet.

Large amounts of vitamin A are found in beef liver and fish liver oils; smaller amounts are in egg yolks, butter and cream. Milk and some cereals are fortified with vitamin A and, per serving, provide about 10 percent of daily needs. And substances in dark green, leafy vegetables and yellow vegetables and fruits are converted to vitamin A in the body.

Annette Dickinson, acting president of the trade group for supplement makers, the Council for Responsible Nutrition, said the Swedish men had an unusually high intake of vitamin A, even though very few were taking supplements.

"I don't think there's a reason now from the studies we have before us to say that multivitamins containing ordinary amounts of vitamin A are harmful," Dickinson said. She said that in many multivitamins, much of the vitamin A is in the form of beta-carotene, which studies have shown does not weaken bones.

The study had some shortcomings: Blood levels of vitamin A were measured only once, and the participants' reports of diet and supplement use 20 years later did not match well with their earlier vitamin A blood levels.

Day 78

金融财经类词汇

economist /iˈkɔnəmist/ *n.* 经济学家
socialist economy 社会主义经济
capitalist economy 资本主义经济
political economy 政治经济学
protectionism /prəˈtekʃ(ə)niz(ə)m/ *n.* 保护主义
autarchy /ˈɔːtɑːki/ *n.* 闭关自守
infrastructure /ˈinfrəstrʌktʃə(r)/ *n.* 基本建设
purchasing power 购买力
circulating capital 流动资本
investment /inˈvestmənt/ *n.* 投资,资产
transfer /trænsˈfəː/ *n.* 转让,转账,过户
exchange rate 汇率,兑换率
foreign exchange 外汇
speculation /spekjuˈleiʃ(ə)n/ *n.* 投机
share /ʃeə/ *n.* 股份,股票
opening price 开盘
closing price 收盘
rate of interest 利率
insurance /inˈʃuərəns/ *n.* 保险
mortgage /ˈmɔːgidʒ/ *n.* 抵押
article /ˈɑːtik(ə)/ *n.* 物品,商品
by-product 副产品
income tax 所得税
International Chamber of Commerce 国际商会
United Nations Trade and Development Board 联合国贸易与发展理事会
European Economic Community, EEC; European Common Market 欧洲经济共同体
Organization of the Petroleum Exporting Countries, OPEC 石油输出国组织
Economic Commission for Europe, ECE 欧洲经济委员会
London Stock Market 伦敦股票市场
income and expenditure, receipts and expenditure, output and input 支出和收入
marketing /ˈmaːkitiŋ/ *n.* 销售学,销售业务,市场调查
customs /ˈkʌstəms/ *n.* 海关
registered trademark 注册商标

补充读物

The Rent-to-Own Industry

The rent-to-own industry (also known as the rental-purchase industry) consists of dealers that rent furniture, appliances, home electronics, and jewelry to consumers. Rent-to-own transactions provide immediate access to household goods for a relatively low weekly or monthly payment, typically without any down payment or credit check. Consumers enter into a self-renewing weekly or monthly lease for the rented merchandise, and are under no obligation to continue payments beyond the current weekly or monthly period. The lease provides the option to purchase the goods, either by continuing to pay rent for a specified period of time, usually 12 to 24 months, or by early payment of some specified proportion of the remaining lease payments. These terms are attractive to many consumers who cannot afford a cash purchase, may be unable to qualify for credit, and are unwilling or unable to wait until they can save for a purchase. Some consumers also may value the flexibility offered by the transaction, which allows return of the merchandise at any time without obligation for further payments or negative impact on the customer's credit rating. Other consumers may rent merchandise to fill a temporary need or to try a product before buying it. The rent-to-own industry trade association estimated that in 1998 there were 7,500 rent-to-own stores in the United States, serving nearly three million customers, and producing $4.4 billion in revenues

Consumer Protection Issues

A number of consumer protection concerns have been raised about the rent-to-own industry by consumer advocates. The areas of concern have included the prices charged by the industry (which can be two to three times retail prices, and sometimes more), the treatment of customers during the collection of overdue rental payments, the repossession of merchandise after customers have paid substantial amounts towards ownership, the adequacy of information provided to customers about the terms and conditions of the rental agreement and purchase option, and the disclosure of whether merchandise is new or used. Consumer advocates also have argued that rent-to-own transactions are really credit sales, not leases, and should be subject to federal and state consumer credit laws.

Currently, rent-to-own transactions are not specifically regulated by federal law, either by the Truth-in-Lending Act (TILA) or the Consumer Leasing Act (CLA). Federal legislation that would specifically regulate rent-to-own transactions has been proposed several times in recent years. Some of the proposed legislation would apply federal and state credit laws to the rent-to-own industry, while other proposed legislation would regulate rent-to-own transactions as leases.

Forty-six states currently have rent-to-own laws that regulate rent-to-own transactions in a manner similar to leases, mandating a variety of disclosures and other requirements. The state laws generally have been supported by the industry but opposed by consumer advocates who believe that rent-to-own transactions should be treated as credit sales. Currently, no state has a rent-to-own law that specifically regulates rent-to-own transactions as credit sales. But courts in several states, most notably Wisconsin, Minnesota, and New Jersey, have ruled that rent-to-own transactions are credit sales and subject to state laws governing credit sales. Vermont does not regulate rent-to-own transactions as credit sales, but does require disclosure of the "effective-APR."

A key factual issue in the debate over whether rent-to-own transactions are sales or leases has been the extent to which rent-to-own customers purchase the rented merchandise. The industry has consistently maintained that only 25 to 30 percent of rent-to-own merchandise is purchased, and that the rest is returned to the dealer after a relatively short rental duration. Some consumer advocates have presented a sharply different view, maintaining that most rent-to-own transactions result in the purchase of the rented merchandise.

Public Policy

Disclosure of total cost and other terms of purchase. The FTC staff survey found that most rent-to-own merchandise is purchased by the customer. Because most merchandise is purchased, information about the total cost and other terms of purchase is important for consumers entering into rent-to-own transactions. Information on the total cost of purchase, including all mandatory fees and charges, would allow potential customers to compare the cost of a rent-to-own transaction to other alternatives, and would be most useful if it were available while the customer was shopping and making a decision. The best way to provide total cost information that can be seen and used while the customer is shopping would be to provide it not only in the written agreement but also on product labels on all merchandise displayed in the rent-to-own store. The other basic terms of the transaction, including the weekly or monthly payment amount, the number of payments required to obtain ownership, and whether the merchandise is new or used, also should be provided on product labels.

These same disclosures also should be provided in any advertisement or catalog that makes a representation concerning the weekly or monthly rent-to-own payment amount for a specific item of merchandise. All of the terms and conditions of the transaction also should be disclosed in the agreement document.

While disclosures in advertisements and rental agreements are required by law in almost all states, most states do not require label disclosures of the total cost or other terms of purchase. Disclosure of the total cost and other basic terms of purchase on product labels, along with disclosures in advertisements and agreement documents, would substantially benefit rent-to-own customers, providing information on the cost of a rent-to-own purchase while customers are shopping and making a decision, and allowing for an easier comparison to the cost of other alternatives.

APR disclosures. APR disclosures for rent-to-own transactions raise more difficult questions. While an APR disclosure would allow consumers to compare the cost of a rent-to-own transaction to a credit card purchase or other source of credit, APR calculations could be subject to manipulation by rent-to-own dealers, possibly resulting in inaccurate disclosures that mislead consumers. Dealers could inflate cash prices in order to understate the disclosed APR, without suffering a significant loss of business, because rent-to-own stores make few cash sales. The difficulties of implementing and enforcing an APR disclosure requirement for rent-to-own transactions must be compared to the benefits it would yield over and above a simpler disclosure of total cost. Disclosure of the total cost and other terms of purchase on product labels, along with disclosures in advertisements and agreement documents, may provide consumers with the information they need to evaluate the cost of purchasing through a rent-to-own transaction, and may avoid the potential for manipulation, misleading disclosures, and enforcement difficulties. These issues should be considered carefully if APR disclosures are contemplated.

Price restrictions. Similar difficulties also could affect a price restriction policy. Dealers could manipulate cash prices to evade or lessen the impact of price restrictions. The possible impact of effective price restrictions on the availability of rent-to-own transactions also must be assessed. These issues should be considered carefully if price restrictions are contemplated.

Regulation of collection practices. The FTC staff survey found that while some rent-to-own dealers may use abusive practices in the collection of overdue rental payments, abusive collection practices are not widespread and do not represent the typical experience of most rent-to-own customers who are late making a payment. These results suggest that federal regulation of industry collection practices may be unnecessary. The most serious abuses, however, such as unauthorized entry into customers' homes, remain troubling, even if they are not widespread, and warrant continued attention.

Regulation of reinstatement rights. The survey also found that few customers lost merchandise through a return or repossession after making substantial payments towards ownership. These results suggest that federal regulation of reinstatement rights may be unnecessary. Industry-supported federal legislation, however, includes a reinstatement rights provision that is broader than the current requirements in many states, and would extend reinstatement rights to customers in the few states that currently do not mandate such requirements.

Conclusion

Any regulation of the rent-to-own industry should recognize that most rent-to-own customers ultimately purchase the rented merchandise. Regulations should ensure that customers have the information and protections appropriate for a purchase transaction. Clear and accurate disclosure of the total cost and other terms of purchase would allow potential customers to compare rent-to-own transactions to other alternatives, and would help ensure that consumers choosing rent-to-own transactions do so on an informed basis. Disclosure of the total cost and other basic terms of purchase on product labels, along with disclosures in advertisements and agreement documents, would ensure that the information is available to consumers while they are considering the rent-to-own transaction.

Regulation of the rent-to-own industry should also reflect, where appropriate, the differences between rent-to-own transactions and other forms of purchase. Regulatory policies mandated for other types of purchases should be applied to rent-to-own transactions only after careful consideration of the potential costs and benefits. Careful analysis also should be undertaken before adopting policies that would substantially reduce the availability of rent-to-own transactions. Most rent-to-own customers are satisfied with their experience with rent-to-own transactions, suggesting that the rent-to-own industry provides a service that meets and satisfies the demands of most of its customers.

（摘自 *www.fpc.gov*）

Note 前事不忘后事之师 *Remember the past and it will guide your future.*

Day 79

国际关系类词汇

protectorate /prəˈtektərət/ *n.* (被)保护国
asylum /əˈsailəm/ *n.* 庇护;避难
never to attach any conditions 不附带任何条件
non-aligned countries 不结盟国家
consultation /kɔnsəlˈteiʃ(ə)n/ *n.* 磋商
the third world 第三世界
plebiscite /plebisait/ *n.* 公民投票
generally-accepted principles of international relations 公认的国际关系原则
joint action 共同行动
normalization of relations 关系正常化
an established principle of international law 国际法准则
rudimentary code of international relations 国际关系中最起码的准则
mutual understanding and mutual accommodation 互谅互让
territorial sea 领海
territorial air 领空
territorial waters 领水
territorial integrity 领土完整
complete prohibition and thorough destruction of nuclear weapons 全面禁止和彻底销毁核武器
sacred and inviolable 神圣不可侵犯
ecocide /iˈkəusaid/ *n.* 生态灭绝
bilateral and multilateral economic cooperation 双边和多边经济合作
neutralized state 永久中立国
sovereign state 主权国家
mutual non-aggression 互不侵犯
equality and mutual benefit 平等互利
peaceful coexistence 和平共处
community /kəˈmjuːniti/ *n.* 共同体
European Common Market 欧洲共同市场
European Economic Community, EEC 欧洲经济共同体
Asian and Pacific Council, ASPAC 亚洲太平洋地区理事会
League of Red Cross Societies, LRCS 红十字会协会
North Atlantic Treaty Organization, NATO 北大西洋公约组织(北约)

Day 80

宗教法律类词汇

faith /feiθ/ *n.* 信仰
piety /ˈpaiəti/ *n.* 虔诚
fervour /ˈfəːvə(r)/ *n.* 热情 (美作:fervor)
mysticlsm /ˈmistiklzm/ *n.* 神秘主义
temptation /tempˈteiʃ(ə)n/ *n.* 邪念,诱惑
atheism /ˈeiθiiz(ə)m/ *n.* 无神论
Christianity /kristiˈænəti/ *n.* 基督教
Catholicism /kəˈθɔlisizəm/ *n.* 天主教
Protestantism /ˈprɔtistəntizəm/ *n.* 新教,耶稣教
Islamism /ˈizləmizəm/ *n.* 伊斯兰教
Buddhism /ˈbudiz(ə)m/ *n.* 佛教
Daoism 道教
devil /ˈdev(ə)l/ *n.* 魔鬼
paradise /ˈpærədais/ *n.* 天堂
miracle /ˈmirək(ə)l/ *n.* 奇迹
confession /kənˈfeʃ(ə)n/ *n.*忏悔
Government bill 政府议案
to enact a law, to promulgate a law 颁布法律
legislation /ledʒisˈleiʃ(ə)n/ *n.* 立法
jurist /ˈdʒuərist/ *n.* 法学家
jurisprudence /dʒuərisˈpruːdəns/ *n.* 法学
to abolish 废止,取消
immunity /iˈmjuːniti/ *n.* 豁免,豁免权
constitutional law 宪法
criminal law 刑法
administrative law 行政法
civil law 民法
commercial law, mercantile law 商法
international law 国际法
Civil Suit Law, Code of civil law 民事诉讼法
Criminal Law 刑事诉讼法
Copyright Law 著作权法
civil rights 民事权利,公民权利
human rights, rights of man 人权
summons /ˈsʌmənz/ *n.* 传票
sworn statement 誓词
public hearing 公平
acquittal /əˈkwit(ə)l/ *n.* 宣告无罪,开释
bribery, suborning 行贿,受贿,贿赂
marriage certificate 结婚证书
notarial deed 公证书
patent rights 专利权

IELTS 核心词汇

单词索引

A

C

J

K

L

S

T

图书在版编目（CIP）数据

80 天攻克雅思核心词汇/孟飞，江涛主编．—3 版（修订本）．
北京：石油工业出版社，2007.1
ISBN 978-7-5021-5796-8

Ⅰ．8…
Ⅱ．①江…②孟…
Ⅲ．英语－词汇－高等学校－入学考试，国外－自学参考资料
Ⅳ．H313

中国版本图书馆 CIP 数据核字（2006）第 131555 号

80 天攻克雅思核心词汇（第 3 版）（含 MP3）
丛书主编　江涛　　本册主编　孟飞　江涛

出版发行：石油工业出版社
（北京安定门外安华里 2 区 1 号楼　100011）
网　址：www.petropub.com.cn
发行部：（010）64523623　编辑部：（010）64523613
经　销：全国新华书店
印　刷：北京晨旭印刷厂

2007 年 1 月第 3 版　2009 年 9 月第15次印刷
787×1092 毫米　开本：1/16　印张：24.75
字数：739 千字

书　号：ISBN 978-7-5021-5796-8/G·571
定　价：58.00 元（含 3 小时 MP3 光盘 1 张）
（如出现印装质量问题，我社发行部负责调换）

读石油版书，获亲情馈赠

《80天攻克雅思核心词汇》(修订本)意见反馈卡

亲爱的读者朋友，首先感谢您阅读我社图书，请您在阅读完本书后填写以下信息。我社将长期开展“读石油版书，获亲情馈赠”活动，凡是关注我社图书并认真填写读者信息反馈卡的朋友都有机会获得亲情馈赠，我们将定期从信息反馈卡中评选出有价值的意见和建议，并为填写这些信息的朋友**免费**赠送一本好书。

1. 您的年龄：20岁以下□　20~30岁□　30~40岁□　40岁以上□
2. 您的文化程度：大专以下□　本科□　硕士□　博士□
3. 您购买本书的动因：书名、封面吸引人□　内容吸引人□　版式设计吸引人□
4. 您认为本书的内容：很好□　较好□　一般□　较差□
5. 您认为本书书名反映内容的程度：很高□　较高□　一般□　较差□
6. 您认为本书在哪些方面存在缺陷：内容□　封面□　装帧设计□
7. 您认为本书的定价：较高□　适中□　偏低□
8. 您考雅思前学过哪些英语教材：

    ____

9. 您曾参加过哪个学校的培训班，效果如何？

    ____

10. 您考雅思时除了用此书外还用了哪些其他雅思书：

    ____

11. 您还需要哪些雅思方面的教材：

    ____

12. 您对本书的综合评价：

    ____

13. 您在哪里购买的本书？

    ________省________市________书店

您的联系方式：

姓名 ________

单位 ________　邮政编码 ________

地址 ________　电话 ________

手机 ________　E-mail ________

回信请寄：北京安定门外安华里二区一号楼　石油工业出版社

社会图书出版中心　刘玮收

邮政编码：100011

电子信箱：LW@cnpc.com.cn　(复印有效)